Down by the Riverside

Religion, Race, and Ethnicity

General Editor: Peter J. Paris

Public Religion and Urban Transformation: Faith in the City
EDITED BY LOWELL W. LIVEZEY

Down by the Riverside: Readings in African American Religion
EDITED BY LARRY G. MURPHY

Down by the Riverside

Readings in African American Religion

EDITED BY

Larry G. Murphy

New York University Press

NEW YORK AND LONDON

NEW YORK UNIVERSITY PRESS
New York and London

Library of Congress Cataloging-in-Publication Data
Down by the riverside : readings in African American religion / [edited by] Larry G. Murphy.
p. cm.—(Religion, race, and ethnicity)
Includes bibliographical references.
ISBN 0-8147-5580-1 (alk. paper) — ISBN 0-8147-5581-X (pbk. : alk. paper)
1. Afro-Americans—Religion.   I. Murphy, Larry (Larry G.)   II. Series.
BR563.N4 D69 2000
200'.89'96073—dc21   00-061294

New York University Press books are printed on acid-free paper,
and their binding materials are chosen for strength and durability.

Manufactured in the United States of America

10 9 8 7 6 5 4 3 2 1

To my wife, Jean,
by whose steady-flowing river of love
I have found the grace of joy.

Contents

Introduction

Larry G. Murphy

A good way to understand a people is to study their religion, for religion is addressed to that most sacred schedule of values around which the expression and the meaning of life tends to coalesce.

This quote from the preface of the landmark publication by C. Eric Lincoln and Lawrence H. Mamiya[1] illuminates the rationale for the present volume. Religion has, indeed, been a determinative dynamic in the unfolding life of the African American community in the United States. This does not suggest an unqualified assent to the common assertion that African Americans are "a religious people." Rather, it is a recognition of the fact that it is impossible to achieve an adequate understanding of this people's, or any people's, historical identity apart from a serious consideration of religion as both a motive force and an organizing framework for their efforts toward a secure, equitable inclusion in the human community.

While this volume focuses on the collective body of persons of African descent who have made their abode in the United States, the writer is aware that the plenary identifier *African American* includes a multitude of subidentities, related to such distinctions as one's heritage within the larger African Diaspora (e.g., Central America, the Caribbean); region of residence within the United States; social class; particular family or denominational traditions; gender; urban versus rural formative influences in one's life; and so forth. Thus, our subject is not a monolithic entity whose religious life can be addressed as a single sociocultural thread unreeling in simple linear fashion. Instead, we will examine a rich array, a variegated panorama of people, practices, and theological positions. At the same time, themes and practices exist that *are* pervasive, which enable the designation of this diversity as a discreet group. This volume will attempt to present for consideration both the continuities and divergences.

The composite subject of *African American* and *religion* calls for some further commentary as background to what follows. The subject people are persons of *African* descent, who arrived in this country under circumstances peculiar to their history: violent, forcible uprootage, enslavement, and transplantation. That beginning has been a key factor in the nature of their subsequent religious development. Particular points of impact and modes of influence are yet being discerned, but the impact, itself, is certain. The meaning and mode of their continuing *African*-ness has also been a matter of scholarly research and debate. Familiar to many is the contention of African American sociologist E. Franklin Frazier that enslavement and acculturation in the United States effectively stripped Africans of their remembered religio-cultural past. This was countered by anthropologist Melville Herskovits, who dubbed this reading of Africans' past a *myth*, and who laid out his identification of African cultural retentions in the Western Hemisphere, including the United States, in a series of publications. Subsequent researchers have demonstrated that, in fact, much of African religion and general culture survived the "Middle Passage" and reasserted itself on this side of the Atlantic. This is particularly evident in Central and South America and in the Caribbean, where some whole West African religious systems seem to have been reconstructed—though, perhaps, in "creolized"[2] form—and are in regular practice. In these places one also can readily see examples of the merger of African and European cultural elements in aspects of national cuisine, dress, language, dance, the arts, and the like.

In colonial and national United States, such cultural reassertion was expressly stifled, in part for fear of its potential for contributing to any sense of unity or connectedness among slaves, which might, in turn, support joint efforts of rebellion. Nonetheless, students of Africans in North America have uncovered substantial instances of Africanisms in diet, dress, language, music, styles of labor, thought patterns, and religious belief and practice. Anthropologist Margaret Mead asserted the resilience of culture, even in the face of violent social disruption. She also spoke of the ability of cultures to readapt to changed circumstances, appropriating new cultural forms to carry old meanings, or ascribing new meanings to old forms, thus allowing culture to remain viable and existentially relevant under changed conditions. In what ways and to what extent this process was operative among African Americans will be addressed, implicitly and explicitly, in the present work.

As to religion, the second part of our composite subject, the discussion above accounts for the practice, from earliest slave days, of elements of traditional African ceremonies and conjuring arts. It accounts, as well, for researchers' increasing encounter with African slave practitioners of Islam and slave archaeology's discoveries of Qur'anic fragments and other artifacts of Islamic devotions. But Africans, whether in the homeland or in Diaspora, have been confronted by the same fundamental questions that face all peoples—existential questions of origins, identity, security, ontological meaning, and destiny. Religions emerge as human intentional responses to these questions, responses that are lodged in some cosmic, or transhuman, or overarching verity. For Africans in the United States, the questions were writ large, the urgency for answers intensified, by a confused Protestant social milieu that could not make peace with human bondage in the way that Catholic Latin America had, but that nevertheless could not/would not expunge the practice from its midst. This social psychosis, this religious schizophrenia, had the result, variably, of denying authentic human or religious identity to black people; of imposing a denigrated, self-effacing identity; of adding, with legal sanction, arbitrary white willfulness to the natural forces that threaten human security; of seeking to make the meaning and the aims of black life contingent upon white self-interest. As a consequence, much of the focus and the energy of African American religious practice, as with its theology, has been directed toward responding to the white assault on black existence. Yet, African American religion has retained its own internal integrity. That is to say, it is not simply, or even primarily, a dependent, reactive enterprise. Rather, it has involved persons addressing those fundamental human questions, out of the particularities of their life circumstances, drawing from the insights of their own religious sensibilities, resourced by the strength of the inherent will to affirm the sanctity of being.

Plan of the Volume

The present volume offers a vista onto the religious mosaic of African America. Through its arrangement, it provides a thematic overview of the unfolding religious life of this people, with emphasis on the nineteenth and twentieth centuries. It does not intend to be a religious history, as such, but rather to set forth a representative sampling of major institutional, theological, and social/religious developments in historical sweep. The opening essays by Charles H. Long, Gayraud S. Wilmore, Albert J. Raboteau, and co-authors C. Eric Lincoln and Lawrence H. Mamiya, all pre-eminent scholars in this arena of inquiry, address the general subject of African American religiosity in terms of the ideational framework for the events, actors, issues, and movements that emerge in the story. They present the authors' conceptions of the threads that hold the disparate, sometimes incongruous elements of the story in one thematic whole. They attempt to offer some cues both for discerning a narrative line and for understanding its meanings.

In the next section, several authors examine aspects of the religious developments among African Americans, starting from the African religious heritage and making transition into various forms of Christian profession—some of which incorporated elements from the traditions of the Motherland. Richard Brent Turner's piece reminds us, however, that Islam, as part of the African heritage, continued in practice among a small but devoted contingent of the slave population. Monroe Fordham's work on Christian missions is very revealing of the complex motive forces resulting from African Americans' acculturation to American Christianity, with its assumptions concerning Africa as a religiously/culturally benighted continent.

Although it would not be accurate to assert Western notions of gender equality to have pertained among the peoples from whom African Americans derived, one could find in their sacred cosmos conceptions of deity as female, respected female religious practitioners, and women as social leaders and civil rulers. The situation of enslaved Africans in the United States proscribed the reestablishment of traditional African social structures. As Africans became acculturated to the ways of the West, they appropriated much of its styles of gender relationships in family, institutional structures, and the public sphere. Thus, while women were highly visible and instrumental in the development of black religious life, they were excluded from positions of official public leadership, especially from ordained clerical status, the arenas from which historical narrative typically has been drawn. An adequate, accurately gendered presentation of African American religious history therefore requires intentional deconstructive/reconstructive research and interpretation. Delores C. Carpenter offers one of several pieces in this volume that contribute in this direction.

With the cessation of hostilities, the legal and social impediments to Northern black evangelization in the South were removed. Emissaries of the black denominations took full advantage of this opening: with vigor, they recruited among the newly freed, receiving for their use the major boon of numerous choice church properties seized by the Union troops from congregations supporting the Rebellion. The response to their initiatives was overwhelming: in the years immediately following the war, the rolls of the black denominations quadrupled in size. Leon F. Litwack offers a look at the intense, hope-filled work of Northern black and white missionaries in fostering literacy and "moral reformation" among the newly free, as a means of enabling their economic and social elevation. Manning Marable allows us to see some interior dimensions of African American religious life in this time period through the contemporary eyes of noted scholar, editor, and rights advocate W. E. B. Du Bois. Du Bois himself represented an element of the diversity of black religiosity as one who eschewed traditional Christian piety in favor of a posture that ranged between agnosticism and a kind of theo-humanism. Larry G. Murphy discusses some of the important personal and communal roles filled by the black church as the century wound down, while St. Clair Drake chronicles the recurrent issue among African Americans of whether or not to emigrate from the United States to redeem their hopes for a usable future, particularly to return to Africa where they might also "redeem" that place.

Section IV explores some of the religious developments attendant upon the migration of African Americans from the rural areas of the South to the cities of the South and North at the turn of the twentieth century. St. Clair Drake provides the case of Chicago, a major terminal on the northward procession, while Lawrence W. Levine speaks of the shift in sacred music that accompanied the rural-urban relocation.

Section V touches upon the variety of religious expressions to which the urban challenge and modernity gave rise: from the resurfacing of Islam in several renditions; to new syntheses of African, Christian, and Judaic elements; to full-blown humanism.

In the twentieth century, African Americans continued to particularize their religiosity to the vital realities of their life context, giving rise to various initiatives of protest and agitation for social justice, as well as modes of adaptation and accommodation. Three of the authors in Section VI glimpse some of the ways individuals and organized groups pursued these initiatives. They speak to social advocacy as a pervasive current in African American religion and to the continuing instrumental roles of women in what transpires. C. Eric Lincoln and Lawrence H. Mamiya address the "either/or" question of African American religious social activism. They offer a perspective on the black church that incorporates the spectrum of potential activist/quietist postures into one dialectical religious identity.

Section VII enables the reader to gain an image of black Christian churches today, both urban and rural, in terms of their demography, staffing, devotional life, and daily functioning. Survey data as well as specific cases are presented.

One of the more significant developments in religion in this century has been the emergence of Black Theology. It had ample, forceful precursors in the pronouncements of nineteenth-century black religionists such as David Walker, the Reverend Nathaniel Paul, Ms. Maria W. Stewart, and the Reverend Henry McNeal Turner. In the second half of the twentieth century, however, it came to be named and consciously to be articulated as an appropriate, indeed essential, contextualization of African American Christian faith. Black Theology has inspired similar formulations among other identity groups—racial, ethnic, gender, class, and so on—here and abroad. In Section VIII, James H. Cone, modern inaugurator of the form, chronicles the emergence of Black Theology, from its nurturing in the Civil Rights/Black Power ferment to its renderings in the writings of several theologians through the 1970s. Then two important early Black Theology statements of clergy groups from the late 1960s are presented. M. Shawn Copeland brings to the conversation the theological visions that have come from the black Catholic tradition. And Toinette M. Eugene gives a very helpful exposition of the kinds of theological concerns and emphases of black feminist and "womanist" theologians, representing the particularities of women's existence within the generality of African American social and religious history.

Finally, Gayraud S. Wilmore and Vincent Harding, in separate writings, review the narrative of African America's religious unfolding, critically illuminating both the "agony and the ecstacy" of this pilgrimage toward freedom and wholeness, and seeking to discern lessons and meanings that may serve as crucial resources for the fulfillment of that abiding quest.

The two appendixes to the text provide a timeline of people, places, and events in African American religious history, and a listing of currently available films for further study.

N O T E S

1. *The Black Church in the African American Experience* (Durham: Duke University Press, 1990), p. xi.

2. See William Watty, "Black Religion in the Caribbean—Present and Future." Paper delivered at the Annual Meeting of the Society for the Study of Black Religion, Kingston, Jamaica, November 25, 1976.

Part I

Thematic, Contextual Prisms for Understanding African American Religion

Chapter One

Perspectives for a Study of African American Religion in the United States

Charles H. Long

Charles H. Long offers an analysis of African American religion from his vantage point as an historian of religion. He describes the development of a mode of religion that draws upon, but is not defined by, either an Hebraic or a Christian identification but that, rather, draws from the enduring heritage of an African past in concert with the experience in the United States. The result is a religion that emphasizes the transforming power of the deity, who enables them to sustain an integrous, empowered existence in which they have been able to hold together "eschatological hopes and the archaic religious consciousness."

•

Americans of African descent have for some time been the subject of countless studies and research projects—projects extending from the physical through the social sciences. The religion of this culture has not been overlooked.[1]

Most of the studies of religion have employed the methodology of the social sciences; hardly any of them have come to terms with the specifically religious elements in the religion of black Americans. We have not yet seen anything on the order of Pierre Verger's[2] study of African religion in South America or of Alfred Metraux's[3] study of the same phenomenon in the Atlantic islands.

On the contemporary scene, a group of younger blacks are about the task of writing a distinctively "black theology." I refer here to the works of Joseph Washington (*Black Religion* [Boston, 1961], James Cone (*Black Theology and Black Power* [New York, 1969]), and to Albert Cleage's sermons (*The Black Messiah* [New York, 1968]). In this enterprise, these men place themselves in the religious tradition of David Walker, Henry Garnett, Martin Delaney, and W. E. B. Du Bois. They are essentially apologetic theologians working implicitly and explicitly from the Christian theological tradition.

What we have in fact are two kinds of studies: those arising from the social sciences, and an explicitly theological apologetic tradition. This limitation of methodological perspectives has led to a narrowness of understanding and the failure to perceive certain creative possibilities in the black community in America.

One of the most telling examples of this limitation of perspectives in the study of black religion is to be found in Joseph Washington's work cited above. Washington has correctly seen that black religion is not to be understood as a black imitation of the religion of the majority population. His religious norm is Christianity, and the internal norm for Christianity is faith expressing itself in theology. From his analysis he concludes that black religion is not Christian, thus does not embody faith, and therefore has produced no theology. Black religion has, in his view, been more concerned with civil rights and protest, and hardly, if ever, concerned with genuine Christian faith.

I do not wish to take issue with Washington regarding his understanding of Christian faith and theology, for this lies outside the scope of our concerns in this chapter. However, a word or two must be said in passing. Washington seems to conceive of Christianity and theology in static terms unrelated to historical experience. He seems to be unaware of the historical situations that were correlative to European and American theology, and he seems equally unaware of the fact that Americans have produced few theologians of the variety that would meet his norm. In short, his critique of black religion from the stance of Christian theology is blunted by the lack of his historical understanding of theology.

But now, to the point that is most relevant for our discussion: the distinctive nature of black religion. Washington's insights here are very accurate, for he shows in his work how folkloric materials, social protest, and Negro fraternalism, along with biblical imagery, are all aspects of black religion. He experiences a difficulty here, for he is unable to deal with religion outside of the normative framework of Christian theology. But even if one is to have a theology, it must arise from religion, something that is prior to theology.

I have felt the need for some time to present a systematic study of black religion— a kind of initial ordering of the religious experiences and expressions of the black communities in America. Such a study should not be equated with Christianity, or any other religion for that matter. It is rather an attempt to see what kind of images and meanings lie behind the religious experiences of the black communities in America. While recognizing the uniqueness of this community, I am also working as a historian of religious, and thus the context for my interpretation is the variety of the religious traditions of mankind.

I should like in this chapter to present three interrelated perspectives for a study of black religion from the point of view of a historian of religion. These perspectives constitute symbolic images as well as methodological principles. They are:

A. Africa as historical reality and religious image.
B. The involuntary presence of the black community in America.
C. The experience and symbol of God in the religious experience of blacks.

A. Africa as Historical Reality and Religious Image

It is a historical fact that the existence of the black communities in America is due to the slave trade of numerous European countries from the seventeenth to the nineteenth centuries (slaves were still being illegally smuggled into the United States as late as the 1880s). The issue of the persistence of African elements in the black community is a hotly debated issue. On the one hand, we have the positions of E. Franklin Frazier and W. E. B. Du Bois,[4] emphasizing the lack of any significant persisting elements of Africanism in America. Melville Herskovitz held this same position but reversed his position in the *Myth of the Negro Past* (Boston, 1958), where he places a greater emphasis on the persistence of African elements among the descendants of the slaves in North America. One of the issues in this discussion had to do with the comparative level of the studies. Invariably, the norm for comparison was the black communities in the Atlantic islands and in South America. In the latter the African elements are very distinctive, and, in the case of Brazil, Africans have gone back and forth between Africa and Brazil.[5] African languages are still spoken by blacks in Brazil. Indeed, Pierre Verger first became interested in Yoruba religion when he saw it being practiced in South America!

It is obvious that nothing of this sort has existed in the United States. The slave system of the United States systematically broke down the linguistic and cultural pattern of the slaves, but even a protagonist for the loss of all Africanisms, such as E. Franklin Frazier, acknowledges the persistence of "shout songs," African rhythm, and dance in American culture. Frazier, and in this matter, Du Bois, while acknowledging such elements did not consider them to be of ultimate significance, for they could not see these forms playing an important role in the social cohesion of the black community. Without resolving this discussion, another issue needs to be raised. The persistence of elements of what some anthropologists have called "soft culture" means that given even the systematic breakdown of African cultural forms in the history of North America slavery, the slaves did not confront America with a religious *tabula rasa*. If not the content of culture, a characteristic mode of orienting and perceiving reality has probably persisted. We know, for example, that a great majority of the slaves came from West Africa, and we also know from the studies of Daryll Forde that West Africa is a cultural as well as a geographical unit.[6] Underlying the empirical diversity of languages, religions, and social form, there is, according to Forde, a structural unity discernible in language and religious forms.[7] With the breakdown of the empirical forms of language and religion as determinants for the social group, this persisting structural mode and the common situation as slaves in America may be the basis for the persistence of an African style among the descendants of the Africans.

In addition to this, in the accounts of the slaves and their owners we read of "meetings" that took place secretly in the woods. It is obvious that these "meetings" were not the practice of the masters' religion. They were related to what the slaves themselves called "conjuring," and the connotation reminds one of Voodoo rites in Haiti.

Added to this is the precise manner in which, by being a slave and a black man, one was isolated from any self-determined legitimacy in the society of which one was a part and was recognized by one's physiological characteristics. This constituted a complexity of experience revolving around the relationship between one's physical being and one's origins. So even if he had no conscious memory of Africa, the image of Africa played an enormous part in the religion of the black man. The image of Africa, which is related to historical beginnings, has been one of the primordial religious images of great significance. It constitutes the religious revalorization of the land, a place where the natural and ordinary gestures of the black man were and could be authenticated. In this connection, one can trace almost every nationalistic movement among the blacks and find Africa to be the dominating and guiding image. Even among religious groups not strongly nationalistic, the image of Africa or Ethiopia still has relevance.[8] This is present in such diverse figures as Richard Allen, who organized the African Methodist Episcopal Church in the early nineteenth century, through Martin Delany in the late nineteenth century, and then again in Marcus Garvey's[9] "back to Africa movement" of the immediate post—World War I period, and finally the taking up of this issue again among black leaders of our own time.

The image of Africa as it appears in black religion is unique, for the black community in America is a landless people. Unlike the American Indian, the land was not taken from him, and unlike the black Africans in South Africa or Rhodesia, his land is not occupied by groups whom he considers aliens. His image of the land points to the religious meaning of land even in the absence of these forms of authentication. It thus emerges as an image that is always invested with historical and religious possibilities.

B. The Involuntary Presence of the Black Community in America

Implied in the discussion concerning the land and the physiological characteristics of the black is the significance attributed to his meaning in America. His stance has, on the one hand, been necessitated by historical conditions, and on the other hand, been grasped as creative possibility. From the very beginning, he was brought to America in chains, and this country has attempted to keep him in this condition in one way or another. His very presence as a *human being* in the United States has always constituted a threat to the majority population. From the point of view of the majority population, he has been simply and purely a legal person, first as a slave defined in terms of property, and then, after the abolition of chattel property, as a citizen who had to seek legal redress before he could use the common facilities of the country—water fountains, public accommodations, restaurants, schools, etc. There is no need to repeat this history; it is too well known, and the point I wish to make is more subtle than these specific issues, important as they may be.

In addition to the image and historical reality of Africa one must add, as another persisting datum, the involuntary presence and orientation as a religious meaning. I have stated elsewhere the importance of the involuntary structure of the religious consciousness in the terms of oppugnancy.[10] In the case of the slaves America presented a bizarre reality, not simply because of the novelty of a radical change of status and culture, but equally because their presence as slaves pointed to a radical contradiction within the dominant culture itself. The impact of America was a discovery, but one had little ability to move from the bizarre reality of discovery to the level of general social rules of conduct, which happens in the case of other communities presented with an ultimate discovery. In addition to this, to normalize the condition of slavery would be to deny his existence as a human being.

The slave had to come to terms with the opaqueness of his condition and at the same time oppose it. He had to experience the truth of his negativity and at the same time transform and create *an-other* reality. Given the limitations imposed upon him, he created on the level of his religious consciousness. Not only did this transformation produce new cultural forms, but its significance must be understood from the point of view of the creativity of the transforming process itself.

Three short illustrations of this phenomenon must suffice at this point. Listen to this spiritual:

> He's so high, you can't get over him
> He's so low, you can't get under him
> So round, you can't get around him
> You got to go right through the door

or this poem by a black poet:

> Yet do I marvel at this curious thing
> To make a poet black and bid him sing

or a folk aphorism:

> What do you mean I gotta do that
> Ain't but two things I got to do—Be black and die.

The musical phenomenon, the blues, is another expression of the same consciousness. What is portrayed here is a religious consciousness that has experienced the "hardness" of life, whether the form of that reality be the slave system, God, or simply life itself. It is from such a consciousness that the power to resist and yet maintain one's humanity has emerged. Though the worship and religious life of blacks have often been referred to as forms of escapism, one must always remember that there has always been an integral relationship between the "hardness" of life and the ecstasy of religious worship. It is, in my opinion, an example of what Gaston Bachelard described in Hegelian language as the lithic imagination. Bachelard had reference to the imaginary structure of consciousness that arises in relationship to the natural form of the stone and the manner in which the volitional character of human consciousness is related to this imaginary form.[11] The black community in America has confronted the reality of the historical situation as immutable, impenetrable, but this experience has not produced passivity; it has, rather, found expression as forms of the involuntary and transformative nature of the religious consciousness. In connection with this point, let me illustrate by returning to the meaning of the image and historical reality of Africa.

Over and over again this image has ebbed and flowed in the religious consciousness. It has found expression in music, dance, and political theorizing. There has been an equally persistent war against this image in the religion of black folk. This war against the image of Africa and blackness can be seen in the political and social movements connected with the stratagems of segregation and integration. Even more telling is the history of the names by which this community has chosen to call itself. From African to colored, Negro, Afro-American, and, presently, black. The history of these designations can be seen as a religious history through which this community was coming to terms with a primary symbol of opacity.

Recall the words of G. van der Leeuw. In speaking of religious experience, he said, "Religious experience, in other terms, is concerned with a 'somewhat.' But this assertion often means no more than this 'Somewhat' is merely a vague 'something,' and in order that man may be able to make more significant statements about this 'Somewhat,' it must force itself upon him, oppose it to him as being Something Other. Thus the first statement we can make about religion is that it is a highly exceptional and extremely impressive 'Other.' "[12] From the point of view of religious history, one could say that this community in its own self-interpretation has moved from a vague "somewhat" to the religious experience of a highly exceptional and *extremely impressive* "Other." The contemporary expressions of black power attest to this fact, and the universalizing of this notion in terms of pan-Africanism, negritude, or neo-Marxian and Christian conceptions must equally be noted.

The meaning of the involuntary structure or the opacity of the religious symbol has within this community held together eschatological hopes and the archaic religious consciousness. In both secular and religious groups, new expressions such as Moorish Temple, Black Jews, Black Muslims retain an archaic structure in their religious consciousness, and this structure is never quite settled for; it is there as a datum to be deciphered in the context of their present experience.

C. The Experience and Symbol of God

The sources for my interpretation of the experience of the holy in this community are from the folkloric tradition. By this, I mean an oral tradition that exists in its integrity as an oral tradition, the writing down of which is a concession to scholarship.

These sources are slave narratives, sermons, the words and music of spirituals and the blues, the cycle of Brer Rabbit, and High John the Conqueror stories. These materials reveal a range of religious meanings extending from trickster-transformer hero to High Gods.

To be sure, the imagery of the Bible plays a large role in the symbolic presentations, but to move from this fact to any simplistic notion of blacks as slaves or former slaves converted to Christianity would, I think, miss several important religious meanings.

The biblical imagery was used because it was at hand; it was adapted to and invested with the experience of the slave. Strangely enough, it was the slave who gave a religious meaning to the notions of freedom and land. The deliverance of the children of Israel from the Egyptians became an archetype that enabled him to live with promise.

God for this community appears as an all-powerful and moral deity, though one hardly ever knows why he has willed this or that. God is never, or hardly ever, blamed for the situation of man, for somehow in an inscrutable manner there is a reason for all this. By and large a fundamental distinction is made between God and Jesus Christ. To the extent that the language of Christianity is used, black Americans have held to the Trinitarian distinction, but adherence to this distinction has been for experiential rather than dogmatic reasons. Historians of religion have known for a long time that the Supreme Being appears in differing forms. To be sure, God, the first person of the Trinity, is a powerful creator deity.

It is not so much the dogma of the trinity as it is the modalities of experience of the Trinity that are most important. The experience of God is thus placed within the context of the other images and experiences of black religion. God, as first person of the Trinity, is, of course, a powerful Creator Supreme deity. Though biblical language is used to speak of his historical presence and intervention in history, we neither have a clear Hebraic nor what has become a Christian interpretation of history. I am not implying that the deity is a *deus otiosus* for there is an acceptance of historical reality, but neither in its Hebraic nor traditional Christian mode. We must remember that the historicity of these two traditions was related to the possession of a land, and this has not been the case for blacks in America. In one sense, it is possible to say that their history in America has always presented to them a situation of crisis. The intervention of the deity into their community has not been synonymous with the confirmation of the reality of their being within the structures of America. God has been more often a transformer of their consciousness, the basis for a resource that enabled them to maintain the human image without completely acquiescing to the norms of the majority population. He provided a norm of self-criticism that was not derivative from those who enslaved them. I cite two examples as illustrations:

> When I was very small my people thought I was going to die. Mama used to tell my sister that I was puny and that she didn't think that she would be able to raise me. I used to dream nearly all the time and see all kinds of wild-looking animals. I would nearly always get scared and nervous.
>
> Some time later I got heavy one day and began to die. For days I couldn't eat, I couldn't sleep; even the water I drank seemed to swell in my mouth. A voice said to me one day, "Nora you haven't done what you promised." And again it said, "You saw the sun rise, but you shall die before it goes down." I began to pray. I was making up my bed. A light seemed to come down from heaven, and it looked like it just split me open from my head to my foot. A voice said to me, "Ye are freed and free indeed. My son set you free. Behold, I give you everlasting life."
>
> During all this time I was just dumb. I couldn't speak or move. I heard a moaning sound, and a voice said, "Follow me, my little one, and I will show you the marvelous works of God." I got up, it seems, and started to traveling. I was not my natural self but a little angel. We went and came to a sea of glass, and it was mingled with fire. I opened my mouth and began to pray, "Lord, I will perish in there." Then I saw a path that led through the fire, I journeyed in this path and came to a green pasture where there were a lot of sheep. They were all of the same size and bleated in a mournful tone. A voice spoke to me, and it sounded like a roar of thunder; "Ye are my workmanship and the creation of my hand. I will drive all fears away. Go, and I go with you. You have a deed to your name, and you shall never perish."[13]

Everybody seemed to be getting along well but poor me. I told him so, I said, "Lord, it looks like you come to everybody's house but mine. I never bother my neighbors or cause any disturbance. I have lived as it is becoming a poor widow woman to live and yet, Lord, it looks like I have a harder time than anybody." When I said this, something told me to turn around and look. I put my bundle down and looked towards the east part of the world. A voice spoke to me as plain as day, but it was inward and said, "I am a time-God working after the counsel of my own will. In due time I will bring all things to you. Remember and cause your heart to sing."

When God struck me dead with his power I was living on Fourteenth Avenue. It was the year of the Centennial. I was in my house alone, and I declare unto you, when his power struck me I died. I fell out on the floor flat on my back. I could neither speak nor move, for my tongue stuck to the roof of my mouth; my jaws were locked and my limbs were stiff.[14]

These two narratives are illustrative of the inner dynamics of the conversion experience. The narratives combine and interweave the ordinary events with the transformation of the religious consciousness. It is not merely a case of God acting in history, for the historical events are not the locus of the activity, but then neither do we have a complete lack of concern for historical events in favor of a mystification of the consciousness. It is the combination of these two structures that is distinctive in these narratives; clues such as these might help us to understand the specific nature of the black religious consciousness.

But this structure of the deity is present in non-Christian movements among the blacks; the transforming power of the deity may be seen among the Black Muslims and the Black Jews. This quality of the presence of the deity has enabled blacks to affirm the historical mode by seeing it more in terms of an initiatory structure than in terms of a progressivistic or evolutionary understanding of temporality.

Continuing with the Christian language of the Trinity, Jesus has been experienced more in the form of a dema-deity[15] than as conquering hero. One could make the case that this understanding of Jesus Christ has always been present in the history of the Western church, but it is clear that this image of the Christ has not been experienced as a symbol of the total Western culture since the seventeenth century. Christ as fellow sufferer, as the little child, as the companion, as the man who understands—these symbols of Christ have been dominant. For example, the spirituals:

> I told Jesus it would be all right if he changed my name
> Jesus told me that the world would hate me if he changed my name

or

> Poor little Jesus boy, made him to be born in a manger.
> World treated him so mean
> Treats me mean too. . . .

But there is more than the biblical imagery as a datum. In the folklore we see what appears as the trickster, transformer hero. More than often he appears in the Brer Rabbit cycle of stories, which seem related to similar West Africa stories of Ananse, the Spider.

This is one of the cycles of the Brer Rabbit stories:[16] Brer Rabbit, Brer Fox, and Brer Wolf were experiencing a season of drought. They met to decide the proper action to take. It was decided that they should dig a well so that they would have a plenteous supply of water. Brer Rabbit said that he thought this was a very good plan, although he did not wish to participate in the digging of the well because he said that he arose early in the morning and drank the dew from the grass, and thus did not wish to participate in the arduous task of digging. Brer Fox and Brer Wolf proceeded with their task and completed the digging of the deep well. After the well was dug, Brer Rabbit arose early each morning and went to the well and drank his fill, pretending all the time that he was drinking the morning dew. After a while, Brer Fox and Brer Wolf became suspicious of Brer Rabbit and set about to spy upon him. Sure enough, they caught him one morning drinking from their well. They subjected him to some punishment, which we need not go into for the point of the story has been made.

Brer Rabbit is not simply lazy and clever; it is clear that he feels he has something else to do—that life cannot be dealt with in purely conventional terms and commit-tee meetings. In many respects the preacher in the black community exhibits many of the traits of Brer Rabbit, and it was often the preacher who kept alive the possibility for another life, or who protested and affirmed by doing nothing.

One other instance should be mentioned: High John, the Conqueror. Now it is stated explicitly in the folklore that High John came dancing over the waves from Africa, or that he was in the hold of the slave ship. High John is a flamboyant character. He possesses great physical strength and conquers more by an audacious display of his power than through any subtlety or cunning. He is the folkloric side of a conquering Christ, though with less definite goals.

The essential element in the expression and experience of God is his transforming ability. This is true in the case of God as absolute moral ruler as well as in Brer Rabbit or High John the Conqueror. Insofar as society at large was not an agent of transformation, the inner resources of consciousness and the internal structures of his own history and community became not simply the locus for new symbols but the basis for a new consciousness for the black.

It is therefore the religious consciousness of the black in America that is the repository of who he is, where he has been, and where he is going. A purely existential analysis cannot do justice to this religious experience. Probably a new interpretation of American religion would come about if careful attention is given to the religious history of this strange American.

NOTES

1. W. E. B. Du Bois, ed., *The Negro Church* (Atlanta, Ga.: Atlanta University Press, 1903); Carter G. Woodson, *The History of the Negro Church* (Washington, D.C.: Associated Publish-ers, 1921); Benjamin E. Mays and Joseph Nicholson, *The Negro Church* (New York: Russell & Russell, 1969); Arthur Fauset, *Black Gods of the Metropolis* (Philadelphia: University of Penn-sylvania Press, 1944; London: Oxford University Press, 1944; E. Franklin Frazier, *The Negro*

Church in America (New York: Schocken Books, 1962); Howard M. Brotz, *The Black Jews of Harlem* (New York: Schocken Books, 1970); C. Eric Lincoln, *The Black Muslims in America* (New York: Beacon Press, 1961); and E. U. Essien-Udom, *Black Nationalism: A Search for an Identity in America* (Chicago: University of Chicago Press, 1962).

2. Pierre Verger, *Notes sur le culte des Orisa et Vodum à Bahia la Baie de tous les saints au Bresil et à l'ancienne Côtes des esclaves en Afrique* (Dakar, 1957).

3. Alfred Metraux, *Le Vaudou haitien* (Paris, 1958).

4. See W. E. B. Du Bois, *The Souls of Black Folk* (Chicago, 1903).

5. See Verger.

6. Daryll Forde, "The Cultural Map of West Africa: Successive Adaptations to Tropical Forests and Grassland," in *Cultures and Societies of Africa*, ed. S. and P. Ottenborg (New York, 1960).

7. Joseph Greenberg makes a similar argument for the structural similarity of West African languages in his *Studies in African Linguistic Classification* (New Haven, Conn., 1955).

8. See especially Edward W. Blyden's *Christianity, Islam and the Negro Race* (London, 1887). Blyden, though born in the Virgin Islands and ordained as a Presbyterian minister, was one of the early leaders in pan-Africanism. It is interesting to note that he set the problem within a religious context. The publication of his work is directly related to the problems created in the 1840s by the passage of the Fugitive Slave Law and the Dred Scott decision of the United States Supreme Court.

9. See Edmund D. Cronon, *Black Moses* (Madison: University of Wisconsin Press, 1962).

10. See Charles H. Long, "Prolegomenon to a Religious Hermeneutic," *History of Religions*, 6, no. 3 (February 1967): 254–64.

11. See Gaston Bachelard, *La Terre et les reveries de la volonte* (Paris, 1948).

12. G. van der Leeuw, *Religion in Essence and Manifestation*, trans. J. E. Turner (London, 1933), p. 23.

13. Clifton H. Johnson, ed., *God Struck Me Dead, Religious Conversion Experiences and Autobiographies of Ex-Slaves*, with a foreword by Paul Radin (Philadelphia: Pilgrim Press, 1969), pp. 62–63.

14. Ibid., pp. 58–59.

15. Adolf E. Jensen defined this religious structure as a result of his researches in Ceram. See his *Hainuwele* (Frankfurt, 1939) and *Myth and Cult among Primitive People* (Chicago, 1963). I do not wish to say that Jesus Christ is understood in any religious structure that one should begin the deciphering of the meaning of Jesus. Essential to this structure is the notion of the deity as companion and creator, a deity related more to the human condition than deities of the sky, and the subjection of this deity to death at the hands of men.

16. See T. F. Crane, "Plantation Folklore," in *The Negro and His Folklore* (Austin, Tex., 1967), pp. 157–67.

SELECTED BIBLIOGRAPHY FOR FURTHER READING

Asante, Molefi K. *The Afrocentric Idea.* Philadelphia: Temple University Press, 1987.

Long, Charles H. *Significations: Signs, Symbols, and Images in the Interpretation of Religion.* Philadelphia: Fortress, 1986.

Marks, Morton. "Uncovering Ritual Structures in Afro-American Music" in *Religious Movements in Contemporary America.* ed. Irving I. Zaretsky and Mark P. Leone. Princeton: Princeton University Press, 1974.

Smith, Theophus H. *Conjuring Culture: Biblical Formations of Black Culture*. New York: Oxford University Press, 1994.

Thompson, Robert Farris. *Flash of the Spirit: African & Afro-American Art & Philosophy*. New York: Vintage, 1983.

Chapter Two

African Americans, Exodus, and the American Israel

Albert J. Raboteau

The biblical story of the departure of Israelites from Egyptian bondage, the "Exodus," has frequently been deployed by beleaguered Christian groups as a hope-inspiring paradigm of the divine will to effect deliverance and justice for the oppressed. In this piece, historian Albert J. Raboteau explores the use of this paradigm in American religious history and, in particular, its appropriation among African American Christians.

•

Exodus

No single story captures more clearly the distinctiveness of African American Christianity than that of the Exodus. From the earliest days of colonization, white Christians had represented their journey across the Atlantic to America as the exodus of a New Israel; slaves identified themselves as the Old Israel, suffering bondage under a new Pharaoh. White American preachers, politicians, and other orators found in the story of Exodus a rich source of metaphors to explicate the unfolding history of the nation. Each section of the narrative—bondage in Egypt, rescue at the Red Sea, wandering in the wilderness, and entrance into the Promised Land—provided a typological map to reconnoiter the moral terrain of American society. John Winthrop, the leader of the great Puritan expedition to Massachusetts Bay Colony, set the pattern in his famous "Modell of Christian Charity" sermon composed on board ship in 1630. Having elaborated the settlers' covenantal obligations to God, echoing the Sinaitic covenant of Israel with Yahweh, Winthrop concluded his discourse with a close paraphrase of Moses' farewell instruction to Israel (Deuteronomy 30):

> Beloved there is now sett before us life, and good, deathe and evill in that wee are Commaunded this day to love the Lord our God, and to love one another, to walke in his wayes and to keepe his Commaundements and his Ordinance, and his lawes, and the Articles of our Covenant with him that wee may live and be multiplied, and that the Lord our God may blesse us in the land whither we goe to possesse it: But if our heartes shall turne away soe that wee will not obey, but shall be seduced and worship . . . other Gods, our pleasures, and proffitts, and serve them; it is propounded unto this day, wee shall surely perishe out of the good Land whither wee passe over this vast Sea to possesse it.[1]

Notice the particular application that Winthrop draws from the Exodus story: possession of the land is contingent upon observing the moral obligations of the covenant with God. It is a mark of the greatness of Winthrop's address that the obligations he emphasizes are justice, mercy, affection, meekness, gentleness, patience, generosity, and unity—not the qualities usually associated with taking or keeping possession of a land. Later and lesser sermons would extol much more aggressive virtues. But even in Winthrop's address, there is an explicit notion of reciprocity between God's will and American destiny: "God has made a contract with us. If we live up to our part of the bargain, so will he." The idea of reciprocity between divine providence and America's destiny had tremendous hortatory power, and Puritan preachers exploited it to the full over the next century and more in the jeremiad. In sermon after sermon, a succession of New England divines deciphered droughts, epidemics, Indian attacks, and other misfortunes as tokens of God's displeasure over the sins of the nation. Unless people took the opportunity to humble themselves, repent, and reform, they might expect much more of the same. Implicit, however, in this understanding was the danger of seeing the will of God in the actions of America's settlers. Winthrop was too good a Puritan to succumb to this temptation. Protected by his belief in the total sovereignty of God, he knew that the relationship between God's will and human action was one-sided and that the proper human attitude was trust in God, not confidence in man. God's will was the measure of America's deeds, not vice versa. Of course, no American preacher or politician would have disagreed, but as time went on the salient features of the Exodus story changed. The farther Americans moved from the precariousness of Egypt toward the security of the Promised Land, the greater the danger of relaxing the tension between America's destiny and God's will.

The change is clear when we compare the tone of Winthrop's "Modell of Christian Charity" with that of an election sermon entitled "The United States Elevated to Glory and Honor," preached by Ezra Stiles in 1783. Flushed with excitement over the success of the Revolution, Stiles dwelled at length on the unfolding destiny of the new nation. Quoting, like Winthrop, from the book of Deuteronomy, Stiles struck a celebratory rather than a hortatory note:

> And to make thee high above all nations which he hath made, in praise, and in name, and in honour; and that thou mayest be an holy people unto the Lord thy God." . . . I have assumed [this] text as introductory to a discourse upon the political welfare of God's American Israel, and as allusively prophetic of the future prosperity and splendour of the United States. . . . Already does the new constellation of the United States begin to realize this glory. It has already risen to an acknowledged sovereignty among the republicks and kingdoms of the world. And we have reason to hope, and I believe to expect, that God has still greater blessings in store for this vine which his own right hand hath planted, to make us "high among the nations in praise, and in name, and in honour.[2]

Stiles went on at great length to identify the reasons for his optimism about America's present and future preeminence, including the fact that "in our civil constitutions, those impediments are removed which obstruct the progress of society towards perfection." It's a long way from Winthrop's caution to Stiles's confidence, from an

"Errand in the Wilderness" to "progress towards perfection." In Stiles's election sermon we can perceive God's New Israel becoming the Redeemer Nation. The destiny of New Israel was to reach the pinnacle of perfection and to carry liberty and the gospel around the globe. In tandem with this exaggerated vision of American destiny came an exaggerated vision of human capacity. In an increasingly confident and prosperous nation, it was difficult to avoid shifting the emphasis from divine sovereignty to human ability. Historian Conrad Cherry has succinctly summarized the change in perception of American destiny: "Believing that she had escaped the wickedness of the Old World and the guilt of the past, God's New Israel would find it all too easy to ignore her vices and all too difficult to admit a loss of innocence."[3] Except for the presence of another, a darker, Israel:

> America, America, foul and indelible is thy stain! Dark and dismal is the cloud that hangs over thee, for thy cruel wrongs and injuries to the fallen sons of Africa. The blood of her murdered ones cries to heaven for vengeance against Thee. . . . You may kill, tyrannize, and oppress as much as you choose, until our cry shall come up before the throne of God; for I am firmly persuaded, that he will not suffer you to quell the proud, fearless and undaunted spirits of the Africans forever; for in his own time, he is able to plead our cause against you, and to pour upon you the ten plagues of Egypt.[4]

So wrote Maria Stewart, a free black reform activist in Boston during the 1830s. These words, written in 1831, were addressed to an America that projected itself as the probable site of the coming millennium, Christ's thousand-year reign of peace and justice. Slaves and free blacks like Maria Stewart located themselves in a different part of the Exodus story than white Christians. From their perspective America was Egypt, and as long as it continued to enslave and oppress black Israel, America's destiny was in jeopardy. America stood under the judgment of God, and unless it repented, the death and destruction visited upon biblical Egypt would be repeated here. The retribution envisaged was quite literal, as Mary Livermore, a white govern- ess, discovered when she overheard a prayer uttered by Aggy, the housekeeper, whose daughter had just been brutally whipped by her master:

> Thar's a day a comin'! Thar's a day a comin' . . . I hear de rumblin' ob de chariots! I see de flashin' ob de guns! White folks' blood is a runnin' on de ground like a riber, an' de dead's heaped up dat high! . . . Oh, Lor'! hasten de day when de blows, an' de bruises, an' de aches, an' de pains, shall come to de white folks, an' de buzzards shall eat 'em as dey's dead in de streets. Oh, Lor'! roll on de chariots, an' gib de black people rest an' peace.[5]

Nor did slaves share the exaggerated optimism of white Americans about human ability. Trapped in a system from which there seemed little, if any, possibility of deliverance by human actions, they emphasized trusting in the Lord instead of trusting in man. Sermon after sermon and prayer after prayer echoed the words that Moses spoke on the banks of the Red Sea: "Stand still and see the salvation of the Lord." Though the leaders of the main three slave revolts, Gabriel in 1800, Denmark Vesey in 1822, and Nat Turner in 1831, all depended on the Bible to justify and motivate rebellion, the major import of Exodus was to nurture internal resistance, not external revolution, among the slaves.

The story of Exodus contradicted the claim made by white Christians that God intended Africans to be slaves. Exodus proved that slavery was against God's will and that slavery inevitably would end, even though the when and the how remained hidden in the providence of God. Christian slaves thus applied the Exodus story, whose end they knew, to their own experience of slavery, which had not yet ended, and so gave meaning and purpose to lives threatened by senseless and demeaning brutality. Exodus functioned as an archetypal myth for the slaves. The sacred history of God's liberation of his people would be or was being reenacted in the American South. A white Union Army chaplain working among freedmen in Decatur, Alabama, commented disapprovingly on the slaves' fascination with Exodus: "There is no part of the Bible with which they are so familiar as the story of the deliverance of Israel. Moses is their *ideal* of all that is high, and noble, and perfect, in man. I think they have been accustomed to regard Christ not so much in the light of a *spiritual* Deliverer, as that of a second Moses who would eventually lead *them* out of their prison-house of bondage."[6]

Thus, in the story of Israel's flight from Egypt, the slaves predicted a future radically different from their present. In times of despair, they remembered Exodus and found hope enough to endure the enormity of their suffering.

By appropriating the story of Exodus as their own story, black Christians articulated their own sense of peoplehood. Exodus symbolized their common history and common destiny. It would be hard to exaggerate the intensity of their identification with the children of Israel. AME pastor William Paul Quinn demonstrated how literal the metaphor of Exodus could become when he exhorted black Christians, "Let us comfort and encourage one another, and keep singing and shouting, great is the Holy One of Israel in the midst of us. Come thou Great Deliverer, once more awake thine almighty arm, and set thy African captives free."[7] As Quinn reveals, it was prayer and worship services that made the connection so immediate. Sermons, prayers, and songs recreated in the imagination of successive generations the travail and triumph of Israel.

Exodus became dramatically real, especially in the songs and prayer meetings of the slaves who reenacted the story as they shuffled in the ring dance they called the "Shout." In the ecstasy of worship, time and distance collapsed, and the slaves became the children of Israel. With the Hebrews, they traveled dry-shod through the Red Sea; they, too, saw Pharaoh's army "get drownded"; they stood beside Moses on Mount Pisgah and gazed out over the Promised Land; they crossed Jordan under Joshua and marched with him round the walls of Jericho. Their prayers for deliverance resonated with the experiential power of these liturgical dramas.

Identification with Israel, then, gave the slaves a communal identity as special, divinely favored people. This identity stood in stark contrast with racist propaganda depicting them as inferior to whites, destined by nature and providence to the status of slaves. The Exodus, the Promised Land, and Canaan were inextricably linked in their minds with the idea of freedom. Canaan referred not only to the condition of freedom but also to the territory of freedom, the North or Canada. As Frederick Douglass recalled, "A keen observer might have detected in our repeated singing of 'O Canaan, sweet Canaan,/I am bound for the land of Canaan,' something more than a hope of reaching heaven. We meant to reach the *North*, and the North was our Canaan."[8] Slaveowners, too, were well aware that the Exodus story could be a source of unflattering and perhaps subversive analogies. It took no genius to identify Pharaoh's army in the slave song "My army cross ober, My army cross ober,/O Pharaoh's army drownded."

The slaves' faith that God would free them just as he had Israel of old was validated by Emancipation. "Shout the glad tidings o'er Egypt's dark sea,/Jehovah has triumphed, his people are free!" the former slaves sang in celebration. But it did not take long for the freedmen to realize that Canaan Land still lay somewhere in the distance. "There must be no looking back to Egypt," a band of refugee slaves behind Union lines were instructed by a slave preacher in 1862. "Israel passed forty years in the wilderness, because of their unbelief. What if we cannot see right off the green fields of Canaan, Moses could not. He could not even see how to cross the Red Sea. If we would have greater freedom of body, we must free ourselves from the shackles of sin. . . . We must snap the chain of Satan, and educate ourselves and our children."[9] But as time went on and slavery was succeeded by other forms of racial oppression, black Americans seemed trapped in the wilderness no matter how hard they tried to escape. Former slave Charles Davenport voiced the despair of many when he recalled, "De preachers would exhort us dat us was de chillen o' Israel in de wilderness an' de Lord done sent us to take dis land o' milk and honey. But how us gwine-a take land what's already been took?"[10] When race relations reached a new low in the 1880s and 1890s, several black leaders turned to Africa as the Promised Land. Proponents of emigration, such as Alexander Crummell and Edward Wilmot Blyden, urged African Americans to abandon the American wilderness for an African Zion. Few black Americans, however, heeded the call to emigrate to Africa; most continued to search for their Promised Land here. And as decade succeeded decade, they repeated the story that had for so many years kept their hopes alive. It was, then, a very old and evocative tradition that Martin Luther King echoed in his last sermon:

> We've got some difficult days ahead. But it really doesn't matter with me now. Because I've been to the mountaintop. Like anybody I would like to live a long life. Longevity has its place. But I'm not concerned about that now. I just want to do God's will. And He's allowed me to go up to the mountain. And I've *seen* the Promised Land. And I may not get there with you. But I want you to know tonight that we as a people will get to the Promised land.[11]

Between King's vision and Winthrop's vision of this American Promised Land, there stretches a period of more than three hundred years. The people who Winthrop addressed long ago took possession of their Promised Land. The people who King addressed still wait to enter theirs. For three centuries, white and black Americans have dwelled in the same land. For at least two of those centuries, they have shared the same religion. And yet during all those years, their national and religious identities have been radically opposed. It need not have been so. After all, Winthrop's version of Exodus and King's were not far apart. Both understood that charity is the charter that gives title to the Promised Land. Both taught that mercy, gentleness, and justice are the agreed upon terms for occupancy. Both remembered that the conditions of the contract had been set by God, not man. Occasionally, the two visions have come close to coinciding, as they did in the antislavery stance of the early Evangelicals, or in the abolitionist movement, or in Lincoln's profound realization that Americans were an *"almost* chosen people," or in the civil rights movement of our own era. Yet despite these moments of coherence, the meaning of Exodus for America remained fundamentally ambiguous. Was it Israel or was it Egypt?

NOTES

1. Reprinted in Conrad Cherry, ed., *God's New Israel: Religious Interpretations of American Destiny* (Englewood Cliffs, N.J.: Prentice-Hall, 1971), 43.

2. Reprinted in ibid., 83–84.

3. Ibid., 66.

4. Maria W. Stewart, *Religion and the Pure Principles of Morality, the Sure Foundation On Which We Must Build* (Boston, 1831); reprinted in Marilyn Richardson, ed., *Maria W. Stewart, America's First Black Woman Political Writer: Essays and Speeches* (Bloomington: Indiana University Press, 1987), 39.

5. Mary A. Livermore, *My Story of the War* (Hartford, Conn., 1889), 260–61.

6. W. G. Kephart, letter of May 9, 1864, Decatur, Ala., American Missionary Association Archives, Amistad Research Center, Tulane University, New Orleans.

7. W. Paul Quinn, *The Sword of Truth Going "Forth Conquering and to Conquer..."* (1834); reprinted in Dorothy Porter, ed., *Early Negro Writing, 1760–1837* (Boston: Beacon Press, 1971), 635.

8. Frederick Douglass, *The Life and Times of Frederick Douglass*, rev. ed. (1892); reprint, London: Collier-Macmillan, 1962), 159–60.

9. *American Missionary* 6, no. 2 (February 1862):33.

10. Norman R. Yetman, ed., *Voices from Slavery* (New York: Holt, Rinehart and Winston, 1970), 75.

11. Sermon of April 3, 1968, delivered at Mason Temple, Memphis, Tennessee; reprinted in James M. Washington, ed., *A Testament of Hope: The Essential Writings and Speeches of Martin Luther King, Jr.* (San Francisco: Harper and Row, 1986), 286.

Chapter Three

What Is African American Christianity?

Gayraud S. Wilmore

In the emergent "black consciousness" days of the 1960s and 1970s, many socially critical African Americans disparaged black affiliation with Christianity, declaring it to be "the white man's religion," imposed in distorted, truncated form upon African slaves as a means of social control. At the same time, some black Christians began articulating a statement of their faith which located African Americans equitably within the divine vision of human community, indeed which, because of their historical condition of oppression, identified blacks as particular objects of God's concern. In addition, scholars of the religions of blacks in the United States began writing and speaking of the characteristic ways that blacks expressed their religiosity and gave voice to their faith convictions. However, some African American Christians took exception to what they seemingly saw as segregating and thereby redistorting, retruncating the truth of the faith. They denied the legitimacy of a "black Christianity." In the following piece, noted black scholar and author Gayraud S. Wilmore responds to these issues and objections.

•

Before the reader turns another page, we need to address the problem of terminology. When words such as *African American, Euro-American, White,* and *Black* are used to modify nouns such as *religion* or *Christianity,* many folks are quickly turned off. Most of us like to believe that because we live in the modern world, where everyone wants first to be recognized as a human being who is created in the image of God, there is no reason to classify each other in ways that draw attention to our differences. Why is it necessary, many will ask, to throw up artificial barriers between us by insisting on a Black or African American Christianity instead of just plain Christianity, or Black or White Presbyterians instead of just plain Presbyterians? One might have used these terms in the 1960s and made sense, but why should anyone read this book at the start of the third millennium of the Christian era?

Some will have an even more basic objection. "What," they will ask, "does the Bible have to say about a *Black* Christianity or a *White* Christianity? Show me those terms in my family Bible, Preacher! Then maybe we'll have something to discuss. Otherwise, just talk to me about Christianity, pure and simple, and leave out all that racial and ethnic stuff."

Of course, such a request is not unreasonable; it just happens to be pointless if we're really interested in examining the state of the Christian faith in the world we read about every day in the newspaper. If ever there was anything about Christianity that was "pure and simple," it evaporated sometime before the end of the first century A.D. The way Christianity has come down to us today makes it a very mixed bag of racial/ethnic, or cultural and religious, traditions and understandings that may or may not—depending how they are transmitted and by whom—help someone to know who Jesus Christ is and what he wants his modern-day disciples to believe and do.

Nor is it possible to run to the Bible every time we try to escape this problem. We cannot even hear or tell a simple biblical story about the birth of Jesus, his first sermon in his hometown of Nazareth, or his parable about the man who was robbed on the Jericho road without consciously and unconsciously filtering it through the sieve of our different languages, the time and place of our rearing, our age and gender cohort, our racial, ethnic, and cultural locations in the biosphere, the level of our education, our psychosomatic condition, our economic and social status, our political convictions, and so forth.

The Bible does not speak to us as if we were purely disembodied spirits floating around in some celestial vacuum, but in the only way human beings can hear God's voice and recognize it as truth for themselves. The Bible speaks to us in a way that takes into account all the dirt and grime of our personal and social existence, who we really are in the bathroom as well as the sanctuary, our given time and place in history. If we insist, therefore, that the Scriptures must be the exclusive judge of how the term *Christianity* should or should not be modified, we should at least be aware that the word *Christian* appears only three times in the Bible (Acts 11:26; 26:28; and 1 Peter 4:16), and the word *Christianity* does not appear! We use both these terms to describe the peculiar religion that formed itself, albeit by the power of the Holy Spirit, around the personality and ministry of Jesus long after both he and those who knew him in the flesh had passed off this earthly scene.

So where does all that leave us?

It leaves us with the difficulty that when we use the term *Christianity* we are speaking, whether we intend to or not, as if we were primarily concerned with history, with systems of beliefs, practices, and social structures that have grown up around the memory and teachings of the man called Jesus. Take it or leave it.

Someone will retort, more or less angrily: "Hold on there, Preacher! You're not talking about *me*. I have absolutely no concern about such things. I'm only interested in the pure and unadulterated gospel!"

Well, it's hard to know how to satisfy such a "pure and unadulterated" interest. Because the gospel, that is, the good news about Jesus, comes packaged in the wrappings of so many different kinds of languages, cultures, and ways of looking at reality—some ancient, some modern, and some postmodern—not even its essential message can be extracted without an interpretive posture (something biblical scholars call *hermeneutics*) that comes preliminary to comprehension and involves much more than reading a series of words on a printed page.

Both in ordinary conversation and in technical writing we use the word *Christi-

anity to connote the particular system of beliefs, ritual practices, and sociological characteristics of the religion about Jesus as understood in various contexts. When we speak of Early Christianity, we imply that system in its first two or three centuries; when we speak of Western Christianity, we mean that system as it developed with Rome as its center instead of Constantinople; when we speak of Black Christianity, we refer to that system as it predominates in African and African American communities rather than in European or Euro-American (we'll sometimes use the term *North Atlantic*) communities.

Thus, in the first instance we focus on the religion from the perspective of time; in the second, from the perspective of geographical or geopolitical factors; and in the third, from the perspective of race ethnicity or culture.

In none of these contexts can we pretend that the Bible is the primary and exclusive source of the information we seek. We may, of course, consult Scripture about the particular features of the church in, say, the late first century A.D. But what we learn in the text will tell us very little about Christianity in the Middle Ages, in Puritan New England, or among Negroes in the United States at the beginning of the Civil War. Let us not ask the Bible to do what it was never intended to do.

A Social and Cultural Fact of Life

So it makes little sense to insist that there is no such thing as a Black or an African American Christianity. Even if you want to argue that we're talking about Jesus Christ and not about Christianity, and that Jesus Christ is "the same yesterday and today and forever," as the writer of Heb. 13:8 tells us, we must concede that the way the religion (or faith, if you prefer) about him developed in different times, in various parts of the world, and among diverse peoples is a cultural and societal fact that reasonable people have to take seriously.

We may *profess* that we are interested only in some unadulterated form of the faith that takes no account of these things, but upon an honest investigation we would find it practically impossible to describe that form without certain social and cultural accretions sticking to our description.

We may as well be honest about it. Both the sins and the virtues of humankind are all too obvious in any study of Christianity. There is really no point in being so coy about why and how it developed among African Americans as to reject out of hand the idea of a Black or African American Christianity among other forms of the faith. Is there any reason to doubt that the Holy Spirit, given to lead us into the truth, has been able to use our form as well as other forms? The apostle Paul confessed, "I have become all things to all people, that I might by all means save some" (1 Cor. 9:22).

To speak or write about an African American Christianity is to refer to a social and cultural reality for more than four hundred years in what used to be called the New World; that during most of those years—like it or not—85 to 90 percent of all Black Christians have worshiped with their own race in all-Black conventicles or congregations. Certain characteristics of faith and life, belief and behavior, have resulted from that simple (we probably should say complex) fact. To acknowledge those characteristics and study them is to neither condemn nor commend them. Here we attempt to establish the reasonableness, even the correctness, of this terminology.

The Christianization of Africans in America

In this small study we cannot hope to survey the whole history of Christianity among African Americans in the United States, much less among African Americans in Canada, the Caribbean, and Central and South America. And unfortunately, we have to leave out altogether what Christianity looked like in Africa, particularly in Egypt, Ethiopia, and Nubia, almost a thousand years before Europeans began in earnest to explore the west and east coasts of the continent of our ancestors. Even apart from these important considerations, we would have more than could be contained in a much larger work if we were to discuss Black religion that has existed in all parts of our Western Hemisphere for hundreds of years—sometimes as Christianity, sometimes in forms assumed to be antagonistic to Christianity, sometimes as a mixture of Christianity and some other religion—notably as neo-African cults and sects. All of that is a part of the whole story, but the whole story will have to be left for another book.

Slavery and Christianity

At first the English settlers of the North American colonies did not intend to make their slaves Christians. That was considered a dangerous practice, for a baptized slave might get the foolish idea that freedom in Christ (Gal. 5:1) had to include freedom from bondage. The conversion of slaves was also thought to be unreasonable, because who would suppose that people who were believed to be little more than savages could understand the Christian religion well enough to be benefitted by it?

There were, however, always a few White people who insisted on trying to convert African slaves. The bishops of London, prelates of the Anglican Church, felt some responsibility and instructed priests of the Church of England in the colonies to minister to Black slaves. The Society of Friends, or Quakers, tried to give them religious instruction. Beginning with Reverend Samuel Davies in Virginia, even the Presbyterians showed some interest. By 1757, Davies reported that he had baptized at least 150 Negroes, after preaching to them for about eighteen months.

The major credit for getting a revival started among the slaves in the South must go to the Separatist Baptists. They were rough-hewn, evangelistically minded frontier preachers, many of whom came from New England, who built many churches in the plantation country of the Carolinas and Georgia. There was also a group called "Methodist societies" that broke away from the Church of England after the Revolutionary War and encouraged the slaves to join them and even preach to White people. These two denominations, the Baptists and the Methodists, made the most consistent and enthusiastic effort to Christianize the Africans in North America. After 1750, they were attracting increasing numbers of slaves to their services—mostly to the displeasure of many slaveholders who correctly suspected that only mischief could come out of this kind of imprudent evangelism.

Scholars are now fairly confident that the first slaves to become Christians, and many who came after them, held on to certain features of the religions they or their parents had practiced in Africa. In Africa, they had recognized a Supreme or High God. That concept was not new to them. They also had practiced assembling for prayer, ritual worship, and a form of water baptism, so some aspects of Christian belief and practice were not difficult for them to accept.

Where they adopted new ideas and rituals that were similar to the old ones they knew back home, the African forms were strengthened rather than discarded, although it is more accurate to say that they were gradually transformed. The Africanized Christianity that flourished on southern plantations, often to the disgust and dismay of the White missionaries, included some characteristics that were unfamiliar to White Christians. For example, there was much dancing and singing in the African style of "call and response"; drumming (whenever permitted, for the masters were afraid that drums might signal revolt); elaborate nighttime funeral customs; spirit possession (or what we later called "getting happy"); and conversion experiences that involved flying, traveling great distances, or encountering spirit guides, of one kind or another, in dreams and visions.

Bishop Daniel A. Payne of the African Methodist Episcopal Church found the "ring shout," an unmistakable retention from the African past, being practiced in urban African Methodist Episcopal (AME) congregations well into the late nineteenth century.[1] It is now the twenty-first century, but we wouldn't have to search very hard in most American cities to find something very close to the ring shout today.

Black Christianity continued to retain African features, particularly where the Whites granted Black preachers the freedom to organize "independent" Black congregations. The African Baptist or Bluestone Baptist Church appeared in 1758 near present-day Mecklenburg, Virginia; and in 1773, slave preachers David George and George Lisle had a slave congregation at Silver Bluff, South Carolina, just across the Savannah River from Augusta, Georgia. There was a flourishing congregation in Williamsburg, Virginia, as early as 1776. We can assume that these were all Christian churches that had a decided African twist!

In the North, Black Methodist and Episcopal churches were founded in Philadelphia by Richard Allen and Absalom Jones before 1794. A group of African Methodists had split from the White St. George's Methodist Church in Philadelphia seven years before and were quickly followed by Black members of White congregations in Baltimore, New York City, Wilmington, Charleston, and elsewhere. A fever for independent churches, under the leadership of Black pastors, was abroad in the free African American communities of the North. Such freedom was, of course, violently repressed in the south for many years before the Civil War, although a few independent churches flourished under White surveillance. But in the North most African American converts increasingly became members of churches led by preachers of their own color. In the South, where the slaves continued to worship with their masters in segregated pews, many nonordained Black preachers carried on an "invisible institution" behind the backs of the slaveowners and were ready to claim their people as soon as emancipation came.

NOTE

1. The author and publisher have made every attempt to document and research the quoted material included in this revised edition. Since the publication of the first edition, most of the author's research, which was conducted at the Presbyterian Historical Society in Philadelphia and the Schomburg Center in New York City, is now inaccessible. "When I wrote the book in 1980," says Wilmore, "I was probably influenced by the success of Nathan T. Huggins's *Black Odyssey: The African American Ordeal in Slavery* (New York: Random House, 1978), which has no notes. . . . The style is conversational and storytelling rather than a work of 'scientific historiography.' "

Chapter Four

The Religious Dimension
"The Black Sacred Cosmos"

C. Eric Lincoln and Lawrence H. Mamiya

Much of the discussion concerning the spirituality of African Americans has centered around their identity as descendants of Africa, and the question of their religio-cultural inheritance from that source. C. Eric Lincoln and Lawrence H. Mamiya enter the discussion with the affirmation that there is a pervasive residual African organizing framework that informs ways of knowing, ways of apprehending and managing reality; it influences devotional options and expressive behaviors. It is in large measure constitutive of African American identity, especially their religious identity. Scholar and author Leonard Barrett refers to this as "soul force"; Charles Long speaks of "the archaic religious consciousness."[1] Lincoln and Mamiya adopt the terminology of author Mechal Sobel and designate this factor as the "black sacred cosmos."

•

The black sacred cosmos or the religious world view of African Americans is related both to their African heritage, which envisaged the whole universe as sacred, and to their conversion to Christianity during slavery and its aftermath. It has been only in the past twenty years that scholars of African American history, culture, and religion have begun to recognize that black people created their own unique and distinctive forms of culture and world views as parallels rather than replications of the culture in which they were involuntary guests.[2] As slaves on the farms and plantations, then as domestic servants in white households, black people were privy to some of the most intimate aspects of white life and culture, from worship to sexual behavior; but very few whites knew anything about black people or their culture, or cared to. In fact, some scholars have viewed aspects of black cultural creations as aberrational attempts to mimic mainstream white culture.[3] Other scholars have claimed that "The Negro is only an American and nothing else. He has no values and culture to guard and protect."[4] Such arguments seem unwilling to grant to African Americans the minimum presuppositions all other hyphenated Americans are permitted to take for granted, which is to say that their origins were elsewhere, and that coming from elsewhere, if they have a viable history, they must also have an effective culture. That a large gulf separated the black world from the expectations of the white is undeniable, but hardly inexplicable. Culture is the sum of the options for creative survival. Two hundred and fifty years of slavery were followed by one hundred years of official and unofficial segregation in the South and the North. Even today the gulf persists, bolstered in large measure by racial segregation in the place of residence, education, religion, and social life.[5] However, the more limited the options for approved participation in the cultural mainstream, the more refined and satisfying become the alternatives to those excluded from the approved norms.

Depending on the culture and history of a particular African-related religious tradition, different sacred object(s) or figure(s) will be at the center of the black sacred cosmos. For the more African-based syncretic religions of the Caribbean and Latin America like the Voudou of Haiti, the Obeia of Jamaica, the Santeria of Cuba, and the Candomble and Umbanda of Brazil, African deities and spiritual forces played a more prominent role in the rituals and worship of the people.[6] For African American Christianity, the Christian God ultimately revealed in Jesus of Nazareth dominated the black sacred cosmos. While the structure of beliefs for black Christians were the same orthodox beliefs as of white Christians, there were also different degrees of emphasis and valences given to certain particular theological views. For example, the Old Testament notion of God as an avenging, conquering, liberating paladin remains a formidable anchor of the faith in most black churches. The older the church or the more elderly its congregation, the more likely the demand for the exciting imagery and the personal involvement of God in history is likely to be. The direct relationship between the holocaust of slavery and the notion of divine rescue colored the theological perceptions of black laity and the themes of black preaching in a very decisive manner, particularly in those churches closest to the experience. Nonetheless, as Henry Mitchell, James Cone, and Gayraud Wilmore have all agreed, throughout black religious history the reality of Jesus as the Son of God made flesh finds a deep response in black faith and worship. The experience of oppression is more likely to find immediate resonance with the incarnational view of the suffering, humiliation, death, and eventual triumph of Jesus in the resurrection than with an abstract concept of an impersonal God.[7] Another example of this difference in emphasis concerned the greater weight given to the biblical views of the importance of human personality and human equality implicit in "children of God."[8] In light of the trauma of being officially defined by the U.S. Constitution as "three-fifths" human, and treated in terms of that understanding, the struggle of the African American people to affirm and establish their humanity and their worth as persons has a long history. The black Christians who formed the historic black churches also knew implicitly that their understanding of Christianity, which was premised on the rock of antiracial discrimination, was more authentic than the Christianity practiced in white churches.

A major aspect of black Christian belief is found in the symbolic importance given to the word "freedom." Throughout black history the term "freedom" has found a deep religious resonance in the lives and hopes of African Americans. Depending on the time and the context, the implications of freedom were derived from the nature of the exigency. During slavery it meant release from bondage; after emancipation it meant the right to be educated, to be employed, and to move about freely from place to place. In the twentieth century, freedom means social, political, and economic justice. From the very beginning of the black experience in America, one critical denotation of freedom has remained constant: Freedom has always meant the absence of any restraint that might compromise one's responsibility to God. The notion has persisted that if God calls you to discipleship, God calls you to freedom. And that God wants you free because God made you for Himself and in His image. Although generations of white preachers and exhorters developed an amazing complex of arguments aimed at avoiding so obvious a conclusion, it was a dictum securely anchored in the black man's faith and indelibly engraved on his psyche. A well-known black spiritual affirms that:

> Before I'll be a slave
> I'll be buried in my grave
> And go home to my Father
> and be free. . . .

Implicit is the notion that unfreedom puts at risk the promise of salvation. No person can serve two masters, and freedom as a condition of spiritual readiness was no less critical to the religious strategies of Martin Luther King, Jr., than to those of Richard Allen, Nat Turner, Sojourner Truth, and Fannie Lou Hamer. Each person developed a modus vivendi consistent with their times and the resources at hand. Their objectives were the same: freedom to be as God had intended all men and women to be. Free to belong to God.

For whites, freedom has bolstered the value of American individualism: to be free to pursue one's destiny without political or bureaucratic interference or restraint. But for African Americans, freedom has always been communal in nature. In Africa, the destiny of the individual was linked to that of the tribe or the community in an intensely interconnected security system. In America, black people have seldom been perceived or treated as individuals; they have usually been dealt with as "representatives" of their "race," an external projection. Hence, the communal sense of freedom has an internal African rootage curiously reinforced by hostile social convention imposed from outside on all African Americans as a caste. But Dr. Martin Luther King's jubilant cry of "Free at last, free at last, thank God Almighty, we are free at last," echoed the understanding black folk always had with the Almighty God, whose impatience with unfreedom matched their own.[9] In song, word, and deed, freedom has always been the superlative value of the black sacred cosmos. The message of the Invisible Church was, however articulated, *God wants you free!*

Above all, the core experience of the black sacred cosmos was the personal conversion of the individual believer. The Christianity that was spread among slaves during the First and Second Awakenings was an evangelical Christianity that stressed personal conversion through a deep regenerating experience, being "born again." The spiritual journey began with an acknowledgment of personal sinfulness and unworthiness and ended in an emotional experience of salvation by God through the Holy Spirit. The rebirth meant a change, a fundamental reorientation in the approach to life. While white Christians also stressed personal conversion, the historical and narrative evidence indicate that the black conversion and visionary experience was of a qualitatively different level. As Mechal Sobel has argued in her analysis of the black Baptist's cosmos, "black religious experiences began to be singled out as particularly ecstatic by white Baptists, signifying consciousness of a difference."[10] As time passed, the black-white difference intensified. "Analysis of the black visionary experiences indicate," wrote Sobel, "that they were very different from the outset, and that their uniqueness was highlighted as the whites grew less concerned with spiritual journeys."[11]

We can also extend Sobel's argument about the forging of a new cosmos from the seventeenth to the early nineteenth centuries that "united African and Baptist elements in a new whole."[12] What was really created was a black sacred cosmos that cut across denominational lines—largely Baptist and Methodist at first, but also Roman Catholic, Pentecostal, and others in later years. Wherever black people were gathered in significant enough numbers, the distinct quality of a shared Afro-Christian religious world view and faith was felt. Even in predominantly white denominations with a million or more black members like the United Methodist Church and the Roman Catholic Church, the surges and eruptions of the black sacred cosmos were constant and influential.[13] A qualitatively different cultural form of expressing Christianity is found in most black churches, regardless of denomination, to this day.

Culture is the form of religion and religion is the heart of culture. Paul Tillich's insight about the relationship between religion and culture is important in a discussion of the black sacred cosmos.[14] Religion is expressed in cultural forms like music and song, styles and content of preaching, and modes of worship, to give a few examples. But religion is also the heart of culture because it raises the core values of that culture to ultimate levels and legitimates them.[15] The relationship between the black sacred cosmos and black culture in general is similar. The core values of black culture like freedom, justice, equality, an African heritage, and racial parity at all levels of human intercourse, are raised to ultimate levels and legitimated by the black sacred cosmos. Although this cosmos is largely Afro-Christian in nature due to its religious history, it has also erupted in other black militant, nationalistic, and non-Christian movements.[16] The close relationship between the black sacred cosmos and black culture has often been missed by social analysts who impose sacred/secular distinctions too easily upon the phenomena of black culture.[17] What is often overlooked is the fact that many aspects of black cultural practices and some major social institutions had religious origins; they were given birth and nurtured in the womb of the Black Church.

NOTES

1. See Leonard Barrett, *Soul Force: African Heritage in Afro-American Religion* (Garden City, NY: Anchor Press/Doubleday, 1974); Charles Long, "Perspective for a Study of African American Religion in the United States," reprinted in this volume.

2. A good sociological analysis of the process of creating world views is found in Peter L. Berger and Thomas Luckmann, *The Social Construction of Reality: A Treatise in the Sociology of Knowledge.* The historical work of Melville Herskovits, John Blassingame, Eugene Genovese, Herbert Gutman, and Albert Raboteau are a few examples of the recent trend in scholarship

which recognized that black slaves were not merely robots responding to the demands of the slave system, but they were also active creators of their own forms of culture and world view.

3. Examples of this view are found in the works of E. Franklin Frazier and Gunnar Myrdal.

4. Nathan Glazer and Daniel Patrick Moynihan, *Beyond the Melting Pot*, p. 51.

5. For the tenacity of residential and educational segregation, see the studies by Gary Orfield, *Public School Desegregation in the United States 1968–1980;* and Gary Orfield and William Taylor, *Racial Segregation: Two Policy Views.*

6. As scholars like Melville Herskovits have pointed out, more of African culture survived in the Caribbean and Latin American countries like Brazil than in the United States. See Melville J. Herskovits, *The Myth of the Negro Past.* For an overview of the influences of African religious traditions in the New World, see George Eaton Simpson, *Black Religions in the New World.*

7. See the following: Henry H. Mitchell, *Black Belief: Folk Beliefs of Blacks in America and West Africa;* James Cone, *A Black Theology of Liberation;* and Gayraud Wilmore, *Black Religion and Black Radicalism: An Interpretation of the Religious History of Afro-American People.* Also see Theo Witvliet, *The Way of the Black Messiah.*

8. See Wilmore, *Black Religion and Black Radicalism*, pp. 75–78.

9. See the ending of Dr. King's "I Have a Dream" speech in James M. Washington, editor, *A Testament of Hope: The Essential Writings of Martin Luther King, Jr.*, p. 220. For an attempt to construct a black theology of freedom, see Charles H. Long, *Significations: Signs, Symbols, and Images in the Interpretation of Religion* chapters 9–12. For Long, freedom is a fundamental construct of both the human condition and religion.

10. Mechal Sobel, *Trabelin' On: The Slave Journey to an Afro-Baptist Faith*, p. 107.

11. Ibid., p. 108.

12. Ibid., p. 109.

13. One example of this is the formation of caucuses of black priests, nuns, and bishops who are attempting to include more of their Afro-Christian heritage in their services. See the issue on "The Black Catholic Experience," in *U.S. Catholic Historian* 6 (1986), no. 1.

14. Tillich's theology of culture involved a dialectical relationship between religion and culture. His broad definition of religion as "ultimate concern" or "ultimate value" makes it possible to see how religion sacralizes the central values of a culture or a group of people. In Tillich's view of Christianity, however, he also provided for the possibility of religion transcending culture and providing a critique of it in his notion of the "Protestant principle." For a general summary of Tillich's view of religion and culture, see James Luther Adams, *Paul Tillich's Philosophy of Culture, Science, and Religion.* For the self-transcendence of the Spirit, see Paul Tillich, *Systematic Theology*, 3:50–98.

15. Much of the discussion and debate about American civil religion and the religious quality of political nationalism have tended to miss this point.

16. For examples, see Lawrence H. Mamiya and C. Eric Lincoln, "Black Militant and Separatist Movements," in the *Encyclopedia of the American Religious Experience*, 2:755–71.

17. In the sphere of black music, one example of the attempt to impose rigid sacred/secular distinctions is found in the work of LeRoi Jones (Amiri Baraka), *Blues People: Negro Music in White America.* For example, Jones traces the origins of the blues to the "secular" work songs and field hollers of the slaves, instead of what he calls their "sacred" Afro-Christian music. Clearly the distinctions represent Jones's own modern divisions rather than those of the slaves. Charles Keil in *Urban Blues*, pp. 32–41, has criticized Jones for failing to see the interactive and dialectical nature of black music, the constant interchanges between spirituals, gospel, blues, and jazz. Keil has argued that Jones seems to feel that gospel and blues are worlds apart;

consequently, he (Jones) has missed the important role of storefront churches in the development of the blues tradition since so many blues musicians received their musical training in these churches. The musicians often move back and forth between church and nightclub. Scholars of black music have often missed the "mutual malleability" of that music and the "flexibility of African cultural systems."

Part II

From the Motherland to Another Land
*The Emergence of African American Religion in the
Antebellum United States*

Tireli, Mali, 1993. "Dogon dancers perform the ceremonial Kanaga Dance. These men dressed as woodcutters represent some of the figures of the Dogon creation myth and show the Dogon cosmology in which the world oscillates between chaos and order." Text and photo from *Feeling the Spirit* by Chester Higgins. Copyright © 1994 by Chester Higgins. Used by permission of Bantam Books, a division of Random House, Inc.

Chapter Five

Black Religion
The African Model

Maulana Karenga

Professor Maulana Karenga, who in the 1960s conceived and inaugurated the celebration of the Kwanzaa festival which is based on traditional African themes and practices, here provides an overview of some central elements in African Traditional Religion.

•

Introduction

Religion has always been a vital part of Black life in both Africa and the United States. In Africa, religion was so pervasive that distinctions between it and other areas of life were almost imperceptible (Mbiti 1970). In the United States, the extent of Black religiousness is clear and has been well documented (Lincoln 1974). Although there are numerous definitions for religion, for the purpose of this chapter, *religion can be defined as thought, belief, and practice concerned with the transcendent and the ultimate questions of life* (Karenga 1980:23). Among such questions are those concerning human death, relevance, origin, destiny, suffering, and obligations to other humans and in most cases, to a Supreme or Ultimate Being. Within the context of the concern with the ultimate is also the clear division between the sacred, that is, the set apart and exalted, and the profane, the common and nonexalted (Yinger 1970).

The religion of Black people in the United States is predominantly Judeo-Christian, but Islam, both Black and orthodox, and ancient African religious and ethical traditions, are growing among African Americans (Wilmore 1989). Among these other varied traditions are the Black Hebrew tradition (Ben Yehuda 1975), the Rastafarian tradition (Barrett 1988; Morrison 1992), and the Yoruba tradition which is an international tradition including a Continental Yoruba practice (Lucas 1948; Abimbola 1976; Awolalu 1979; Thompson 1983; Drewal 1992), a Santería Yoruba practice (Murphy 1988; Gonzalez-Wippler 1982; Gleason 1975), and a Candomblé Yoruba practice (Bastide 1978; Richards 1976). Also in recent years, the Maatian tradition from ancient Egypt has emerged (Karenga, 1984, 1988).

Given the fact that Black religion is so predominantly Judeo-Christian, the tendency is to see it as "white religion in Black face." However, as Lincoln (1974) and Wilmore (1983) contend, such an interpretation is grossly incorrect. For regardless of what external details of white Christianity are similar to Black Christianity, the essence of Black Christianity is different. The essence of a people's religion is rooted in its own social and historical experiences and in the truth and meaning they extract from these and translate into an authentic spiritual expression that speaks specifically to them. Thus, Black religion represents in its essence not imitation but "the desire of Blacks to be self-conscious about the meaning of their Blackness and to search for spiritual fulfillment in terms of their understanding of themselves and their experience of history" (Lincoln 1974:3).

Ancient African Traditions

General Themes

Black religion, like Black people, began in Africa and thus it is important to discuss its historical forms before turning to its current expressions. The study of traditional African religions is made difficult by Europeans' interpretations which exhibit a need to make Christianity seem superior and African religions primitive (Evans-Pritchard 1965) and by African Christian interpretations which strive to make African religions more "normal" by making them look more Christian or Western (Idowu 1975; Mbiti 1970). To appreciate African religions, one must admit similarities and differences without seeing the similarities as "less developed" and the differences as evidence of psychological or cultural defectiveness.

Thus, if African stories of creation and divinities are myths, so are Christian, Jewish, and Islamic ones. However, a better category for both African and other creation stories would be"narratives." Moreover, Jehovah, Yahweh, and Allah are no more arguable than Nkulunkulu, Oludumare, and Amma. And the abasom of the Ashanti and the orisha of the Yoruba are no less effective as divine intermediaries than Catholic saints like Jude and Christopher. All nonscientific approaches to the origin of the world and the forces operative in it are vulnerable to challenge. And the choice of one over the other is more a matter of tradition and preference than proof of any particular one's validity. Therefore, my use of Western religious examples will not be to force comparisons or contrasts, but to demonstrate parallels where appropriate that would help to lessen a person's tendency to reductively translate African religions in a mistaken assumption of superiority for his/her own.

Although African religious traditions are complex and diverse, some general themes tend to appear in all of them (Mbiti 1970, 1991; Ray 1976; Zahan 1979; Wright 1984; Gyekye 1987). First, there is the belief in one Supreme God: Oludumare among the Yoruba, Nkulunkulu among the Zulu, and Amma among the Dogon. This God is the Father in most societies, but also appears as Mother in matriarchal societies like the Ovambo in Namibia and the Nuba in Kenya. Moreover, in Dogon religion, Amma has both male and female characteristics, reflecting the Dogon concept of binary opposition as the motive force and structure of the universe (Ray 1976:28–29; Griaule 1978).

Second, in ancient African religious traditions, God is both immanent and transcendent, near and far. In this framework, then, Africans engage in daily interaction with divinities, who are seen as God's intermediaries and assistants (Mbiti 1970, 1991). These divinities are both similar to and different from Jesus, angels, and Catholic saints as intermediaries and assistants to the Supreme Being. It is this deference and exchange with the divinities that made the less critical assume Africans were polytheistic rather than monotheistic. However, evidence clearly argues against this assumption.

Third, African religions stress ancestor veneration. The ancestors are venerated for several reasons that reinforce the concepts of linkage, heritage, and spiritual relevance (Richards 1989:7,8). They "are venerated because they are: (1) a source and symbol of lineage; (2) models of ethical life, service, and social achievement to the community; and (3) because they are spiritual intercessors between humans and the Creator" (Karenga 1988: 20; see also Mbiti 1970: 108; 1991). The Ashanti have a special Day of Remembrance of the Ancestors called *Akwasidae* in which ceremonies focus on linkage between those who have passed, the living, and the yet unborn. As Mends (1976:8) notes, by participating in the ceremony to honor ancestors, one is stressing "the common bonds of kinship and association which make for solidarity among the people." And it is also a way to reinforce the value and honor due those whose ethical life and service make them worthy members of the community.

Fourth, ancient African religions stress the necessary balance between one's collective identity and responsibility as a member of society and one's personal identity and responsibility. Like religion itself, a person is defined as an integral part of a definite community, to which she/he belongs and in which she/he finds identity and relevance. Summing up this conception, Mbiti (1970:141) states that "I am because we are, and since we are, therefore I am." The Dinka have captured this stress on the moral ideal of harmonious integration of self with the community in their word *cieng*, which means both morality and living together. In this conception, the highest moral ideal is to live in harmony, know oneself and one's duties through others, and reach one's fullness in cooperation with and through support from one's significant others (Deng 1973).

Another key theme in African religions is the profound respect for nature. Because humans live in a religious universe, everything that is has religious relevance (Richards 1989:6–7). The whole world as God's creation is alive with His/Her symbols and gifts to humans, and bears witness to His/Her power, beauty, and beneficence. Thus, there are sacred trees, rivers, mountains, and animals (as in Western religions). Nature is not only respected because of its association with God, but also because of its relevance to humankind. This respect is grounded in the belief that there is an unbreakable bond between the divine, the human, and the natural and that therefore damage to one is damage to the other and likewise respect and care for one is respect and care for the other. The stress, then, is to show nature due respect, not abuse it in any way, and to live in harmony with it and the universe. Dona Marimba Richards (1989:10) notes that African culture is a "culture that perceives the interrelationships and interdependence of all beings within the universe." Thus, she says the African approach is that "if we take or destroy, we must give or rebuild; for there is one spiritual unity that joins us all. . . ."

Finally, the conception of death and immortality is an important theme in African religions. Death in African religions is seen in several ways. First, it is seen as another stage in human development. Humans are born, live, die, and become the ancestors. Death is thus not the end, but a beginning of another form of existence as ancestor and spirit. Therefore, it is seen as a transition in life rather than an end to it. After a period of mourning there is celebration for the human conquest of death, for after the funeral, the dead are "revived" in the spirit world and, as ancestors, are close and relevant. Second, death is seen as reflective of cosmic patterns, that is the rising and setting of the sun, and often graves are dug east and west to imitate this pattern.

Third, death is seen as a transition in life to personal and collective immortality. Personally, one lives after death through four media: (1) children; (2) other relatives; (3) rituals of remembrance; and (4) great works or significant deeds. The living remember and speak one's name and deeds, and one's works speak of one's significance throughout time. Thus, without relatives to keep one's memory alive or significant achievements and deeds, one is what Africans call "utterly dead." Collective immortality is achieved through the life of one's people and through what one means to them. For as long as they live, the person lives and shares in their life and destiny.

The Dogon Tradition

One of the most complex and impressive African religious systems is that of the Dogon. The Dogon, who live in Mali, have astounded the world by their astronomical knowledge and impressed it with the logic and intricacy of their thought. So impressive is their knowledge, especially of the Sirius star-system, that some Europeans have argued that the Dogon's knowledge was given to them by space beings (Temple 1976) or by mysterious Europeans (Sagan 1979). However, Europeans did not know themselves until the 1800s what the Dogon knew about the Sirius star-system 700 years ago (Adams 1979).

The socioreligious thought of the Dogon evolves from an elaborate cosmogony and an extremely complex cosmology (Griaule 1978; Griaule and Dieterlen 1965). It is these constructions around which the Dogon understand and organize their world and seek to carry out their social and spiritual tasks. For the sake of brevity and clarity, I have tried to reduce the story of creation to its most basic elements while at the same time trying to remain faithful to its logic and content.

In the beginning everything that would be already potentially was. The substances and structure of the universe were in Amma, the Supreme God, who was in the image of an egg and divided into four quarters containing the four basic elements—air, earth, fire, and water, and the four cardinal directions—north, south, east, and west. Thus, Amma was the egg of the universe, and the universe and Amma were one. As egg, Amma symbolized and was fertility and unlimited creative possibility. Through creative thought, Amma traced within himself the design and developmental course of the universe using 266 cosmic signs which contained the essence, structure, and life-principle of all things. Placing the four basic elements and sacred signs and seeds on a flat disk, Amma set the disk revolving between the two cosmic axes. But the spinning disk threw off the water, drying up the seeds. The first creation was thus aborted and Amma began again, deciding that this time he would make humans the preservers of order and life in the world.

Placing a seed at the center of himself, the cosmic egg, he spoke seven creative words. From this, the seed (matter) vibrated seven times unfolding along a spiral path, conserving itself on one hand and transforming itself on the other through alternations between opposites. Thus, the principal of twinness or binary opposition directed its movement and its form and established a pattern for the structure and functioning of the universe, that is, up/down, man/woman, action/inaction, hot/cold, etc. From the infinitely small (seed, atom) the infinitely large (universe) evolved. The seed, vibrating seven times and turning in a spiral fashion, extended itself in seven directions in the womb of the world, prefiguring the shape of a human being, that is, two directions for the head, two for the arms, two for the legs, and one for the genital. The world was thus created in the image of humans and would later be organized around them.

Transforming the egg into a double placenta, Amma placed two sets of twins, male and female in each, again underscoring the principle of opposites which informs the structure and functioning of the universe. In the twins, He placed the sacred signs, words, and seeds of creation. Before gestation was completed, however, one of the male twins, Yurugu (Ogo), feeling lonely and incomplete, burst through the womb to seize his female twin. Unable to acquire his twin, he rebelled against the established order of things. Imposing disorder on an orderly process, Yurugu descended into the void in an attempt to create a world himself. But his knowledge was incomplete and he could not speak the creative words. Then Amma, using the piece of placenta which Yurugu took as he broke from the celestial egg-womb, created the earth. This creation of earth restored the human shape of the world. The celestial egg became the head of man; the lower incomplete placenta, now earth and forming an incomplete circle, became the hips and legs; and the space and lines which divide and connect heaven and earth became the trunk and arms. Binary opposition is thus again established in that heaven is the head (mind, spirit), and earth, the lower region of the body (the physical). Joined together, they form the structure and essence of humans.

To restore order in the world, Amma scattered Yurugu's male twin, Nommo, that is, creative word, over the expanse of the universe. Also, He created four other Nommo spirits from Nommo and their offspring became the eight ancestors of the Dogon. Amma then sent Nommo and the eight ancestors down to earth, with all species of animals and plants, and all the elements of human culture, thus laying the basis for human development and a prosperous earth. Descending, Nommo shouted out the creative words, therefore transmitting the power of creative speech and thought to earth, making it available to humankind. Through this power, they would be able to push back the boundaries of ignorance and disorder and impose creative order on the world. To punish Yurugu for his disorder and revolt, Amma transformed him into a Pale Fox. Deprived of his female half, the Pale Fox is an incomplete and lonely being wandering though the world in a vain quest for wholeness. But as he wanders, he leaves tracks through the mysteries of life, revealing the dangers humans must avoid. Finally, sending rain to earth, Amma made the earth flourish and humans began to cultivate the land and cover it with ever-increasing numbers. Possessing creative intelligence through Nommo, humans walk the way of Yurugu as well, alternating between disorder and order, destruction and creation, rationality and irrationality, conformity and revolt.

There are several aspects of this cosmogonical construction that reveal the profundity of Dogon thought and its susceptibility to interesting and expansive interpretations. First, it stresses the binary oppositional character and functioning of the universe—creation/destruction, order/disorder, male/female, perfection/imperfection, self-conscious action/unconscious action, and so on. This is essentially an African dialectic, posing opposites necessary to the explanation and functioning of the world. In fact, each opposite explains and necessitates the other. Thus, Yurugu rebels because he feels deprived of his female half which he needs for his wholeness. He fails because he represents action without critical consciousness, and Nommo, who reflects the creative thought and action of Amma, succeeds in establishing order and promoting development. Second, the concept of God as the cosmic womb, already containing in the beginning everything that would come into being in Him, suggests a concept of God as the universe and of its already having at the beginning all the building material (matter) for everything in it. This reflects the scientific principle that matter was always and already here, and only its forms changed and change.

Third, the concept of God as egg is reflective of His fertility, productiveness, and infinite creative possibilities, as well as the idea of them. As infinite creative possibility in the universe and of the universe, God is infinite in a logical and meaningful way. Fourth, the Dogon pose God as making a mistake in the first creation and thus maintain logical consistency even in discussing God. For God is both perfect and imperfect, male and female, thought and action and therefore reflects and reinforces the principle of binary opposition.

Also, there is a clear contention that the world is not perfect either and is in the process of perpetual becoming. This process again is marked by binary opposition in structure and functioning and strives toward the creative and ongoing harmonizing of the two opposites. Especially profound and far-reaching is the concept that becoming of necessity requires rebellion or oppositional thought and action against the established order. Yurugu comes into being by breaking through the cosmic egg and thus sets up conditions for a new world. Breaking from Amma, God, he becomes truly man rather than a cosmic baby. In this action, he reminds one of the young adult leaving his/her parents' house in order to build a world for him/herself. In a word, independence and development require a break from the established state of things. And even though Yurugu fails to make the world, he contributed to its origin and still leaves tracks through the mysteries of life which humankind can read and from which they can learn vital lessons.

Finally, Dogon thought is clearly impressive in its stress on humans as the indispensable element in the world's becoming and functioning. As previously noted, the universe was created in the image of the human personality; he/she is the world in microcosm, containing its basic elements, the four cardinal directions, and the sacred cosmic seeds, signs, and words. Moreover, Amma/God could not make the world without humans, for not only did the world need man/woman to flourish, but so did God. For if God is idea and creative possibility, only man/woman can know and appreciate it. Only humans are capable of creative thought; trees will not pray or praise, and dogs do not discuss spiritual or social duties. But if God needs man/woman, the binary oppositional logic of Dogon thought requires that man/woman also needs God. For if idea and creative possibility (God) cannot exist without man/woman, man/woman cannot exist without idea and creative possibility (God).

REFERENCES

Abimbola, Wande. (1976) *Ifa: An Exposition of Ifa Literary Corpus.* Ibadan: Oxford University Press.

Adams, Hunter III. (1979) "African Observers of the Universe: The Sirius Question." *Journal of African Civilization*, 1, 2 (November): 1–20.

Awolalu, J. O. (1979) *Yoruba Beliefs and Sacrificial Rites.* London: Longmans.

Barrett, Leonard E. (1988) *The Rastafarlans.* Boston: Beacon Press.

Bastide, Roger. (1978) *The African Religions of Brazil: Towards A Sociology of the Interpretations of Civilizations.* Baltimore: John Hopkins University, Book Associates.

Ben Yehuda, Shaleak. (1975) *Black Hebrew Israelites: From America to the Promised Land.* New York: Vantage Press.

Deng, Francis. (1973) *The Dinka and Their Songs.* Oxford: Clarendon Press.

Drewal, Margaret T. (1992) *Yoruba Ritual.* Bloomington: Indiana University Press.

Evans-Pritchard, E. E. (1965) *Theories of Primitive Religion.* London: Oxford University Press.

Gleason, Judith. (1975) *Santeria*, Bronx, NY: Atheneum Press.

Gonzales-Wippler, Migene. (1982) *The Santeria Experience.* Bronx, NY: Original Publications.

Griaule, Marcel. (1978) *Conversations with Ogotemmeli.* New York: Oxford University Press.

Griaule, Marcel, and Germain Dieterlen. (1965) "The Dogon." In Daryll Ford (ed.) *African Worlds.* London: Oxford University Press, pp. 83–110.

Gyekye, Kwame. (1987) *An Eassy on African Philosophical Thought: The Akan Conceptual Theme.* New York: Cambridge University Press.

Idowu, E. Bolaji. (1975) *African Traditional Religion*, Maryknoll, NY: Orbis Books.

Karenga, Maulana. (1980) *Kawaida Theory: An Introductory Outline.* Inglewood, CA: Kawaida Publications.

———. (1984) *Selections From the Husia: Sacred Wisdom of Ancient Egypt.* Los Angeles: University of Sankore Press.

———. (1988) *The African American Holiday of Kwanzaa: A Celebration of Family, Community, and Culture.* Los Angeles: University of Sankore Press.

Lincoln, C. Eric. (1974) *The Black Church Since Frazier.* New York: Schocken Books.

Lucas, J. O. (1948) *The Religion of the Yoruba.* Lagos: C.M.S. Bookshop.

Mbiti, John S. (1970) *African Religions and Philosophy.* Garden City, NY: Anchor Books.

———. (1991) *Introduction to African Religion*, 2nd ed. Oxford: Heineman International Literature and Textbooks.

Mends, E. H. (1976) "Ritual in the Social Life of Ghanaian Society." In J. M. Assimeng (ed.) *Traditional Life, Culture and Literature in Ghana.* New York: Cinch Magazine Limited.

Morrison, Silburn M. (1992) *Rastafari: The Conscious Embrace.* Bronx, NY: Itality Publishing House.

Murphy, Joseph. (1988) *Santeria: An African Religion in America.* Boston: Beacon Press.

Ray, Benjamin C. (1976) *African Religions.* Englewood Cliffs, NJ: Prentice-Hall.

Richards, Dona Marimba. (1976) "A Community of African Descendants: The Afro-Bahian Candomble." *The Proceedings of the Conference on Yoruba Civilization, 26–31 July,* Ife, Nigeria: University of Ife.

———. (1989) *Let the Circle Be Unbroken: Implications of African Spirituality in the Diaspora.* New York: Dona Marimba Richards.

Sagan, Carl. (1979) *Broca's Brain-Reflections on the Romance of Science.* New York: Random House.

Temple, Robert. (1976) *The Sirius Mystery.* New York: St. Martin's Press.

Thompson, Robert F. (1983) *Flash of the Spirit.* New York: Random House.

Wilmore, Gayraud S., ed. (1989) *African American Religious Studies.* Durham, NC: Duke University Press.

———. (1983). *Black Religion and Black Radicalism.* 2nd ed. Garden City, New York: Anchor Books.

Wright, Richard A. (1984) *African Philosophy: An Introduction.* 3rd ed. New York: University Press of America.

Yinger, Milton. (1970) *The Scientific Study of Religion.* New York: Macmillan.

Zahan, Dominique (1979) *The Religion, Spirituality, and Thought of Traditional Africa.* Chicago: University of Chicago Press.

Chapter Six

"The Rule of Gospel Order"
Religious Life in the Slave Community

Albert J. Raboteau

Among the "peculiar cargo" of "twenty negars" borne by the Dutch Man O'War that sailed into Jamestown harbor in 1619, some apparently were associated with the Christian faith, as evidenced by their European names—traditionally given at baptism as "Christian" names. In any case, colonial records shortly thereafter begin to list baptisms of African servants. By the turn of the nineteenth century, some 20 to 25 percent of all Methodists and Baptists in the country were black. Yet, the task of converting the enslaved to Christianity was impeded by logistical problems as well as ecclesiastical debate over the social meaning of the category of Christian slave. On the other hand, it was encouraged by the prevailing social notion of an hierarchical society ordered and governed according to a supposedly Christian theological model. Albert J. Raboteau offers a vista into aspects of the effort to bring this model into effect.

•

The intense emphasis upon conversion, which was the primary characteristic of evangelical, revivalistic Protestantism, tended to level all men before God as sinners in need of salvation. This tendency opened the way for black converts to participate actively in the religious culture of the new nation as exhorters, preachers, and even founders of churches, and created occasions of mutual religious influence across racial boundaries whereby blacks converted whites and whites converted blacks in the heat of revival fervor. This egalitarian tendency could push, as it did in the case of early Methodism, toward the condemnation of slavery as inconsistent with the gospel of Jesus. However, very few white Christians in the South were willing to be pushed that far. Increasingly, slavery was not only accepted as an economic fact of life, but defended as a positive good, sanctioned by Scripture and capable of producing a Christian social order based on the observance of mutual duty, slave to master and master to slave. It was the ideal of the antebellum plantation mission to create such a rule of gospel order by convincing slaves and masters that their salvation depended upon it.

Plantation Missions

The closing years of the eighteenth and the early decades of the nineteenth centuries witnessed an unprecedented spread of Christianity among Afro-Americans, slave and free.

Although the numbers of black Christians, particularly among the Baptists and Methodists, increased rapidly, and while those slaves living in or close to towns and cities had opportunities to attend church with their masters, and even in rare instances to worship at independent black churches, the great majority of rural slaves remained outside the reach of the institutional church. In the 1830s and 1840s, some Southern churchmen became increasingly concerned about this neglect and determined to remedy it. In 1834, Charles Colcock Jones, one of the leading proponents for the establishment of plantation missions, explained why more needed to be done:

> It is true they [slaves] have access to the house of God on the Sabbath; but it is also true that even where the privilege is within their reach, a minority only (and frequently a very small one) embrace it. There are multitudes of districts in the South and Southwest, in which the churches cannot contain one-tenth of the Negro population; besides others in which there are no churches at all. It must be remembered also that in many of those churches there is preaching only once a fortnight, or once a month, and then perhaps only one sermon. To say that they fare as well as their masters does not settle the point; for great numbers of masters have very few or no religious privileges at all.[1]

The distance of many plantations from churches meant that it was not possible to reach numerous plantations through ordinary pastoral care. It was necessary to carry the gospel to slaves at home. Planters had generally become accustomed to the idea that slaves should be converted, but mere passive permission was not enough. An aggressive program of plantation missions was needed to bring the slaves under Church care. Missionaries were required who could devote at least part-time energy to improving religious conditions for slaves. Monetary support for plantation missions was to come from denominational missionary societies, from local churches, and from slaveholders. It was recommended that one church or a single planter associate with others to share the expense of paying a missionary and building a mission station or chapel.[2]

In the antebellum South, the plantation mission was widely propagated as an ideal whose time had come. Techniques similar to those used by Bible, Temperance, Tract, and other reform societies were employed to raise Southern Christian consciousness about the cause of plantation missions. Addresses before planter associations, printed sermons and essays, committee reports and resolutions of clerical bodies, meetings of concerned clergy and laymen, annual reports of associations, interdenominational cooperation, and networks of correspondence were all devoted to spreading the message. Through the circulation of pamphlets and papers, plantation missions were brought to the attention of thousands. Religious journals such as *The Gospel Messenger* (Episcopal) of Charleston, *The Christian Index* (Baptist), and *The Southern Christian Advocate* (Methodist), to name only three, gave favorable coverage and editiorial support to missions for slaves. *The Charleston Observer* (Presbyterian) even ran a series in 1834 on the "Biographies of Servants mentioned in the Scripture: with Questions and Answers," as a practical aid to the religious instruction of slaves.[3]

Pamphlets with such titles as "Detail of a plan for the Moral Improvement of Negroes on Plantations," "Pastoral Letter . . . on the Duty of Affording Religious Instruction to those in Bondage," and "The Colored Man's Help, or the Planter's Catechism" were published and distributed widely. A Baptist State Convention actually sponsored a contest for the best essay on the topic "Conversion of the slaves," which was won by Holland N. McTyeire with a paper entitled "The Duties of Christian Masters to Their Servants." The aim of most of this literature was succinctly described in a pamphlet published in 1823 by an Episcopal clergyman from South Carolina: "to show from the Scriptures of the Old and New Testament, that slavery is not forbidden by the Divine Law: and at the same time to prove the necessity of giving religious instruction to our Negroes." These attempts to mold public opinion in favor of plantation missions were evaluated optimistically by Jones: "As an evidence of the increase of feeling and effort on the subject of the religious instruction of the colored population we state, that *more has been published and circulated* on the general subject, within the last two years [1833–34] than in ten or twenty years' preceding. . . ."[4] Various denominational bodies frequently urged support for plantation missions in official resolutions. Not only churchmen but also laymen spoke out for religious instruction of the Negro. The prominent planters Charles Cotesworth Pinckney, Edward R. Laurens, and Whitemarsh B. Seabrook, in 1829, 1832, and 1834, respectively, stressed the benefits of a Christian slave population before South Carolina agricultural societies.[5]

Writing pamphlets and making speeches for the plantation missions did not exhaust the efforts of proponents of the cause. Missionary societies and associations were actually founded. In 1830, the Missionary Society of the South Carolina Conference was founded as an auxiliary branch of the Missionary Society of the Methodist Episcopal Church under William Capers, superintendent of missions and, later, bishop. In 1830–31, two associations of Georgia planters were formed for the religious instruction of slaves. One of these, in Liberty County, Georgia, became famous. Formed by the Midway Congregational Church, pastored by Robert Quarterman, and the local Baptist church, under Samuel Spry Law, the Liberty County Association, with Presbyterian Jones as missionary, served as a model plantation mission.[6] In the association's twelve annual reports, printed and distributed in pamphlet form throughout the slave states, planters and clergy could read of the practical programs and experience of a working mission. The annual reports served also as a clearinghouse for information about the mission activities of Baptists, Methodists, Presbyterians, and Episcopalians throughout the South by publishing progress reports and letters from as far away as Louisiana, Tennessee, and Arkansas. The geographical center of the plantation mission movement was lowland South Carolina and Georgia. Letters printed in the Liberty County Association Reports indicate that there was growing interest but much less concrete achievement in other areas of the South. Methodists seemed the most active, but the efforts of smaller churches, such as the Moravians and German Lutherans, were duly noted. It was hoped that example would move the inactive to missionary zeal.

The conversion of slaves occupied an important place on the agendas of denominational meetings and sometimes was the topic for whole conferences. In 1839, an assembly of Presbyterians from the slave states met to consider religious instruction of slaves. In 1845, a meeting was held at Charleston that was attended by some of the most prominent planters and ministers of the state. A circular had been sent out in preparation for the meeting asking interested parties in all the Southern states what was being done in their areas for slave conversion. The *proceedings* of the three-day meeting as well as answers to the circular were published. Aiming to mold public opinion, slaveholders were exhorted in the *Proceedings* to realize that a "moral agency . . . gains strength by action. The efforts of masters to afford religious instruction to their negroes, will act upon others, and react upon themselves."[7]

Charles Colcock Jones, the leading theoretician and chief publicist of the plantation mission, tried to portray the movement as part of the national fervor for reform which was articulated institutionally in the interlocking group of benevolent societies known corporately as the United Evangelical Front. In Jones's view, in the interdenominational efforts to make America holy by means of home and foreign mission societies, Bible and tract societies, and temperance and Sabbath School societies, the urgent need of the heathen slaves at home to have the Gospel preached to them should not be neglected.

Several catechisms had been specially prepared for teaching slaves. Two of the most popular were Capers' *A Short Catechism for the Use of the Colored Members on Trial of the Methodist Episcopal Church in South Carolina* (1832) and Jones's *A Catechism for Colored Persons* (1834), though sometimes regular catechisms were employed. (Jones's *Catechism* proved so popular that it was eventually translated into Armenian and Chinese for use in the foreign mission field.)[8] The oral method of instruction also created a demand for collections of homilies, such as that of Episcopalian bishop Meade, *Sermons, Dialogues and Narratives for Servants, To Be Read to Them in Families* (1836). Audiovisual aids, such as hymns and Scripture cards— illustrations of Bible stories with texts, questions, and answers printed on the back— were also used.

In moments of doubt about his own salvation, the slaveholder perhaps found some compensation in zeal for the conversion of his slaves. Moreover, as the *North Carolina Christian Advocate* of December 15, 1859, argued, the Southern Christian conscience was caught in a bind: "Everybody who believes in religion at all, admits that it is the duty of Christians to give religious instruction to the slave population of the Southern States. To deny the safety and propriety of preaching the Gospel to the negroes, is either to abandon Christianity, or to admit that slavery is condemned by it."[9]

The effectiveness of the antebellum plantation mission is difficult to measure. Undoubtedly, the publicity generated by sponsors of the mission contributed to an increased awareness of their cause as a current issue in Southern society. As the century wore on into the decade of the 1850s, institutional efforts were increased. However, the resolutions of some clerical bodies remained simply that. For example, in 1834 an impressive-sounding "Kentucky Union for the moral and religious improvement of the colored race" was formed as "a union of several denominations of

RULES
For the Society of
NEGROES. 1693.

WE the Miserable Children of *Adam*, and of *Noah*, thankfully Admiring and Accepting the Free-Grace of GOD, that Offers to Save us from our Miseries, by the Lord Jesus Christ, freely Resolve, with His Help, to become the Servants of that Glorious LORD.

And that we may be Assisted in the Service of our *Heavenly Master*, we now Join together in a SOCIETY, wherein the following RULES are to be observed.

I. It shall be our Endeavour, to Meet in the *Evening* after the *Sabbath*; and *Pray* together by Turns, one to Begin, and another to Conclude the Meeting; And between the two *Prayers*, a *Psalm* shall be Sung, and a *Sermon* Repeated.

II. Our coming to the Meeting, shall never be without the *Leave* of such as have Power over us: And we will be Careful, that our Meeting may Begin and Conclude between the Hours of *Seven* and *Nine*; and that we may not be *unseasonably Absent* from the Families whereto we pertain.

III. As we will, with the Help of God, at all Times avoid all *Wicked Company*, so we will Receive none into our Meeting, but such as have sensibly *Reformed* their Lives from all manner of Wickedness. And therefore, None shall be Admitted, without the Knowledge and Consent of the *Minister* of God in this Place; unto whom we will also carry every Person, that seeks for *Admission* among us; to be by Him Examined, Instructed and Exhorted.

IV. We will, as often as may be, Obtain some Wise and Good Man, of the *English* in the Neighbourhood, and especially the Officers of the Church, to look in upon us, and by their Presence and Counsil, do what they think fitting for us.

V. If any of our Number, fall into the Sin of *Drunkenness*, or *Swearing*, or *Cursing*, or *Lying*, or *Stealing*, or notorious *Disobedience* or *Unfaithfulness* unto their Masters, we will *Admonish* him of his Miscarriage, and Forbid his coming to the Meeting, for at least *one Fortnight*; And except he then come with great Signs and Hopes of his *Repentance*, we will utterly Exclude him, with Blotting his *Name* out of our List.

VI. If any of our Society Defile himself with *Fornication*, we will give him our *Admonition*; and so, debar him from the Meeting, at least *half a Year*: Nor shall he Return to it, ever any more, without Exemplary Testimonies of his becoming a *New Creature*.

VII. We will, as we have Opportunity, set our selves to do all the Good we can, to the other *Negro-Servants* in the Town; And if any of them should, at unfit Hours, be *Abroad*, much more, if any of them should *Run away* from their Masters, we will afford them *no Shelter*: But we will do what in us lies, that they may be discovered, and punished. And if any *of us*, are found Faulty, in this Matter, they shall be no longer *of us*.

VIII. None of our Society shall be *Absent* from our Meeting, without giving a *Reason* of the Absence; And if it be found, that any have pretended unto their *Owners*, that they came unto the *Meeting*, when they were otherwise and elsewhere Employ'd, we will faithfully *Inform* their Owners, and also do what we can to Reclaim such Person from all such Evil Courses for the Future.

IX. It shall be expected from every one in the Society, that he learn the *Catechism*; And therefore, it shall be one of our usual Exercises, for one of us, to ask the *Questions*, and for all the rest in their Order, to say the *Answers* in the *Catechism*; Either, The *New-English* Catechism, or the *Assemblies* Catechism, or the Catechism in the *Negro Christianized*.

Reprinted from Thomas J. Holmes, *Cotton Mather: A Bibliography of His Works* (Cambridge, Mass., 1940).

christians in the State." Five years later, according to the chairman of the Union's executive committee, the "Union had not accomplished much," despite ten vice presidents and a seven-man executive committee. The opposite was true of the Liberty County Georgia Association, which was an effective organization for catechizing slaves, though its successes were dwarfed by the size of the black population in the area where it worked.[10]

In the field of plantation missions the Southern Methodists proved to be the most active, although Baptists, Presbyterians, and Episcopalians also increased their efforts toward slave conversion. From 1846 to 1861 the Methodist Episcopal Church, South, is said to have raised its black membership from 118,904 to 209,836. Methodist contributions to plantation missions grew from about $80,000 in 1845 to $236,000 in 1861. However, Methodist claims to increased membership due to mission work must be viewed with caution. It has been pointed out that "The apparent rapid growth of missions, compared to that of the regular work, was not as impressive as it appears ... many city churches put their Negroes into missions, thus swelling the mission statistics without any actual growth in Church membership." It has been estimated that between the years 1845 and 1860, the black membership of the Baptist Church increased from 200,000 to 400,000.[11] But figures of church membership are not generally noted for their accuracy. It should be remembered also that church membership is not the only measure of evangelization. Undoubtedly, many slaves learned the tenets of Christianity, accepted them, and attended church, without actually appearing on the official rolls of any church. In 1857, the white Methodist minister, John Dixon Long, described the class of slaves most likely to be so enrolled, "such as are owned by the less extensive slaveholders and farmers ... have no overseer, live in the kitchen, mingle with the master's family, eat the same kind of food ... Their children are raised with their master's children, play with them, and nurse them ... A strong attachment frequently exists between them and their masters and mistresses. From this class we derive most of our church members ..." (Significantly Long adds: "Notwithstanding the superior physical condition of this class of slaves, they are generally more unhappy and restless than the more degraded classes. Their superior advantages only serve as a lamp to show them their degradation.")[12]

How did slaves respond to plantation missions? For some, the novelty of religious instruction exerted an appeal. Other slaves met the missionary's instruction with arguments he did not expect. Novice missionaries were forewarned:

> He who carries the Gospel to them ... discovers deism, skepticism, universalism ... all the strong objections against the truth of God; objections which he may perhaps have considered peculiar only to the cultivated minds ... of *critics* and *philosophers!*[13]

Some slaves resented the message of docility preached by the missionaries and rejected it out of hand as "white man's religion." Still another attitude toward religious practice was expressed by those slaves who complained that they were too weary to attend church, and that it was "hard for them to serve their earthly and heavenly master too."[14] And, of course, there were slaves who found meaning in the message spread by plantation missionaries, accepted it on faith, and tried their best to incorporate it in their lives.

It is important to realize that slaves learned about Christianity not only from whites but from other slaves as well. Some slave children received their first instruction in Christianity from parents, kinfolk, or elder slaves. According to Jones, "The Negroes on plantations sometimes appoint one of their number, commonly the old woman who minds the children during the day to teach them to say their prayers, repeat a little catechism and a few hymns, every evening."[15] Slave preachers, licensed and unlicensed, black exhorters, and church-appointed watchmen—or "overseers," as they were also called—instructed their fellow slaves in the rudiments of Christianity, nurtured their religious development, and brought them to conversion in some cases without the active involvement of white missionaries or masters. Then, too, it was in the nature of Protestant evangelicalism to de-emphasize the role of mediators between the person and God. As Luther Jackson perceptively observed: "Experimental religion by its very nature is an inward, subjective, experience so that the slave who was convinced of sin in his own heart might seek baptism and church membership without the intervention of any white Christians whatsoever."[16] At the core of this piety was the Reformation insight that salvation was based not on external observance and personal merit, nor on the intercession of church and clergy, but on the relationship of the individual to the sovereign will of God. With this view of the religious life the person inevitably turned inward and searched his or her own heart to discern the workings of God's Spirit there.

Coupled with the notion that ultimate authority rested on God's Word as expressed in the Bible, the stress on inner personal experience encouraged individual autonomy in matters of religious conscience, an autonomy difficult to control, as the fissiparous tendencies of Protestantism have frequently shown. Among the evangelical churches the Baptists, in particular, institutionalized the spirit of Gospel freedom by insisting upon the autonomy of each congregation. Black Protestants, as well as whites, imbibed this spirit of religious freedom, and proved, to the extent possible, not at all reluctant about deciding their own religious affairs. Baptists, precisely because of their independent church polity, offered more opportunity than any other denomination for black members to exercise a measure of control over their church life. In some mixed churches committees of black members were constituted in order to oversee the church order of black members. These committees listened to applicants relate their religious experience and heard the replies of those members charged with breach of discipline. They were usually restricted to an advisory role, as their recommendations had to be approved by the general church meeting. Still, committees of "the brethren in black," meeting once a month, conducting business, and reporting their recommendations to the general meeting, gave to black church members experience in church governance, and so laid a foundation upon which freedmen would rapidly build their own independent churches after emancipation.[17]

Long before that day, however, as discussed earlier, both slaves and free blacks in some towns of the South had already begun to exercise control over religious organizations. The early independence of black churches and preachers had been curtailed in law and in fact by the reaction of Southern whites to slave conspiracies and to abolitionist agitation. By 1832, some separate African Baptist churches were required to merge with white churches. The African Baptist Church at Williamsburg, Virginia, was closed, and slave members at Elam Baptist in Charles City were transferred by their owners to a church under white control.[18] Despite harassment and legal restriction, there were black churches and black preachers who managed, now and then, to successfully evade limits to their autonomy. Decried as a dangerous anomaly by some Southern whites, black congregations—a few led by black pastors— not only survived but even thrived. In 1845, the Baptist Sunbury Association of Georgia had 4,444 black members (and 495 whites) served by seven black churches with four ordained black ministers and at least one more black member licensed to preach. In Virginia, several African church choirs gave concerts and organized fairs to raise funds for their churches. Black churches engaged in benevolent activities as well. According to one traveler, "In 1853, fifteen thousand dollars were contributed by five thousand slaves in Charleston, to benevolent objects." One benevolent cause which black Christians took up was the foreign missions. As early as 1815, the Richmond African Baptist Missionary Society was formed, and in 1821, two members of the society, Lott Carey and Colin Teague, were sent as missionaries to Liberia. In 1843, the slaves of J. Grimke Drayton of South Carolina "planted in their own time, a *missionary* crop" which netted sixteen dollars for "the extension of the gospel." Another benevolent cause sponsored by black churches was self-help. The Gillfield Baptist Church, in Petersburg, Virginia, received a "petition of a member from a sister church for funds with which to buy her self and her children"—a common request. By the time of emancipation there were black churches in the South with histories that extended back fifty—and in a few cases, seventy-five—years.[19]

For slaves, either in mixed or in separate black churches, to participate in the organization, leadership, and governance of church structures was perceived as "imprudent," and attempts were made to carefully limit black participation. Surely it was inconsistent, argued the more thoroughgoing defenders of slavery, to allow blacks such authority. As Charles Cotesworth Pinkney declared before the Charleston Agricultural Society in 1829, the exercise of religious prerogatives opened to slaves a sphere of freedom from white control. "We look upon the habit of Negro preaching as a wide-spreading evil; not because a black man cannot be a good one, but . . . because they acquire an influence independent of the owner, and not subject to his control; . . . when they have possessed this power, they have been known to make an improper use of it."[20] By active if limited participation in the institutional life of the church, black preachers and church members seized opportunities to publicly express their views and to direct themselves. The problem with including slaves in church fellowship was that it was difficult to control their efforts toward autonomy, particularly when the churches stressed an inner, personal, experimental approach to religion and thus encouraged individualism. The difficulty was augmented by the participatory character of church government which did not, among evangelical Protestants, depend solely upon the clergy but involved the voices and votes of individual members of the congregation in such important matters as "calling" ministers, electing representatives to meetings of larger church bodies, disciplining fellow members, and admitting new ones. There were, then, two conflicting tendencies in the biracial religious context: one encouraged black independence; the other, white control.

NOTES

1. Charles Colcock Jones, *The Religious Instruction of the Negroes in the United States* (Savannah, Ga.: 1842), p. 176.

2. *Proceedings of the Meeting in Charleston, S.C.*, May 13–15, 1845, *On the Religious Instruction of the Negroes* (Charleston, S.C.: 1845), p. 6–7.

3. Jones, *Religious Instruction*, p. 79; Luther P. Jackson, "Religious Instruction of Negroes, 1830–1860, With Special Reference to South Carolina," *Journal of Negro History*, Vol. 15, No. 1 (January 1930), p. 84.

4. Lewis M. Purifoy, Jr., "The Methodist Episcopal Church, South and Slavery, 1844–1865," (Ph.D. diss., University of North Carolina, Chapel Hill, 1965), pp. 127–28; *Jones Religious Instruction*, p. 69; *Second Annual Report of the Missionary to the Negroes in Liberty County*, Ga. (Charleston, S.C.: 1835), p. 11.

5. Jones, *Religious Instruction*, pp. 70–72, 77–79.

6. James Stacy, *History of Midway Church* (Newman, Ga. [1899]), pp. 168–70.

7. *Proceedings of the Charleston Meeting, May 13–15, 1845* (Charleston, S.C.: 1845), pp. 6–7.

8. R. Q. Mallard, *Plantation Life Before Emancipation* (Richmond, Va.: 1892), p. 117.

9. Cited by Guion Griffis Johnson, *Antebellum North Carolina: A Social History* (Chapel Hill, N.C.: University of North Carolina Press, 1937), p. 543.

10. Jones, *Religious Instruction*, pp. 78–79. In 1830, Liberty County, Ga., had a population of 1,544 whites and 5,729 blacks.

11. Luther P. Jackson, "Religious Development of the Negro in Virginia, From 1760 to 1860," *Journal of Negro History*, Vol. 16, No. 2 (April 1931), pp. 95, 103; Purifoy, pp. 151–52. For example, "the Virginia Annual Conference . . . between 1858 and 1860 showed an increase in the number of missions from four to seventeen and an increase in Negro membership in mission of 1,661, whereas, the net gain in Negro membership for the entire Conference was only 648," because missions "had been established to take over . . . Negro membership" (Purifoy, 155n).

12. Rev. John Dixon Long, Pictures of Slavery in Church and State; Including Personal Reminiscences, Biographical Sketches, Anecdotes, etc., etc.: *With an appendix, Contains the views of John Wesley and Richard Watson on slavery* (Philadelphia: self-published, 1857), pp. 20–21.

13. *Proceedings of the Charleston Meeting*, p. 56; Jones, *Religious Instruction*, p. 127.

14. *Tenth Annual Report*, Liberty County Association (1845), pp. 24–25; see also W. G. Hawkins, *Lunsford Lane*, 1st publ. Boston, 1863 (Miami, Fla.: Mnemosyne Publishing Co., 1969), p. 65; Jones, *Religious Instruction*, p. 129.

15. Jones, *Religious Instruction*, p. 114.

16. Jackson, *"Religious Development,"* pp. 217–18.

17. Jones, *Religious Instruction*, pp. 94–95; *Tenth Annual Report, Liberty County Association* (1845), p. 10; James B. Sellers, *Slavery in Alabama* (University: University of Alabama Press, 1950), pp. 299–300; Noah Davis, *A Narrative of the Life of Rev. Noah Davis* (Baltimore, Md.: 1859), p. 27; Jeremiah Bell Jeter, *The Recollections of a Long Life* (Richmond, Va.: 1891), pp. 105, 211.

18. Jackson, "Religious Development," pp. 203–5.

19. *Proceedings of the Charleston Meeting*, pp. 50, 70; Nehemiah Adams, *A South-Side View of Slavery*, 3rd ed. (Boston: 1855), p. 54; Jackson, "Religious Development," pp. 200–2, 230, 230n, 232.

20. Quoted by J. Carleton Hayden, "Conversion and Control: Dilemma of Episcopalians in Providing for the Religious Instruction of Slaves, Charleston, South Carolina, 1845–1860," *Historical Magazine of the Protestant Episcopal Church*, Vol. 40, No. 2 (June 1971), p. 143.

Left. Mt. Zion Baptist Church, Vienna, GA. Constructed by one of the congregation's leading members, Mr. Henry Kendrick (1869–1955), it is characteristic of the small, simple worship structures of African American congregations throughout the rural South. Photo by Larry Murphy, great grandson to Mr. Kendrick. *Right.* Mother Bethel Church, 1804–1841. Lithograph drawn on stone by W. L. Brenton, 1829. Courtesy of the Mother Bethel Church Historical Commission.

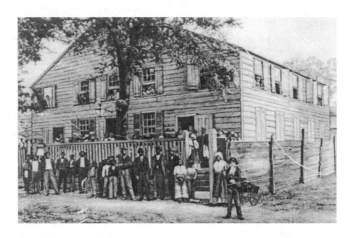

Above Left. Andrew Bryan (1737–1812) formally organized the First African Baptist Church of Savannah in 1788. From Emanuel K. Love, *History of the First African Baptist Church from its Organization, January 20th 1788 to July 1st 1888* (New York, 1969). Courtesy of Howard University, Moorland-Spingarn Research Center. *Above right.* First African Baptist Church of Savannah, erected in 1794. From James M. Simms, *The First Colored Baptist Church in North America* (Philadelphia, 1888). *Left.* John Street Methodist Episcopal Church, New York, with Peter Williams, Sr., the black sexton, in the doorway. Courtesy of the Library of Congress.

Chapter Seven

Sources of Black Denominationalism

Mary R. Sawyer

Today there are eight historically black Christian confessional bodies in the United States, divided among Baptist, Methodist, and Church of God in Christ affiliation. Professor Mary R. Sawyer carefully follows the unfolding of denominational diversity among African American Christians, giving attention to the theological as well as sociological factors that gave rise to independent black communions. She also looks helpfully at issues of differentiation within the various bodies, such as class and sectional identity.

•

Unlike their brethren of European ancestry, African Americans brought to the shores of the New World no sectarian preferences. They came, rather, as a mosaic and fettered representation of the religious diversity of West Africa, which, while including an unknown number of devotees of Islam, in all probability was devoid of practitioners of the Christian faith.[1] Through the sparse ventures of the Society for the Propagation of the Gospel and the more fruitful evangelism of the early nineteenth-century revivals, Africans denied opportunity to practice the rituals of their homelands were introduced to the fundamentals of Christianity.[2] The result was a "congregation" of enslaved believers furtively clustered across the South in what came to be known as the "invisible institution."[3]

In the free North, the first formal congregating of African believers separate and apart from white churches occurred in the self-help and benevolent associations called African Societies, the most famous of which was the Free African Society of Philadelphia organized by Richard Allen and Absalom Jones in 1787. As quasi-religious bodies, the Societies frequently gave rise to one or more churches, the well-known products of the Philadelphia Society being St. Thomas Episcopal Church and Bethel Church, the Mother Church of the African Methodist Episcopal denomination. Either through the medium of the Societies or the process of schism—or both—the number of congregations grew until in 1810, A.M.E. minister Daniel Coker reported the existence of fifteen African churches representing four denominations in ten cities from South Carolina to Massachusetts.[4] Those early separate churches, Will Gravely has suggested, point to "the emergence of an Afro-American community in the new United States." Implicit in this early movement of independent churches was the possibility of a "community or union church," in contradistinction to the phenomenon of denominationalism then taking hold in the larger society.[5] It was a possibility that was never realized.

The process of denominationalism among blacks occurred over a period of a century in three major stages: the Methodist stage at the turn of the nineteenth century, the Baptist stage in the second half of that century, and the Holiness-Pentecostal stage at the turn of the twentieth century.

The initial steps to denominationalism were taken when the constituency of the Philadelphia Free African Society, upon deciding to organize a church, determined also to model the church on an existing polity. Unable to agree on whether to emulate the Anglicans or the Methodists, the Society was divided into two churches, one of which *affiliated* with the white Episcopal denomination, while the other *became* the nucleus of a new, if still Methodist, denomination.

The first black denomination to be formed, however, was the Union Church of Africans organized by Peter Spencer in Dover, Delaware, in 1813, eight years after he and other members had withdrawn from Asbury Methodist Episcopal Church in Wilmington.[6] The Union Church was later renamed Union American Methodist Episcopal Church. Spencer, though among the delegates attending the 1816 meeting in Philadelphia convened by Richard Allen to organize the African Methodist Episcopal (A.M.E.) Church, declined to become a part of Allen's new denomination. Similarly, the New York A.M.E. Zions, following discussions with Allen in 1820, opted to organize a separate denomination, which they did the following year. This decision—predicated largely on resentment of Allen's use of a former Zion member to do mission work in New York for Allen's own denomination—suggests that the implications of proliferating black denominations was not a matter that weighed heavily on the minds of church leaders. That is not to imply that the formation of additional denominations was undertaken in a frivolous or cavalier fashion; rather, it argues a certain "taken for grantedness" about the phenomenon of denominationalism that blacks never challenged.

If the separation of black churches from white had a theological impetus—namely, the belief that the demeaning treatment accorded blacks was an affront to God and to all those created in the image of God—the explanations for the creation of multiple black denominations are more decidedly sociological. Gravely identifies three circumstances that undoubtedly contributed to the pattern of church organization established by the antebellum black Methodists. To begin with, freedom of religion had officially been guaranteed only as recently as 1791 with the adoption of the Bill of Rights. The first black denominations thus emerged in an era when the legal structures pertaining to religious independence were just beginning to be defined; it was the opportunity to participate in this early litigation that even made possible the separation of black churches from white denominations. Bethel Church, for example, became free of the control of the Methodist Episcopal Church only after appealing to the state Supreme Court.[7]

The corollary of this process of developing a body of legal precedents was the formalizing of denominational boundaries within American society.

In the post-Revolutionary generation, there was a fluidity in the process of forming denominations because of the new context of religious freedom. All of the denominational polities and structures within which African churches were formed were being shaped, revised, challenged, defended, and implemented. In the 1780s Episcopalians and Methodists were moving from a colonial to an American organization of church government. Presbyterians did not hold their first general assembly until 1789. Baptists were only regionally organized until 1813, when they established the first national network for the purpose of missionary cooperation.[8]

By and large, as black congregations within these new bodies split off, they retained the name and polity and doctrines of the denomination from which they separated. Those black churches organized as free-standing congregations took on the identity of the particular representatives most significant in introducing their members to the gospel. In this evangelical era of the Second Great Awakening, they were primarily Methodists and Baptists.

Many black congregations, of course, chose to remain within the white denominations, and in those denominations where blacks were relatively few or the mission outreach to blacks tepid, no separate black bodies materialized. This pattern, in turn, was related to a third factor, which Gravely suggests influenced the course of black denominationalism. In those white denominations in which the numbers of black members were small, slavery was a far less divisive issue than in the denominations having substantial black memberships. In this the Presbyterians were an exception, joining the Methodists and Baptists in splitting into northern and southern segments over the issue of slavery, while the Episcopalians and Congregationalists and Lutherans remained intact. But even before these formal divisions occurred, the diminution in opposition to slavery within these churches may well have encouraged black separatism. Gravely points out that

> in the case of the Methodists, . . . all three African separations occurred *after* the failure of the general conferences between 1800 and 1808 to remove slaveholders from membership and from clerical orders. Indeed, the conferences of 1804 and 1808 printed expurgated copies of the Church's *Discipline* for the southern states without the legislation on slavery. Even Asbury, who had despised slavery from the first, gave in to proslavery pressures, conceding in his journal that it was more important to save the African's soul than to free his body.[9]

These three factors, then—access to legal authority condoning a multiplicity of religious expressions, the "fashionableness" of denominationalism, and diminishing anti-slavery sentiment—all conjoined to foster the establishment of black denominations. At that, the overwhelming majority of black Methodists initially remained within the white denomination. Of the 42,300 blacks in the Methodist Episcopal Church in 1816, only 1066 withdrew to follow Allen into the new A.M.E. Church. The A.M.E. Zion Church was organized in 1820 with but 1406 Methodists. In short, "at no time was there a wholesale rush out of the Methodist Church."[10] This situation changed dramatically after the Civil War, however, when former slaves, for the first time, had a choice of religious affiliation.

In 1860, shortly before Emancipation, the total black population of the United States was 4.4 million. Of these, 4.2 million were in the South, while a mere 200,000 were in the North.[11] With the abolition of slavery, the factors already operative in black separatism and denominationalism became even more pronounced. In addition to those cited, C. Eric Lincoln identifies the "longing to be rid of the unremitting stress of living in a white-dominated world," the "dearth of leadership opportunities elsewhere in the society," and the heterogeneity among blacks that generated both a capacity and a need for diverse religious expressions.[12]

The importance of this heterogeneity for black denominationalism was greatly magnified following Emancipation. Indeed, internal differences within the black population became as compelling, if not more so, than the external factors involved in denominationalism. Among these categories of differentiation—each of them products of the slave system—were legal status, role assignment, and skin color.[13] Class divisions within the white-defined black caste stemmed from prior status of free or slave and, within the former slave population itself, from relationships and skills that had been developed in their capacity either as house servants or field hands. Often a correlation obtained between these assignments and skin complexion. Thus, light-skinned blacks were more likely to have had contact with whites, to have cultivated social and artisan skills, to have been exposed—if tangentially—to white churches and to educational systems. These differences became the source of considerable elitism and conflict in the years and decades following Emancipation, a divisive circumstance not substantially modified until the black consciousness movement of the 1960s.

Nor did these divisions among blacks bypass the church, which too often became a mirror of the distorted values bequeathed to blacks by the larger society. George Simpson maintains that "the blacks who were attracted to the Presbyterian and Episcopal Churches tended to be closer in class affiliation and complexion with the whites than was the case among the black Baptists and Methodists,"[14] and Lincoln adds that "while black churches attached to white denominations tended to be more color-conscious than others, the problem was not unknown in the authentic Black Church of independent tradition, although it was considerably less pronounced."[15]

The class divisions took on sectional dimensions as tensions developed between better-educated northern blacks who were a generation or more removed from slavery—or who had never been slaves—and newly liberated southern blacks. Many of the northern black leaders had been engaged in the abolitionist movement and were accustomed to political activism. Southern blacks had a different experience and agenda, preoccupied, as they were, with learning how to live free in a virulently hostile climate. Furthermore, the intense resentment of southern whites toward northern missionaries, as well as northern politicians and military personnel, made identification with radical northern elements—black or white—a dangerous proposition for southern blacks.

In spite of these realities, thousands of freed slaves did respond to the overtures of A.M.E, A.M.E Zion, and Methodist Episcopal emissaries from northern churches. But the social and political circumstances also played a major part in the formation of yet another black Methodist denomination—the Colored (now Christian) Methodist Episcopal Church, organized in Jackson, Tennessee, in 1870. The members of this new body represented the residual black membership of the Methodist Episcopal Church, South, which declined to come under the jurisdiction of any of the other Methodist bodies, partially out of resentment of the northerners' aggressive tactics of taking over established congregations, along with their church property.[16]

Some of the same sectional hostilities and tensions served to prolong the process of achieving a united black Baptist denomination. Independent black Baptist churches began separating from white Baptist bodies in the North as early as 1805. These churches, of course, were preceded by black Baptist congregations in the South dating from the early 1770s; indeed, by far the majority of black Baptists were in the South, most of them gathered within the "invisible institution" of slave religion. Upon gaining their independence, they clung fiercely to it, declining to come under the episcopacy of the Methodist churches.

The first black Baptist associations were formed in Ohio in 1834 and 1836, and in Illinois in 1839. These were followed in 1840 by the first regional convention. A second regional convention organized in 1864 joined with the first in 1866 to form the first national black convention, called the "Consolidated American Baptist Missionary Convention." But financial difficulties and regional differences over such issues as the political role of church leaders and emotionalism in worship services caused this effort to be short-lived.[17] Disbanded in 1879, it was succeeded in 1880 by the Baptist Foreign Mission Convention and in 1886 by the American National Baptist Convention. Not until 1895 did these two groups join with yet a third, the National Baptist Educational Convention, to become the first enduring national black Baptist denomination: the National Baptist Convention, U.S.A. Class and sectional divisions again entered into the formula of black denominationalism, however, when two years later the Lott Carey Foreign Missionary Convention was organized by some of the more highly educated members of the National Convention from North Carolina, Virginia, and the District of Columbia.

The year 1897 also marked the founding of what has become the largest of the black Holiness-Pentecostal denominations, the Church of God in Christ. COGIC, along with numerous other black denominations, was initially a product of the Holiness Movement dating from the 1860s. As the Methodists had become more middle class, they also had become disparaging of the old "folk" ways of worship, in reaction to which a reform movement was initiated within the churches. The movement gradually became schismatic, however, as the "come-outers" among Methodists, Baptists, and other denominations—black and white alike—formed their own independent congregations and associations, some of which then became new denominations.[18]

While social class conflicts were a distinctive feature of the movement, this stage of denominationalism—in this instance more aptly termed "sectarianism"—did have a theological dimension as well. The complaint was that Methodists had abandoned the Wesleyan doctrine of sanctification, or spiritual perfection, an experience deemed as necessary to salvation as conversion, or spiritual rebirth. It was from this emphasis that the appellation "holiness" derived as a description of those who participated in the protest.

The Pentecostal Movement, then, stemming from the Azusa Street Revival held in

TABLE 7.1
Major Black Denominations' Membership

	Est. U.S. Members
African Methodist Episcopal	1,700,000
African Methodist Episcopal Zion	1,100,000
Christian Methodist Episcopal	850,000
Church of God in Christ	3,500,000
National Baptist Convention of America, Inc.	*
National Missionary Baptist Convention of America	*
National Baptist Convention, U.S.A., Inc.	7,100,000
Progressive National Baptist Convention, Inc.	1,000,000
TOTAL	17,450,000

SOURCE: Executives and published reports of the respective denominations and conventions. Figures are estimates for 1984.

* The membership of the National Baptist Convention of America before dividing into these two groups was estimated to be 2.2 million. The distribution of the membership in the two groups was unclear as of the early 1990s, but it appeard the majority had affiliated with the newly incorporated body.

Los Angeles from 1906 to 1908 under the leadership of a black minister, W. J. Seymour, was distinctly theological in origin.[19] The Pentecostals posited a "third work of grace" designated as "baptism in the Holy Ghost" and evidenced by the phenomenon of "speaking in tongues," or glossolalia. Yet the movement also had class overtones and held particular appeal for the masses of blacks migrating to the North and West during the War and Depression decades in search of a brighter future.

In its nearly ninety-year history, the Pentecostal Movement has produced as many as seventy separate black groups, most of them with memberships of less than a thousand. Many of these groups are both Holiness and Pentecostal, COGIC being a case in point. The Pentecostals, in turn, have divided—again on doctrinal grounds— into Trinitarian churches and Apostolic, or "oneness," churches.[20]

There are, of course, other Methodist and Baptist communions as well. The National Baptist Convention, U.S.A., experienced schism a second time in 1915, which produced the National Baptist Convention of America, and again in 1961, which resulted in the Progressive National Baptist Convention, Inc. In both instances, the conflicts revolved around matters of personality and organizational control, although in the case of PNBC a theological difference over the appropriateness of political activism was also at issue.[21] In 1988 yet another division occurred when the National Baptist Convention of America split into the National Baptist Convention of America, Inc. and the National Missionary Baptist Convention of America. These four Baptist Conventions, together with the three largest Methodist Churches and the Church of God in Christ, accounted for nearly 17.5 million church members in the late 1980s (see Table 7.1).

To these could be added approximately 1.2 million church members in smaller black communions. Among them are the National Primitive Baptist Convention of the U.S.A.; the United Free Will Baptist Church; the National Baptist Evangelical Life and Soul Saving Assembly of the U.S.A.; the Union American Methodist Episcopal Church; the Church of the Living God (or Christian Workers for Fellowship, known locally as C.W.F.W.); the National Convention of the Churches of God, Holiness; the Apostolic Overcoming Holy Church of God; Triumph the Church and Kingdom of God in Christ; Pentecostal Assemblies of the World; Bible Way Churches of Our Lord Jesus Christ, World Wide; the United Holy Church of America; and the Church of the Lord Jesus Christ of the Apostolic Faith, Inc.—all of which had memberships ranging from 25,000 to 100,000.[22]

An additional 1.8 million blacks were estimated to be members of predominantly white denominations, ranging from 48,000 black Lutherans to 400,000 black United Methodists. The highest rate of growth in recent decades may be in the Roman Catholic Church, which as of 1990 counted some 1.2 million black members in the United States. The American Baptist Churches and Southern Baptist Convention also reported substantial increases in black membership, although in many instances these undoubtedly entail dual affiliation with one of the National Baptist conventions (see Table 7.2).

Significantly, over 80 percent of all black church members are gathered in the eight largest black denominations. These, in turn, represent but three different orientations—namely, those orientations corresponding to the three major stages of denominationalism among black Christians. Thus, if a single united church has eluded African Americans, the dynamic of denominationalism has never fragmented this population as extensively as has been the case for Euro-Americans. One may see in this circumstance an extraordinary holding in tension of inheritances from vastly differing cultural sources. Black denominationalism, in its moderation, is at once an acknowledgment of diversity within the black nation and an emphatic statement of ethnic solidarity.

TABLE 7.2
Blacks in White Denominations/Sects, U.S.

Orientation	Estimated Members
Protestant	
United Methodist	400,000
American Baptist	580,000*
Southern Baptist	147,000
Presbyterian	62,000
Episcopal	49,000
United Church of Christ	70,000
Evangelical Lutheran Church of America	48,000
Seventh-day Adventist	122,000
Jehovah's Witnesses	170,000
Assemblies of God	63,000
Church of the Nazarene	8,000
Various Pentecostal and Spiritual	50,000
	1,769,000
Catholic	1,200,00
	2,969,000

SOURCE: Denomination officials and reports. Figures are variously for 1988 and 1989.
* This figure includes some double counting, since many black Baptists dual affiliate with a black Convention and American Baptist Churches.

NOTES

This chapter appeared previously in *Phylon: The Clark Atlanta University Review of Race and Culture 49*, nos. 3–4 (Fall and Winter 1993–94), and is reprinted with permission.

1. C. Eric Lincoln, "The American Muslim Mission in the Context of American Social History," in E. H. Waugh et al., eds., *The Muslim Community in North America* (Edmonton, Alberta, Canada: University of Alberta Press, 1983).

2. Milton C. Sernett, *Black Religion and American Evangelicalism* (Metuchen, N.J.: Scarecrow Press and the American Theological Library Association, 1975).

3. Albert J. Raboteau, *Slave Religion: The "Invisible Institution" in the Antebellum South* (New York: Oxford University Press, 1978).

4. Will B. Gravely, "The Rise of African Churches in America (1786–1822): Re-examining the Contexts," *Journal of Religious Thought* 41, no. 1 (Spring–Summer 1984):58.

5. Ibid., 58, 64–65.

6. Lewis V. Baldwin, "The A.U.M.P. and U.A.M.E. Churches: An Unexplored Area of Black Methodism," *Methodist History* 19 (April 1981): 177–78. Baldwin writes: "In September 1813, Spencer and 26 of his followers organized the Union Church of Africans, which was incorporated at Dover, Delaware. By December of 1813, this church had become a connectional body with the addition of two small congregations in New York and Pennsylvania. By 1816, the year the A.M.E. Church was incorporated as an independent African Methodist connection, the number of congregations comprising the Union Church of Africans had increased to five."

7. Gravely, "The Rise of African Churches," 66–67.

8. Ibid., 68.

9. Ibid., 71.

10. Harry V. Richardson, *Dark Salvation: The Story of Methodism as It Developed among Blacks in America* (Garden City, N.Y.: Anchor Press/Doubleday, 1976), 148.

11. Ira Berlin, *Slaves without Masters* (New York: Oxford University Press, 1974), 46–47, 136–37, Appendix 1.

12. C. Eric Lincoln, *Race, Religion, and the Continuing American Dilemma* (New York: Hill and Wang, 1984), 81.

13. Ibid., 74–77.

14. George E. Simpson, *Black Religion in the New World* (New York: Columbia University Press, 1978), 228.

15. Lincoln, *Race, Religion, and the Continuing American Dilemma*, 77.

16. Richardson, *Dark Salvation*, 195–98, 235–36.

17. James M. Washington, *The Origins and Emergence of Black Baptist Separatism*, 1863–1897 (Ann Arbor, Mich.: University Microfilms, 1983). See chapter 4, "The Dissolution of the Consolidated Convention, 1869–1879."

18. For an overview of the emergence of the Holiness Movement, see chapter 2 in Vinson Synan, *The Holiness-Pentecostal Movement in the United States* (Grand Rapids, Mich.: Wm. B. Eerdmans Publishing Co., 1971).

19. The Azusa Street Revival is treated in chapter 4 of Synan, entitled "The American Jerusalem—Azusa Street."

20. James Tinney, "Selected Directory of Afro-American Religious Organizations, Schools, and Periodicals," in Dionne J. Jones and Wm. H. Matthews, eds., *The Black Church: A Community Resource* (Washington, D.C.: Howard University Institute for Urban Affairs and Research, 1977), 199–200, 214–15.

21. Specifically, the conflict revolved around the opposition of the Convention's president, Joseph Jackson, to the direct action protest tactics of the civil rights movement. It was Martin Luther King's supporters in the Convention who challenged Jackson and ultimately led the schismatic movement to form the PNBC.

22. Tinney, "Selected Directory of Afro-American Religious Organizations, Schools, and Periodicals," 160–215, passim.

Omar Ibn Said (1770–1864), African Muslim slave in North Carolina. Courtesy of the Library of Davidson College. Used by permission.

Chapter Eight

Pre–Twentieth Century Islam

Richard Brent Turner

Scholar of African American Islam Richard Brent Turner documents the long association of blacks and Islam, a heritage transported from the African continent from the earliest days of U.S. slavery. Though never numerically extensive, pre–twentieth century Islam was a distinctive presence and demonstrated the ability of African religious and cultural elements to survive intact through the enslavement process.

•

In the New World, African Muslim slaves were noteworthy for their sometimes violent resistance to the institution of slavery. In Brazil, hundreds of African Muslim slaves planned and executed a major slave uprising in Bahia, in 1835, fighting soldiers and civilians in the streets of Salvador. Moreover, at least one African Muslim participated in the revolt on the Spanish slave ship the *Amistad* in the Caribbean, in 1839. The slaves' knowledge of Arabic and of the religion of Islam were key factors in their identification as African Muslims. In other locations, African Muslims were noted for their bold efforts both to resist conversion to Christianity and to convert other Africans to Islam. Mohammed Sisei, an African Muslim in Trinidad in the early nineteenth century, noted that the Free Mandingo Society there was instrumental in converting a whole H. M. West Indian Regiment of blacks to Islam. At the same time, prominent African Muslim slaves in Jamaica in the early 1800s circulated a letter urging other African Muslims in their communities to adhere to their religion. Muhammad, an African Muslim slave in Antigua, was manumitted by his master because of his stubborn adherence to Islam and returned to Africa in 1811.[1]

Resistance, then, was a global theme in New World black Islam in the eighteenth and nineteenth centuries.[2] In the United States, however, African Muslims practiced more subtle forms of resistance to slavery. Some of them kept their African names, wrote in Arabic, and continued to practice their religion; others used the American Colonization Society to gain their freedom and return to Africa. All of this constituted intellectual resistance to slavery, as African Muslims, who had been members of the ruling elite in West Africa, used their literacy and professional skills to manipulate white Americans. This peculiar form of resistance accounts in part for the compelling and provocative nature of the life stories of the known African Muslim slaves in America.[3]

Even the slave community noted the compelling presence of African Muslims in its midst. Ex-slave Charles Ball, one of the first African Americans to publish an autobiography, was struck by the religious discipline and resistance to Christianity of a nineteenth-century African Muslim slave on a plantation in North Carolina. He wrote,

> At the time I first went to Carolina, there were a great many African slaves in the country. . . . I became intimately acquainted with some of these men. . . . I knew several, who must have been, from what I have since learned, Mohammedans; though at that time, I had never heard of the religion of Mohammed. There was one man on this plantation, who prayed five times every day always turning his face to the East, when in the performance of his devotions.[4]

Signification is the analytical key that explains resistance in the lives of the African Muslims noted previously and in the biographical sketches that follow, for African Muslim slaves preserved their Islamic identities by refusing to internalize the Christian racist significations that justified the system of exploitation. These were profound acts of resistance to an institution that, in setting the terms for pre–twentieth century racial discourse in America, attempted to eradicate all aspects of African heritage in the slave quarters by stripping slaves of their culture, thus leaving them powerless. As African Muslims signified themselves as the people they wanted to be in America, they transformed Islam to meet the demands of survival and resistance in this "strange Christian land." Their signification turned their history, religion, and genealogies into "an instrument of identity and transformation."[5]

In this context, writing in Arabic, fasting, wearing Muslim clothing, and reciting and reflecting on the Quran were the keys to an inner struggle of liberation against Christian tyranny. Thus, for African Muslim slaves, their significations became "the ultimate test of their faith" in America and a "paradigm for the liberation struggles" of other oppressed blacks in the New World. Their stories reveal that African slaves had ethnic and religious identities that could not be erased by the trauma of slavery.[6]

Fascinating portraits of a few influential African Muslims slaves exist in the historical literature. Excerpts from several of their life stories follow.

Bilali and Salih Bilali were two of at least twenty black Muslims who were reported to have lived and practiced their religion in Sapelo Island and St. Simon's Island during the antebellum period. The Georgia Sea Islands provided fertile ground for Islamic and other African retentions because of their relative isolation from Euro-American influences. Both Bilali and Salih Bilali remained steadfast in the struggle to maintain their Muslim identities in America. Both men were noted for their devotion to their religious obligations, for wearing Islamic clothing, and for their Muslim names, and one was noted for his ability to write and speak Arabic, which he passed on to his children. Moreover, available evidence suggests that they might have been the leaders of a small black Muslim community in the Georgia Sea Islands.[7]

Georgia Conrad, a white American resident of one of the Sea Islands, met Bilali's family in the 1850s and was struck by their religion, dress, and ability to speak Arabic. She wrote:

On Sapelo Island near Darcen, I used to know a family of Negroes who worshipped Mohamet. They were tall and well-formed, with good features. They conversed with us in English, but in talking among themselves they used a foreign tongue that no one else understood. The head of the tribe was a very old man named Bi-la-li. He always wore a cap that resembled a Turkish fez.[8]

Bilali, who was also known as Belali Mahomet, Bu Allah, and Ben Ali, was a Muslim slave on the Thomas Spalding plantation on Sapelo Island, Georgia from the early to the mid-1800s. His great grandchildren told his story to Works Progress Administration writers in Georgia in the 1930s. Bilali maintained his identity by giving his nineteen children Muslim names and teaching them Muslim traditions. When he died, he left an Arabic manuscript he had composed, and had his prayer rug and Quran placed in his coffin.[9]

Only a few facts are known about Bilali's pre-American history. Although his surname is unknown, we do know that his first name represents the West African Muslim fascination with Bilal, the Prophet Muhammad's black companion and the first muezzin. Bilali was born in Timbo, Futa Jallon. Like other Fulbe Muslim compatriots in America, he was probably raised in a prominent scholarly family, for the Arabic manuscript that he composed in America was undoubtedly the product of someone who wrote and read Arabic at an advanced level. The manuscript was a compilation of pieces from the Malikite legal text, *ar-Risala*, which was originally written by Abu Muhammad' Abdullah ibn, Abi Zaid al-Qairawani. Bilali's work, "First Fruits of Happiness," attempts to reconcile the law of Islam with a wholesome daily life. It suggests that Bilali was struggling to uphold his faith in America.[10]

Bilali's leadership ability, reflecting his elite roots in West Africa, was legendary on Sapelo Island. He was the manager of his master's plantation, which included close to five hundred slaves. During the War of 1812, Bilali and approximately eighty slaves who had muskets prevented the British from invading their island. Some of these slaves were undoubtedly Muslim, since Bilali forewarned Thomas Spalding that, in battle, "I will answer for every Negro of the true facts, but not for the Christian dogs you own." Moreover, in 1824, during a hurricane, Bilali saved the slaves on Sapelo Island by leading them into cotton and sugar shacks constructed of African tabby.[11]

Perhaps the most fascinating aspect of Bilali's Islamic legacy was that his descendants on Sapelo Island remembered him in the 1930s, when they were interviewed by the Savannah Unit of the Georgia Writer's Project. These interviews also brought to light other nineteenth-century blacks who practiced Islam on the Georgia Sea Islands. Although they have been criticized for inaccuracy and contextual problems, these interviews are an invaluable source of information on Bilali and his descendants.[12]

According to Shadrack Hall, who was Bilali's great grandson, the African Muslim slave was brought to Georgia from the Bahamas with his wife Phoebe and maintained Islamic names and traditions in his family for at least three generations:

Muh gran wuz Hestah, Belali's daughter. She tell me Belali wuz coal black, wid duh small feechuhs we hab, and he wuz very tall. . . . Belali hab plenty daughtahs, Medina, Yaruba, Fatima, Bentoo, Hestah, Magret, and Chaalut.

Ole Belali Smith wuz muh uncle. His son wuz George Smith's gran. He wuz muh gran Hestuh's son an muh mudduh Sally's brudduh. Hestah an all ub um sho pray on duh head. Dey weah duh string uh beads on duh neck. Dey pray at sun-up and face duh sun on duh knees an bow tuh it tree times, kneelin' on a lill mat.[13]

Finally, Katie Brown, another one of Bilali's great grandchildren, recalled her Muslim grandmother Margret, who wore a Muslim headdress and made rice cakes for the children at the end of a fast day:

Yes'm, I membuh gran too. Bilali he from Africa but muh gran she came by Bahamas. . . .

She ain tie uh head up lak I does, but she weah a loose wite clawt da she trow obuh uh head lak veil an it hang loose on uh shoulduh. I ain know wy she weah it dataway, but I tink she ain lak a tight ting roun uh head.

She make funny flat cake she call "saraka." She make um same day ebry yeah, an it big day. Wen dey finish, she call us in, all duh chillun, an put in hans lill flat cake an we eats it. Yes'm, I membuh how she make it. She wash rice, an po off all duh watuh. She let wet rice sit all night, an in mawnin rice is all swell. She tak dat rice an put it in wooden mawtuh, an beat it tuh paste wid wooden pestle. She add honey, sometimes shuguh, an make it in flat cake wid uh hans. "Saraka" she call um.[14]

James Hamilton Couper, a Georgia aristocrat who owned a plantation on St. Simon's Island with several hundred slaves, contributed a paper to the American Ethnological Society about one of his Muslim slaves, Salih Bilali, also known as Tom:

He is a strict Mahometan; abstains from spiritous liquors, and keeps the various fasts, particularly that of Rhamadan. He is singularly exempt from all feeling of superstition; and holds in great contempt the African belief in fetishes and evil spirits. He reads Arabic and has a Koran . . . in that language but does not write it. . . . Mr. Spaulding of Sapelo has, among his Negroes, one named Bul-Ali who writes Arabic and speaks the Fonlah language. Tom and himself are intimate friends. He is now old and feeble. Tom informs me that he is from Timboo.[15]

Salih Balali, born in Massina in 1765, was probably a member of a prominent Mandingo Fulbe clerical family. When he was twelve years old, he was taken into slavery while he was returning home from Jenne, one of the major black Muslim intellectual centers of West Africa. In his African reminiscences, Salih Bilali remembered well the racial and cultural differences between the black Muslims in his land and the white Arab Muslim traders who sold them goods in Jenne, Timbuktu, Kouna, and Sego.[16]

Salih Bilali's odyssey in the New World brought him first to the Bahamas, where he was purchased by the Couper family around 1800. By 1816, he had become the overseer of the family's St. Simon's plantation, which had more than four hundred slaves. By all accounts, Salih Bilali was an impressive figure in the Georgia Sea Islands. His steadfast religiosity may have been the result of Islamic training under Bilali in the Bahamas and Georgia.[17] Together they formed the nucleus of a small Muslim community, of which the members can only be suggested by the interviews with Salih Bilali's grandchildren, conducted by the Georgia's Writer's Project on the Georgia Sea Islands in the 1930s.[18]

Salih Bilali's grandson, Ben Sullivan, remembered that his father had received his Arabic name—Bilali—from his own father. Bilali was the butler on another Couper plantation until the end of the Civil War, when he chose the surname Sullivan. Bilali Sullivan also made saraka (rice cakes) at certain times of the year. Ben Sullivan was one of several of Couper's slaves who practiced Islam. This group included Alex Boyd, his maternal grandfather, and a light-skinned man named Daphne, and Israel: "Ole Israel he pray a lot wid a book he hab wit he hide, and he take a lill mat and he say he prayuhs on it. He pray wen duh sun go up and wen duh sun go down. . . . He alluz tie he head up in a wite clawt."[19]

At the same time Rosa Grant, who may have been descended from Salih Bilali, recalled her Muslim grandmother, who lived in Possum Point: "Muh gran came from Africa too. Huh name wuz Ryna. I membuh wen I wuz a chile see in muh gran Ryna pray. Ebry mawnin at sun-up she kned on duh flo in uh ruhm an bow abuh an tech uh head tuh duh fo tree time."[20]

Finally Grant remembered one more Muslim woman in Darien:

> Baker told us that many people in the section refused to eat certain foods, believing bad luck would follow if they ate them.
>
> Deah's lots dataway now. Lots uh folks dohn eat some food cuz ef dey did dey say it would bring bad luck on duh parents. Some dohn eat rice, some dohn eat egg, an some dohn eat chicken.
>
> Muh gran, she Rachel Grant, she use tuh tell me bout lot uh deze tings. I membuh she use tuh pray ebry day at sunrise, at middle day and den at sunset. She alluz face duh sun an wen she finish prayin she alluz bow tuh duh sun. She tell me bout duh slaves wut could fly too. Ef dey didn lak it on duh plantation, dey just take wing an fly right back tuh Africa.[21]

In the biographical sketches of Bilali and Salih Bilali, there is fragmentary evidence of a small African Muslim slave community that attempted to preserve Muslim identities and traditions in the nineteenth century. In these sketches, we also have evidence of how African Muslim women were involved in the struggle to preserve Muslim identities in America. It appears that they played a significant role in this struggle, for their preparation of Muslim foods, their Muslim clothing, and their disciplined devotion to their religion deeply impressed their children and grandchildren. And their families' memories of their Muslim identities have influenced the significations of nineteenth-century Islam that African Americans have preserved in their folklore in the twentieth century.

But now, to the point most relevant to our discussion. What did African Muslim slaves' retention of Muslim names and traditions signify in American racial discourse in the nineteenth century? We know that identity was important to this discourse for both blacks and whites. The act of taking away an African's name and religious traditions and assigning him a new name and a new religion in an alien land imposed on the black a rite of passage, an unholy confirmation—"branding a mark" into his consciousness that symbolized his depersonalization and his subordinate state in a new social order. These measures placed the slave in a state of permanent marginality, for his old identity was lost forever and he could not acquire a new one on his own. Therefore, he was positioned as an "acquired stranger" or a "non-person" in the structure of the racial discourse. In that discourse, only the master had the power to define who or what the African slave could signify. For a slave to retain Muslim names and traditions must have been perceived by some whites as an intolerable threat to the social order.[22]

For some whites, slaves had to remain "the unspoken invisible other" in the racial discourse. Who they were was not important. What they could signify, however, was. Therefore, some white Americans used the power of signification and characterized the Muslim slaves as "overly tanned" Arabs or referred to them as "Moors" instead of Africans.[23] For people of European descent, the term "Moor" signified their Muslim enemies wherever they encountered them in the world. Indeed the term Moor held complex and longstanding religious and political significations for Euro-Americans. In the Middle Ages, Europe was significantly threatened by the political, military, and cultural power of the Moors from Morocco. It was not until the eve of the modern era that Spanish, Portuguese, and southern Italian Christians achieved the reconquest of their own lands after centuries of domination by Moroccan Muslims; around the same time, Russian Christians finally conquered the Tatar Muslims who had ruled and/or threatened them for centuries. Partly because of the long-standing history of warfare between Christians and Muslims during the Crusades in the holy lands, other European peoples welcomed the Christian reconquest of Europe and connected it ideologically to the new voyages of discovery and exploration in the New World. It was not until 1683, however, that the "Moorish" Muslim threat to Europe really ended. On September 12 of that year, Turkish Muslims finally withdrew from the outskirts of Vienna after a failed attempt to seize the city. In 1699, the Treaty of Carlowitz officially signaled the hegemony of the Hapsburgs over the Muslim Ottoman empire. Because of this history of conflict between Europe and Muslims, Europeans "continued to name all of their Muslim enemies 'Moors.' "[24]

By the time of the antebellum period in America, Europeans had finally surpassed global Islam in terms of technology and military power, but the image of the "Moor" or the Muslim enemy was still a powerful signification for people of European descent everywhere. It explained the awe and respect that some African Muslim slaves received from some white Americans, as well as the repeated attempts by whites to facilitate these slaves' return to Africa as a means of ridding America of Islam.[25]

According to Charles H. Long, encounters between the enslaver and the enslaved, the colonizer and the colonized, the conqueror and the conquered produced during the modern period a "structure of experience" and an intellectual problem for both the signified and the signifier. The signifier created new intellectual categories, such as "race" and "Moor," to objectify people who were "novel" and "other." At the same time, the signifier used these intellectual formulations to obscure the culture's real economic, political, and military objectives among black people. The signified had to cope with these new names and categories in order to survive in the context of European domination. However, especially in the nineteenth and early twentieth centuries, they began to reformulate their racial and cultural identities through "a signification upon this legitimated signifying."[26]

For blacks, both slave and free, slave names were a metaphor for the cultural pain inflicted on Africans. The purpose of this pain was to destroy the African's ethnicity and to replace it with a racial identity. This is one of the reasons why naming the African American was such a controversial issue for black political leaders and intellectuals in the nineteenth century. Some of those leaders were attempting to come to terms with their own slave names and to reconstruct their ethnicity. They proposed many names for their race: Free African, African, Children of Africa, Sons of Africa, Ethiopian, Negro, Colored American, Colored, people of color, free people of color, Afro-Saxon, African, Afro-American, Africo-American, African American, Aframerican, and Afmerican.[27]

African Muslim slaves established a unique position in this discourse. They constituted the first Islamic group in America, and their original ethnic identities and names had remained intact in the eighteenth and nineteenth centuries. They were Songhai-Hausa, Mandingo, Fulani, Kanuri-Mandara, Sereculeh, and Tukolor. In Africa, most of them had been professionals: teachers, doctors, traders, translators, religious scholars, and military and political leaders. Their positions in the racial discourse of their time were complex, since their names, dietary laws, rituals, dress, literacy in Arabic, former social status, and ethnicity set them apart from other slaves.[28]

Moreover, the very qualities that distinguished African Muslims from other slaves impressed their black compatriots, both slave and free, because they represented resistance, self-determination, and education. Vincent P. Franklin has shown that resistance, self-determination, and education were the "core values" of African American culture from slavery to the present. Indeed, in the antebellum period, no other group of blacks in America had a religion that articulated these values more uniquely and effectively than African Muslims. Aspects of global Islam—literacy in Arabic and signification—equipped them with the tools for a liberation struggle in America that in many cases resulted ultimately in their emigration back to Africa. Furthermore, resistance, self-determination, and education connected the religion of the African Muslim slaves ideologically to the Pan-Africanist impulse that bridged ethnic differences binding slaves together and sustaining them under brutal conditions of oppression. This Pan-Africanist impulse, which became more pervasive and influential in black America as the nineteenth century progressed, was the ideological link between the "old Islam" of the original African Muslim slaves and the "new American Islam" that developed at the turn of the century.[29]

At the same time, by the eve of the Civil War, the old Islam of the original African Muslim slaves was, for all practical purposes, defunct because these Muslims were unable in the nineteenth century to develop institutions that would perpetuate their religion. With no community of believers for them to connect with outside of the slave quarters, they were religious oddities, mavericks. When they died, their version of Islam, which was private and individually oriented, disappeared. Unfortunately, the historical record does not provide us with a holistic picture of their religious life. They were important, nevertheless, because they brought the religion of Islam to America.

Pan-Africanism and black bitterness towards Christian racism were new seeds planted in the consciousness of nineteenth-century African Americans that in turn flowered into a new American Islam in the early twentieth century. This new American Islam in the African American community was at once anti-Christian and multicultural; and it developed a distinct missionary and internationalist political agenda. It was also part of a new era in American religious history as Eastern religions began to flourish in the United States. Noble Drew Ali's Moorish Science Temple of America was the first mass-based version of this new American Islam among African Americans in the early twentieth century.

NOTES

1. João José Reis, *Slave Rebellion in Brazil*, trans. Arthur Brakel (Baltimore: The Johns Hopkins University Press, 1993). This work is based on transcripts of the trials of the rebels at Conceicão da Praia, Brazil. At the Amistad Trial in New Haven, Connecticut, Richard R. Madden identified one of the African mutineers as a Muslim by saying an Islamic prayer to him. The African Muslim responded to the prayer in Arabic: "Allah Akbar"—God is Great. Howard Jones, *The Mutiny on the Amistad* (New York: Oxford University Press, 1987), 108; Madden deposition, November 20, 1839, 133 U.S. District Court Records for Connecticut, Federal Archives and Record Center, Waltham, Massachusetts.

2. John Washington, "Some Account of Mohammed Sisei, a Mandingo, of Nyani-Mara in the Gambia," *Journal of the Royal Geographical Society* VIII (1838): 449–54; Richard R. Madden, *A Twelve Month's Residence in the West Indies, During the Transition from Slavery to Apprenticeship, with Incidental Notices of the State of Society, Prospects and Natural Resources of Jamaica and Other Islands*, 2 vols. (Philadelphia: Carey, Lea, and Blanchard 1835); Folarium Shyllon, *Black People in Britain, 1555–1833* (New York: Oxford University Press, 1977), 60.

3. For a brilliant analysis of intellectual resistance to slavery, see William D. Piérsen, *Black Legacy* (Amherst: University of Massachusetts Press, 1993). Janet D. Cornelius has analyzed slave literacy as resistance in *When I Can Read My Title Clear* (Columbia: University of South Carolina Press, 1991). This section of the chapter is a challenge to Orlando Patterson's major thesis in *Slavery and Social Death* (Cambridge: Harvard University Press, 1982) that slave systems erase social identity. Patterson fails to distinguish between what slave systems attempt to do and what they succeed in doing; he forfeits agency to the ruling/master classes and their appurtenances, thus concealing entirely the possibilities that the enslaved have any choices in the matter.

4. Charles Ball, *A Narrative of the Life and Adventures of Charles Ball, A Black Man*. 3d ed. (Pittsburgh: John T. Skyrock, 1854), 143.

5. Reis, *Slave Rebellion in Brazil*, 154. Sidney W. Mintz and Richard Price present a pathbreaking study of how African slaves were acculturated in America in *The Birth of African-American Culture* (Boston: Beacon Press, 1992), first published by Institute for the Study of Human Issues, 1976.

6. Vincent J. Cornell, "Jihad: Islam's Struggle for the Truth," 18; Adbul Khatib, "The Need for Jihad," *Gnosis Magazine* (Fall 1991), 24.

7. Allan D. Austin, *African Muslims in Antebellum America: A Sourcebook* (New York: Garland Press, 1984), 386.

8. Georgia Bryan Conrad, *Reminiscences of a Southern Woman* (Hampton, VA: Hampton Institute, n.d.), 13.

9. Charles Spalding Wylly, *The Seed That Was Sown in Georgia* (New York: Neale, 1910). Wylly, the grandson of Thomas Spalding, recalled that his grandfather owned slaves of

"Moorish or Arabian descent, devout Mussulmans, who prayed to Allah . . . morning, noon, and evening."

10. William B. Hodgson, *Notes on Northern Africa, the Sahara and Sudan* (New York: Wiley and Putnam, 1844), 73; Joseph H. Greenberg, "The Decipherment of the 'Ben Ali Diary,' a Preliminary Statement," *Journal of Negro History* (July 1940); Ella May Thornton, "Bilali—His Book," *Law Library Journal* XLVIII (1955): 228–29. Bilali's diary is in the library of Georgia State University in Atlanta. Recently, Ronald A. T. Judy has translated Bilali's (Ben Ali's) diary and analyzed the various accounts of his life in *(Dis) Forming: The American Canon: African-Arabic Slave Narratives and The Vernacular* (Minneapolis: University of Minnesota Press, 1993). Also see William S. McFreely, *Sapelo's People: A Long Walk Into Freedom* (New York: W. W. Norton, 1994).

11. Zephaniah Kingsley, *Treatise on the Partiarchal or Co-operative System of Society*, 2d ed. (1829); reprint (Freeport, New York: Books for Libraries, 1970), 13–14; Wylly, *The Seed That Was Sown in Georgia, 52; E. Merton Coulter, Thomas Spalding of Sapelo* (Baton Rouge: Louisiana State University, 1940), 190–193; Caroline Couper Lovell, *The Golden Isles of Georgia* (Boston: Little Brown, 1933), 103–104.

12. Savannah Unit of the Georgia Writer's Project on the Works Projects Administration, *Drums and Shadows* (Athens: University of Georgia, 1940; Garden City, NY: Doubleday-Anchor, 1972); Charles T. Davis and Henry Louis Gates, Jr., eds., *The Slave's Narrative* (New York: Oxford University Press, 1985).

13. Savannah Unit of the Georgia Writer's Project *Drums and Shadows*, 158–170.

14. Ibid.

15. "Letter of James Hamilton Couper, Esq.," in Austin, *African Muslim Slaves in Antebellum America*, 321–325; originally published by William Brown Hodgson in *Notes on Northern Africa, the Sahara, and the Sudan* (New York, 1844), 68–75; also see Philip D. Curtin, ed., *Africa Remembered: Narratives by West Africans from the Era of the Slave Trade.* (Madison: University of Wisconsin Press, 1967), 145–151. See Judy, *(Dis) Forming The American Canon*, 187–207, for detailed analysis of James Hamilton Couper's writings about Salih Bilali.

16. Ibid.

17. Ibid.

18. Savannah Unit of Georgia Writer's Project, *Drums and Shadows*; Lydia Parrish, *Slave Songs of the Georgia Sea Islands* (Athens: University of Georgia Press, 1992), first published in 1942. She also met and got stories of Salih Bilali and Bilali's descendants. No one has systematically analyzed the impact of these Muslims and their traditions on Gullah culture.

19. Ibid., 154, 168–169, 170–173.

20. Ibid., 166–167.

21. Ibid., 148.

22. Sterling Stuckey, *Slave Culture: National Theory and the Foundations of Black America* (New York: Oxford University Press, 1987) 198; Suzanne Miers and Igor Kopytoff, eds. *Slavery in Africa* (Madison: University of Wisconsin Press, 1977), 14–18.

23. Austin, "Kunta Kinte's Fellows," 6.

24. Bernard Lewis, *Islam and the West* (New York: Oxford University Press, 1993), 15–19.

25. Ibid. Judy argues that the "African-Arabic" Muslim slave narratives "challenge the claim of traditional Enlightenment discourse that literacy and reason are the privileged properties of Western culture." See *(Dis) Forming the American Canon*.

26. Long, *Significations*, 4.

27. Stuckey, *Slave Culture*, 198–200.

28. Austin, "Kunta Kinte's Fellows," 6. Michael Mullin, in *Africa in America* (Chicago:

University of Illinois Press 1992), has demonstrated that slaves who preserved their African ethnicity "retained a more collective identity and were more likely to be treated as a people and to resist by organizing with others" (15).

29. Vincent P. Franklin, *Black Self-Determination*, 2d ed. (New York: Lawrence Hill, 1992), first published 1984. For a distinctive study as a widespread and important tool of resistance to slavery, see Janet Duitsman Cornelius, *When I Can Read My Title Clear* (Columbia: University of South Carolina Press); Stuckey, *Slave Culture*, ix. Sterling Stuckey believes that "African religions and ethnic differences were considered a handicap and steadily lost ground before the need for unity against overwhelming odds" in the nineteenth century (119). The evidence that I have gathered demonstrates the opposite trend: that preservation of specific African identities in America, in some cases, served as a paradigm for Pan-Africanist resistance and unity in the nineteenth century.

Baptism of the Negroes. Engraving by Johann Jakob Bossart, 1757. From the Archiv der Brüder-Unität, Herrnhut, Germany.

Chapter Nine

Memoir of Abraham

Jon F. Sensbach

Translated by Erika Huber

The African American religious experience has exhibited a broad diversity, finding black adherents in virtually all American faith traditions. Jon F. Sensbach reveals one of the lesser known black religious affiliations in his volume, A Separate Canaan: The Making of an Afro-Moravian World in North Carolina, 1763–1840, *from which the following vignette is taken.*

•

Our Dear Brother Abraham, otherwise called Sambo, a Negro from the Mandingo Nation on the coast of African Guinea, was born about the year 1730. It appears that his father was a respected man among his countrymen. Through diligent praying he established a religious way of thinking himself, though this was mixed with heathen superstition. When he grew up and was already father of several children, he went to war like others in the frequent hostilities with the neighboring tribes. In one of those wars he was wounded severely in head and face and was taken prisoner, and then sent back to his father with mutilated ears. He, the father, became so angry about this that he stirred the inhabitants of the community to another war to get his revenge. They started at once, and Sambo, wounded though he was, did not let them keep him from following them. Now he was taken prisoner for the second time and sold to European slave traders, who brought him to the West Indies and sold him on a French island. He was there for several years. Later he was brought to Virginia. In August of 1770, his master (H. Lyon)[1] intended to sell him again and brought him with two other Negroes to Brother Herbst (tanner here). For several days they stayed under his supervision. One of them was sold to Hope not far from here, was baptized and called Paul. In the beginning Brother Herbst was not willing to keep one of them, because at that time already there were important reasons for not keeping any Negroes in the Salem Community. However, his attention was called mainly to Sambo, who seemed to be of good humor, and who perhaps could be won for the Lord, and he could not get rid of this thought. Therefore, he decided to pay the price for him and to keep him here for a time on approval.

At that time Sambo suffered severely from the Guinea worm on his big toe, which had to be taken off. For quite a while he stayed in his former heathen ways and mores. We could not give him the right instruction because he understood only his native language and a little French. After he had been here for three years, he ran away from his master quite unexpectedly, but was, however, returned to Salem, after he had suffered much from hunger, and of his own free will he admitted that he ought to be punished. Since that time he started to think about the status of his soul, attended diligently the Congregation meetings, and was eager to learn German and verses. He asked the Brethren *how* one can become happy eternally, and his attention was called to the Gospel, that a poor and oppressed sinner through faith in Jesus Christ can be relieved from the burden of sins and sinning. Still some time passed until he learned to see himself as the poorest sinner and to realize this evil. Finally, however, he came to the thorough perception of his lost condition, and admitted openheartedly and repentantly to a Brother what a slave of sin he had been up to now and how much he would like to be saved and become happy. It was a comforting word for him that Jesus Christ had come into this world to make sinners happy. He prayed to the Lord for mercy and pardon. We took special care of him, and he paid attention to the exhortations of the Brethren. Since we noted distinctly that his heart had truly changed and that he was longing for the washing of his sins with the blood of Christ, he received holy baptism through our dear Brother Graff on December 26, 1780, and afterwards we saw with joy that he had not received the mercy of God in vain. In June of 1787 he received the Holy Communion, and he received it in the perception of Jesus Christ and himself. Simple like a child, he kept to the Lord and he testified daily that he would always ask that the Lord would cleanse him now with his blood. He had some weaknesses in his character, which required the patience of his master and all those who were around him. On the whole he was loved by the congregation and recognized as a special example of the mercy of Jesus Christ. He enjoyed the news from our missions in the West Indies very much, thought of it daily in his prayer, and also contributed his part.

On July 30, 1785, he married Sarah, at present his widow, about whose soul he was very troubled, and he often mentioned his concern about her unhappy state of heart. Though he could hardly express himself in matters concerning his soul, he used opportunities to announce to other Negroes the truths of the Gospel.

On March 27, he became sick and showed at once that at this time he would go to the Lord, to which he was looking forward. It was really edifying to see him with his pains which he felt mainly in his abdomen, so quiet, patient, and free from all fright of death, yea, the calmness and the well-being of his soul sparkled in his countenance. When he was asked what would be mainly comforting to him, he prayed like a child the verse: The blood and righteousness of Christ are my adornment and dress of honor.

He asked to be blessed before his death, which happened on April 6, 1797, and on the 7th he passed away calmly, at the age of about 60 years.

NOTE

1. Identified as Edmund Lyne in a bill of sale from Aug. 24, 1771.

Above. Graduates of the Missionary Training Department of Spelman Seminary, 1893. Those prepared by this program offered religious and moral instruction across the State of Georgia. *Right.* Lott Carey (1780–1829). In 1821, Carey and the congregation he had organized, the Providence Baptist Church, sailed to Liberia, West Africa, to establish an African mission. Courtesy of the First African Baptist Church, Richmond, Virginia.

Chapter Ten

The Idea of Missions

Monroe Fordham

Historically, Christianity has been an evangelistic religion, actively advancing across the globe its theological vision and corresponding way of life. This has been no less true of African American Christianity, though black Christians have felt an especial burden to begin their fideistic charity, as it were, "at home." Less than a decade after the establishment of the first officially independent black denominations, missionaries had already set sail for the African continent. Monroe Fordham gives insight into some of the religious and cultural motive forces and specific initiatives in this movement.

•

From its very inception, the black Christian church began to reach out beyond itself and the local black community to other communities of blacks. Initially, missionary efforts by black churches were restricted to home missions. That is, their first efforts were aimed at establishing new congregations in the northern United States. That the effort to establish home missions was successful is indicated by the tremendous expansion of black independent and aligned churches throughout the northern and western states during the first half of the nineteenth century. As the black church matured and gained stability, it focused on the foreign fields. While the actual success in the foreign field during the first half of the nineteenth century were much more limited than those in the area of home missions, the foreign efforts were nonetheless important, and enthusiasm for foreign missions among many of the northern black clergy remained high. In the foreign missionary field, black American Christians were drawn particularly to labors among other people of African descent. The geographic areas receiving the most emphasis were Africa, the Caribbean Islands, and black settlements in Canada.

The predominant scriptural basis for the idea of missions in the black churches was basically the same as it was for most Protestant Christian churches of the period. The scriptural passage most often cited in connection with the idea of missions was the command given by Jesus to his disciples to "Go ye into all the world and preach the gospel, teaching all nations and baptizing them in the name of the Father, and the Son, and the Holy Ghost." In addition, the idea of missions among American Protestants was greatly influenced by the Hopkinsian views on disinterested benevolence. Samuel Hopkins was one of the first New England Calvinists to advocate foreign Christian missions. Hopkins reasoned that by assisting the "heathen" in "coming to a knowledge of the truth," the Christian missionary was thereby contributing to the alleviation of human suffering. According to the Hopkins doctrine, that was disinterested benevolence. Only benevolence would lead a man "to suffer one degree of pain and misery, in order to save another from a hundred degrees of pain . . . "[1] The effort to promote foreign missions was deemed a sign of "true holiness." The idea of missions among nineteenth-century white and black Christians alike was influenced by the Hopkinsian views.

In addition to the scriptural and theological basis, the idea of Christian missions in antebellum northern black thought was shaped and conditioned by two other factors. On the one hand, the black concept of Christian missions was influenced by American evangelical Protestant beliefs concerning "manifest destiny" and the millennium. On the other hand, the idea of Christian missions among northern blacks was shaped by the strong feelings of kinship and commitment that northern blacks felt toward African peoples.

The belief that America had a special and providential mission to lead in the reformation and redemption of the world goes back to the seventeenth century. The first settlers to New England believed that God sent them on an "errand into the wilderness" to build a "city on the hill." Such a city was expected to be a beacon of light which would guide the rest of the world.[2] The belief that America had a unique mission was held in varying degrees of intensity by Americans during most of the seventeenth and eighteenth centuries.[3]

By the beginning of the nineteenth century, numerous factors combined to produce a national spirit of "manifest destiny." In the religious sense, "manifest destiny" represented an expansion and nationalization of the Puritan vision of American as the "city on the hill." The concept was millennial in that it was predicated on the belief that the millennium would begin in the United States and spread to the rest of the world.[4] Some Protestant Evangelists believed that the revivalistic reform movement of the early nineteenth century would lead to the perfection of society in the United States. It should be emphasized here that antebellum revivalists recognized that America was not a perfect society. Far from it, they often supported reform movements premised on the notion that sin, corruption, and immorality were widespread in the nation, and they believed that Protestant evangelism was the best means of reforming and perfecting society. They further believed that after fulfilling its mission in America, Protestant evangelism would eventually effect the completion of the reformation and thus lead to the regeneration of the world.

At the root of the antebellum conception of America's religious mission were certain very important assumptions. On the one hand, there was the assumption that spiritual salvation and regeneration could be achieved only through the gospel of Christ. Second it was assumed that human progress and civilization were directly related to and even dependent on the presence of the spirit of Christianity. Using those assumptions, Americans reasoned that Protestant Christianity was the most appropriate vehicle for uplifting "backward" and "uncivilized" peoples. After all, the economic prosperity and the spread of democracy in the United States, coupled with the widely held belief that the millennium was about to dawn in America, were proof enough that Christianity was indeed the key to the uplift and perfection of a society. The acceptance of those assumptions by northern blacks was a major factor in shaping the idea of Christian missions in northern black thought. Again, it seems important to state that northern blacks did not believe that American was a perfect society; they believed that the true means by which a society could achieve perfection had been revealed in America. Northern blacks believed that those "true means" to perfection could be utilized in effecting the uplift of all African peoples.

The idea of missions in black thought was also influenced tremendously by the strong ties of kinship that many northern blacks felt toward Africa and African peoples. Those spiritual and cultural ties were contributing factors in the major wave of black nationalist-emigrationist sentiment and activities during the 1840s and 1850s.[5] It is significant that some of the leading black emigrationist of the period were ministers of the gospel. The black emigrationist movement, that is, the effort by northern blacks to promote selective emigration of American blacks to Africa or the Caribbean, was not an escapist movement as some of its critics (both contemporary and modern) charged. Leading black nationalist-emigrationist spokesmen like the Reverend James Theodore Holly and Martin Robinson Delany believed that the "rape" of Africa and the enslavement and oppression of African peoples could be ended if a strong black nation could be established in Africa or the Caribbean. The black nationalist-emigrationists believed that a strong black nation could use its economic, diplomatic, and military powers to rescue and protect Africa and African peoples from the destructive aims and policies of other nations. Of course, not all nationalist-emigrationists had the long-range sense of history that was demonstrated in the ideas of Holly and Delany. Some were motivated simply by the belief that they could contribute to the "uplift" and "progress" of Africa.

In defining the concepts of "progress" and "civilization," northern blacks accepted those definitions that were dominant in American (Western) culture. That is, "progress" and "civilization" were measured and defined in terms of Christianity, democracy, and scientific development. Using those gauges, a nation that was unchristian, undemocratic, and "primitive" could be duly defined as "backward" and "uncivilized." In the minds of most Protestants in antebellum America, Christianity was the most important component in the trilogy. Consequently, most Americans, including northern blacks, were left with the assumption that human progress and civilization were directly dependent on the presence of the spirit of Christianity. It was, therefore, quite logical for northern black Christians with a sense of duty and commitment to contribute to the "uplift" of African and African peoples, to advocate Christian missions as one means of effecting that "uplift."

One of the most representative full-length statements on the duties of black Americans in the missionary field is an essay by the Reverend Alexander Crummell entitled "The Relations and Duties of Free Colored Men in American to Africa."[6] Episcopal minister who spent twenty years in missionary and educational work in Liberia and Sierra Leone. The essay was written on the eve of the American Civil War. In the essay, he presented most of the standard reasons why it was believed that Africa was in need of aid. The Reverend Crummell described Africa as a nation that was wasting away under the accretions of civil and moral miseries.[7] The whole continent, he argued, "with its million masses of heathen, presents one broad, almost unbroken, unmitigated view of moral desolation and spiritual ruin."[8] The Reverend Crummell concluded that the widespread "social evils" and "licentiousness" were due to the fact that Africa was un-Christian.[9] Assuming the existence of a positive correlation between Christianity and civilization, the Reverend Crummell concluded that the main remedy for the "heathenism and benightedness" of Africa was the spreading of Christianity throughout the continent.[10]

In addition to what he described as Africa's spiritual need, the Reverend Crummell emphasized the need for economic development in Africa and the need for Africa's descendants throughout the world to develop economic ties with the motherland.[11] He believed that such ties would lead to the development of black commercial power in Africa as well as in other lands where Africans were in residence.[12] The Reverend Crummell maintained that if the natural resources and wealth of Africa were properly developed, and if Africa and her transplanted descendants could gain a sort of monopoly on that development and the benefits therefrom, progress and prosperity in Africa would be assured.[13] Thus, economic and commercial development was associated with progress and civilization. In defining the task at hand, the Reverend Crummell explained that the charge was "to wrest a continent from ruin; to bless and animate millions of torpid and benighted souls; to destroy the power of the devil in his strongholds, and to usher therein light, knowledge, and blessedness, inspiring hope, holy faith and abiding glory."[14]

In presenting "proof" that African-Americans were able to perform the necessary tasks, the Reverend Crummell summarized some of the achievements of the A.M.E. Church. He explained that the A.M.E. Church had established home missions among free blacks in America and had gathered into its fold "tens of thousands of the sons of Africa on American soil." In addition, that denomination had established schools, built churches, founded a college, and "saved the United States the shame of hundreds of thousands of black heathens."[15] The Reverend Crummell expressed confidence that the black Christians of America could do for Africa what the A.M.E. Church had done for free black communities in the northern and western states of the United States.[16] He made a special plea to the A.M.E. Church to get involved in missionary labors in Africa. As a concluding challenge, the Reverend Crummell maintained that "never before in human history has such a grand and noble work been laid out in the divine providence before the Negro race."[17]

More than thirty years before the statement by the Reverend Crummell, the Reverend Nathaniel Paul expressed sentiments that were very similar. The Reverend Paul's contentions, like those of the Reverend Crummell, were based on the belief that the regeneration of Africa was dependent on the spread of Christianity in that land and that African Americans had a special duty to contribute to that regeneration. Speaking in 1827, the Reverend Paul, pastor of the African Baptist Society of Albany, New York, expressed optimism that the day would come when the sons and daughters of Africa who had been transplanted in America would go back to the land of their fathers and spread the gospel of Jesus Christ.[18] The Reverend Paul believed that Africa, by yielding to the spread of the Christian gospel, would be restored to her original greatness.

Prior to 1840, most of the missionary labors by blacks were sponsored by individual churches or denominations. There had been no sustained effort by blacks to establish any kind of national missionary organization. In early 1841, a major campaign was launched to create such an organization. One of the leading spokesmen in the movement to establish a national missionary society was the Reverend James W. C. Pennington.

In a letter to the editor of the *Colored American,* the Reverend Pennington argued that the *Amistad* incident "has brought us under solemn obligations to commence missionary operations in Africa."[19] He stated that he had waited for more than ten years for an opening to promote missionary work in Africa "without countenancing colonization." The Reverend Pennington, like most northern blacks, opposed the idea of colonization. Colonization, in their minds, suggested domination, exploitation, and subjugation of Africans by outsiders. The Reverend Pennington was aware that Christian missions were frequently used by European powers to soften foreign peoples for political, economic, and military domination. In a letter to the *Colored American,* the Reverend Pennington expressed the belief that the time was then right for the African people of America to move toward Christianizing Africa. However, he made it clear that that effort should not be connected in any way with colonization. The letter concluded with an appeal for further dialogue on the subject of African missions.

Encouraged by the replies and reactions to his initial statements and queries on the subject of African missions, the Reverend Pennington organized a temporary committee and called a public meeting for May 5, 1841, in Hartford, Connecticut. The stated purpose of the meeting was to explain and discuss "the obligations of Christians, colored Christians, to do something in relation to carrying the gospel to Africa."[20]

The meeting was held as scheduled. During the proceedings, numerous ministers and deacons gave speeches and remarks supporting African missions. The Reverend Pennington maintained that black Americans had a special obligation to become involved in African missions. A. W. Hanson expressed the belief that the destiny of black Americans "was ultimately connected with the regeneration of Africa." After the speeches, those assembled passed several resolutions expressing their support of a preamble which stated that: "It is a matter of vital importance to the spiritual interests of Africa, and the honor and success of the Gospel in that country, that a mission should be established in the interior, disconnected with the stations on the coast."[21] The last phrase indicates the group's opposition to being connected with colonization and European control. The group voted to call a national missionary convention for August 18 and 19, 1841. That convention was to be held in Hartford, Connecticut, for the purpose of devising measures for launching the African missions.

On July 3, the *Colored American* published the first in a series of public announcements regarding the proposed missionary convention. The "Call For a Missionary Convention" began with a reminder that "it is designed by our Creator that we should not be indifferent to the condition and necessities of our fellow creatures." The call contained an open invitation to "all our brethren, who feel an interest in the subject of missions." In his initial letter to the editor, published in the *Colored American,* the Reverend Pennington asked the readers to respond by sending their views on African missions to the editor.

Even though the letters to the editor of the *Colored American* suggested the existence of widespread support for African missions among American blacks, there was some opposition to such missions. Many blacks associated African missions with colonization. Northern blacks, as a group, were overwhelmingly opposed to colonization.[22] The opposition to colonization had several grounds. On the one hand, northern blacks thought of colonization as a scheme by proslavery forces to rid America of free blacks by sending them back to Africa. Second, northern blacks were well aware of how European powers utilized Christian missions as a vehicle in the subjugation and exploitation of African peoples. Although the Reverend Pennington, in his initial call for African missions, pointedly and publicly explained that his ideas and aspirations regarding African missions were in total opposition to colonization, many people had reservations about endorsing his proposals. In addition to the Reverend Pennington, many other advocates of missions who were sensitive to the arguments by anticolonizationists took pains to reject colonization as they argued for African missions.

In addition to anticolonization, there were other problems with which missionary-minded black Christians had to contend. The Reverend Alexander Crummell described some of those difficulties. One was the lack of missionary zeal among American black lay Christians. "Our religion is not diffusive, but rather introversive."[23] He described religiosity among black Americans as the "piety of self-satisfaction," that is, a proneness to "enjoy the religious experience themselves, but not being inclined to spread it to others." A second obstacle to the promotion of the idea of African missions among American blacks was what the Reverend Crummell described as "inhabitativeness"; "As a people, we cling with an almost deadly fixity to locality."[24] He maintained that because of the first factor, Americans were not missionary-minded, and because of the second they were generally opposed to emigration to Africa.

The points mentioned by the Reverend Crummell undoubtedly contributed to what black contemporaries of that period often described as a lack of enthusiasm among black laymen generally and many black clergy for establishing and supporting foreign missions. However, the objective reality faced by free people of color was certainly equally as important. It would indeed be difficult for a people who experienced severe political, economic, and social restrictions and disadvantages to focus a prolonged and intense effort toward "rescuing" Africa. This would be even more true since many northern blacks either had friends or relatives who were still slaves in the southern United States. Nevertheless, many perceptive black ministers, emigrationists, and reformers made a determined effort to generate enthusiasm among free people of color for the idea of foreign missions.

Four days prior to the convening of the missionary convention at Hartford, an editorial in the *Colored American* called upon all Christians to support the cause of

African missions. The editorial claimed that the time had come for the God of Abraham, Isaac, and Jacob to replace the "graven images and false Gods" of Africa.[25] Here is an obvious manifestation of the fact that northern black Christians accepted the belief that spiritual salvation and regeneration could be achieved only through the gospel of Christ. In essence, they were accepting the premise that Christianity was the only true religion.

The Hartford Missionary Convention of 1841 convened as scheduled on August 18. The convention was opened with a sermon by the Reverend Pennington. The text of the sermon came from Isaiah, chapter fifty-eight, verse ten: "And if thou draw out thy soul to the hungry, and satisfy the afflicted soul, then shall thy light rise in obscurity, and thy darkness be as the noonday."[26] Six states and six Christian denominations were represented by delegates to the convention. Joseph Cinque and four other Africans connected with the Amistad were also enrolled as members. In addition, a number of white persons were in attendance as delegates.[27]

One of the major actions taken by the Hartford convention was the formation of a national missionary society, of which the Reverend Pennington was elected president. Other officers included: the Reverend Amos G. Beman of New Haven; the Reverend Theodore S. Wright of New York; and Charles W. Gardner of Philadelphia.[28] In other action, the convention voted unanimously to support the establishment and maintenance of African missions. A resolution was also passed "disavowing the fellowship of the colonization scheme, and showing reasons why."[29]

Following the Hartford Missionary Convention, the officers and supporters of that convention continued their effort to stimulate interest in and support for African missions by appealing to the conferences and governing bodies of the various churches. The Baltimore Conference of the African Methodist Episcopal Church in 1842 reportedly received a petition from the committee elected at the Hartford convention calling for their support of "The African and Foreign Home Missionary Society." The Baltimore Conference voted to direct its preachers to devote attention to the promotion of the work of the missionary society.[30]

Being the first independent black religious denomination to be established in the United States, the A.M.E. Church became a leader among black churches in the home and foreign missionary fields. The first missionary work by the A.M.E. Church was in the home field. Almost immediately upon being established, the connection launched an effort to spread African Methodism to black communities throughout the northern and western states as well as to free black communities in the South. By 1822, the A.M.E. Church membership had grown to 9,888.[31] Of that total, 1,400 were listed as part of churches in South Carolina.[32]

A number of A.M.E. ministers went to Africa in the early nineteenth century in the capacity of missionaries. Several attempts were made to organize a branch of the A.M.E. in Liberia but failed because of insufficient support. The ministers often stayed on by connecting themselves with missions established by white denominations. One such example was the Reverend Daniel Coker, a founder of the A.M.E. Church, who served as a minister in Liberia and Sierra Leone in missions established by white denominations.[33]

In 1822, the Philadelphia A.M.E. Conference dealt with the question of establishing an African mission. It was proposed that the Reverend Charles Butler be appointed and sent to Africa as a missionary. However, the church as an independent denomination was only six years old and was not yet up to the task of acting in the foreign field. The result in that instance was but a "paper mission."[34] The first successful foreign mission to be established by the A.M.E. Church was in Hayti. In 1827, Scipio Beanes was sent to that island republic under the auspices of the A.M.E. denomination. Elder Beanes was able to establish several mission stations there.[35]

If one man can be singled out for his dedication to the idea of building a strong black Christian nation in Hayti that man would be the Reverend James T. Holly. The Reverend Holly was a clergyman of the Protestant Episcopal Church. For several years he was pastor of a church in New Haven, Connecticut. During the 1850s, the Reverend Holly along with Martin Delany were the two leading black nationalist-emigrationist spokesmen in the United States. In 1859, Holly wrote six essays on Hayti for the *Anglo-African Magazine*.

One of the primary assumptions underlying the six essays was stated in the first of the series. The Reverend Holly expressed his belief that "whatever is to be the future destiny of the descendants of Africa, Hayti certainly holds the most important relation to that destiny."[36] Given that premise, he maintained that for African descendants to "refuse to make any and every sacrifice to advance the interests and prosperity of that nation is to be a traitor both to God and humanity."[37]

The Reverend Holly praised Hayti for having achieved her political sovereignty. He added, however, that independence was only one of the necessary components of a truly great national state. In his view: "The dissemination of sound religious morality as the basis of public virtue, and the cultivation of Literature, the Arts and Sciences, as the sources of national prosperity, are inseparable concomitants of political sovereignty in making up true national greatness."[38] The Reverend Holly maintained that Hayti was suffering under two great disabilities. He believed that if those disabilities were not corrected, Hayti would have difficulty reaching her potential as a great nation. The two disabilities, according to Holly, were the lacks of "Christianity and Science." Holly maintained that Protestant Christian missionaries had bypassed Hayti and left her to "swelter in darkness, deprived of the enlightening influences of the pure religion of Jesus." He concluded that the Haytian people were "perishing for want of the light of the Gospel."[39]

The Reverend Holly envisaged emigration to Hayti as a vehicle for carrying Christianity and science to the island. He believed that science, together with Hayti's rich natural resources, would enable the republic to develop economically and thus emerge as a strong political and commercial power. Moreover, the Reverend Holly acted on the premise that Christian values and morality would provide the spiritual and moral power that was essential for a people to survive, prosper, and progress toward a higher level of civilization.

Missionary-minded black Christian Americans believed that the command of Jesus to his disciples to "Go ye into all the world and preach the gospel, teaching all nations and baptising them in the name of the Father, and the Son, and the Holy Ghost" was equally applicable to them. In addition to the scriptural command, northern black advocates of missions were motivated by other factors as well. They believed that spiritual salvation and regeneration were possible only through the Christian gospel. Through their Christian missionary activities they could feel that they were contributing toward the alleviation of human suffering among those "benighted souls" who were being crushed under the weight of "moral desolation" and "spiritual ruin." In addition, black Christians believed that progress and civilization were largely dependent on the presence of the spirit of Christianity. Perceiving of themselves as having acquired the knowledge of the Christian gospel and the "true" means of progress and perfection, and perceiving Africa and her descendants as a depressed and un-Christian people, northern black advocates of missions reasoned that because of kinship ties, they had a special and providential duty to evangelize and promote the uplift of their African brethren. To that extent, northern blacks were extending to other African peoples the same kind of adaptive religion that they were applying to themselves.

NOTES

1. Oliver W. Elsbree, "Samuel Hopkins and His Doctrine of Benevolence," *New England Quarterly*, 8 (1935), 534–550.

2. Perry Miller, *Errand into the Wilderness* (New York, 1956), chap. I.

3. Ernest Lee Tuveson, *Redeemer Nation* (Chicago, 1968), pp. 91–124.

4. Charles I. Foster, *Errand of Mercy* (Chapel Hill, 1960), chaps. VIII–XI.

5. See the following articles by Howard H. Bell: "The Negro Emigration Movement, 1849–1854: A Phase of Negro Nationalism," *Phylon*, XX (Summer, 1959), 132–142; "American Negro Interest in Africa, 1858–1861," *The Journal of Social Science Teachers*, VI (November, 1960), 11–18; "Negro Nationalism: A Factor in Emigration Projects, 1858–1861," *The Journal of Negro History*, XLVII (January, 1962), 42–53.

6. Alexander Crummell, *The Future of Africa* (reprint ed., New York, 1969), pp. 213–281.

7. Ibid., pp. 219, 220.

8. Ibid., p. 257.

9. Ibid., p. 220.

10. Ibid.

11. Ibid., pp. 221–257.

12. Ibid., pp. 257–258.

13. Ibid., p. 256.

14. Ibid., p. 280.

15. Ibid., pp. 265, 266.

16. Ibid., p. 270.

17. Ibid., p. 281.

18. Carter G. Woodson, *Negro Orators and Their Orations* (New York, 1969), p. 76.

19. *Colored American*, 17 April 1841. The *Amistad* was a slave ship carrying captured Africans to the markets in the Americas. Black captives, led by a fellow black Joseph Cinque, revolted and took control of the ship. The ship was eventually captured by an American navy vessel and taken to port at New London, Connecticut. A legal battle followed over the status of the Africans and the question of how the matter should be resolved. It was eventually decided that the Africans should be taken back to their homeland and released. Some suggested that the Africans should be "educated" and Christianized and sent back as evangelists.

Others suggested sending American missionaries back to Africa with the group. For more detailed discussion, see Bertram Wyatt-Brown, *Lewis Tappan* (New York, 1969), pp. 205–225.

20. *Colored American,* 15 May 1841.

21. Ibid.

22. Benjamin Quarles, *Black Abolitionists* (New York, 1969), pp. 4–8.

23. Crummell, *Future of Africa,* p. 274.

24. Ibid., pp. 274–276.

25. *Colored American,* 14 August 1841.

26. Ibid., 4 September 1841.

27. Ibid.

28. Ibid., 28 August 1841.

29. Ibid., 4 September 1841.

30. L. L. Berry, *A Century of Missions of the African Methodist Episcopal Church, 1840–1940* (New York, 1942); see introduction by Charles H. Wesley, p. vii.

31. Daniel A. Payne, *History of the African Methodist Episcopal Church* (reprint ed., New York, 1968), p. 38.

32. Ibid., p. 33.

33. Ibid., pp. 483–484.

34. Ibid., p. 33.

35. Ibid., pp. 66, 67.

36. *Anglo-African Magazine,* vol. 1 (1859), p. 186.

37. Ibid., p. 187.

38. Ibid., p. 220.

39. Ibid., p. 221.

The seven deaconesses in the first graduating class of the first training school for colored deaconesses in the United States, 1902. Deaconesses were prepared to extend aid to the poor, the physically suffering, and the socially disabled. Reprinted from Rev. Christian Golder, *History of the Deaconess Movement in the Christian Church* (Cincinnati: Jennings and Pye, 1903).

Above. Nannie Helen Burroughs (1883–1961), influential Baptist laywoman. *Right.* Mrs. Florence Randolph, Evangelist. Licensed to preach by the African Methodist Episcopal Zion Church in 1897.

Chapter Eleven

Black Women in Religious Institutions
A Historical Summary from Slavery to the 1960s

Delores C. Carpenter

In the nineteenth century, American women, African American women included, began to assert their sense of call into public religious vocation. Over a century later that assertion, resisted in its first emergence, is yet contested in many quarters, though significant advances have been in made women's ordination and deployment in positions of ordained and lay ministry. Delores C. Carpenter here highlights African American women's key participation in early missions, as well as in the broader range of activities contributing toward the personal and institutional development of Christianity among blacks prior to the Civil War.

•

Black women have played an important role in giving leadership to the Black Church. It is a happy circumstance that there is now an increasing body of research to familiarize individuals and groups with the names and history of noteworthy black women ministers. One such study is that of Dr. Jualynne Dodson, which focuses upon black women in African Methodist Episcopal church history. Her study appears in *Women in New Worlds: Historical Perspectives on the Wesleyan Tradition.*[1] The United Methodists produced one of the pioneering publications on black women, a collaboration by Carter, Curry, Gray, McCallum, and Strother entitled *To a Higher Glory:The Growth and Development of Black Women Organized for Mission in the Methodist Church, 1940–1968.*[2] It documents the contributions of African American women in the Methodist Episcopal tradition from the time of slavery to the 1960s. Dr. Cheryl Gilkes continues her sociological research on women in the Church of God in Christ. Some of Gilkes's work has already been published in the *Journal of Religious Thought.*[3] *Sisters of the Spirit* by William L. Andrews chronicles the ministries of Jarena Lee, Julia Foote, and Zilpha Elaw.[4] We shall have occasion to cite other studies as our historical summary unfolds. It is encouraging that numerous scholars are now delineating the historical, sociological, biblical, theological, and preaching contributions of black women, both past and present.[5]

Late Nineteenth-Century Black Women in Ministry

We begin this report on some of the exciting results of the research on black women ministers by giving attention to less well known personalities, and to other black female preachers, pastors, and their predecessors. Also, it is impossible to study black women in ministry without mentioning some lay women. This we do because it is highly probable that lay women, such as Nannie Helen Burroughs, would have become ministers had that opportunity been available to them. This is attested to by more recent developments wherein a woman such as Pauli Murray sought and received ordination, after many years as an active Episcopal lay woman, even though she did so toward the end of her life.

The United Methodists have traced the religious contribution of black women to slaves such as Mother Suma, who converted her mistress, one of the Boston Hancocks, and thereby raised the prestige of Methodism in Boston. Still another slave, Aunt Hester of Franklin, Louisiana, preached and prayed so constantly that she influenced all of the slaves owned by her master. The master sold her but soon bought her back again. She continued to spread the Word, however, causing even the young mistresses in the house to become serious about religion. Again Aunt Hester was sold, but there was so much consternation in the household that the master bought her back once again, complaining that he would have to put up with her religion and the spoiling of the Negroes.[6]

Much has been written already about the two religious giants, Harriet Tubman, the black female "Moses" of her people, and Sojourner Truth, the famous black Methodist preacher and abolitionist. The accounts of their religious faith and church affiliation are well documented elsewhere.[7] Other black abolitionists also spoke as ministers. An illustrous example is Maria Stewart, who was born in Hartford, Connecticut, in 1803. An orphan at five years old, she was bound out to a clergyman's family. She left this home at the age of fifteen. Although she had been previously denied an education, she spent the next five years in Sabbath Schools and wrote of her religious conversion in 1830. While preaching against slavery and teaching pride and self-help among blacks, she called, "O ye daughters of Africa, awake! Awake! Arise! No longer sleep or slumber, but distinguish yourselves, store thy mind with useful knowledge."[8] Eloquently and convincingly, she emphasized piety and knowledge.

> I have borrowed much of my language from the Holy Bible. During childhood and youth, it was the book that I mostly studied and now, while my hands are toiling for their daily sustenance, my heart is most generally meditating upon its divine truth.[9]

Because Maria Stewart spoke out on behalf of black women, she was hissed and reproached. She called upon the women to make mighty efforts to raise their sons and daughters from servitude and degradation. She criticized the male clergy for crying "Peace, peace when there was no peace, they have plastered us up with untempered mortar, and have been as it were blind leaders of the blind."[10]

Stewart repeatedly had to defend her right to preach in the churches.

I believe, that for wise and holy purposes, best known to [God], [God] hath unloosed my tongue and put [divine] word into my mouth, in order to confound and put all those to shame that have rose up against me. For [God] hath clothed my face with steel, and lined my forehead with brass. [God] hath put [divine] testimony within me, and engraven [the divine] seal on my forehead. And with these weapons I have indeed set the fiends of earth and hell at defiance . . . Among the Greeks, women delivered the Oracles; the respect the Romans paid to the Sybils is well known. The Jews had their prophetesses. The prediction of the Egyptian women obtained much credit at Rome, even under the Emperors. And in the most barbarious nations, all things that have the appearance of being supernatural, mysteries of religion, the secrets of the psychic, and the rites of magic, were in the possession of women. Why cannot a religious spirit animate us now?[11]

Even before Maria Stewart began her ministry in New England, another black woman preacher had arisen. Jarena Lee was born in 1784 at Cape May, New Jersey. She joined the African Methodist Episcopal (A.M.E.) Church after hearing Reverend Richard Allen and experiencing conversion. When she felt called to preach, Reverend Allen told her of another Methodist woman, a Mrs. Cook, who had done well in exhortation and holding prayer meetings by verbal license of the preacher in charge. However, he said, there was no provision for women to preach. Nonetheless, eight years later, Bishop Allen affirmed Jarena Lee's calling, and she became the first female preacher in the A.M.E. Church. She worked in the Bethel Church in Philadelphia and travelled extensively. In four years, she travelled 1,600 miles, of which she walked 1,100 miles to carry out her ministry. Bishop Allen wanted to give her an appointment at Bethel Church, but the opposition against a woman preaching blocked her appointment. Still, she preached in schoolhouses, slave camp meetings, and in homes as well as churches in Pennsylvania, New York, New Jersey, Virginia, and Maryland. She was sometimes asked to fill in when the preacher did not show up, but she also faced enormous aversion from elders and local magistrates in her travels. Mrs. Lee wrote, "At times I was pressed down like a cart beneath its shafts—my life seemed as at the point of the sword—my heart was sore and pained me in my body."[12]

Early in church history, black women took a particular interest in missionary work in Africa. Thus, they assumed leadership positions years ago. Francis Burns in 1834, Lavinia Johnson in 1845, and Sarah Simpson in 1860 were missionaries to Liberia. In 1902 Susan Collins and in 1906 Martha Drummer went to Angola as Methodist missionaries. All these women worked in the mission field until they retired.[13]

Many black women began their ministries as evangelists. Such a woman was Amanda Smith. Born a slave, Amanda Smith was working as a washerwoman in 1870 when she felt led by God to go to an evangelistic meeting. Converted as a young woman, she found "sanctification"—the perfection of holiness—in September of 1868 under John Inskip's preaching at his Greene Street Church in New York. She began to attend camp meetings around the East, testifying and singing, mostly with white Pentecostals. She said God saved many from prejudice under her ministry. Once, she attended a national camp meeting in Knoxville, Tennessee, where the session had been in progress for three days without success. However, after she gave her testimony, one of the leading opponents of holiness began to weep. Stepping onto the platform, he told how many years he had been a Methodist minister and how prejudiced against the subject of holiness he had been.

> When I heard this colored sister tell how God had led her and brought her into this blessed experience, the darkness swept away and God has saved me, and I see truth as I never did before. Glory to God![14]

Amanda Smith took her message of holiness to the British Isles as well. She also traveled to India where the Methodist bishop observed,

> She possessed a clearness of vision which I have found seldom equalled. . . . During seventeen years that I have lived in Calcutta, I have found many famous strangers to visit the city, but I have never known anyone who could draw and hold so large an audience as Mrs. Smith.[15]

She also spent a number of years in Africa, particularly in Liberia. When she finally felt too old to travel, Amanda Smith returned to the United States in 1890 and founded an orphanage near Chicago, where she served until her death in 1915.

In the latter part of the nineteenth century, some black women volunteered to teach in the Freedmen's. Late in the last century Aid Societies through their denominations. Some went to work in the South. Realizing that they could not serve on the Freedmen's Board of Directors, the Methodist women turned their minds to playing a larger role. The activities of their Woman's Home Missionary Society supplemented the Freedmen's, Aid Society and won acclaim for its accomplishments, including providing for the education of black girls, for childcare, and for general evangelism.

Many black congregations supported these types of activities, although women's rights in church were hotly debated in both the late nineteenth and early twentieth centuries. For example, the highest legislating bodies of the three denominations that eventually made up the United Methodist Church did not officially seat women until 1892, 1900, and 1902. Full clergy rights for women in this church were not achieved until 1956.

Beginning in 1888, a small number of black women were commissioned as deaconesses. Their ministries stressed work with destitute persons and groups in urban areas. An outstanding example of such a worker, Anna Hall was the first black graduate deaconess of the African Methodist Episcopal Church. Commissioned in 1901, she started a city mission in Atlanta and supervised the field work of Clark College female students. After five years, Anna Hall went to Liberia, where she stayed for twenty-four years. She was "everything to the people—farmer, teacher, preacher, doctor, dentist, nurse and evangelist."[16] The Liberian Church named a mission station for her in 1952. In 1954, the Anna E. Hall Apartments for married students were dedicated at Gammon Theological Seminary in Atlanta.

In 1909, Viola Mae Young wrote, "And from a child I have loved the church and have felt I was a preacher's friend!"[17] Miss Young echoes the great host of black women who have endeavored to work in the area of pastor's aid and pastoral relations. She joined the A.M.E. Church in 1899 at the age of twelve and worked to better help laymen understand the minister's message. She established the practice of repeating the minister's text to members after service until many others in the congregation began to pay closer attention to it and frequently recall it. She also began to keep a calendar of all the minister's appointments so that the members would not forget them. Her book, *Little Helps for Pastors and Members*, a practical guide to pastors and members, was published in Rosebud, Alabama, in 1909.

Baptist women were recognized in the early 1900s as elocutionists, lecturers, field secretaries for the Women's Conventions, missionary workers, teachers, writers, training school directors, Bible Band workers, and orators. Included in *Who's Who Among the Colored Baptists in the United States* in 1913 was Ida Becks of Missouri, a fearless advocate of woman's suffrage and defender of African Americans.[18] She became secretary of the Colored Women's League of Dayton, Ohio. Also listed is Mrs. M.A.A. Smith of Texas, who was director of the Guadalupe Training School. Women of the Baptist churches supported the teacher for this school. Ella Whitfield, Matron at Guadalupe College, became a field worker in Miss Joanna Moore's Bible Band. Remarkably, she delivered 491 addresses, visited 823 homes and 312 churches, and collected $2,009 for the church.[19] L. J. McNorton, who took millinery and dressmaking classes in Chicago and St. Louis, taught these skills to other black women. She eventually operated a successful business in Ft. Worth, Texas.

Minnie Moxley, who became a high school teacher in Waco, Texas, was famous for her ability to inspire her students. Annie Wilkins became head teacher at Hearne Academy, Houston College, after serving as industrial teacher at Bishop College, Mrs. T. Castle, founder of Rescue Home in Byram, Texas, was an apostle of temperance. She enrolled over 160 clients and raised, with the help of the church, $6,000 to purchase eleven acres of land with a nine-room residence for her young people. Josie B. Hall taught public schools when she was only sixteen, and she also distinguished herself as a poet and writer. All the women mentioned here gave great energy and time to the Baptist Church. Although the information about them is sketchy, it remains a tribute to their varied contributions that they are remembered as prominent church women.

One famous Baptist woman about whom much more is recorded is Nannie Helen Burroughs. Born in 1897 in Washington, D.C., Nannie Burroughs founded the first Girl's Literary Society of the public high schools, and wrote for leading newspapers and journals of the day. Converted at the age of fifteen, she joined the Nineteenth Street Baptist Church and held many offices in the congregation. Working as a stenographer, she was elected President of the National Training School for Women. She traveled throughout America giving brilliant speeches that emphasized listeners must "Do ordinary things in an extraordinary manner."[20] By way of example, in three years she raised the assets of her school from $6,000 to $35,000. She took a vital interest in Africa and was the leader of the Young Women's Department of the National Association of Colored Women's Clubs. Under her leadership much was done to get blacks to vote. Burroughs urged black women to take their families to the polls to vote for those issues and persons who were working on behalf of the uplift of the race. Thus, she became a political as well as religious leader.[21]

In the religious arena, probably the most enduring contribution of Nannie Helen Burroughs was encouraging churches to establish Woman's Day observances. Writing in a monograph, she described how this great tradition started within the Black

Church. She first presented the idea, purpose, and plan of Woman's Day in Memphis, Tennessee, in September 1906 as part of her report as Corresponding Secretary of the Woman's Convention Auxiliary to the National Baptist Convention. Since the work of the convention had hardly begun, Nannie Burroughs was dubbed an "upstart," to which unkind thrust she was provoked to answer, "I might be an 'upstart,' but I am also starting up." The convention eventually voted to accept the "Woman's Day" resolution. The purpose of this national observance day was to interest women of the local churches in raising money for Foreign Missions, the chief interest of the Woman's Convention at that time. It was not intended to be a scheme for raising money, but an effort primarily designed for "raising" women. Nannie Helen Burroughs suggested that in order to interest and develop the women, the Secretary be permitted to prepare and send out the Woman's Day program and three special addresses (short but challenging) on missions or on some kindred phase of that subject and that the speeches be based on firsthand, current information about the missionary enterprise. It was pointed out that the material for the addresses furnished would be committed to memory by speakers selected by the Missionary Society and, thus, the convention could discover and develop public speakers for church programs, particularly for Woman's Day.

Woman's Day eventually proved to be equally successful in raising money as in expanding the ranks of black women church leaders. Dr. Adam C. Powell, Sr., Pastor of Abyssinian Baptist Church, New York City, had the following to say to a great Sunday morning audience: "As much as the churches have gained from Nannie Burroughs's idea of WOMAN'S DAY and from her famous play 'THE SLABTOWN CONVENTION,' every church ought to set aside one Sunday in the year to be known as 'NANNIE BURROUGHS' DAY,' and send this woman every dollar they raise on that one day in the year to endow and operate the school which she founded for women and girls at Washington, D.C."

Continuing, Dr. Powell said:

> The churches owe it to her because we are all getting more money off of her idea of WOMAN'S DAY and her play "THE SLABTOWN CONVENTION," than we are getting from any other idea given to the churches in this generation.[22]

The Nannie Helen Burroughs School stands today as a community center in the far northeast Washington, D.C. as a monument to this great church woman. Another tribute, the Nannie Helen Burroughs Scholarship Fund, established at Howard University School of Divinity, has assisted many female seminarians. For many years it was the only scholarship available to women at this institution.

Over time, Woman's Day came to be referred to as Women's Day. The institution of Women's Day is very significant for African American female ministers, because when pulpits first opened to women preachers, it was usually within the context of Women's Day. Well over half their preaching was done in the course of traveling to different churches to speak for Women's Day. This, coupled with the evangelistic preaching of revivals, was the only opportunity for most women to preach until recently. At present, there are still many black congregations that hear a woman speak only on Women's Day. Initially, professional lay women were preferred speakers on this day. During the 1960s, 1970s, and 1980s, it became more and more common to invite an ordained or licensed woman minister, frequently referred to as "a lady preacher."

NOTES

1. Jualynne Dodson, "A.M.E. Preaching Women in the Nineteenth Century: Cutting Edge of Women's Inclusion in Church Polity," in Hilah Thomas and Rosemary Thomas, *Women in New Worlds: Historical Perspectives on the Wesleyan Tradition* (Nashville, TN: Abingdon Press, 1988).

2. United Methodist Church (United States), Board of Global Ministries, Women's Division, Task Force on the History of the Central Jurisdiction Women's Organization; Ruth C. Carter, Willa Curry, Mai H. Gray, Thelma McCallum, and Emma Wilson Strother, *To a Higher Glory: The Growth and Development of Black Women Organized for Mission in the Methodist Church, 1940–1968* (Cincinnati, Ohio: The Methodist Church, Education and Cultivation Division, 1968).

3. Cheryl Townsend Gilkes, "The Role of Women in the Sanctified Church," *The Journal of Religious Thought*, vol. 43 (Spring–Summer 1986), pp. 24–41.

4. William L. Andrews, *Sisters of the Spirit* (Bloomington: Indiana University, 1986).

5. Several of the recent works include Delores Causion Carpenter's dissertation, *The Effects of Sect-typeness Upon the Professionalization of Black Female M. Div. Graduates, 1972–1984* (Ann Arbor: University Microfilms International, 1986); Ella Pearson Mitchell, *Those Preaching Women*. vols. 1 and 2 (Valley Forge, PA: Judson Press, 1988); Suzan D. Johnson, ed., *Wise Women Bearing Gifts: Joys and Struggles of Their Faith* (Valley Forge: Judson Press, 1988); Cain Hope Felder, *Troubling Biblical Waters: Race, Class and Family* (Maryknoll, NY: Orbis Books, 1989). (See Chapter Two, "Ancient Ethiopia and the Queen of Sheba," and Chapter Eight, "The Bible, Black Women, and Ministry.")

6. United Methodist Church Board of Global Ministries, *To a Higher Glory*, p. 13.

7. Works on Harriet Tubman include John Blassingame, *Slave Testimony* (Baton Rouge: Louisiana State University Press, 1977); David H. Bradley, *A History of the African Methodist Episcopal Zion Church* (Nashville, TN: The Parthenon Press, 1956); Earl Conrad, *Harriet Tubman* (Washington, D.C.: The Associated Publishers, 1944); Adam Clayton Powell, Jr., *Marching Blacks* (Charlotte, NC: The A.M.E. Zion Publishing House, 1974). Works on Sojourner Truth include: Hertha Pauli, *Her Name Was Truth* (New York: Appleton-Century-Crofts, 1962); Arthur Huff Fauset, *Sojourner Truth: God's Faithful Pilgrim* (Chapel Hill: The University of North Carolina Press, 1938); G. Vale, *Fanaticism: Its Influence, Illustrated by The Simple Narrative of Isabella in the Case of Matthias, Mr. & Mrs. B. Folger, Mr. Mills, Catherine Isabella etc.* (New York–Roosevelt Street: G. Vale, 1835); Sojourner Truth, *Narrative of Sojourner A Northern Slave* (Boston, n.p. 1850); Olive Gilbert, *Narrative of Sojourner Truth: A Bondswoman of Olden Time*, with a *History of her Labors and Correspondence* (Boston: n.p. 1875); and Victoria Ortiz, *Sojourner Truth, A Self-Made Woman* (Philadelphia: J. P. Lippincott Co., 1974).

8. Maria Stewart, *Productions of Mrs. Maria Stewart* (Boston: Friends of Freedom and Virtue, 1835), p. 11.

9. Stewart, *Productions*, p. 24.

10. Ibid., p. 60. (This quotation comes from the scriptural references Ezekiel 13:10 and Jeremiah 6:14.)

11. Ibid., p. 75.

12. Jarena Lee, *Religious Experience and Journal of Mrs. Jarena Lee: Giving an Account of her Call to Preach the Gospel* (Philadelphia: n.p., 1849).

13. United Methodist Church Board of Global Ministries, *To A Higher Glory*, section entitled "Foreign Missions," pp. 36–40.

14. Rosemary Reuther and Eleanor McLaughlin, *Women of Spirit* (New York: Simon and Schuster, 1979), p. 237. Dr. Jualynne Dodson wrote an "Introduction" for *The Story of the Lord's Dealing with Mrs. Amanda Smith, Colored Evangelist*, rpt. (New York: Oxford University Press, 1988).

15. Ibid.

16. United Methodist Church Board of Global Ministries, *To A Higher Glory*, p. 37.

17. Viola Mae Young, *Little Helps for Pastors and Members* (Rosebud, AL, n.p., 1909), p. 1.

18. Samuel Wm. Bacote, *Who's Who Among the Colored Baptists in the United States* (Kansas City: Franklin Hudson, 1913).

19. Ibid., pp. 101–103 (Ella Whitfield); pp. 249–250 (T. Castle); pp. 258–260 (Josie B. Hall).

20. Ibid., p. 240.

21. Evelyn Brooks, *The Women's Movement in the Black Baptist Church*, 1880–1920, Ph.D. dissertation, University of Rochester, 1984.

22. Nannie Helen Burroughs, *Who Started Women's Day?* (Washington, D.C.: Nannie Helen Burroughs Publications, 1968).

Part III

"Slavery's Chains Done Broke At Las'"
African American Religion in the Aftermath of Slavery

Following the Civil War, the Freedman's Bureau sponsored women to come to the South to provide for the education of newly-emancipated African Americans. Here a New England schoolmarm leads a class, with its typical enrollment of boys and girls and adult men and women. Reprinted from Langston Hughes and Milton Melzer, *A Pictorial History of the Negro in America* (New York: Crown Publishers, 1956).

Chapter Twelve

The Gospel and the Primer

Leon F. Litwack

Evangelical Protestantism's fervor for social reform, which was largely an outgrowth of religious revivalism and of women's initiatives in pursuing their religious vocation in their "appropriate" "sphere of usefulness," had challenged the institution of chattel slavery and contributed to the onset of the Civil War. At War's end, the fervor continued in the effort to provide for the newly freed a foundation, through education, for a viable future of citizenship. At the same time, African Americans, particularly through their churches, took advantage of the opportunity now afforded to address the broad range of needs among their people, with education as one priority for enhancing piety and ensuring socioeconomic sustainability.

•

Wealth, intelligence and godliness combined, make their possessors in dispensable members of a community.
—Address of the Bishops of the African Methodist Episcopal Church, May 2, 1866[1]

Wat's de use ob niggers pretendin' to lurnin? Dey's men on dis yeah plantation, old's I am, studyin' ober spellin'- book, an' makin' b'lieve 's if dey could larn. Wat's de use? Wat'll dey be but niggers wen dey gits through? Niggers good for nothin' but to wuck in de fiel' an' make cotton. Can't make white folks ob you'selves, if you is free.
—Black Driver, Fish Pond Plantation, Louisiana, April 1866[2]

When the Civil War ended, Henry McNeal Turner sensed that his work had only begun. He thought he knew how and where he could best serve his people. Two years earlier, he had preached his farewell sermon as pastor of Israel Bethel Church in Washington, D.C., and within weeks he had returned to his native South as a chaplain assigned to the 1st Regiment, United States Colored Troops. While serving in that post, he manifested a racial pride that would distinguish his thoughts and actions for the remainder of his life. Never would he relent in the conviction that the

African race possessed the capacity for intellectual and material greatness. "I claim for them," he wrote in August 1865, "superior ability." None of the renowned orators, ministers, and statesmen he had heard in the North, not even a Henry Ward Beecher or a Charles Summer, compared in his estimation with the simple eloquence he had once heard from the lips of a black slave in South Carolina. Nor did he consider the celebrated work of architects and mechanics in the North superior to the skills demonstrated by many slave artisans. While conceding that these were "exceptional" blacks who had "mastered circumstances," Turner liked to think of them nevertheless as "extraordinary projections" who suggested the still largely unrealized potential unrealized of his people.

Even with emancipation, he realized, this vast potential would be difficult to tap. No matter how often he celebrated the achievements of individual blacks, he remained deeply troubled in 1865 by the condition of the great mass of recently freed slaves, especially those outside of the urban centers who had spent a lifetime laboring in the fields, sustained only by the will to survive. Almost everywhere he traveled in the postwar South, Turner found freedmen still embracing and cherishing the old slave habits, exhibiting little of the racial pride he felt so intensely; some of them were too "timid," "doubtful," and "fearful" to exercise their freedom, preferring instead to defer to their old masters or to transfer their feelings of dependency to their new Yankee masters.

> That old servile fear still twirls itself around the heart strings, and fills with terror the entire soul at a white man's frown. Just let him say stop, and every fibre is palsied, and this will be the case till they all die. True, some possessing a higher degree of bravery may be killed or most horribly mutilated for their intrepidity, but should this be the case, the white man's foot-kissing party will be to blame for it. *As long as negroes will be negroes* (as we are called) *we may be negroes.*

That so many of his brethren should behave in this way came as no surprise to him. "Oh, how the foul curse of slavery has blighted the natural greatness of my race!" he wrote in early 1865, while his regiment was camped in North Carolina. "It has not only depressed and horror-streaked the should-be glowing countenance of thousands, but it has almost transformed many into inhuman appearance."

Since early in the war the black South had loomed as a fertile field for missionary labor. None recognized this potential more readily than did the black churchmen of the North. "*The Rubicon is passable,*" exulted the Reverend James Lynch in September 1861, after noting how his African Methodist Episcopal Church had been compelled for years to operate on the northern side of the Potomac River. "With God for our guide, and his promises for our specie currency, *we will cross*, and carry there the legacy of the sainted Allen, our church government, and the word of God." Although the black church acted initially with caution, pending a clarification of the war's objectives, the Emancipation Proclamation and the enlistment of blacks in the Union Army removed any lingering doubts. Within several months of these developments, James Lynch was on his way to South Carolina. "My own heart has been fired by our brethren here," he soon reported. "Ignorant though they be, on account of long years of oppression, they exhibit a desire to hear and to learn, that I never imagined. Every word you say while preaching, they drink down and respond to, with an earnestness that sets your heart all on fire, and you feel that it is indeed God's work to minister to them."[3]

Although other denominations were no less zealous in bringing the freed slaves into their respective folds, the Methodists and the Baptists enjoyed a clear advantage from the outset. If the Baptists offered greater organizational flexibility and more easily accommodated native black preachers, the Methodists provided, as the founder of the A.M.E. Church once explained, "the plain simple gospel" which "the unlearned can understand, and the learned are sure to understand." Both of these pietistic sects also found it necessary to spend less time in conversion than in simply providing the organizational structure that would accommodate the tens of thousands of slaves already committed to their faiths. When the Reverend Lynch, for example, sought to organize the 800 black residents of Helenaville, into the A.M.E. Church, he would report that "they all readily assented, with the exception of a few Baptists." At the same time, he continued, "I licensed two local preachers, and two exhorters who had been previously verbally licensed; I never saw men appreciate anything so much in my life."[4]

No matter what denominations they represented, the black missionaries found upon entering the South a ready confirmation of the marvelous workings of the Divine Spirit. To look around them, to witness at first hand this "most terrible retribution" which God had inflicted on the white South for the "cruel barbarities" of slavery, more than fulfilled the warnings they had hurled against Babylon from their pulpits in the North. What more dramatic proof of His presence and the triumph of His justice than to see for themselves Pharaoh's hosts engulfed and vanquished. After the Reverend Richard H. Cain walked through the streets of Charleston and gazed at the ruins that were once "the dwellings of the proud and defiant man-stealers," he could only conclude that this city had become "a monument of God's indignation and an evidence of His righteous judgments." For the slave, he added, a new era had dawned, the day of redemption was at hand, and the prophet's proclamation had come to be realized: "Arise, shine: for thy light is come, and the glory of the Lord has risen upon thee." And those who wished to oversee the fulfillment of this prophecy had only to "go among this redeemed people; enter their humble homesteads; sit down with them and listen to their stories of wrong and their songs of rejoicing; [and] gain their confidence." For the Reverend Cain, Charleston was the place to establish his church for the freedmen.[5]

Although some of the black missionaries had once resided in the South as slaves or free Negroes, many of them were native Northerners who had formed their impressions of slavery in the abolitionist movement. Upon entering the South, then, they expected to find a people degraded and scarred—physically and psychically—by a lifetime of bondage and in desperate need of "regeneration and civilization." No proclamation or legislative act, they assumed, could get at the evils that had accumulated and festered over many decades. "As a malignant cancer leaves its roots after being apparently cured," the Reverend James W. C. Pennington observed from Jacksonville, Florida, "so Slavery has left its barbarisms which are in danger of being mixt up with all that is now being done for the advancement of christian civilization among the people." The breakup of slavery, he believed, had uncovered "a fearful moral chaos" in the South, and only education and "the *Remedial power of the Gospel*" could accomplish for the African race in the United States what they had already achieved for the Anglo-Saxon race. Repeatedly, clerics and teachers alike would define the task before them as undoing the moral depravity, self-debasement, and dependency which slavery had fostered in its victims, and the Reverend Cain, for one, thought no vestiges of bondage more resistant to reform then these. "*The people are emancipated but not free!*" he wrote from Charleston. "*They are still slaves to their old ideas,* as well as to their masters. The great masses have, by the old systems, been taught that they were inferior to the whites in everything, and they believe it still."[6]

If instruction in the spelling book could be left to the teacher, the work of moral reformation belonged properly to the clergyman, but in the post-emancipation South such distinctions in roles were seldom deemed necessary or even desirable and the teacher and the minister in some instances were the same person. In any event, both the school and the church declared open war on the "rum-suckers, bar-room loafers, whiskey-dealers, and card players among the men, and those women who dressed finely on *ill-gotten* gain." The best weapon by which to combat these evils was instruction at every level in the virtues of temperance, marital fidelity, chastity, and domestic economy. The larger and the more urgently this task loomed, the more frequently went out the appeals for assistance—for more individuals like themselves who would dedicate their lives to the work of redemption. "The only thing I regret is, that there are not more Baptist and Methodist ministers down here," the Reverend Arthur Waddell wrote from Beaufort, South Carolina. "When I say this, I mean *colored ministers,* and I do not mean the *silk-gloved* kind, and those who come down here to buy farms, and to cheat these poor people out of their rights. But I mean those who come down here to preach Christ in the way that St. Paul commanded Timothy."[7]

Not the least of the "barbarisms" associated with slavery that dismayed both white and black missionaries was, in fact, the excessive emotionalism, frenzy, and "heathenism" they claimed to find in the religious practices of the freedmen. Neither the Methodists nor the Baptists were strangers to emotional fervor in worship; indeed, that had been a source of their appeal to the slaves. What many of the missionaries now appeared to suggest, however, was that emancipation demanded a new dignity and decorum in religious worship, and that these objectives could best be attained through instruction by an educated clergy.

Until such order prevailed in the freedmen's worship, both black and white northern missionaries would share some common concerns. Upon visiting their first black prayer meeting in the South, white ministers conceded a certain admiration for the "simple and childlike" faith of the freedmen, their evident "sincerity and earnestness," their "implicit belief in Providence," their demonstrated love of prayer, and the powerful emotional impact of their music and hymns. "It took me nearer to heaven than I had been for years," one missionary said of the singing he had heard. Still another spectator at a black religious service came away impressed not only by the "purity and simplicity" of the slaves' faith but also by its practicality. "They believe simply in the love of Christ, and they speak of Him and talk to Him with a familiarity that is absolutely startling. They pray as though they thought Christ himself was standing in the very room." Even though he considered the preachers "very rude and uncultivated," exhibiting little understanding of the Bible, he would conclude from his observations that the freedmen were "the only people I ever met whose religion reacted on their daily life."[8]

What appalled the white missionaries and visitors about black religious worship made by far the deeper impression—the emotional wildness and extravagance, the unlettered preaching, the "incoherent speeches and prayers," the "narrowness" of the religious knowledge, and the evidently strong survivals of superstition and paganism. "My spirit," said one missionary, "sinks within me in sorrow to think of their noisy extravagance around the altar of my blessed Lord, who is the God of *order* not confusion." While some observers claimed to be deeply moved by the *"soul thrilling"* hymns and the "melodious responses" to the sermons, others found them "ludicrous." While some thought the shuffling, clapping, cries, shouts, and groans blended into "a kind of natural opera of feeling," others considered them a vulgar display of paganism without any redeeming religious virtue. Rather than try to understand the role of tone, gesture, and response in the blacks' worship, it would be far easier to ridicule it or to dismiss it altogether. "I never saw anything so savage," the usually tolerant Laura Towne wrote of the first "shout" she witnessed after coming to the Sea Islands. No less dismayed, Lucy Chase came away from her first prayer meeting convinced that the religious feeling of the freedmen was "purely emotional, void of principle, and of no practical utility"; at the same time, her supervisor seized every opportunity to impress upon black worshippers "that boisterous Amens, wild, dancing-dervish flourishes . . . and pan-demoniamics generally, do not constitute religion."[9]

What the well-intentioned northern emissaries failed to appreciate was precisely the degree to which the freedmen considered the emotional fervor inseparable from worship because it brought them that much closer to God. It was almost as though white people wished to maintain a distance.

> White folks tells stories 'bout 'ligion. Dey tells stories 'bout it kaise dey's 'fraid of it. I stays independent of what white folks tells me when I shouts. De Spirit moves me every day, dat's how I stays in. White folks don't feel sech as I does; so dey stays out. . . . Never does it make no difference how I's tossed about. Jesus, He comes and saves me everytime. I's had a hard time, but I's blessed now—no mo' mountains.

The testimony of this former South Carolina slave suggests what so many of the missionaries appeared to have missed—that the slaves over more than a century had fashioned a Christianity adapted to their circumstances. Thomas Wentworth Higginson, a missionary of a very different sort as commander of a black regiment, may have been unique in this respect. Unlike Lucy Chase, he had no difficulty in finding a "practical utility" in black religious worship; in fact, he would be forced to conclude, in retrospect, that "we abolitionists had underrated the suffering produced by slavery among the negroes, but had overrated the demoralization. Or rather, we did not know how the religious temperament of the negroes had checked the demoralization."[10]

Although nearly every postwar black convention and newspaper praised the white benevolent societies for their efforts, these same spokesmen insisted that "the great work of elevating our race" properly belonged to black people. If the freedmen were to be taught self-respect, if they were to be inculcated with pride in their race and begin to view themselves as the equals of whites, what better examples for them to follow than those who had already demonstrated in their own lives the capacity for improvement and leadership. If the freedmen were to be introduced to new forms of church government and worship, would not black ministers be the ideal guides, since they would at once remove "the greatest stigma" that could be attached to such reforms—"that of being a 'white man's religion.'" And if the freedmen were to be encouraged to drop "the old broken brogue language" of slavery, they should listen to "enlightened" and educated ministers of their own color who spoke "in plain English."[11]

The black missionary moved quickly to exploit a critical advantage he had over his white denominational rivals. He could offer the freedmen an immediate alternative to the white man's church and to the white minister. "The Ebony preacher who promises perfect independence from White control and direction carries the col[ore]d heart at once," an officer in the American Missionary Association observed. Near Columbia, Kentucky, a newly freed slave who had some years before been ordained as a deacon and elder in the white Methodist Episcopal Church needed little persuasion to transfer his loyalties to the African Methodist Episcopal Church. "I was offered liberal inducements to continue in the M.E. Church and preach to my people," he explained, "but I preferred to come out from under the yoke. I had been there long enough." That was reason enough for tens of thousands of freedmen and freedwomen to abandon the white-dominated churches for their own facilities, organizations, and preachers; indeed, such a move became for some as important and symbolic an assertion of freedom as the decision to separate from the scene of their bondage.

With some four million souls at stake, the struggle for supremacy among the several Protestant denominations often took on the spirit and the language associated with the prosecution of a war. Into the breach left by departing and deposed "rebel" ministers poured native black preachers and both white and black northern missionaries, and each congregation captured would be hailed as though an enemy had been routed. "Our cause has been gaining daily," the Reverend Cain reported from South Carolina. "In Columbia, the capital of the State, we have captured all the Methodists, and are laying the foundation for an immense congregation." Less than forty-eight hours after General Sherman entered Savannah, the Reverend James Lynch was in the city to claim Andrew's Chapel, previously affiliated with the Methodist Episcopal Church; the white minister had fled, and under the Reverend Lynch's exhortations the black congregation voted overwhelmingly to align itself with the African Methodist Episcopal Church. Consolidating the gains made by previous missionaries, the Reverend Henry M. Turner reported in early 1866 that Georgia had been secured for the A.M.E. Church. "I have visited every place it was safe to go, and sent preachers where it was thought I had better not venture. Last night was the first quiet night I have had for five weeks in succession."[12]

Few triumphs, however, were more gratifying to the African Methodist Episcopal Church than the day in September 1865 when the cornerstone was laid for a new church building in Charleston. Not only did this mark the return of the A.M.E. Church to a city from which it had been banished some forty years earlier for complicity in the Denmark Vesey insurrection plot, but the new building would be erected exclusively by black labor and the architect was none other than Robert Vesey, the son of the executed insurrectionist. Some three thousand black Charlestonians listened that day to speeches from a group of black clergymen who would for the next decade play a dominant role in both the religious and the political history of the state. By September 1866, a black Charlestonian could proudly describe eleven colored churches in his city—five Methodist (two of them affiliated with the A.M.E. Church), two Presbyterian, two Episcopalian, one Congregational, and one Baptist. "The flower of the city," he also noted, worshipped at the Episcopalian Church (St. Mark's), some of "the wealthiest colored families" attended the Methodist Episcopal Church (which had been reorganized by northern white missionaries), and the Reverend Cain's A.M.E. Church was made up largely of newly freed slaves. In Charleston, as in other urban centers where a free Negro community had thrived before the war, church affiliation often reflected divisions of class, status, and color within the black community. And if the experience of Ed Barber some years after the war was in any way typical, those who crossed those lines in choosing a church might come away disappointed.

> When I was trampin' 'round Charleston, dere was a church dere called St. Mark, dat all de society folks of my color went to. No black nigger welcome dere, they told me. Thinkin' as how I was bright 'nough to git in, I up and goes dere one Sunday. Ah, how they did carry on, bow and scrape and ape de white folks.... I was uncomfortable all de time though, 'cause they was too "hifalootin" in de ways, in de singin', and all sorts of carryin' ons.[13]

Almost conceding defeat at the outset, the Methodist Episcopal Church (South) did little to check the mass withdrawal of blacks from its ranks. Within a year after the end of the war, in fact, it had already lost more than half of its black membership; those who remained would soon be reorganized into a separate Colored Methodist Episcopal Church.[14] To win over the departing black Methodists, an often furious battle ensued between the Methodist Episcopal Church (North) and the African Methodist Episcopal Church. Despite the impressive number and quality of the missionaries dispatched South by the northern Methodist and their clear superiority in financial resources, the black Methodist organizations also did quite well, demonstrating to their satisfaction that "blood is always more potent than money." In some communities, the rivals worked out a "compromise" by which preachers of both denominations used the same building and took turns at the pulpit. But at least one black minister who experimented with that arrangement found it unworkable. "The Apostle said, 'Be not unequally yoked together with unbelievers.' But in an accommodating sense, I say be not unequally yoked together with a white man." Even less charitable, the Reverend Richard H. Cain viewed his Methodist rival in Charleston as "this Judas, who comes here to rule over our people with his Yankee rod of iron," acting "more like Barnwell Rhett with his slaves, than a minister of Christ."[15]

What exacerbated the denominational rivalries was the unresolved question of who had the legal and moral right to the property of those churches which had formerly serviced the slaves. Although blacks had often built them, title to the land and the building had invariably been held in trusteeship for the black congregations by the whites. This issue assumed particular importance now that black congregations were searching for places in which to meet. Wherever possible, they would seek to establish new church structures to make absolutely clear their break with the past and their new independence in religious affairs. But even where the will and the labor existed to build their own churches, the resources were not always available. Until land could be acquired by purchase or rental and a building erected, blacks would be forced to hold their services in improvised "brush arbors," abandoned warehouses, and in their own cabins. On a plantation in Louisiana, a double cabin which had previously housed two slave families was subdivided so that black worshippers could meet in one of the rooms. "As you entered," a visitor noted, "you had your choice—you could visit the family or go to church." In many communities, moreover, the black preacher might be kept in quarters and food by his parishioners but he would have to appeal elsewhere for anything approaching a salary. "We are not doing so Well here," one such preacher wrote to the nearest Freedmen's Bureau officer, "the People of Smithville are very Poor so much so that they cannot support me as their Preacher. For the last three month I have not had but $8.78 cents from my congregation. I do not know how I shall get along at this rate."[16]

The spectacle of overwhelming numbers of blacks withdrawing from the established churches in order to worship by themselves provoked a mixed response in the white South. Faced with the choice of permitting the black congregations to depart or granting them equal privileges and seating within the old churches, most whites preferred separation. But the social convenience this afforded them would have to be weighed against the risks incurred, and these covered an assortment of fears. If black laborers without white supervision reverted to indolence and vagrancy, as many whites expected, black worshipers freed from white surveillance might presumably fall into the vices of heathenism. Recalling the exodus of blacks from the white churches, Myrta Lockett Avary thought that was precisely what happened.

> With freedom, the negro, *en masse*, relapsed promptly into the voodooism of Africa. Emotional extravaganzas, which for the sake of his health and sanity, if for nothing else, had been held in check by his owners, were indulged without restraint. It was as if a force long repressed burst forth. "Moans," "shouts" and "trance meetings" could be heard for miles. It was weird.

Voicing an even more common concern, she noted how the blacks who had participated in these orgies would return to their homes late at night or at dawn, "exhausted, and unfit for duty."[17]

With the withdrawal of thousands of blacks from the white-dominated churches, the black church became the central and unifying institution in the postwar black community. Far more than any newspaper, convention, or political organization, the minister communicated directly and regularly with his constituents and helped to shape their lives in freedom. Not only did he preach the gospel to the masses in these years but he helped to politicize and educate them. Many of the black missionaries and clergymen also assumed the position of teachers, and very often the classrooms themselves were housed in the only available quarters in town—the church. While northern black missionaries envisaged in an educated ministry and congregation an end to the excesses that marked the religious worship of southern blacks, even the old slave preachers, many of whom were illiterate, understood the value of knowledge and implored their people to make certain that the new generation learned the word of God in ways that had been denied the parents. "Breddern and sisters!" one such preacher declared. "I can't read more'n a werse or two of dis bressed Book, but de gospel it is here—de glad tidings it is here—oh teach your chill'en to read dis yar bressed Book. It's de good news for we poor coloured folk."[18] If some elderly blacks flocked to the newly opened freedmen's schools in the hope of reading the Bible before they died, the young thirsted for a knowledge not only of the Scriptures but of those subjects that would help them to improve their lot in this world.

"Charles, you is a free man they say, but Ah tells you now, you is still a slave and if you lives to be a hundred, you'll STILL be a slave, cause you got no education, and education is what makes a man free!" Nothing that any missionary educator or Freedmen's Bureau officer might have told Charles Whiteside about the value of schooling could have made as deep an impression as these words with which his master informed him of his freedom. Few freedmen, in fact, would have failed to appreciate the thrust of the slaveholder's remarks. If they looked to any panacea (outside of land) to free them from mental and physical dependency, they fastened their hopes on the schoolhouse. The Reverend Richard H. Cain pronounced education as second in importance only to godliness, but many newly freed slaves might have found it difficult to rank such priorities. "If I nebber does do nothing more while I live," a Mississippi freedman vowed, "I shall give my children a chance to go to school, for I considers education next best ting to liberty."[19]

Although most masters had managed to overcome their fears of religious worship among the slaves, only a very few had dared to extend such toleration to teaching blacks to read and write. "Everything must be interdicted which is calculated to render the slave discontented," was the explanation once offered by a Supreme Court judge in Georgia for the legislative restrictions placed on black literacy. Notwithstanding the elaborate precautions and legislation, some slaves and larger numbers of freeborn blacks managed to acquire a smattering of education, whether in clandestine schools, in the several schools for the freeborn tolerated in certain communities, or because of the indulgence of a member of the master's family. By virtue of their duties and access to the Big House, the plantation slaves most likely to have acquired a competence in reading and writing were the drivers, house servants, and artisans. Whenever the opportunity was there, some blacks had made the most of it.

"These whites don't read and write because they don't want to," a black preacher observed in 1865; "our people don't, because the law and public feeling were against it. The ignorant whites had every chance to learn, but didn't; we had every chance to remain ignorant, and many of us learned in spite of them."[20] At the time of emancipation, however, the vast majority of southern blacks were illiterate—a triumph of sorts for the masters, legislatures, and courts who had deemed such a condition essential to the internal security of their society.

Nothing could have been more calculated to impress upon slaves the value of education than the extraordinary measures adopted by their "white folks" to keep them from it. Even if blacks simply drew on their own experiences and observations, they had come to recognize that power, influence, and wealth in southern society were invariably associated with literacy and monopolized by the better-educated class of whites. "My Lord, ma'am, what a great thing larning is!" a freed slave exclaimed to a white teacher in South Carolina. "White folks can do what they likes, for they know so much more'na we." No less impressed were some "contraband" children at Fortress Monroe early in the war. When placed in schools, one freed slave suggested, these children "thought it was so much like the way master's children used to be treated, that they believed they were getting white."[21]

The practical value of education never seemed clearer than in the aftermath of emancipation, when illiterate black laborers learned from bitter experience, especially on payday and at contract time, how white poeple used "book-larnin' " to take advantage of them. To an elderly Louisiana freedman, that was reason enough to send the children to school, even if their absence from the fields deprived the parents of their earnings. "Leaving learning to your children was better than leaving them a fortune; because if you left them even five hundred dollars, some man having more education than they had would come along and cheat them out of it all." Nearly every convention of freedmen in the postwar years dwelled incessantly on this point, seeking to drive home to every black family that "knowledge is power." Of course, nearly every black family that had survived slavery could readily understand that maxim. "They had seen the magic of a scrap of writing sent from a master to an overseer," a missionary in the Sea Islands noted, "and they were eager to share such power if there were any chance."[22]

To remain in ignorance was to remain in bondage. That conviction alone drew hundreds of thousands, adults and children alike, to the freedmen's schools from the moment they opened, some of the prospective students making a pilgrimage of several miles, and many of them forced to combine their schooling with rigorous work schedules. The very intensity of their commitment caught both teachers and native whites by surprise. "They will endure almost any penance rather than be deprived of this privilege," a missionary educator in North Carolina observed. To a school official in Virginia, trying to convey his thoughts about the freedmen's enthusiasm for education, the phrase "*anxious* to learn" was insufficient; "they are *crazy* to learn," he reported, as if their very salvation depended on it. No doubt many exslaves were certain that it did. When asked why he wished to enroll in a school, an elderly black man quickly replied, "Because I want to read de Word of de Lord." That would permit him, moreover, as an old Mississippi black man noted, to read all of the Bible, not simply the portions the master and mistress had always selected for their slaves.

But no matter how fully committed they might be to the principle of schooling, not all black parents could afford the luxury of losing the labor of their children. As teachers and school officials would quickly discover, the turnover in students and erratic attendance usually reflected work demands and planting seasons, and in some places teachers tried to adjust their instruction to accommodate the laborers. "We work all day," a group of freedmen in Macon, Georgia, explained to the teacher, "but we'll come to you in the evening for learning, and we want you to make us learn; we're dull, but we want you to beat it into us!" Many of her students, a teacher reported from New Bern, North Carolina, were unable to leave work before eight o'clock in the evening but they still insisted on spending at least an hour afterwards "in earnest application to study." Even when at work, however, some freedmen took their primers with them, much to the neglect of their duties. "I don't wonder E. learns so fast and reads so well," one pupil told his teacher, "for while she sits in the field watching the crows, she minds her book so hard they come and eat up her corn."[23]

The demand for schools increased so rapidly that the initial problem lay not in finding willing students but in hiring teachers and locating quarters to house the classes. Until new structures could be built with money raised by the freedmen or donated by the northern benevolent societies, almost any place would have to suffice—a mule stable (Helena, Arkansas), a billiard room (Seabrook plantation, Sea Islands), a courthouse (Lawrence, Kansas), an abandoned white school (Charleston), the plantation cotton house (St. Simon's Island), warehouses and storerooms (New Orleans), and, most commonly, the black church.

Although a few states began to take some faltering steps toward establishing schools for whites and blacks, the development of a system of tax-supported public education would be largely an achievement of Radical Reconstruction. During the interim years, the work of educating the newly freed slaves would have to be undertaken by the freedmen themselves, and by that host of white and black teachers who came to the South in the wake of Union occupation. As the northern emissaries boarded the ships and trains that brought them to their various destinations, and as they began their work, they came increasingly to believe that the very wisdom of emancipation itself was at stake—whether or not black people possessed the capacity for mental improvement and would be able to function as citizens and free workers in a competitive, white-dominated civilization.

NOTES

1. *Christian Recorder*, May 26, 1866.

2. Whitelaw Reid, *After the War: A Southern Tour, May 1, 1865 to May 1, 1866* (Cincinnati: Moore, Wilstach, and Baldwin, 1866), p. 510.

3. *Christian Recorder*, Sept. 7, 1861, June 27, 1863.

4. Eugene D. Genovese, *Roll, Jordan, Roll: The World the Slaves Made* (New York: Pantheon Books, 1974), p. 234; *Christian Recorder*, July 25, 1863.

5. *Christian Recorder*, May 27, 1865.

6. J.W.C. Pennington to "My Esteemed Friend," May 25, 1870, American Missionary Assn. Archives; *Christian Recorder*, June 29, 1867. See also Amos Gerry Berman to Rev. George Whipple, Feb. 25, 1867, in "Documents," *Journal of Negro History*, XXII (1937), 222–26.

7. *Christian Recorder*, June 16, 1866 (H. M. Turner and A. Waddell letters).

8. Rev. Joel Grant to Prof. Henry Cowles, April 10, 1863, H. S. Beals to Rev. S. S. Jocelyn, April 28, 1863, Martha L. Kellogg to Rev. S. S. Jocelyn, Sept. 3, 1863, American Missionary Assn. Archives; *National Freedman*, I (Sept. 15, 1865), 264 (Rev. Henry J. Fox); *New York Times*, Nov. 28, 1863. See also Maria Waterbury, *Seven Years Among the Freedmen* (Chicago: Arnold, 1893), pp. 18–19, and David Macrae, *The Americans at Home* (New York: Dutton, 1952), pp. 353–75.

9. H. S. Beals to Rev. S. S. Jocelyn, April 28, Aug. 18, 1863, William G. Kephart to Lewis Tappan, May 9, 1864, Augustus C. Stickle to Jacob R. Shipherd, July 9, 1867, Timothy Lyman to Rev. W. T. Richardson to Rev. George Whipple, July 3, 1863, Mary E. Burdick to Rev. George Whipple, March 8, 1864, American Missionary Assn. Archives; *National Freedman*, I (Oct. 15, 1865), 285 (M. J. Ringler); Laura M. Towne, *Letters and Diary of Laura M. Towne: Written from the Sea Islands of South Carolina, 1862–1884*, ed. Rupert Sargent Holland (Cambridge: 1912), p. 20; Henry L. Swint, ed., *Dear Ones at Home: Letters from Contraband Camps* (Nashville: 1966), pp. 21–22, 58. See also Elizabeth Ware Pearson, ed., *Letters from Port Royal: Written at the Time of the Civil War* (Boston: 1906), pp. 26–28; Mary Ames, *From a New England Woman's Diary in Dixie in 1865* (Springfield, Mass.: 1906), pp. 81–82; Thomas Wentworth Higginson, *Army Life in a Black Regiment* (Boston: 1870), pp. 17–18.

10. George P. Rawick, ed., *American Slave: A Composite Autobiography*, III: S. C. Narr. (Part 3) (Westport, Conn.: 1972), p. 5; Higginson, *Army Life in a Black Regiment*, p. 253.

11. Sella Martin to M. E. Strieby, March 20, 1866, American Missionary Assn. Archives; *Christian Recorder*, Feb. 11, 1865 (James H. Payne).

12. *Christian Recorder*, Feb. 24, 1866 (R. H. Cain), Jan. 21 and Feb. 4, 1865 (J. Lynch), March 24, 1866 (H. M. Turner). See also *Christian Recorder*, Jan. 29, 1870 ("Our Record").

13. *Christian Recorder*, Oct. 14, 1865, Sept. 8, 1866; Rawick, ed., *American Slave*, II: S. C. Narr. (Part 1), pp. 35–36.

14. H. Shelton Smith, *In His Image, But . . . : Racism in Southern Religion, 1780–1910* (Durham, N.C.: 1972), pp. 229–31; Ralph E. Morrow, *Northern Methodism and Reconstruction* (East Lansing, Mich.: 1956), p. 129; Vernon Lane Wharton, *The Negro in Mississippi, 1865–1890* (Chapel Hill: 1947), pp. 260–61; Joel Williamson, *After Slavery: The Negro in South Carolina During Reconstruction, 1861–1877* (Chapel Hill: 1965), pp. 196–97; Peter Kolchin, *First Freedom: The Responses of Alabama's Blacks to Emancipation and Reconstruction* (Westport, Conn.: 1972), p. 111–13.

15. Morrow, *Northern Methodism and Reconstruction*, p. 136; *Christian Recorder*, March 5, 1870 ("Separate Churches"), March 26, 1864 (J.D.S. Hall), June 17, 1865 (R. H. Cain). For the struggle between the A.M.E. and the Methodist Episcopal Church, including the conflicts over church property, see also *Christian Recorder*, March 12 (J.D.S. Hall), June 25 (J. Lynch), 1864, April 15 ("Arnold"), May 13 (H. M. Turner), June 3 (S.C. Conference), Aug. 5 and Oct. 7 (H.R. Revels), Oct. 21 (J. Lynch), 1865, Sept 21, 1867 ("True Position of A.M.E. Church"); Bishop L. J. Coppin, *Unwritten History* (Philadelphia: 1919), pp. 117–18; Morrow, Northern Methodism and Reconstruction, 139–40; and Williamson, *After Slavery*, pp. 181–91.

16. Reid, *After the War*, pp. 519–20; Rev. A. G. Smith to "Dear Sir," Sept. 25, 1867, Records of the Assistant Commissioners, North Carolina (Letters Received), Freedman's Bureau.

17. Myrta Lockett Avary, *Dixie after the War* (New York: 1906), pp. 203–04.

18. Macrae, *Americans at Home*, p. 368.

19. Jon W. Blassingame, ed., *Slave Testimony: Two Centuries of Letters, Speeches, Interviews, and Autobiographies* (Baton Rouge: 1977), p. 598; *Missionary Record* (Charleston), July 5, 1873; J. W. Alvord, *Eighth Semi-Annual Report on Schools for Freedmen, July 1, 1869* (Washington, D.C., 1869), p. 46.

20. Genovese, *Roll, Jordan, Roll*, p. 562; Reid, *After the War*, p. 145.

21. Elizabeth Hyde Botume, *First Days Amongst the Contrabands* (Boston: 1893), p. 259; Blassingame, ed., *Slave Testimony*, p. 174.

22. John Richard Dennett, *The South As It Is*, 1865–1866, ed. Henry M. Christman (New York: 1965), p. 322; Willie Lee Rose, *Rehearsal for Reconstruction: The Port Royal Experiment* (Indianapolis: 1964), p. 46. On the theme of "knowledge is power," see also, e.g., "State Convention of the Colored People of South Carolina," in *South Carolina Leader*, Nov. 25, 1865; *Loyal Georgian*, Jan. 20, 1866; and 39 Cong., 1 Sess., House Exec. Doc. 70, *Freedman's Bureau*, 334.

23. J. T. Trowbridge, *The South: A Tour of Its Battle-Fields and Ruined Cities, A Journey Through the Desolated States, and Talks with the People* (Hartford: 1866), p. 466; *National Freedman*, I (April 1, 1865), 93 (M. E. Jones and N. J. McCullough); Harriet B. Greeley to Rev. George Whipple, April 29, 1865, American Missionary Assn. Archives. On the difficulty of adjusting work schedules to schooling, see also Rawick (ed.), *American Slave*, XIII: Ga. Narr. (Part 3), 117; XIV: N. C. Narr. (Part 1), 277; XVI: Tenn. Narr., 29; *American Freedman*, III (June 1868), 431 (L. M. Towne); and Helen M. Jones to S. G. Wright, Jan. 13, 1866, American Missionary Assn. Archives.

Chapter Thirteen

The Black Faith of W. E. B. Du Bois

Sociocultural and Political Dimensions of Black Religion

Manning Marable

Manning Marable walks us through the scenario of African American social and religious life at the rounding of the nineteenth into the twentieth century, through the eyes of one of African America's most prolific scholars and most probing cultural critics. W. E. B. Du Bois's researches and analyses of the African American situation have been watersheds for much of subsequent black scholarship. And even though his faith stance sometimes interrogated, sometimes dismissed orthodox Christian belief—both agnostics and humanists might claim him—he had a profound understanding of the spirituality of African Americans, and his writings convey the powerful, moving ruminations from his own wrestlings with the "numinous other." They have provided professional black theologians and lay Christian believers with arresting challenge and illumination.

•

W. E. B. Du Bois—founder of the National Association for the Advancement of Colored People and editor of its journal, the *Crisis*, sociologist, civil rights leader, and "Father of Pan-Africanism"—is seldom viewed as a Christian. His biographers note that he frequently attacked all Christian denominations for their support of racial segregation. In published articles Du Bois described himself as an "agnostic" and questioned the "immortality" of man ("Immortality" 18).[1] As a college student and in later life, he affirmed that "work, systematic and tireless," was his only true faith (*Autobiography* 124). In December 1940 he announced that he worshipped "Truth and Truth only. . . . I will face each sunrise with one prayer: There is no God but Love and Work is his Prophet" ("Crow Flies"). At the end of his public career Du Bois declared, "I believe in communism," renouncing American "free enterprise [as] leading the world to disaster" (*Autobiography* 57), and died as an exile in Ghana. This image of Du Bois reveals only one aspect of his multifaceted character. For also throughout his life he wrote extensively on the black church. His earliest published essays focus on black religious life in his native town, Great Barrington, Massachusetts,[2] one of his final articles, written in 1962, was an introduction to a photographic study of "Store Front Churches" in Buffalo, New York's ghetto. In the intervening years he wrote several hundred articles on religion, the black church, and the social and political function of religious institutions. Du Bois was simultaneously an agnostic and an Anglican, a staunch critic of religious dogma and a passionate convert to the black version of Christianity. His belief in his people was expressed in his own black faith for the world.

Du Bois's religious sensibility was formed early in life. His grandfather, Alexander Du Bois, was senior warden of the black Episcopal Parish of St. Luke, founded by black residents of New Haven, Connecticut, in 1847 (*Dusk* 107–8; *Autobiography* 67). His mother, Mary Burghardt, was deeply religious and frequently but softly chastised her high-spirited son to attend church services regularly and "never to go into a liquor saloon or even near it" (*Autobiography* 81). [3] Life in Great Barrington, Massachusetts, during the Gilded Age was largely defined by the church and its strict moral code. Du Bois and his mother attended two churches: a small Negro Methodist Zion Church, formed by a small colony of " 'contrabrands,' freed Negroes from the South," and Great Barrington's Congregational Church, which was patronized by the leading merchants, farmers, and "professional men" of the community (*Autobiography* 83, 88).[4] Even as a teenager, Du Bois noticed the class divisions within his small community that were manifested in the existence of various denominations. The local Catholic church "was perched across the river beyond the mills, and thither the [Irish] girl servants trudged faithfully early mornings to mass. This and other traits of the Irish became the basis of jokes and ridicule in town. . . ." Colored people, by contrast, despite their lower class status, were cordially welcomed in white middle-class congregations. The Episcopal church catered to "older families and the more well-to-do," and most of Du Bois's extended family in the region belonged to this congregation. In the northern section of the town near the mill was an unpretentious, "small white wooden Methodist church," attended by "the less well-known inhabitants" of Great Barrington (*Autobiography* 82, 89–90).

Du Bois graduated from high school in June 1884 and his mother died several months later. His subsequent academic career would have been in doubt had it not been for the timely intervention of three leading citizens: the Reverend Mr. Scudder, the pastor of the Congregational church; Edward Van Lennep, superintendent of the Congregational church's Sunday school and principal of a local private school; and the Reverend C. C. Painter, a retired Federal Indian Agent and former pastor of several Congregational churches in Connecticut. The church in Great Barrington and Painter's churches agreed to donate one hundred dollars annually for Du Bois's college education. The black youth desired to attend Harvard, but Painter insisted that "the reconstructed South . . . was the place for me to be educated." Over the objections of "my family and colored friends," Du Bois was sent to Fisk University in Nashville in September 1885 (*Autobiography* 103, 105; *Dusk* 22; *Correspondence* 5).

Painter's decision to send Du Bois to the South fundamentally shaped the young man's life. Growing up in New England, Du Bois had known little racial prejudice, and his contacts with other blacks were few and brief. In Nashville, a world of color was revealed, and the young Puritan was sorely out of place at first. "I was thrilled to be for the first time among so many people of my own color. . . . Never before had I seen young men so self-assured and who gave themselves such airs, and colored men at that; and above all for the first time I saw beautiful girls" (*Autobiography*

107). Years of sexual repression and Calvinist training put him at odds with his contemporaries, who had "loose sex morals." Years later Du Bois admitted frankly, "I actually did not know the physical difference between men and women. At first my fellows jeered in disbelief and then became sorry and made many offers to guide my abysmal ignorance. This built for me inexcusable and startling temptations" (*Autobiography* 280). Regarded as a "liar" or "freak"⁵ when he asserted his virginity, he sought familiar refuge in the arms of the church. Dutifully attending church services, revivals, and morning prayers at the beginning of each school day, Du Bois tried desperately to find inner tranquility. Writing to Reverend Scudder in February 1886, the young college freshman observed that he had "united with the Church and hope that the prayers of my Sunday-School may help guide me in the path of Christian duty." Du Bois faithfully continued to correspond with members of the Great Barrington Sunday School class until at least 1892 (*Correspondence* 5, 18–19). But in Nashville, he encountered controversy in his faith from "fundamentalist" quarters. One of Du Bois's classmates, "Pop" Miller, brought him before the congregation and accused him of "a particularly heinous form of sin," public "dancing." Du Bois protested in vain that he had "never attended public dance halls" and had only engaged in the "innocent pastime . . . at the homes of colored friends in the city." Fisk University teachers supported Miller, warning the young sinner "that my dancing might well be quite innocent, but . . . my example might lead others astray." Du Bois deeply resented their intervention, and much later concluded that this little tempest "led to my eventual refusal to join a religious organization." But for the moment, he still "never questioned [his] religious upbringing. Its theory had presented no particular difficulties: God ruled the world, Christ loved it, and men did right, or tried to; otherwise they were rightly punished" (*Autobiography* 110–11, 127).

Another aspect of the black social and religious experience became part of Du Bois's development in the summers of 1886 and 1887. In east Tennessee he obtained a minor position as a rural schoolteacher at twenty-eight dollars per month. At last he encountered "the real seat of slavery . . . I touched intimately the lives of the commonest of mankind—people who ranged from barefooted dwellers on dirt floors, with patched rags for clothes, to rough hard-working farmers, with plain, clean plenty"(*Autobiography* 114). His schoolhouse was nothing but a log hut with no door, "a massive rickety fireplace," and little furniture. "I was haunted by a New England vision of neat little desks and chairs, but alas the reality was rough plank benches without backs, and at times without legs," Du Bois noted. "They had the one virtue of making naps dangerous, possibly fatal, for the floor was not to be trusted" (*Autobiography* 115–16). Among his class of nearly thirty youths, many older than himself, was "a thin, homely girl of twenty," Josie—later to be described as an unforgettable figure in *The Souls of Black Folk* (64).⁵ The crucible of southern black life and labor was opened to Du Bois. Here he found warmth and unpretentious friendship he had not thought possible. Frequently after classes were finished he visited the families of his pupils: sitting on the porch eating fresh peaches with Josie and her talkative mother; visiting Doc Burke's farm, helping himself to fried chicken, wheat biscuits, string beans and plump berries. Here he also discovered the mystery of sex, as Du Bois slept with an "unhappy wife who was my landlady." Time for these folk seemingly stood still. To be sure, life "was dull and humdrum," Du Bois wrote in his last *Autobiography*, "I have called my community a world, and so its isolation made it. There was among us but a half-awakened common consciousness, sprung from common joy and grief, at burial, birth or wedding; from a common hardship of poverty, poor land and low wages; and, above all, from the sight of the Veil that hung between us and Opportunity" (118–20, 280).

But the essence of black life was to be found on Sunday mornings, as the dawn broke above the rural countryside. In the center of Alexandria, Tennessee's, colored district were "the twin temples of the hamlet, the Methodist and Hard-Shell Baptist churches." In these unadorned wooden halls the black rural folk made "the weekly sacrifice with frenzied priest at the altar of the 'old-time religion.' " It was here that the families of his students sang in "soft melody and mighty cadences" the black spirituals of slavery. At first Du Bois was baffled by this experience. "We in Berkshire . . . were very quiet and subdued, and I know not what would have happened those clear Sabbath mornings had someone punctuated the sermon with a scream, or interrupted the long prayer with a loud Amen!" Sensitive about his strict background, and yet alienated from the Congregational church in Nashville, Du Bois was "determined to know something of the Negro in the country districts." Their deep expressions of spirituality were utterly new to him. As a budding scholar, and more importantly as a black man, he was determined to understand their religion, and to integrate it into his own embryonic world view (*Autobiography* 114, 119–20).

The basic anatomy of the black religious experience was expressed in three factors: "the Preacher, the Music, and the Frenzy." The black minister, Du Bois later suggested, "is the most unique personality developed by the Negro on American soil." The black minister during slavery emerged as a powerful force in community life. "He early appeared on the plantation and found his function as the healer of the sick, the interpreter of the Unknown, the comforter of the sorrowing, the supernatural avenger of wrong, and the one who rudely but picturesquely expressed the longing, disappointment, and resentment of a stolen and oppressed people." Thus the social dynamics which produced white clergy and religious institutions differed radically from the organic evolution of the black church and its preachers. The transition from traditional African social systems to the plantation South was nothing less than "a terrific social revolution, and yet some traces were retained of the former group life, and the chief remaining institution was the Priest or Medicineman." This charismatic representative of the *nommo* or essence of his people, a synthesis of "bard, physician, judge, and priest," became within the American South "the Negro preacher." During Reconstruction and after, other basic characteristics were added to his social profile: he was at once "a leader, a politician, an orator, a 'boss,' an intriguer, an idealist. . . . The combination of a certain adroitness with deep-seated earnestness, of tact with consummate ability, gave him his preëminence," Du Bois noted, "and helps him maintain it" (*Souls* 141–42).

The music of black faith "is that plaintive rhythmic melody," Du Bois wrote in The Souls of Black Folk, "which, despite caricature and defilement, still remains the most original and beautiful expression of human life and longing yet born on American soil." Even as a small boy "these songs have stirred me strangely," Du Bois reflected. "They came out of the South unknown to me, one by one, and yet at once I knew them as of me and of mine." The spirituals and the "Sorrow Songs" revealed the anguish and hope of a people in bondage, a mass of illiterate slaves whose spiritual strivings brought together an aspiration of secular emancipation and religious freedom. In such songs, "the slave spoke to the world" in an Aesopian language, partially "veiled and half articulate." "Steal away to Jesus" could mean different things to the masters and the slaves. There was the "cradle-song of death which all men know—'Swing low, sweet chariot . . . ' "; "songs of the fugitive like that which opens 'The Wings of Atlanta . . .'"; and songs which revealed the full glory of the end of life's oppression—" 'My Lord, what a mourning! when the stars begin to fall' . . ." In the Carolina swamplands, the slaves sang:

> Michael, haul the boat ashore,
> Then you'll hear the horn they blow,
> Then you'll hear the trumpet sound,
> Trumpet sound the world around,
> Trumpet sound for rich and poor,
> Trumpet sound the Jubilee,
> Trumpet sound for you and me.

The spirituals were simultaneously sorrowful and yet filled with hope, or as Du Bois expressed it, "a faith in the ultimate justice of things. The minor cadences of despair change often to triumph and calm confidence." In the face of oppression, the music provides a "faith in life"; it offers "sometimes assurance of boundless justice in some fair world beyond." The transition to Jim Crow and lynching was the secular political reality which created the living aesthetic space for such songs to continue to capture "the tragic soul-life" of black people. They express the hope "that sometime, somewhere, men will judge men by their souls and not by their skins" (141–42, 187–91).

The "Frenzy or 'Shouting,' when the Spirit of the Lord passed by, and, seizing the devotee, made him mad with supernatural joy, was the last essential of Negro religion," Du Bois wrote, adding for emphasis, "and the one more devoutly believed in than all the rest." The shout was at once a purgation of the believers' anxieties, fears, and doubts created under slavery and segregation; it was a catharsis, the expression of transcendence, a cry of faith and hope, a physical and collective explosion which was necessary for a people wedged in the permanent vise of social anxiety and frustration. "It varied in expression from the silent rapt countenance or low murmur and moan to the mad abandon of physical fever—the stamping, shrieking and laughing, the vision and trance." The common rapture was expressed by man, but was not of man: the frenzy, for the black Christian, was the "visible manifestation of God." Without this catharsis Du Bois wrote, blacks believed that "there could be no true communion with the Invisible" (*Souls* 143).

The soul-searing experiences in the Tennessee countryside placed Du Bois increasingly at odds with established Christian theology, and with himself. When assigned a text on Christian logic at Fisk, it now "affronted my logic. It was to my mind, then and since, a cheap piece of special pleading." University president Erastus Cravath secured a scholarship for Du Bois's postgraduate work at Hartford Theological

Seminary. But Du Bois could not accept it. "I believed too little in Christian dogma to become a minister. I was not without faith: I never stole material nor spiritual things; I not only never lied, but blurted out my conception of truth on the most untoward occasions; I drank no alcohol and knew nothing of women, physically or psychically, to the incredulous amusement of most of my more experienced fellows" (*Autobiography* 124, 127). His graduate training at Harvard University, under the direction of philosophers William James and George Santayana, pushed the black scholar far from "the sterilities of scholastic philosophy to realistic pragmatism" *Autobiography* 133). While in Boston, however, he pursued his relationship with the black church. On Thanksgiving night, 1891, Du Bois organized and participated in the Aristophanes play, "The Birds," at the black community's Charles Street Church. Nevertheless, he expressed blunt criticisms of the black church in an 1891 paper prepared for the National Colored League of Boston: "A religion that won't stand the application of reason and common sense is not fit for an intelligent dog." But his hostility toward the white Christian church was far more profound. In his diary, Du Bois attacked the Anglo-Saxon's "high Episcopal Nicene creed" as a rationale for white supremacy. Musing on the Biblical image of "Ethiopia [stretching] forth her hands to God," the young Harvard man fumed: "the spectacle [of] the venerable colored dame in this rather unbalanced position in regard to the Anglo-Saxon god has become somewhat nauseating to the average young Negro of today." For the white West, with the possible exception of the "self-forgetful Quakers," God was dead, Du Bois decided (Broderick 18–19, 23).

If racial oppression and segregation had compromised and destroyed the reality of God among most American whites, Du Bois thought, then he would refuse to participate in the charade. In his first teaching post at Wilberforce University, a small black Methodist institution, he "wandered casually" into a local black prayer gathering. "Suddenly and without warning," a student leader of the meeting announced that "Professor Du Bois will lead us in prayer.' I simply answered, 'No, he won't,' and as a result nearly lost my new job." An outraged president forced Du Bois before the school's governing board of bishops, and "it took a great deal of explaining" to convince its members "why a professor in Wilberforce should not be able at all times and sundry to address God in extemporaneous prayer. I was saved only by the fact that my coming to Wilberforce had been widely advertised and I was willing to do endless work . . ." (*Autobiography* 186). He quickly acquired the reputation as a troublemaker, cynic and "agnostic" by refusing "to attend the annual 'revivals' of religion which interrupted school work every year at Christmas time." In May 1896 he threatened the college treasurer in order to receive back payment for his salary (*Autobiography* 187–88).

Such irreverent behavior did not go unnoticed beyond Wilberforce. After a fifteen-month stint at the University of Pennsylvania, where he compiled the first major sociological survey of Afro-American urban life, *The Philadelphia Negro*, Du Bois applied for a position at Atlanta University. The college's president, Horace Bumstead, was by nature and political training a cautious man. Several trustees and prominent friends of Atlanta University expressed "objections and misgivings" to him when learning of Du Bois's possible appointment. Bumstead later wrote that

"Atlanta University has always had a pronounced religious, though undenomina-
tional life," and that its teachers were expected "to help to maintain it." But on that
point, such assurances "were not very easy to get" from Du Bois. When asked of his
religious affiliation, he curtly replied " 'none to speak of.' But though reluctant to
speak of his religion or to say what he would do at Atlanta," and despite grave
"objections and misgivings," he was permitted to join the faculty (*Autobiography*
209–10).

Yet the spiritual commitment Du Bois held for his people, which deepened
and enlarged his analytic critique of the total society, could not be expressed as a
complete rejection of black Christianity. Repeatedly his sociological research focused
on the centrality of religion within black life, not only in *The Philadelphia Negro*,
but also in his 1897 study of black life in Farmville, Virginia, completed for the
U.S. Department of Labor, and in his 1898 study of Atlanta, Georgia (*Some Efforts*). The black "First Baptist" Church in Farmville is described by Du Bois in intimate detail as "a roomy brick edifice seating five hundred or more persons, taste-
fully finished in Georgia pine, with a carpet, a small organ, and stained-glass windows":

> Underneath is a large assembly room with benches. This building is the central club-
> house of a community of a thousand or more Negroes. Various organizations meet
> here,—the church proper, the Sunday-school, two or three insurance societies,
> women's societies, secret societies, and mass meetings of various kinds. Entertainments,
> suppers, and lectures are held beside the five or six regular weekly religious services.
> Considerable sums of money are collected and expended here, employment is found
> for the idle, strangers are introduced, news is disseminated and charity distributed. At
> the same time this social, intellectual, and economic centre is a religious centre of great
> power. Depravity, Sin, Redemption, Heaven, Hell, and Damnation are preached with
> much fervor, and revivals take place every year after the crops are laid by; and few
> indeed of the community have the hardihood to withstand conversion. Back of this
> more formal religion, the Church often stands as a real conserver of morals, a strength-
> ener of family life, and the final authority on what is Good and Right. (*Souls* 144)

Du Bois-the-agnostic confronted the vibrant reality of black spiritual and social life,
and could not stand apart from it. As a Pan-Africanist and as a sociologist, he came
to political terms with the black church in these words: "the Negro church of to-day
is the social centre of Negro life in the United States, and the most characteristic
expression of African character" (*Souls* 144). The uneven and contradictory synthesis
of his religious doubts and faith was expressed, at last, in his famous theory of
"double consciousness." If the Negro was at once "an American, a Negro; two souls,
two thoughts, two unreconciled strivings; two warring ideals in one dark body"
(Meier 190), then his soul for the white world would be expressed in agnosticism, or
at best, only in the most critical and formal guise. The soul of Du Bois confronting
the black world had no choice except to embrace black Christianity.

As a mature scholar and leader of the NAACP, Du Bois maintained his contradictory
position on religion. Before the white world, he made few concessions. Reverting to
the denomination of his paternal grandfather, he was nominally an Episcopalian for

a time (*Correspondence* 13:1). But inside the color line, he gave poetic expression to his love of God in his "Credo," first printed in October 1904:

> I believe in God, who made of one blood all nations that on earth do dwell. I believe that all men, black and brown and white, are brothers. . . . knowing that men may be brothers in Christ, even though they be not brothers-in-law . . . I believe in the Devil and his angels, who wantonly work to narrow the opportunity of struggling human beings especially if they be black; who spit in the faces of the fallen, strike them that cannot strike again, believe the worst and work to prove it, hating the image which their Maker stamped on a brother's soul. I believe in the Prince of Peace. I believe that War is Murder: . . . Finally, I believe in Patience—patience with the weakness of the Weak and the strength of the Strong, the prejudice of the Ignorant and the ignorance of the Blind; patience with the tardy triumph of Joy and the mad chastening of Sorrow; —patience with God!

The black American church was the organizational and spiritual center of black life and as such touched every minute aspect of the segregated community's endeavors. It was a race-conscious organization—it could hardly have been otherwise during the Jim Crow era—yet its strength served to preserve and to defend the basic humanity of American people, and its true vision of itself was one without color or class barriers. Even as a senior at Fisk University, Du Bois recognized that being a Christian meant that "we should not forget the practical side" of Christianity; that is, good works which uplifted the most oppressed groups of society (*Fisk Herald*). A decade later, speaking before a Fisk University graduate audience, he merged the ideals of black faith with the political struggle to transform the material conditions of African Americans. "The German works for Germany, the Englishman serves England, and it is the duty of the Negro to serve his blood and lineage, and so working, each for each, and all for each, we realize the goal of each for all." As the collective expression of all blacks, the church and its clergy were crucial in this process of self-achievement. African American ministers must and "will transform the mysticism of Negro religion into the righteousness of Christianity." Only by "cherish[ing] unwavering faith in the blood of your fathers," could this spiritually moved mass of black humanity achieve political freedom ("Careers").

In late 1900, Du Bois contributed a brief essay on "The Religion of the Negro" to the Boston publication *New World*, which expanded upon these themes. "The Negro church antedates the Negro home," he noted, an historical fact which created "the expression of the inner ethical life of a people in a sense seldom true elsewhere." The church is a haven in a heartless world, as blacks search for meaning in a segregated and politically oppressive society. "Conscious of his impotence, and pessimistic," the Negro "often becomes bitter and vindictive; and his religion, instead of a worship, is a complaint and a curse, a wail rather than a hope, a sneer rather than a faith." And at these moments, "one type of Negro stands almost ready to curse God and die . . ." Yet he finds salvation within the Veil, and a spiritual deliverance from earthly suffering. Silently as ever broods "the deep religious feeling of the real Negro heart, the stirring, unguided might of powerful human souls who have lost the guiding star of the past and seek in the great night a new religious ideal. Some day the Awakening will come," Du Bois predicted, "when the pent-up vigor of ten million souls shall sweep irresistibly toward the Goal, out of the Valley of the Shadow of Death . . . [toward] Liberty, Justice, and Right . . ." (614–25).

NOTES

1. Despite the title of the book which includes his essay (*We Believe in Immortality*), Du Bois observed. "My thought on personal immortality is easily explained, I do not know."

2. Articles under the headings "Great Barrington News" and "From the Berkshire Hills" in the New York *Globe*, 29 Sept. 1883, 29 Dec. 1883 and 22 Nov. 1884.

3. Writing at the age of ninety, Du Bois added: "I never did, and indeed, so strong was the expression of her wishes that never in my life since have I felt at ease drinking at a bar. . . . When the Murphy crusade for total abstinence swept the valley, I as a boy was one of the first to don the blue ribbon. I kept the pledge until I went as a student to Germany" (*Autobiography* 81–82).

4. For a time, Du Bois and his mother lived "next to the horsesheds of the Congregational church." Du Bois's family was Episcopalian, but he and his mother joined the church, becoming its only "colored communicants."

5. "My journey was done, and behind me lay hill and dale and Life and Death. How shall man measure Progress there where the dark-faced Josie lies? How many heartfuls of sorrow shall balance a bushel of wheat? . . . And all this life and love and strife and failure,—is it the twilight of nightfall or the flush of some faint-dawning day?" (*Souls* 64).

WORKS CITED

Broderick, Francis L. W. E. B. Du Bois: *Negro Leader in a Time of Crisis.* Stanford: Stanford University Press, 1959. 18–19, 23.

Du Bois, W. E. B. "As the Crow Flies." *Amsterdam News.* October 24, 1941.

———. *The Autobiography of W. E. B. Du Bois: A Soliloquy on Viewing My Life from the Last Decade of Its First Century.* New York, International, 1969.

———. "Careers Open to College-Bred Negroes." *Two Addresses Delivered by Alumni of Fisk University, in Connection with the Anniversary Exercises of Their Alma Mater.* Pamphlet. June, 1898. Nashville: Fisk U, 1898. 1–14.

———. *The Correspondence of W. E. B. Du Bois: Volume 1, Selections, 1877–1934* Ed. Herbert Aptheker, Amherst: University of Massachusetts Press 1973.

———. "Credo." *Independence 57* (Oct. 6, 1904): 787 Reprinted in *Darkwater* 3–4.

———. *Darkwater: Voices from Within the Veil.* 1920 New York: AMS, 1969, 123–33.

———. *Dusk of Dawn: An Essay Toward An Autobiography of a Race Concept.* New York: Schocken, 1968.

———. "Editorial." *Fisk Herald 5* (Jan. 1888): 8.

———. "Immortality." *We Believe in Immortality.* Ed. Sydney Strong. New York: Coward-McCann, 1929. 18.

———. "The Religion of the Negro." *New World 9* (Dec. 1900): 614–25. Reprinted as "Of the Faith of the Fathers" in *The Souls of Black Folk*, 140–51.

———. ed. *Some Efforts of American Negroes For Their Own Social Betterment: Report of an Investigation under the direction of Atlanta University: together with the Proceedings of the*

Third Conference for the Study of the Negro Proglems, held at Atlanta University, May 25–26, 1898. Atlanta: Atlanta University Press 1898.

————. *The Souls of Black Folk: Essays and Sketches*. 1903. Greenwich: Fawcett, 1961.

Meier, August. *Negro Thought in America, 1880–1915: Racial Ideologies in the Age of Booker T. Washington*. Ann Arbor: University of Michigan Press, 1963. 180, 218–21.

Walters, Alexander. *My Life and Work*. New York: Fleming H. Revell, 1917, 126.

Church Buildings also provided meeting places for schools, fraternal organizations, and other groups. Courtesy of the Library of Congress.

Replica of Sunday School literature used by the AME Church in the 1890s.

Chapter Fourteen

"All Things to All People"
The Functions of the Black Church in the Last Quarter of the Nineteenth Century

Larry G. Murphy

Many commentators on the black church have asserted that the church has been at the center of black community life. To be sure, there is ample historical basis for this ascription of prominence. The work that follows details the way in which the black church in the post–Civil War period served to address the multiple unmet needs and opportunities of a people still very much in a liminal status in American society.

•

Reconfiguring Life in the Post-War Period

The period following the close of hostilities in the Civil War was a time of great ferment for African Americans. Although the uncertainties about new directions were real and formidable, the exciting, energizing fact for black people was that new directions were now actually possible. In a radical departure from the past, their futures now rested largely in their own hands and on their own initiative (or so it seemed). The legal and military arrangements known as Reconstruction laid open the way for emancipated blacks to participate in the institutions and structures of society, as well as to create others of their own choosing. Two observations on this point are in order.

First, the black people who stood at freedom's doorstep had a lot of "catch up" to do, in terms of functioning within American society as it existed. For the most part, they had only observed its political, economic, and social workings from "within the veil," as it were. There was much that hands-on experience had yet to teach. (The same was also true to some extent for large numbers of poor, agrarian whites.)

Second, though, blacks proved to be quick learners. They handled themselves very well in their new role of citizen. As legislators, they helped to write southern State constitutions and laws that are still in effect today. They were prime movers in the erection of the public educational system of the South, and they served with distinction in a variety of local, state, and federal offices.

The Ministries of the Church

During the centuries of chattel slavery, the lives of enslaved blacks had been regimented around the needs of the slavery system. That system provided a common pool of experiences and common points of reference. Though it was a negative context of socialization, it was, nonetheless, the only one available for the vast majority of blacks. It is true that the enslaved developed valuable psychological and spiritual survival mechanisms by which they could resist the degradation and personal disintegration which were so easily slavery's result. Blacks in slavery even managed to fashion a coherent subculture with a full complement of familial, social, and informal religious institutions. Yet, the insidious nature of the slave system was such that it still left a legacy of behaviors, attitudes, and knowledge deficiencies that needed to be addressed and reshaped if blacks were to be equal to the duties and promises of free citizenship. It was the black church that accepted the challenge thus posed. It sought to give caring oversight to each component of the lives of black people. Its primary arenas of ministry may be grouped under four headings: social, political, educational, pastoral.

Social

The church in this late nineteenth-century period was the unchallenged center of black community life. Aside from the black Masonic orders, the church was the only social institution to which blacks enjoyed unhampered access and over which they exercised direct, autonomous control. The church was a valuable symbol to blacks that they *as a people* could manage the structures of civil society. At the same time, it served to train blacks *as individuals* in such management. Learning how to carry on a meeting, conduct financial transactions, administer programs, supervise staff, negotiate individual and group dynamics, work cooperatively toward common goals— for all these social skills, and more, the church was a ready laboratory. Booker T. Washington, a first-hand observer of this period, affirmed that "They [blacks] learned through their churches and their secret orders the art of corporate and united action."[1]

As an open, inclusive institution, the church provided its laity a sense of place and belonging, a point of rootage and identity in a potentially overwhelming, frequently antagonistic social context. Similarly, the church was a source of personal recognition and affirmation. Whereas in the outside world one's personhood might be devalued, the church was a place "where everybody is somebody," as some church slogans go. Furthermore, energetic service, demonstration of abilities, and pious living could gain one even more specific recognition as an officer, or program chair, or "mother of the church," or other designation. Even in small congregations, such personal recognition carried great weight and importance.

Black pastors, were focal figures. Typically rising to their role through their personal charisma and leadership gifts, they were highly respected and admired. They were expected to take the vanguard position in interpreting the complexities of black life and navigating a course for black well-being—both temporal and eternal. They served as advocates for blacks to the white structures of power. For instance, black pastors might be the spokespersons in negotiations with whites for underwriting the erection of a school or recreational facility in the black community. They might intercede with employers to hire given individuals or with law enforcement to release an alleged black offender to their supervision. Common to the times, women generally were excluded from the ranks of the clergy. Nonetheless, they exercised religious and moral agency as laity in initiating and supporting the ministries of the church.

The black church served the community as a center for socializing and recreation, in the absence of access or provisions for the same in the public sector. The singing and preaching were entertaining as well as edifying. The Sunday meeting was a time for visiting with friends, a pleasantry for which the schedule of the work week did not always allow. There was a picnic atmosphere to "dinner on the grounds"—common between Sunday morning and afternoon services services or at revivals and special events; church conventions doubled as vacations and were festive reunions.

The church was also the place where the various talents and skills of blacks could find opportunity for public expression as they were featured in worship or in anniversary day programs and religious holiday stage productions. The church also served as an intellectual and cultural center by sponsoring or hosting lectures, debates, dramatic performances, musical recitals, and similar exhibitions. The church building was usually the only "auditorium" accessible for such events, by reason of costs and restrictive racial customs. But because of the black church's multifaceted concern for the totality of black life, it was a natural and willing fit for the purposes.

Political

Although there may have been persons who denounced "politics in the church," the black church had a distinct political dimension. Holders of office, including, in many congregations, the office of pastor, were selected by popular vote. The leadership was responsible for the governance of the body, as well as for coordinating the competing, sometimes conflicting goals and interests of individual members and auxiliaries. In these and other ways, church members acquired practice in the political process. It was, perhaps, all the more meaningful for them because of the limitations on their participation in the regular civil and governmental processes of the larger society.

Beyond this, the church served as the forum for the discussion of social issues and social action strategies. Whether initiated from the pulpit or brought in from the community, the vital issues facing blacks were aired in the churches and strategies of response were assessed. Clergy were prominent among the lead voices in advancing black concerns or in implementing social strategies in the public arena. In those places where blacks had the opportunity to vote, politicians commonly were granted permission to make their case in speeches to congregations during Sunday morning worship (a practice still typical in black churches, especially around election time). Finally, because of the charismatic nature of their leadership and the expectations of their constituents, clergy were well-represented among those blacks who sought and achieved elective office. And so, both internally and externally, the black church had politics in its portfolio.

Educational

African Americans, enslaved and free, had long felt the need for education. For blacks in slavery, the focus was on literacy, so as to enable one to read the Bible for oneself. For free blacks, whose circumstances were, theoretically, less constricted, the focus was on knowledge and mental cultivation to enable a more profound understanding of scriptural faith, as well as to enhance the prospects for social and economic advancement. However, literacy training for the enslaved was forbidden, by law and custom; access to public education for free blacks was impeded by racially discriminatory local practice.

By the mid-nineteenth century, free blacks were mounting initiatives to achieve educational privileges in their communities, setting up schools on their own and agitating for inclusion in the public school system. With the coming of the Civil War and emancipation, the way was opened for the full black population to be part of the effort.

An 1888 letter from a black clergyman of Mississippi to a church news journal provides a window into the situation.

> Our people must learn many lessons of self-denial before they can successfully compete with the "pale brother." Here the law makes no provision for school houses and school furniture. A school is simply granted, and if you want it you must provide a school house; so we country school teachers teach in a shanty or an old church. I am writing these notes in a Baptist church (which, by the way, is the second best church in the county), where I am teaching. This is one of the best schools in the county and I receive $45.00 per month. The house is minus windows, doors, stove and, I might say, roof. It is a crazy old shanty made of cypress boards—cold and comfortless. I have to make my own fire, and, what is more, I have to get my own wood. Attendance is very irregular and nobody seems interested. This is one case, it is true, but it is a fair sample of a majority of our country schools.[2]

As one can see from this post–Reconstruction quote, the black church was involved in addressing the predicament of black education. As in the above case, black preachers often doubled as school teachers and principals; the church building, or its adjacent property, frequently served as the school site, whether the school was established at black initiative or by governmental bodies. (Reminiscences of this practice can still be seen today in the instances across the American South of small, time-worn schoolhouses standing on the grounds of black churches.) In the organized efforts common in this period aimed at securing full educational rights for African Americans, black clergy were a prominent leadership presence. Equally, if not more, active were lay women. For instance, historian Evelyn Brooks Higginbotham has written of the seminal work of Baptist women in fostering and financing educational initiatives through their churches, seeing education as, perhaps, of singular importance in the moral and social advancement of African Americans. Black women came to outnumber men, by far, in the teaching profession. In the church arena, education became a central component of missions strategies. Higginbotham relates that In the late nineteenth century, "All of the [Baptist] women's state conventions promoted school and black-controlled educational work."[3]

Black denominations modeled a concern for education in their programmatic structures. By the end of the century, the African Methodist Episcopal Church had established at least nine high schools and institutes and twelve schools of higher learning, five of which were in foreign countries. The African Methodist Episcopal Zion Church had at least fifteen high schools, institutes, and academies, and four schools of higher learning, while the Christian Methodist Episcopal Church had two colleges, two seminaries, and an institute. Black Baptists supported some eighty schools, while contributing to several other schools supported by white Baptists.[4]

Finally, the black church performed another service that was educational, not strictly in terms of academics but in terms of keeping African Americans informed about current issues particularly relevant to them, as well as matters of general interest and cultural enrichment. The instruments of this service were the many weekly and monthly news journals and magazines published under the auspices of each of the denominations.

Pastoral

The black church offered to the hopeful yet often beleaguered African American population of the late nineteenth century a significant ministry to their personal and spiritual needs. It was, in the words of a Negro Spiritual, "a shelter in the time of storm." It provided a refuge from the frustration, denigration, and barbarity that interposed itself so recurrently into black life. The black church was, to be sure, a ritual space and a setting for worship. But it was also *community*, a mutual, participatory sharing in a common life. As such, it counteracted the personality-destroying forces of white oppression by an affirmation of the value and worth of the black man and woman, boy and girl. A common expression employed to characterize one's treatment in the world was, "I've been called everything but a child of God." But in the church the converse was true: One *was* called a child of God, and therefore one's authentication was grounded in a higher, transcendent reality. The world did not grant it, so the world could not take it away. By this assurance of the integrity and independence of their selfhood, African Americans were freed from existential despair and personal disintegration.

Further, the black church kept alive a spirit of hope by continually calling its constituents' attention to God's active care for the dispossessed; to the liberative acts of God recorded in scripture; and to the faith claim that the ultimate outcome of the drama of history was not in the hands of their oppressors but was reserved to Godself, who, at the opportune time, would act to effect justice and liberation, as demonstrated in the biblical paradigms.

One might see in this pastoral approach an inducement to social quietism, an accommodationist response to negative social circumstances. There is evidence to suggest such an outcome among some black Christians of the time. One might also see it as enabling a people living in seemingly intractable hostile conditions to carve out of the chaos a space of survivability. At the same time, one can discover persons for whom the church's affirmation of the integrity of black identity, in concert with the biblical/theological notion of God's concern for universal human wholeness and freedom, fueled an activist, rather than a quietist response; resistance, rather than accommodation. For some, religious faith provided models and impetus for challenging their oppressive social reality.

Beyond the social intervention implications of the black church's pastoral ministry, one may note its services in personal counseling; encouragement to members in their aspirations and achievements; helping to mark significant life passages, such as birth, marriage, and progression through the life cycle. Not least, the church provided a framework for meaning during life and a context of dignity at death.

The overall evaluation of the black church by its members and by other observers of the period was that it was generally a positive force, attracting youth, aiding the needy, and raising the quality of life of African Americans, in terms of character, morals, family stability, and social advancement.

NOTES

1. See Herbert Aptheker, *A Documentary History of the Negro People in the United States* (New York: The Citadel Press, 1971), Vol. II, p. 871.

2. This letter appeared in the A.M.E. *Christian Recorder*, May 3, 1888. It was reprinted, in excerpted form, in Aptheker, p. 746f.

3. Evelyn Brooks Higginbotham, *Righteous Discontent: The Women's Movement in the Black Baptist Church, 1880–1920.* (Cambridge, Massachusetts: Harvard University Press, 1993), passim. Quoted material from p. 58.

4. See W. E. B. Du Bois, *The Negro Church* (Atlanta: Atlanta University Press, 1903), pp. 117; 130–33.

Edward Wilmont Blyden (1832–1912), the father of Pan-Africanism. From the collections of the Library of Congress.

Chapter Fifteen

The Redemption of Africa and Black Religion

St. Clair Drake

In several songs in their sacred musical literature, African Americans described them-selves as "pilgrims," "wayfaring strangers," and the like, sojourning in a world that was not their home. Whatever the spiritual meanings intended by black singers, such religious imagery fit well with the mundane interests of certain segments of the white populace who raised the prospect of Africans in America being repatriated to their homeland. But blacks, themselves, generally were not as sanguine about that idea. Most did, in fact, affirm the United States as their earthly home, notwithstanding that it was a pervasively inhospitable and abusive one. These latter realities, however, kept alive among some the notion of relocation for the enlargement of black advancement opportunities and com-munal security. Ties of heritage and identity with the homeland and its people kept the African continent as the destination of choice, though not the only one considered. St. Clair Drake looks at the recurrent initiative by whites and blacks for the repatriation of blacks to Africa. He discusses the related concept of Ethiopianism and highlights one of the most celebrated early proponents of that concept, the Reverend Edward Wilmot Blyden.

•

God's Hand in Black History

The ten years between the Denmark Vesey Conspiracy and the Nat Turner Revolt were among the most important in the history of the Negro in the United States. A well-financed "colonization movement" emerged, designed to encourage free Ne-groes to leave the United States. It was one aspect of the manumission movement for which Thomas Jefferson was the most persuasive spokesman. He took the posi-tion that slaves had every right to use insurrectionary violence to free themselves and that the various plots and insurrections indicated that black men in America would increasingly resort to such means. Prudent men would not wait to have their throats cut; they would free their slaves voluntarily. He believed, however, that black men and white men could never exist in peace or as equals in the same society, and was therefore in favor of providing training for them and assisting them to emigrate outside of the boundaries of the United States, either to the Far West, or to the

Caribbean, or to Africa. Many southern slaveholders who were not manumissionists were disturbed over the presence of the freedmen who were already concentrated in southern cities, and wanted to see them "deported"; others were embarrassed by the presence of the evidence of their miscegenation always around them.

Colonization societies had come into being in Virginia and Maryland by 1800 and were in contact with the British humanitarians who had sponsored a settlement at Freetown in Sierra Leone. They found allies among a group of Quakers and other antislavery leaders in the North whose motivations were quite different, who wanted to see American Negroes going to Africa as teachers and missionaries, and who elaborated the doctrine of "Providential Design" to give sanction to their plans— *"God, in his inscrutable way, had allowed Africans to be carried off into slavery so that they could be Christianized and civilized and return to uplift their kinsmen in Africa."* As one Catholic father eloquently phrased it:

> The branch torn away from the parent stem in Africa, by our ancestors, was brought to America—brought away by Divine permission, in order that it might be engrafted upon the tree of the Cross. It will return in part to its own soil, not by violence or deportation, but willingly, and borne on the wings of faith and charity.

The American Colonization Society was founded in 1817 and the first load of immigrants left on an American naval vessel in 1820. The president of the society was George Washington's brother, General Bushrod Washington. The settlement was eventually called Monrovia in honor of Virginia's former governor, President Monroe.

The colonization movement split the African American leadership group. Some were in favor of cooperation with the white colonizationists in order to achieve "Black Power" goals. As early as 1808, a prosperous Negro shipowner in Boston, bearing a West African name, Paul Cuffee (i.e., Kofi), had begun to study the reports of the settlement of black people at Freetown, Sierra Leone, where some of the slaves who had deserted to the British during the Revolutionary War were taken. He became convinced that a program of selective immigration of American Negro freedmen should be instituted to supply leadership to the 2,000 black people already settled in Africa and the thousands that would be landed by British naval vessels as they captured slave ships on the high seas in the attempt to stop the trans-Atlantic slave trade. He visualized an intensive program of education that would lead eventually to the rise of new sovereign states in West Africa, and foresaw ". . . a vast trade between Negro America and West Africa designed to enhance the wealth and prestige of the race." He made a trip to Sierra Leone in his own boat in 1811, and four years later he carried over thirty eight settlers at his own expense. For a while he was in favor of cooperating with white colonizationists, but then later he refused to do so.

Paul Cuffee reinforced "emigrationist" tendencies among Negroes that never died out, but fluctuated in strength with the rise and fall of economic and social conditions. These were the voluntary, self-financed efforts of Negroes to settle in Africa. Some emigrationists had no uplift ideology but were simply trying to escape from what they felt were intolerable conditions in the United States. The first Negro college graduate in the United States, the editor of the first Negro newspaper, John Russworm, abandoned his *Freedom's Journal* in 1829, two years after he founded it and left for Liberia. Most of the Negro leaders, however, took the position that black men should stay in the United States and fight for their rights, and repudiating the name "African" for their organizations, began to organize *Colored Men's* Conventions. This was not abandonment of interest in Africa, but they felt that to continue to call themselves "African," now, was an invitation to deportation.

In 1829, the year that the editor of *Freedom's Journal* emigrated to Africa, a publication appeared that created consternation in the South. A free Negro, born in North Carolina but living in Boston, published what he called *David Walker's Appeal to the Coloured Citizens of the World, but in the Particular and Very Expressly, to Those of the United States of America.* It was rumored that white citizens in the South immediately placed a price of $3,000 on his head, and a year after Walker published the *Appeal* he was found mysteriously dead in the streets of Boston. Walker had been an agent for *Freedom's Journal* and was disturbed at the "defection" of its editor to Liberia. One of the four chapters in his booklet was on "Our Wretchedness in Consequence of the Colonizing Scheme." Denouncing it as a trick and a plot, he quoted with approval from an article written by Richard Allen, who had said, "Why should they send us into a far country to die? See the thousands of foreigners emigrating to America every year: and if there be ground sufficient for them to cultivate and bread for them to eat, why would they wish to send the first tillers of the land away? Africans have made fortunes for thousands, who are yet unwilling to part with their services; but the free must be sent away and those who remain, must be slaves. I have no doubt that there are many good men who do not see as I do, and who are for sending us to Liberia; but they have not duly considered the subject—they are not men of colour. This land which we have watered with our tears and our blood, is now our mother country, and we are well satisfied to stay where wisdom abounds and the gospel is free."

Although David Walker lauded Richard Allen in the article, its general tone was very different from Allen's. He hinted at a coming insurrection, ". . . I am one of the oppressed, degraded and wretched sons of Africa, rendered so by the avaricious and unmerciful among the whites . . . know ye that I am in the hand of God, and at your disposal. . . . But remember Americans, that, as miserable, wretched, degraded and abject as you have made us . . . some of you (whites) on the continent of America will yet curse the day that you were ever born. . . . My colour will yet root some of you out of the very face of the earth!!!! O! save us, we pray thee, thou God of Heaven and of earth, from the devouring hand of the white Christians!!!!"

David Walker, speaking to "My dearly beloved Brethren and Fellow Citizens," was summoning them to stick together so that they could act effectively to "root out" the oppressors. He assailed ". . . some of my brethren in league with the tyrants, selling their own brethren into hell on earth" by acting as spies and informers and counseling acquiescence in slavery. He spoke glowingly of the revolt in Haiti and commented that "The whites have had us under them for more than three centuries, murdering and treating us like brutes . . . they do not know indeed that there is an uncontrollable disposition in the breasts of the blacks, which, when it is fully awakened and put in motion, will be subdued only with the destruction of the animal existence. Get the blacks started, and if you do not have a gang of tigers and lions to deal with them, I am a deceiver of the blacks and of the whites." Although counseling education, piety, and faith, what he called for most vigorously was racial solidarity: "O! that the coloured people were long since of Moses' excellent disposition, instead of courting favour with, and telling news and lies to our *natural enemies*, against each other—aiding them to keep their hellish chains of slavery upon us. Would we not long before this time have been respectable men, instead of such wretched victims of oppression as we are? . . . The question, my brethren, I leave for you to digest; and may God almighty force it home to your hearts. Remember that unless you are united, keeping your tongues within your teeth, you will be afraid to trust your secrets to each other and thus perpetuate our miseries under the Christians!!!! . . . Never make an attempt to gain our freedom or *natural right* from under our cruel oppressors and murderers, until you see your way clear—when that hour arrives and you move, be not afraid or dismayed; for be you assured that Jesus Christ the king of heaven and of earth and who is the God of Justice and of armies will go before you . . ."

Walker had faith in the power of the written word to stir his people, writing in the preface to his last edition:

> It is expected that all coloured men, women and children, of every nation, language and tongue under heaven, will try to procure a copy of this *Appeal* and read it, or get some one to read it to them. . . . Let them remember that though our cruel oppressors and murderers, may (if possible) treat us more cruel, as Pharaoh did the children of Israel, *yet the God of the Ethiopians, has been pleased to hear our moans in consequence of oppression and the day our redemption from object wretchedness draweth near, when we shall be enabled in the most extended sense of the word, to stretch our hands to the Lord our God.*

To Walker, the God he served was "the God of the Ethiopians."

When Nat Turner brought down a Day of Wrath upon Southampton County, there was a widespread tendency to blame Walker's agitation for his act, as well as for other disturbances throughout the South. The *Appeal*, and what was interpreted as Walker's martyrdom, probably had its greatest influence, however, among educated freedmen in the North, moving a larger number of them in the direction of sanctioning violence.

In 1833, slavery was abolished in the British Empire. Hope for abolition in America burgeoned, and that same year the American Anti-Slavery Society was founded, supporting a two-pronged program: an Underground Railroad for helping as many slaves as possible to steal away to the North, and the mobilizing of support for a political solution by electing candidates of a national party committed to the abolition of slavery. During the next thirty years the national crisis deepened, building up toward what has been called "The Irrepressible Conflict."

Some Northern Negroes felt that the Underground Railroad helped individuals but could not operate on such a massive scale as to destroy the slave system. They believed that the slaves must revolt. Three years after Nat Turner's death, a highly educated Northern free Negro Presbyterian preacher, Henry Highland Garnet, speaking before a national convention of coloured leaders in 1843, sounded a call for revolt:

> Brethren, arise, arise! Strike for your lives and liberties. Now is the day and the hour. Let every slave throughout the land do this, and the days of slavery are numbered. You cannot be more oppressed than you have been—you cannot suffer greater cruelties than you have already. *Rather* die freemen than live to be slaves. Remember that you are FOUR MILLIONS! . . . In the name of God, we ask, are you men? Where is the blood of your fathers? Has it all run out of your veins? Awake, awake. . . . Let your motto be resistance! resistance! RESISTANCE!

A resolution of support for this policy lost by only one vote, but those who would have to pay the price did not respond. In fact insurrectionary plotting diminished as the Underground Railroad became more efficient. The most militant slaves went North, and spirituals such as "Steal Away" became signals for action instead of mere escapist songs used in worship services.

When aggressive attempts were made to enforce the Fugitive Slave Act of 1850, disillusionment and despair increased the ranks of those free Negroes who wanted to go to either the Caribbean or Africa. The Dred Scott decision of 1857 also generated widespread feelings of disgust with the United States that caused many Negroes to decide it would be better to leave, though only a few did. One eminent Negro physician, Dr. Martin R. Delany, actually traveled to Nigeria to negotiate with a group of Yoruba chiefs for land and made arrangements for establishing a cotton growing scheme. He hoped to dump cotton on the world market at a low price and break the plantocracy.

While the black leadership was becoming polarized into those who counseled emigration and those who said, "Stay here," the white antislavery forces suffered a similar sharp rift in the North. Both the Negro and white anticolonizationists were further polarized between those who were in favor of escalation of slave revolts and those who would only sanction nonviolent means. The latter group, led predominantly by Quakers and including Unitarians, Methodists, and Baptists, was shocked by one of the Southern responses to insurrections and antislavery propaganda. This was the activity of their fellow white Christians in the South who attempted to strengthen their control over the minds of the slaves by tightening up the supervision of their religious training, including attempts to prevent slaves from holding worship unless white people were present. Some southern theologians were also circulating manuals with material for masters and mistresses to read to their slaves containing admonitions such as:

> Almighty God hath been pleased to make you slaves here, and to give you nothing but labour and poverty in this world, which you are obliged to submit to, as it is his will that it should be so. Your bodies, you know, are not your own; they are at the disposal of those you belong to . . .

> When correction is given you, you either deserve it or you do not deserve it. But whether you deserve it or not, it is your duty, and almighty God requires, that you bear it patiently.

A "Catechism to be Taught Orally to Those Who Cannot Read" informed slaves that "to disobey your master is to yield to the temptation of the devil." All of this gave Christianity a bad name, and Walker rubbed the salt in the wounds, referring sarcastically to "*Christian* America" and to "the perverters" of the teachings of Christianity.

As Cotton gradually became King in the South after 1793, the humanitarians and religious sectarians had been thrown on the defensive by southern "scholars" who were arguing that black skin was "the sign of the curse placed on Cain and his descendants" because he killed his brother Abel. The myth was already embedded in the mass culture of the nation as early as the time when Phyllis Wheatley who lived in Massachusetts pleaded with her fellow Christians:

> Remember Christians, Negroes black as Cain
> May be refined, and join the angelic train.

The keystone of the theological argument, however, rested upon the curse that Noah was said to have placed upon the sons of Ham, dooming them to be hewers of wood and drawers of water to the sons of Shem and Japheth. Illiterate Negro preachers tried to counterattack by insisting that Noah was drunk when he pronounced the curse and therefore it was invalid. The white antislavery ministers either took the position that the coming of Christ wiped out the curse or just stubbornly reiterated the argument that God is father and all men are brothers.

The Negro preachers, whether literate or illiterate, whether they believed in insurrections or did not, whether they approved of emigration or disapproved, felt impelled to counterattack on a more basic front. They were not only convinced that God would eventually destroy the slave system in one way or another, but also that the Bible did not support the position that black men were cursed or inferior. Out of their offensive efforts a retrospective myth of a glorious past and a prospective myth of eventual divine deliverance took form, backed up by Biblical "proof-texts." As soon as a semi-literate group emerged among the slaves, interpreting the "open Bible" in the Protestant tradition, the possibilities were present for developing a mythology to counter that used by white Christians to degrade them.

Negro folk theologians were able to find the texts to counter the derogatory scriptural interpretations. Black preachers may have been advising the slaves to obey their masters and wait for the Lord to show his hand, but they were also building group pride and self-respect by naming their churches "African" and painting a verbal picture of a glorious past. As soon as they became aware that Egypt and Ethiopia were in Africa, they were able to preach and teach along these lines: God's own chosen people had to go into Africa once, long ago, when the famine came, and Joseph became a great man in a black folks' kingdom. And then, when a Pharaoh arose "who knew not Joseph" it was black men, wicked ones but powerful ones, who put the Jews in slavery, forcing them to make bricks without straw. Finally, when God raised up a deliverer among the Hebrew children he was educated by a kind black princess, Pharaoh's daughter, and he married an Ethiopian woman. When his own brother and sister "murmured against him" because of the marriage, God struck them down with leprosy until they apologized. And how did they *know* these ancient people were not *white* men? All of them were made out of the dust of the earth and that's brown not white. And as for the Ethiopians, they were the darkest of all, for did not the prophet Jeremiah ask, "Can the Ethiopian change his skin? Can the leopard change his spots?"

The preachers talked about how the light browns sometimes looked down on the darker ones even in those biblical days, for the great King Solomon's black woman who loved him—and who got him—had to sing at those jealous women, "I am black but[1] comely, oh ye daughters of Jerusalem." And black women sometimes got "the dirty end of the stick" just like it happened on the plantation. When Father Abraham had a baby, Ishmael, by the bondservant, his wife, Sarah, made him put both the mother and the child out. That's why we call ourselves "Aunt Hagar's children."

But nothing could keep the black man down. Ethiopia was right there in the Bible alongside Egypt and Babylon and Assyria with her chariots and her mighty men of war. And when the wicked men threw the prophet of God, Jeremiah, into a dungeon, it was one of the "highups" at King Zedekiah's court, Ebed-Melech, the Ethiopian eunuch, who took him out and hid him.

There were New Testament passages too, to provide them with texts and stories for their sermons. Did not Joseph take Mary and the infant Jesus into Africa so the prophecy could be fulfilled, "Out of Egypt have I called my son?" And was it not an African, Simon of Cyrene, who picked up the cross and carried it when Jesus stumbled? Ethiopia was still a great kingdom in those latter days, because the Apostle Philip met the treasurer of Queen Candace riding home from Jerusalem in a chariot, converted him, and baptized him. We were not always white men's slaves and *our* time will come again, for the Bible says, "Princes shall come out of Egypt and Ethiopia shall soon stretch forth her hand unto God." Walker cited the prophecy in his *Appeal.*

This myth was a comforting morale builder and steeled those black people who believed it against those who tried to "rob them of their past." But it left unanswered a question, "Why was this ancient glory lost?" Insofar as they were believers in the Judaeo-Christian religion, they saw the same answer for themselves as for the Jews: "When a people forgets God and sins He'll bring them down! When they turn back to God again they'll be redeemed."

One educated minister preaching in the early 1800s sounded the call to repentance, "Oh ye sons of Ethiopia, awake unto righteousness, for Jesus saith, 'Come unto me.' ... Upon the wicked he shall rain fire and brimstone."

This Biblical myth is the core of a thought-style that might be called "Ethiopianism," and which became more complex and secularized as it developed during the nineteenth and twentieth centuries. It emerged as a counter-myth to that of southern white Christians (and many northern ones). It functioned on a fantasy level, giving feelings of worth and self-esteem to the individual, but also as a sanction for varied types of group action. It generated concern for the "redemption" of black men in the Motherland as well as the Diaspora so that the ancient state of power and prestige could be restored. It was the duty of black men who were "saved" to try to "convert" and "save" others—to preach the Gospel to their brothers wherever they might be, to enlighten them, to "civilize" them, to lift them from "their fallen state," to "redeem" them. Black Christians began at home working on the "sinners" in their midst. When their masters took them to the Caribbean, they extended their evangelizing activity there. White Baptists had initiated some activity among the slaves in Jamaica by the middle of the eighteenth century, but the work did not begin to grow until a slave from America was brought there by his master after the Revolutionary War and so aroused his fellows that a distinctive Jamaican variety of the Baptist faith took root. As early as 1787, the first black American left for Africa to preach to his kinsmen there. Eventually, a Negro missionary movement gathered strength.

It was also not difficult for some black Christians to give an Ethiopianist twist to the white men's doctrine of Providential Design and to thus find a *modus vivendi* for cooperating with the colonization societies. One of the first Negro missionaries to Liberia, Daniel Coker, son of a Negro man and an English mother, taught to read and write by the son of his master, and who ran away to New York where he earned enough money to purchase his freedom, later opened an "African School" in Baltimore. Upon becoming a preacher he helped Richard Allen to organize the African Methodist Episcopal Church in 1816 and was elected its first bishop. Historian Hollis Lynch states that " . . . he declined the honor in order to go to Africa to help in laying of the foundation for a strong Negro nation." After a harrowing sea voyage to Africa under the auspices of the American Colonization Society he wrote in his journal, "O God! Why were we spared? Surely because this expedition is in the care of God—My soul travails that we may be faithful. And should God spare us to arrive in Africa that we may be useful." Lott Cary, a well-to-do Baptist minister in Richmond, Virginia, left for Liberia in 1815, with his family, declaring that "I am an African and in this country, however meritorious my conduct and respectable my character, I cannot receive the credit due either. I wish to go to a country where I shall be estimated by my merits not by my complexion." Although he went to Liberia under the colonization society, the American black Baptists eventually founded a missionary convention that bears his name. Another American Negro, Alexander Crummell, took a degree at Cambridge in England in 1853, and emigrated to Liberia. In a sermon delivered in Monrovia 40 years after the establishment of the republic, he gave eloquent expression to the Doctrine of Providential Design, referring to:

> the forced and cruel migration of our race from this continent, and the wondrous providence of God, by which the sons of Africa by hundreds and by thousands, trained, civilized, and enlightened, are coming hither again, bringing large gifts, for Christ and his Church, and their heathen kin.

He envisioned black history rising to a climax: "The day of preparation for our race is well nigh ended; the day of duty and responsibility on our part, to suffering, benighted, Africa, is at hand. In much sorrow, pain, and deepest anguish, God has been preparing the race, in foreign lands, for a great work of grace on this continent. The hand of God is on the black man in all the lands of his sojourn for the good of Africa." Crummell was not the only American Negro preacher who felt this way during the post– Civil War period. Bishop B. W. Arnett of the church founded by anticolonizationist, Richard Allen, organized a company for trading with Africa in 1876, and favored the selective emigration of Negroes with some capital in order to help "... build up a New Christian Nationality in the Fatherland ... that would cause Negroes everywhere to be respected."

By 1880, Alexander Crummell, disillusioned with the way in which the emigrants from America were conducting the affairs of Liberia, had returned home. Although Crummell returned to the United States, there were other black ministers who remained ardent emigrationists. In fact, increasing discrimination against the Negro during the 1890s gave new impetus to Back-to-Africa movements and in 1901, Bishop Henry M. Turner of the A.M.E. Church wrote, in *Voice of the People:*

> The Negro Race has as much chance in the United States ... of being a man ... as a frog has in a snake den ... Emigrate and gradually return to the land of our ancestors. ... The Negro was brought here in the providence of God to learn obedience, to work, to sing, to pray, to preach, acquire education, deal with mathematical abstractions and imbibe the principles of civilization as a whole, and then to return to Africa, the land of his fathers, and bring her his millions.

To give effect to these ideas, he organized the Colored Emigration and Commercial Association, which had a large following in some areas of the rural South, but sent no exiles home. The historian August Meier reminds us that "The persistence of emigrationist sentiment and the later mass appeal of the Garvey Movement suggests that perhaps the desire for colonization was more widespread among the masses than is generally believed ..."

The mainstream of sentiment within the Negro church, however, was not emigrationist, but it was always concerned with Africa. The concern found institutional expression through the mission boards of the Negro denominations which, in addition to their programs of evangelization, attempted to implement Bishop Arnett's dream of fostering trade with Africans, brought Africans to the United States for an education, and injected strong Ethiopianist elements into the doctrine of Providential Design. Negro missionaries, like their white counterparts, believed that Africa must be regenerated through the Gospel. The report of the Ecumenical Missionary Conference meeting in New York in 1900 contained a section on "A Work for American Negroes" with both white and Negro delegates stating that they thought black Americans had a special role. One Negro Baptist preacher castigated white missionaries for hampering the spread of the Gospel by importing race prejudice into Africa, citing this as one of the reasons why more Negro missionaries were desirable, but revealed his own *cultural* prejudices by his remarks about the "backwardness" of the Zulu people. He was expressing the general view of educated American Negroes, as revealed in the Indianapolis *Freeman*, a Negro newspaper, that had called for American intervention in the Congo in 1885, with the use of Negro settlers, for since "Africa is our Fatherland ... we must prepare to enter upon the elevation of Africa with other races ... civilizing our brethren ... as well as Christianizing it."

The belief that Africa had a glorious past and that the people of the Diaspora were destined to help "redeem" it and "regenerate it" lent powerful impetus to the missionary movement of the Negro Methodist and Baptist churches and to Back-to-Africa movements that arose from time to time. The people involved believed that they were helping to speed the day when "Princes shall come out of Egypt and Ethiopia shall soon stretch forth her hand unto God." But this combination of Ethiopianism with the doctrine of Providential Design also stereotyped Africa as "heathen," "dark," and "benighted." Although there was a tendency for black missionaries to differ from whites by trying to use the mission movement to stimulate commercial relations between Africans and American Negroes, and, occasionally, a black missionary put up a defense for some aspects of African culture, in general Negro missionaries were as censorious of African customs as white missionaries were. This troubled some of the more sensitive black secular intellectuals, but among preacher-scholars there was little sensitivity of this sort.

But of the theologically trained emigrants to Africa, one was very different from his fellows. Edward Wilmot Blyden did not return to the land of the Diaspora, but, "playing for keeps," he not only achieved the international renown that Crummell never attained, but also transformed the doctrine of Providential Design and the myth of Ethiopianism into something of greater significance for the black world.

Ethiopianism and Religious-Political Movements

Edward Wilmot Blyden's Ethiopianism was utilized only incidentally as a sanction for the Christian missionary movement. He utilized it primarily as a sanction for New World emigration to Africa. Near the end of his life, Blyden abandoned his interest both in emigration from the New World and in the missionary movement. The logical end of Ethiopianist thinking is the position that Africans, themselves, are thoroughly competent to chart their own course of development and to manage their own affairs. When shorn of Christian beliefs about "degeneration" and "redemption" through conversion to Christ, Ethiopianist thinking leads to a belief that the forces are latent within Africa itself to "redeem" it. Blyden came to believe that the most potent forces lay in the African variety of Islam, but that Africans could adapt Christianity to their needs just as they had with Islam. This would mean, however, the replacement of the missionary movement—especially where controlled by whites—with an autonomous African church. The history of Christianity in ancient North Africa and Ethiopia—and especially in Ethiopia—was cited as proof of African religious genius. In 1890, he formed a close and enduring friendship with a Nigerian, Majola Agbebi, who was one of the main architects of the Independent Baptist Native Church, the forerunner of what eventually came to be called "separatist" and "independent" churches in Africa.

Hollis Lynch describes the Nigerian movement briefly: "Agbebi had continued to strive for an African Church free of foreign trappings; thus in 1898 he excluded the use of wine as a sacrament in the services of the Native Baptist Church, partly as a protest against the trade in liquor in West Africa. . . . In 1895, he persuaded a West Indian couple, the Rev. J. E. Ricketts and his wife, to join his church as 'Industrial Missionaries.' . . . In his missionary and educational work Agbebi refused to recognize the territorial boundaries drawn by the European imperialist powers. . . . He pointed out to prospective converts that conversion to Christianity would not entail the disruption of the social fabric by giving up such wholesome customs as polygamy . . . several chiefs became Christian converts and placed their sons and nominees under his instruction. Agbebi's drive and organizing ability can be estimated by the fact that by 1903 he had organized and become President of the Native Baptist Union of West Africa which included churches in Sierra Leone, Ghana (Gold Coast), Nigeria, and the Cameroons." Blyden encouraged him in his ambition to merge the Native Baptist Church with another group, the United Native African Church, to form the African Church of Lagos, and to eventually organize "a united West African Church." In commenting on a sermon by Agbebi he wrote to him: "No one can write on the religion of the African as an African can . . . and you have written thoughtfully and with dignity and impressiveness . . . 'Africa is struggling for a separate personality' and your discourse is one of the most striking evidences of this. The African has something—a great deal to say to the world . . . which it ought to hear." One of Blyden's favorite expressions, probably coined by him, was "The African Personality." Kwame Nkrumah revived it in the twentieth century.

The West African separatist and independent church movement was "Ethiopianist" in spirit although it did not use the word. During the same period, however, a similar movement in South Africa explicitly designated itself as such. Here, a group of preachers, some of whom had studied at Negro schools in the United States, expressed their dissatisfaction with white missionary controls by setting up their own congregations, some of which sought affiliation with the African Methodist Episcopal Church of the Negroes in America. The story has been told by Bengt Sundkler in *Bantu Prophets* and he divides the churches into two groups: the other-worldly nonpolitical "zionist" sects that became affiliated with a white denomination in the United States, and the "Ethiopianists," who took as their slogan, "Princes shall come out of Egypt and Ethiopia shall soon stretch forth her hand unto God." The government viewed the Ethiopian churches as subversive; the missions defined them as semi-pagan and blasphemous, except for the Church of England which tried to contain and channel the protest by wooing congregations back into its orbit as affiliates of "The Order of Ethiopia" sanctioned by the Anglican Church. The term "Ethiopianism" became embedded in the literature of journalists and scholars to apply to this particular movement, and it has been generalized and extended as a concept referring to a thought-style in this work.

The popularity of the term in the 1890s was enhanced by events actually occurring in Ethiopia. Black nationalists had clung to Liberia and Haiti as symbols of black sovereignty even when they disapproved of the internal politics in those countries or were embarrassed by their "lack of progress." Now, in the 1890s, a new symbol of black nationalism pushed Liberia and Haiti into the background. While Blyden was using his quite considerable scholarship to prove that *all* black Africans were Ethiopians and therefore that any Biblical prophecies that referred to Ethiopia referred to black Africa as a whole and that her "redemption" was certain, the one spot left that bore the name, the inheritor of the ancient glory, stirred the whole black world. Most of the continent had been partitioned between 1884 and 1890 by England, France,

Germany, Portugal, and Belgium. Italy had secured a foothold on the Red Sea in what is now Eritrea and Somalia. In 1889, she had aided Menelik in establishing himself on the imperial throne of Ethiopia and the two countries signed a treaty of friendship. In 1891, Britain signed a treaty with Italy recognizing Ethiopia as being in that European country's "sphere of influence." With some encouragement from France, Menelik denounced the treaty as a trap. England then encouraged Italy to assert its authority and to declare a protectorate over Ethiopia. In 1895, Italy crossed the border and started advancing into the Ethiopian highlands. On March 1, 1896, Menelik and his forces struck back and shattered the Italian army at Adowa. For the first time in modern history an African nation had defeated a white nation. When the peace treaty was signed, Italy paid Ethiopia an indemnity of $2 million and recognized the "absolute independence" of the ancient empire. Menelik became a hero throughout the black world. He was the harbinger of the "redemption of Africa" that would someday come to pass. Ethiopia replaced Haiti and Liberia as the master symbol of Black Power and Black Nationalism.

Between the end of the nineteenth century and the outbreak of World War I in 1914, there was a gradual secularization of black leadership in the United States, the West Indies, and Africa. As increasing numbers of college graduates emerged who were not trained in theology, the "vindication of the Race" passed from the hands of those who believed in Providential Design and biblically sanctioned "Ethiopianism" into the hands of professionally trained historians, anthropologists, and archaeologists. After 1900, Pan Africanism gradually became the dominant political myth of the black world—replacing the Ethiopianist pre-political myth. But Ethiopianism was by no means dead. It has persisted in its oldest and most theological form in the churches of the unsophisticated in the United States and South Africa. It became a basic subsidiary reinforcing myth for the great black nationalist mass movement of the 1920s, Marcus Garvey's Universal Negro Improvement Association (UNIA). By the mid-1920s, Ethiopianist ideas were so deeply imbedded in the urban subcultures of the African American urban communities, from the impact of the Negro church and the UNIA, that an apperceptive mass was present to which founders of cults and social movements could appeal. All of these cults provide meaningful schemes of living and answers to the identity quest for a small fraction of the black population in the United States. Their political significance as organized groups is minimal, but their influence on ghetto thinking has sometimes been significant.

NOTE

1. Many of the more modern translations indicate that the original language really meant "black *and* comely."

Part IV

A Shift of Locus and Focus

African American Religion and the Transition into the Twentieth Century

Chapter Sixteen

"Everyone Is Welcome"
North to the Promised Land

Martha Fowlkes

If the great majority of African Americans had determined not to relocate outside of the country to seek a better life, they did not dismiss the option of relocation across the country. Henry Adams, of Shreveport, Louisiana, found post–Civil War conditions for blacks to be sufficiently discouraging that in 1874 he led in the organization of a "colonization council," which eventually numbered some 98,000 supporters in several states. By 1879, failing to garner any assistance from the U.S. president or Congress for ameliorating these conditions, some 50,000 of the council supporters undertook an exodus from their southern home region to the state of Kansas. The leader of the migration, Benjamin "Pap" Singleton, said, "The great God of glory has worked in me. I had open interviews with the living spirit of God for my people; and we are going to leave the South." Singleton was sometimes referred to by his followers as "Moses," and their migration is known as the "Colored Exodus."[1] In a speech in 1887, the Reverend M. Edward Bryant, of Alabama, decried the continuing, daily oppression of black citizens and called upon the Negro to ". . . march his own army across the Red Sea."[2] Then in an 1890 address to the founding convention of the Afro-American League, black newspaper publisher T. Thomas Fortune called for the establishment of a bureau of emigration, based on his belief that blacks would benefit by being more dispersed throughout the country.[3] The movements initiated by Adams and Singleton and called for by persons such as Bryant and Fortune came into full force in the opening decades of the twentieth century. A confluence of circumstances, including severe economic reversals in the South, continuing vile racial abuse there, and exciting economic opportunities opened up by greatly increased labor needs in northern industry, set in motion what became the largest internal migration in the country's history.

•

In 1910, more than 90 percent of African Americans live in the South. Between the turn of the century and 1930, nearly two million will make their way north in a mass exodus. They are "led as if by some mysterious unseen hand which was compelling them on," reports Charles S. Johnson, an African American sociologist in Chicago at the time. A group of nearly 150 Southerners, crossing the Ohio River, a divide "between Dixie and the rest of the creation," kneels together and prays. Other journeys north are marked by rituals, such as men stopping their watches. Often, voices join together in spirituals and hymns learned from grandparents, and their grandparents before them, during the many years of slavery:

> When Israel was in Egypt's land,
> Let my people go;
> Oppressed so hard they could not stand,
> Let my people go.
>
> Go down, Moses,
> 'Way down in Egypt land,
> Tell ole Pharaoh,
> Let my people go.
>
> No more shall they in bondage toil,
> Let my people go;
> Let them come out with Egypt's spoil,
> Let my people go.
>
> Go down, Moses,
> 'Way down in Egypt land,
> Tell ole Pharaoh,
> Let my people go.

Their reasons for leaving are legion: segregation that severely limits black citizenship, economic hardship exacerbated by the boll weevil's devastation of the cotton crop, a rise in white violence (754 lynchings of African Americans in the decade between 1900 and 1910 alone). Many are desperate, a mother in Biloxi writes, "to get out of this land of suffrin'." Yet the migration seems to catch many in the nation by surprise. Federal investigators describe a frenzy of activity at southern railroad stations. People move about "like bees in a hive," one says. A couple climbs aboard a car, then finds a seat, "patting their feet and singing. A man nearby asks, 'Uncle, where are you going?' The old man replies, 'Well, son, I'm gwine to the Promised Land.' " An investigator for the Department of Labor reports, with amazement, that crowds of blacks are leaving Alabama with nothing except the confidence that God has opened up this path. "Moving out," he concludes, "is an expression of their faith."

One stream of these northward migrants makes Chicago its destination. Upon arrival, many head for the only address they know: the corner of 27th and Dearborn, site of the Olivet Baptist Church.

Olivet was established in 1850 and at the time was one of only two black churches in the city. By 1910, Olivet's 3,100 members comprise the largest Baptist congregation in the nation. It is among a rapidly growing number of African American churches which, notes social worker Fannie Barrier Williams in 1905, are more than centers of preaching and religious education. They are "regarded by the masses as a sort of tribune of all their civic and social affairs." Black churches might seek to address parishioners' needs for housing and employment, or offer programs in homemaking and employment skills. Some also became involved in policies and protest movements, although among the larger and more established black churches of the North, this was more unusual. Scholars C. Eric Lincoln and Lawrence Mamiya argue that many black church leaders at this time share the economic views of Booker T. Washington:

> The gospel of wealth that Washington preached espoused the major values of the Protestant ethic: thrift, industry, and self-help. He felt that "economic accumulation" and the "cultivation of morality" were the major means of black acceptance in American society. By demonstrating their worth through frugality, hard work, and achievement, the African American's economic progress would lead to social equality and political rights; Washington eschewed political protests and did not press for the franchise.

W.E.B. Du Bois, writing of black Philadelphians at the time, divides the (potential) congregants into four groups: "the well-to-do," who attend "Presbyterian, Episcopal, and Congregational" churches; the "working class strivers," who tend to be Baptist and Methodist; the working poor, sometimes unemployed, who may attend Baptist services but not at the "better" Baptist churches; and "the criminal element."

Into this environment comes a flood of poor, rural, largely uneducated, Southerners carried north by faith. It is, as the Reverend Reverdy Ransom of Chicago's Institutional A.M.E. Church says, "an epochal moment." This moment gives rise not only to changes within established churches but to new forms and venues of religious experience including storefront churches (especially in the Holiness-Pentecostal movement) and the emergence of gospel music.

In the summer of 1916, the Chicago *Defender*, one of the most widely read African American newspapers in the nation, begins inviting black Southerners north. The United States is being steadily drawn into the war abroad and the flow of immigrants from Europe has slowed. Northern factories—auto plants, meat packing industries, steel mills—are opening their doors to African Americans. The black churches of the North announce in the *Defender*: "Everyone is welcome and made to feel at home."

The southern response is overwhelming. Olivet's pastor, the Reverend Dr. Lacey Kirk Williams (himself a migrant from Texas), already leads a congregation of 4,000 people, in a church built to seat 1,800. Now, he is flooded with letters and appeals, some addressed simply to "Oliver" or "Olvlivet." "All we want," one writer says, "is a chanst." Over the next three years, 100,000 migrants will arrive in Chicago alone.

Train after train arrives, loaded with passengers weary from days of travel, carrying their belongings in a single suitcase or satchel. Some travel alone, some with family members or neighbors. Reverend Williams sends parishioners to the train station to wait for arrivals, load them into trucks, and drive them through town in search of temporary lodging. Church members with room to spare flash their house lights as a signal for the driver to stop and let off passengers.

Not all church members support these "gospel wagons," as they are called. We hear from established Chicagoans who are nervous about the arrival of the migrants, fearful that this less educated, less sophisticated group will hinder their own efforts at advancement and render them less fit in the eyes of white America. The migrants, too, are wary of their neighbors in church and dismayed by the sheer numbers

A family, just arrived in Chicago from the South, c. 1915. Between 1910 and 1920, Chicago's African-American population more than doubled. Many migrants wrote ahead to churches asking for assistance with employment, housing, and child care.

involved. Reverend Williams and his assistants hold three simultaneous services on Sunday morning, squeezing people into the kitchen, the auditorium, the hallways—and still there are crowds on the sidewalk. "I don't care how early we'd go," one woman complains to her southern family, "you wouldn't get in."

Once in, many newcomers find themselves in a foreign world. Worship in the urban North is not what it was in the South. One migrant recalls that she "couldn't understand the pastor and the words he used. I couldn't sing their way. The songs were proud-like." Williams' sermons paint a picture of a large, urban ministry in the World War I era. The tone of the sermons is intellectual and the style is somewhat formal and staid. In the South, increasing urbanization was among the factors leading to new worship styles, such as that described by Mahalia Jackson, born into a devout Baptist family in New Orleans in 1911:

> I know now that a great influence in my life was the Sanctified or Holiness Churches we had in the South. I was always a Baptist, but there was a Sanctified church right next door to our house in New Orleans.
>
> Those people had no choir and no organ. They used the drum, the cymbal, the tambourine, and the steel triangle. Everybody in there sang and they clapped and

stomped their feet and sang with their whole bodies. They had a beat, a powerful beat, a rhythm we held on to from slavery days, and their music was so strong and expressive it used to bring the tears to my eyes.

Through the stories, letters, and writings of followers from this period, and through the words of scholars, we see the growth and appeal of the Holiness and Pentecostal traditions in the cities, particularly in "storefront churches"—places of worship established in parlors, basements, and storefronts. These churches form an oasis in a large, unfamiliar city, allowing migrants to recapture some of the intimacy of rural life. As sociologist E. Franklin Frazier noted, back home worshippers "had a seat in church that everyone recognized as theirs and if that seat were empty on Sunday the pastor came to their homes to find out the cause of their absence." In a church like Olivet, one lonely newcomer would be lost in a crowd of 8,000. In a tiny storefront, that lonely newcomer has a name and, most likely, a role.

NOTES

1. See Herbert Aptheker, *A Documentary History of the Negro People in the United States.* Two volumes. (New York: The Citadel Press, 1970), Vol. II, p. 723.

2. Ibid., p. 673.

3. Ibid., p. 705.

Chapter Seventeen

The Grip of the Negro Church

St. Clair Drake

The cities of the North introduced African Americans formerly of the rural South to a world they had not known before: bustling urban landscapes, integrated schools and public accommodations, substantial hourly wages that were paid as promised, and many other things that seemed to bear out the correctness of their decision to migrate. There was another side, though: The racial harmony was not nearly what it appeared to be at first glance; and city life posed formidable challenges to physical, economic, and psycho-emotional sustainability. St. Clair Drake offers and informative case study of how black churches related themselves to those facing the urban challenges.

•

The Negro newspaper is a business institution which Bronzeville expects to "serve The Race." The Negro church is ostensibly a "religious" organization, but Bronzeville expects it, too, to "advance The Race." There are nearly 500 churches in Black Metropolis, claiming at least 200,000 members and distributed among over thirty denominations (see Table 17.1). Almost half of the churches, and over two thirds of the people who claim church membership, are affiliated with one of the two Negro National Baptist Conventions. These congregations and their ministers have virtually no face-to-face relationships with any of their white co-religionists. The first Negro Baptist Convention arose as a split from white organizations primarily because colored preachers felt that they were being denied an opportunity to express their talents without discrimination. Negro Baptists think of their organization as a "Race church," and their leaders concern themselves with such matters as fighting the Job Ceiling and demanding equal economic opportunity as well as "serving the Lord." There are also three Negro Methodist denominations represented in Bronzeville, and the colored Holiness, Spiritualist, and Community churches. There are also a number of small denominations indigenous to Bronzeville and such all-Negro "cults" as the African Orthodox Church, the Christian Catholics, the Temple of Moorish Science, and numerous fly-by-night groups organized around enterprising but untrained preachers.

About 10 percent of the churches and less than 10 percent of the church-goers in Bronzeville are affiliated with predominantly white denominations, such as the Meth-

TABLE 17.1
Negro Congregations in Chicago: 1928[a] and 1938[b]

Group	Denomination	1928 Number	1928 Percent	1938 Number	1938 Percent
1	Baptist (No special designation)	98	33.2	141	29.7
	Missionary Baptist	30	10.2	68	14.3
	Primitive Baptist	5	1.7	6	1.3
	Total	133	45.1	215	45.3
2	African Methodist Episcopal	24	8.2	27	5.7
	African Methodist Episcopal Zion	5	1.7	8	1.7
	Colored Methodist Episcopal	6	2.0	7	1.5
	Total	35	11.9	42	8.9
3	Methodist Epicsopal	8	2.7	6	1.3
	Episcopal	3	1.0	3	.6
	Presbyterian	3	1.0	4	.9
	Congregational	2	.7	2	.4
	Disciples of Christ	2	.7	3	.6
	Seventh-Day Adventists	2	.7	3	.6
	Catholic (Roman)	1	.3	3	.6
	Lutheran	1	.3	2	.4
	Church of Christ, Scientist	—	—	1	.2
	Total	22	7.4	27	5.6
4	Community Churches, Inc.	3	1.0	10	2.1
5	Church of God in Christ	24	8.2	27	5.7
	Church of Christ (Holiness USA)	3	1.0	3	.6
	Church of Christ (No designation)	5	1.7	1	.2
	Church of the Living God	2	.7	4	.9
	Church of God (Holiness)	1	.3	7	1.5
	Church of God (no designation)	6	2.0	10	2.1
	Church of God and Saints of Christ	1	.3	4	.9
	Apostolic and Pentecostal	11	3.8	27	5.7
	Pentecostal Assemblies of World	2	.7	3	.6
	Old-Time Methodist	1	.3	1	.2
	Holiness (Miscellaneous Groups)	—	—	20	4.2
	Total	56	19.0	107	22.6
6	Spiritual and Spiritualist	17	5.8	47	9.8
	I.A.M.E. Spiritual	—	—	4	.9
	Total	17	5.8	51	10.7
7	Cumberland Presbyterian	2	.7	1	.2
	African Orthodox	1	.3	1	.2
	Christian Catholic	—	—	1	.2
	Liberal Catholic	1	.3	1	.2
	Others	25	8.5	19	4.0
	Total	29	9.8	23	4.8
	Grand Total	295	100.0	475	100.0

[a] Adapted from Robert Lee Sutherland, "An Analysis of Negro Churches in Chicago," Ph.D. Dissertation, University of Chicago, 1930.

[b] Compiled from a field survey of the Cayton-Warner Research.

odist Episcopal Church, the Episcopal, Presbyterian, Congregational, Roman Catholic, Lutheran, Christian Scientist, Seventh-Day Adventist, and Disciples of Christ. Though in the state and national organizations of these churches Negroes wield very little influence, a number of the churches have extensive educational and social welfare projects for Negroes throughout the United States. Some people in Bronzeville who would prefer to be identified with these relatively powerful white groups have found that individual white congregations in these sects do not welcome Negro members, even though the Negro church officials and the white church officials often have very close ties. On the whole, Bronzeville sticks to the "Race churches."[1]

As we have noted previously, Negroes purchased the white churches and synagogues in the Black Belt area as the white population moved out. These financial deals often embittered Negroes against their white brethren, whom they accused of unloading church property on them at exorbitant rates during the Fat Years. In 1933, Chicago Negro churches were carrying the second highest per capita indebtedness among all urban Negro churches in the country. Some of these were fine buildings in good repair. Others were deteriorating. Many had formerly been maintained by well-to-do white congregations, and the Negroes found difficulty in keeping the properties in good condition. Thus, during the last twenty years all the larger Negro churches have been forced to spend a great deal of their income on paying off mortgages and maintaining church property. Some have also spent a great deal upon interior decoration. All this financial activity brings Negro church trustees into contact with white businessmen and sharpens somewhat the antagonisms between Negroes and whites in Midwest Metropolis.

There are five churches in Bronzeville seating over 2,000 persons and claiming more than 10,000 members, and some fifty church buildings seating between 500 and 2,000 persons. Seventy-five percent of Bronzeville's churches are small "storefront" or house churches, with an average membership of fewer than twenty-five persons. Many of these represent survivals from the period of the Great Migration. Others are the result of leadership conflicts within the larger churches. The proselytizing drive in certain denominations has also helped to swell the number. Although there were "missions" in the Black Belt prior to the Great Migration, the prevalence of storefront churches seems to have resulted from the lack of available edifices during the first years of the influx. Church memberships skyrocketed during this period, and competition between congregations for the abandoned white churches and synagogues resulted, on the one hand, in the payment of exorbitant prices for church property, and, on the other, in the proliferation of makeshift churches. In many cases, pastor and congregation hoped some day either to build or to move into a larger edifice. Many of them did one or the other. In other cases the congregation remained where it was, or moved into another store. Several large congregations boast of their evolution from storefronts, and in their anniversary souvenir programs proudly display "before and after" photographs. The enterprising pastor who leads his congregation from storefront to edifice is well on his way to success in the church world. If he ever pays off the mortgage, he is a hero.

Church service in Illinois, c. 1941 (The altar cloth on the podium reads "Langley Avenue All Nations Pentecostal Church, Elder Lucy Smith.")

Serving the Lord (and Man)

While about a third of Bronzeville's churches have only worship as an activity, the majority of them also sponsor some associated activities, if no more than a Sunday School and an usher board or several money-raising clubs. The key activity for all is what the people call "Sunday service." An average Sunday morning probably finds at least 65,000 of Bronzeville's 300,000 persons in some church, and many persons who do not themselves attend church hustle their children off to Sunday School as a part of their "right raising."

Sunday morning in Bronzeville is a colorful occasion. At 9 o'clock, little knots of children and adolescents, in their Sunday best, begin to gather around the doors of the storefronts in the poorer neighborhoods to joke and play before going inside for two hours of singing, studying the lesson, and lifting the collection—all amid a great deal of friendly banter. At the larger churches the picture is similar, except that once inside the building the various groups of pupils are more likely to study the lesson in separate classrooms with teachers who boast certificates from the Interdenominational Council of Religious Education, and the teachers are likely to stray from the Bible to discuss current events, the race problem, or questions of personal adjustment. It has been estimated that an average of 60,000 Negro children attend Sunday School each week. Sunday School out, most of the youngsters are ready to spend the rest of the day in play at some park or on the streets. Many of them, too, begin to queue up for the opening of the movies. A few may "stay for church," especially those who attend the one or two congregations that have a special "junior church."

"Eleven o'clock service" is the main event of the day, and some of the larger churches are filled by 10:45 A.M., when the older members start the pre-service prayer meeting. Jitneys, streetcars, and buses do a rushing business. Rows of automobiles, freshly polished, line the streets around all the larger churches and many of the smaller ones. "Church mothers," their little gray caps perched on their heads and secured by chin straps, mingle around the door with the younger folks clad in their stylish Sunday best. On special occasions such as Easter and Christmas it is impossible, at 10:45 A.M., to secure a seat in any of the five largest Protestant churches. (These churches each seat more than 2,500 persons.) A surprisingly large number of young people attend these morning services, and special usher boards and junior choirs provide them with specific functions.

Afternoon services, though not a definite part of most church programs, are by no means rare. These are usually "special services"—lodge turnouts, rallies, "Women's Day," "Children's Day," etc. Most churches also have a young people's society, which meets late in the afternoon, though it draws comparatively few youngsters.

Some of the higher-status churches have dispensed with night services entirely, especially in the summer months. Others, in order to meet the competition of Chicago's night life, have evolved the custom of giving "special programs" in addition to, or instead of, preaching. These take the form of dramas, musical extravaganzas, or occasional movies. These Sunday night services are usually entertaining enough to appeal to a circle far wider than the membership of the church. In fact, a great deal of interchurch visiting takes place without regard to denominational lines, and many persons will attend services of this type who make no claim to being religious. It is good entertainment with no cover charge and no compulsion even to drop a nickel in the "free-will offering."

Throughout the week, most churches are centers of activity—singing and praying in the smaller, lower-status churches, and club meetings, socials, plays, concerts, movies, and mass meetings in the larger ones. Community organizations may ordinarily have access to a church building, provided the church itself has nothing scheduled for the night. Bronzeville's churches are centers of free speech, and many a bulletin board is just as likely to list a meeting of a left-wing labor union, or even of a Communist organization, as a meeting of an American Legion post.

Church *attendance*, however, is not a reliable index to church membership in Bronzeville. A careful study of the four largest churches, each averaging over a thousand Sunday morning worshipers and claiming more than 5,000 members—indicates that the actual duespaying membership may hardly exceed 1,500 persons. Church rolls are seldom pruned, and a boasted "10,000 members" may include the dead, "backsliders," and persons who have shifted to other churches. The largest proportion of people who maintain relationships with the church probably do so, except in very small congregations, through sub-organizations. In fact, many persons have their only relationship in this indirect manner. Such associated organizations, range from purely social clubs to cooperative stores. Yet were it not for the primacy of the worship service, and for the hard labor of the "sustaining members" (predominantly women), the average church could not maintain itself. As it is, all the larger churches are saddled with heavy mortgages, and much of the money raised through frequent rallies must be applied to debts. Those interested in "serving the Lord" provide an institution for "serving man."

A Bone of Contention

Forty years ago, church news was "big news" in Negro newspapers. Today, churches and preachers seldom make the front page unless some sensational incident is involved. In total bulk, too, church news falls far behind club news. The church is not the *center* of community life as it was in Midwest Metropolis before the Great Migration or as it is today in the small towns of the South. Yet the church is the oldest and wealthiest institution in the community, and in competition with a wide range of secular organizations it has managed to remain an important element in the life of Bronzeville. The southern migrants brought to Chicago a tradition of church membership which has persisted in the metropolitan setting. The preachers have adjusted speedily to rapid changes in the urban community, and have thus been able to compete with the "worldly" organizations in an environment notorious for its secular emphasis.

For many people the church is still the center of attention. For an even larger number it is an interesting topic of conversation. Commanding the allegiance of so many people and handling such a large amount of Bronzeville's money, the church inevitably becomes a matter for public discussion. The Cayton-Warner Research staff collected thousands of random comments during the Depression years. The most striking thing about these comments was the prevalence of grumbling against preachers and the church—a habit found among members and nonmembers alike. The major criticisms ran somewhat as follows:

(1) Church is a "racket," (2) Too many churches, (3) Churches are too emotional, (4) There's no real religion among the members, (5) Churches are a waste of time and money, (6) Ministers don't practice what they preach, (7) Ministers don't preach against "sin," (8) Church places too much emphasis upon money, (9) Negroes are too religious.

During the Depression, the charge that the church was a "racket" was encountered everywhere in Bronzeville. This typically Chicago reaction expressed a doubt of motives that did not necessarily mean refusal to cooperate with the church but did indicate disapproval of the emphasis placed upon money by the preachers. It also implied a suspicion that funds were being used dishonestly or unproductively; non-church members made the latter charge more frequently than did the "faithful." The proprietor of a gambling establishment, for instance, observed: "The church is getting to be too big a racket for me. I'd rather support my own racket." A flat-janitor who attended church infrequently confided to an interviewer, "You know churches are nothing but a racket." The proprietor of a small business said: "I just don't care anything about the churches because I think they are rackets." An optometrist was caustic in his comment: "I was baptized in a Baptist church but I don't go regularly. . . . It's just racketeering on people's emotions anyway." A young business woman used the same term: "I used to be a member of the Flaming Sword Baptist Church, but I've dropped my membership. One of my brothers is a deacon. My other brother, like myself, thinks the church is just a racket." A housewife in the lower income brackets states that her husband objects to her attendance at church. He calls the church "nothing but a racket" and insists that "nobody gets anything out of it but the preachers." His wife is inclined to agree.

Even when Bronzeville's people do not bluntly characterize churches as "rackets," they often make the charge by implication. Thus, a hotel maid states: "I just haven't made up my mind to join a church. Of course I was a Baptist at home in the South, but most of these churches are full of graft. You pay and pay money and the church is still in debt." A WPA worker stated that he didn't attend church because "they don't help anybody, and all they want is money to keep the big shots going."

Inevitably the criticisms focus on the preaches. "Blood-suckers!" snapped a skilled laborer; "they'll take the food out of your mouth and make you think they are doing you a favor."

"You take some of these preachers," observed a steel-mill worker; "they're living like kings—got great big Packard automobiles and ten or twelve suits and abunch of sisters putting food in their pantry. Do you call that religion? Naw! It ain't nothing but a bunch of damn monkey foolishness."

Church members, too, while retaining their membership, are sometimes as caustic as the "unbelievers," making statements like the following:

> I'm a church member. I believe churches are still useful. But like everything else, there's a lot of racketeering going on in the church.

> The preachers want to line their pockets with gold. They are supposed to be the leaders of the people, but they are fake leaders.

> Ministers are not as conscientious as they used to be. They are money-mad nowadays. All they want is the almighty dollar and that is all they talk about.

> When you are making plenty of money and share it with them you are all right, you're a fine fellow. When the crash comes and you are not doing so well, they forget all about you.

Closely related to the charge that churches are a racket is the contention that there are too many churches. One businessman expresses a very general complaint when he says: "I am a churchman and I believe that the church occupies an important

CHART 17.1
Where the Church Dollar Goes

REPAIRS AND UPKEEP
CHURCH OVERHEAD
SALARIES
6.3%
6.6%
43.2%
21%
BENEVOLENCE AND
MISCELLANEOUS
ITEMS
22.9%
INTEREST AND REDUCTION
OF CHURCH DEBT

From table in Benjamin E. Mays and Joseph W. Nicholson, *The Negro's Church,* Institute for
Social and Religious Research, 1933.

place in the life of any community. But I'm also positive that there are too many
Negro churches in Chicago and too many false preachers."

Large numbers of people combine a belief in religion with a denunciation of the
church, as in the case of the woman who said: "I thinks there's only one heaven
where we all will go, but the biggest thieves are running the churches, so what can
they do about saving us? Nothing!"

These criticisms express the annoyance and frustration of a group trying to survive
on a subsistence level during a depression. The church, too, was trying to survive,
and the ministers were forced to emphasize money-raising to keep their doors open
and to gather sufficient funds to meet obligations incurred during the Fat Years.[2]
(see chart 17.1). Except for a dozen pastors of the largest churches, ministerial salaries
averaged less than $2,000 a year, but most preachers, whether in charge of big
churches or of small, were conspicuously better off than most of the laity, and hence
served as convenient targets for attack. Few churches have adequate systems of
accounting and it was virtually impossible to verify or disprove charges of stealing
and misappropriation of funds. The truth of such charges is, however, largely irrelevant, since antagonism to the church seems to lie deeper than mere hostility toward
preachers or concern over clerical probity.

Bronzeville's loyal church members, thrown on the defensive by these criticisms,
usually defend the institution in conventional terms. A "racial angle" (note the
italicized passages) is sometimes added. The following expressions are typical of the
"defense":

I am a member of the Solid Rock A.M.E. Church. Churches are a necessity, for I believe
that *it is through them that our people first got the idea that we must co-operate with each*

other. Take the church away with its teachings and I'm afraid we would not be able to live because it is fear of the beyond that causes one to think of his fellow man and respect his feelings.

My opinion is that the church is a good influence on the community. People seem to have a certain amount of respect for the church that no other institutions can enjoy. People who are members of churches are the ones that you find trying to accomplish something worth while and are very seldom in the clutches of the law.

My wife and I are members of Pleasant Green Baptist Church and get a lot of pleasure out of attending services. I think the church is a great necessity, for the people get something from it that is resting and gives them a feeling of peace.

My family and I are members of Zion's Star A.M.E. Church. I think the church is a good influence. The store-front churches are all right too, and I am sure they are able to interest some people that otherwise would not go to church at all.

My whole family belongs to St. Simon's Baptist Church. I am of the opinion that the church fills a great need. It is hard to picture the amount of evil that would take hold of the world if the church were done away with. *I also believe that many of our folks have learned from the church that big things can be accomplished only by the joining of forces of a large group of people.*"

What the Church Has to Offer

"Why," it may be asked, "in the face of widespread criticisms and such apparent dissatisfaction, does the church still flourish?" Underlying the conventional reasons which the faithful give for supporting the church are more fundamental satisfactions that bind them to the institution. Churches offer a wide variety of activities, and a person may take his choice.

The collective ceremonies lend a certain rhythm to existence, and there is little emphasis upon theology. If a person has talent, is a Race Leader, or even a moderately successful business or professional man, he can believe anything he chooses, so long as he "supports the church." In the South, people are sometimes "churched" (i.e., accused publicly) when they have breached the moral code or the church rules, verbally or in their conduct. In Bronzeville this hardly ever happens. One critic commented cynically, "The only thing they might put you out of church for up here is not paying dues." One of the most striking aspects of Bronzeville's church life is a mutually shared core of religious custom that cuts across denominational lines. People "feel at home" in any of the major Protestant denominations, and interdenominational visiting and shifts in church membership are widespread. Bronzeville's churches provide a congenial environment for the thousands of people who were taught as children that they "ought to go to church."

Many people who attend church offer no "religious" reasons at all in explaining their behavior. They attend church, they say, because they "like good singing" and "good speaking," or because the services are "restful and beautiful." Bronzeville's churches are centers of entertainment as well as places of worship. Popular preachers and a wide variety of musical offerings draw large crowds both on Sundays and on week nights. It is not unusual to find a total of over 10,000 people attending Sunday evening musicales in the four largest churches, and an equal number distributed among the smaller churches. The most popular pastors in the Black Belt are excellent showmen. Their sermons are replete with humor and apt illustration, as well as pithy epigram, good jokes, and rousing flights of oratory. Preachers who can flay sin in an original manner, who can denounce iniquity with a "knowing" air and with some sexual innuendo, attract large crowds. In addition to this incidental entertainment, all of Bronzeville's churches are continually offering concerts, pageants, plays, suppers, and other similar activities. Many people without formal membership in any church might be attracted, for example, to the horse shows and fashion shows featuring Joe Louis's wife, Marva, which some Bronzeville churches have sponsored within the last few years.

It is probable, however, that the church's main attraction is the opportunity it gives for large masses of people to function in an organized group, to compete for prestige, to be elected to office, to exercise power and control, to win applause and acclaim. Even church fights, although dubbed "unchristian," are interesting.

The Church as a Race Institution

Much of the grumbling against the church is on the basis of "race loyalty." Both members and nonmembers expect the church to play a prominent part in "advancing The Race," and they often judge the institution from this angle alone. As we have mentioned, segregation of Negroes from Whites at the congregational level is almost absolute. Negroes seldom see white people in their congregations. The great mass denominations—the Baptists and Negro Methodists—have separate state and national organizations. The relations between white and Negro ministers are rare and formalized. The larger white denominations have a tendency to look upon the Negro churches as a field for "home mission" work. Negroes, as a low-income group, are somewhat dependent upon these white groups for assistance in paying off mortgages, and whenever large community programs are contemplated, Negro churches must either approach these white boards for assistance or seek assistance from other white people.

In enlisting support for their special projects, Bronzeville's churches have had to develop a technique for extracting donations from "white friends." At one extreme is the attractive folder written by a sociologist to get money for a new church building and community center. The appeal is directed to high-status whites as

> an opportunity to build a model, influential Negro church that can serve as an example and standard for institutions of similar kind throughout the country. The need of such a high example of intelligent ministry, rational religious services, adequate recreational and community social service, is imperative as the Negro gropes for an intelligent, sincere, and fearless religion.

At the other extreme is the almost illiterate plea of a Negro Pentecostal evangelist, soliciting funds and gifts over the radio each Sunday night:

Now you white folks in my radio audience mus' have some ol' pianos an' sewin' machines up in yo' attic that yuh kin sen' me. We need 'em. Our church kin use 'em.

In between is the pastor of one of Bronzeville's largest churches, who has noticed some white people at the Sunday evening musical:

Now, Mr. ———— of the ———— Steel Company is here tonight. I didn't know he an' his frien's were coming, but since they're here we're gonna make them pay for it. [Laughter.] Pass those baskets, ushers! We're tryin' to build up a church here that will make good citizens out of these Negroes on the South Side. I've got 15,000 members and they're all spillin' outa the place. We need a building on that lot we've bought over there, an' if you white folks will put up the building we can save the South Side.

    Now, Deacon ———— works for this steel company. Stand up over there, Deacon. He may have told these visitors to come. I didn't. But we're glad you're here. You know Negroes always did love white folks, anyhow ———— that is, we love the *men*. [Laughter from the audience at this daring play on a socially tabooed subject, the relations between Negro men and white women ———— a type of joke that could not have been used in addressing white visitors in the South.]

Such "begging from white folks" is distasteful to many of Bronzeville's church people, but it is mixed with admiration for those preachers who can do it with finesse and without "Uncle Tomming" or sacrificing their dignity.[3] The following incident illustrates the mixed reactions of Negroes, dependent upon whites for financial support but desirous of preserving their independence of action. In this case the trustee board of a small school for training storefront preachers was in session. The funds for the experiment had been supplied by a white denominational board, and the Negroes were trying hard to meet a pledge they had made. They felt, however, that they would have more success if they had a concrete objective such as buying a building to house the school. They planned a large money-raising campaign around this financial project. The white co-sponsors felt that the purchase of a building was too ambitious a goal. After the enthusiastic speeches of Bronzeville's ministers had all been delivered, a young white minister representing the Home Mission Board of his denomination rose. He was very blunt.

Before you brethren start discussing the purchase of a building, I think we should pay some attention to the fact that we are running a $300 deficit on this year's budget. I am sure Dr. ———— [the white president of the Home Mission Board] would want this wiped out before we make any further commitments.

The Negro ministers were incensed. It was a fact that they had fallen behind on their pledges for the year, but the white speaker had touched a raw spot: He had reminded them of their subordinate position. He had implied that they were putting nonessentials first. He had assumed the air of a missionary or a tutor lecturing his improvident wards. The chairman of the meeting, a well-educated Negro minister, rose to defend the honor of The Race.

I think the time has come [he said] when Negroes ought to take up their own responsibilities and maintain their own organizations. There are 126 churches in our denomination on the South Side. I think we can support this institution by ourselves. White people have helped me. They gave me money to go to Harvard. They helped me pay the mortgage on my church. But I think the time has come when Negroes can handle their own affairs. Now, I feel we should pay these brethren[the whites] what we owe them, then buy our building, and run this institution by ourselves.

The atmosphere was tense. The three white board members were embarrassed and disconcerted, the Negro ministers uneasy. At this point a skillful and eloquent Bronzeville preacher took the floor and began to restore the atmosphere of "good-will," using all the techniques of handling white folks which Negroes in the South have developed—humor, a little "stooping to conquer," playful denunciation of Negroes. At the same time he threw in some concessions to race pride to appeal to the Negroes. His approach is a striking illustration of the technique of a Race Leader handling a mixed audience in a crisis situation:

> Brother Chairman, you may be ready to cut loose from the white folks, but I'm not. I'm going to get all the money I can out of them. [Laughter from both Negroes and whites.] I'm going down *tomorrow* to see about getting some money for *my* church. You know it's the *duty* of white folks to help their colored brothers, and I'm going to do anything to stand in the way of letting a man do his Christian duty.[4]
>
> Negroes are poor. You know the white folks have all the money. Just because Negroes ride around in fine automobiles and wear good clothes doesn't mean that they've got any money. You said that we have 126 churches. Now, you know as well as I do that if we come right down to it, there are only about 26 real churches, and every one of them is so interested in taking care of his own corner that they can't get together.
>
> Now, I'm tried of so much talk. Negroes can preach longer, pray louder, and make more noise than any folks on God's earth. [Both Negroes and whites laughed at this bit of racial depreciation.] I think we ought to pay that $300 deficit just to show the brethren that we are co-operating with them. I think we ought to put up or shut up. I have a check for $50 in my pocket that I was getting ready to use to pay another bill. I'm going to give that $50. Who'll match it?

At this point the chairman was forced to pledge $25 in order to save face. Within ten minutes $125 had been pledged. The peacemaker assured the white members of the board that the Negroes would have the remainder by the next Sunday. He then turned to the subject of the building:

> Now I think that if the colored brethren want a building they ought to have it. I think that the finance committee should look the site over and report back to us. We've got a great future and, Brother Chairman, I believe we can buy that building if we want want to.

Despite the dependence of Negro congregations upon the occasional friendly aid of white co-religionists, the Negro church is largely free of white control. Negro preachers have the greatest "freedom" of any Race Leaders. Politicians must fit themselves into machine politics. Most "civic" leaders are dependent upon white philanthropy. Most of Bronzeville's preachers are answerable to no one except their congregations. They can say what they please about current affairs and race relations; there are no church superiors to discipline them and no white people to take economic reprisals. Because they are so largely free of the political and economic controls of the white community, Bronzeville expects them to be *real* Race Men. Preachers are subjected to continuous community criticism, and to retain the allegiance of their followers they are forced to concern themselves with a wide range of secular activities—political action, protest against discrimination, advice on securing jobs and legal aid, and the encouragement of Negro business enterprises.

Yet, when a preacher responds to these demands, he immediately risks being accused of "racketeering."[5] For instance, most of the larger churches advertise Negro-owned businesses on the theory that successful colored businessmen are "advancing The Race." They try to throw business toward certain Negro undertakers, physicians, and retail stores. Church newspapers carry ads of colored enterprises in Bronzeville and of white stores that employ Negroes. Sometimes a pastor will appoint special agents or representatives within his church to plug specific stores or products.[6] Naturally, the community assumes that the ministers get "kickbacks" and special considerations from these businessmen.

Bronzeville is very critical of its preachers when accusing them of tying up too much money in church property or in other "noneconomic" uses. Ordinarily these sentiments are expressed in rather vague and general terms, such as one man's comment:

> I used to be active in the church; I thought we could work out our salvation that way. But I found out better. These Negro preachers are not bothered about The Race— about all they think of is themselves.

The ministers counter with the argument that the church is not *primarily* a business or political institution, and insist that if they weren't meeting the people's "needs" they couldn't survive. Often the criticisms are by no means vague—they are an insistent demand that the Negro churches should encourage the support of Negro businessmen who "make jobs for The Race."

NOTES

1. During the last ten years an intensive drive by the Roman Catholic Church has met with considerable success in Bronzeville. There are three large Catholic Churches in the Black Belt, and the Masses are well attended. Interviews with Negro Catholics, and with non-Catholics whose children go to parochial schools, seem to indicate that one of the primary attractions of the Catholic Church is its educational institutions. With the public schools running on double shifts during those years, many parents felt that the parochial school offered a more thorough education in a quieter atmosphere with adequate discipline and personal attention for all students. The Catholic approach to the Negroes has been aided by the establishment of a small community house, by the extensive athletic program of the Catholic Youth Organization, and by the forthright stand against race prejudice taken by an auxiliary Bishop of the Chicago diocese. In 1944, the Catholics purchased the most imposing piece of church property in Bronzeville—Sinai Temple, a wealthy Jewish synagogue—and converted it into a school and community center.

2. Frequent newspaper accounts of mortgage-burning ceremonies in the autumn and winter of 1943–44 indicated that churches in Bronzeville were taking advantage of the war boom to institute drives for clearing off their debts.

3. One of the authors observed another case of flattering powerful white people. A large church was giving its annual music festival. The Chicago postmaster had been invited to attend, since many Negroes worked under his supervision, including the choir director. Near the end of the program, while the audience was expectantly awaiting the *Hallelujah Chorus*, all postmen in the audience were asked to stand. The postmaster proceeded to deliver a 45-minute harangue while the audience twisted, squirmed, and muttered in disapproval. After "honoring" the postmaster, the choir director announced that a prominent white banker was present. He explained that this man had flown to Chicago from New York especially to attend this service. Both the pastor and the choir director praised him fulsomely. The banker was the main mortgage-holder on the church property!

4. In 1939 only two or three Negro churches were receiving aid from white church boards in paying off mortgages, but the number has been much larger in the past. At a state convention of one large Negro denomination in 1939, the moderator was heard telling the delegates: "They[the whites] will help us if we help ourselves. The whites are looking at what we are doing. . . . If you need help go down and tell them. Some arrangement will be made."

5. This charge is very frequently made with respect to political campaigns. The ministers are accused of promising to "deliver the vote" for a sizable financial reward or for the promise of some position. The ministers, on the other hand, are likely to insist that they accept donations for the church but no personal gifts from politicians. There have been ministers in Bronzeville who were actively engaged in politics. One of them, Bishop Archibald J. Carey, held several high appointive positions under Major Thompson and finally secured a post on the state Civil Service Commission. He was accused of accepting bribes, although there was widespread belief that he had been "framed." Any minister who does business with the political machines lays himself open to criticism. Yet many people in Bronzeville feel that their preachers should go into politics. The popularity of clerico-politicians in Negro communities is illustrated by the elections of 1944 in which a Negro preacher was elected from New York's Harlem to represent the area in Congress, another was made Recorder of Deeds in Washington shortly before the election, and still another was elected to the state legislature in Ohio.

6. The following ads have been selected as typical of hundreds appearing in church newspapers of Bronzeville's largest churches:

———— ELECTRIC SERVICE COMPANY——Inquire about our special plan to the members of ———— Baptist Church. Miss ————, Representative. At your own authorized dealer.

———— SHOE AND DRY GOODS STORE——Headquarters for Florsheim Shoes. Men's, Ladies', Children's Ready to Wear. We Employ Colored Salesmen.

WHEN IN NEED OF FURNITURE SEE REV. WM. P. ————, Representative of the ———— FURNITURE COMPANY.

Thomas Dorsey, "Father of Gospel Music." Here, Dorsey directs a choir at the Pilgrim Baptist Church, Chicago, where he was affiliated from the early 1920s. From the Archival Collection of the Institute for Black Religious Research.

Chapter Eighteen

The Development of Gospel Song

Lawrence W. Levine

The Negro Spiritual is said to be among the unique contributions of the United States to modern musical literature. They were the creative synthesis of African musical forms and Judeo-Christian concepts contextualized around the lived experiences and resilient spirits of an enslaved population. The transition from slavery to freedom, then from the rural South to the cities, engendered new creative musical expressions as bearers of religious meanings. Gospel songs were one important result.

•

Changes in religious consciousness and world view are clearly delineated in the gospel songs, which from the 1930s on displaced the spirituals as the most important single body of black religious music. There were, to be sure, a number of important points of continuity in the consciousness of the gospel songs and the spirituals. In both, God was an immediate, intimate, living presence. Such gospel titles as *I am Walking With My Jesus, I Had a Talk With Jesus, I Know God, He's Holding My Hand, He Has Never Left Me Alone, He Answers Me, Jesus Is Real to Me, I Want Jesus to Walk With Me, I'm Going to Move in the Room With the Lord*, abounded.[1] Like the spirituals, the gospel songs were songs of hope and affirmation. Explaining why she refused to give up gospel music for blues, Mahalia Jackson exclaimed: "Blues are the songs of despair, but gospel songs are the songs of hope. When you sing them you are delivered of your burden. You have a feeling that here is a cure for what's wrong. It always gives me joy to sing gospel songs. I get to sing and I feel better right away."[2] In song after song the singers affirmed: "There's a crown at the end of your road," "Going to live with God," "I've got a home, a home in heaven, I've got a home," "Some day I'm goin' to see my Jesus," "There'll be joy on tomorrow . . . When my work on earth is through," "I've got heaven in my view Hallelujah."

> I can sing I can shout I can work joyfully
> I can pray I can smile I can feel Christ in me
> I can love I can live I can die peacefully
> For Jesus lives in me.[3]

As important as these similarities are, they are overshadowed by the differences. The overriding thrust of the gospel songs was otherworldly. Emphasis was almost wholly upon God with whom Man's relationship was one of total dependence. These typical gospel titles set the tone: *He's Everything to Me, Only God, He's Everything You Need, He's Got Everything You Need, Give God the Credit, He'll Fill Every Space in Your Life, I Don't Care What the World May Do, The Lord Will Provide, He'll Fix it All, The Lord Will Make a Way Some How.*

> I don't know what I'd do without the Lawd,
> I don't know what I'd do without the Lawd,
> When I look around and see
> What the Lawd has done for me,
> I don't know what I'd do without the Lawd.[4]

> I'm not worried about lov'd ones
> I'm not worried about friends
> Because He makes all my decisions for me;
> Yes, for me.
> He's a mighty good doctor
> I'm so glad that He's a lawyer
> Because He makes all my decisions for me.[5]

Jesus rather than the Hebrew Children dominated the gospel songs. And it was not the warrior Jesus of the spirituals but a benevolent spirit who promised His children rest and peace and justice in the hereafter. Again, titles are instructive: *The Lord Jesus Is My All and All, Christ Is All, Jesus Is All, Jesus Knows and Will Supply My Every Need, Jesus, the Perfect Answer, More of Jesus and Less of Me, Wait on Jesus, I'm Goin' to Bury Myself in Jesus' Arms, Jesus Is the Answer to Every Problem, I Live for Jesus, Jesus Will Make It Alright.* The focus was on heaven, and in the gospel songs, unlike the spirituals, the concept of heaven remained firmly in the future, largely distinct from Man's present situation: "I'm not working for earthly fame / My deeds are not for material gain / . . . in heaven I'll find my reward."[6] There was, asserted one of the songs sung by the Golden Gaters and other gospel quartets in the 1940s, *No Segregation in Heaven.*[7] Where the spirituals proved their point by analogy, precedent, and concrete example, the gospel ethos was largely one of pure faith:

> The Lord will provide,
> The Lord will provide,
> Sometimes another, the Lord will provide.

> It may not be in my time;
> It may not be in yours,
> But sometimes another, the Lord will provide.[8]

> I don't know why I have to cry sometime
> I don't know why I have to sigh sometime
> It would be a perfect day but there's trouble in the way
> I don't know why but I'll know by in by.[9]

The religion of the gospel songs remained a sustaining, encouraging, enveloping creed. Nevertheless, it differed markedly from the beliefs of the spirituals. Certainly it recognized and discussed the troubles, sorrows, and burdens of everyday existence, but its immediate solutions tended to be a mixture of Christian faith and one variety or another of positive thinking. Touches of American popular culture were increasingly evident:"The best things in life are free," "Just look around and take what God is giving you," "Life can be beautiful."

> If we put away our worries
> And think of good along the way
> Just take the whole world as you find it
> And try to live one day each day
> Life can be beautiful if you live it right today.[10]

In terms of long-range solutions for Man's problems, the gulf between this world and the next had grown wider. There were few songs about the Old Testament heroes, few songs portraying victory in this world. Ultimate change when it came took place in the future in an otherworldly context. Christ, with His promise of a better tomorrow "sometime, somewhere, someday, somehow," was the dominating figure upon whom Man was almost wholly dependent. No longer were temporal and spatial barriers transcended. This world had to be suffered; one had to take comfort from the blessings one had and from the assurances of the Almighty. The world had become increasingly compartmentalized. Thomas Wentworth Higginson's dictum that black religion exhibited "nothing but patience for this life,—nothing but triumph in the next," was far truer of the gospel songs than it had ever been of the spirituals. The sacred world of the antebellum slaves had been diluted if not dissolved. The literacy, the education, the conditions of the outside world had brought with them a cosmology more familiar to modern Western culture.

Gospel songs, of course, no less than the spirituals that preceded them, were more than collections of verbalized ideas and attitudes. As important as the lyrics were, to leave our discussion there without some consideration of the nature of the music and the mode of performance would lose the essence and distort the experience of gospel song. Consideration of these matters necessitates a brief discussion of the relationship between sacred and secular music after slavery. Though the slaves' blurred lines between sacred and secular song persisted after emancipation, as I have shown, the decline of the sacred world view inevitably created increasingly rigid distinctions among large numbers of black religious folk. In the early 1870s Helen Ludlow asked Harry Jarvis, a forty-year-old exslave and one-armed veteran of the Civil War, if he would sing some songs other than spirituals—songs he had used to accompany himself at work. His reply was to become familiar to scores of folklorists in the ensuing decades: "Not o' dem corn shuckin' songs, madam. Neber sung none o' dem sence I 'sperienced religion. Dem's wickid songs.... Nuffin's good dat ain't religious, madam. Nobody sings dem cornshuckin' songs arter dey's done got religion."[11]

The young William Handy discovered the force of these distinctions in the 1880s when he saved his money and bought himself a cheap guitar. Though his father, an Alabama minister, had sent him for organ lessons, his tolerance ended at the sight of the stringed instrument. "A box," he roared. "A guitar! One of the devil's playthings. Take it away. Take it away, I tell you. Get it out of your hands. Whatever possessed you to bring a sinful thing like that into our Christian home? Take it back where it came from." Handy's ambitions were similarly dampened at school when he told his teacher he wanted to be a musician. Musicians, the latter informed him coldly, were idlers, dissipated characters, whisky drinkers, rounders, social pariahs. Southern white gentlemen—who should serve as the youngster's models—looked upon music as a parlor accomplishment, not as a way of life. That evening his father told him: "Son, I'd rather see you in a hearse. I'd rather follow you to the graveyard than to hear that you had become a musician." When he arrived to sing with the church choir with his violin or cornet under his arm, Handy was convinced he heard one of the old sisters whisper: "Yonder goes de devil."[12]

This combination of religious and social resistance was to plague another black youngster, William Henry Joseph Bonaparte Bertholoff Smith, who, as Willie the Lion Smith, was to become an important jazz pianist. Smith had first learned music at the turn of the century by hearing his mother play the piano and organ in church and then broadened his education by listening to streetcorner quartets and frequenting the local saloons, dance halls, and theaters. When his mother finally bought a piano so her son could practice, he attempted to amalgamate the two styles. After listening to his mother play the familiar hymns he would tell her: "That's all right, but it can be beautified," and then would sit down and play *Sweet and Low* to a ragtime beat: "She actually would run me away from the piano when I'd play a blues or make the tunes she enjoyed playing into ragtime," Smith recalled.

> Back in those early days churchgoing Negro people would not stand for ragtime playing; they considered it to be sinful. Part of that feeling was due to the fact that the popular songs you heard played around in the saloons had bawdy lyrics and when you played in a raggy style, folks would right away think of the bad words and all the hell-raising they heard, or had heard about, in the red-light district.
> Yeah, in the front parlor, where the neighbors could hear your playing, you had to sing the proper religious words and keep that lilting tempo down![13]

These attitudes lived on well into the twentieth century. In 1933, John Lomax asked a cotton picker in Texas to sing the ballad of the boll weevil and was told: "Boss, dat a reel. If you wants to get dat song sung, you'll have to git one of dese worl'ly niggers to sing it. I belongs to de church." Lomax was in a better position to get his way when he asked a prisoner in the Nashville State Penitentiary to sing a levee camp holler. The prisoner, known as Black Samson, refused, explaining that as a Hard-Shell Baptist he would be in danger of hell-fire if he sang such a song. With the insensitivity that too frequently characterized the folklorists of the period, Lomax persisted, but the prisoner continued to refuse even when the white chaplain promised he would make it all right with the Lord. He gave in only when the warden, in Lomax's words, "especially urged him to sing." Even then he manifested his uneasiness by prefacing the song he sang into Lomax's recording equipment with a protest: "It's sho hard lines dat a poor nigger's got to sing a wor'ly song, when he's tryin' to be sancrified; but de warden's ast me, so I guess I'll have to."[14] As late as 1937, when the Reverend Zema Hill of Nashville's Primitive Baptist Church organized a choir and added to it a "rhythmic piano," he was accused of heresy.[15]

It was within this context of a sharpening dichotomy between sacred and secular music that black gospel song developed. No matter how seriously many church folk took the distinctions between these two large genres of black song, the barriers were never complete. One has only to examine the recorded music of the 1920s and 1930s to see how permeable they were in terms of musical style. It was not uncommon during these decades for such blues singers as Charley Patton, Blind Willie McTell, Barbecue Bob, and Blind Lemon Jefferson to record religious songs as well as blues. Thus Patton did not find it incongruous to record blues with such suggestive lines as:

> You can shake it, you can break it, you can hang it on the wall,
> Throw it out the winder, catch it 'fore it falls, . . .
> My jelly, my roll, sweet mama don't you let it fall.

at the same time that he recorded fourteen sides of such religious songs as:

> Some day, some happy day, crying praise, praise be.
> I'll live with Christ for ages, some day.[16]

Accompanying themselves on the guitar, the style these singers brought to both types of music was often indistinguishable. Conversely, the recordings of such sacred singers as Arizona Dranes and Blind Willie Johnson and such groups as the Cotton Top Mountain Sanctified Singers and the Memphis Sanctified Singers were commonly marked by the rocking, driving beat that characterized the blues and jazz of the period. Recording for a black audience, they made no concessions to the "developed" singing of the jubilee songs as they cried out in harsh, urgent, unpolished tones: "Sweet Heaven is my home," "Trouble will soon be over," "I know I got religion and I ain't ashamed," "God don't never change," "I know His blood can make me whole," "Ain't it grand to be a Christian," incorporating all of the musical influences and sounds they had grown up with.[17]

Within the church these amalgamated sounds first became prominent in the Holiness and Spiritualist sects that developed at the turn of the century. While many churches within the black community sought respectability by turning their backs on the past, banning the shout, discouraging enthusiastic religion, and adopting more sedate hymns and refined, concertized versions of the spirituals, the Holiness churches constituted a revitalization movement with their emphasis upon healing, gifts of prophecy, speaking in tongues, spirit possession, and religious dance. Musically, they reached back to the traditions of the slave past and out to the rhythms of the secular black musical world around them. They brought into the church not only the sounds of ragtime, blues, and jazz but also the instruments. They accompanied the singing which played a central role in their services with drums, tambourines, triangles, guitars, double basses, saxophones, trumpets, trombones, and whatever else seemed musically appropriate. The spirit of their music was summed up years later by a church patriarch who paraphrased Martin Luther: "The devil should not be allowed to keep all this good rhythm."[18]

That the Devil was not allowed to is attested to by many contemporary black observers. In Chicago around the time of World War I, Langston Hughes, then still in his teens, encountered the music of the Holiness churches for the first time: "I was entranced by their stepped-up rhythms, tambourines, hand clapping, and uninhibited dynamics, rivaled only by Ma Rainey singing the blues at the old Monogram Theater. . . . The music of these less formal Negro churches early took hold of me, moved me and thrilled me."[19] The jazz bassist Pops Foster found musical inspiration in the Holiness churches: "Their music was something. They'd clap their hands and bang a tambourine and sing. Sometimes they had a piano player, and he'd really play a whole lot of jazz. . . . The first time I heard one of their bands was about 1930 in Washington, D.C. We used to hurry to finish our theater job so we could go listen to them play. They really played some great jazz on those hymns they played."[20] The blues singer T-Bone Walker had a similar experience: "The first time I ever heard a boogie-woogie piano was the first time I went to church. That was the Holy Ghost Church in Dallas, Texas. That boogie-woogie was a kind of blues, I guess. Then the preacher used to preach in a bluesy tone sometimes. You even got the congregation yelling 'Amen' all the time when his preaching would stir them up—his preaching and his bluesy tone."[21] During the 1930s Zora Neale Hurston, collecting folklore for the WPA in Florida, reported: "In Jacksonville there is a jazz pianist who seldom has a free night; nearly as much of his business comes from playing for 'Sanctified' church services as for parties. Standing outside of the church, it is difficult to determine just which kind of engagement he is filling at the moment."[22] The clarinetist Garvin Bushell, speaking of the jazz scene in New York City when he arrived there in 1919, also testified to the musical interaction with the church: "They sang the blues in church; the words were religious, but it was the blues. They often had a drummer and a trumpet player."[23]

The music of the early Holiness churches comprised a wide variety of traditional and newly created songs, including a group of songs written by a Philadelphia Methodist, C. H. Tindley, during the first decade of this century. Neither spirituals nor hymns, Tindley's creations were prototypes of the gospel songs of the post–World War I years:

> When the storms of life are raging, stand by me,
> When the storms of life are raging, stand by me,
> When the world is tossing me,
> Like a ship upon the sea,
> Thou who rulest wind and water, stand by me.[24]

The music of the Holiness churches first penetrated the established denominations through the storefront Baptist and Methodist churches that grew rapidly in the urban centers whose black migrants found the older and larger churches unresponsive to their needs. The development of black gospel music can be understood by looking briefly at the careers of two of its leading early practitioners: Thomas A. Dorsey and Mahalia Jackson.

The son of a Baptist minister, Thomas A. Dorsey was born in Georgia in 1899. Musically precocious, he mastered several instruments by the time he was in his teens and played and sang in the dance halls, theaters, and house parties in and around Atlanta as well as in the church. After World War I he migrated North, settling eventually in Chicago, which he was to help make the mecca of gospel music. Inspired by Tindley's music, he began to write gospel songs early in the 1920s, but throughout that decade he pursued a successful career as a blues musician as well. Known as "Georgia Tom," he was the piano accompanist for the Classic Blues singer Ma Rainey for several years and wrote, according to his own account, some two hundred blues and other secular songs. In 1928, just two years after composing what was to become his first successful gospel song, *If You See My Saviour, Tell Him That You Saw Me*, he wrote his most popular and lucrative secular song. Together with Tampa Red, he published and recorded *It's Tight Like That*, a song whose sexually charged lyrics helped to sell almost a million recordings and were to return to haunt Dorsey in his later years:

> Now the girl I love is long and slim,
> When she gets it it's too bad, Jim.
> It's tight like that, beedle um bum,
> It's tight like that, beedle um bum,
> Hear me talkin' to you, it's tight like that.

Dorsey's success in the church took a bit longer. For years he printed his religious songs on single sheets in the traditional manner and sold them himself for fifteen cents a copy in the face of a church leadership which found his style of music anathema. "Many are the times I walked from church to church seeking a chance to introduce my songs, my feet soaked from snow, sleet and rain." His first break-through came at the National (Negro) Baptist Convention in 1930. His gospel song, *If You See My Saviour*, was performed and swept the convention, leading to orders from black Baptist churches throughout the nation. From that time Dorsey devoted himself to gospel music, composing over four hundred songs. So prolific was he that among church people gospel songs were often referred to as "Dorseys." He solidified his success in 1932 with his most famous gospel song, *Precious Lord*, which ultimately was translated into thirty-two languages. Dorsey's description of how he composed that song is similar to the slaves' insistence that their spirituals were inspired by visions: "De Holy Spirit done revealed 'em." A week after the death of his wife and infant son, he sat before a piano seeking consolation: "There in my solitude, I began to browse over the keys like a gentle herd pasturing on tender turf. Something happened to me there. I had a strange feeling inside. A sudden calm—a quiet stillness. As my fingers began to manipulate over keys, words began to fall in place on the melody like drops of water falling from the crevices of a rock:

Precious Lord take my hand,
Lead me on, let me stand,
I am tired, I am weak, I am worn.
Through the storm, through the night,
Lead me on to the light,
Take my hand precious Lord, lead me home."

Though Dorsey abandoned the world of blues after 1929, the blues did not abandon him, as he admitted in later years: "Blues is a part of me, the way I play piano, the way I write." "I was a blues singer, and I carried that with me into the gospel songs." "I started putting a little of the beat into gospel that we had in jazz. I also put in what we called the riff, or repetitive (rhythmic) phrases. These songs sold three times as fast as those that went straight along on the paper without riffs or repetition." If his music came from the entire black world around him, his lyrics came from the hope of the Christian message, and it is not a coincidence that his first great successes came during the Great Depression. "I wrote to give them something to lift them out of that Depression. They could sing at church but the singing had no life, no spirit. . . . We intended gospel to strike a happy medium for the downtrodden. This music lifted people out of the muck and mire of poverty and loneliness, of being broke, and gave them some kind of hope anyway. Make it anything but good news, it ceases to be gospel."[25]

What Dorsey was to gospel composition Mahalia Jackson was to its performance. Born into a devout Baptist family in 1911, she spent the first sixteen years of her life in New Orleans absorbing the musical sounds of her family's church, the local brass bands, Dixieland jazz, and the blues—especially the records of Bessie Smith, which her worldly cousin Fred brought into the house and which she listened to when no one was at home. She was particularly impressed by the music of the Sanctified church next door to her home, which she contrasted with the "sweet" singing of her own Baptist church: "Those people had no choir and no organ. They used the drum, the cymbal, the tambourine, and the steel triangle. Everybody in there sang and they clapped and stomped their feet and sang with their whole bodies. They had a beat, a powerful beat, a rhythm we held on to from slavery days, and their music was so strong and expressive it used to bring the tears to my eyes." All of these sounds blended into the music she brought with her when she migrated to Chicago in 1928. She experienced the same opposition to her style of gospel singing that Dorsey had: "In those days the big colored churches didn't want me and they didn't let me in. I had to make it my business to pack the little basement-hall congregations and store-front churches and get their respect that way. When they began to see the crowds I drew, the big churches began to sit up and take notice."

Again and again Jackson had to resist attempts to change her singing style. In 1932, a Negro music teacher she consulted stopped her in the midst of her rendition of the spiritual *Standing in the Need of Prayer* and told her to stop hollering: "The way you sing is not a credit to the Negro race. You've got to learn to sing songs so that white people can understand them." Thirty years later she still recalled her reaction vividly: "I felt all mixed up. How could I sing songs for white people to understand when I was colored myself? It didn't seem to make any sense. It was a battle within me to sing a song in a formal way. I felt it was too polished and I didn't feel good about it. I handed over my four dollars to the Professor and left." It was her first and last music lesson. But it was hardly her last criticism. On one occasion a minister rose after she had finished singing and denounced her from the pulpit for lacking dignity. Her response to denunciations of her rocking, swaying rhythm, her shouting, her use of her hands, her feet, her hips, her entire body while singing was always the same: "I had been reading the Bible every day most of my life and there was a Psalm that said: 'Oh, clap your hands, all ye people! Shout unto the Lord with the voice of a trumpet!' If it was undignified, it was what the Bible told me to do. . . . How can you sing of Amazing Grace? How can you sing prayerfully of heaven and earth and all God's wonders without using your hands? I want my hands, . . . my feet . . . my whole body to say all that is in me. I say, 'Don't let the devil steal the beat from the Lord! The Lord doesn't like us to act dead. If you feel it, tap your feet a little—dance to the glory of the Lord.' "[26]

It was a reaction common to the gospel singers of the period. "I'll sing with my hands, with my feet," Willie Mae Ford Smith declared, "—when I got saved, my feet got saved too—I believe we should use everything we got."[27] "Don't let the movement go out of the music," Thomas A. Dorsey warned. "Black music calls for movement! It calls for feeling. Don't let it get away."[28] Many black churchgoers agreed with these exhortations. Anna Wilson of Rosedale, Mississippi, was convinced that only a shouting religion could command the attention of the Lord: "Ef you doan' stamp in de 'ligion hit woan' git no further dan de ceilin'."[29] For many it was this quality that marked the difference between black religion and the more staid practices of the whites. "I stays independent of what white folks tells me when I shouts," Anderson Jackson of South Carolina affirmed. "De Spirit moves me every day, dat's how I stays in. White folks don't feel sich as I does."[30]

Members of the Sanctified churches in Florida felt that whites were ridiculous figures in church, Zora Neale Hurston reported in the 1930s. Negro ministers who emulated the pulpit style of their white colleagues were the objects of derision: "Why he don't preach at all. He just lectures." "Why, he sound like a white man preaching."[31] The superiority of black religious practices was underscored in a number of jokes. One told of a black man on his death bed who, although he had never been a churchgoer, requests that a preacher be sent for. His wife who was a Catholic calls in her priest. Focusing on the white skin of the cleric as he enters the room, the sick man cries out in anguish: "I don't want him. I need a real preacher, honey. I'm dying."[32] The white evangelist Sam Jones was the subject of a widely told anecdote that made the same point. After delivering a sermon to a large gathering of Negroes, Jones was approached by an old woman, who shook his hand vigorously and exclaimed: "Gawd bless you, Brudder Jones. You is everybody's preacher, black as well as white! You may have a white skin, Brudder, but you is sho got a black heart."[33] From the time it was first collected in 1909, through the Great Depression, Negroes in the South sang variants of the lines:

> White man go tuh meetin'.
>   Can't get up a smile;
> Nigger go tuh meetin'.
>   Boys, yuh hyeuh him shout a mile.[34]

Mahalia Jackson's insistence upon uninhibited religion, then, reflected a commonly held attitude among the black folk. Jackson's un-self-conscious musical and kinetic style, her interpolated cries of "Lord," "Lord have mercy," "My Lord," "Well, well, well," "Yeah, yeah, yeah," her interaction with her audiences—"sometimes I get right down off the stage on my knees and sing with the folks"—prompted Robert

Anderson, one of her fellow gospel singers, to comment: "Mahalia took the people back to slavery times."[35] Dorsey, Jackson, and the many talented gospel singers and composers around them revitalized black religious music by extending the developments that had taken place within the Holiness churches to the more established Negro denominations. They helped bring back into black church music the sounds and the structure of the folk spirituals, work songs, and nineteenth-century cries and hollers; they borrowed freely from the ragtime, blues, and jazz of the secular black world; they helped to keep alive the stylistic continuum that has characterized African American music in the United States. Put simply, the antebellum songs of the praise house and field strongly influenced in the work songs, blues, and jazz of the postbellum years which were incorporated into the gospel song that in turn helped to shape the secular rhythm and blues, jazz, and soul music of the post–World War II era. All of the developments that have marked black music since the antebellum era took place within the context of a traditional African American musical matrix. Increasingly, as John Szwed has suggested, social function alone became the primary means of distinguishing one black musical genre from another.[36]

To say this is not to deny that black gospel style and performance differed in important ways from that of the slave spirituals. There was, to begin with, the matter of composition. Where spirituals were created and disseminated in folk fashion, gospel music was composed, published, copyrighted, and sold by professionals. Nevertheless, improvisation remained central to gospel music. One has only to listen to the recorded repertory of gospel song to realize that gospel singers rarely sang a song precisely the same way twice and never sang it according to its exact musical notation. Each rendition was a new creation. Gospel singers produced what jazz musicians referred to as "head arrangements" proceeding from their own feelings, from the way in which "the spirit" moved them at the time. This improvisatory element was reflected in the manner in which gospel music was published. In 1956 Kenneth Morris, one of the leading composers and publishers of black gospel music, told an interviewer:

> We don't write it too difficult by including all of the harmony. The people who play it are not interested in harmony. There is no attempt to include perfect cadences and the like. It's not written for trained musicians. . . . A musician is a slave to notes. It's not written for that kind of person. It's written for a person who can get the melody and words and interpret the song for himself. We give only the basic idea and the person suits his own concept. If it were written correctly, we would go out of business. They wouldn't buy it.[37]

Black gospel composers scored the music intended for white consumption fully, indicating the various vocal parts—soprano, alto, tenor, and bass—and the accompaniment, while the music produced for the Negro market included only the minimum ingredients of a vocal line and piano accompaniment. Dorsey estimated that some 60 percent of his sheet music was purchased by whites. "Negroes don't buy much music," he explained. "A white chorus of one hundred voices will buy one hundred copies of a song. A Negro chorus of the same size will buy two. One for the director and one for the pianist."[38] Most of Dorsey's published sheet music includes the admonition: "Do not print ballads of these songs—Penalty," reflecting the fact that formal publishing and copyrights did not end the Negro practice of circulating new songs in cheaply printed single-sheet versions. That these sheets or "ballits" included only the words and not the music is a further indication of the improvisation characterizing black gospel singing.

A more important distinction between gospel music and spirituals is that the former increased the distance between performer and audience. Where slave spirituals were almost always performed antiphonally by the entire congregation, gospel music was frequently marked by solo and choir singing with the majority of the congregation in the role of audience—a role that did not really exist in slave religious music. This development is undeniably important and again manifests a strong degree of acculturation, yet it needs to be examined more closely. Even in the setting which most clearly distinguished between the singers and their audience—that of the gospel concert in a theater—the audience participated in the music in terms of motor behavior—nodding, tapping, clapping, bodily movement, and dancing in the aisles—and commonly shouted assents and comments. In both the theater and the church, gospel singers reached out to their listeners in a dialogue that embraced familiar topics of concern and reminded everyone present of their roots. Thus, the lead singer for the Pilgrim Jubilee Singers would tell his listeners between numbers: "You know I didn't always come from Chicago. Didn't always have it easy. My brothers and I grew up in a little three-room shack in Houston, Mississippi. We didn't have much back then, church, but we had a family altar. Aw, you all don't know what I'm talking about. . . ." The latter phrase, commonly used in sermons by black preachers, was, of course, a signal to the audience to demonstrate that indeed they did know. Similarly, Sister Rosetta Tharpe would introduce her songs by speaking of her youth in Cotton Plant, Arkansas: "I remember when I was a girl, how much love we had. Why, I used to be busy all day, carrying Aunt Lucy and Aunt Jane some po'k chops. You can't get them fresh no more, now they put them in the deep freeze and *embalm* them for months and months. Seems to me, church, the sweetness has gone out of the land."

This dialogue often included specific remembrances of baptisms and conversions— "I got my religion one Tuesday evening in the clay hills of Alabama,"—and such nostalgic songs as Rosetta Tharpe's *Bring Back these those Happy Days*:

> We healed the sick, we cared for the poor,
>   And we even raised the dead
> We greeted each other with a holy kiss,
>   Lord bring back those happy days.

In this manner gospel singers invoked a strong sense of communality and helped to perpetuate tradition among a people who had recently uprooted themselves in pursuit of a dream which, in the disillusioning years of post–World War I race riots, lynchings, and discrimination and the poverty of the Great Depression, seemed increasingly hollow.[39]

NOTES

1. Unless otherwise noted, the gospel music used in this discussion can be found in the extensive collection of gospel sheet music in the Music Division of the Library of Congress.

2. Mahalia Jackson, *Movin' On Up* (New York, 1966), 72.

3. Thomas Dorsey, *Jesus Lives in Me*, copyright 1937, Thomas Dorsey.

4. WPA manuscripts, South Carolina File, Archive of Folk Song.

5. Alex Bradford, *He Makes All My Decisions For Me*, copyright 1959, Martin and Morris.

6. Alex Bradford, *My Reward Is in Heaven*, copyright 1953, Martin and Morris.

7. Tony Heilbut, *The Gospel Sound* (New York, 1971), 13, 323.

8. WPA manuscripts, Florida File, Archive of Folk Song.

9. Thomas Dorsey, *I Don't Know Why I Have To Cry Sometime*, copyright 1942, T. A. Dorsey Publishing Co.

10. Thomas A. Dorsey, *Life Can Be Beautiful*, copyright 1940, T. A. Dorsey Publishing Co.

11. Mary Frances Armstrong and Helen W. Ludlow, *Hampton and Its Students, by two of its teachers, Mrs. M. F. Armstrong and Helen W. Ludlow; with Fifty Cabin and Plantation songs, arranged by Thomas P. Fenner* (New York: Putnam's Sons, ©1874), 113.

12. W. C. Handy, *Father of the Blues: An Autobiography* (1941; Collier Book ed., 1970), 5, 9–13, 134.

13. Willie the Lion Smith, *Music on My Mind: The Memoirs of an American Pianist* (London, 1965), 25–26.

14. John A. Lomax, "Sinful Songs of the Southern Negro," *Musical Quarterly*, 20 (1934), 181; John and Alan Lomax, *American Ballads*, 49.

15. John W. Work, "Changing Patterns in Negro Folk Songs," *JAF*, 62 (1949), 138–39.

16. John Aloysius Fahey, *A Textual and Musicological Analysis of the Repertoire of Charley Patton* (unpublished M.A. thesis, University of California, Los Angeles, 1966), 88, 148; Paul Oliver, *Aspects of the Blues Tradition* (New York, 1970), 199; Robert M. W. Dixon and John Godrich, *Recording the Blues* (New York, 1970), 57–58; Roots Recording, RL-304.

17. Examples of their music can be found on the following recordings: Roots, RL-304 and RL-328; Historical, HLP-34; RBF 10; Atlantic 1351.

18. Work, *JAF*, 62 (1949), 140.

19. Langston Hughes, "Gospel Singing," newspaper clipping dated Oct. 27, 1963, in Music Division, Library of Congress.

20. *Pops Foster: The Autobiography of a New Orleans Jazzman*, as told to Tom Stoddard (Berkeley, 1971), 20–21.

21. Nat Shapiro and Nat Hentoff, eds., *Hear Me Talkin' to Ya: The Story of Jazz by the Men Who Made It* (Penguin Books ed., 1962), 247.

22. WPA manuscripts, Florida File, Archive of Folk Song.

23. Nat Hentoff, "Jazz in the Twenties: Garvin Bushell," in Martin Williams, ed., *Jazz Panorama: From the Pages of the Jazz Review* (New York, 1964), 76.

24. Heilbut, *Gospel Sound*, 60.

25. This account of Dorsey's career was derived from the following: Thomas A. Dorsey, "The Precious Lord Story and Gospel Songs," mimeographed ms. in Music Division, Library of Congress; Thomas A. Dorsey, "Gospel Music," in Dominique-René de Lerma, ed., *Reflections on Afro-American Music* (1973), 189–95; Hollie I. West, "The Man Who Started the Gospel Business," newspaper clipping dated Dec. 7, 1969, in Music Division, Library of Congress; Heilbut, *Gospel Sound*, Chap. 2; George Robinson Ricks, *Some Aspects of the Religious Music of the United States Negro: An Ethnomusicological Study with Special Emphasis on*

the Gospel Tradition (unpublished Ph.D. dissertation, Northwestern University, 1960), Chap. 4; Eileen Southern, *The Music of Black Americans* (New York, 1971), 402–4; Samuel B. Charters, *The Country Blues* (London, 1960), 92–93. A conveniently available selection of Dorsey's gospel songs can be found on the recently released two-record album, Columbia KG 32151, *Precious Lord: New Recordings of the Great Gospel Songs of Thomas A. Dorsey.*

26. This account of Jackson's career is derived from her autobiography, *Movin' On Up,* passim. Also Heilbut, *Gospel Sound,* Chap. 4. Jackson's singing can be sampled on her many recordings including: Columbia CL 644, *World's Greatest Gospel Singer*; Columbia CL 1643, *Every Time I Feel the Spirit*; Kenwood 474, *In the Upper Room*; Kenwood 486, *Mahalia.*

27. Heilbut, *Gospel Sound,* 224–25.

28. Dorsey, "Gospel Music," in de Lerma, ed., *Reflections on Afro-American Music,* 190–91.

29. Newbell Niles Puckett, "Religious Beliefs of Whites and Negroes," *JNH,* 16 (1931), 26.

30. WPA Slave Narratives (S.C.).

31. WPA manuscripts, Florida File, Archive of Folk Song.

32. Langston Hughes, *The Book of Negro Humor* (New York, 1966), 264.

33. Sterling Brown, "Negro Jokes," unpublished ms.; William Pickens, *American Aesop: Negro and other Humor.* (New York: AMS Press, 1969), 33.

34. E. C. Perrow, "Songs and Rhymes From the South," *JAF,* 28 (1915), 140; Scarborough, *On the Trail,* 168; John A. and Alan Lomax, *Folk Song U.S.A.* (New York, 1947), 337.

35. Mahalia Jackson, *Movin' On Up,* 66; Heilbut, *Gospel Sound,* 94.

36. John F. Szwed, "Negro Music: Urban Renewal," in Tristram P. Coffin, ed., *Our Living Traditions* (New York, 1968), 282.

37. Kenneth Morris, interview with George Robinson Ricks, 1956, in Ricks, *Some Aspects of the Religious Music of the United States Negro,* 143.

38. Thomas A. Dorsey, interview with George Robinson Ricks, 1956, in ibid., 143–44.

39. Heilbut, *Gospel Sound,* 19–20, 216, 231–32.

Right. Bishop C. H. Mason, founder of the Church of God in Christ. Courtesy of *The Whole Truth Magazine. Below.* The church in Lexington, MS, where Bishop Mason pastored. From the Archival Collection of the Institute for Black Religious Research.

Chapter Nineteen

The Black Roots of Pentecostalism

Iain MacRobert

The Pentecostal churches represent one of the more vibrant church movements in the twentieth century. They have garnered millions of adherents across racial and ethnic lines, both across the United States and across many continents. Iain MacRobert offers an examination of the history of the movement and of the instrumental role of African Americans, especially William J. Seymour, in that history.

•

In 1965, at a time when most white American Pentecostal authors had either written William Joseph Seymour and his black prayer group out of their movement's history or trivialized his central role, Walter Hollenweger recognized that:

> The Pentecostal experience of Los Angeles was neither the leading astray of the Church by demons . . . nor the eschatological pouring out of the Holy Spirit (as the Pentecostal movement itself claims) but an outburst of enthusiastic religion of a kind well-known and frequent in the history of Negro churches in America which derived its specifically Pentecostal features from Parham's theory that speaking with tongues is a necessary concomitant of the baptism of the Spirit.[1]

The historical origins of Pentecostalism in the United States lie primarily in the Wesleyan-Holiness, Keswick and Higher Life Movements, and in the black American church.[2] While the white influences on the early Pentecostal Movement have been recognized by Pentecostal historians, they have often disparaged and sometimes completely ignored the crucial influences of African American Christianity. White pioneers and early leaders like Charles Fox Parham or Ambrose Jessup Tomlinson have been recognized—even eulogized—whereas Seymour, one of the most influential of the pioneers, has generally been marginalized and his important role even denied by the myth of no human leadership, and this in spite of the recognition accorded him by such diverse people as Frank Bartleman in the United States, Alexander A. Boddy in Britain, and G. R. Polman in the Netherlands.[3] Parham may have been accused of homosexuality and Tomlinson of financial mismanagement and megalomania, but Seymour was less acceptable to most North American Pentecostal historians than either of them. They were white, he was black.

A more scholarly and rigorous historian, James R. Goff, continues to maintain that "Parham, more than Seymour, must be regarded the founder of the Pentecostal movement," because "it was Parham who first formulated the theological definition of Pentecostalism by linking tongues with the Holy Spirit baptism."[4] For Goff, glossolalia as the initial evidence of Spirit baptism is "the *sine qua non* of the experience" and "the central theological corpus which has always defined the movement."[5] To characterize Pentecostalism in terms of the evidence doctrine is, however, to accept a narrow, inadequate, white, North American definition which is belied, not only by Pentecostals in the two-thirds world, but also by some white classical Pentecostals in Britain, and by many black-majority Pentecostal churches both in Britain and in the United States itself.[6]

Because Pentecostalism is primarily found not on a theological proposition, but on a shared perception of human encounter with the divine, it has roots in many Christian traditions and in a diversity of cultures; but it is first and foremost an experiential rather than a cognitive movement. Goff maintains that "the primacy of theological formulation" labels Parham as chronologically the founder of Pentecostalism.[7] While doctrine was important to some early Pentecostals (though generally less so to black worshipers), all theological formulations were both secondary to their pneumatic experience and, to a greater or lesser extent, inadequate in their attempts to understand or explain the Pentecostal phenomena. The Pentecostal movement did not spread to fifty nations within two years of the Azusa Revival or grow to its current size of some 360 million adherents worldwide as a result of Pentecostal "theology" or Parham's evidence doctrine, although his understanding of tongues as *xenoglossa* did encourage early Pentecostal foreign missions.[8]

The particular attraction of Pentecostalism to people around the world and the ease with which it has been indigenized in non-Western societies lies in its black experiential roots which provide a substratum of enduring values and themes for the bulk of the Movement outside of white North America and Europe.

One historian who has taken Seymour's role seriously is the Methodist clergyman, Douglas J. Nelson. In 1981, Nelson completed his thesis—under Hollenweger's supervision—on "The Story of Bishop William J. Seymour and the Azusa Street Revival."[9] His historical and biographical research made Seymour's crucial role clear. Seymour, however, was not simply an American with a black skin. Nor was his socialization solely determined by his negative encounters with the aftermath of American slavery and enduring discrimination and racism. Seymour and the other black worshippers who brought to birth the Azusa Street revival and the worldwide Pentecostal Movement which flowed from it shared an understanding and practice of Christianity had developed in the African diaspora out of a syncretism of West African primal religion and culture with Western Christianity in the crucible of New World slavery.

African Roots and the Black Leitmotif

Africans, brought as slaves to the Americas, did not arrive *tabula rasa* nor did forced acculturation totally eradicate their primal religious beliefs. On the contrary, both in Africa and in the Americas, these preliterate beliefs were transmitted from generation to generation by oral tradition and symbolism. In narratives—myths, legends, and folk tales—songs, parables, and other aphorisms, ritual, drama, dance, and the rhythms and tones of "talking" drums, African religious ideas were preserved to be syncretized with the Christianity of white America and thus produce a distinctively black form of Christianity. Albert J. Raboteau has well summarized this process:

> Shaped and modified by a new environment, elements of African folklore, music, language, and religion were transplanted to the New World by the African diaspora. . . . One of the most durable and adaptable constituents of the slave's culture, linking African past with American present, was his religion. It is important to realise, however, that in the Americas the religions of Africa have not been merely preserved as static "Africanisms" or as archaic "retentions" . . . African styles of worship, forms of ritual, systems of belief, and fundamental perspectives have remained vital on this side of the Atlantic, not because they were preserved in a "pure" orthodoxy but because they were transformed. Adaptability, based upon respect for spiritual power wherever it originated, accounted for the openness of African religions to syncretism with other religious traditions and for the continuity of a distinctively African religious consciousness.[10]

The primal religious beliefs brought from Africa with the diaspora included a powerful sense of the importance of community in establishing and maintaining both the personhood of individuals and an experiential relationship with the spirit world of ancestors and divinities. They inhabited a world in which the sacred and profane were integrated and the ability to tap into the *force vitale* by means of divination and spirit possession was considered essential to the welfare of the community, the wholeness of the individual, and the success of any major undertaking in the material world.[11]

To attune themselves to the power of the spirits, both in Africa and in the New World, they used rhythm and music. Polyrhythmic drumming, singing, dancing, and other motor behavior opened up the devotee to spirit possession. In Africa, these were understood as the spirits of the ancestors and divinities. In the Americas new understandings grew out of the pragmatic syncretism of their primal religion with Western Christianity. The possessing spirits of Africa became identified with the apostles, prophets, saints, angels, and Holy Spirit of the white missionaries but phenomenologically there was considerable continuity.[12]

In spite of missionary attempts to demythologize the perceptions of slaves, literacy brought them into contact with the world of the Bible which, like their own, was concerned with the relationship between the spiritual and the natural. The biblical accounts of miracles, healings, exorcisms, spiritual power, and the presence of the Holy Spirit in peoples' lives did not seem so different from their own experiential ancestral religion. Furthermore, their identification with the story of Israel's bondage in Egypt and their subsequent Exodus to the promised land meant that freedom was understood as more than liberation from the power and consequences of personal sin. An African concept of sin as antisocial activities was reflected in an understanding of the work of the devil as predominantly in the concrete realities of enslavement. The Lord of Hosts who delivered his people from Pharoah's oppression was the God of liberation from political and social evil.[13]

The adventism of evangelical revivalism was also particularly attractive to black Christians for it proclaimed an apocalyptic revolution to be inaugurated by the Second Coming of Christ. The high, the mighty, and the oppressor were to be put down, while the humble, the powerless, and the oppressed—the Saints—were to be exalted. This eschatological status-reversal was believed to be immanent. Thus, the black church in the Americas embraced an inaugurated eschatology that was congruent with an African sense of the future which is so close that it has almost arrived. And if at any moment they were to put on their golden slippers "to walk the golden streets" it was because—in spite of their bondage and subhuman status—they were the children of God now! Others were inspired by the scriptures and their Christian faith to plan insurrections during Sunday services and other ostensibly religious gatherings.[14]

The revivalism of the late eighteenth and early nineteenth centuries attracted black people because it stressed an experiential conversion of the heart rather than an intellectual or catechetical religion. "The powerful emotionalism, ecstatic behavior, and congregational responses of the revival," writes Raboteau, "were amenable to the African religious heritage of the slaves, and forms of African dance and song remained in the shout and the spirituals of Afro-American converts to evangelical Protestantism." "In addition," continues Rabateau, "the slaves' rich heritage of folk belief and folk expression was not destroyed but was augmented by conversion."[15]

Thus, much of the primal religion of West Africa was syncretized with Western Christianity and, in particular, with those themes were of primary importance to the survival and ultimately the liberation of an oppressed people. Certain leitmotifs which echo both their African origins and their sojourn in the "Egypt" of chattel slavery surface again and again in the black church of the Americas. An integrated holistic world view, the immanence of the divine, belief in spirit possession, spirit healing and spirit power, the importance of dreams and trances, the extensive use of rhythm, certain types of motor behavior, antiphonal participation in worship, baptism (immersion) in water, and the centrality of community all had African antecedents and reemerged during the revivalist camp meetings of the eighteenth and nineteenth centuries where they also influenced whites.[16]

Other leitmotifs of white evangelical or biblical origin became particularly important in the black Christian community: the imminent Parousia, an inaugurated eschatology, and an "Exodus" theology which perceives freedom in sociopolitical as well as spiritual terms. These leitmotifs were expressed, not in systematic propositions but in the oral, narrative, sung, and danced liturgy and theology of the black Christian community.[17]

By the beginning of the twentieth century, many of the black churches in the United States—particularly in the North—had largely conformed to white, middle-class, conservative evangelicalism. Both the black and white Holiness people—who were mainly proletarian—were dissatisfied with the "deadness" and "worldliness" in many churches and looked for a worldwide revival as the harbinger of the imminent Second Advent of Christ. One such Holiness preacher was William J. Seymour.[18]

William Joseph Seymour and the Azusa Street Revival

Born in the South in 1870, the son of emancipated slaves, Seymour grew up in the midst of violent racism. Nelson writes that during his first twenty-four years of life:

> Seymour receives little or no formal schooling but works hard, educates himself . . . drinks in the invisible institution of black folk Christianity, learns to love the great Negro spirituals, has visions of God, and becomes and earnest student of unfulfilled scriptural prophecy.[19]

That invisible institution of black folk Christianity with its black leitmotif formed the cultural and religious basis for Seymour's subsequent role as the leader of the Azusa Street Revival.

Seymour was "seeking for interracial reconciliation" but was aware that this could only be brought about with the aid of divine power.[20] Leaving the interracial Methodist Episcopal Church, he joined another less bourgeois interracial group, the Evening Light Saints, who taught—in addition to holiness, divine healing, racial equality, and a kind of ecumenism—that a final great outpouring of the Spirit was about to take place before the end of world history. Their holiness doctrine, like that of the rest of the Holiness Movement, was based on a simplistic understanding of Wesley's teaching and stressed that a second crisis experience of entire sanctification should follow conversion. Some, following the teaching of Charles G. Finney, also stressed the social aspects of Wesley's teaching and defined sanctification as a willingness to become involved in social action as an outworking of personal faith and consecration.

After recovering from smallpox, which left him blind in one eye, Seymour was ordained by the Evening Light Saints and, during the summer of 1905, was serving as the pastor of a black Holiness church in Jackson, Mississippi. In October he received reports that glossolalia as an evidence of the power of the Holy Spirit was being experienced at the Bible School of Charles F. Parham in Houston, Texas. While outbursts of glossolalia have recurred again and again throughout the history of the Church from the day of Pentecost to the present, in 1901 Parham was responsible for the teaching that it is both the initial evidence of Spirit baptism and the ability "to preach in any language of the world."[21] While the former tenet has become widely, but by no means universally, accepted by Pentecostals, the latter, like his Anglo-Saxon Israel, antimedicine, and conditional immortality teaching, has been largely rejected.[22]

Seymour enrolled at Parham's Bible School. At nine o'clock each morning, he attended classes "segregated outside the classroom beside the door carefully left ajar by Parham," who "practices strict segregation."[23] Leaving Houston, Seymour traveled to the cosmopolitan city of Los Angeles to become pastor of a small black (Church of the Nazarene) Holiness mission on Santa Fe Street. At nightly meetings he preached on conversion, sanctification, divine healing, and the imminent Second Advent; and on Sunday morning he spoke on glossolalia as a sign accompanying Spirit baptism, and this in spite of the fact he had not yet spoken in tongues himself. Returning to the mission for the evening service, he found the doors locked against him. He lived and worshipped in the home of Edward S. Lee and his wife and later with Richard and Ruth Asbury. Both couples were black. On Friday the sixth of April, Seymour and a small group began a ten-day fast. Three days later Lee asked Seymour to pray for his recovery from illness. After anointing and prayer, Lee felt better and requested that Seymour pray for him to receive the Holy Spirit with the evidence of tongues. He was not disappointed.[24]

Later that night in the Ashbury home, a group of black "sanctified wash women" were singing, praying, and testifying. As Seymour rose to preach on *Acts* 2:4, he recounted the events that had taken place earlier that evening but could preach no longer because as soon as he had completed his account of Lee's experience, Lee burst forth in tongues. Nelson describes what followed:

> The entire company was immediately swept to its knees as by some tremendous power. At least seven—and perhaps more—lifted their voices in an awesome harmony of strange new tongues. Jennie Evans Moore, falling to her knees from the piano seat, became the first woman thus to speak. Some rushed out to the front porch, yard, and street, shouting and speaking in tongues for all the neighborhood to hear. . . . Teenager Bud Traynor stood on the front porch prophesying and preaching. Jennie Evans Moore returned to the piano and began singing in her beautiful voice what was thought to be a series of six languages with interpretations.[25]

Within three days the original all-black group was receiving visits from whites as well as blacks to witness and experience glossolalia, trance, and healing. On the twelfth of April, Seymour spoke in tongues himself.[26]

The revival rapidly outgrew the Asbury home, and a rundown former African Methodist Episcopal chapel was leased at 312 Azusa Street. Cleared of construction materials that had been stored there, sawdust was spread on the dirt floor and pews fabricated from odd chairs, nail kegs, and boxes with planks laid across them. The three services that were conducted each day often overlapped. Some meetings only attracted about a dozen people, but within a month Sunday attendance had risen to 750 or 800 with a further 400 or 500, for whom there was no room, crowding outside.[27] Nelson declares that "multitudes converged on Azusa including virtually every race, nationality, and social class on earth, for Los Angeles contained the world in miniature. . . . Never in history had any such group surged into the church of a black person."[28] Multiracial congregations were unusual. Black leadership of such congregations, while not unheard of, was extremely rare.

Spirit baptism was, for Seymour, more than a glossolalic episode. It was the power to draw all peoples into one Church without racial distinctions or barriers. Seymour's newspaper, *The Apostolic Faith* of September 1906, declared that "multitudes have come. God makes no difference in nationality. Ethiopians, Chinese, Indians, Mexicans, and other nationalities worship together."[29] Black witnesses to those events recalled that "everybody went to the altar together. White and colored, no discrimination seemed to be among them."[30] "Everybody was just the same, it did not matter if you were black, white, green, or grizzly. There was a wonderful spirit. Germans and Jews, black and whites, ate together in the little cottage at the rear. Nobody ever thought of color."[31] White witnesses echoed the same theme: "The color line was washed away in the blood."[32] Visiting from England, the Church of England clergyman, Alexander A. Boddy, recorded that

> It was something very extraordinary, that white pastors from the South were eagerly prepared to go to Los Angeles to the Negroes, to have fellowship with them and to receive through their prayers and intercessions the blessings of the Spirit. And it was still more wonderful that these white pastors went back to the South and reported to the members of their congregations that they had been together with Negroes, that they had prayed in one Spirit and received the same blessings as they.[33]

Within five months of the birth of this Movement, thirty-eight missionaries had gone out from Azusa. In only two years it had spread to over fifty nations worldwide, but the radical challenge to racism was by this time being subverted and rejected by some arrogant and pusillanimous whites. Parham, who propagated the Anglo-Saxon Israel teaching of white supremacy and wrote for the notoriously racist Ku Klux Klan, was horrified at the desegregation and the adoption of black liturgy by whites which had taken place and castigated Azusa for having "blacks and whites mingling" and "laying across one another like hogs."[34] In 1912 he wrote:

> Men and women, whites and blacks, knelt together or fell across one another; frequently, a white woman, perhaps of wealth and culture, could be seen thrown back in the arms of a big "buck nigger," and held tightly thus as she shivered and shook in freak imitation of Pentecost. Horrible, awful shame![35]

Dissociation and Replication

In 1914, the white-dominated Assemblies of God was formed, thus ending, in the words of Vinson Synan, "a notable experiment in interracial church development."[36] Two years later, the "new issue" controversy over the baptismal formula and the nature of the Godhead resulted in the withdrawal of the "Jesus Name" Oneness Pentecostals and the further purging of black people and elements of the black leitmotif from the Assemblies of God. Thus, writes Robert Mapes Anderson, "the Assemblies became an all but 'lily white' denomination . . . Since 1916, except for a few black faces here and there in urban congregations in the Northeast, the Assemblies has remained a white man's church."[37] The moralistic Oneness Pentecostals fared little better. The same desire for white "respectability," racial segregation, and the rejection of the black leitmotif tore them apart so that by 1924 there were separate white and black organizations. When the Pentecostal Fellowship of North America was set up in 1948 with the ostensible purpose of demonstrating to the world the fulfillment of Christ's prayer for Christian—in this case Pentecostal Christian—unity, only white organizations were invited to join. In 1965, having added a further nine organizations to the original eight, it was still exclusively white.[38]

What began in April 1906 as a black revival under Seymour's leadership incorporated the leitmotif of black Christianity in the Americas and Parham's distinctive doctrine of glossolalia as an evidence of Spirit baptism and the instrument of world evangelization. Almost immediately it became interracial and spread at a phenomenal rate, both in the United States and throughout the world. White Pentecostals in the United States, however, exploited doctrinal disagreements to dissociate themselves from their black brethren, to distance themselves from the black origins of the Movement, and to purge it of its more obviously black and radical elements which, however, re-emerge again and again wherever Pentecostals of the African diaspora meet for worship.

In Britain, for example, the black Pentecostal congregations that have been established by settlers from the Caribbean from the early 1950s, fall into three broad categories. Those that are part of the white-dominated, three-stage, Trinitarian organizations in the United States, like the Church of God (Cleveland) [known in Britain as the New Testament Church of God] and the Church of God of Prophecy, or the white-dominated, moralistic United Pentecostal Church, tend to be culturally ambivalent and there is often considerable tension between white-defined fundamentalist "orthodoxy" and "orthopraxis" and the black leitmotif which can never be totally stifled. Other three-stage, Trinitarian, "Church of God" type congregations have broken free from white headquarters in the United States and are significantly more "black" in their beliefs, liturgy, and practice. But the congregations that demonstrate the most overt commitment to the black leitmotif tend to be the Oneness groups with black headquarters in the United States or the Caribbean which pre-date the West Indian migrations of the late 1940s and early '50s.

These groups continue to pulsate most clearly with the liturgical characteristics of the Azusa Revival:[39] orality, narrativity, dance, and liturgical motor behavior with the extensive use of music and rhythm; an integrated and holistic world view incorporating Spirit possession[40] and trances; the importance of dreams, healing, and the need for spiritual power to change the material (and social) world; the importance of community and human relationships—including the abolition of the color line—if life and religion are to be worthwhile; freedom as a sociopolitical as well as a spiritual issue; the imminence of a revolutionary world order inaugurated by the Second Advent of Christ, which is already to some extent present in an inaugurated eschatology. These themes were all in evidence at Azusa as they had been in the church of the African diaspora in the United States and they are replicated among black Pentecostals in Britain and in the two-thirds world where the overlay of white, North American "orthodoxy" is often quite superficial and in many situations—when the North Americans have gone home—totally absent. Parham's evidence doctrine, while of real importance to most white North American Pentecostals, some European Pentecostals, and a few mission churches, is largely irrelevant to most Pentecostals in the underdeveloped and developing nations and serves only as a redundant symbol of Pentecostal "orthodoxy" for most black Pentecostals in Britain.

Does it Matter?

"Directly or indirectly," writes Synan, "practically all of the Pentecostal groups in existence can trace their lineage to the Azusa Mission."[41] If this is true, then Seymour rather than Parham or Tomlinson is the most significant historical figure in the early Pentecostal Movement. But does it actually matter who the person primarily responsible was: Parham, who taught that glossolalia is the evidence of Spirit baptism and who advocated and practiced racial segregation; Tomlinson, who forbade political involvement and led a racially divided church;[42] or Seymour who, as part of the African diaspora, believed in and lived out a Pentecostal experience with socially revolutionary implications? It matters to many black Pentecostals in the United States, Britain, and South Africa who have to confront the social, economic, and political sins of racism, discrimination, and apartheid.[43] It matters—though they may not realize it—for many white Pentecostals who in the denial of their Movement's roots perpetuate the racial arrogance and support for an oppressive sociopolitical and economic status quo that makes them the enemies of the Gospel to the poor. And it matters so that Pentecostalism does not become—or indeed remain—an individualistic ideology used by the powerful to control the powerless, or an alien ideology internalized by the powerless to control themselves, but returns to its original emphasis on God's pneumatic empowering of the powerless to be agents of transformation in both the Church and the wider society.

NOTES

1. Walter J. Hollenweger, *The Pentecostals* (London: SCM Press, 1972), 23–24; originally in his ten-volume *Handbuch der Pfingstbewegung* (Geneva, 1965–67).

2. See Vinson Synan, *The Holiness-Pentecostal Movement in the United States* (Grand Rapids, Michigan: William B. Eerdmans, 1961), and Vinson Synan (Ed.), *Aspects of Pentecostal-Charismatic Origins* (Plainfield, NJ: Logos International, 1975).

3. Frank Bartleman, *Azusa Street* (Plainfield NJ: Logos International, 1980 [originally 1925]), especially 46; A. A. Boddy in *Confidence* (September 1912); G. R. Polman, letter to G. A. Wumkes, 27th February 1915.

4. James R. Goff, *Fields White Unto Harvest: Charles F. Parham and The Missionary Origins of Pentecostalism* (Fayetteville: University of Arkansas Press, 1988), 11.

5. Ibid.

6. The Elim Pentecostal Church in Britain, following the teaching of George Jeffreys, maintains that any of the gifts of the Spirit are evidence of Spirit baptism. While most of the black Pentecostal organizations have articles of faith—largely inherited from their white co-relgionists—which state their belief in glossolalia as the initial evidence—in practice they are largely ignored and displaced by an implicitly inclusive charismatology.

7. Goff, *Fields White*, 15.

8. Barrett's estimate of 360 million Pentecostals may be a little too high for the narrower definitions of Pentecostalism because it includes traditions that predate both Parham (1901) and Seymour (1906). David B. Barrett, "The Twentieth Century Pentecostal/Charismatic Renewal in the Holy Spirit, with its Goal of World Evangelization" in *International Bulletin of Missionary Research*, Vol. 12, No. 3 (July 1988).

9. Douglas J. Nelson, "For Such Time As This: The Story of Bishop William J. Seymour and the Azusa Street Revival" (unpublished Ph.D. dissertation, University of Birmingham, 1981).

10. Albert J. Raboteau, *Slave Religion: The Invisible Institution in the Antebellum South* (Oxford: Oxford University Press, 1978), 4–5.

11. Iain MacRobert, *The Black Roots and White Racism of Early Pentecostalism in the USA* (Bassingstoke: Macmillan Press, 1988), 9–14.

12. Ibid., 14–15.

13. Ibid., 15–18.

14. Ibid., 20–23, 33–36.

15. Raboteau, *Slave Religion*, 149.

16. Melville J. Herskovitz, *The Myth of the Negro Past* (Boston: Beacon Press, 1958), 227–31.

17. MacRobert, *Black Roots*, 31–34.

18. Ibid., 38–42.

19. Nelson, "For Such Time As This," 31, 153–58.

20. Ibid., 161.

21. Sarah E. Parham (Comp.), *The Life of Charles F. Parham: Founder of the Apostolic Faith Movement* (Joplin, MO: Tri-State Printing Co, 1930), 51–52.

22. On Parham's theories of racial supremacy, see Charles Fox Parham, *A Voice Crying in the Wilderness* (Joplin, MO: Joplin Printing Co, 1944 [originally 1902]), 81–84, 92–100, 105–18; and Charles Fox Parham, *The Everlasting Gospel* (Baxter Springs, KS, 1942), 1–4.

23. Nelson, "For Such Time As This," 35.

24. Ibid., 187–90; MacRobert, *Black Roots*, 51–52.

25. Nelson, "For Such Time As This," 191.

26. Ibid., 191–92.

27. Ibid., 192–94, 196; *The Apostolic Faith* Vol. 1, No. 1 (September 1906), 1, col. 1; Bartleman, *Azusa Street*, 47–48.

28. Nelson, "For Such Time As This," 196.

29. *The Apostolic Faith, op. cit.*, 3, col. 2.

30. Quoted in Synan, *Aspects*, 133.

31. Quoted in Nelson, "For Such Time As This," 234, n. 91.

32. Bartleman, *Azusa Street*, 54.

33. *Confidence* (September 1912).

34. Parham, *Everlasting Gospel*, 1–3.

35. Charles Fox Parham, *Apostolic Faith*, Baster Springs, Kansas (December 1912).

36. Synan, *Holiness-Pentecostal*, 153.

37. Robert Mapes Anderson, "A Social History of the Early Twentieth Century Pentecostal Movement" (Ph.D. Thesis, Columbia University, 1969), 319–20; published in a revised form as *Vision of the Disinherited: The Making of American Pentecostalism* (New York: Oxford University Press, 1979).

38. Synan, *Holiness-Pentecostal*, 179–80.

39. Iain MacRobert, "Black Pentecostalism: Its Origins, Functions and Theology with special reference to a Midland Borough" (unpublished Ph.D. dissertation, University of Birmingham 1989), 39.

40. Even Bartleman, a white Pentecostal pioneer, constantly refers to the baptism with, in, or of the Holy Spirit as "possession." Bartleman, *Azusa Street*, 72 ff.; see also Seymour in *The Apostolic Faith* Vol. 1, No. 4 (December 1906), 1, col. 4.

41. Synan, *Holiness-Pentecostal*, 114.

42. A. J. Tomlinson, *Answering the Call of God*, 9–10, quoted in Lillie Dugger, *A. J. Tomlinson* (Cleveland, TN: White Wing Publishing House, 1964), 21; A. J. Tomlinson, quoted in C. T. Davidson, *Upon This Rock* (Cleveland, TN: White Wing Publishing House and Press, 1973), 437–38, 448, 518, 552–53, 594; "Minutes of 45th Assembly (1950)," quoted in *Church of God of Prophecy Business Guide* (Cleveland, TN: White Wing Publishing House and Press, 1987), 45.

43. See, for example, Nico Horn, "The Experience of the Spirit in Apartheid South Africa" in *Azusa Theological Journal*, Vol. 1, No. 1, Durban, South Africa: Relevant Pentecostal Witness Publications (March 1990), 19–42.

SELECTED BIBLIOGRAPHY FOR FURTHER READING

Cox, Harvey. *Fire From Heaven: The Rise of Pentecostal Spirituality and the Reshaping of Religion in the Twenty-first Century*. Reading, MA.: Addison-Wesley, 1995.

Hurston, Zora Neale. *The Sanctified Church*. Berkeley: Turtle Island, 1981.

Nelson, Douglas J. "For Such a Time As This: The Story of Bishop W. J. Seymour and the Asuza Street Revival." Ph.D. dissertation, University of Birmingham, England, 1981.

Paris, Arthur. *Black Pentecostalism: A Southern Religion in an Urban World*. Amherst: University of Massachusetts Press, 1982.

Tinney, James S. "Exclusivist Tendencies in Pentecostal Self-Definition: A Critique from Black Theology." *The Journal of Religious Thought* 36 (1979): 32–49.

Part V

Expanding the Options
Diversification in African American Religious Expression

Noble Drew Ali, founder of the Moorish Science Temple of America.
From the collection of Sheila Harris-El.

Chapter Twenty

The Second Emergence of Islam

Gordon Melton

Names such as Elijah Muhammad, Malcolm X, and Louis Farrakhan have added a Muslim dimension to the popular picture of African American religiosity, though often this is seen as a recent and statistically unsubstantial, if not also less than fully genuinely Islamic dimension. But as Richard Brent Turner has shown in an earlier piece in this volume, the association of African Americans and Islam has deep roots. And beyond the reality that other particularizations of Islam have long pertained in the Middle East, there is the fact that Elijah Muhammad's son, Wallace Deen Muhammad, heads a predominantly black United States organization of some two million Orthodox Muslims.

Gordon Melton describes how Islam emerged from its relative obscurity to provide for large numbers of African Americans an alternative piety to traditional Judeo-Christianity.

•

The Second Emergence of Islam

Islam began to make a reappearance in the United States in the late nineteenth century with the arrival of individual Muslim immigrants from the Middle East Asia. The first prominent advocate was Alexander Russell Webb, the American consul in the Philippines. Converted during his stay in the Islands, Webb resigned his post and worked his way home by lecturing on his newfound faith. He arrived in Chicago in time to be the only Muslim speaker at the 1893 World's Parliament of Religions that summer.

In the early twentieth century, Islam reappeared within the African American community through several movements which had drawn significant inspiration from Muslim themes. Among the first was the Moorish Science Temple of America founded in 1913 by Noble Drew Ali (1886–1929). Ali developed a myth of the origins of Black people whom he considered Moors whose homeland was Morocco. He claimed that the Moors had been systematically stripped of their identity by Whites during the eighteenth century. Their actions culminated in George Washington's cutting down the cherry tree, their bright red flag, which he had hidden away in

Independence Hall in Philadelphia. During the first decade the Temple spread across the African American communities of the urban North and Midwest.

To Ali, the national religion of Black people was Islam. In 1927, he introduced Temple members to a new volume, *The Holy Koran*, which laid out Ali's beliefs about the origin of Black people and the problems created by their acceptance of Christianity. This *Koran*, however, was not the orthodox Islamic sacred text, the *Qur'an*, but a small book he had put together from, among other sources, *The Aquarian Gospel of Jesus Christ*, a Spiritualist text authored by one Levi Dowling.

Ali was still a relatively young man when he died in 1929. His movement continued (and is still in existence), but had peaked. The thrust initiated by the Temple was picked up within a few months by a former Temple member, Wallace Fard Muhammad. Making his appearance in Detroit, Muhammad claimed to be Noble Drew Ali reincarnated. He claimed that he had come all the way from Mecca, Saudi Arabia, to lead the Black people of America to freedom, justice, and equality. He called his new movement the Nation of Islam.

Fard attracted a small following, among whom was his most capable lieutenant, Elijah Poole, soon reborn as Elijah Muhammad. Like Ali, Wallace F. Muhammad taught a myth to explain the condition of the African American. He attributed it to Yakub, a mad scientist, who created White people. In return, Allah has allowed the White beast to reign for six thousand years, a period which ended in 1914. It was now time for Black people to regroup, reorganize, and regain their ascendant position.

Less heralded, but possibly more successful in its first generation, was the Muslim Mission of America established by Sheikh Daa'wud Faisal in Brooklyn, New York, in 1920. Shaikh Daa'wud moved to the United States from Bermuda in that same wave that brought so many West Indians to the New York area in the early decades of the twentieth century. His more orthodox form of Islam, though later overshadowed by the Nation of Islam, also took root in the African American communities, and mosques were founded across the Eastern half of the United States as far away as Ft. Worth, Texas.

Wallace F. Muhammad sent Elijah Muhammad to Chicago to begin a second temple of the Nation of Islam. After only a brief period, however, Elijah Muhammad was forced to return to Detroit and quiet a disturbance which threatened to split the Temple. In the process he moved his teacher to Chicago and soon emerged as the visible authority. Wallace Muhammad faded into obscurity and to this day his eventual fate is unknown. Elijah Muhammad began the long process of growing a national movement whose time was yet to come.

Meanwhile, among the Asian immigrants to America, a third Islamic movement had appeared. The Ahmadiyya movement had been founded by Hazrat Mirza Ghulam Ahmad in the nineteenth century. From India (present-day Pakistan) Ahmad saw himself as leading a revival of true Islam. Welcomed at first as an energetic teacher of the faith, Ahmad gradually departed from a number of orthodox Muslim teachings. He, for example, taught in contradiction to the *Qur'an* that Jesus had not died on the cross, but had survived his ordeal and retired quietly to India where he lived a long life and where he was eventually buried. More important, he began to assume the prerogatives of the "Madhi," the promised Prophet who would come to revive the faith when it was at a low ebb. In that regard, he seemed to be placing himself in the same level as Muhammad, a position angrily rejected by Muslims.

The followers of Ahmad differed from other Muslims in that they initiated a mission to proselytize Europe and North America. Thus, while orthodox Muslims were moving to the American Midwest and creating cultural ghettos, the Ahmadiyyas sent missionaries. The first to arrive was Dr. Mufti Muhammad Sadiq, who settled in Chicago in 1921 and who published a small magazine, *Muslim Sunrise.*

As the Ahmadiyya movement began to grow, it attracted primarily African Americans. Comparative religious scholar Charles Braden, who tracked the Ahmadiyyas for a generation, noted that one of its most appealing aspects was its message of racial brotherhood. Braden noted in 1959, after a quarter of a century of evangelizing, that the majority of Ahmadiyyas were Black people, and that Islam was demonstrating a much greater ability to handle the racial question than was Christianity. In any case, over its first generation, the Ahmadiyya version of Islam spread through the Black communities of the northern United States.

Since World War II

Through the 1920s and 1930s, Islam, though of an unorthodox variety, established itself within the African American world. Not yet ready to challenge the Christian hegemony, it offered African American an alternative and saw the formation of a core group through which it could reach a mass following in future decades. The last World War proved a trauma for the Nation of Islam. With membership then numbering in the thousands, Elijah Muhammad planned to purchase property and establish permanent headquarters in Chicago. However, in 1942, he was arrested for preaching sedition and avoiding the draft. Convicted, he sat out the rest of the War in the Federal Penitentiary in Marion, Indiana. There was some compensation for the disaster of the early 1940s by the acquisition of Malcolm Little, later to be known as Malcolm X, as a member. Malcolm soon proved to be the Nations' most effective evangelist-spokesperson. Sent to New York, he built one of the strongest temples in the organization and through his travels was responsible for the founding of a number of other centers.

The Nation of Islam grew steadily through the 1950s. With the exception of a few scholars of religious and/or fringe groups in the African American community, the movement was virtually unknown in the White community. Then in 1959, Black journalist Louis Lomax initiated a television documentary on the Nation. It introduced its racial teachings to the American public. It was soon followed by two books, one by Lomax and one by scholar C. Eric Lincoln. While White people were concerned, if not horrified, the bad publicity made them famous and attracted many African Americans to the movement. The next fifteen years were ones of unexpected growth.

By 1970, as the flow under the new immigration law stabilized, the Nation of Islam was the voice of Islam within the Black community. It became the center of controversy as the White media attacked the anti-White teachings, and Blacks argued the degree of its correctness. The Nation's membership surpassed the 100,000 mark, and many suggested it was even larger. It challenged the Christian church members to leave the White man's religions and some did.

While it departed from Muslim orthodoxy to a large extent, it held the major Islamic symbols before its members, and provided a context in which some would begin to explore and accept orthodox Islam. Data has yet to be assembled detailing the openings provided by the Nation of Islam for the development of both orthodox and unorthodox forms of Islam among African Americans. Not the least of the sources of change within the movement was its insistence upon study of the *Qur'an*, which brought many up against the many statements which contradicted the Nation's racialist teachings.

Among the people attracted to orthodox Islam was Elijah Muhammad's own son, Wallace Muhammad (now known as Warith Deen Muhammad). Raised within the movement, as early as 1961 he questioned the teachings and on two occasions left the movement altogether. However, he was reinstated as a minister in 1974 and the following year assumed control as his father's successor. Within the first year he began to change the movement's teaching on race, an initial step that would over the next decade lead to the integration of the Nation into the larger orthodox Islamic community.

Other people initially attracted to Islam by the Nation could not wait for Wallace to gradually make the transition to orthodox Muslim life. They left the Nation (or never joined) and affiliated with orthodox Islamic centers. The emerging Muslim Student Association, annually adding new chapters on college campuses, provided the conduit through which African Americans could find their way to other orthodox Muslims. Islam welcomed all converts.

A few left to found rival movements. Malcolm X soon paid with his life for founding the competing Muslim Mosque, Inc. in New York. Haamas Abdul Khaalis was not at home the day the assassins arrived, but he lost several children, and his wife was permanently crippled. However, through the 1970s and into the 1980s, the majority of Black Muslims discovered the orthodox center of the faith.

While the great majority of African American Muslims slid over into the orthodox camp, new heterodox movements appeared. Several years after the changing of leadership in the Nation of Islam, Louis Farrakhan, possibly the most gifted speaker/leader with the movement, rejected the changes initiated by Wallace Muhammad and left the organization and reorganized the several thousand who left with him as the reconstituted Nation of Islam. Since his becoming independent in the late 1970s, Farrakhan has become the most notable of the several revived Nation of Islam groups (such as those led by John Muhammad or Silis Muhammad).

Though having the support of only a relatively small membership (5,000–10,000). Farrakhan has forced one Black leader after another (from Jesse Jackson to Mayor Tom Bradley of Los Angeles) to choose between him and solidarity with the African American community and their ties with the White power base they must have to survive as viable political voices.

The Future of Islam in the African American Community

Islam has become an established minority voice within the African American community. It shows no signs of challenges the overwhelming support still given to the several large Christian denominations. It has also lost much of the controversial focus which carried it through the civil rights/Black Power era, but has been able to find common cause with the larger multiracial American Muslim Community, now numbering in the millions and growing.

SUGGESTED BIBLIOGRAPHY FOR FURTHER READING

Austin, Allan D. *African Muslims in Antebellum America: A Sourcebook*. New York: Garland Publishing, 1984.

Davis, Charles H., Jr. *Black Nationalism and the Nation of Islam*, 4 parts. Los Angeles: The John Henry and Mary Louisa Dunn Bryant Foundation, 1962.

Diara, Agadem I. *Islam and Pan-Africanism*. Detroit: AGASCA Productions, n.d.

Essien-Udom, E. U. *Black Nationalism: A Search for an Identity in America*. University of Chicago Press, 1962. Rept.: New York: Dell, 1964.

Goldman, Peter Louis. *The Death and Life of Malcolm X*. Urbana, IL: University of Illinois Press, 1979.

Lee, Martha F. *The Nation of Islam, An American Millenarian Movement*. Lewiston, NY: Edwin Mellen Press, 1988.

Lincoln, C. Eric. *The Black Muslims in America*. Boston, MA: Beacon Press, 1961.

Lomax, Louis. *When the Word Is Given . . .* Cleveland, OH: World Publishing, 1964.

Marsh, Clifton E. *From Black Muslims to Muslims: The Transition from Separation to Islam, 1930–1980*. Metuchen, NJ: Scarecrow Press, 1984.

al-Talal, Faissal Fahd, and Khalid Abdullah Tariq al-Mansour. *The Chalolenges of Spreading Islam in America*. San Francisco, CA: The Authors, 1980.

Chapter Twenty-one

The Voodoo Cult among Negro Migrants in Detroit

Erdmann Doane Beynon

Erdmann Doane Beynon provides a second look at Islam Among African Americans, revealing details and nuances of the movement's development and suggesting some of the motive factors in its appeal, including the growing discontent of African American migrants with the conditions of their life in the city.

•

The Negro sect known to its members as the "Nation of Islam" or the "Muslims,"[1] but to the police as the Voodoo Cult,[2] has significance for social science research partly because of its synthesis of heterogeneous cultural elements and partly because of its unique expression of race consciousness. If the movement be viewed as the life cycle of a cult, however, its various phases tend to show an orderly progression through which the attitudes of its devotees were molded to a common pattern. There developed among them a way of living which isolated them to a certain extent from all persons not members of their cult, even though they themselves remained scattered among an urban population of their own race and color. In their trade relations the members of this cult have continued to live, like other Negroes, within the ecological organization of the Negro community of Detroit. Their principal occupational adjustment has been factory labor, and thus the cult members have maintained a functional relationship with the metropolitan economy outside of the Negro community. At the same time, however, they have severed contacts with the social organization of the community in which they live, so that they have gained isolation almost as effectively as did the members of agricultural religious communities who migrated to new homes.

The Beginning of the Movement

The prophet and founder of the cult made his first appearance among the Negroes of Detroit as a peddler. Like other Arab and Syrian peddlers, he went from house to house carrying his wares.

He came first to our houses selling raincoats, and then afterwards silks. In this way he could get into the people's houses, for every woman was eager to see the nice things the peddlars had for sale. He told us that the silks he carried were the same kind that our people used in their home country and that he had come from there. So we all asked him to tell us about our own country. If we asked him to eat with us, he would eat whatever we had on the table, but after the meal he began to talk: "Now don't eat this food. It is poison for you. The people in your own country do not eat it. Since they eat the right kind of food they have the best health all the time. If you would live just like the people in your home country, you would never be sick any more." So we all wanted him to tell us more about ourselves and about our home country and about how we could be free from rheumatism, aches and pains.[3]

At the stranger's suggestion a group of people was invited to one of the houses visited by him, so that on a particular evening they all might hear the story in which all alike were so much interested. Accustomed as these people were to the cottage prayer meetings of the Negro Methodist and Baptist churches, they found no difficulty in holding informal meetings in their homes.

The former peddler now assumed the role of prophet. During the early period of his ministry he used the Bible as his textbook, since it was the only religious book with which the majority of his hearers were familiar. With growing prestige over a constantly increasing group, the prophet became bolder in his denunciation of the Caucasians and began to attack the teachings of the Bible in such a way as to shock his hearers and bring them to an emotional crisis. Brother Challar Sharrieff told of the crisis through which he himself passed after hearing the prophet's message:

> The very first time I went to a meeting I heard him say: "The Bible tells you that the sun rises and sets. That is not so. The sun stands still. All your lives you have been thinking that the earth never moved. Stand and look toward the sun and know that it is the earth you are standing on which is moving." Up to that day I always went to the Baptist church. After I heard that sermon from the prophet, I was turned around completely. When I went home and heard that dinner was ready, I said: "I don't want to eat dinner. I just want to go back to the meetings." I wouldn't eat my meals but I goes back that night and I goes to every meeting after that. Just to think that the sun above me never moved at all and that the earth we are on was doing all the moving. That changed everything for me.[4]

The report of the prophet's message spread through the Negro community. Many of those who heard him invited their friends and relatives to come to the meetings, appealing either to their curiosity or to deeper interest. The attendance at the house meetings increased so much that the prophet was compelled to divide his hearers into several groups, the members of each of which were permitted to hear his message only at the time assigned to their group. The inconvenience was so obvious that the prophet's followers readily contributed money sufficient to hire a hall which was fitted up as the Temple.

The Prophet

Although the prophet lived in Detroit from July 4, 1930, until June 30, 1934, virtually nothing is known about him, save that he "came from the East" and that he "called" the Negroes of North America to enter the Nation of Islam. His very name is uncertain. He was known usually as Mr. Wali Farrad or Mr. W. D. Fard, though he used also the following names: Professor Ford, Mr. Farrad Mohammed, Mr. F. Mohammed Ali. One of the few survivors who heard his first addresses states that he himself said: "My name is W. D. Fard and I came from the Holy City of Mecca. More about myself I will not tell you yet, for the time has not yet come. I am your brother. You have not yet seen me in my royal robes."[5] Legends soon sprang up about this mysterious personality. Many members of the cult hold that the prophet was born in Mecca, the son of wealthy parents of the tribe of the Koreish, the tribe from which Mohammed the Prophet sprang, and that he was closely related by blood to the dynasty of the Hashimide sheriffs of Mecca who became kings of the Hejaz. He is said to have been educated at a college in England,[6] in preparation for a diplomatic career in the service of the kingdom of the Hejaz, but to have abandoned every thing to bring "freedom, justice and equality"[7] to "his uncle"[8] living "in the wilderness of North America, surrounded and robbed completely by the Cave Man."[9]

There has grown, however, among the members of the cult a belief that the prophet was more than man, as Brother Yussuf Mohammed claimed: "When the police asked him who he was, he said: 'I am the Supreme Ruler of the Universe.' He told those police more about himself than he would ever tell us."

The Negroes Who Heard the "Call"

Not all who attended the meetings and heard the stranger's message accepted him as a prophet. Many ridiculed his attacks against the Caucasians and were angered by his criticisms of the churches and the preachers. During the four years of his ministry, however, approximately eight thousand Negroes[10] in Detroit "heard the call" and became members of the Nation of Islam. Interviews with more than two hundred Moslem families showed that with less than half dozen exceptions, all were recent migrants from the rural South, the majority having come to Detroit from small communities in Virginia, South Carolina, Georgia, Alabama, and Mississippi. Investigations of cult members by the Wayne County Prosecutor's office also indicated the same origin. The interviews disclosed that the Moslems not only had migrated recently from the South, but also had visited their old homes in the South one or more times after their migration and before they had come into contact with the Nation of Islam. Through these visits they had become more conscious of race discrimination on the part of the Caucasians. After their brief sojourn in the North, they tended to reinterpret with sinister implications incidents of race contact in the South. They began to realize that lynchings and the indignities of the Jim Crow system were perpetrated by Caucasians who worshiped the same God as they did and worshiped Him in the same way. In many of its parts the Secret Ritual of the cult reflects the aroused feelings with which these Negroes returned from their visits to the South. "Me and my people who have been lost from home for 379 years have tried this so-called mystery God for bread, clothing and and a home. And we receive nothing but hard times, hunger, naked and out of doors. Also was beat and killed by the ones that advocated that kind of God."[11]

The illiteracy of the southern Negroes now seemed due to Caucasian "tricknollogy."[12] "Why does the devil keep our people illiterate? So that he can use them for a tool and also a slave. He keeps them blind to themselves so that he can master them."[13]

Awakened already to a consciousness of race discrimination, these migrants from the South came into contact with militant movements among northern Negroes. Practically none of them had been in the North prior to the collapse of the Marcus Garvey movement. A few of them had come under the influence of the Moorish-American cult that succeeded it. The effect of both these movements upon the future members of the Nation of Islam was largely indirect. Garvey taught the Negroes that their homeland was Ethiopia. The Noble Drew Ali, the prophet of the Moorish-Americans, proclaimed that these people were "descendants of Morrocans."[14] The newer migrants entered a social milieu in which the atmosphere was filled with questions about the origin of their people. Long before their new prophet appeared among them, they were wondering who they were and whence they had come.

The migrants did not find life in the North as pleasant as they had expected it to be, when first they came to the "land of hope," as the North was known in Negro poetry and song. The depression deprived them of their means of livelihood, and they suffered their first experience of urban destitution. Though public relief came to their rescue, the attitudes shown by the welfare agents increased their hatred of the Caucasian civilization. Forced to stand waiting for hours to receive their dole, these people began to believe that race discrimination was evident in the North as well as in the South. The welfare workers—including those even of their own race—became symbolic of all that these people hated.

> An Asiatic trend among Negro dole recipients of the Elmwood district, noted at the time as a passing whim, to-day came back with horror to two women welfare workers on learning that the fanatical Robert Harris had intended them for human sacrifices as infidels.... Harris stated to the police that each of these was a "no good Christian," and that they would have been sacrificed if he knew where he could have found them.[15]

A further disillusionment came from their own physical discomfort resulting from life in crowded quarters in a northern city. Unaccustomed to the climate of the North, and especially to its winters, these people soon developed many bodily ailments. Their condition is described by the Prophet Fard in his teaching:

> He had fever, headaches, chills, grippe, hay fever, regular fever, rheumatism, also pains in all joints. He was disturbed with foot ailment and toothaches. His pulse beat more than eighty-eight times per minute: therefore he goes to the doctor every day and gets medicine for every day in the year: one after each meal and three times a day, also one at bedtime.[16]

The migrants realized that they suffered much more physical pain than they had in their old homes. They connected this suffering with the civilization of the white man to whose cities they had come. Even before they met the prophet, they had begun to blame the Caucasian for their aches and pains.

The Organized Cult

Maladjusted migrant Negroes came into contact with the prophet at the informal meetings in their own homes. With the change to temple services, the movement took on a more formal character. The teaching became systematized. Membership was recognized and "registered." The movement itself became organized in a hierarchical manner.

The prophet's message was characterized by his ability to utilize to the fullest measure the environment of his followers. Their physical and economic difficulties alike were used to illustrate the new teaching. Similarly, biblical prophecies and the teaching of Marcus Garvey and Noble Drew Ali were cited as foretelling the coming of the new prophet. As additional proofs of his message, the prophet referred his followers to the writings of Judge Rutherford, of Jehovah's Witnesses, to a miscellaneous collection of books on Freemasonry and its symbolism, and to some well-known works, such as Breasted's *Conquest of Civilization* and Hendrik van Loon's *Story of Mankind*. Since many of these people were illiterate, it became necessary to organize classes in English so that they might be able to read "the proofs about themselves." They were also instructed to purchase radios in order that they might listen to the addresses of Judge Rutherford, Frank Norris, the Baptist fundamentalist, and others. The prophet explained to the people that the recommended books and addresses were symbolic and could be understood only through the interpretation which he himself would give at the temple services. The Koran itself was soon introduced as the most authoritative of all texts for the study of the new faith. The prophet, however, used only the Arabic text which he translated and explained to the believers. Here too they were completely dependent upon his interpretation.

To give more systematic character to his teaching, the prophet himself prepared certain texts which served as authoritative manuals of the religion and were memorized verbatim by all who became members of the Nation of Islam.

The prophet's teaching was in substance as follows:

The black men in North America are not Negroes, but members of the lost tribe of Shebazz, stolen by traders from the Holy City of Mecca 379 years ago.

> The prophet came to America to find and to bring back to life his long lost brethren, from whom the Caucasians had taken away their language, their nation and their religion. Here in America they were living other than themselves. They must learn that they are the original people, noblest of the nations of the earth. The Caucasians are the colored people, since they have lost their original color. The original people must regain their religion, which is Islam, their language, which is Arabic, and their culture, which is astronomy and higher mathematics, especially calculus. They must live according to the law of Allah, avoiding all meat of "poison animals," hogs, ducks, geese, 'possums

and catfish. They must give up completely the use of stimulants, especially liquor. They must clean themselves up—both their bodies and their houses. If in this way they obeyed Allah, he would take them back to the Paradise from which they had been stolen—the Holy City of Mecca.[17]

Those who accepted this teaching became new men and women, or, as the prophet expressed it, were restored to their original and true selves. As a mark of this restoration the prophet gave them back their original names which the Caucasians had taken from them. Since a sum of money—usually ten dollars—was required to secure the original name, this work must have been extremely profitable to the prophet. Each new believer wrote a separate letter asking for his original name, which the prophet was supposed to know through the Spirit of Allah within him. Examples of the changed names are:

> Joseph Shepard became Jam Sharrieff
> Lindsey Garrett became Hazziez Allah
> Henry Wells became Anwar Pasha
> William Blunt became Sharrieff Allah.

Apparent mistakes sometimes occurred when three or more brothers applied for new names, neglecting to mention in their letters that they were blood brothers. Thus, despite his omniscience, the prophet once gave the surnames of Sharrieff, Karriem, and Mohammed to the three Poole brothers. The prophet explained this seeming mistake as due to his divine knowledge of the different paternity of the three brothers.

The people who secured the new names value them as their greatest treasure. "I wouldn't give up my righteous name. That name is my life."[18] They became so ashamed of their old slave names that they considered that they could suffer no greater insult than to be addressed by the old name. They sought to live in conformity with the Law of Islam as revealed to them by the prophet, so that they might be worthy of their original names. Gluttony, drunkenness, idleness, and extramarital sex relations, except with ministers of Islam, were prohibited completely. They bathed at least once a day and kept their houses scrupulously clean, so that they might put away all marks of the slavery from which the restoration of the original name had set them free.

The rapid increase in membership made necessary the development of a formal organization. Subsidiary organizations had been established as the need for them arose. Chief of these was the University of Islam to which the children of Moslem families were sent rather than to the public schools. Here they were taught the "knowledge of our own," rather than the "civilization of the Caucasian devils." Courses were given in "higher mathematics," astronomy, and the "general knowledge and ending of the spook civilization." That women might keep their houses clean and cook food properly, there was established the Moslem Girls' Training and General Civilization Class. Fear of trouble with the unbelievers, especially with the police, led to the founding of the Fruit of Islam—a military organization for the men who were drilled by captains and taught tactics and the use of firearms. Each of these organizations was under the control of a group of officers trained specially by the prophet for their task. Finally the entire movement was placed under a Minister of Islam and a corps of assistant ministers, all of whom had been selected and trained by the prophet. Within three years the prophet not only began the movement but organized it so well that he himself was able to recede into the background, appearing almost never to his followers during the final months of his residence in Detroit. This was undoubtedly an important factor in the cult's survival after the prophet's departure.

Schisms and Persecutions

Inherent apparently in the prophet's message were certain teachings which, from the very beginning of the movement, led to schisms within the membership of the cult and to persecution from without.

The prophet proclaimed that his followers did not belong to America. They were citizens of the Holy City of Mecca and their only allegiance was to the Moslem flag. Their children must be removed from the public schools and sent to the University of Islam. In revolt against this position, Abdul Mohammed, one of the first officers in the temple, seceded and organized a small Moslem group of his own in which the cardinal principle was loyalty to the Constitution of the United States and to its flag. The attendance officers of the Board of Education and the police attempted to break up the University of Islam and to compel the children to return to the public schools. This led to a severe riot in which the members of the cult tried to storm the police headquarters. Fearful of race riots, the judges of the recorder's court released with suspended sentence almost all of the rioters. Since that time the University of Islam has continued its classes.

More serious difficulties arose over the question of human sacrifice. The prophet's position on this question was never made clear. He taught explicitly that it was the duty of every Moslem to offer as sacrifice four Caucasian devils in order that he might return to his home in Mecca.[19] The prophet also taught that Allah demands obedience unto death from his followers. No Moslem dare refuse the sacrifice of himself or of his loved ones if Allah requires it. On November 21, 1932, the people of Detroit became conscious of the presence of the cult through its first widely publicized human sacrifice. A prominent member, Robert Harris, renamed Robert Karriem, erected an altar in his home at 1249 Du Bois Street and invited his roomer, John J. Smith, to present himself as a human sacrifice, so that he might become, as Harris said, "the Saviour of the world." Smith agreed, and at the hour appointed for the sacrifice—9:00 A.M.—Harris plunged a knife into Smith's heart. After constant recurrences of rumors of human sacrifice or attempted sacrifice, on January 20, 1937, Verlene McQueen, renamed Verlene Ali, brother of one of the assistant ministers, was arrested as he prepared for the ceremonial slaying and cooking of his wife and daughter. This sacrifice was, as he said, to have "cleansed him from all sin."

These cases of human sacrifice have directed to the cult much attention from the Police Department so that the cult has been forced to pursue many of its activities in secret. The question of sacrifice has led also to serious internal clashes. "Rebels against the Will of Allah," as they are called, have left the Temple and organized another Temple of Islam, desiring to remain within the framework of the cult but to avoid human sacrifice, the necessity of which as an expiation of sin forms one of the most hotly debated subjects among the cult members.

Persecutions and schisms alike have tended to increase the cultural isolation of the members of this group. The effect of the schisms was selective, leaving within the parent organization those who were bound together by common attitudes and common loyalties. Attacks made on the cult by the Police Department have been instigated usually by the leaders of Negro organizations. These persecutions have led naturally to a greater solidarity among the cult members and to a constantly increasing isolation of the Moslems from the other residents of the Detroit Negro community.

Efforts to Exploit the Movement

The solidarity and cultural isolation of the Moslems have rendered ineffectual the various attempts made by interested parties to redirect the activities of the cult in order to further their own particular purposes. The first of these efforts was made by the Communists in 1932, but the cult members rebuffed their appeal. Then came Major Takahashi, a reserve Japanese officer, who sought to lead the Moslems to swear allegiance to the Mikado. Only a small minority of the members followed him into the new movement he organized—The Development of Our Own. With his deportation, this schismatic movement came to nought. An Ethiopian, Wyxzewixard S. J. Challouehliczilczese, sought in June 1934, to reorganize the movement as a means of sending financial support to Ethiopia. This too, was unsuccessful. At present the members of the cult have come under the influence of certain anti-Union interests and talk violently of the war of the C.I.O. against Allah and the need of removing from the Planet Earth all Union organizers. While this trend seems very pronounced at present, it is unlikely to leave any permanent impression upon the movement, and still less likely to detach from the Nation of Islam any of its members.

Adjustments of Cult Members in the Urban Economy

At the time of their first contact with the prophet, practically all the members of the cult were recipients of public welfare, unemployed, and living in the most deteriorated areas of Negro settlement in Detroit. At the present time,[20] there is no known case of unemployment among these people. Practically all of them are working in the automobile and other factories. They live no longer in the slum section around Hastings Street, but rent homes in some of the best economic areas in which Negroes have settled. They tend to purchase more expensive furniture, automobiles, and clothes than do their neighbors, even in these areas of higher-class residence. This improved economic adjustment is due, doubtless, partly to post-depression conditions of employment and to the increased hiring of Negroes as a result of recent labor troubles. The members of the cult, however, claim that they have secured work much more easily than have other Negroes. They offer thanks to Allah for this evidence of his favor. To some extent their claim appears to be justified, though no statistical study has yet been made of comparative unemployment of cult members and other recent Negro migrants. Through the Nation of Islam they have gained a new status and a new confidence in themselves. When they meet Caucasians, they rejoice in the knowledge that they themselves are superiors meeting members of an inferior race. Employment managers tend to accept more readily persons whose appearance gives evidence of clean living and self-reliance than those who show the marks of debauchery, defeat, and despair.

The ascetic manner of life of the Moslems also has contributed to their economic improvement. No money whatever is spent by them on liquor, tobacco, or pork. Their one meal of the day consists almost entirely of vegetables and fruits. Consequently, their expenditure on food is significantly smaller than is that of other Negroes in Detroit. This economy is consumption, however, is not extended to visible marks of status, such as houses, automobiles, and clothes. The prophet taught them that they are the descendants of nobles in the Holy City of Mecca. To show their escape from slavery and their restoration to their original high status, they feel obliged to live in good houses and to wear good clothes. Despite their expenditure on these items, members of the cult constantly declare that they are ashamed that they have not been able to purchase better commodities or to rent finer homes. "This furniture is the best we could afford to buy here in the wilderness of North America, where we have to live other than ourselves. When we go home to Mecca, we will be able to get really good furniture, just like all our people who live there use."

Relation to Other Negro Cults

The story of the Nation of Islam cannot be considered as complete in itself. Militant and cultist movements among migrant Negroes in the cities of the North have formed a sort of tree. After one branch has grown, flourished, and begun to decay, another shoots up to begin over again the same cycle, though always with an increasing degree of race-consciousness and anti-Caucasian prejudice.

Out of the wreck of the Marcus Garvey movement there sprang Phoenix-like the Moorish-American cult of which the prophet was Noble Drew Ali. After this prophet's disappearance and the stabilization of the movement as a formally organized denomination there sprang up the Nation of Islam. Although the cultural isolation of the members of this cult has not declined during the three years of their prophet's absence, there are many evidences of the loss of militant aggressiveness which once characterized this group. The organization also is tending to become more amorphous. From among the larger group of Moslems there has sprung recently an even more militant branch than the Nation of Islam itself. This new movement, known as the Temple People, identifies the prophet, Mr. W. D. Fard, with the god Allah. To Mr. Fard alone do they offer prayer and sacrifice. Since Mr.

Fard has been deified, the Temple People raise to the rank of prophet the former Minister of Islam, Elijah Mohammed,[21] now a resident of Chicago. He is always referred to reverently as the "Prophet Elijah in Chicago." A former assistant of his, the Haitian Theodore Rozier,[22] has become the minister and director of the new movement.

Thus continues the chain of these movements, each running through its cycle of growth and decay and all of them interwoven as strands of a web. Fundamental to them all is the effort of migrant Negroes to secure a status satisfactory to themselves after their escape from the old southern accommodation of white and Negro.

NOTES

1. Spelling: "Moslem"; pronounced: "Muslim." This is one of the changed pronunciations by which initiates recognize each other. The Moorish-Americans also are "Moslems," but pronounce the word as spelled.

2. No effort is made in this chapter to trace relationship between this cult and Voodooism in Haiti and other West Indian islands. The cult received the name "Voodoo" solely because of cases of human sacrifice.

3. Sister Denke Majied, formerly Mrs. Lawrence Adams.

4. Brother Challar Sharrieff, formerly Mr. Charles Peoples.

5. Interview with Mrs. Carrie Peoples (Sister Carrie Mohammed).

6. Sister Carrie Mohammed and certain others claim that the prophet graduated from the University of Southern California in Los Angeles.

7. Symbolized by the letters F J E on the Muslim flag hanging in the home of every cult member.

8. The American Negroes—"the black men in the wilderness of North America"—are referred to symbolically in the cult ritual as "the uncle of Mr. W. D. Fard." Moslems of the East—Syrians, Turks, and others—are referred to as "the second uncle of Mr. W. D. Fard."

9. Prophet W. D. Fard, *Teaching for the Lost Found Nation of Islam in a Mathematical Way*, Problem No. 30.

10. Estimated by officials of the cult. Detectives of the Special Investigation Squad of the Detroit Police Department estimate 5,000.

11. W. D. Fard, *Secret Ritual of the Nation of Islam*, Part II, sec. II. This has been preserved as an oral tradition, memorized verbatim by the pupils at the University of Islam. Only a few manuscript copies are extant.

12. A cult term pronounced "trickenollogy."

13. Wallace D. Fard, *Secret Ritual of the Nation of Islam* Part I, see. VI.

14. *Koran Questions for Moorish Americans* (Chicago, 1928), p. 1, question 14.

15. *Detroit Times*, November 22, 1932.

16. *Teaching for the Lost Found Nation of Islam in a Mathematical Way*, Problem No. 6.

17. Compiled from the three texts issued by the prophet: *Teaching for the Lost Found Nation of Islam in a Mathematical Way*, consisting of 34 problems. This text was printed, but given only to registered Moslems. *Secret Ritual of the Nation of Islam*, Part I, in 14 secs.; ibid., Part II, in 40 secs.

The *Secret Ritual* was, and still is, transmitted orally. The entire teaching is symbolic and can be understood only by the initiates.

18. Mrs. William McCoy, renamed Sister Rosa Karriem.

19. Fard, *Secret Ritual*, Part I, sec. 10.

20. Written in August 1937.

21. His slave name was Elijah Poole. The prophet conferred on him the name of "Elijah Karriem." The Temple People claim that Mr. W. D. Fard himself changed this name later to "Elijah Mohammed" to indicate the higher status to which the minister was called. Moslems opposed to the Temple People deny this and continue to speak of "Brother Elijah Karriem."

22. One of the newer converts, Brother Theodore Rozier, admits that he never saw the "Savior," Mr. W. D. Fard, and that he learned of Islam solely through his contact with the "Prophet Elijah Mohammed." Opponents of the Temple People contend that Brother Theodore Rozier is not qualified to be minister of Islam since he received the revelation "second-hand."

"I have mastered the economic situation!" (Father Divine) from *Black Gods of the Metropolis: Negro Religious Cults in the Urban North* by Arthur Huff Fauset. Copyright 1944, 1971 by the Trustee of the University of Pennsylvania. Reprinted by permission of the University of Pennsylvania Press.

Chapter Twenty-two

Father Major Jealous Divine

Gary L. Ward

Islam, in its several versions, was one alternative to traditional Protestant piety for African Americans. Another was centered around charismatic figures who claimed transcendent powers, even deity, for themselves, coalesced their followers into communities defined out of the leaders' own teachings and which offered the hope of personal socioeconomic amelioration. The Father Divine Peace Mission Movement added participation in the present in a racially reconciled community.

•

Father Major Jealous Divine (1877?–September 10, 1965), founder of the Peace Mission Movement, was one of the more mysterious and elusive of public figures. He did not discuss his origins, and neither did his followers. There is some evidence that he was born George Baker in 1877 in Savannah. Georgia, but nothing conclusive. His followers claim that he married his first wife, Penninah (Sister Penny), on June 6, 1882. At various times he is considered to have been associated with Sam Morris (Father Jehoviah), and with John Hickerson (Bishop St. John the Divine). All three men were in Brooklyn, New York, shortly before 1919, when reliable biographical information about Divine is first available.

In 1919, Divine established himself, his wife, and twenty followers in Sayville, Long Island, New York, the substantive beginning of his Peace Mission Movement, though that name was not used until the 1930s. He was able to find many of his followers domestic jobs in the surrounding estates, and he preached a gospel of hard work, honesty, sobriety, equality, sexual abstinence, and himself as the Second Coming of Christ. He was known for "forbidding" sickness and death in his home, and providing free, or nearly free, meals and shelter for anyone who asked. Whites were invited to join, and some did, including some with wealth. In 1930, formerly known as Major Jealous Divine, he took the name Father Divine.

As his fame grew, literally busloads of people would travel to see him on the weekends, and the police took him and some eighty followers to court on November 15, 1931, as a "public nuisance." Divine pleaded not guilty, and after a jury trial ending May 25, 1932, found him guilty, the judge sentenced him on June 4 to the maximum one year in jail and a $500 fine. Three days later, on June 7, 1932, the apparently healthy judge, Lewis J. Smith, died of a heart attack, and Divine was quoted as saying, "I hated to do it." The conviction was soon reversed, and Divine's reputation as one who personally controlled cosmic forces was set. His followers still celebrate June 7.

In 1933, Divine moved the headquarters to Harlem, New York City, and on November 4, mayoral candidate Fiorello LaGuardia walked into a banquet and announced, "I came here tonight to ask Father Divine's advice and counsel," indicating significant political influence. The Peace Mission (no real estate or bank accounts were in Divine's name) became the owner of many hotels and businesses in several states, adding to the ability to provide jobs, shelter, and income. Divine attempted to alleviate social ills not only through these means, but through various forms of social agitation as well. In January 1936, he proposed a "Righteous Government Platform," and over 6,000 delegates from many social and political backgrounds came to a meeting to develop and sign the platform. Between 1936 and 1940, he lobbied strongly for a federal antilynching law. Divine's strength was such that he emerged relatively unscathed from a number of lawsuits, allegations, and scandals. In 1938, the Peace Mission acquired the Krum Elbow estate in Hyde Park and Divine became a neighbor of the Roosevelts. In 1941, he moved to a Philadelphia mansion on seventy-three acres, through the generosity of a White disciple, John De Voute, who sold the property to the Church in 1953.

The Peace Mission did not hold traditional worship services; at meals there were songs and occasional sermons. He promised his followers heaven on earth, and the rich, communal banquet table was the major religious symbol. The feasts were intended to recreate the daily communions of early Christianity, which time, for Divine, provided the defining practices of the religion. On April 29, 1946, several years after the death of his first wife, Divine married a young, White, Canadian woman named Edna Rose Ritching. Following his own teaching, their marriage was platonic. He said that the spirit of his first wife was transferred to her, as was his own spirit. This laid the foundation for her leadership after his death, at which time the movement's holdings were estimated to be worth $10 million.

SUGGESTED BIOGRAPHY FOR FURTHER READING

Burnham, Kenneth E. *God Comes to America*. Boston: Lambeth Press, 1979.

Divine, Mother. *The Peace Mission Movement*. Philadelphia, PA: Imperial Press, 1982.

Harris, Sara and Harriet Crittenden. *Father Divine, Holy Husband*. Garden City, NY: Doubleday, 1953. Revised as *Father Divine*. New York: Collier Books, 1971.

Hoshor, John. *God in a Rolls Royce*. New York: Hillman, Curl, 1936.

Parker, Robert A. *The Incredible Messiah: The Deification of Father Divine*. Boston: Little, Brown, 1937.

Weisbrot, Robert. *Father Divine and the Struggle for Racial Equality*. Urbana, IL: University of Illinois Press, 1983.

Rabbi Yhoshua Ben Yahonatan and his wife, Leana Yahonatan, in their synagogue in Mount Vernon, New York, 1989. From *Feeling the Spirit* by Chester Higgins. Copyright © 1994 by Chester Higgins. Used by permission of Bantam Books, a division of Random House, Inc.

Commandment Keepers Synagogue, New York City, 1989. From *Feeling the Spirit* by Chester Higgins. Copyright © 1994 by Chester Higgins. Used by permission of Bantam Books, a division of Random House, Inc.

Chapter Twenty-three

Black Judaism in the United States

Merrill Singer

As with some of the Islamic movements, Black Judaism addressed the issue of African American identity, a significant struggle for a people variously defined in society as "three-fifths of a person," a nonperson, a human degenerate, a cultureless pariah. William Christian told African Americans that they were of the same race—black race— as Abraham, David, and Jesus. Prophet Cherry and others took this identification with scriptural personages a step further to assert that African Americans were actually Jews, or the "real" Jews, or the "Lost Tribes of Israel," or some similar Jewish identity. Issues of racial/cultural integrity and self-esteem were thus addressed through re-identifying African Americans, revealing their "true," valuable selves. Some, of course, might see in this approach an inadvertent assent to what whites had claimed, namely, that being black was a degraded, undesirable thing. Merrill Singer provides a look at the emergence of Black Judaism, in several of its organizational expressions. Though it was not in the author's purview to address, it should be noted that, like Islam, Judaism has African American adherents to its traditional, orthodox wings.

•

According to James Landing, the earliest groups to express some form of black Judaism antedate World War I and thus represent "the first sectarian-based brand of black nationalism . . . which was not explicitly Christian." While black Jewish groups never gained the membership of some of the Islamized black nationalist movements, they have had, nonetheless, a significant if subtle impact on black culture and identity.

Black Judaism developed initially in the South in the period after the Civil War. In *The Black Jews of Harlem*, Howard Brotz notes that by the late 1800s, itinerant black preachers "were traveling through the Carolinas preaching the doctrine that the so-called Negroes were really the lost sheep of the House of Israel" (1).[1] During this period, there appeared scattered newspaper and magazine references to black members of Jewish congregations in Charleston, New Orleans, and elsewhere in the South. Black identification with the Biblical Israelites is undoubtedly far older. Deprived of their African history, many slaves probably adopted the Biblical history of the Israelites as their own history (see Powdermaker). Certainly black slaves recognized the parallels between their bondage and that of their Hebrew counterparts. And it was in the deliverance of the Israelites from Egypt that they found an idiom in which to speak and to sing about their own emancipation.

One of the earliest Jewish-oriented black sects was called the Church of the Living God the Pillar Ground of Truth for All Nations. Organized by a black seaman and railroad worker named F. S. Cherry, this group was founded in Chattanooga in the late 1880s. Cherry preached that both Adam and Eve, and Jesus as well, were black, white people being described as descendants of Gehazi, a servant cursed by the prophet Elisha with skin "as white as snow" for his greed and misrepresentation.[2] Additionally, Cherry taught his followers that blacks were systematically stripped of their Hebraic heritage during slavery, but in the year 2000 the Battle of Armageddon would restore black Jews to their land and their true identity. Cherry's church survived his passing and is now led by his son, who heads the main congregation in Philadelphia.

A second black Jewish group to emerge prior to the turn of the century was called the Church of the Living God. Initiated in Lawrence, Kansas, it moved to Philadelphia in 1900 and later to its present location in Belleville, Virginia. The founder, William S. Crowdy, was, like Cherry, a railroad worker who claimed a revelation from God to lead black people back to their true heritage. In Crowdy's formulation blacks were the rightful heirs of the Ten Lost Tribes of Israel, while caucasian Jews were seen as the unfortunate product of miscegenation with white people. Various Jewish ritual symbols, such as the performance of circumcision, use of the Jewish calendar, wearing of skull caps, observance of Saturday as the Sabbath, and the Passover celebration, were adopted by Crowdy's church. These were blended with certain Christian rites, including baptism, the sacrament of Holy Communion, and foot washing. At the thousand-acre Belleville headquarters, members live collectively while operating a farm, several cottage industries, a school, and homes for orphans and seniors.

Following the First World War, the epicenter of black Judaism shifted from the South to the ghettos of the North, carried by black migrants to New York, Cleveland, Chicago, and other cities. Over the years, a myriad of ideologically diverse black Jewish groups appeared in the North, as either local congregations or as federations united around a particular charismatic individual. Some of these leaders, like Warren Robinson, claimed divine status, while avidly mixing beliefs and rituals from farflung sources (Landes). Others held more modest claims or attempted to cleave to mainstream Jewish practices. In certain instances, this led to formal conversion into the Jewish religion (Shapiro 180–217). Although most of the black Jewish groups have been short-lived, often succumbing to internal bickering and power struggles among rival claimants to leadership, several have had greater longevity, most notably the Commandment Keepers Congregation of the Living God, which has been active in Harlem since 1930 (Brotz 15–45). A concern with land and communalism has been a hallmark of a number of black Jewish groups. Some, like Adat Beyt Moshe, started by Abel Respes in the early 1950s, established their own residential communities, while others, such as the Negro Israelite Bible Class headed by Lucius Casey, purchased land and attempted to organize communal farms (Berger 134–37). Finally, an interest in Africa has enlivened a few groups. Central to the ideology of the Beth B'nai Abraham congregation led by Arnold Josiah Ford was a desire for return to Africa. Ford and a number of his followers in fact emigrated to Ethiopia in the 1920s and 1930s (King).

Among the various motifs found in these sects, several stand out as expressions of the essence of black Judaism: (1) repudiation of the denegrated image of the subservient "Negro"; (2) rejection of certain social features of the inner city black community, especially female-headed households; (3) substitution of an alternative identity founded on a belief in a glorious black history; (4) adoption of various rituals and symbols from the Bible or contemporary Judaism; (5) vocal opposition to racism and white political-economic dominance; (6) a strong nationalist orientation; (7) interest in communalism; (8) concern for and pride in black culture; (9) charismatic leadership; and (10) chiliastic and messianic expectation. Given these features, black Judaism has been termed a *messianic-nationalist* reaction to racism and racial stratification in U.S. society (Baer and Singer).

The most noticed black Jewish group in recent years is known as the Black Hebrew Israelite Nation, now centered in Dimona, Israel. This group, called the Nation or the Kingdom by its members, incorporated a large body of traditional black religious songs into its musical repertoire, while promoting an interpretation of their meaning that both rationalizes group existence and underpins their conversionary efforts.

This group's origin can be traced to the ghettos of Chicago, although many of its founding members were migrants from the South. The group coalesced in the early 1960s around a rented hall called the Abeta Hebrew Cultural Center. The Center was under the leadership of a number of "elders," men in their forties and fifties who had a long-standing involvement in black Judaism. Central to group ideology was a belief in African repatriation. To further this aim, the elders sought to acquire land on the African continent for the eventual relocation of the group. Because of this effort, the Abeta Center proved to be quite popular with individuals involved in the African American cultural renaissance of the 1960s. For many of these new members, young men and women who were recent converts to black Judaism, African repatriation was an immediate rather than an eventual goal. Reviewing the following brief life history of one of these new members, a woman who is now a prominent singer with the group in Israel, gives some insight into the type of individual attracted to the Abeta Center; a fuller examination of the relationship between personal history and musical involvement will be provided in the next section.

Alice Thompson, who was given the name Bat Sheva when she became involved in black Judaism, was born in Georgia in 1940.[3] Her family was quite religious and active in the Baptist Church: "The church was our life, going to church, singing and praising." While she was still young, her family migrated to the Midwest in search of employment, and Alice eventually moved to Chicago to attend a secretarial school. But she began to grow disillusioned: "I guess it started with the assassination of President Kennedy. I liked President Kennedy and thought he was a good man. After that, I stopped going to church. I started to see the lies and hypocrisy there." Then Alice's uncle told her about a black Jewish group that he had encountered. Out of curiosity she began to attend meetings, and later, when she learned that the Abeta Center was discussing a migration to Africa, she switched to that group. She felt that her questions about her identity and role in life were answered by the leaders of the Abeta Center, and the idea of returning to Africa seemed an exciting alternative to life as a secretary.

This case is indicative of a more general pattern among Abeta members. Many were southern-born but had migrated to the North in the years after World War II. Generally, these recruits were of working-class background but held strong upward mobility desires or other goals that they felt they were unable to achieve. Some saw racism or the bureaucratization and depersonalization of society as the cause of their plight. Most came from religious backgrounds; however, even prior to their involvement with Abeta, they had grown dissatisfied with established black religions. The emigration talk at Abeta was appealing because the members felt alienated from the United States, which they came to refer to as Babylon or the "land of captivity."

In May 1967, three members of the Abeta Center flew to Liberia to investigate the possibilities for relocation. Believing that God was soon to punish the United States for the maltreatment of black people, the group hoped to establish a farming settlement that would serve as a beachhead for what they thought would be a massive wave of black immigrants. With the aid of a black expatriot from Cincinnati who had already acquired Liberian citizenship, the three scouts were able to acquire three hundred acres of thickly forested land at fifty cents per acre.

To raise funds for the migration, the Abeta members sold all of the possessions they would not need or could not transport to their new home. In July, the first emigrés boarded a Pan American jet bound for Monrovia, Liberia. By the end of the year, over two hundred men, women, and children had joined this vanguard. Thus, the largest black-organized Return-To-Africa migration in U.S. history was initiated.

In addition to their supplies and personal possessions, group members carried with them a pioneering spirit and high hopes for their adventurous undertaking. While they recognized that only a few members had farming skills, they felt, as one Black Hebrew man expressed at the time, it "doesn't take much to live on dedication" (McCahill 38). Events proved this assessment to be woefully premature.

Preliminary clearing of the dense forest was hampered by the heavy rains characteristic of the Liberian summer. Using machetes and other hand tools, they struggled to cut back the stubborn vegetation covering the Camp, as the black Hebrews dubbed their fledgling settlement. As the weeks passed, the harsh realities of jungle life dampened their early euphoria, allowing underlying tensions to boil to the surface. Recalled one man, "In the land of captivity, you light a match and you have a gas flame. In Liberia, if you wanted to eat, you had to chop your tree down, bring it back, chop it up, build a fire. Even building a fire was hard and it was smoky. We didn't know how to build no fire. In the rainy season, the shelters wasn't properly covered. . . . We ran into many difficulties." The settlers began to argue over the distribution of food and the organization of the communal kitchen. Several women rebelled when their husbands, following in the footsteps of the Biblical patriarchs, took plural wives. Disputes among the leaders also threatened to splinter the embryonic collective. Various tropical diseases and a number of tragic accidents also took their toll on group health and morale. Ultimately, the Camp was threatened with complete collapse.

Under these trying conditions, a number of individuals defected from the group and sought work and housing in Monrovia, while others gave up completely on the Liberian venture and returned to the United States. By the end of the second year, at least one hundred ex-members had recrossed the Atlantic, including a number of early leaders and advocates of the migration. But a hard core of devoted settlers did not succumb to their misfortune. Instead, a young man who had been a secondary leader at Abeta now rose to the fore. This man, Ben Carter, or Ben Ami (Son of My People) as he was known in the group, claimed divine inspiration for a number of solutions he offered to the Black Hebrews' dilemma. Under his direction, the group appealed to the Liberian government for assistance and was able to secure a government subsidy and jobs at a number of factories. The group started several businesses to bring in much-needed capital. Moreover, Ben Ami began to institute various rules to tighten up group organizations. Finally, he instructed one of his lieutenants to travel to Israel to investigate possibilities for a second migration.

Although a handful of Black Hebrews continued to arrive in Liberia throughout the early part of 1969, members increasingly looked to Israel as the ultimate destination of their migration. This view was supported by encouraging letters sent to the settlers from their compatriots in Israel. To test the waters for this alternative, Ben Ami dispatched five more members to "scout out the land." These new arrivals were provided housing and jobs in the Israeli development town of Arad overlooking the Dead Sea.

On December 12, 1969, thirty-nine Black Hebrews, mostly women and children, arrived at Lod airport outside Tel Aviv and requested admittance under the Law of Return, an Israeli statute that insures the rights of citizenship and government assistance to all officially confirmed Jewish applicants. Despite the acceptance into Israel of Jews from the four corners of the world, several immigration officials at the airport questioned the validity of the Black Hebrews' claim to Jewish roots. Eventually, the would-be immigrants were provided temporary visas, assigned apartments in the Negev Desert town of Dimona, and extended other privileges of citizenship. The permanent status of the group was left unresolved, a volatile circumstance that continues into the present.

The following March, Ben Ami and his remaining seventy followers in Liberia departed for Israel. This new contingent was admitted into the country and given tourist visas on the basis of their U.S. passports, but, as a result of a government determination that the Black Hebrews did not qualify under the Law of Return, they were not provided with housing or employment. In response, Ben Ami and the other newcomers crowded into the existing apartments held by the group in Arad and Dimona.

Over the next fourteen years, relations between the Black Hebrews and the government of Israel have gone through periods of intense hostility and relative calm. The government has never officially recognized the group nor accepted its presence in the country. On the other hand, the long period of residence and growing size of the group (from both natural increase and continued migration) have afforded the Black Hebrews a kind of de facto legitimacy. While there have been periods when the government actively has pressured the group, hoping to encourage its return to the United States, the Black Hebrews have steadfastly refused to budge.

Presently, the Black Hebrew Nation has over 1,500 members in Israel, as well as additional followers in the United States and several African countries. The group has evolved a highly organized community, a communitarian residential and economic system, national dress and customs, and a markedly hierarchical authority structure, with Ben Ami at the pinnacle. As the paramount leader, Ben Ami has achieved near deification in the eyes of his followers. Members commonly refer to him as "the true and living God" and have adorned him with titles such as Adonenu Rabbenu (Our Lord and Master) or Rabbey for short. Ben Ami is credited by the Black Hebrews with delivering them from Babylon and they believe that at "the appointed time" he will restore them to their rightful place as the rulers of the Land of Israel.

NOTES

1. On black Judaism, also see Shapiro, Berger, and Gerber. Evidence of an early identification with Judaism among southern blacks is also found in the beliefs and names of a number of the oldest black Spiritual churches, such as the Spiritual Israel Church and its Army, which teaches that black people are the biological descendants of the Biblical Israelites. On black Spiritual churches, see Baer.

2. II Kings 5:27, *The Holy Bible*, King James Version. The elaborate names of some of these congregations reflect a peculiarly African American place naming pattern, as discussed by Dillard.

3. The names cited in the text for this individual are pseudonyms.

WORKS CITED

Baer, Hans. *The Black Spiritual Movement*. Knoxville, Tenn.: University of Tennessee Press: 1984.

Baer, Hans, and Merrill Singer. "Toward a Typology of Black Sectarianism as a Response to Racial Stratification." *Anthropological Quarterly* 54 (1981): 1–14.

Berger, Graenum. *Black Jews in America*. New York: Commission on Synagogue Relations, 1978.

Brotz, Howard. *The Black Jews of Harlem*. New York: Shocken, 1970.

Dillard, J. L. "On the Grammar of Afro-American Naming Practices." *Mother Wit From the Laughing Barrell*. Ed. Alan Dundes. New York: Garland, 1981. 175–81.

Gerber, Israel J. *The Heritage Seekers: Black Jews in search of Identity*. Middle Village: Jonathan David, 1977.

King, K. L. "Some Notes on Arnold J. Ford and New World Black Attitudes on Ethiopia." *Journal of Ethiopian Studies* 10 (1972): 81–87.

Landes, Ruth. "Negro Jews in Harlem." *The Jewish Journal of Sociology* 9 (1967): 175–89.

Landing, James. "The Spatial Expression of Cultural Revitalization in Chicago." *Proceedings of the Association of American Geography* 6 (1971): 27, 50–53.

Levine, Lawrence W. *Black Culture and Black Consciousness: Afro-American Folk Thought From Slavery to Freedom.* New York: Oxford University Press, 1977.

McCahill, Dolores. "Black Hebrews Cook up a Land of Promise in Liberia." *Chicago Sun Times* 11 Apr. 1969: 38.

Powdermaker, Hortense. *After Freedom.* New York: Viking, 1939.

Shapiro, Deanne Ruth. *Double Damnation, Double Salvation: The Sources and Varieties of Black Judaism in the United States.* MA thesis. Columbia University, 1970.

Chapter Twenty-four

The Historical Development of Black Spiritual Churches

Hans Baer and Merrill Singer

An eclectic weaving together of diverse religious and ethnic traditions, the Black Spiritual Churches were another creative response to issues of personal and existential security elicited by the challenge of living in the urban context. The following excerpt from the seminal work by Hans Baer and Merrill Singer outlines some of the prominent persons and events in this movement's development, in which women played key leadership roles.

•

The origins of the Black Spiritual movement remain obscure, but it appears to have emerged in various large cities of both the North and the South—particularly Chicago, New Orleans, New York, Detroit, and Kansas City—during the first quarter of this century. Apparently during this period the movement began to combine elements of Spiritualism, Roman Catholicism, and Voodooism or hoodoo, as well as other esoteric belief systems. Furthermore, elements from these diverse traditions seemed to have been grafted onto or merged with a Black version of Protestantism that began in antebellum times and came to maturity in a wide array of Baptist, Methodist, Holiness, and Pentecost denominations and sects.

According to Spear (1967: 96), several "Holiness and Spiritualist churches" were established in the Black community of Chicago during the first decade of the twentieth century. While many of the storefront churches that appeared in Chicago during the early migration years called themselves Baptists, they often closely resembled Holiness and Pentecostal groups in their exuberant and demonstrative form of worship. Others called themselves "Spiritualist," a "vague term used to identify those religious groups that believed in 'communication of the spirit' and that attempted to relay messages and spirits through mediums" (Spear 1967: 177). While indeed there may have been several Black Spiritualist groups, particularly of the storefront variety, at this time in Chicago and possibly elsewhere, the earliest specific congregation that Spear mentions is the Church of the Redemption. The *Chicago Defender*, a well-known Black newspaper, carried an advertisement on August 28, 1915, noting that the Church of the Redemption held regular services on State Street. Elsewhere, Kaslow (1981: 61) fleetingly notes that Mother Leafy Anderson, a Black Spiritualist who was destined to play an instrumental role in the development of the Spiritual religion in New Orleans, established the Eternal Life Christian Spiritualist Church in Chicago in 1913. At any rate, according to Spear (1967: 177) several "true" Black Spiritualists churches were organized between 1915 and 1920, adding elements of the Baptist, Holiness, and Pentecostal storefronts to those of Spiritualism.

New Orleans and the Beginnings of the Spiritual Movement

If indeed the Black Spiritual movement started in Chicago, its development in New Orleans appears to have been of vital importance in determining its present content. Although there was much opposition in the South to American Spiritualism, it nevertheless spread to cities such as Memphis, Macon, Charleston, and New Orleans (G. Nelson 1969). Perhaps in part because its doctrines were favorable to equality and liberalism, as well as compatible with African religions, Spiritualism found adherents among the Black population of the South. According to G. Nelson (1969: 16–17):

> A stronghold of Spiritualism in the south seems to have been New Orleans, where many circles were held not only by the white but also by the coloured population, and many coloured persons were found among the mediums. Dr. Barthet who became a leading spiritualist in the city was known to have experimented with animal magnetism in the early eighteen-forties, and Dr. Valmour, a free creole, attained great celebrity as a healing medium.

Although there seems to be a consensus that Mother Leafy Anderson, a woman of Black and Indian ancestry, started the first Black Spiritualist or Spiritual church in New Orleans, there are conflicting reports as to when she actually founded the Eternal Life Spiritualist Church in the Crescent City. Zora Hurston (1931: 319), a well-known Black anthropologist, folklorist, and novelist who studied under Franz Boas for several years, reported that this congregation was established in 1918. Tallant (1946: 173), however, placed Mother Anderson's arrival in New Orleans in 1921 and adds that she had previously operated several Spiritualist churches in Chicago. More recently, Kaslow (1981: 61) has stated that the Black Spiritual churches of New Orleans" were officially established in 1920, under the leadership of Leafy Anderson." Because Hurston was intimately involved in various cultic circles in New Orleans and was also the apprentice of a Voodoo practitioner there, I suspect—though without means of confirmation—that her date is the most reliable one.

Mother Anderson was popular not only among Blacks but also some poor Whites. She trained several other women, who established congregations of their own in New Orleans, and eventually she became the head of an association that included the New Orleans congregations plus others in Chicago, Little Rock, Memphis, Pensacola, Biloxi, Houston, and some smaller cities (Kaslow and Jacobs 1981). Although Leafy Anderson herself detested Voodoo, other Spiritualist churches that were established in New Orleans—some of which were outgrowths of her own—did incorporate elements of the Voodooism, as well as the Catholicism that was indigenous to

TABLE 24.1
A Partial Listing of Early Black Spiritual Churches in New Orleans

Church	Founder	Founding Date	Mother Church
Eternal Life Spiritualist Church	Mother Leafy Anderson	c. 1918–21	Eternal Life Christian Spiritualist Church (Chicago)
Temple of the Inno-cent Blood	Mother Catherine Seals	1922	N.A.[a]
St. James Temple of Christian Faith	Mother C. J. Hyde	1923	N.A.
Church of the Helping Hand and Spiritual Faith	Mother L. Crosier	1923	N.A.
St. James Temple of Christian Faith No. 2	Mother E. Keller	N.A.	St. James Temple of Christian Faith
Spiritualist Church of the Southwest	Bishop Thomas B. Watson	1920s	N.A.
St. Michael's Church No. 1	Mother Katherine Francis	late 1920s	Spiritualist Church of the Southwest
St. Anthony's Daniel Helping Hand Di-vine Chapel	Mother Shannon	late 1920s	Spiritualist Church of the Southwest
St. Michael's Church No. 9	Father Daniel Dupont	1932	St. Michael's Church No. 1

[a] Information not available.

southern Louisiana; according to Hurston (1931: 319), the "strong aroma of hoodoo" clung to a number of these. Mother Anderson passed away in 1927.

Another of the earliest and best-known Spiritual churches in New Orleans was the Temple of the Innocent Blood, established in 1922 by Mother Catherine Seals (*New Orleans City Guide* 1938: 199). Like the Eternal Life Spiritualist Church, this congregation was the forerunner of several other Spiritual groups in the city. The church incorporated many aspects of Catholicism, including the ritualistic use of the sign of the cross, votive candles, holy pictures, elaborate altars, and statues. The Catholic religious articles found in the church were in large part gifts from those Mother Catherine had healed; she used castor oil to cure people and gave spiritual advice to Whites as well as Blacks (Tinker 1930). Before she died on August 9, 1930, Mother Catherine, who claimed to be inspired by the Holy Spirit, prophesied that she would rise from the dead (Saxon, Dreyer, and Tallant 1945: 21). She was succeeded by Mother Rita, who renamed the renowned temple on the outskirts of New Orleans the Church of the True Light. Shortly before her death, however, Mother Catherine had completed a "Manger" near the church building proper, which reportedly could seat up to three hundred people (*New Orleans City Guide* 1938: 200). The Manger, used for banquets and musical festivals, was adorned not only by an altar and Stations of the Cross but also in later years with several small clay figurines and a five-foot statue of the revered prophetess herself.

Several other Spiritual temples were established in New Orleans during the early 1920s (see Table 24.1). Upon the "instructions" of the Blessed Virgin Mary, Mother L. Crosier started the Church of the Helping Hand and Spiritual Faith in 1923 (*New Orleans City Guide* 1938: 204–07). Even earlier that year, Mother C. J. Hyde organized the St. James Temple of Christian Faith (*New Orleans City Guide* 1938: 206–07). Several of her followers received subcharters under her city charter and went forth to found congregations of their own, among them Mother E. Keller, who established the St. James Temple of Christian Faith No. 2. Prior to turning to the Spiritual religion and becoming a disciple of Mother Hyde, Mother Keller claimed that she "received training in Voodooism from a Mohammedan prince in New York, met some of the greatest Voodoo doctors in the country, and became well versed in this mysterious art" (*New Orleans City Guide* 1938: 208).

The Growth of the Spiritual Movement in the Urban North

Like many other sectarian groups in the Black community, the Spiritual movement apparently underwent a tremendous growth during the 1920s and 1930s in various northern cities. Drake and Cayton (1945) note that the Spiritual movement flourished in Bronzeville, the Black section of Chicago, during this period. Although there was a wide variety of esoteric religions in Bronzeville at the time—Black Jewish groups, the Nation of Islam, the Moorish Science Temple, the African Orthodox Church, the Liberal Catholics—most of these sects were small compared to the Spiritual groups. "In 1928 there were seventeen Spiritualist storefronts in Bronzeville; by 1938 there were 51 Spiritualist churches, including one congregation of over 2,000 members. In 1928 one church in twenty was Spiritualist; in 1938, one in ten" (Drake and Cayton 1945: 642). A perusal of the telephone directories of the metropolitan areas with large concentrations of Blacks and my conversations with members of Spiritual churches indicate that Chicago is today the largest center of the movement.

The Spiritual movement diffused to many other cities in both the North and the South during the 1920s and 1930s. Ira A. Reid, a well-known early Black sociologist, notes its presence in the Black section of Harlem by the 1920s. Among the various "esoteric cults," he notes the activities of "a large number of exploiters and charlatans," including those "who dabble in spiritualism, exhibiting their many charms and wares in the form of Grand Imperial incense, prayer incense, aluminum trumpets, luminous bands and other accessories" (Reid 1926: 107). Although it is not clear which of the various congregations listed by Reid were part of the early Spiritual movement, names that he mentions—such as the Metaphysical Church of the Divine Investigation, and St. Matthew's Church of the Divine Silence and Truth—bear a striking resemblance to the names of churches that I have come across in my own fieldwork.[1]

Another Black writer, Claude McKay (1940: 74), remarks upon the "innumerable cults, mystic chapels and occult shops" that existed in Harlem during the Depression. Although he does not specifically refer to any of these as "Spiritual" or "Spiritualist," his narrative strongly suggests that at least some of them fit into this category. Many distraught persons resorted to the services of these institutions in seeking comfort and solace, employment, love, friendship, and marriage. McKay (1940: 77) notes that "heavy aromas of burning oils and incense" filled the atmosphere of a chapel that he visited. On the white altar in the front, he found a cross, a star, a crescent, a bouquet of roses, colored candles, and a painting of the Tree of Life and Hope. The audience, consisting primarily of women, was led by a "priestess," who wore a black and white robe and a headdress. In addition to giving public prophecies from the spirits, for a nominal donation the pastor offered private revelations and "consecrated numbers."

Brief sketches of three Spiritual associations of varying size will serve to illustrate the diversity of development within the Spiritual movement in the urban North. The first, the Metropolitan Spiritual Churches of Christ, is significant because it is probably the largest of the Spiritual associations and includes several congregations in West Africa. The second, Spiritual Israel Church and Its Army, is of medium size but adds elements from Black Judaism and Ethiopianism to the general core found in most Spiritual groups. Finally, although a relatively small association, Mt. Zion Spiritual Temple is, with its colorful founder and leader, an excellent example of the type of Spiritual church that is organized as a "kingdom."

1. Metropolitan Spiritual Churches of Christ, Incorporated

The mother congregation of the Metropolitan Spiritual Churches of Christ was established on September 22, 1925, in Kansas City, Missouri; its founders were Bishop William F. Taylor, a former Methodist minister, and Elder Leviticus L. Boswell, a former Church of God in Christ (Pentecostal) preacher. According to Tyms (1938: 112–14), by 1937 the group had grown to encompass thirteen congregations and some seven thousand members: in addition to its national headquarters, the association had two congregations in Chicago, one in Gary, two in St. Louis, one in East St. Louis (Illinois), one in Detroit, one in Tulsa, one in Oklahoma City, one in Omaha, and two in Los Angeles.

In 1942 a new organization, called the United Metropolitan Spiritual Churches of Christ, was established as the result of a merger between the Metropolitan Spiritual Churches of Christ and the Divine Spiritual Churches of the Southwest, based in New Orleans under the leadership of Bishop Thomas B. Watson.

> The Southwest organization had saved the considerable assets of Metropolitan (esti-mated at between one and two million dollars) from reverting to the family of the late Bishop Taylor, who founded the association in 1925. Metropolitan had no bona fide state charter, unlike Southwest, and thus entered the merger for somewhat opportunis-tic reasons. Bishop Watson quickly assumed a somewhat autocratic rule of the United organization, leading to a split only three years later, after he unilaterally called a conference in New Orleans without consulting with the national executive board. Two groups emerged as a result: the United Metropolitan, under Watson, and the Metro-politan under Cobbs and the Kansas City people. (Kaslow and Jacobs 1981: 100)

The United Metropolitan group experienced yet another schism in 1951, resulting in the establishment of the Israel Universal Spiritual Churches of Christ with Bishop E. J. Johnson as its head.

Under the leadership of Reverend Clarence Cobbs (who moved the headquarters of the association to Chicago), the original Metropolitan organization prospered and grew. Cobbs, who had been ordained by Bishop Taylor, had started the First Church of Deliverance with four members in a storefront on Chicago's South Side in 1929 (*Ebony 1960*). From these humble beginnings, the First Church of Deliverance grew into a large religious center with a community hall and a convalescent facility. By 1968, the Metropolitan Spiritual Churches of Christ had 125 churches and some ten thousand members (Melton 1978, II: 106). My data on the association indicated that the group's congregations today are heavily concentrated in Illinois and Michigan, but it also has churches in many other parts of the country, as well as several in Liberia and Ghana.[2]

According to Melton, the Metropolitan Spiritual Churches of Christ draw elements from Christian Science and Pentecostalism and emphasize a "foursquare gospel" consisting of preaching, teaching, healing, and prophecy. My own visits to three congregations affiliated with the association indicate that it is a reflection *par excellence* of the Spiritual movement, adding elements of Spiritualism, Catholicism, Black Protestantism, Voodooism or hoodoo, astrology, and probably others to those mentioned by Melton.

Cobbs's appeal to lower-class Blacks was manifested by several events, such as one "candlelight service" at Comiskey Park (the baseball stadium of the Chicago White Sox), to which he drew nearly 3,000 spectators on a cold, rainy night; and a service attempting to vindicate him of alleged wrongdoings, which packed an audience of nearly 10,000 people into a downtown auditorium (Drake and Cayton 1945: 646). Cobbs was a classical example of the "prophet" found in the Black community who assures the hopeful that they will receive a blessing if they engage in certain magico-religious rituals. One account (Carter 1976: 87) describes a service in Baltimore at the end of which he gave those in attendance an opportunity to be the beneficiaries of his spiritual powers: after each believer came forward to confide to Cobbs his innermost desires, he or she received a candle from the prophet; as compensation for this favor, each one was expected to place a monetary offering on the altar. Cobbs, who resided in a mansion until his death, was in a sense the informal leader of the diffuse Spiritual movement.

2. Spiritual Israel Church and Its Army

As is true of the Spiritual movement in general, the roots of Spiritual Israel Church and Its Army are obscure. My interviews with several leaders of the group—including its present "King," Bishop Robert Haywood, and its "Overseer," Bishop George Coachman[3]—provided me with only fragmentary data on its origin. It is not clear whether the group emerged as early as the mid-1920s or as late as the late 1930s. The forerunner of the Spiritual Israel Church and Its Army was the Church of God in David, which was established by Bishop Derks Field in Alabama. At some point, either in Alabama or in Michigan, Derks Field met W. D. Dickson, who had arrived at similar ideas about Israel from studying the Bible. According to one informant, Field was forced to leave Alabama by Whites who became agitated by his doctrines on Israel. Another informant, however, stated that W. D. Dickson moved the Church of God in David to Detroit after being instructed to do so by the Spirit of God. Regardless of who moved the group to Michigan, after the death of Field, Dickson emerged as the leader of the Church of God in David. Bishop Dickson, who became known as "the King of All Israel" (a title also carried by his successors), pulled Spiritual Israel "out of David" upon instructions from the Spirit. His leadership had been unsuccessfully opposed by the two surviving Field brothers, Doc and Candy. Both were pastors of congregations affiliated with Spiritual Israel in Detroit, and both established their own organizations, but they did not survive. One informant claimed that several other groups, all retaining the word "Israel" in their titles, also broke away from Spiritual Israel Church and Its Army.

Because of the severe winters in Michigan, Dickson moved the church to Virginia for a while, but returned it to Detroit upon further instructions from the Spirit. Since the death of Bishop Dickson, the line of succession in Spiritual Israel has included Bishop Martin Tompkin and Bishop Robert Haywood, the current King. The leader of Spiritual Israel is also reverently referred to by members as the "Holy Father." The largest concentration of the about thirty churches and several missions of Spiritual Israel Church is located in southeastern Michigan: the Detroit metropolitan area, Ann Arbor, Flint, and Saginaw. There are other congregations in New York City, Chicago, Milwaukee, New Orleans, Florida, Alabama, Mississippi, Georgia, and three cities in Indiana (Gary, Fort Wayne, and Muncie).

While like other Spiritual groups, Spiritual Israel Church and Its Army has incorporated various elements of Spiritualism, Black Protestantism, Catholicism, and possibly Voodooism and/or hoodoo, its inclusion of certain dimensions of Judaism gives it, at least in theory, a strong nationalist tone. In this regard, Spiritual Israel shares certain traits not only with various Black Muslim and Black Jewish sects, but also with the Universal Hagar's Spiritual Church.

Members of Spiritual Israel Church view themselves as the spiritual descendants of the ancient Israelites or "spiritual Jews," and their organization as a restoration of the religion of the ancient Israelites. In their belief, "Ethiopian" is the "nationality" name of Black people whereas "Israel" is their "spiritual" name. The original Ethiopians were "pure" Blacks, they say, but the Ethiopians of today are in large measure of mixed racial ancestry. Furthermore, the first human beings were Black people, starting with Adam, who was created from the "black soil of Africa." All of the great Israelite patriarchs and prophets, including Noah, Abraham, Isaac, Solomon, David, and Jesus, were Black men. In time, however, with the sons of Isaac, a division in humanity arose. Jacob became the progenitor of the Ethiopian nation and Esau of the White nation. Although these two nations have been in constant struggle with one another since their creation, they must learn to live in harmony and peace because they are "close kin."

According to the doctrine of the church, being an "Israelite" is more a matter of spirituality than of race and nationality. A Gentile, or "unbeliever," may be White or Black; and although most members of Spiritual Israel Church are Black, the group reportedly has some White members as well. Spiritual Israelites maintain that most Whites who identify themselves as "Jews" are actually the descendants of Gentiles who intermarried with the original Jews or Israelites. Unlike traditional Jews, however, members of Spiritual Israel Church do not observe any particular dietary prohibitions.

Spiritual Israel Church and Its Army, often simply referred to by members as "Israel," is regarded to be the "one true Spiritual church." Spiritual Israelites believe that God is not "something in the sky" but the Spirit that dwells in all people. When one's body dies, one's spirit or soul does not go to heaven or hell, both of which are merely projections of the human mind, but simply rejoins the all-pervasive Spirit of God. Spiritual Israelites also believe in reincarnation, or the return of one's spirit to earth in a new body. The Christ Spirit, which is simply the "anointed power" of God, has occupied the bodies of the many kings of Israel, including Bishops Field, Dickson, Tompkin, and Haywood, as well as Jesus. As a consequence, the present head of Spiritual Israel is on occasion referred to as "Christ Haywood."

3. Mt. Zion Spiritual Temple

One of the most colorful Spiritual associations is the Mt. Zion Spiritual Temple, Inc., which was founded in 1943 (and incorporated in 1945) by King Louis H. Narcisse, D.D. The "International Headquarters" of the group is in Oakland, California, where King Narcisse maintains one of his two residences; the "East Coast Headquarters" of the association is the King Narcisse Michigan State Memorial Temple in Detroit. In addition to these two temples, the association has seven other congregations, including a second temple in Detroit and temples in Sacramento, Richmond (California), Houston, Orlando, New York City, and Washington, D.C.

On the occasion of one of my visits to his eastern headquarters, I had the opportunity to meet King Narcisse, a tall stately man who appeared to be in his late sixties. He was dressed in a most regal manner, wearing a golden toga and cape with a white surplice, a white crown with glitter and a golden tassel, eight rings on his fingers, and a ring in his left ear. In a style befitting a potentate, King Narcisse was chauffeured to the temple in a shiny black Cadillac limousine with his title and name inscribed upon the door. As he proceeded down the center aisle of the sanctuary, the congregation stood to welcome its majestic leader. During the remainder of the service, except when he was preaching and conducting various rituals, King Narcisse sat on a throne in the front, occasionally sipping a beverage from a golden goblet.

For those occasions when King Narcisse cannot be with his flock in Detroit, a large picture of "His Grace" faces the congregation, reminding its members of their spiritual leader. Below the picture is a sign which reads as follows:

GOD IS GREAT AND GREATLY TO BE PRAISED IN THE SOVEREIGN STATE OF MICHIGAN IN THE KINGDOM OF "HIS GRACE KING" LOUIS H. NARCISSE, DD WHERE "ITS'S [*sic*] NICE TO BE NICE, AND REAL NICE TO LET OTHERS KNOW THAT WE ARE NICE."

Ironically, in contrast to the massive sanctuary with its elaborate altar and chandeliers, the presence of only thirty or so individuals at the service suggested that perhaps the Kingdom of Louis H. Narcisse has seen better days.

NOTES

1. Dillard (1973) argues that while the individual words in the names of Black storefront churches may be standard English ones, the combinations of these words appear to be distinctly African American. For example, as opposed to the names of most White religious groups, many Black storefront churches are characterized by long titles with three to five premodifiers (St. Anthony's Daniel Helping Hand Divine Chapel) and/or postmodifiers consisting of one or prepositional phrases (the United House of Prayer for All People or the Church on the Rock of the Apostolic Faith).

2. Another concentration of congregations affiliated with the Metropolitan Spiritual Churches of Christ is located in the New York–New Jersey megalopolis, where it has eight congregations in New York City proper and another three on the New Jersey side of the Hudson River.

3. The main duties of the Overseer appear to be to visit and provide guidance to the various congregations in the association.

REFERENCES

Carter, Harold A.
  1976 *The Prayer Tradition of Black People*. Valley Forge, Pa.: Judson Press.
Dillard, J. L.
  1973 "On the Grammar of Afro-American Naming Practices." In *Mother Wit from the Laughing Barrell: Readings in the Interpretation of Afro-American Folklore*, ed. Alan Dundes, 175–81. New York: New Garland.
Drake, St. Clair, and Horace R. Cayton
  1945 *Black Metropolis*. New York: Harcourt, Brace.
Ebony
  1960 October: 69.
Hurston, Zora
  1931 "Hoodoo in America." *Journal of American Folklore* 44: 317–417.
Kaslow, Andrew J.
  1981 "Saints and Spirits: The Belief System of Afro-American Spiritual Churches in New Orleans." In *Perspectives on Ethnicity in New Orleans*, 61–68. New Orleans: Committee on Ethnicity.
Kaslow, Andrew J., and Claude Jacobs
  1981 *Prophecy, Healing, and Power: The Afro-American Spiritual Churches of New Orleans*. A Cultural Resources Management Study for the Jean Lafitte National Historical Park and the National Park Service. Dept. of Anthropology and Geography, University of New Orleans.
McKay, Claude
  1940 *Harlem: Negro Metropolis*. New York: Dutton.
Melton, J. Gordon
  1978 *The Encyclopedia of American Religions*, vols. I, II. Wilmington, N.C.: McGrath.
Nelsen, Geoffrey K.
  1969 *Spiritualism and Society*. London: Routledge and Kegan Paul.
New Orleans City Guide
  1938 Federal Writers Project. Boston: Houghton Mifflin.

Powdermaker, Hortense
  1939 *After Freedom.* New York: Atheneum.
Reid, Ira De A.
  1926 "Let Us Prey." *Opportunity* 4: 274–78.
Saxon, Lyle, Edward Dreyer, and Robert Tallant
  1945 *Gumbo Ya-Ya.* Louisiana Writers Project Publications. Cambridge, Mass.: Riverside.
Simpson, George Eaton
  1978 *Black Religions in the New World.* New York: Columbia Univ. Press.
Spear, Allan H.
  1967 *Black Chicago: The Making of a Negro Ghetto, 1890–1920.* Chicago: University of Chicago Press.
Tallant, Robert
  1946 *Voodoo in New Orleans.* New York: Collier.
Tinker, Edward Laroque
  1930 "Mother Catherine's Castor Oil." *North American Review* 230 (2): 148–54.
Tyms, James Daniel
  1938 "A Study of Four Religious Cults Operating among Negroes." Thesis, Howard University.

Worshipers perform sacred dancers at the Yoruba Shrine of Obatala in Harlem. New York City, 1991. From *Feeling the Spirit* by Chester Higgins. Copyright © 1994 by Chester Higgins. Used by permission of Bantam Books, a division of Random House, Inc.

Chapter Twenty-five

Orisha Worship in the United States

Anthony B. Pinn

If the Spiritual Churches incorporated some aspects of the African heritage, Santería—in both Cuba and the United States—affirmatively asserted the religious and cultural traditions of Africa. In this, it paralleled the reconstruction of African rites and practices such as one finds in the candomble and macumba of Brazil, obeah in Jamaica, and Vodun in Haiti. Anthony B. Pinn offers a helpful survey of Santería in the United States.

•

Without doubt, the twentieth century witnessed a large movement of believers to North America, but it would be wrong to assume that religious practices resembling Santería did not exist in the United States before the late twentieth century. Although the United States is more influenced by Congo-Angolan populations of slaves than by the Yorùbá and Dahomey, I contend that substantial "retention" provided fertile ground for the development of traditions such as Santería within African American communities.

By the late nineteenth century, the vast majority of slaves in the United States had been born in the States. There were African-born slaves, of course, but as of 1776 this number only represented about 20 percent of the slave population. Yet it was possible for African religion—particularly deities who had been associated with natural forces—to survive in vital and vibrant ways.[1] In fact, the historical record demonstrates the persistence of religious beliefs and practices associated with Yorùbá tradition. For example, Raboteau writes that "hints in the historical record suggest that some slaves in Virginia in the 1830s thought of Christian conversion and baptism as similar to the initiation rituals of spirit possession. Henry Brown, a former slave from Virginia, remarked that when his sister 'became anxious to have her soul converted' she 'shaved the hair from her head, as many of the slaves thought they could not be converted without doing this.' . . . Shaving the head of the initiate, according to African custom, prepared the individual for possession by his or her patron god." This certainly shows some consistency in terms of ritual reenactment with the African traditions brought to the New World, including those of Yorùbá, Dahomey, Congo, Angola, and so on.[2]

Hyatt's *Hoodoo—Conjuration—Witchcraft—Rootwork* contains other examples applicable here. Regarding the Mother of Perpetual Help, Hyatt's informant told him: "And the Mother of Perpetual Help, she opens the way, she gives you bread when you got children like I have—she opens the way for you to have success. Well, you give her a blue candle—that's for children. And you pray twice a day to her . . . And whatever you promise her when you get your wish, why you give her that."[3] The reader will notice strong similarities between this saint as recognized in the United States and the Santería divinity, Yemaja. The color blue is the color of both, and the association with children—the divine mother—is consistent. In addition, in both Santería and U.S. practices, saints are, at times, given strong drink. This certainly is consistent with the representation of *orishas* for whom cigars and drink are important. One of Hyatt's informants had this to say about approaching St. Anthony with drink and cigars:

> An' Yo' put 'im [St. Peter] ovah de do'
> If Yo' ain't got but a nickel
> Try tuh git a nickel's wuth of beer
> an' when Yo' gittin' up in de mawnin'
> an' Yo' want a good time in yore house
> an' some fellahs come in an' give yo' money
> Yo' jes' throw beer on 'im [St. Peter]
> jes' throw plenty beer on 'im an' light a white light
> an' ah bet chew St. Peter gon'a open dat do'
> Yo' git St. Anthony, yeah, a brown candle . . .
> Yo' git a cigar . . .
> Yo' git 'bout a little whiskey glass of whiskey see
> 'cause St. Anthony he's a Saint he laks cigahs
> an' he wus a good-time man . . .
> an' yo' wake up de nex' mawnin' an' Yo' see
> de glass dry an' de cigah half smoked.[4]

Elements of the cosmology and theology associated with Santería are noticeably maintained. The movement of Santería to other areas of the Caribbean and the United States served to *strengthen* appreciation for African-based religious practices, an appreciation forged through centuries of retention. Many have minimized the importance of such findings by arguing that African deities could not significantly survive in the United States because of the dominance of Protestantism. Such scholars contend that these gods are best able to survive in Catholic countries because of the saint cults and accompanying ritual practices that resemble African attitudes toward the *orisàs*. I think, however, that Erika Bourguigeon's argument is useful for its refutation of this assumed direct relationship between Catholicism's presence and the presence of African-derived religions:

> [A]n explanation for the presence or absence of Afro-Christian spirit cults cannot simply be found by asking what the dominant form of Christianity in a given area is. It is true that these cults have incorporated into their liturgy and ritual certain elements of Catholic practice, and the Africans could not have done so without having been

taught rudiments of the Catholic religion. But this fact in itself is not enough, it seems, to explain the existence of the cults. It merely provides a necessary element for their development. Some Catholic countries such as Cuba . . . have Afro-Catholic cults. Others such as Martinique . . . do not have them.[5]

The presence of *botánicas* on the streets of many urban areas such as New York, Boston, West St. Paul, and Los Angeles point to the existence of Santería in these locations.[6] These are shops for practioners of this religion. Careful observers may see Shango's wooden axe or Ògûn's blacksmith's tools and tools of war on the shelves of these shops. The *botánicas* I have entered in Manhattan, Boston, and elsewhere are full of these items as well as of lithographs of the various saints, the *eleke*, statues, herbs, and so on. The fact that these shops are typically located in Spanish-speaking communities indicates that Cuban and Puerto Rican practitioners from the core of the Santería community. Joseph Murphy reports that Oba Ifa Morote (Francisco Mora) brought Santería to New York in 1946, when he came from Havana where he had become a *babalao* in 1944. With time, his knowledge and the interest of those living in New York resulted in the development of a house (*ile*). His reputation grew and he produced over six thousand "godchildren" (those he brought into the religion), who represent a committed group that provides for the house's needs based upon a sense of faith and family.[7] According to Steven Gregory:

> The relationship between godparent and godchild lies at the core of the social organization of Santería. Symbolically, it connotes the bonds existing between parents and children, and the living and their ancestors, and the Orisha and mankind. Practitioners of Santería conceive this relationship to be reciprocal. The godparent directs the spiritual development of the godchild and provides an array of supportive assistance. In return, the godchild contributes labor and resources in support of the ritual and secular activities of the house.[8]

Such was the relationship between Mora and his godchildren. Mora asserts that he was commissioned by the *Asociación de San Francisco* (a group of *Babalawos*) to bring the tradition to the United States. It is possible, however, that there were some practitioners here prior to this, but not with the influence that Mora would exert.[9]

Although Cubans began making their way to North America in the nineteenth century (perhaps informing early North American religious practices in some ways), it was not until the demand of the 1950s that the ritual substance of the tradition found strong expression on U.S. soil, as more than fifty thousand Cubans moved to the United States before 1970. Those moving during this period, whether or not they followed the *orishas* in Cuba, found the *orishas* a stabilizing force in the United States, which was then troubled by human rights struggles.

During these earlier years ritual focus was still on Cuba, where many went to receive initiation when this was possible (Puerto Rico when Cuba was not a possibility). Many contended that proper Santería initiation ceremonies could only be held in Cuba because of materials such as sacred stones that were not present in the United States. Others argued that the location was unimportant; otherwise the tradition would not have survived in the New World.[10] It is said, however, that *babalao*

Carlos Ojeda of Miami possessed important ritual items taken from Cuba. This, combined with the presence of consecrated *batá* drums, made initiations and ceremonies possible.

Levels of involvement correspond to levels of knowledge and training, beginning with the receiving of beads, then receiving of the warriors, and ending with initiation into the priesthood. Those who receive the beads are referred to as *alejo* and are protected by the godparents' saint. They are then able to move to receiving the warriors and perhaps the priesthood. One's position within the house is based upon years initiated rather than chronological age. These houses, for the most part, are within the living space of the priest or priestess; various rooms serve the ritual and theological needs of the community.

Marta Moreno Vega argues that before 1960 there were only twenty-five persons in New York City who followed the way of the saints. But although small in numbers, their work was enhanced by the presence of two traditional drummers from Cuba living in New York City, Julito Callazo and Francisco Aguabella. Other musicians also entered the world of Santería that was developing in New York City. In addition to Cuban participants, there was a growing number of Puerto Ricans.[11] And although some African Americans participated at this point, Chief Medahochi K. O. Zannu argues that African Americans who might have been interested assumed that these *ile* were Spanish clubs and that the activities were limited to Spanish speakers because Spanish was the dominant language.[12]

It is commonly held that many African Americans in the twentieth century first became acquainted with the superficial aspects of Santería through the music of figures such as Mongo Santamaria, Ray Barretto, and Tito Puente, and through dance.[13] George Brandon claims that the first devotee to be initiated in the United States was Julia Franco (1962); the initiation was done by Cuban-born priestess Mercedes Noble. Yet Brandon and others recognize that the first African American priestess, Margie Baynes Quiniones, was initiated in New York in 1961 by Cuban priestess Leonore Dolme.[14] She subsequently developed a house that consisted of twenty-one priests.

As of 1986, there were as many as ten thousand African American practitioners in New York City alone. Some African Americans, after initiation and proper training, began establishing their own *iles* (houses) with their own godchildren, while others remained in "multiethnic" houses. Murphy's description of one encounter in the house of Oba Ifa Morote on the day of Ifa's (Orunmila's) feast sheds light on African American involvement in Santería:

> As I move back from these senior priestesses, I fall into conversation with Olatutu, a black American man in his fifties. As the priestesses radiate strength and worldly wisdom, Olatutu is small and gentle and only newly initiated into the way of the *orishas*. But his story is that of many other seekers who find themselves in Padrino's *ile*. Olatutu is a self-taught scholar of the mystical traditions of the world. He has found in santería a grand synthesis of his reading in Egyptology and his participation in Moorish Science and Masonry. For him, the *orishas* are the purest expression of the primordial African wisdom that gave birth not only to Egypt and Ethiopia but to human life itself in the Rift Valley.[15]

Steven Gregory also provides useful information concerning the involvement of African Americans in Santería, based upon field work done in the Bronx, New York. One *ile*, referred to as "Fernando's house," had, in 1972, roughly twenty-five African American members, most of whom were in their twenties and thirties and had moved into the tradition through the influence of friends and acquaintances. Although this tradition has its deepest roots in the black African practices of the Yorùbá, some African American members of "Fernando's house" claim that racism on the part of Hispanic members often prevents them from progressing in the tradition.[16] As one of the first African American members of the house noted, many objected to his early involvement at the house; and he attributed this animosity to racial prejudice. His initial discomfort was increased through the heavy use of Spanish as the house's language. He overcame these difficulties, however, and his reputation and responsibilities have grown. In addition, he has also begun producing godchildren of his own.[17] Despite these difficulties, the number of African Americans continues to grow.

In addition to joining Cuban and Puerto Rican houses, African Americans established a good number of houses that reflect the "unique" needs and concerns of African Americans. One such house, "Peter's and Katherine's house," was studied by Mary Curry during the completion of her dissertation. It was understood as an important house in the African American sections of New York City and is a fairly good size house, with Peter numbering his godchildren at roughly two hundred (with beads). There are at least nineteen priests within the house who have godchildren of their own. According to Curry, Peter was initiated in 1973 and began producing godchildren three years later, while Katherine was initiated in 1974 and began producing godchildren in 1977. As with all houses, growth results from the reputation of the padrino or madrina and his or her knowledge. Those who have needs they believe the padrino or madrina can meet begin to attend, first casually.

Mary Curry asserts that notable ritual differences between African American houses, like Peter's and Katherine's, and other Santería houses do not exist. Nonetheless, there are differences in that nationalistic tendencies and race-based issues inform theology and ritual activities. One sign of this is the tendency of African Americans to call the tradition "Yorùbá religion" instead of using the term *Santería*. For nationalistically minded African American, their own term provides a much wanted and much stronger link to an "African past" and allows for attention to race-based issues. In some African American houses the religion is practiced without any attention to spiritist influences present in Cuban and Puerto Rican houses, and without attention to Christian (Catholic) influences also present elsewhere.[18] In many of these cases there is a concern with ritual and theological orthodoxy using Nigerian practice as the standard. These are, for the most part, conceptual differences undoubtedly fueled by the Black Power Movement, civil rights movement, and an overarching rethinking of African American identity.[19] Concerning this, early African American priests made an effort to think through the *odus* and the *orishas* and there find significance for black life.[20] For example:

It was these same . . . priests . . . who also thought about Olokun . . . The great *Orisha* of the sea. They reasoned that Olokun was the *Orisha* of the dark and unknowable *bottom* of the sea, that mysterious harbinger of the secrets of creation and in whose murky but stabilizing wetness is the actual support of all of life. They saw the bottom of the sea as being in principle the same as the layer of fluid that supports the human brain at its bottom . . . "Ancestral memory," as we have since come to call it, is a [*sic*] ability that refers back to the Middle Passage itself and recalls the many millions of Africans who in defiance of the *thought* of "slavery" dove or rebelled and were thrown into the sea—ultimately to form a spiritual collective that could forever be sympathetic to children of their comrades who did survive the journey. The assumption is that that body of souls forms a kind of *collective unconsciousness* in the psyche of Black Americans in general and is totally essential to Orisha Worship in the New World. That collective unconscious is seen as a manifestation of *Olokun*.[21]

Unlike the majority of other priests, many African American priests have organized themselves into societies. As of 1991, the following societies were active: the Society of the Children of Obàtálá, the Society of the Children of Yemaya, the Society of the Children of Oshun, and the Society of the Children of Oya.[22]

Julia Franco; the first African American initiated in the United States, was not the first African American to make the tradition her own. In fact, the first African American to seek religious selfhood through this religion was Walter Eugene King (b. 1928), a priest of Obàtálá, in 1959 in Mantanza, Cuba.

King recounts that as a member of the Baptist Church, baptized at age twelve, he had an interest in African dance, which he pursued at the Detroit Urban League. This sparked an interest in African studies, which ultimately resulted in his break with Christianity at the age of sixteen.[23] This interest in African philosophy and nationalism was not simply a result of external stimulation, but also of his family's orientation. King's father had moved to Detroit from Georgia in 1912 and became involved in the Moorish Science Temple and the Garvey movement. Yet, in addition to the exposure to alternate religious systems provided by his father, King recounts that his reading of Somerset Maugham's *The Razor's Edge* and Mbono Ajiki's *My Africa* moved him in the direction of Eastern traditions and African religion.[24]

At age twenty, King danced with the Katherine Dunham dance troupe for two months in late 1950. Shortly after this he married and became entrenched in the culturally eclectic world of Greenwich Village.[25] With his wife he developed a coffee house and, with those who frequented the shop, he developed an organization called the Order of Dambala Hwedo. This was a nationalist group practicing Akan and Dahomean religion.[26] Under the leadership of Fritz Vincent, the group was small but interested in deepening its understanding of African religion. But the group began to move in a direction with which Nana Oseijeman (King's new name) was not comfortable. It was a movement away from pure commitment to establishing African religion and society. According to Carl Hunt, "[The group] did not want to worship more than one god, though they would salute such deities as Damballa, Ògûn and Shango. They argued that black Americans could not understand and would not accept more than one god. Nana Oseijeman disagreed because blacks understood and accepted Christian emphasis [on the Trinity]."[27]

Nana Oseijeman's progress from casual training to his interest in the priesthood was, in part, motivated by what he understood as a need for leadership within the black nationalist movement. But he was only interested in a religious priesthood that would leave him free to speak to the unique ontological and epistemological concerns of African Americans in ways Christian clergy did not.[28] Having done initial readings in voodoo and other African religious traditions, he was convinced that priesthood in the Yorùbá religion and the espousing of its importance to African Americans would provide the type of nationalist movement and vision African Americans needed. With time, he became convinced that he should train for priesthood in the cult of Obàtálá in Mantanzas, Cuba. At first Nana Oseijeman resisted the idea of initiation because as a black nationalist he did not like the idea of incorporating Catholic saints into an African religion. Finally, convinced that it is an African religion with a necessary Catholic covering, he decided to seek initiation. This initiation took place on August 26, 1959, in Mantanzas, under the guidance of a *santero* named Sonagba.[29] Initiated (to the deity Aganju) with him was Christopher Oliana, whose parents owned a *botánica* in New York and who thus was familiar with the rituals and theology of Santería.

King describes the process this way:

[W]hen we got there[Mantanzas] they took us into a room, as I recall, and they then began to divine. They wanted to do their own. . . . They read me as Obàtálá. . . . It took a week then to buy all kinds of stuff that we needed, to purchase the animals and other live stock and to get us psychologically prepared. . . . I understood absolutely nothing because I was waiting for them to ordain me some kind of way but with words. But they got everything together. . . . So they did then my entire initiation without interruptions. . . . Then we [he and Chris] stayed in the room for six days. We had to perform and everything like that. . . . I wanted everything to be African. They had some type of Spanish clothes they wanted us to wear. I didn't want to wear those, not on a daily basis. So I [wrapped] my sheet around me the way the Akan people do. . . . The only part that I didn't really find African there was, one final day when we had to visit a church. We had to get some holy water.[30]

The Shango Temple

Upon his return to the United States, Nana Oseijeman, as King was now called, was removed from the Order of Dambala Hwuedo. And after another name change, to Adefunmi, he developed the Shango Temple in 1959 on East 125th Street. The charter members of Shango Temple were Adefunmi, Oliana, Clarence Robbins, Henry Maxwell, Royal Brown, Bonsu, and Mama Keke. During this period, his efforts to organize cultural events resulted in his recognition as an important cultural nationalist. He also developed and incorporated the African Theological Archministry Inc., in 1960, and an African market in 1961 that sold cloth and other goods as well as books written by Adefunmi, such as *The Yorùbá State, Tribal Origins of the Afro-Americans*, and *The Gods of Africa*.[31]

Adefunmi held nationalist leanings that would eventually result in a split with

Christopher Oliana, who rejected a removal of Catholic influences on the tradition. Adefunmi remained convinced that a more authentic form of religious expression, one that was Yorùbá in nature and action, was possible and desirable. His goal was to acquaint African Americans with their heritage and provide them with a strong sense of community through mutual respect and kindness, by introducing them to Yorùbá culture as a means of ending their "cultural amnesia." According to Adefunmi:

> African and Western cultures were fundamentally opposed. The purpose of Western culture is to perfect the physical world. Africans want to perfect the spiritual environment. Our achievement is "human technology." Here in America we have been briefly conquered by European culture, but we are Africans nonetheless. The Italians have their festivals. The Chinese have their New Year.... We're just "Negroes." What does that mean? Afro-Americans are suffering from cultural amnesia. They don't know which nation they belong to.[32]

The temple responds to two major needs. For black nationalists, it provides a sense of cultural identity and a unified community. The use of dashikis and other indications of an African connection sparked the interest of nationalists who wanted to add a religious dimension to their agenda. And for others it provided a response to pressing personal issues by taking into consideration their explicitly articulated spiritual questions. Adefunmi and the members of the temple were committed to regenerating African American cultural life. He renamed Harlem "New Oyo," in order to highlight the regeneration of Yorùbá culture exemplified by the temple.[33]

Tension naturally developed between the Santería community and the Shango Temple because the temple openly expressed the more delicate elements of the tradition.[34] As Stephen Clapp records, African American devotees associated with Adefunmi advertised their beliefs by placing a sign outside of the temple and parading through Harlem wearing African attire while carrying statues of the orìsàs. In addition, they openly performed ceremonies during the World's Fair and on film in "Only One New York." Furthermore, the temple organized such high-profile events as the Afro-American Day, which attracted roughly six hundred people wearing African attire.[35] The alterations advocated by the temple extended beyond this level of display in that the traditional secrecy observed with respect to ceremonies and knowledge was questioned by African American participants, who proselytized openly and aggressively. African Americans were clearly doing away with traditional protocol and religious sensibilities. Also notable among these alterations was the removal of Christian influences. Adefunmi believed that the maintenance of the Catholic cover, which was no longer necessary, compromised the purity of practice.

Many within the larger Santería community believed that misunderstandings concerning animal sacrifice and a general assumption that Santería lacked values (i.e., Christian values) already made Santería dangerously vulnerable to attack from self-righteous and fear-driven officials and community leaders. Thus, African Americans who openly altered the religion to meet their nationalistic goals might bring even more pressure from the authorities. Many practitioners of Santería acted upon their concerns by questioning the authenticity of the temple's ceremonies and thereby distancing the temple from the larger religious community. For example, it was argued that the drums used were not consecrated and, as a result, the participants were not actually possessed by the *orishas*.[36] In addition, restrictions were placed upon Adefunmi's function as a priest. In this way, his activities were monitored because he had to work with Puerto Rican and Cuban priests in order to gain a better knowledge of the rituals and to perform important ceremonies such as initiation. This allowed Santería houses to keep practitioners away from Adefunmi by claiming that his knowledge was too limited and that he preserved a sense of racism that should be offensive to true devotees. Nonetheless, clients came from cities such as Philadelphia, Chicago, and Washington for consultations with him, primarily over money concerns.[37] According to Hunt, a common ritual solution to this problem involved the following: "the person [burns] orange leaves and peels together with brown sugar. Another remedy for money problems . . . is for a person to mix some parsley with honey, cinnamon and grains of dried corn and leave it in a high place."[38]

By 1964, the division between the temple and the larger Santería community was irreconcilable.[39] Again, *santeros* objected to his overt ritualism and nationalism and Adefunmi rejected their Catholic-Yorùbá synthesis. Those involved in Santería were not the only ones to question the feasibility of "purifying" the tradition. Others questioned the ability of Adefunmi and his group to fully understand and connect with the actual culture of Nigeria, a culture that had itself undergone alterations.[40]

Adefunmi was not alone in his quest for "authentic" Yorùbá culture. John Mason and Edward Gary also refer to a return to precolonial Yorùbá tradition. Although many argue against the potential of such an endeavor, Mason and Gary maintain a vision of a "Yorùbá Reversionism," a tradition free of Catholic and slave-trade connotations. This process permits the preservation of an oral tradition that is slowly disappearing and fosters a "re-Africanizing" of the religion in a way that allows blacks in the diaspora to maintain an epistemological and cultural connection with their African heritage. Finally, Gary contends, this process provides otherwise inaccessible educational resources to interested persons.[41]

In response to the larger Santería community, Adefunmi and the members of the temple, eventually renamed the Yorùbá Temple, asserted that the religious is political and the political is religious; it is impossible to separate the two. As part of this reenvisioning, it was necessary to redefine various terms, including religion itself. Baba Oseijeman understood it as encompassing "the ethnic heritage of a particular people." As such, it entails their collective and complete history and philosophical outlook as a response to their environment. In short, it is an "ethnic celebration" inseparable from what it means to be alive. Understood in this way, each community possesses its own tradition, and it is dangerous to embrace that of another group. To do this, according to Baba Oseijeman, is equivalent to cultural suicide.[42] Very early in his practice of this tradition, Adefunmi indicated a strong connection between the self and the community's religious practices. He argued that religious practice is actually "worship of one's own personality" with the goal of controlling the forces that influence one's being. In this way the tradition provided ground rules and models for living properly in the world. Acceptance of these rules is first marked by the receiving of a new name symbolizing one's move toward the essential self.[43] The religion was idolatrous, but this idolatry allowed for the reconstitution of self-identity and self-worth based upon a close connection to cosmic forces and energies. This tradition provided African Americans with a connection to Africa that is deeper than rhetoric and mere aesthetic appeal; it is spiritual, a connection to energies that can never be understood strictly in light of material appearances.[44]

The name given to the practices of the Yorùbá Temple, Orisa-Vodu, reflects the theological and ritual break with the larger Santería community noted above. Chief Adenibi Edubi Ifamyiwa Ajamu, an early leader in this movement, explains that the temple's cultural practices, as of 1966, were dominated by the Yorùbá reality. There are also, however, a Dahomean and Congolese influence. According to Chief Ajamu, there is no conflict in incorporating these various cultural elements. The task of building a cultural complex that speaks directly to the needs of African Americans (a mixture of various African cultural groups) requires the blending of various cultural realities.

Although the temple's language was strongly racial, it took time for restrictions on white participation in the religion to be fully enforced. And so, during the first phase, the 1960s, white Americans were free to attend some of the functions. The collection of elders, the Ogboni council, decided that white Americans can attend all but the Night of Oshun, which is a secret rite.[45] According to Baba Oseijeman, "There is no room for racism in our religion. . . . If the religion is valid for blacks, it applies to whites as well. We teach that when an Afro-American has self-respect, he has no need to fear or hate the white man."[46] Stephen Clapp offers an account of his visit to a Friday evening meeting called the *Bembé*:

> On the second floor landing was a door painted in triangles of red, yellow and blue. Beyond a small hallway a dozen or so people sat on folding chairs and low stools along two walls. A team of drummers was ranged along another wall. At the base of the fourth wall a waist-high altar had been fitted out with statues and squat, flickering candles. The walls themselves were decorated with drawings of the five-footed fowl whom Obatala sent to mix earth and water in the Yorùbá myth of Creation. There were paintings of carved columns and inscriptions in an alphabet that Adefunmi had concocted from symbols used in the phonetic alphabet. . . . The bembe began with the "cleaning" of the temple with incense. The priests went around the circumference of the room with incense and water in order to seal off those inside from negative forces. Next Adefunmi petitioned the Yorùbá ancestors for permission to hold the ceremony: Through divination he determined whether quarrels in the room were likely to break up the ceremony. . . . Adefunmi called upon Elegba, the spirit guardian of the door, to protect the room. Permission to hold the bembe was asked of Obatala, patron god of the temple. When this was secured, those present were invited to salute the statue of the god that dominated the altar. Men prostrated themselves on the floor. Women lay at full length on one hip and one elbow. Adefunmi then blessed the drummers, asking the orishas to allow the drummers' rhythms to reach them without mistake. The heart of the service was a series of dances, with accompanying chants and drumming, that honored the twelve major orishas in the Yorùbá pantheon. . . . The first gods honored were the male orishas—Ogûn, Oshosi, Obatala, Shango, Babalu-aiye, Agunju, and Irenle. Those were followed by dances honoring Yemoja, the mother of the gods,

Oshun, Ibeji, and Oya, the female orishas. The cycle closed with another invocation to Elegba, the messenger. Throughout the bembe various onlookers rose and danced along with the priests. . . . Frequently dancers went into trances of possession.[47]

The average day within the life of a temple member was less dramatic than these celebrations might indicate. According to Adefunmi, a typical day began with the presentation of water to the *orishas*. Other ritual activities might include a reading by Adefunmi.[48] For the average person the tradition enabled material gain and social status. For those with a stronger interest in the religion, the first step in becoming a member involved gaining a new African name, which, as noted above, marked the awareness of one's African self and the necessary break with the cultural perspective of white America. If interest remained strong after this point, the person was given the opportunity to purchase proper African clothing. The next stage was the receiving of *ileki* (*eleke*), or the beads. After receiving these initial beads, the person received the warriors—Elégbá Ògún, and Oshosi.

The work of the temple was not without problems and internal strife as the questionable intent of some "clients" might suggest. For example, conflict over Adefunmi's marriage to a white American and his decision to take a second wife from within the temple resulted in the secession of many members. Other problems surfaced, which ultimately resulted in the closing of the temple except for necessary rituals. Adefunmi, along with a few families who participated in the temple, gave some thought to moving out of New York since it was hopelessly devoted to the ways and world view of white Americans.

NOTES

1. George Eaton Simpson, *Black Religions in the New World* (New York: Columbia University Press, 1978), 19.

2. Albert J. Raboteau, "The Afro-American Traditions," Ronald and Darrel W. Amundsen, eds., *Caring and Curing: Health and Medicine in the Western Religious Traditions* (New York: Macmillan, 1986), 546.

3. Harry Middleton Hyatt, *Hoodoo—Conjuration—Witchcraft—Rootwork*, vol. 1 (Washington, D.C.: Distributed by American University Bookstore, 1970 [Hannibal, Mo.: Western Pub.]), 870.

4. Ibid. 2:1220–21.

5. Erika E. Bourguigeon, "Afro-American Religions: Traditions and Transformations," 191–202, in John F. Szwed, ed., *Black America* (New York: Basic Books, 1970), 196.

6. Joseph M. Murphy, *Santería: African Spirits in America* (Boston: Beacon Press, 1993), chap. 3.

7. Ibid., 50.

8. Steven Gregory, *Santería in New York City: A Study in Cultural Resistance* (dissertation, New School for Social Research 1986), 67.

9. Ibid., 55. Some of this information is available in Steven Gregory, "Afro-Caribbean Religion in New York City: The Case of Santería," in Constance R. Sutton and Elsa M. Chaney, eds., *Caribbean Life in New York City: Sociocultural Dimensions* (New York: Center

for Migration Studies of New York, Inc., 1994): 287–302. Also see Migene Gonzalez-Wippler, *The Santería Experience: A Journey into the Miraculous*, rev. and expanded ed. (St. Paul, Minn.: Llewellyn Publications, 1992). Canizares claims that he has evidence suggesting that Afro-Cuban groups practiced in Florida as early as 1939 (*Walking with the Night*, 122–23).

10. Canizares, *Walking with the Night*, 125.

11. Marta Moreno Vega, "The Yorùbá Orisha Tradition Comes to New York City," in *African American Review* 29 (November 2, 1995): 201–2. An interesting popular account of Santería is Karl Vick, "Gods Help Us All," *The Washington Post* (July 2, 1995): F1, F5. Another story in this issue of the *Post* is also worth noting: William Booth, "At a Miami Courthouse: A Chicken in Every Spot," F1, F2.

12. Interview with Chief Medahochi K. O. Zannu, February 1996, Milwaukee, Wisconsin.

13. See Vega, "The Yorùbá Orisha Tradition Comes to New York City." Readers should also be aware of the Caribbean Cultural Center, 408 W. 59th Street, New York, NY 10019, which published *African Religion in the Caribbean: Santería and Voudon* (New York: Caribbean Cultural Center, n.d.).

14. George Brandon, *Santería from Africa to the New World: The Dead Sell Memories* (Bloomington: Indiana University Press, 1993), 104–5, 107. For interesting work on an African American house, see Mary Elaine Curry, "Making the Gods in New York: The Yorùbá Religion in the Black Community," Ph.D. dissertation, City University of New York, 1991. Curry asserts that most African American initiates are descendants of either Omi Duro or Osa Unko; both have their roots in Ofun Che in Regla, near Havanna (151).

15. Murphy, *Santería*, 54.

16. Gregory, "Afro-Caribbean Religion in New York City," 295. For more information on this particular house see Gregory, "Santería in New York City," 70–102.

17. Gregory, "Santería in New York City," 72, 77–78, 79.

18. Ibid., 69.

19. Curry, "Making the Gods in New York," 154, 159; Steven Gregory, "Santería in New York City," 5.

20. For extensive information on particular African American houses see, e.g., Gregory, "Santería in New York City"; Curry, "Making the Gods in New York"; Brandon, *Santería from Africa to the New World*, chap. 5; Canizares, *Walking with the Night*, 121–26; Vega, "The Yorùbá Orisha Tradition Comes to New York City."

21. Curry, "Making the Gods in New York," 48.

22. Ibid., 139, 142–53.

23. Biographical sketch of H. R. H. Oseijeman Adefunmi I provided by Oyotunji African Village.

24. Stephen C. Clapp, "A Reporter at Large: African Theological Arch-Ministry, Inc." (New York Public Library: Schomburg Collection), 10.

25. Carl M. Hunt, *Oyotunji Village: The Yorùbá Movement in America* (Washington, D.C.: University Press of America, 1979), 24.

26. Clapp, "A Reporter at Large," 11.

27. Hunt, *Oyotunji Village*, 25.

28. Interview with H. R. H. Oba Adefunmi I, April 1996, the Palace of Oyotunji African Village.

29. Biographical sketch made available by Oyotunji African Village and also based upon an interview with Oba Adefunmi I, April 1996, for which I am grateful.

30. Interview with Oba Adefunmi I, April 1996.

31. Biographical sketch provided by Oyotunji African Village.

32. Clapp, "A Reporter at Large," 5.

33. Ibid., 4.

34. As Raul Canizares indicates, however, this secrecy is questioned by many non-Cuban priests who want to adapt the tradition to its new U.S. context. See *Walking with the Night*, "Secrecy and Survival," beginning on p. 26.

35. Clapp, "A Reporter at Large," 3.

36. Gregory, "Santería in New York City," 62; S. Cohn, "Ethnic Identity in New York City: The Yorùbá Temple of Harlem," M.A. thesis, New York University, 1973.

37. Hunt, *Oyotunji Village*, 30.

38. Ibid., 30–31.

39. Adefunmi would separate from his wife in 1965 due to the demands of his nationalist perspective. In 1962, Adefunmi helped two practitioners establish a Yorùbá Temple in Gary, Indiana. One of these two men would be among the first persons initiated by Adefunmi in Oyotunji Village, in 1970.

40. Clapp, "A Reporter at Large," 25–26.

41. Gary Edwards and John Mason, *Black Gods: Orisa Studies in the New World* (Brooklyn NY: Yorùbá Theological Archministry, 1985).

The Yorùbá Theological Archministry sponsors classes on Yorùbá cooking, language, theology, and songs. Mason, along with others, is responsible for putting much of this information into English. Adefunmi's group considers itself orthodox and Mason as moderate because of his work outside African American communities.

42. H. R. H. Oseijeman Adefunmi I, "Keynote Address," Columbia University, New York: January 16, 1993.

43. Clapp, "A Reporter at Large," 16.

44. Ibid., 16.

45. Ibid., 18.

46. Ibid., 5–6.

47. Ibid., 6–8.

48. Ibid., 20.

African American Yorubas in Harlem and the Transition to Oyotunji Village

Tracey Hucks

One of the more prominent expressions of Santería in the United States added an overtly nationalistic dimension, including withdrawal into a separate community. Tracey Hucks provides a vista into this separate Santería community, called Oyotunji Village, in South Carolina.

•

Walter Serge King was the first African American initiated into Santería priesthood, by way of Cuba. Taking the name His Royal Highness Oba Oserjeman Adefunmi I, he became one of U.S. Santería's most noted spokespersons. According to Adefunmi:

> [W]hen the Gods of Africa (Yoruba Pantheon) arrived in Harlem in late September 1959, powerful currents began to circulate. Black suddenly became beautiful, the shout for Black Power echoed across America. From the Yoruba Temple in Harlem where the Gods were kept, the dashiki was first produced and introduced into Afro-American culture. The gele, a colorful headwrap for women, was de riguer for rites and ceremonies. The idea of the African Boutique, where African attire could be purchased, started in its storefront location. Books of African names and classes in African languages were organized in the Temple. The rhythm of conga drums began to be heard, not only in professional orchestras as previously, but also in the streets and in the parks of Harlem. Then throughout the 1960s African nationalists, dressed in full African attire, vied with the integrationists for news headlines. During the memorable 1960s scores of black young men and women from Harlem, the Bronx, Brooklyn, New Jersey, Philadelphia, Gary, Chicago and elsewhere, who had received word of the presence of Orisha-Vudu, began to make the same journey of initiation into the priesthoods of the Black Gods. Some went to Cuba, and when political problems with the United States prevented such travel, Puerto Rico, where large numbers of Cubans had migrated, became the new arena for initiation. Later the Bronx, El Barrio, became the center for an onslaught of initiations of Afro-Americans into "Santo Africana" or "Ocha" as the Cubans called it.

By 1959, Adefunmi established Shango Temple in Harlem with Christopher Oliana, which eventually evolved into his own singular enterprise, Yoruba Temple, by 1960. Its mission was to restore West African cultural institutions in America, to function as an educational resource, and, more importantly, to inform African Americans of the ancient religion of Orisha-Voodoo. During these early years, a written promotion for the Temple was made available highlighting the question, "What is the Yoruba Temple?" In response to this question the promotion read, "The Yoruba Temple is the first purely African institution . . . in the United States since the Emancipation of Africans from slavery . . . A renaissance of African culture has commenced among African Americans. It is a monument to the thousands of Yorubas who perished during the slave era . . . Those traditions of ancient ways have filtered down to the present generation and fired [up their] spirit. It is the proud achievement of young African Americans who take pride in their ancestry . . . and the increasing need [of] African Americans for a fundamental cultural identity and a living expression of their racial genius." The promotion then went on to draw connections between the Temple and its ritual and ceremonial activities in relationship to the gods of Africa. It read as such: "The Yoruba Temple is the 'home' of the Gods of Africa in America. For here the worship of Obatala, Ogun, Shango, Elegba, Babalu, and the rest of the great Gods of the Yoruba pantheon is maintained in all its vitality, symbolism, and ritual. Day and night great chants rise to the Yoruba Gods, Temple drummers play Sacred Drums, and Harlemites, young and old, dressed in Nigerian clothes, arrive and dance for the gods of their Fathers. These Yoruba Americans have been organized, and support the Yoruba Temple under the leadership of their young American-born Chief and Priest (Nana) Oserjeman Adefunmi."

Although Adefunmi's understanding of Yoruba religion was greatly indebted to that of Cubans and to some degree Puerto Ricans, his black nationalist vision of the religion and its function for African Americans extended (and at times caused great tension) beyond that of his forerunners. Ultimately, Adefunmi saw Yoruba religion as a window for nationhood for African Americans. As the founder of the African National Independence Party and a member of the Republic of New Africa, Adefunmi's focus throughout the 1960s became that of cultural redemption of African Americans and the establishment of an "African State" in America. By 1962, Adefunmi had announced at a public rally that by 1972 an African State would exist in America. According to Adefunmi, "the foundation of the state will be African, and it will be purely African in culture." By 1970, Adefunmi's nationalist impulses and vision of Yoruba religion for African Americans were reconciled in the Village of Oyotunji.

The Rise of Oyotunji Village

"Iya mi ile odo, iya mi ile odo" resound the chants for Oshun, the Goddess of the river. *"Iya mi ile odo,"*—In the House of my Mother, the River. With the call and response of the chant, the ritual moment in honor of Oshun begins. We stand outdoors before the golden altar where gifts of music, dance, and food are offered to Oshun. Soon sacred space shifts from the golden altar of Oshun to the golden shrine of Oshun, a small building housing the ritual offerings permissible only to those who have consecrated their lives and heads to Oshun. A great procession leads the

devotees to this new sacred space. Oshun, the river goddess, personifying beauty, goodness, and sensuality, is offered sweet candy and fruit. Praises of dance are offered to Oshun. And suddenly she appears. A human figure dressed in elaborate gold ashoke and a gold covering about the face appears before the crowd. Praises in Yoruba are offered to her presence. *"Ko wa ni yeko wa ni ye ye to ko nta,"* Teach us to have understanding. *"Oshun ala si rere o maa,"* Oshun we dream of uncovering goodness always. *"Omi o akete oba Oshun,"* Water is throne of Oshun. Sweet honey is offered to Oshun. Sweet honey is then offered to all the practitioners present— African, African Caribbean, African American—in order to solidify the sacred community.

The goddess Oshun is honored once again but this time not in Oshogbo, her sacred home in Nigeria, or even in the presence of El Caridad de Cobre in Cuba, but in her new home in Oyotunji African Village in South Carolina under the leadership of His Royal Highness Oba Oserjeman Adefunmi I, his royal family, chieftancy, and council of elders.

Oyotunji African Village was founded in 1970. It was originally located on one of the South Carolina Sea Islands and in 1973 was moved and reestablished in its current location in Sheldon, South Carolina, located in Beaufort County. It was formed as a cultural and religious community for African Americans. Its purpose was twofold. One purpose of the Village was to carry on the black nationalist teachings that Adefunmi and others adhered to in Harlem, namely black separatism, economic self-determination, and cultural redemption. The second and most important of the Village's purposes was to create a space where West African Yoruba religion and culture could be established and practiced as a societal norm. Adefunmi chose the name "Oyo Tunji" to "rise again" as part of his larger vision that African religion and culture would one day rise again among "Africans" in America.

In terms of the physical appearance and structure of Oyotunji Village, Adefunmi himself gives a very vivid description.

> One enters the struggling 'village state' occupying perhaps 27 acres, through a larger wooden, [now cement] arch. Its facade is decorated with painted figures at an African forge with the red, yellow and green of the Yoruba flag as a background. Its dusty main road is posted with traffic signs in Yoruba and English. To the left is a collection of circular structures with thatched roofs which serves as the village market place. Opposing this across the road is another thatched shed sheltering a large blood-stained clay phallus, which is the shrine of Eshu-Elegba: Eshu-in-charge-of-the-gate. Further along, the road is bounded by thatched roofed guest houses belonging to His Royal Highness the King of Oyotunji. Presently one arrives at the village square which features a grove of tall pines, a heavily decorated village drum house, and the largest structure in the entire village, the brightly pained Royal Palace facade. From this center of the village one can see tucked beneath the oppressive forest, the clusters of small wooden houses that compose the family compounds of the villagers. Flocks of goats, chickens, ducks, geese, and half naked children scamper to and fro. Groups of novice priestesses, wrapped in white as a sign of devotion to the Orisha-Vudu Gods, carry pails of water on their heads, and young men with axes, machetes, and shovels, repair palace buildings and fill in holes in the dirt streets. As most tourists conclude, the effect of Oyotunji is of suddenly being some place strange and misplaced.

From its inception, Oyotunji African Village has indeed been viewed as "some place strange and misplaced" in America. It stands in South Carolina as an anachronism, a reminder of a time decades ago when African Americans were struggling through a tumultuous and often painful social history. Through layers of issues surrounding race, identity, and religion, African Americans were able to forge a space for themselves within the Orisha tradition. It functioned for them between these early years from 1960 to 1970 as a form a resistance against a society in the United States some African Americans believed held no place for them. Therefore, not only did African Americans attempt to create a new culture and homeland during this ten-year period; many of them made a commitment to dedicate their lives to the "Gods of Africa."

Chapter Twenty-seven

The Other Kind of Doctor
Conjure and Magic in Black American Folk Medicine

Bruce Jackson

A persistent presence among African Americans from the earliest days of slavery has been those practitioners of "alternative medicine," persons believed to be repositories of skills and knowledge—passed down from pre–American days—to ward off evil and achieve beneficial aims for their clients. These quasi-religious conjure doctors were called upon in slave revolts to provide protective amulets for the insurrectionists. Before and after slavery's end, they would be consulted for assistance with illness, financial matters, and romantic pursuits. Blacks who became Christians might dismiss the power of conjure, or "hoodoo"; they might affirm its efficacy but assert the superior efficacy of Christianity; they might forthrightly deploy both systems; or they might find in their Christian belief the grounding for the ability of persons to exercise "power." A former slave interviewed by the staff of the Federal Writers' Project in the 1930s said:

> *"There is some born under the power of the devil and have the power to put injury and misery on people, and some born under the power of the Lord for to do good and overcome the evil power. . . . When the Lord gives such power to a person, it just comes to 'em. . . . The old folks in them days knows more about the signs that the Lord uses to reveal His laws than the folks of today. It am also true of the folks in Africa, they native land. Some of the folks laughs at their beliefs and says it am superstition, but it am knowing how the Lord reveals His laws."*[1]

•

There is a remarkable account of conjure work in the *Narrative of the Life Adventures of Henry Bibb: An American Slave Written by Himself*, originally published in 1849. Bibb tells of slaves who adopted various techniques to avoid whippings. "The remedy is most generally some kind of bitter root; they are directed to chew it and spit towards their masters when they are angry with the slaves. At other times they prepare certain kind of powders, to sprinkle about their master's dwellings."[2] Bibb says he got into a scrape for slipping off one time. He expected to be flogged; so he went to a conjurer who gave him both a powder to sprinkle and a root to chew, and "for some cause I was let pass without being flogged that time."[3] The next week, encouraged by his apparent power over the master, Bibb stayed away most of the weekend and on his return talked back to the master. "He became so enraged at me for saucing him, that he grasped a handful of switches and punished me severely, in spite of all my roots and powders."[4] Bibb went to another conjure doctor who told him the first doctor was a quack; the second supplied him with a sneezing powder to sprinkle about the master's bed; it would, he said, turn feelings of anger to love. The only effect was the master and his wife both suffered violent sneezing fits. Bibb "was then convinced that running away was the most effectual way by which a slave could escape cruel punishment."[5]

His interest in flight was suspended for a while when he got interested in women. Even though he'd been ill-served by conjure doctors before, he once again turned to them for help. "One of these conjurers, for a small sum agreed to teach me to make any girl love me that I wished. After I had paid him, he told me to get a bull frog, and take a certain bone out of the frog, dry it, and when I got a chance I just step up to any girl whom I wished to love me, and scratch her somewhere on her naked skin with this bone, and she would be certain to love me, and would follow me in spite of herself, no matter who she might be engaged to, nor who she might be walking with."[6] One Sunday, Bibb saw a woman he liked walking with her lover. He "fetched her a tremendous rasp across her neck with this bone, which made her jump." It also made her rather angry. He went to still another conjure adviser, an old slave who told him to place a lock of his lady's hair in his shoes, an act which would "cause her to love me above all other persons." He was by that time interested in another girl, but she refused him the hair. "Believing that my success depended greatly upon this bunch of hair, I was bent on having a lock before I left that night let it cost what it might. As it was time for me to start home in order to get any sleep that night, I grasped hold of a lock of her hair, which caused her to screech, but I never let go until I had pulled it out. This of course made the girl mad with me and I accomplished nothing but gained her displeasure."[7]

To the modern reader, Bibb's experience must seem absurd on at least two major counts: how could he believe such devices would function? and after he saw they didn't help him, why didn't he learn from experience that the conjure doctor's advice was not only not helpful but sometimes downright dangerous to him?

We must change the logic a bit, shift the basic premises. What if we assume that events in this world are *causally* rather than *randomly* linked? What if we assume the world has a sense to it greater than accident and less than total divine plan? Then the only real problem is to find out how to influence the various operations. The *donnée* would be that the world *can* be influenced for good or ill, that both events and persons can be directed in significant ways. The various failures Bibb reports could then be viewed as resulting from incompetence on the part of the practitioners or some mistake on Bibb's part, but they do not themselves invalidate the theory, the process, the art.

The curious thing about the stuff so often referred to as "primitive" medicine or magic is that it is terrifically logical. It assumes the operation of the universe is causal, not gratuitous. The educated executive in New York may attribute his fall down a flight of steps to bad luck, his missing a plane to uncommon traffic congestion, but the so-called primitive would ask why he—rather than someone else—had the mass of cars in his way that afternoon and why he should have missed that top step he had always found in the past. The "logical" answer is that something caused it to happen.

A. B. Ellis, writing of Gold Coast folklore, said:

> To the uncivilized man there are no such deaths as those we term natural or accidental. All deaths are attributed directly to the actions of men or to the invisible powers. If a man be shot or his skull be fractured by another man, the cause of death appears to the uncivilized man obvious. Such and such an injury has been inflicted by So-and-so, and experience, either personal or derived, has shown him that death results from such injuries. But should a man be drowned, be crushed by a falling tree in the forest, or be killed by lightning, such an occurrence would not be considered an accident; and a man who met his death in one of these modes would be believed to have perished through the deliberate act of a malignant being. And such, to us, accidental deaths, prove to the uncivilized man both the existence and the malignancy of these beings. A man is drowned. Who has killed him? So-and-so, a local spirit of the sea or a river has dragged him down. . . .
>
> Thus far for violence and sudden deaths; but the same belief is held with regard to deaths which are really due to disease or old age. These are likewise attributed to the action of the invisible powers directly, or to witchcraft, that is to say, to the indirect action of the same powers; for it is from them that wizards and witches obtain assistance and mysterious knowledge.[8]

An extraordinary amount of folk culture is devoted to ways of dealing with what highly literate groups like to consider luck. If there are potent beings in the universe, they can do well or ill; if they exist, they can probably be influenced; if they can be influenced for good, they can be influenced for ill; if someone has caused an evil influence, perhaps someone else can cause a good one, or at least undo the evil. The world of folk magic and medicine, as many commentators have noted, assumes a total coherence in the operation of the world.

What has been assumed to be learned fatalism among lower-class American blacks in the seventeenth, eighteenth, and nineteenth centuries wasn't fatalism at all: most *knew* quite well that whatever happened was *caused*. Some things were beyond their power of influence. That didn't mean it was beyond anyone's influence—only theirs, in that place at that time.[9]

If the magic didn't work, it meant either that it was done imperfectly or that someone else was working something stronger. It is curious that a high degree of learning is directed away from the "logical" and toward the gratuitous. But the random and gratuitous are far harder to accept and live with, far more fearful exactly because one cannot cope with them.[10]

In an article on folk medicine, Don Yoder writes:

> Of folk medicine there are essentially two varieties, two branches: (1) natural folk medicine, and (2) magico-religious folk medicine. The first of these represents one of man's earliest reactions to this natural environment, and involves the seeking of cures for his ills in the herbs, plants, minerals, and animal substances of nature. Natural medicine, which is sometimes called "rational" folk medicine, and sometimes "herbal"

folk medicine because of the predominance of herbs in its material medica, is shared with primitive cultures, and in some cases some of its many effective cures have made their way into scientific medicine. The second branch of folk medicine is the magico-religious variety, sometimes called "occult" folk medicine, which attempts to use charms, holy words, and holy actions to cure disease. This type commonly involves a complicated, prescientific world view.[11]

The important difference between the two kinds of folk medicine is that the first assumes a direct cause and effect between application of some substance to some somatic problem, while the other attempts to influence some agent other than the doctor or patient or subject. The first is quite close to what we usually consider proper medical practice; the second is closer to what we consider religious manipulation.

In Old World black culture, the two were often combined. The medicine man or voodun in Africa or Haiti would not only cure with herbs but would also act as intermediary with various divinities in the manipulation of a variety of situations. What is curious about the American situation is that the second aspect survived, but it survived without the theological framework upon which it was based. George J. McCall, for example, reports:

> "Hoodoo" represents the syncretistic blend of Christian and Nigritic religious traditions in the United States, corresponding to *vodun* ("voo-doo") and *obeah* in Haiti, *shango* in Trinidad, *candomble* and *macumbo* in Brazil, *santería* in Cuba, and *cumina* in Jamaica. In twentieth-century hoodoo, however, Catholic elements are less prominent than in the other variants, and Nigritic collective rituals have largely disappeared. Instead, hoodoo has been assimilated to the bewildering variety of store-front spiritualist churches in its truly religious aspect, leaving a heavy residue of sorcery and fetishism as the remaining native elements.
>
> As with sorcery among other peoples, the major foci of hoodoo sorcery lie in the realms of health, love, economic success, and interpersonal power. In all these cases, hoodoo doctors—after careful spiritual "reading" of the client—prescribe courses of action (which always include some hoodoo ritual) and gladly sell him the charms, potions, and amulets the ritual requires.[12]

At its most fully developed, as in Haiti and nineteenth-century New Orleans, voodoo is a system which explains the world; it has various deities assigned a variety of tasks, deities who may be supplicated or motivated in various ways. The voodoo doctors are trained in such manipulation. But rootwork, the more common form found in the rest of the United States, is only technique; much of the work done by root doctors and conjure men has to do with common folk remedies and with good luck (or bad luck for others) charmers. The voodoo doctors sometimes engaged in simple medical work, but they originally did such work through the agency of a powerful outsider, a god.

The function of the voodoo doctor in the Haitian and Louisiana traditions is close enough to the function of the African medicine man that we may cite John S. Mbiti's long description of the medicine man's work:

> First and foremost, medicine-men are concerned with sickness, disease and misfortune. In African societies these are generally believed to be caused by the ill-will or ill-action

of one person against another, normally through the agency of witchcraft and magic. The medicine-man has therefore to discover the cause of the sickness, find out who the criminal is, diagnose the nature of the disease, apply the right treatment and supply a means of preventing the misfortune from occurring again. This is the process that medicine-men follow in dealing with illness and misfortune: it is partly psychological and partly physical. Thus, the medicine-man applied both physical and "spiritual" (or psychological) treatment, which assures the sufferer that all is and will be well. The medicine-man is in effect both doctor and pastor to the sick person. His medicines are made from plants, herbs, powders, bones, seeds, roots, juices, leaves, liquids, minerals, charcoal and the like; and in dealing with a patient, he may apply massages, needles or thorns, and he may bleed the patient, he may jump over the patient, he may use incantations and ventriloquism, and he may ask the patient to perform various things like sacrificing a chicken or goat, observing some taboos or avoiding certain foods and persons—all these are in addition to giving the patient physical medicines. In African villages, disease and misfortune are religious experiences, and it requires a religious approach to deal with them. The medicine-men are aware of this, and make attempts to meet the need in a religious (or quasi-religious) manner—whether or not that turns out to be genuine or false or a mixture of both. . . .

On the whole, the medicine-man gives much time and personal attention to the patient, which enables him to penetrate deep into the psychological state of the patient. Even if it is explained to a patient that he has malaria because a mosquito carrying malaria parasites has stung him he will still want to know why that mosquito stung him and not another person. The only answer which people find satisfactory to that question is that someone has "caused" (or "sent") the mosquito to sting a particular individual, by means of magical manipulations. Suffering, misfortune, disease and accident, all are "caused" mystically, as far as African peoples are concerned. To combat the misfortune or ailment the cause must be found, and either counteracted, uprooted or punished. This is where the value of the traditional medicine-man comes into the picture.[13]

The most complex and highly structured voodoo work in this country apparently occurred in and around New Orleans because both the black and white populations there had strong ties with Haiti. One of the most interesting descriptions of that scene is offered by Zora Neale Hurston. In the second half of *Mules and Men*, she describes how, while doing research as a Columbia graduate student, she was several times initiated as a voodoo doctor. She offers formulas for various influences: "Concerning Sudden Death," "To Rent a House," "For Bad Work," "Court Scrapes," "To Kill and Harm," "Running Feet," "To Make a Man Come Home," "To Make People Love You," "To Break Up a Love Affair";[14] and she quotes some "Prescriptions of Root Doctors."[15]

The tradition she describes is essentially Caribbean and African; it operates with the claimed mediation of deities and through the application of chemicals, and some of the practitioners claim temporary apotheosis as the source of their power. Luke Turner, descendant of famed voudooienne Marie Leveau, gives Hurston a long description of Levau's work and says, "Marie Leveau is not a woman when she answer one who ask. She is a god, yes. What ever she say, it will come so."[16]

Turner described in some detail Leveau's method of affixing a curse:

She set the altar for the curse with black candles that have been dressed in vinegar. She would write the name of the person to be cursed on the candle with a needle. Then she place fifteen cents in the lap of Death upon the altar to pay the spirit to obey her orders. Then she place her hands flat upon the table and say the curse-prayer.

"To the Man God: O great One, I have been sorely tried by my enemies, and have been blasphemed and lied against. My good thoughts and my honest actions have been turned to bad actions and dishonest ideas. My home has been disrespected, my children have been cursed and ill-treated. My dear ones have been backbitten and their virtue questioned. O Man God, I beg this that I ask for my enemies shall come to pass:

"That the South wind shall scorch their bodies and make them wither and shall not be tempered to them. That the North Wind shall freeze their blood and numb their muscles and that it shall not be tempered to them."

There follows a catalog of bodily afflictions and diseases and infirmities that make the plagues of Exodus seem a mild sentence in comparison.[17]

It is difficult to estimate the actual spread of voodoo worship in Louisiana in the nineteenth century, but the practice was extensive enough to get wide contemporary coverage in popular magazines in other parts of the country. George Washington Cable, for example, told the urban readers of *Century Magazine* in April 1886 of the potency of voodoo worship:

Whatever the quantity of Voodoo *worship* left in Louisiana, its superstitions are many and are everywhere. Its charms are resorted to by the malicious, the jealous, the revengeful, or the avaricious, or held in terror, not by the timorous only, but by the strong, the courageous, the desperate. To find under his mattress an acorn hollowed out, stuffed with the hair of some dead person, pierced with four holes on four sides, and two small chicken feathers drawn through them so as to cross inside the acorn; or to discover on his door-sill at daybreak a little box containing a dough or waxen heart stuck full of pins; or to hear that his avowed foe or rival has been pouring cheap champagne in the four corners of Congo Square at midnight, when there was no moon, will strike more abject fear into the heart of many a stalwart negro or melancholy quadroon than to face a leveled revolver. And it is not only the colored man that holds to these practices and fears. Many a white Creole gives them full credence.[18]

But outside of the curious situation in southern Louisiana, black folk medicine on the mainland United States has in general lacked an overarching theory or any coherent organization of deities. Much of what Hurston's doctors do is simply the uttering of folk superstitions, many of which are common to European traditions. ("If you kill and step backwards over the body, they will never catch you. . . . If you are murdered or commit suicide, you are dead before your time comes. God is not ready for you, and so your soul must prowl about until your time comes . . . Bury the victim with his hat on and the murderer will never get away . . .")[19] Her root doctor prescriptions cover common diseases—bladder trouble, rheumatism, swelling, blindness, lockjaw, upset stomach, loss of mind, poisons. Though some of the salves for swelling might work well enough, it is hard to see how some of the treatments for gonorrhea ("parch egg shells and drink the tea" or "fifty cents iodide potash to one quart sarsaparilla; take three teaspoons three times a day in water") or for syphilis ("ashes of one good cigar, fifteen cents worth of blue ointment; mix and put on the sores" or "get the heart of a rotten log and powder it fine; tie it up in a muslin cloth; wash the sores with good castile soap and powder them with the wood dust")[20] would help sufferers much. (Of course, the techniques of medical doctors at the time weren't any better for treating those diseases.)

Although there was—and still is in some rural areas—much belief in the efficacy of various magical practices and the potency of folk doctors and the existence of certain supernatural beings, that body of belief does not form a system so much as a great mass of techniques varying widely from place to place; and just about everywhere in this country, it is the technological, rather than the theological, aspect which is operative.

The most spectacular collection of black folk medicine is Dr. Harry M. Hyatt's *Hoodoo—Conjuration—Witchcraft—Rootwork*.[21] The first four volumes of this projected five-volume work consist of almost thirty-eight hundred pages of interviews with hoodoo doctors and thousands of samples of techniques for various situations and afflictions. The fifth volume, an index being done under the direction of Wayland D. Hand, should make this enormous mass of rare data more easily accessible and approachable. At present, it is pretty much like wandering in a cataloged but unindexed archive, where we have the names and titles of performers but can only sense the holding by experiencing the entire collection. Dr. Hyatt is quite aware of his collection's value and limitations. "Though *Hoodoo* is full of magic rites and cures," he wrote me recently,

> always I sought the professional operator, the *doctor*, his appearance, personal mannerisms, origin of his power, possible descent from a predecessor, activities, beliefs, methods and the atmosphere surrounding him. The latter also means a study of his clients. As you can see, *Hoodoo* is an archive, not a logical presentation of material or a *Golden Bough* trying to prove a theory; but a picture of living people, talking, demonstrating rites in front of you, 1600 of us, asking study by the scholar.

The literature on black folk medicine and magic, on conjure and such, is quite extensive.[22] In the nineteenth century, long before F. J. Child began his monumental library work at Harvard, gifted amateurs were already hard at work in the field collecting Negro folk tales (Joel Chandler Harris's first Remus book was published in 1880)[23] and folk song (Thomas Wentworth Higginson's influential article "Negro Spirituals" was published in *The Atlantic Monthly* in June 1867, and the first book-length collection of black American songs, *Slave Songs of the United States*, was published in the same year.)[24] There were numerous articles about black superstition, magic, and medicine in the third quarter of the nineteenth century,[25] and when the American Folklore Society was organized in the late 1880s, its founders set forth as one of its areas of special concern the folklore of the Negro.

But there is another reason why there is so much material on black folk medical and magical practices and customs: there was in fact a great deal of such material around. There were few other sources of power available to the slaves and ex-slaves; there was no justice in the courts for them and no regular source of financially reasonable medical aid from the white doctors in town. Because of custom and the policy of the controlling class, those practices among the folk survived long after they had become moribund in other groups. It is still difficult to know how much of that nineteenth-century material was African survival and how much was European material translated into black idiom and style. Just as with spirituals, there remains something of both. But those things remained because they were necessary, because more sophisticated devices of control were absent. I think John Dollard expresses this as well as anyone else:

> There is another means of accommodating to life when it is not arranged according to one's wishes. This is the use of magic. Of course, one can think of magical practices among the Negroes as lagging culture patterns, which they are, but one can also think of them as forms of action in reference to current social life. Magic accepts the *status quo*, it takes the place of political activity, agitation, organization, solidarity, or any real moves to change status. It is interesting and harmless from the standpoint of the caste system and it probably has great private value for those who practice it. . . . Magic, in brief, is a control gesture, a comfort to the individual, an accommodation attitude to helplessness. There is no doubt that magic is actively believed in and practiced in Southern-town and country.[26]

I think it is clear that one of the reasons many of these practices have become rarer in the past three decades is that those lacks Dollard notes have become realities: there has been considerable "political activity, agitation, organization, solidarity, [and other] real moves to change status." But the remembrance of such time is still with us. Mrs. Janie Hunter told Guy and Dancie Carawan in the early 1960s:

> We didn't go to no doctor. My daddy used to cook medicine—herbs medicine: seamuckle, pine top, lison molasses, shoemaker root, ground moss, peachtree leave, big-root, bloodroot, read oak bark, terrywuk.
>
> And you hear about children have worm? We get something call jimsey weed. You put it in a cloth and beat it. And when you done beat it, you squeeze the juice out of it, and you put four, five drop of turpentine in it, give children that to drink. You give a dose of castor oil behind 'em. You don't have to take 'em to no doctor. . . .
>
> All this from old people time when they hardly been any doctor. People couldn't afford doctor, so they have to have and guess. Those old people dead out now, but they worked their own remedy and their own remedy come out good.[27]

But it wasn't just for medical problems that people visited the folk doctors. Social affairs were just as much in their domain. There are many reports similar to the story told by Henry Bibb about people visiting hoodoo or conjure doctors to try to get help in managing the difficulties of simply getting on in the world. John Dollard wasn't the first observer to understand how such belief compensated for a sense of impotence or for a lack of other kinds of organization. Leonora Herron and Alice M. Bacon, writing in the *Southern Workman* in 1895, said:

> Overt and natural means of obtaining justice being forbidden the Negro, was it surprising that, brought up in ignorance, and trained in superstition, he should invoke secret and supernatural powers to redress his wrongs and afford him vengeance on those of his follows whom envy, jealousy or anger prompt him to injure?

The agent of this vengeance was usually the Conjure Doctor. This individual might be a man or a woman, white or colored, but was found in every large Negro community, where though held in fear and horror, his supernatural powers were still implicitly believed in. The source of these powers is but ill defined.[28]

As the source of power some of their informants cite the devil; some God; some, education. Basically, they say, "The conjure doctor's business was of two kinds: to conjure, or 'trick,' a person, and to cure persons already 'conjured.' "[29]

The conjure doctor is simply a library of folk beliefs and techniques in the areas of contagious and homeopathic magic. Many people know of these matters and can cite a limited number of cures or techniques, but he is the man (or woman) one goes to for the best technique for a specific situation. He is known by various names, but his functions are relatively constant. Richard Dorson describes categories of such operators when he discusses the term *two-head*: "Although 'two-head' designates any person with esoteric gifts, the Southern Negro speaks of three separate kinds. The hoodoo doctor diagnoses and treats diseases caused by hoodoo evil. The fortuneteller, like renowned Aunt Caroline Dye of Newport, Arkansas, prophesies the future, and locates lost persons and property. The healer cures natural ailments that baffle doctors through his secret arts. Some of the most graphic stories told by Negroes involve these two-header practitioners."[30]

Dorson is no doubt correct that there are three separate kinds of practitioners in this area, but the boundaries dividing them are sometimes rather amorphous. Most of the reports in this century suggest that the practitioners assume a variety of functions which seem to depend as much on neighborhood needs as on professional divisions of labor.

Carl Carmer, for example, describes an Alabama conjure woman whose name is Seven Sisters. "It's a spirit in me that tells," she told Carmer, "a spirit from the Lord Jesus Christ. Used to be old voodoo woman lived next to my mammy's cabin. She tol' me how to trick. She say her mammy in Africa teached her. But she was a bad ol' woman—a voodoo conjure woman. I tricks in the name o' the Lord."[31] She offers recipes and techniques for various conjure acts. One will "keep your wife from flirting around; take a persimmon sprout about six inches long and bury it under the doorstep while her flirting spell is on." Other cures have to do with getting good crops, inflicting revenge on an enemy, knowing when you've been tricked by another conjurer, or curing warts. You can get a girl to sleep with you if you "steal something dirty from being next to her skin—a string from her drawers, moisture from under her right arm, best of all a menstruation cloth—stick nine pins in it and bury it under the eaves of the house" or "take hair from her head, make it into a ball, sew it up, and wear it under your right arm."[32] Norman Whitten, reporting on such practices in North Carolina, found a similar combination of activity. The conjurer, he said, "is the professional diviner, curer, agent finder, and general controller of the occult arts. Local synonyms for the conjurer are " 'root doctor,' 'herb doctor,' 'herb man,' 'underworld man,' 'conjure man,' and 'goofuhdus man.' [This last is probably *gooferdust man*, referring to the graveyard dust such doctors sometimes use.] The principal function and role of the conjurer is to deal with and control the occult. This he does for a fee."[33] And Loudell F. Snow, reporting on a voodoo practitioner in Tucson, Arizona, says her informant will treat any sort of disorder: "I don't turn down nothin'," the practitioner said to Snow, "I don't care what's wrong with 'em, I just have confidence. I tell you what. I believe in God. I believe God can do anything and everything. That is a high power, faith and the belief. I never lose faith, I never doubt myself. I know there's nothin' I can do *without* him, and I feel like He's with me at all times."[34]

This last is in many ways close to the white Fundamentalist preacher who some-times also assumes the power of healing; she is clearly a long way from the complex theological framework of the African slaves and New Orleans devotees of Haitian voodoo of the last century. It would be difficult to separate which of her techniques derive from European and white American tradition and which derive from African and black American tradition. Clearly some significant melding has occurred, and many old contexts have disappeared. I don't think this informant is anomalous; although there are remnants of those older traditions still around, one would now be hard put to duplicate the monumental fieldwork of Hyatt or the important collection of Puckett.

But it isn't completely dead. Although these practices are not much in evidence in modern American cities (and the majority of America's population—white and black—lives in urban centers now), there are occasional reports that suggest some of the old power is still there, that it still influences behavior in significant ways. Though fewer people may be involved in the various levels of practice than in previous years (as is the case with most rural folk traditions brought to the city), many still take them with as much seriousness as ever, with deadly seriousness. Both the folk remedies and the techniques for control still surface as significant elements in certain communities. Consider the following item, an Associated Press dispatch datelined Miami, February 12, 1974:

COURT REFUSES TO APPOINT VOODOO DOCTOR

The court was bedeviled when a defense lawyer asked to have the defendant examined by a voodoo doctor or an exorcist.

"What's a voodoo doctor?" Circuit Court Judge Dan Satin asked at a hearing Monday.

"One who by training has learned about the powers of voodoo," replied defense lawyer David Cerf.

Mr. Cerf pointed out that the defendant, Harvey Lee Outler, has been determined component for the murder of his common law wife but the evaluating doctor said Outler believed he was under a curse.

Mr. Cerf said Outler, 36, believed that Mable Young, 31, had put a curse on him. Police say Outler shot Mrs. Young with a pistol April 13.

"Your honor, a voodoo curse is just as deadly as a threat with a gun," Mr. Cerf said.

Judge Satin said: "I respect any man's rights. But if you think I'm going to appoint a voodoo doctor, you've got another thing coming."

Mr. Cerf's motion was denied.

NOTES

1. See B. A. Botkin, *Lay My Burden Down* (Chicago: The University of Chicago Press, 1945), 36–37.

2. In Gilbert Osofsky, ed., *Puttin' On Ole Massa: The Slave Narratives of Henry Bibb, William Wells Brown, and Solomon Northup* (New York: Harper and Row, 1969), p. 70.

3. Ibid.

4. Ibid., p. 71.

5. Ibid.

6. Ibid., p. 73.

7. Ibid.

8. A. B. Ellis, *The Tshi-Speaking Peoples of the Gold Coasts of West Africa: Their Religion, Manners, Customs, Laws, Languages, Etc.* (London: Chapman and Hall, 1887), p. 13.

9. See, for example, Norman E. Whitten, Jr., "Contemporary Patterns of Malign Occultism Among Negroes in North Carolina," *Journal of American Folklore*, 75 (1962), 311–325; reprinted in Alan Dundes, ed., *Mother Wit from the Laughing Barrel* (Englewood Cliffs, N.J.: Prentice-Hall, 1973), pp. 402–418. Whitten notes: "Everything has its antithesis. For instance, for every disease there is an antidote if man can only find it" (p. 413). See also Ruth Bass, "Mojo," in *Scribner's Magazine*, 87 (1930), 83–90, reprinted in Dundes, *op. cit.*, pp. 380–387. Bass writes: "So far as I have been able to discover, there seems to be a trick for every kind of occupation and desire in life. To the swamp Negroes nothing is inanimate, incapable of being tricked. I have heard a swamp Negress talking about her pot because it was slow about boiling. She begged it to boil, pointed out the advantages of boiling over not boiling, and when it remained obstinate she resorted to a trick which consisted of rubbing her belly. The pot promptly cooked faster" (p. 383).

10. The story of Job, which is one of the most popular stories in the Old Testament, is of course an attempt to deal with exactly this problem: it suggests the Lord acts in ways which are not for man to question. The problematic nature of the solution put forth in Job is attested to by the fact that it is the most frequently analyzed book of the Old Testament.

11. Don Yoder, "Folk Medicine," in Richard M. Dorson, ed., *Folklore and Folklife: An Introduction* (Chicago: University of Chicago Press, 1972), p. 192.

12. George J. McCall, "Symbiosis: The Case of Hoodoo and the Numbers Racket," in Dundes, *op. cit.*, p. 420.

13. John S. Mbiti, *African Religions and Philosophy* (Garden City, N.Y.: Doubleday Anchor, 1970), pp. 221–222.

14. Zora Neal Hurston, *Mules and Men* (New York and Evanston, Ill.: Perennial Library, 1970), pp. 332–335.

15. Ibid., pp. 340–343.

16. Ibid., p. 243.

17. Ibid., pp. 245–246.

18. George Washington Cable, "Creole Slave Songs," *Century Magazine*, 11 (April, 1886); reprinted in Bruce Jackson, ed., *The Negro and His Folklore in Nineteenth Century Periodicals* (Austin: University of Texas Press and the American Folklore Society, 1967), pp. 237–238.

19. Hurston, *op. cit.*, p. 332.

20. Ibid., pp. 340–341.

21. Harry M. Hyatt, *Hoodoo—Conjuration—Witchcraft—Rootwork*, 4 vols. (Hannibal, Mo.: Memoirs of the Alma Egan Hyatt Foundation, 1970–1975).

22. See, for example, quoted material and reference in Dundes, *op. cit.*: Jackson, *op. cit.*;

Richard M. Dorson, *American Negro Folktales* (New York: Fawcett, 1967); Newbell Niles Puckett, *Folk Beliefs of the Southern Negro* (Chapel Hill: University of North Carolina Press, 1926); Georgia Writers' project of the Works Project Administration, *Drums and Shadows* (Athens: University of Georgia Press, 1940); Robert Tallant, *Voodoo in New Orleans* (New York: Macmillan, 1946).

23. Joel Chandler Harris, *Uncle Remus: His Songs and His Sayings* (New York: D. Appleton, 1880).

24. *Slave Songs of the United States*, ed. William Francis Allen, Charles Pickard Ware, Lucy McKim Garrison (New York, 1867; reprint ed., (New York: Peter Smith, 1951).

25. See Jackson, *op. cit.*, p. 134 ff.

26. John Dollard, *Caste and Class in a Southern Town* (Garden City, N.Y.: Doubleday Anchor, 1957), p. 265.

27. Guy and Candie Carawan, *Ain't You Got a Right to the Tree of Life?* (New York: Simon and Schuster, 1966), p. 45. The photograph on the opposite page (p. 44) shows an old woman (who may not be Mrs. Hunter, since the photos and interviews were arranged separately) sitting in a wooden chair before an old iron stove. The walls beyond her are papered with pages of newspapers. It may be that the newspapers serve because nothing else is at hand— but anyone from that area knows full well that *hants* (spirits, ghosts, demons), who sometimes possess people at night, are compulsive counters, and grains of salt or pages of a newspaper will serve as adequate protection because it takes so long to count the grains or letters that dawn comes before the hants can do any harm. I am reminded of a visit to the Massachusetts Hospital for the Criminally Insane at Bridgewater about ten years ago. A guard tried to prove to me how batty one particular old black inmate was. He called the man over and asked him about the devils in his room at night. The man said there weren't any devils in his room; "The devils in your army, not mine." That seemed rational enough a position. The guard urged the man to tell me how he kept the devils out, and the man said it wasn't devils he kept out.

"Is it hants?" I asked.

He said it was hants and looked at the guard, who at that point was starting to look oddly at me.

"Tell him what you do," the guard said, "about the newspapers."

"You put newspapers on the floor to keep them out?" I asked.

"That's right."

"Where are you from? South Carolina? Georgia?"

He named a coastal town in northern Florida.

I asked the guard just what it was about the man that was supposed to be so batty. He scowled and asked, "How'd you know where he was from?"

"Because of the hants." I pointed out that no southern doctor would consider that sort of superstition adequate grounds for incarceration. "Lots of the old people there used to do that." The guard, obviously no student of folklore, looked at me as if I were as batty as the inmate and walked way, shaking his head.

28. Leonora Herron and Alice M. Bacon, "Conjuring and Conjure Doctors," in Dundes, *op. cit.*, p. 360 (originally in *Southern Workman*, 24).

29. Ibid.

30. Dorson, *op. cit.*, p. 187.

31. Carl Carmer, *Stars Fell on Alabama* (1934; reprint ed., New York: Hill and Wang, 1961), p. 218.

32. Ibid.

33. Whitten, *op. cit.*, p. 409.

34. Loudell F. Snow, " 'I Was Born Just Exactly With the Gift': An Interview with a Voodoo Practitioner," *Journal of American Folklore*, 86 (1973): 277–278.

SELECTED BIBLIOGRAPHY FOR FURTHER READING

Baer, Hans A. *The Black Spiritual Movement: A Religious Response to Racism.* Knoxville: University of Tennessee Press, 1984.

Hurston, Zora Neale. *Mules and Men.* New York: Harper & Row, 1970.

Murphy, Joseph. *Working the Spirit: Ceremonies of the African Diaspora.* Boston: Beacon Press, 1993.

Puckett, Newbell Niles. *Folk Beliefs of the Southern Negro.* Chapel Hill: University of North Carolina Press, 1926.

Snow, Loudell F. *Walkin' over Medicine: Traditional Health Practices in African-American Life.* San Francisco: HarperCollins, 1993.

Chapter Twenty-eight

African Americans and Humanism

Anthony B. Pinn

Among the diverse expressions of African American piety, there have been persons whose "faith" is embodied in nontheistic formulations. W. E. B. Du Bois exemplified such a posture, though he always seemed to linger at the borders of theism. There have been others, perhaps of lessor name but of no less integrity of conviction. Anthony B. Pinn illuminates this alter religiosity of African America.

•

African slaves in the United States used versions of theism to make sense of life's absurdities; but this was not the case for all slaves, for the hypocrisy of some slave owners, and the contradictions between the political and economic-driven interpretations of the gospel and Africans' essential sense of self, caused some to question the validity of theism. In 1839, Daniel Payne expressed his concern that slaves would completely give up faith if they were not introduced to the true gospel message:

> The slaves are sensible of the oppression exercised by their masters and they see these masters on the Lord's day worshipping in his holy Sanctuary. They hear their masters professing Christianity; they see these masters preaching the gospel; they hear these masters praying in their families, and they know that oppression and slavery are inconsistent with the christian religion; therefore they scoff at religion itself—mock their masters, and distrust both the goodness and justice of God. Yes, I have known them even to question his existence. I speak not of what others have told me, but of what I have both seen and heard from the slaves themselves . . . A few nights ago between 10 and 11 o'clock a runaway slave came to the house where I live for safety and succor. I asked him if he was a christian; "no sir," said he, "white men treat us so bad in Mississippi that we can't be christians." . . . In a word, slavery tramples the laws of the living God under its unhallowed feet—weakens and destroys the influence which those laws are calculated to exert over the mind of man; and constrains the oppressed to blaspheme the name of the Almighty.[1]

Thus it seems fairly clear that the early presence and rationale for humanism within African American communities is based on the hypocrisy of nominally Christian slave owners. They turned to a nontheistic solution to the challenge of reorienting human destiny and fostering equality.

It is possible that hush arbor meetings, secret slave gatherings, and field work arrangements allowed for conversation that was humanistic in orientation; however, little evidence of this has been recorded, because it would have been considered unimportant. Payne's statement, along with allusions in, for example, some blues tones and African American folk wisdom, point to the presence of humanism in early African American communities, but it is not until the African American renaissance (i.e., the "Harlem Renaissance" of the twentieth century) that nontheistic orientations are widely presented.

The Great Migration and the First World War, for example, questioned the sense of progress and optimism that marked the pre-war period. Some who questioned the war were still willing to participate in the U.S. war effort because they hoped that it would result in democratic rule throughout the world. Yet, as history proved, the war did not change the oppressive nature of U.S. social relations or reduce the inequality of U.S. ecopolitical interactions. Disillusionment with U.S. religious and political rhetoric naturally resulted from this failure, and it was amplified by what has been noted elsewhere as the "de-radicalization" of African American churches. Based on this inward gaze of African American churches, an inversely proportional relationship between outreach and social problems developed. Consequently, answers to the questions posed by life in the United States took on a harder and rougher texture through the development of the Harlem Renaissance (or, more accurately, the African American Renaissance) and its characteristic rejection of sanitized depictions of life. This Renaissance also opened discussions concerning the impotence of traditional religious practices. According to Arthur Fauset, "The church, once a *sine qua non* of institutional life among American Negroes, does not escape the critical inquiry of the newer generations, who implicitly and sometimes very explicitly are requiring definite pragmatic sanctions if they are to be included among church goers, or if indeed they are to give any consideration at all to religious practices and beliefs."[2]

James Weldon Johnson developed a perspective revolving around the human condition and the human, alone in the world, as responsible for correcting societal problems. He spoke, nonetheless, of the church and its life because it was familiar and had touched him early. Yet, the culture of African Americans and others as chronicled in his *God's Trombones: Seven Negro Sermons in Verse* did not assert an embrace of God; rather it was a mark of his respect for the work of human hands. Logically speaking, an appreciation for cultural production as such is not an endorsement of the doctrinal assumptions and theological stance of the African American church. Johnson was concerned with maintaining the cultural identity and value of African Americans as shapers of American cultural reality, and this required a response to minstrel-like caricatures of African American culture. Hence, Johnson's *God's Trombones* is better understood as a defense of African American folk art than as a testimony of personal belief. Johnson is quite clear on this point.

> My glance forward reaches no farther than this world. I admit that I throughout my life have lacked religiosity. I do not know if there is a personal God; I do not see how I can know; and I do not see how my knowing can matter. As far as I am able to peer into the inscrutable, I do not see that there is any evidence to refute those scientists and

philosophers who hold that the universe is purposeless: that man, instead of being the special care of a Divine Providence, is dependent upon fortuity and his own wits for survival in the midst of blind and insensate forces. . . . All that is clearly revealed is the fate that man must continue to hope and struggle on. To do this, he needs to be able at times to touch God; let the idea of God mean to him what ever it may.[3]

Johnson developed this perspective fairly early. Although his grandmother, and later his father, attempted to secure his involvement in church, Johnson rebelled. The church held little appeal for Johnson:

As he grew older, James became increasingly discontented with the whole business of religion. He was irked by the constant round of church-going forced upon him by his well-meaning grandmother. . . . When he was nine, James allowed himself to be "saved" at a revival meeting, but, he admitted later, he acted largely out of a desire to please his grandmother. . . . His doubts concerning religion and the church increased with each year. He could not, however, resolve the tension solely out of his narrow experience with his family or church. It would take a few years, and a sense of life styles beyond the provincialism of Jacksonville, for Johnson to find his answer in agnosticism.[4]

Johnson's agnosticism was most likely enhanced, prior to his years at Atlanta University, through his work with Dr. Thomas Osmond Summers, who embraced science and rejected religion. Through Summers's library, Johnson "found the works of Thomas Paine and Robert G. Ingersoll, America's best known agnostics. He read Paine and Ingersoll avidly as nourishment for his earlier vague dislike of conventional religion. By his freshman year, Johnson was one of the two acknowledged agnostics at Atlanta University."[5]

James Baldwin also contributed to the advancement of humanism as a system with ramifications for daily conduct, while advancing African American culture. Again, he acknowledged African American religious (Christian) expression as an undeniable fixture within African American culture, but he also regarded it as problematic in ways that prevent personal involvement. For Baldwin, the Church offered a means of dealing with his fears: "all the fears with which I had grown up, and which were now a part of me and controlled my vision of the world, rose up like a wall between the world and me, and drove me into the church."[6] He hoped that church involvement would also provide comfort from the sense of depravity that pervaded his mind with respect to his sexuality and general life as a second-class citizen. He sought affirmation of his value and his "beauty." He felt himself needing "to belong" somewhere, to someone; and he felt that he could not hold out much longer. Like everyone around him, he would surrender to something; and if surrender was inevitable, why not to the church? Reflecting on his turn to the church, Baldwin says:

My friend was about to introduce me when [the pastor] looked at me and smiled and said, "Whose little boy are you?" Now this, unbelievably, was precisely the phrase used by pimps and racketeers on the Avenue when they suggested, both humorously and intensely, that I "hang out" with them. Perhaps part of the terror they had caused me to feel came from the fact that I unquestionably wanted to be *somebody's* little boy. I was so frightened, and at the mercy of so many conundrums, that inevitably, that summer, someone would have taken me over; one doesn't, in Harlem, long remain standing on any auction block. It was my good luck—perhaps—that I found myself in the church racket instead of some other.[7]

From Baldwin's perspective, this turn to the church was logical and relatively safe in light of the other options available in Harlem.

After some years, Baldwin came to realize that the church did not provide the solace he had sought as he lay on the church floor on the day of his conversion. He was "able to see that the principles governing the rites and customs of the churches in which I grew up did not differ from the principles governing the rites and customs of other churches, white. The principles were Blindness, Loneliness, and Terror, the first principle necessarily and actively cultivated in order to deny the two others."[8] He could fool himself and others only for so long; even preaching and the excitement (and acceptance) he found in the pulpit could not ultimately satisfy his needs and push aside his sociotheological questions. He was still lonely and afraid. Hence, Baldwin writes, "when I faced a congregation, it began to take all the strength I had not to stammer, not to curse, not to tell them to throw away their Bibles and get off their knees and go home and organize, for example, a rent strike."[9] Baldwin preached for three years, but he ultimately left the church and found what the church could not provide: orientation and meaning through his writing. For him, "religion" in general and Christianity in particular failed to meet the basic needs of believers. It was equipped to offer them what only pushed them further into absurdity, alienation, and race-based demise. As Baldwin expressed his orientation, he belonged to nothing other than his writing. Thus humanity is his concern and the humanizing of life his orientation. This comes through in a conversation he had with Elijah Muhammad:

> I said, at last, in answer to some other ricocheted questions, "left the church twenty years ago and I haven't joined anything since." . . . "And what are you now?" Elijah asked. I was in something of a bind, for I really could not say—could not allow myself to be stampeded into saying that I was a Christian. "I? Now? Nothing." This was not enough. "I'm a writer. I like doing things alone." . . . "I don't, anyway," I said, finally, "I think about it a great deal."[10]

In addition to Johnson and Baldwin, the work of J. Saunders Redding is important.[11] Redding asserts that God and the Christian faith have played a dubious role in the development of the United States. Both social transformation and the oppressive status quo have been proclaimed "God's will." In this capacity, God has served to both humanize and dehumanize. And what is so striking about all of this is that God resides in the collective consciousness as an "implicit assumption." That is, according to Redding, God "is a belief that operates just by being, like a boulder met in the path which must be dealt with before one can proceed on his journey. . . . God is a catalyst, and He is also a formulated doctrine inertly symbolized in the ritual and dogma of churches called Christian."[12] Yet even in light of the manner in which god is woven into the fabric of American life, Redding has his doubts:

> I do not know how long I have held both God and the Christian religion in some doubt, though it must have been since my teens. . . . I can only think that it came as a result of some very personal communion with God, established perhaps by a random

thought, a word, or a certain slant of light through the yellow and rose and purple windows.[13]

Also, reflecting on the energetic worship and hysterics of black worship, "realized with deep shame that what the Negroes did on this holy day made a clowns' circus for the whites. The Negroes' God made fools of them. Worship and religiosity were things to be mocked and scorned, for they stamped the Negro as inferior."[14]

Although he was not fully aware of the exact progression of thought that led to his final rejection of religion, it seemed the inevitable response to the existential realities of life as an African American. There is an air of comfort accompanying his admission that he "simply rejected religion. I rejected God. Not my instincts, but my deepest feelings revolted compulsively—not because I was I, a sort of neutral human stuff reaching directly to experience, but because I was a Negro."[15] Even with this admission the continued appeal to God within his own family and a significant segment of the African American community required an understated rejection, or a truce with the notion of God, a truce that emerged not from a reversal of opinion but as a means of maintaining community connections:

> It was also years before I made a sort of armed truce with religion and with God. I stepped around God determinedly, gingerly, gloating that I was free of Him and that He could not touch me. Indeed, I had to step around Him, for He was always there. He was there, foursquare and solid, at the very center of my father's life. . . . He was in various people I met and felt affection for. He was in the affable, tremulous sweetness of the first love I felt; in the drowning ecstasy of the first sexual experience; in the joy of imaginative creation. But I moved around Him warily, laughing, mocking His pretensions, determined that He would not betray me into Negroeness. If there lingered still in the deep recesses of my real self some consciousness of a religious spirit, then the ideal self—the Negro-hating me—did all it could to exorcise it.[16]

For Redding, religion short circuited the drive toward social transformation. Whereas religion was virtually absent from social issues, God is, unfortunately, present and supportive of the status quo. Redding appears to regard God as a human construct that holds promises of liberation that it can never fulfill.[17]

The development of humanism among African American writers is not limited to males; figures such as Alice Walker have also worked along these lines. According to Trudier Harris, Alice Walker and others make use of this orientation in constructing their characters; they

> pattern their [characters'] lives according to values Peter Faulkner recognizes as humanism in "its modern sense of an ethic which places human happiness as its central concern and is skeptical about the supernatural and transcendental. . . . The emphasis is on mutual human responsibility. . . . The spirit of humanism is flexible and undogmatic, refusing to sacrifice human happiness to any rigid orthodoxy. . . . Humanism is a philosophical position, not a matter of casual goodwill, and its basis is the belief in human responsibility and human potentiality."[18]

This position comes across in Alice Walker's work—for example, in novels such as *The Color Purple* and *The Third Life of Grange Copeland*—and in her own life. Walker recalls:

> I seem to have spent all of my life rebelling against the church or other people's interpretations of what religion is—the truth is probably that I don't believe there is a God, although I would like to believe it. Certainly I don't believe there is a God beyond nature. The world is God. Man is God. So is a leaf or a snake.[19]

Alice Walker's humanism is deeply contemplative. It is, in essence, a worshipful appreciation for humanity and for the earth in general. This type of reverence for life gives it god-like status in that it must remain at the forefront of our thoughts and actions, centering our every move within a profound sense of awe. What is called for, according to Walker, is a recognition of life as beautiful and beautifully connected to all things. Such a system, I believe, is not a broadened theism; but it is in keeping with the basic principles of humanism as outlined here: healthy existence for all as the goal and proper ethical conduct with respect to nature (i.e., radical environmentalism) directs humanity toward that goal. Walker speaks to this appreciation for nature with respect to the silencing of women in the Christian church:

> The truth was, we already lived in paradise but were worked too hard by the land-grabbers to enjoy it, this is what my mother, and perhaps the other women knew, and this was one reason why they [women] were not permitted to speak. They might have demanded that the men of the church notice Earth. Which always leads to revolution. In fact, everyone has known this for a very long time.[20]

Walker's appreciation of the well-being of all creation as the center of religious life and devotion is present in her reflections on her baptism at age seven. She recounts:

> The "God" of heaven that my parents and the church were asking me to accept, obscured by the mud, leaves, rot, and bullfrog spoors of this world [*sic*]. How amazing this all is, I thought, entering the muddy creek. And how deeply did I love these who stood around solemnly waiting to see my "saved" head reappear above the murky water. *This experience of communal love and humble hope for my well-being was my reality of life on this planet.* I was unable to send my mind off into space in search of a God who never noticed mud, leaves, or bullfrogs. Or the innocent hearts of my tender, loving people.[21]

Some humanists find it useful, if not necessary, to find a body of "believers." That is, their conversion experience is often furthered by communal interaction that affirms the conversion as the correct decision. Many African Americans logically looked for a like-minded community in the academy, others moved toward political involvement in, for example, the Communist Party:

> Doubt, frustration, and denial of God's existence arise also from social crises. God must not be interested in helping the group to achieve the needs necessary for existence. God does not exist; if He does, He is indifferent to the needs of the group. They arise at the point where physical security is denied; economic privilege cut off; the free exercise of the ballot prohibited; segregation in every area sustained by custom and law; and, the free development of spiritual powers almost completely stifled. . . . The negation of the idea of God may . . . drive Negroes into the communistic camp, whereby more militant or violent means would be used to achieve political and economic status.[22]

Within this camp one can include the early Langston Hughes. Although I believe he changed his opinion as a consequence of the "Red Scare," it is clear that his communist leanings facilitated an independence from the Christian faith as outlined in pieces such as "Goodbye Christ."[23] Although many debate whether Hughes was personally committed to communism, this poem provides a critique of Christianity and a rejection of its theological underpinnings and instead reflects a humanism held by many African Americans.[24] Granted, there is a tension between this early poem and his later work, but Faith Berry explains it this way:

> His attraction to communism has been as misinterpreted as his posture toward Christianity. His reaction to both was to what each proclaimed: He watched communism hail the classless society, the distribution of wealth, the equality of all, regardless of race or color; he saw Christianity preach the brotherhood of man, alms for the poor, freedom to the oppressed, the kingdom of God. He found Christianity full of broken promises and communism unable to fulfill its promises. Christianity was old. Communism was young. He reached out to both in his youth only to find two Gods that failed. Those who see a dichotomy, a bifurcation, a contradiction, between an early poem such as "Goodbye Christ" in 1932 as opposed to his more reverent religious works of later years should remember he was always searching for justice for all.[25]

I wish to suggest that the atheistic stance of the Communist Party and its rhetorical appeal to African Americans (thin as it was) provided a forum and "home" for African American humanists who found churches hopelessly out of touch with the times. Documents preserved at the Schomburg Center for Research in Black Culture, in New York City (e.g., Universal Negro Improvement Association Papers) and other locations document party organizing activities in African American communities such as Harlem during the 1920s and 1930s.[26] The Communist Party was reluctant to "attack" African American churches because of their strength within African American communities which could hamper Communist efforts; nonetheless, some African Americans who joined the Party were more than willing to critique Christian churches even when they were church members. According to Robin D. G. Kelley,

> Afro-American Communists shared with the rest of the black working-class community a grass-roots understanding of exploitation and oppression which was based more on scripture than anything else. The prophetic Christian tradition, so characteristic of the Afro-American experience, has historically contained a vehement critique of oppression. Ironically, this radical, prophetic tradition of Christianity was a major factor in drawing blacks into the Communist Party and its mass organizations.
>
> References to God and the bible were not uncommon among Alabama's black radicals. In 1933 the Daily Worker (13 April) received an interesting letter from a black Communist from Tallapoosa County, thanking "God and all the friends of the Negro race that are working for the defense and rights of the Negroes. I pray that they may succeed in our struggle for Bread, Land and Freedom." . . . Furthermore, not only were most black Communists in Alabama churchgoing Christians; for quite some time, Communists in Montgomery opened all their meetings with a prayer.[27]

Furthermore, some churches actively worked with the Communist Party: "Although the Communists never had a sympathetic ear from the larger, well-established black churches, several ministers and working-class congregations of smaller Baptist churches in and around Birmingham provided critical support for the Communists and the International Labor Defense in opposition to a state-wide-anti-sedition bill."[28] Kelly points out, however, that this support was mixed with a critique of clergy, who spent their time gaining wealth and preaching against transformation.[29]

Some took this critique further and rejected the Christian church and its doctrine as nonliberating.[30] Communist Party member Hosea Hudson's reflections on his Communist involvement support this point: Some African American communists were atheists or humanists. Although black communists such as Hudson were active in the church, some ministers attempted to prevent the use of churches for what they considered "trouble-making" speeches and activities. At one point Hudson stopped attending church because of such sentiments, but he recalls starting to attend again between 1937 and 1938. His comments to church members, most likely meant to spark discontent with the Church's otherworldly stance, remained troubling:

> I challenged one or two deacons one Sunday afternoon. We all sitting around talking. I told them, I said, "It ain't no such thing as no God. You all go around here singing and praying," I said, "and they regular lynching Negroes, and you ain't doing nothing about it."[31]

Hudson recalls that this stance was even shared by some Party members who never attended church:

> I had heard other Party people talking. Some of them had never been members of no church, talking about there wont no such thing as God: "Where is he at? You say it's a God, where is he at? You can't prove where he's at." Negro Party people said that to me, Murphy and Horton and Raymond Knox. We'd have big discussions. One Sunday I said I was going to church. "What you going for? What you going for?" I said, "I'm going to serve God." They said, "Where is God at? You can't prove it's no God nowhere." They said, "Where is God?" I said, "In heaven." "Well, where is heaven?"[32]

In rejecting God, the humanists Hudson knew in the Party assigned humanity responsibility for social transformation. Hudson found it difficult to respond to these charges. In his words:

> I just didn't have a [sic] answer. And them was the kind of questions they put. "If God is such a just God, and here you walking around here, ain't got no food. The only way you can get food is you have to organize. So if you have to organize to demand food, why you going to pray to God about it? Why don't you go on and put your time in organizing and talk to people?"[33]

Hudson found these arguments challenging, but he never lost his belief in God. His remarks, however, suggest agnosticism:

> I never did finally stop believing in God. I haven't stopped believing yet today. I don't argue about it. I don't discuss it, because it's something I can't explain. I don't know whether it's a God, I don't know whether it's not a God. But I know science, if you take science for it, and all these developments, I can't see what God had much to do with it. . . . So it's something beyond my knowledge to deal with. And I don't deal with it. I don't try to deal with it.[34]

As the disillusionment with the Communist Party expressed in Ralph Ellison's *The Invisible Man* and the work (and life) of Richard Wright indicate, the Party—by the time African Americans participated in noticeable numbers—had withdrawn from a strong interest in the "negro question" and were concerned primarily with the "Moscow line."[35] Although some African Americans undoubtedly remained within the Party hoping for a change, others moved in the direction of black nationalism as a means by which to embrace a materialist critique of U.S. society and the question of race.[36]

In the late twentieth century the Black Power Movement, particularly the second wave of the Student Non-violent Coordinating Committee (SNCC) and the Black Panther Party, served as an example of this turn toward black cultural nationalism. I believe that the shift away from the Christian-based civil rights movement marked by the second wave of SNCC and its thundering call for black power point to deep theological differences between SNCC and the larger civil rights movement. It is more than likely that the theistic motivations espoused by Dr. Martin Luther King, Jr., and others, did not adequately address the concerns of some of the more radical elements of the movement. The break, therefore, marks a transition from the theism of the civil rights movement toward materialist analysis and human-centered solutions. Although I am unwilling to stress this point too forcefully, I suggest that SNCC's underlying framework was humanist in nature regardless of whether this term was actually employed.

The late 1960s witnessed a methodological and epistemological shift within SNCC. Gone were the integrationist goals that made it compatible with the civil rights movement; gone was its reliance upon Christian doctrine and paradigms for action. The rhetoric found in early issues of SNCC's newspaper, *Student Voice*, was replaced with calls for self-determination through black power. But in 1960, SNCC described its philosophy in the following terms:

> We affirm the philosophical or religious ideal of nonviolence as the foundation of our purpose, the pre-supposition of our faith, and the manner of our action. . . . Love is the central motif of nonviolence. Love is the force by which God binds man to himself and man to man. Such love goes to the extreme; it remains loving and forgiving even in the midst of hostility. . . . By appealing to conscience and standing on the moral nature of human existence, nonviolence nurtures the atmosphere in which reconciliation and justice become actual possibilities.[37]

Veering away from this agape paradigm, SNCC embraced its own version of black nationalism predicated upon a strong appeal to the acquisition of power. According to Stokeley Carmichael and Charles Hamilton:

> [Black power] is a call for Black people in this country to unite, to recognize their heritage, to build a sense of community. It is a call for black people to begin to define their goals, to lead their own organizations and to support those organizations. It is a call to reject the racist institutions and values of this society. The concept . . . rests on a fundamental premise. *Before a group can enter the open society, it must first close ranks.* By this, we mean that group solidarity is necessary before a group can operate effectively from a bargaining position of strength in a pluralistic society.[38]

Although inadequately defined in terms of social transformative thrusts and foci, black power, for some of its advocates, did adopt rather clearly defined theological assumptions based on humanist leanings and articulated in the language of self-determination. One example is the thought of James Forman, an important member of SNCC.

In his autobiography, *The Making of Black Revolutionaries*, James Forman describes his "conversion" to humanism as a move that did not hamper but rather informed his praxis. He notes that during his time at Wilson Junior College in Chicago his doubts concerning the existence of God grew and were intensified by contact with questionable black preachers whose self-centered ways sparked his distaste for ministry and the church, Says Forman, "God was not quite dead in me, but he was dying fast."[39]

After returning from military service some years later, Forman came to a final conclusion concerning the existence of God:

> The next six years of my life were a time of ideas. A time when things were germinating and changing in me. A time of deciding what I would do with my life. It was also a time in which I rid myself, once and for all, of the greatest disorder that cluttered my mind—the belief in God or any type of supreme being.[40]

Outlining the rationale for his "disbelief," Forman notes that during a philosophy course he set firm upon the following:

> I reject the existence of God. He is not all-powerful, all-knowing, and everywhere. He is not just or unjust because he does not exist. God is a myth; churches are institutions designed to perpetuate this myth and thereby keep people in subjugation.[41]

Foreman did not reach this conclusion because God had not responded to his petitions; rather, his conclusion was based on the historical condition and needs of a large community. His rejection of God was not a surrender to absurdity but a call to arms. For him humanism required a strong commitment on the part of people to change their present condition:

> When a people who are poor, suffering with disease and sickness, accept the fact that God has ordained for them to be this way—then they will never do anything about their human condition. *In other words, the belief in a supreme being or God weakens the will of a people to change conditions themselves.* As a Negro who has grown up in the United States, I believe that the belief in God has hurt my people. *We have put off doing something about our condition on this earth because we have believed that God was going to take care of business in heaven.* . . . My philosophy course had finally satisfied my need for intellectual as well as emotional certainty that God did not exist. I reached the point of rejecting God out of personal experience and observations.[42]

Critiques of the African American churches based on materialist approaches to social transformation were also present in the ideological platform of the Black Panther Party. In fact, the attraction of some SNCC workers to the Black Panther Party led by Huey Newton, Bobby Seale, Eldridge Cleaver, and others, was based on a common concern with transformative activity that held as its measuring stick the welfare of African Americans and other oppressed groups. The Party, however, had a more clearly materialist platform and was much more certain of its armed and revolutionary stance. This commitment to human struggle as the key to social transformation reveals theological underpinnings that are humanistic in nature. Reflecting on the ultimate demise of many Black Panthers, Bobby Seale sums up the goals of the Party, goals that speak to humanist desires:

> We need activists who cross all ethnic and religious backgrounds and color lines who will establish civil and human rights for all, including the right to an ecologically balanced, pollution-free environment. We must create a world of decent human relationships where revolutionary humanism is grounded in democratic human rights for every person on earth. Those were the political revolutionary objectives of my old Black Panther Party. They must now belong to the youth of today.[43]

Drawing heavily from Marx, Fanon, Engels, Lenin, Mao, and others, the Party initially denounced the church, labeling it counterproductive. In the words of Huey P. Newton:

> As far as the church was concerned, the Black Panther Party and other community groups emphasized the political and criticized the spiritual. We said the church is only a ritual, it is irrelevant, and therefore we will have nothing to do with it. We said this in the context of the whole community being involved with the church on one level or another. That is one way of defecting from the community, and that is exactly what we did. Once we stepped outside of the whole thing that the community was involved in and we said "You follow our example; your reality is not true and you don't need it."[44]

The Party softened its position, however, when it recognized the central role the church played in the African American community's life. Like the Communist Party, the Panthers recognized that recruitment would be difficult if open hostility existed between the Party and the black churches. Therefore, the Panthers fostered a relationship of convenience and sociopolitical necessity, but without a firm commitment to the church's theology. Newton rationalized this involvement by arguing a different conception of God, God as the "unknown" whom science will ultimately eliminate. In this sense, God does not exist in the affirmative; God is the absence of knowledge:

> So we do go to church, are involved in the church, and not in any hypocritical way. Religion, perhaps is a thing that man needs at this time because scientists cannot answer all of the questions. . . . the unexplained and the unknown is God. We know nothing about God, really, and that is why as soon as the scientist develops or points out a new way of controlling a part of the universe, that aspect of the universe is no longer God.[45]

Another voice from the Black Panther Party that denounced claims of God's existence and involvement in human affairs was Eldridge Cleaver. Although Cleaver would later give attention to the Mormon Church and Reverend Moon, his earlier thoughts on God and humanity are still worth noting. Reflecting on his incarceration in 1954, he writes:

> In Soledad state prison, I fell in with a group of young blacks who, like myself, were in vociferous rebellion against what we perceived as a continuation of slavery on a higher plane. . . . While all this was going on, our group was espousing atheism. Unsophisticated and not based on any philosophical rationale, our atheism was pragmatic. I had come to believe that there is no God; if there is, men do not know anything about him. Therefore, all religions were phony. . . . Our atheism was a source of enormous pride to

me. Later on, I bolstered our arguments by reading Thomas Paine and his devastating critique of Christianity in particular and organized religion in general.[46]

Although Cleaver at one point became a Muslim "chained in the bottom of a pit by the Devil," his sense of religion was utilitarian. He writes: "To me, the language and symbols of religion were nothing but weapons of war. I had no other purpose for them. All the gods are dead except the god of war."[47] His connection to the black Muslims would give way as soon as it failed to provide a useful political tool.

Whether successful or misguided, the Black Panther Party's humanism is notable. The notion of divine assistance is rejected and humans given sole responsibility for altering the world. In the words of Bobby Seale:

> It is necessary for young people to know that we must use organized and practical techniques. We cannot let ourselves continue to be oppressed on a massive scale. We are not trying to be supermen, because we are not supermen. We are fighting for the preservation of life. We refuse to be brainwashed by comic-book notions that distort the real situation. The only way that the world is ever going to be free is when the youth of this country *moves* with every principle of human respect and with every soft spot we have in our hearts for human life. . . . We know that as a people, we must seize our time. . . . Power to the People! Seize the Time![48]

Some may question what distinction, if any, this study suggests between humanism and atheism. I acknowledge that in this text the line between the two is blurred, but I do not hold that a humanist must necessarily be an atheist. As I demonstrated in *Why, Lord? Suffering and Evil in Black Theology*, humanism does come in a theistic form called "soft humanism."[49] Much of the religious stance embraced in the various forms of liberation theology involves the type of partnership between humans and God promoted by "soft humanism." Hence, humanists can be theists; humanism is not necessarily reducible to atheism. Within this study, a blurring of the boundary exists between the two because my concern is with what they share in common: the basis for both humanism and atheism is belief in the need for humans to act in responsible ways that do not assume the presence of a superhuman force.

NOTES

1. Daniel Alexander Payne, "Daniel Payne's Protestation of Slavery," in *Lutheran Herald and Journal of the Franckean Synod* (August 1, 1839): 114–15.

2. Arthur Fauset, *Black Gods of the Metropolis: Negro Religious Cults of the Urban North* (Philadelphia: University of Pennsylvania Press, 1944), 7.

3. In Roy D. Morrison II, "The Emergence of Black Theology in America," *The A.M.E. Zion Quarterly Review*, vol. 94, no. 3 (October 1982): 6.

4. Eugene Levy, *James Weldon Johnson: Black Leader, Black Voice* (Chicago: University of Chicago Press), 15.

5. Ibid., 19.

6. James Baldwin, *The Fire Next Time* (New York: Dell Books), 42.

7. Ibid., 43–44.

8. Ibid., 47.

9. Ibid., 56–57. Also see pp. 64–67.

10. Ibid., 97.

11. Faith Berry, ed. *A Scholar's Conscience: Selected Writings of J. Saunders Redding, 1942–1977* (Louisville: University Press of Kentucky, 1992).

12. Ibid., 49.

13. Ibid.

14. Ibid., 52.

15. Ibid.

16. Ibid.

17. Ibid., 53–54.

18. Trudier Harris, "Three Black Women Writers and Humanism: A Folk Perspective," in R. Baxter Miller, ed., *African-American Literature and Humanism* (Lexington, Ky.: University Press of Kentucky), 54.

19. In ibid., 72. See Alice Walker, *The Color Purple: A Novel* (New York: Harcourt Brace Jovanovich, 1982); Alice Walker, *The Third Life of Grange Copeland* (New York: Harcourt, Brace, Jovanovich, 1970).

20. According to Alice Walker, "the only reason you want to go to heaven is that you have been driven out of your mind (off your land and out of your lover's arms): clear seeing inherited religion and reclaiming the pagan self" (*On the Issue* 6, no. 2 [Spring 1997]: 19–20).

21. Ibid., 23.

22. Benjamin E. Mays, *The Negro's God As Reflected in His Literature* (New York: Russell and Russell, 1968), 243.

23. Langston Hughes, "Goodbye Christ," quoted in ibid., 238.

24. See Langston Hughes, "Concerning 'Goodbye Christ.' " in *Good Morning Revolution: Uncollected Writings of Social Protest by Langston Hughes* (Carol Publishing Group, 1992), 147–49. Hughes also denies being an atheist in "Concerning Red Baiting," 159–61.

25. Hughes, *Good Morning*, xvi–xvii.

26. See Mark Naison, *Communists in Harlem During the Depression* (Urbana: University of Illinois Press, 1983).

27. Robin D. G. Kelley, "Comrades, Praise Gawd for Lenin and Them! Ideology and Culture among Black Communists in Alabama, 1930–1935," *Science and Society* 52, no. 1 (Spring 1988): 61–62. Also see Robin Kelley, " 'Afric's Sons with Banners Red,' " in Sidney J. Lemelle and Robin D. G. Kelley, eds., *Imagining Home: Class, Culture, and Nationalism in the African Diaspora* (New York: Verso, 1994).

28. Kelley, "Comrades," 63.

29. Ibid., 64.

30. Ibid., 65–66.

31. Ibid., 133.

32. Nell Irvin Painter, *The Narrative of Hosea Hudson: His Life as a Negro Communist in the South* (Cambridge, Mass.: Harvard University Press, 1979), 133–34.

33. Ibid., 134.

34. Ibid., 134–35.

35. See Harold Cruse, "Jews and Negroes in the Communist Party," in *The Crisis of the Negro Intellectual: A Historical Analysis of the Failure of Black Leadership* (New York: William Morrow and Company/Quill, 1967, 1984), 147.

36. Others who combined humanism with political involvement include A. Philip Randolph, T. Thomas Fortune, and Paul Robeson. Harold Cruse's comment on Robeson's romanticization of the "negro worker" indirectly reveals Robeson's nontheistic leanings: Robe-

son and [his] middle-class-leftwing ethos truly idealized . . . nice, upright Negro workers; who, even if they did go to church and worship God and not Russia, at least tilled the Southern soil as solid citizen sharecroppers. (Ibid., 236)

37. Rev. J. M. Lawson, Jr., "Statement of Purpose," *The Student Voice* 1, no. 1 (June 1960), in Clayborne Carson, ed., *The Student Voice, 1960–1965: Periodical of the Student Nonviolent Coordinating Committee* (Westport, Conn.: Meckler, 1990), 2.

38. Stokeley Carmichael and Charles Hamilton, *Black Power* (New York: Vintage Books, 1967), 44, quoted in Norman Harris, *Connecting Times: The Sixties in Afro-American Fiction* (Jackson, Miss.: University Press of Mississippi, 1988), 91.

39. James Forman, "Corrupt Black Preachers," in *The Making of Black Revolutionaries* (Washington, D.C.: Open Hand Publishing, 1985), 58.

40. James Forman, "God Is Dead: A Question of Power," in *The Making of Black Revolutionaries*, 80–81.

41. Ibid., 82.

42. Ibid., 83. Italics added.

43. Bobby Seale, *Seize the Time* (New York: Random House, 1991), 3. Although on the individual level the objectives often gave way to problematic and abusive behavior, the humanist tone of the Black Panther Party's platform is still noteworthy:

1. We want freedom. We want power to determine the destiny of our Black Community.

2. We want full employment for our people

3. We want an end to the robbery by the white man of our Black Community.

4. We want decent housing, fit for shelter of human beings.

5. We want education for our people that exposes the true nature of this decadent American society. We want education that teaches us our true history and our role in the present-day society.

6. We want all black men to be exempt from military service.

7. We want an immediate end to POLICE BRUTALITY and MURDER of black people.

8. We want freedom for all black men held in federal, state, county and city prisons and jails.

9. We want all black people when brought to trial to be tried in court by a jury of their peer group or people from their black communities, as defined by the Constitution of the United States.

10. We want land, bread, housing, education, clothing, justice, and peace. And as our major political objective, a United Nations—supervised plebiscite to be held throughout the black colony in which only black colonial subjects will be allowed to participate, for the purpose of determining the will of black people as to their national destiny.

44. *To Die for the People: The Writings of Huey P. Newton*, ed. Toni Morrison (New York: Writers and Readers Publishing, Inc., 1995), 63–64.

45. Ibid., 64.

46. Eldridge Cleaver, "On Becoming," in *Soul on Ice* (New York: McGraw-Hill, 1967), 4–5.

47. Clever, " 'The Christ and His Teachings," in *Soul on Ice*, 34.

48. Seale, *Seize the Time*, 429.

49. Anthony B. Pinn, *Why, Lord? Suffering and Evil in Black Theology* (New York: Continuum Publishing Group, 1995), chaps. 5 and 6.

Part VI

"Didn't My Lord Deliver Daniel?"
African American Religion and Social Advocacy

Twenty-nine

In Search of the Promised Land

Albert J. Raboteau

In his noted volume Black Religion and Black Radicalism, *Gayraud Wilmore takes the position that there was in black folk religion a radical dimension with a definite tendency toward protest for social justice. Wilmore speaks of the clergy who took the lead in such protest. But coming into the twentieth century, says Wilmore, the radicalism of the folk religion was defused by a growing social conservatism among the black clergy. Social activism came more and more to be channeled into secular agencies such as the NAACP and the Urban League. Albert J. Raboteau perhaps makes a more moderate assessment of black clergy activism than Wilmore as he points up the continuing religious underpinning of black protest in the twentieth century. He offers his reading of Martin Luther King, Jr., and the unfolding of the civil rights movement as illustrative of his point.*

•

Black protest in the twentieth century has not been as "secular," nor has the black church been as quiescent about protest, as has sometimes been claimed. Black clergy played active roles in the Garvey movement, the NAACP, and in local political affairs, not only in the North, but in the South as well. Granted, much of their political activism would not appear "radical" from the perspective of the 1960s, but protest demonstrations did occur. In 1935, for example, Martin Luther King, Sr., led several thousand black demonstrators on a march from Ebenezer Baptist Church to the city hall of Atlanta in support of voting rights for blacks. And even earlier, the Reverend Adam Daniel Williams, the maternal grandfather of Martin Luther King, Jr., organized rallies at Ebenezer to protest a municipal bond issue that contained no plans for high school education for black youth. The activism of some black ministers and the legal struggles of the NAACP and the Urban League lay the groundwork for the movement that began in Montgomery. In this movement, the themes of black religious protest found their most eloquent expression.

As the son, grandson, and great-grandson of Baptist ministers, Martin Luther King, Jr., was deeply rooted in the African American religious tradition. Though he briefly considered careers in medicine and law, he decided as a teenager that he, too, would enter the ministry. Already, it was apparent that he was, as his father bragged, a magnificent preacher. Throughout the civil rights movement, King instinctively drew upon that black church tradition to inspire the movement's nonviolent wing. He, and others as well, perceived his leadership as fundamentally religious. His style of speaking, the cadence of his voice, the choice of words and images all echoed his church background and evoked, no less than the substance of his message, the rich tradition of black religion. In King, social justice and religion seemed inseparable. It was important that this connection be made, because many whites and some blacks felt that civil rights was really a political not a religious issue. Christian ethics was personal, not social. King was a living contradiction of that position.

According to King, the means blacks had to use to save the nation was nonviolence. "The spiritual power that the Negro can radiate to the world comes from love, understanding, goodwill, and nonviolence."[1] King's first contact with the theory of nonviolence came from reading Thoreau, but a lecture by Mordecai Johnson, president of Howard University, on the life and thought of Mahatma Gandhi inspired King to study the Indian leader and to commit himself to nonviolence. Nonviolence, he thought, was the perfect method for translating the love ethic of Christianity into social reform. With the advice of Bayard Rustin, a black veteran of the Fellowship of Reconciliation, a pacifist organization, King fitted a theory of nonviolent resistance to the tactics of the civil rights movement, although for him nonviolence was far more than a tactic. Along with his conviction that suffering is redemptive, it represented an entire way of life.

King's doctrine of redemptive suffering awakened old themes within African American religious culture, in particular the theme of the suffering servant, with all its associations in the slave past. The prayers, sermons, and especially the traditional songs "brought to mind the long history of the Negro's suffering," he noted. A simple reference to freedom as the "Promised Land," for example, stirred racial memories and triggered religious emotion. The biblical quotations and allusions that studded King's speeches served to locate the protestors in the long train of prophets and martyrs. The connections between the civil rights movement and the early Christian movement are explicit in King's two epistles in the style of the New Testament, "Letter from Birmingham Jail" and "Paul's Letter to American Christians."[2]

The demonstrations themselves took on the feel of church services. Invariably, they began with rallies in the black churches (which as a consequence became primary targets for white terrorist bombings). These rallies followed a pattern consisting of song, prayer, Scripture reading, discussion of goals and tactics, and an exhortation that frequently sounded like a sermon. From the churches, the demonstrators moved out into the public arena to bear witness with their bodies to the gospel of freedom and equality. Some gave their lives.

By 1966, the cry "black power" could be heard, signifying that some black activists were disappointed with the slow pace of racial change and disillusioned with the tactics of nonviolence. Black power quickly became a rallying cry for those who adopted a more radical position than King's. While King rejected the demand for black power as a slogan without a program, in 1966 the National Committee of Negro Churchmen (later renamed the National Conference of Black Churchmen) distanced itself from King by issuing an extended theological defense in the July 31 issue of the *New York Times*. The assassination of King in 1968 led to massive rioting in urban areas around the country and seemed to confirm that the period of nonviolent protest had passed. Self-determination, community control, and liberation replaced desegregation and integration as the catchwords of the movement. Radical militants joined the black Muslims in attacking the black church for being otherworldly, compensatory, and reactionary. Assertions of black pride and celebrations of black cultural identity marked a new mood of independence among black Americans. Separatism was on the rise while integration seemed discredited even in ecumenical circles.

In 1967, for example, black delegates to a National Council of Churches conference on urban problems insisted on splitting the meeting into two caucuses, one black and one white. Black Christians in white churches established ongoing caucuses to deal with issues of black identity and black autonomy. Between 1968 and 1970, black Catholics organized the Black Catholic Clergy Caucus, the National Black Sisters Conference, the Black Catholic Lay Caucus, and finally the National Office of Black Catholics, which proceeded to characterize the Catholic Church in America as primarily a white racist institution. In 1969, tensions between black clergy and white churches were exacerbated further when the civil rights activist James Forman presented a "Black Manifesto" demanding that white Christian churches and Jewish synagogues pay out $500 million for black economic development in reparation for slavery and racial oppression. Support for the manifesto by the National Conference of Black Churchmen led to bitter controversy between black clergy and white denominational boards over how much money should be given and to whom.[3]

Even before King's assassination, for reasons too numerous to summarize here, the civil rights movement had lost momentum, but his death, more clearly than anything else, marked the end of an identifiable movement for racial equality on the national level. No black leader of national stature arose to take his place, although the Reverend Jesse Jackson attempted to revive the spirit of the movement in his 1984 and 1988 political campaigns for the Democratic Party's presidential nomination. Significantly, black churches played a strategic role in the local organization of his campaign nationwide. The absence of a national black political movement has distracted observers from considering the activity of black churches on the local level, where issues of community organization, housing, education, economic development, and employment have troubled black Americans for the past fifty years and more. A highly successful and widely imitated model of church-sponsored black economic development on the local level was the Opportunities Industrialization Center (OIC) founded in 1964 by Leon H. Sullivan, author of the "Sullivan Principles" and pastor of Zion Baptist Church in Philadelphia. The OIC trained unemployed and underemployed black and white workers for skilled positions in industry and assisted them in finding jobs to match their newly acquired skills. By the end of the decade, similar OIC programs were established across the country. OIC was preceded by a "selective patronage campaign" in which, on a given Sunday, four hundred black ministers urged their congregations not to patronize a particular company because it discriminated against blacks in employment. An estimated twenty-nine selective patronage campaigns between 1959 and 1963 opened up many jobs formerly closed to blacks in Philadelphia and inspired the Southern Christian Leadership Conference to establish a similar program, Operation Breadbasket, in 1962. In numerous black communities, black churches have sponsored housing improvement and neighborhood development programs, health care clinics, day-care centers, and senior citizen facilities.

For most of the past fifty years, scholars have asserted that secular alternatives were diminishing the extent of the black church's power in the black community—a difficult assertion to verify. Evidence is conflicting, and what type of evidence to use is unclear. Recently, for example, social analysts have listed the waning influence of religious values upon inner-city blacks as a contributing factor to the current crises of teenage pregnancies, illegitimate births, absent-father households, drug abuse, and "black on black" crime. Yet the same social planners looked to the black church as the primary community agency to deal with these intractable problems of America's black underclass. Certainly black Americans, like whites, have been exposed to modern secular culture. But, statistically at least, the black church has remained strong. In 1936, the United States Census for Religious Bodies estimated that there were 5.7 million church members in a black population of 12.8 million. According to the 1986 edition of the *Yearbook of American and Canadian Churches*, black Baptists numbered more than 9 million, black Methodists roughly 4 million, and the black Holiness-Pentecostal family probably exceeded 4 million members. While these figures, based on church reports, were surely inflated, there is no reason to doubt that a large percentage of the approximately 28 million black Americans are church members. Yet the efficacy of social programs and the size of membership rolls are not the only, nor necessarily the most revealing measures of the black church's significance over the past five decades. The centrality of the church in the black American's quest for identity and meaning has demonstrated its ongoing resilience and creativity during a period of tumultuous change.

NOTES

1. Martin Luther King, Jr., *Stride toward Freedom: The Montgomery Story* (New York: Harper and Row, 1958), 224.

2. Ibid., 86. "Letter from Birmingham Jail," dated April 16, 1963, was first published as a pamphlet by the American Friends Committee and then appeared in *Why We Can't Wait* (1963). It has been frequently reprinted. "Paul's Letter to the American Christians" was preached by King in 1955 as a radio sermon and was published in Martin Luther King, Jr., *Strength to Love* (Cleveland: Collins and World, 1977; reprint, Philadelphia: Fortress Press, 1981).

3. Reprinted in James M. Washington, ed., *A Testament of Hope: The Essential Writings and Speeches of Martin Luther King, Jr.* (San Francisco: Harper and Row, 1968), 231–44.

Chapter Thirty

The Black Church and Black Politics
Models of Ministerial Activism

Mary R. Sawyer

Mary R. Sawyer chronicles the activist/social advocacy thrust of the black church. She is particularly informative in the area in which she has done seminal work: black ecumenism. Sawyer shows that the ecumenical agenda for black churches has not been so much concerned with either doctrinal or organizational unity as it has been with cooperative action around issues of justice and social advancement for African Americans.

•

From its inception in the 1700s, when the first tentative steps were taken toward autonomy from white Protestantism, the Black Church has been set on freedom. Inasmuch as the first requiste of freedom is survival, the church has been compelled to attend to that condition as well. Accordingly, its "activism" has followed a meandering course: sometimes subterranean and silent, sometimes vocal, visible, and urgent. One may surmise, however, that even when survival was the task of the day, freedom was the longing of the heart, and in that longing were nourished the seeds of black political action.

The politics of African American religion, defined in this context as systematic and spiritually grounded programs of social change, presents two primary models—protest politics and electoral politics—along with an array of secondary models. The present treatment of this range of activity is by no means exhaustive. In particular, where secondary models are concerned, the discussion is limited to activities that are characteristic of black ecumenical organizations.

Electoral Politics

The intent and expectation of civil rights workers was that the securing of voting rights would lead to the election of black representation. Participation in electoral politics in this manner constituted a primary model for seeking social change, for the objective was never representation for representation's sake, but rather reallocation of resources. Recognizing that a landless, moneyless people could not compete in a capitalist economy where resources were controlled by the private sector, African Americans determined to involve the government in the distribution of both public and private resources. The strategy was twofold: first, to position black officials to participate in public policy decision making; second, to increase black voter participation in the jurisdictions of white officials who, recognizing their dependence on black votes, presumably then would become more sensitive to black needs and concerns.[1]

The electoral model had been tested briefly during Reconstruction and its aftermath; even in those few short years, the symbiosis of church and politics was made clear. Of the twenty-two African Americans who served in Congress from 1870 to 1901, at least two and possibly three were ministers, one was a seminary graduate, and others were known to have strong religious sentiments and church ties. Aside from Congress, ministers served as secretaries of state, state legislators, and elected education officials in states across the South.[2]

It was left to a congressman from the North, however, to refine the conjoining of church and electoral politics—and, for that matter, of the church and protest politics. Decades before his 1944 election to the U.S. House of Representatives—and thus long before the emergence of the modern civil rights movement—Adam Clayton Powell Jr. was leading protest marches and economic boycotts in New York City. But it was in the arena of electoral politics that the pastor of Abyssinian Baptist Church made his most substantial contribution.

Using his church as his political base, Powell remained in Congress for twenty-four years. Fearless and constant in his outspokenness against discrimination and segregation, he was the bane of the white establishment and the delight of the black masses who found in Powell a sorely needed symbol of black empowerment. With his elevation in 1961 to chair of the influential House Education and Labor Committee, Powell became a power not only in symbol, but also in substance. Over a five-year period, Powell was responsible for the passage of some sixty major pieces of social legislation, including fair employment practices, manpower development training, public school aid, vocational training, school lunch programs, and the War on Poverty. Powell was thus uniquely qualified to serve as a role model for civil rights activists who by the mid-1960s were beginning to view electoral politics as the next stage of the civil rights movement.

In 1964, 280 African Americans were elected to public office in the entire United States. In 1967, when the National Conference of Black Elected Officials was organized, 600 African Americans held public office. In 1970, black elected officials nationwide still numbered less than 1,500, but by 1975—ten years following the passage of the Voting Rights Act—the figure increased to 3,500. The overwhelming preponderance of these officials were in the South, and large numbers of them were veteran civil rights activists. Many were ministers or church lay leaders, most were young, and virtually all had been conditioned by the religious ethos that permeated the turbulent social climate in which they had come to adulthood. Although only one of the twenty-eight individuals elected to Congress between 1954 and 1980 represented a southern district, the group exhibited much the same profile as the body of black politicians concentrated in local and state offices:three were ordained ministers, one was an active lay leader, three others were the sons or daughters of ministers, and five came to Congress with a history of civil rights organizing.[3]

By the mid-1980s, a new generation of officials was coming into office for whom the civil rights movement was a less immediate experience, and a smaller proportion of whom were ordained ministers—which is not to say that the black religious experience ceased to be a formative influence. But especially in the first decade of political development, electoral politics was viewed quite literally as an extension of the civil rights movement, which in turn was viewed in its essence as a moral campaign. In light of that circumstance, it is scarcely surprising that a study of white and black officials would revealed marked differences in values and objectives between the two groups. James Conyers and Walter Wallace, in their pioneering research, found

> a consistently stronger liberal tendency on the part of Black officials than on the part of White officials . . . Some 70 percent of Black officials, but only 26 percent of White officials, agreed that "true democracy is limited in the United States because of the special privileges enjoyed by business and industry."

Furthermore, 76 percent of black officials agreed that "it is the responsibility of the entire society, through its government, to guarantee everyone adequate housing, income, and leisure," while only 30 percent of white officials concurred. White officials placed a higher premium on the protection of property rights than did black officials. White officials were more concerned that the country had moved close to socialism, while black officials were more concerned that the country had moved close to fascism.[4]

> [White officials seemed to] perceive a sharp incompatibility between correcting social injustices and serving the country, and they make their choice; Black officials did not perceive so sharp an incompatibility. To some Black officials at least, correcting social injustices may have been a way of serving the country. This possibility seems to have its complement in the finding that associations between the desires to correct social injustices and to have personal prestige and income are more positive among White respondents than among Black respondents. Thus, Black officials were less likely to see a contradiction between serving the country and correcting social injustices, but more likely to see a contradiction between seeking personal prestige and correcting social injustices. The net implication of all this seems to be that Black officials may have been motivated to correct social injustices less for immediately self-gratifying reasons than were White officials.[5]

On a more personal and theological note, Andrew Young summed up his vision—and the view of many of his colleagues—in the following manner:

> The gospel is not just good history, it's good news. It's good history that the master fed 5,000 people 2,000 years ago, but it's good news when His followers of today act in the living present to feed the hungry, and set at liberty the captives. Black religion in America, like few religious communions in this century, has taken very seriously the commission of the prophet Isaiah that "we are anointed of God to preach good news to the poor, to bind up the broken hearted and set at liberty those who are captive."[6]

Challenging, as they did, the twin pillars of the Western world order—namely, racial superiority and white economic dominance—the new black officials inevitably tasted the venom spewed a century earlier at black Reconstruction politicians. Since 1975, a pattern of harassment of black elected officials has been noted, which ranges in tactics from character assassination, to inflammatory media coverage, to law enforcement investigation and selective prosecution.[7] Beginning in the late 1980s, a response to that pattern surfaced in local communities around the country in the form of organized protest, mobilization of resources, and even a renewal of economic boycotts. Not untypically, local ministers and church members are leading the movements in defense of public officials who are perceived to be unjustly assailed. In that activity a new stage has unfolded in what is a long-standing tradition of local church involvement in electoral politics.

The historical fight for voting rights and the offering of candidates for public office are two components of the Church's relations to electoral politics. A third key component is the engagement of the local church in the "nuts and bolts" of electoral politics. It remains the case that no other social institution outranks the church as a gathering place for the black community. As the church was the rallying point for the civil rights movement, so, too, it very often serves as an avenue for politicians to gain access to the resources and votes of the black masses. Any doubt that the Black Church continues to perform that function was allayed by the 1984 and 1988 presidential campaigns of the Reverend Jesse Jackson. Many lesser known, and nonministerial, candidates for elective office have had a similar relationship with the Church.

In the ritual that attends political campaigning, it is not uncommon for the candidate to be given access to a podium, or even the pulpit, to address the congregation as it is gathered for Sunday worship. While the pastor may not explicitly direct the church members with regard to their vote, his or her sentiment and preference are often anything but subtle. As individual citizens, of course, pastors sometimes do publicly endorse a particular candidate, lending their names to campaign brochures or newspaper ads. Often, too, endorsements will be issued through local ministerial alliances or associations.

While electoral campaigns increasingly rely on direct mail or media spots, the individual volunteer remains indispensable. Church congregations are a vital source of envelope stuffers, phone caller, and door-to-door canvassers. Churches organize transportation systems to deliver voters to the polls; churches also use their space to house the precinct polling booths. Typically, churches work both ends of the campaign, serving as a vehicle first for voter registration and then for get-out-the-vote drives. Indeed, it is probably safe to venture that if one randomly attended ten black mainstream Protestant churches on a given Sunday, one would hear two announcements at least once: "Join the NAACP," and "Don't forget to register to vote as you exit through the door!"

Finances are the lifeblood of any campaign. Regarding fund-raising, the church must exercise caution, for to be financially involved on a partisan basis as an organization would potentially jeopardize the church's tax-exempt status. However, nothing precludes individuals making contributions in response to appeals issued during a meeting held within the church walls. Many campaigns in urban areas include within their structures a ministerial committee, which can be an important source of fund raising as the committee members sponsor prayer breakfasts or benefit gospel concerts.

The relationship established between pastor and candidate, or congregation and candidate, typically extends beyond the duration of the campaign, and the benefits of campaign involvement ostensibly accrue to all parties concerned. The need of the church or of the neighborhood may be for freedom. But the need commonly manifests itself as a lack of childcare centers, or senior citizen programs, or playgrounds, or traffic signals. By the time candidates are elected to office, they will be aware of the need; if their interest is in reelection, they will not forget. In other words, the engagement of the local church in electoral politics fosters reciprocal relationships that provide a means of communicating the concerns and priorities of the people to the "system." In this relationship, the church might properly be regarded as an enabler of democracy.

Although electoral politics is deemed a necessity, the African American religious community has never considered politics alone sufficient to the task of gaining freedom. The Church has always reserved to itself the right of direct involvement in the project of seeking change. Another important precipitate of the civil rights movement, in addition to electoral empowerment, was a concept of ecumenical, or cooperative, interdenominational action to address social, economic, an political concerns. That organizational strategy for mobilizing the resources of black churches has produced an array of social change modalities, as well as linked the primary models of protest and electoral politics.

Ecumenism

African Americans have been present at the national and international levels from the earliest days of the Protestant ecumenical movement. At the local level, interdenominational ministerial alliances have long provided "ecumenical" forums for enhanced fellowship and for shared liturgical activity. As already intimated, an ecumenical spirit permeated the entire civil rights movement, and the SCLC, in particular, exhibited many ecumenical features. But with one major exception, that being the Fraternal Council of Negro Churches organized in the 1930s, intentional, self-defined black ecumenism of a more overtly political nature was a development of the latter half of the 1960s.

Far smaller in scale than the civil rights organizations, the memberships of these new organizations consisted of individual ministers and lay persons affiliated either with congregations of the larger black denominations or of the predominantly white mainline denominations. By design, the memberships were interdenominational, the strategy was cooperative action to address persistent social inequities, and the organizational authority was independent of denominational structures.

Only twice has black ecumenism assumed a conciliar form, in which the unit of membership is the denomination rather than the individual. The first instance was the Fraternal Council of Negro Churches, which was organized by black churchmen who had gained ecumenical experience in the predominantly white Federal Council of Churches. The Fraternal Council functioned with varying degrees of effectiveness until the early 1960s, when it was overshadowed by the newer National Council of Churches and by the emergent civil rights movement.

The second conciliar effort was initiated in 1977 as the Congress of National Black Churches. In contrast to the Fraternal Council, the membership of the Congress is limited to black denominations having a national constituency, thereby excluding black components of white denominations, as well as smaller black denominations and sects. But like the Fraternal Council, the Congress claims institutional investment on the part of its member denominations, which pay annual dues and the officers of which constitute the representational members of the Congress.

A variation on the conciliar model is the Interdenominational Theological Center (ITC) in Atlanta, which is a consortium of six seminaries representing as many denominations, and which was chartered in 1958. ITC is unique among black ecumenical bodies in that its central mission is education and training for ministry.

The structural relationships with denominations evident in ITC, the Fraternal Council of Negro Churches, and the Congress of National Black Churches are absent in other black ecumenical organizations. Thus, much like the ministerial leaders of the civil rights movement, the members of these organizations may be viewed as a prophetic remnant of the Church family. Though modest in size, this remnant nevertheless has been prolific. It has yielded a steady stream of organizations, both locally and nationally, for the past twenty-five years. Among those may be counted the National Conference of Black Christians (NCBC), National Black Evangelical Association (NBEA), Black Theology Project (BTP), Partners in Ecumenism (PIE), National Black Pastors Conference (NBPC), Black Ecumenical Advocacy Ministry (BEAM), The Gathering of Los Angeles, Alamo Black Clergy in the Bay Area, Philadelphia Council of Black Clergy and the more recent Black Clergy of Philadelphia and Vicinity, Black Ecumenical Commission of Massachusetts, African American Clergy Action Network in Chicago, and Concerned Black Clergy in Atlanta.[8]

The longevity of those groups has varied greatly, from a mere year or two to as much as a decade or more. Factors in success, on the other hand, are nearly uniform, with most efforts floundering on the shoals of adequate and independent financing and leadership succession. Yet, for all their tenuousness, the organizations have generated a marvelous array of alternative models for action.

Theological Development

It is impossible to discuss black ecumenism without reference to the black theology movement of the late 1960s and 1970s. To one degree or another, black liberation theology provides the frame of reference for all ecumenical organizations; indeed, black ecumenical activism might be defined as the attempted actualizing of the mandates of black theology for social, political, and economic liberation. But some ecumenical organizations have also had as a primary focus of activity the systematic formulation of black theology, or the use of black theology for purposes of reflection and critique. Such was the case for the National Conference of Black Christians

(NCBC) and later for the Black Theology Project, which in the late 1970s took over the theological functions of NCBC. The Black Ecumenical Commission of Massachusetts played an important role in those early conversations by way of its magazine, *The Black Church*, which was published for two years. The Philadelphia Council of Black Clergy established an Institute for Black Ministers, which for most of the 1970s offered courses on black theology. Alamo Black Clergy was instrumental in creating a Center for Urban Black Studies, which continues to function as a unit of the Graduate Theological Union in Berkeley, California. Throughout the 1970s, the National Black Evangelical Association was engaged in theological deliberations that then served to infuse its urban ministries with a social concerns dimension.

Consciousness-Raising

Integrally related to the task of theological development was the process of consciousness-raising. The role of the Southern Christian Leadership Conference in this regard has been noted. For those organizations that emerged in the context of the black power movement, consciousness-raising meant the interpreting of that movement both to the white religious establishment and to the more conservative clergy in black denominations. Such was the role of the NCBC. In the late 1970s and throughout the 1980s, Partners in Ecumenism, an entity of the National Council of Churches, sought in deliberate fashion to increase the awareness of white churches and church councils with regard to the needs and concerns of the black community. The National Black Evangelical Association has made similar attempts with its white counterparts in the National Evangelical Association.

Protest

In addition to the SCLC—which continues to function in the 1990s—several local ecumenical groups have engaged in programs of social protest. Such groups as the Philadelphia Council of Black Clergy, the Black Ecumenical Commission, The Gathering, and Alamo Black Clergy took on such issues as school desegregation and police brutality before the backlash of the 1970s set in. A renewal of such activity occurred in the mid- to late-1980s in the Black Clergy of Philadelphia and Vicinity and the Concerned Black Clergy in Atlanta. At the national level, the short-lived National Black Pastors Conference (1979–1981) envisioned a mechanism whereby local ministers could be mobilized to register protest regarding national policies and practices affecting the black community.

Electoral Politics

Other groups have cast their roles as more formal lobbying organizations. The Fraternal Council of Negro Churches maintained a Washington Bureau from the 1940s to the 1960s, the specific function of which was to lobby the federal government on issues affecting the welfare of blacks nationally. Staff members not only corresponded with successive presidents of the United States and testified at congressional committee hearings, but also organized "Committees of 100" in Washington and other cities to communicate concerns to congressional representatives. Thirty years after the Bureau became inactive, a new group called Black Ecumenical Advocacy Ministry, also based in Washington, D.C., began developing a network of local congregations across the country to lobby Congress on legislative matters affecting the black community. For a number of years, Partners in Ecumenism (PIE) set aside one day in its annual Washington meeting for PIE members to visit Capitol Hill. It was also part of PIE's vision—never realized—to develop regional structures to work for political objectives through local campaigns.

International Concerns

Black ecumenism has been concerned not only with domestic affairs, but also with international matters. The Fraternal Council of Negro Churches spoke eloquently on behalf of peace throughout World War II. At the same time, the Council was formally authorized by the federal government to send representatives overseas to visit black troops. A spirit of Pan-Africanism was strong in the National Conference of Black Christians, which organized meetings with African church leaders and scholars to explore mutual theological concerns and to strengthen ties between Africans and African Americans. The Congress of National Black Churches was outspoken on U.S. policy toward South Africa, while the Black Theology Project— which originated with Theology in the Americas—established ties in Cuba.

Economic Development

One of the frustrated objectives of the Philadelphia Council of Black Clergy was the creation of a black-owned bank. Similarly, the National Conference of Black Christians proposed a National Renewal and Development Corporation and an Economic Development Bank, both of which presumed federal and industrial involvement and neither of which came to fruition. The approach to economic development taken by the Congress of National Black Churches has been to generate revenues by creating its own institutions. An insurance component is now operational; a mortgage banking component, in which the Congress will act as an agent to secure reduced rate mortgages for local churches, is being developed; and a press and communications network is on the drawing boards. At one time, the Congress envisioned the formation of "Ecumenical Business Development Groups"—that is, the clustering of churches in urban areas for banking purposes to achieve better interest rates and stronger customer status. Those clusters would then serve as vehicles for collective purchasing, for negotiating community development projects, and for establishing minority businesses. However, such a complex venture awaits the development of proposed subsidiary components, which would be separately incorporated and managed by a for-profit entity separate from the Congress itself. Those assets, in turn, would pass to the Church Missions Trust, a nonprofit body created by the Congress, and would ultimately be used to support the Congress, to finance denominational projects, and to create an endowment for the Trust.

Social Development

While the economic component unfolds, the Congress of National Black Churches has concentrated on generating social development models, particularly around the black family, which can then be appropriated and adapted by local churches. Project SPIRIT, which has been implemented in several urban areas, emphasizes teenage parenting skills, tutoring, ethnic and cultural awareness, and pastoral counseling. Health care, particularly in the area of drug abuse, is prominent among other issues on the organization's agenda. Ultimately, the Congress envisions establishing relations with municipal interdenominational alliances so it can transfer its programs to the local level. "Family" was also a major focus of the Black Ecumenical Commission of Massachusetts, through its federally funded Foster Grandparents Program. Partners in Ecumenism envisioned a comprehensive human services program using black church clusters and local ecumenical bodies. The idea—which was never actually tested—was to provide emergency food and clothing, day care for children and seniors, counseling, tutoring, recreation, and voter education and registration on a scale beyond the capacities of individual congregations. In this manner, PIE hoped to address, at least nominally, the crisis of black survival in urban areas.

While the foregoing examples of ecumenical endeavor are by no means exhaustive, they are indicative of the scope of the planning and programming undertaken in recent decades. Some projects have been more effective than others; some have been more practical than others. But all are searching for means to maximize the resources of the Black Church, and to bring those resources to bear on the life conditions of the Church constituency—which encompasses the whole of the black population. If the visions sometimes exceed organizational capabilities, the benefits are nevertheless myriad.

In such ecumenical efforts, religious leaders have an opportunity to demonstrate theology in action. In the process, linkages are built with secular components of society, political skills are honed, and the information base of congregations and the larger community is enlarged. Admittedly, to a substantial degree, the consequences of those activities are intangible. The tangibles remain large in potential, however, so that it seems reasonable to advocate that the ecumenical framework remain a significant feature of black political activism.

Conclusion

For more than 200 years, the Black Church has engaged the prevailing principalities and powers, faithfully seeking to honor the mandates of Christianity and democracy alike. From the mid-1700s to the mid-1800s, the central quest was for personhood; from the 1860s to the 1960s, citizenship. Half-century by half-century, the circumstances defining black life in America have grown less oppressive, more hopeful—until the past two and a half decades. Although this quarter-century has produced an African American middle class of unprecedented dimensions, it has engendered, as well, an anomic state of despair for the vast populations of America's drug—and violence-ridden central cities. Today the challenge to the Black Church is thus qualitatively different from days past.

The goals of black America today extend beyond personhood and citizenship to full economic, political, and social empowerment. The implicit tasks of institution building—whether in the electoral arena or within the church body itself—are immeasurably larger, and correspondingly more tedious and trying, than the tasks of yesteryear. If the church, or its remnant visionaries, is the beneficiary of an abundance of models for change, the adequacy of resources to fully implement those models is marginal to say the least. The economic shifts of recent years that have gutted the black working class—namely, overseas capital investment and exploitation of cheap international labor—have reduced proportionately the capital available to black churches to support programs of change. Add to this circumstance the task of creating infrastructures adequate to the chore of institution building, next add the task of developing a collective style of democratic and gender-inclusive leadership in a traditionally patriarchal and charismatic milieu, and then add the devising of a palatable mode of criticism that any successful social change effort requires. The odds seem formidable indeed.

Still, the Church has known greater odds, and in the face of those odds, not only has endured, but has substantively advanced the cause of freedom. The idea that religiously motivated political action by Black Church leaders will continue to be a feature of the American landscape seems a projection scarcely subject to debate.

NOTES

1. See R. P. Browning, D. R. Marshall, and D. H. Tabb, *Protest Is Not Enough* (University of California Press, 1984). I am indebted to Nicholas Alozie for his interpretation of the transition from black protest to electoral politics.

2. Mary R. Sawyer, "Black Politics, Black Faith," M. R. Thesis, Howard University Divinity School, Washington, D.C. 1982, chapter 3.

3. Ibid., chapter 5. The three ministers were Andrew Young, Walter Fauntroy, and William Gray. Congresswoman Shirley Chisholm similarly acknowledged functioning politically from a strong religious frame of reference. The lay leader was Parren Mitchell. Civil rights organizers included Mitchell, Young, Fauntroy, Mickey Leland, and William Clay.

4. James E. Conyers and Walter L. Wallace, *Black Elected Officials: A Study of Black Americans Holding Governmental Office* (New York: Russell Sage Foundation, 1976).

5. Ibid.

6. W. Schemmel, "Andrew Young Goes to Washington," *Christian Century*, 24 January 1973, 102.

7. See Mary R. Sawyer, "The Dilemma of Black Politics: A Report on Harassment of Black Elected Officials," National Association of Human Rights Workers, Sacramento, CA 1977, and "Harassment of Black Elected Officials: Ten Years Later," Voter Education and Registration Action, Inc., Washington, DC, 1987. In November 1989, the National Council of Churches adopted a resolution that called for a congressional investigation of this problem.

8. For brief descriptions of the national groups identified here, see Mary R. Sawyer, "Black Ecumenical Movements: Proponents of Social Change," *Review of Religious Research* 30, no. 2 (December 1988): 152–61. For a more elaborate discussion, see Mary R. Sawyer, *Black Ecumenism: Implementing the Demands of Justice* (Valley Forge, PA: Trinity Press, Int., 1994).

Thirty-one

Black Religion and Social Change
Women in Leadership Roles

Mary R. Sawyer

As she did with her earlier piece in this volume on the role of women in the development of the institutional black churches, Mary R. Sawyer makes more adequate the picture of black religious activism by correcting for the virtual—though inaccurate—invisibility of women in the story. Here we learn of their pivotal work both in black ecumenism and in the implementation of the efforts for civil rights.

•

The story of women's leadership in black religion may be viewed as an intertwining of two strands: one strand is composed of women in the church and related religious institutions, the other of women engaged in social change activities having religious underpinnings but whose connections to the church vary in degree and intensity. In an issue of the *Journal of Religious Thought*, Delores C. Carpenter addressed the first strand, providing a valuable historical overview of black women in religious institutions.[1] The objective here is to profile in an initial way personalities prominent in the second strand. In some instances, of course, the strands converge, with individual activist women being prominent both in religious institutions and in social movements tangential or external to the formal institution.

Religiously based social action actually presents a continuum of forms. At one end of the continuum is the "secular" arena, including social protest and reform movements, electoral politics, and service organizations. The secular veneer, however, in no way precludes participation by individuals acting out of religious motivations. At the other end of the continuum are transchurch organizations, that is, interdenominational or ecumenical organizations whose objectives are also social change but whose agendas are overtly anchored in a religious framework. In between are religiously grounded nonchurch organizations (e.g., the YWCA), marginal religious movements (e.g., the Shakers), and quasi-church organizations (e.g., benevolent associations and missionary societies). In all of these, women have played key roles. This particularly the case in the secular and ecumenical arenas, which constitute the primary focus for this inquiry.[2]

Appropriate classification of a given movement or organization on this continuum is not always easy. For example, while some regard the civil rights movement as a secular movement, others regard it as a church-based, or ecumenical movement.[3] Further, conventional understandings of "leadership" may not adhere. In the present context, no assumptions are made with regard to formal credentials. The women are ordained and lay, formally educated and self-educated, well known and little known. The women identified—and the women they represent—may be regarded as "leaders" to the extent that they were moved by religious tenets, or enabled by religious faith, to take action to address inequities and injustice. For the most part, however, they are the more visible leaders connected to formal organizations. The multitudes of women playing critical leadership roles in an informal capacity in local communities and neighborhoods are inevitably more difficult to name, but surely no less to be valued.

The "Secular" Arena

A distinguishing feature of black religion is its historic concern with racial liberation. Throughout the nineteenth century, slave revolts, the abolitionist movement, the Negro convention movement, and the nationalist emigration movement all provided testimony to the inextricable relation of black religion and black politics (i.e., organized social change).[4] The relationship has held not only in protest politics but also in electoral politics, as both the Reconstruction era and the post–civil rights movement era attest.[5]

Heretofore scholars have tended to examine the arenas of political and religious intersection by focusing on the role of clergy and lay church leaders, who more often than not were men. As in increasingly being acknowledged, women, because of the patriarchal structure of the church, have historically been compelled to take their organizing skills and social consciousness into secular avenues without the benefit of church identity and authority. These extra-church involvements were sometimes in exclusively female organizations, sometimes in male-dominated organizations, and sometimes fiercely independent of any organization.

The antebellum period offers up three powerful examples of women in pursuit of justice: Maria Stewart (1803–1879), Harriet Tubman (c. 1823–1913), and Sojourner Truth (c. 1797–1883). Maria Stewart, upon her religious conversion, took up public speaking on behalf of women and the enslaved, addressing, as well, the severe restrictions imposed on "free" blacks. Without fail, her exhortations were couched in the language of religious morality.[6] The religious symbolism surrounding Tubman is apparent in the popular reference to her as the Moses of her people. That she operated out of a personal religious frame of reference is documented in Sarah Bradford's biography. Tubman's own words attest to her abiding faith:

> I had reasoned dis out in my mind; there was one of two things I had a *right* to, liberty, or death; if I could not have one, I would have de oder; for no man should take me alive; I should fight for my liberty as long as my strength lasted, and when de time came for me to go, de Lord would let dem take me.[7]

That the social activism of Sojourner Truth on behalf of women and slaves was solidly anchored in her mystical experiences is even more amply documented. Indeed, the very name taken by this outspoken Methodist preacher (in replacement of her birth name, Isabelle Baumfree) was a product of her recurring visions and dreams. No less were her public political stances rooted in an abiding spirituality.

Few activists were as well known as these three women. But neither were activists so few as conventional histories would lead us to believe. Sara Evans, in her *Born for Liberty: Women in American History*, traces a progression from the evangelical revivals of the Second Great Awakening, to the social reform movements of the eighteenth and nineteenth centuries, to the women's suffrage movement.[8] For free black women before the Civil War, evangelical reform took the shape of missionary, benevolent, and literary societies, an example being the Afric-American Female Intelligence Society of Boston. On a more overtly political plane, black women were active in interracial organizations such as the Philadelphia Female Antislavery Society.[9]

From the late 1800s to the 1950s, social activism was carried out largely through women's organizations. Women's auxiliaries and missionary societies of the Baptist and Methodist denominations, respectively, constituted one important avenue for expressing moral concern. In the first two decades of this century, for example, the Women's Convention of the National Baptist Convention, under the leadership of Nannie Helen Burroughs, took political positions on lynching, disenfranchisement, stereotyping of blacks in the media and entertainment industries, and segregation in public transportation, as well as on women's suffrage and the sexism of black men.[10] But more often the opportunities resided in extra-church vehicles. Perhaps most significant of these was the multitude of clubs that began forming after the Civil War and that were brought together in the 1890s as the National Association of Colored Women under the leadership of Mary Church Terrell. Devoted to community service and racial uplift, the clubs provided avenues for leadership and organizing too often denied in the church proper.[11]

In addition to Burroughs and Terrell, prominent names of this period include Francis E. W. Harper, Ida B. Wells-Barnett, and Mary McLeod Bethune. Frances Ellen Watkins Harper is remembered as a strong advocate of the right of women to vote and as one of the most prominent black participants of the women's suffrage movement in the last decades of the nineteenth century. As a nationally respected public lecturer, however, she consistently advanced a holistic civil rights agenda which encompassed the imperative of voting rights for black men. She was equally constant in presenting her ideas in the imagery and rhetoric of the faith, as this brief sample attests:

> Let the hearts of the women of the world respond to the song of the herald angels of peace on earth and good will to men. Let them throb as one heart unified by the grand and holy purpose of uplifting the human race, and humanity will breathe freer, and the world grow brighter. With such a purpose Eden would spring up in our path, and Paradise be around our way.[12]

Ida B. Wells-Barnett, of course, is best known for her unrelenting campaign against lynching, but her journalistic critiques extended over the range of civil rights concerns of the early twentieth century. Although a founder of the NAACP and an early contributor to the women's club movement, she was by and large a solo crusader. The origins of her feminist stance, and of her audacity in challenging the accommodationist ideology of Booker T. Washington, are obscure. But her appeals to moral conscience and to law as well as pragmatic economic interests as remedies for injustice were no doubt at least a partial result of her formal education at Rust College, a Methodist school in Mississippi.[13]

The entirety of Mary McLeod Bethune's extraordinary career was anchored in her deep religious faith. Intending to serve as a missionary in Africa, Bethune attended Moody Bible Institute for two years. When those aspirations were thwarted, she turned to her own country, finding in the mission field at home a rich harvest. She served as president of the National Association of Colored Women (NACW), then founded and presided over the National Council of Negro Women (NCNW), the umbrella organization that brought together most of the organizations of black women, including the NACW. The only woman member of the "Black Cabinet" under President Franklin Roosevelt's administration, she played a unique role as both spiritual and political adviser in the crucial New Deal years. She is perhaps best known as the founder of Bethune-Cookman College, a Methodist school, which became her own denominational affiliation.[14]

These individuals, each remarkable in her way, are only suggestive of the contributions made by the multitude of black women in the years of segregation. Nevertheless, they begin to hint of the religiously derived power that infused their collective actions. As B. J. Loewenberg and Ruth Bogin have noted:

> Black American women were persuaded that new attitudes could in fact be nurtured. They wished to awaken new understanding among blacks as well as in the general population. Will they had in overflowing measure, and likewise a limitless faith in their own powers to quicken the feelings of others as they themselves had been stirred. They could hardly feel otherwise. They were Americans. They were democrats. And they were Christians. Christianity and its Bible were their justifications for belief, the warrant for reform.[15]

Transitions

By the 1940s, the mood and methods of the black community began to turn, and the options for activist women shifted accordingly. While the exemplary women's organizations continued to function, the advent of the civil rights movement provided new forums as well. In contrast to the women's reform movements and clubs, the civil rights movement and the subsequent black power movement dictated women's entrance into a stage of participation in decidedly male-dominated organizations. Nevertheless, women did play important roles, as is increasingly being documented. Before turning to the prominent personalities in this period, however, it would be appropriate to mention an organization that contributed much to laying a foundation for the civil rights movement, the Young Women's Christian Association (YWCA).

From the time of its formation in the 1860s, the YWCA provided an avenue for Christian women to act on their moral commitments. Sadly, those moral commitments did not extend initially to the problem of race and the conditions of black Americans. In consequence, black participation was for several decades effectively restricted to a parallel YWCA. Only after years of protest by black leaders was the situation remedied. From 1946, however, when an "interracial charter" was adopted, through 1970, when the elimination of racism became its "one imperative," the YWCA was an important training ground for civil rights activists.[16]

One author has noted that the language of the YWCA was evangelical Christian language, and that it was partly for that reason that it became an accessible forum wherein black women could express their concerns to white women.[17] No one was more pivotal in this process of directing the energies of the YWCA toward racial injustice than Dorothy Height, who from 1944 to 1977 served on the national staff of the YWCA as director of the District Action Program on Integration. Height remains an influential personality, of course, as president of the National Council of Negro Women (NCNW).

A second religiously based organization was also a significant predecessor of the civil rights movement. The first black ecumenical organization, the Fraternal Council of Negro Churches, organized by African Methodist Episcopal (AME) Bishop Reverdy Ransom in 1934, had an explicit agenda of social change and racial uplift, framed in a religious context. Ransom and other black church leaders had despaired that the predominantly white Federal Council of Churches would ever address black concerns in any substantive way. As they envisioned the new Fraternal Council, it would be the "authoritative voice" of the "united Negro church" to speak on "social, economic, industrial and political questions."[18] Organized on a conciliar model, the Fraternal Council had representation from sixteen predominantly black communions as well as a half-dozen predominantly white denominations. Significantly, members of the executive committee were not required to be ministers, which enabled the appointment of women. In fact, two of the original thirty-nine members of the executive committee were women—Belle Hendon from Chicago, representing the National Baptist Convention of America (NBCA), and Ida Mae Myller, of Gary, Indiana, from the Community Center Church.[19]

Not until the Fraternal Council entered its second stage, under the leadership of Baptist minister William Jernagin, however, is there again evidence of participation by women in any capacity. Jernagin—for many years the president of NBC, Inc.'s National Sunday School and Baptist Training Union Congress—served variously as president of the Council, chair of the executive committee, and director of the Council's Washington bureau, which he created. Jernagin maintained a close working relation with Nannie Helen Burroughs, who headed NBC's National Training and Professional School for Women and Girls in Washington, D.C. Burroughs served on at least one committee of the Council,[20] and spoke at the 1949 meeting of the Council in Richmond, Virginia. Significantly, her address was given during the "women's hour." At that same meeting, the Council voted to "authorize the establishment of women's auxiliaries in various states."[21] Except for a group in St. Louis, no evidence exists that such appendages ever became active. In 1950, however, a women's auxiliary was organized at the national level and was for several years headed by Mrs. Jernagin. In keeping with this typical Baptist model, the participation of women outside the auxiliary was limited, although the same year the auxiliary was formed, a woman, Berta L. Derrick, did serve as associate director of the Council.[22] Several women were involved in the planning of the Prayer Pilgrimage held in Washington, D.C., under the sponsorship of the Fraternal Council following the 1954 Supreme Court decision *Brown v. Topeka Board of Education*. Burma Whitted, Dorothy Ferebee, and Jane Spaulding were all co-chairs of major committees.[23]

Beset by internal decline and overshadowed by the emergent civil rights movement, the Fraternal Council became inactive in the early 1960s. That it supported the objectives of the civil rights movement is certainly evident in the invitation it extended to a young man named Martin Luther King to become its executive director.[24] Had King accepted, the course of the civil rights movement might have been very different. The Southern Christian Leadership Conference (SCLC), for example, might never have come into being, and that loss certainly would have extended to activist women. SCLC, like the Fraternal Council in its later years, was a Baptist-dominated and therefore male-dominated organization, which accounted for the establishment of a "women's auxiliary," known as "SCLC Women." In spite of structural and philosophical obstacles, women still found ways to make substantive contributions.

Septima Clark, who as a staff member of Highlander Folk School was responsible for citizenship education training, ultimately became a member of the board of directors of SCLC. Perhaps more than any one other individual, Clark was responsible for blacks in the South challenging the denial of voting rights. When the Highlander citizenship education program was taken over by SCLC, it came under the direction of Dorothy Cotton, a talented musician who trained citizenship instructors to use the singing of spirituals to teach their students to read and write.[25] An equally prominent member of the SCLC staff was Ella Baker. Baker was one of three people—the other two being Bayard Rustin and Stan Levinson—who conceived of the SCLC following the Montgomery bus boycott and worked with King and his lieutenants to develop the organization. Baker then served as the first staff director of SCLC, although her official title was "associate director," a concession to the preponderance of Baptist ministers on the SCLC board. Throughout her tenure, Baker had serious philosophical disagreements with King over leadership styles, arguing for a more participatory and less Baptist model. She lost, of course. But it was partially this difference that led her to urge student participants to form their own organization, separate from SCLC. The result was the Student Nonviolent Coordinating Committee, or SNCC, which Baker is credited with founding.[26]

Many of the women in the civil rights movement—whether affiliated with SCLC, SNCC, or other organizations—brought with them strong ties to the church. It was Baker's early ambition to become a missionary.[27] In her singing, her teaching, her preaching, her organizing and marching, the religious grounding of Fannie Lou Hamer was ever apparent.[28] Septima Clark, in her autobiography, states simply, "I've been working in the church all my life."[29] In this, the known leaders of the movement differed little from the thousands of nameless women who carried the movement. One need only view any film on the civil rights protest rallies held in black churches of the South to be reminded that it was women, as much if not more so than men, who dropped their coins in the collection plate, who spread the word of coming events, who encouraged and prayed for male spokespersons, who planned and marched, and agonized and celebrated.

One of the signal accomplishments of the movement was the passage of the 1965 Voting Rights Act, which opened the door for black voter registration and election of black public officials in numbers that had not been seen since Reconstruction. A key difference, of course, was that during Reconstruction black women could neither vote nor hold public office. Although individuals such as Burroughs and Bethune were active in the Republican Party in their day, the contemporary era of black electoral politics afforded women the first opportunity to express their social consciousness in the system of representative government. As of 1989, some eighteen hundred black women held public office, accounting for over a quarter of all black elected officials.[30] It is not surprising to find that religious sentiments and values weigh heavily in the public service careers of black elected officials. Certainly this circumstance obtains no less for women than for a men, as the words of one woman politician, former Congresswoman Shirley Chisholm, attest:

> There is no room left in the world today for a narrow and individualistic religion. To talk of building a Christ-like character while one is absolutely complacent about an economic and political system that engenders selfishness, greed and power-lust—all of this is sheer vanity.

Chisholm has acknowledged that it was the realization that "faith alone is not enough" that compelled her to run for public office in the first place.[31]

If the shift from protest politics to electoral politics was one hallmark of the mid- to late 1960s, there were other hallmarks as well. One was the transition from civil rights to black power, with its separatist emphasis on black culture and black consciousness, an emphasis that in turn produced other results. Demand grew for black studies in major colleges and universities, and interest was renewed in black religion and its institutional manifestation, the black church. These two developments converged, then, in a new academic field of black religious studies.[32]

Central to the emergence of black religious studies was the systematic formulation of a black liberation theology. Significantly, the early steps toward clarifying such a theology occurred not in an academic context but in the activist context of black ecumenical organizations concerned with social change, a new generation of which was spawned in the late 1960s. These organizations, which constitute an intermediary between black churches and extra-church agencies, joined the discipline of black religious studies in providing new arenas in which religious women could pursue social change.

Black Ecumenism

The memberships of black ecumenical organizations, with few exceptions, are drawn directly from churches; they tend to represent, however, activists and the more progressive element of the churches. While the organizations are by no means free of the patriarchal presumptions of black churches, collectively they offer an assortment of models that embrace female participation to varying degrees.

The first of these post–civil rights organizations was the National Conference of Black Churchmen (NCBC), organized in 1967 largely in reaction to confrontations with the white religious establishment, which was offended and threatened by black militancy. NCBC sought not only to explain that militancy to the white churches but also to raise the consciousness of the more conservative ranks of the black clergy. NCBC's most significant contribution, through the leadership of Gayraud Wilmore and James Cone, was the formulation of early statements of a black liberation theology.[33] Like the black power movement itself, however, NCBC was male-dominated, with very minimal participation by women—even though one of the five persons present at the group's initial meeting was a woman. Anna Arnold Hedgeman was the associate to Benjamin Payton, then executive director of the National Council of Churches' Commission on Religion and Race, where the initial meeting was held.[34] Not incidentally, Hedgeman began her influential career in civil rights as a staff member of the YWCA.[35]

Those women who did participate labored to raise their colleagues' consciousness. Among them were United Church of Christ minister Yvonne Delk, Erna Ballentine Bryant, A.M.E. minister Mary Ann Bellinger, Jacqueline Grant, and Thelma Adair. As board members in NCBC's latter years, these women were instrumental in bringing about a change in the name of the organization, from National Conference of Black Churchmen to National Conference of Black Christians, so as to include women. Erna Bryant also played an important role as the second executive director of the Black Ecumenical Commission in Massachusetts from 1974 to 1979.

NCBC was only marginally functional from 1973 until the early 1980s, when it became totally inactive. As this group declined, a number of its members turned to the Black Theology Project (BTP) as an avenue for pursuing the theological expressions of black liberation and empowerment. The Black Theology Project was originally organized in 1976 under the auspices of Theology in the Americas, but began meeting on a regular basis only in 1984. Even in its more erratic years, the participation rate of women significantly exceeded that of other organizations. Shawn Copeland, a Catholic sister, became the program director in 1976 and planned the first major consultation, held in 1977. Yvonne Delk served as chairperson in 1981 and 1982, and as cochair from 1987 to 1991. Olivia Pearl Strokes, Baptist minister, was a cochair in 1985 and 1986. As significant a role as anyone's was played by Jualynne Dodson, who served as cochair in 1984, and as the administrative coordinator from 1984 to 1988. Providing committed leadership as a subsequent executive director was Iva Carruthers. Women are well represented on the board of directors, as well as on the programs of BTP's annual convocations.

Women have also played a significant part in a little-known group that predates both the National Conference of Black Christians and the Black Theology Project. The National Black Evangelical Association (NBEA), organized in 1963, is made up largely of members of the evangelical wing of American Protestantism. But in contrast to most evangelicals, members of NBEA place a dual emphasis on spirituality and liberation-oriented social change activity. Of the eight founders of NBEA, one, Dessie Webster, was a woman, and approximately one-third of its members are women.[36] In 1990, five of the twenty-five members of the board of directors were women, as were two of the association's officers.[37] One of NBEA's eight commissions is a women's commission, and among the separate entities spun off from NBEA is one called the Women's Consciousness Raising Seminar. While such a high profile for women may at first glance seem improbable in a group such as this, it is also a reminder that evangelical and pentecostal churches are often more open to leadership by women than are the "progressive" mainstream churches.

Certainly the opposite circumstance is evident in the Congress of National Black Churches (CNBC). One of the younger ecumenical organizations—the Congress was formed in 1978—its agenda differs from those of other groups in that its primary emphases are neither theological formulations nor political activism, but economic development and human services delivery, with particular focus on the black family. The Congress, like the old Fraternal Council of Negro Churches, is organized on a conciliar model, with its membership consisting of five of the seven largest black denominations—two Methodist, two Baptist, and one Pentecostal.[38] According to its constitution, all national officers of the member denominations are members of the Congress. Since most officers are ministers and most ministers are men, this structural arrangement effectively limits the participation of women. All Methodists bishops, for example, by virtue of that office are members of the Congress—but there are no women bishops in any of the black Methodist denominations. In recent years, though, women have assumed significant leadership positions at the staff level. Two of the Congress's three project directors, for example, are women: Vanella A. Crawford and Reverend Alicia D. Byrd.

In contrast to CNBC was another group also organized in 1978, Partners in Ecumenism (PIE). Established as a unit of the National Council of Churches (NCC), its mission was to challenge the white churches, as did NCBC, to be more sensitive to black concerns, and additionally to bring black and white churches into a partnership to address the needs of urban residents in concrete ways. The first national coordinator of PIE was Joan Campbell, a Disciples of Christ minister who held that title from 1978 to 1980. For several years thereafter, Campbell played an important role in PIE as the assistant general secretary of NCC responsible for the Commission on Regional and Local Ecumenism (CORLE). The steering committee of PIE had strong representation by women, including, at one point, the vice president at-large for the national program, two of six regional vice presidents, one of six regional representatives, and four of twenty-two at-large members. An estimated 20 percent of PIE's members were women, a circumstance due in part to PIE's emphasis on lay participation. In addition, one-half of PIE's membership was made up of the historic black denominations and the other half of blacks in predominantly white denominations, which enlarges the pool of ordained women. PIE discontinued operation in 1997.

Recently, a number of individuals previously active in PIE have turned their energies to the newest adventure in black ecumenism, the Black Ecumenical Advocacy Ministry (BEAM), whose purpose is to function as a legislative lobby on behalf of the black community nationally.

Chronicling the presence of women in black religious organizations is an inexact undertaking at best, especially with older organizations for which historical records are scarce and incomplete. What becomes apparent, however, even in this brief review, is that a change is taking place: Women have been conspicuously more prominent in the Black Theology Project and Partners in Ecumenism than in the Fraternal Council of Negro Churches or the hierarchy of the Southern Christian Leadership Conference. It is no longer so easy to exclude women; nor, as many men have come to appreciate, is such exclusion desirable. That change in itself is among the most important contributions women have made, and it portends greater change to come.

A parallel observation may be made with regard to the field of black religious studies. An early critique of black liberation theology was its omission of the experience of women. The black womanist movement, aided by the emergent field of women's studies, inevitably had its impact not only on black theology but on black religious studies as a whole. Today, women are not only theologians, but sociologists of religion, biblical scholars, and ethicists. These individuals are themselves agents of change, for just as male scholars of black religion have sought to raise the consciousness of black church leaders regarding empowerment around the issues of class and race, so womanist scholars are pointing to alternative paths where gender is at issue. In this, they have been joined by activist women in church structures, prominent among whom, in addition to Yvonne Delk, are such personages as Leontyne Kelley, retired United Methodist bishop; Theresa Hoover, for many years associate general secretary of the United Methodist Women's Division; the late Pauli Murray, Episcopal priest and longtime civil and women's rights advocate; and, more recently, Episcopal bishop Barbara C. Harris, and Presbyterian moderator Joan Salmon Campbell.

A development of particular moment within the church institution is the formation of a separate convention of Baptist women ministers. The National Baptist Women Ministers Convention, founded in 1981, presently claims some 250 participants. In 1990, the convention also admitted to its membership a delegation of recently ordained women in the Church of God in Christ. The unmistakable statement of these women is that if they cannot be preachers, pastors, and activists in the patriarchal communions, they will create alternative structures and develop alternative models of ministry.

And so it has been, from the time of Tubman and Truth, to the dawn of the twenty-first century.

NOTES

1. Delores C. Carpenter, "Black Women in Religious Institutions: A Historical Summary from Slavery to the 1960s," *Journal of Religious Thought* 46, no. 2 (1989): 7–27.

2. Particularly where the secular arena is concerned, this essay relies on pioneering efforts to document the contributions of women. The Carlson Publishing Company series, *Black Women in United States History*, edited by Darlene Clark Hine, is comprehensive collection of resources. An older and still useful compendium on black women's activism is Gerda Lerner's *Black Women in White America: A Documentary History* (New York: Vintage Books, 1973).

3. See Aldon Morris, *The Origins of the Civil Rights Movement* (New York: Free Press, 1984). It is my considered opinion that the civil rights movement is appropriately regarded as an ecumenical movement led albeit by a dissenting "remnant" of the church.

4. Gayraud S. Wilmore, *Black Religion and Black Radicalism*, 2d ed. (Maryknoll, N.Y.: Orbis Books, 1983).

5. Mary R. Sawyer, "Black Politics, Black Faith," master's thesis, Howard University Divinity School, 1982.

6. B. J. Loewenberg and Ruth Bogin, eds., *Black Women in Nineteenth-Century American Life* (University Park: Pennsylvania State University Press, 1976), pp. 183–85.

7. Sarah Bradford, *Harriet Tubman: The Moses of Her People* (Secaucus, N.J.: Citadel Press, 1961).

8. Sara M. Evans, *Born For Liberty: A History of Women in America* (New York: The Free Press, 1989).

9. Lerner, *Black Women in White America*, pp. 435, 437–40.

10. Evelyn Brooks, "Religion, Politics, and Gender: The Leadership of Nannie Helen Burroughs," *Journal of Religious Thought* 44, no. 2 (1988): 14–21.

11. See Charles H. Wesley, *The History of the National Association of Colored Women's Clubs: A Legacy of Service* (Washington, D.C.: National Association of Colored Women's Clubs, Inc., 1984). Also, see Lerner, *Black Women in White America*, pp. 435–37, and Cynthia Neverdon-Morton, *Afro-American Women of the South and the Advancement of the Race, 1895–1925* (Knoxville: University of Tennessee Press, 1989), chap. 10. Significantly, Burroughs was also active in the NACW as the head of the Young Women's Department. See Carpenter, "Black Women in Religious Institutions," p. 14.

12. Loewenberg and Bogin, eds., *Black Women in Nineteenth-Century American Life*, pp. 243–44 and 247.

13. See Thomas C. Holt, "The Lonely Warrior: Ida B. Wells-Barnett and the Struggle for Black Leadership," in John Hope Franklin and August Meier, eds., *Black Leaders of the Twentieth Century* (Urbana: University of Illinois Press, 1982).

14. See Clarence G. Newsome, "Mary McLeod Bethune As Religionist," in Hilah F. Thomas and Rosemary Skinner Keller, eds., *Women in New Worlds* (Nashville, Tenn.: Abingdon, 1981).

15. Loewenberg and Bogin, *Black Women in Nineteenth-Century American Life*, p. 28.

16. For an extended treatment of the special role played by the student division of the YWCA in applying social Christianity to racial matters prior to the mid-1940s, see Frances Sanders Taylor, "On the Edge of Tomorrow: Southern Women, the Student YWCA, and Race, 1920–1944" (Ph.D. diss., Stanford University, 1984). For a brief history of blacks in the YWCA up to 1920, see Neverdon-Morton, *Afro-American Women of the South*, pp. 207–22.

17. Sara Evans, "Redefining Public and Private: The History of Women in America," lecture delivered at Iowa State University, Ames, Iowa, March 22, 1990.

18. Reverdy C. Ransom, ed., "The Fraternal Council of Negro Churches in America," *The Year Book of Negro Churches* (Philadelphia, A.M.E. Book Concern, 1939–1940), p. 123.

19. *1972 Heritage Brochure: Brochure of Examples of Work Done by the Fraternal Council of Churches* (Washington, D.C.: Fraternal Council of Churches, 1964), pp. 4–5.

20. Burroughs served on the National Coordinating Committee of the Fraternal Council

in Civilian Defense. Jernagin to Burroughs, April 15, 1942, Nannie H. Burroughs Papers, Library of Congress, Washington, D.C.

21. Press release to the Associated Negro Press, June 8, 1949, Claude A. Barnett Papers, Chicago Historical Society, Chicago, Ill.

22. *1972 Heritage Brochure*, p. 9.

23. "Program," Lincoln Thanksgiving Pilgrimage, September 22, 1954, Claude A. Barnett Papers, Chicago Historical Society.

24. Interview with Rev. George W. Lucas, executive secretary of the Fraternal Council, cited in Spurgeon E. Crayton, "The History and Theology of the National Fraternal Council of Negro Churches" (Master's thesis, Union Theological Seminary, 1979), p. 52.

25. Donna Langston, "The Women of Highlander," lecture delivered at the Conference on Women and the Civil Rights Movement, Atlanta, Ga., October 1988.

26. See Morris, *The Origins of the Civil Rights Movement.*

27. Nydia D. Thomas, "Remembrances: Masters of Coalition Building—Ella Baker, 1905–1987," *Point of View* (Winter 1988): p. 21.

28. See "Fannie Lou Hamer: Prophet of Freedom," *Sojurners* (December 1982).

29. Cynthia Stokes Brown, ed., *Ready from Within: Septima Clark and the Civil Rights Movement* (Navarro, Calif: Wild Trees Press, 1986), p. 97.

30. *Black Elected Officials: A National Roster, 1989* (Washington, D.C.: Joint Center for Political Studies, 1990).

31. Shirley Chisholm, "The Relationship Between Religion and Today's Social Issues," *Religious Education* 69 (March–April 1974): 120, 122; cited in Sawyer, "Black Politics, Black Faith," p. 104.

32. See Mary R. Sawyer, "C. Eric Lincoln, Scholar and Prophet of Black Religious Studies," *Quarterly Review* 10, No. 3, Fall 1990.

33. For early statements on black theology issued by NCBC, see Gayraud S. Wilmore and James H. Cone, eds., *Black Theology: A Documentary History, 1966–1979* (Maryknoll, N.Y.: Orbis Books, 1979).

34. Others present at the July 1986 meeting were Gayraud S. Wilmore, J. Oscar Lee, and H. R. Hughes.

35. Carpenter, "Black Women in Religious Institutions," p. 19.

36. Dessie Webster is a Baptist. The diversity of NBEA is evident in the denominations represented by other founders: Open Bible Pentecostal Churches, Evangelical Friends, Presbyterian, Christian and Missionary Alliance, Church of Christ Holiness, United Holy Church of America, and United Brethren.

37. NBEA differs from other black religious organizations in that approximately one-third of its five hundred members are white; in 1990, one member of its board of directors was white.

38. Presently, the five member bodies are the A.M.E. Church, CME Church, National Baptist Convention of America, Inc., National Missionary Baptist Convention of America, and the Church of God in Christ.

Marcus Garvey. Courtesy of the Moorland-Spingarn Research Center, Howard University.

Chapter Thirty-two

Black Religious Nationalism and the Politics of Transcendence

R. Drew Smith

In a study of religious nationalism, R. Drew Smith sets forth an insightful review of African American religious movements that have sought "spatial and theological reconfiguration," that is, separation of African Americans: from an assaultive, denigrating white context; to geographic and/or religious ideational spaces where self-affirmation and racial advancement could be realized. Smith shows the interplay of this thrust with recurrent themes and issues in African American social and religious life, such as colonization; emigration for social advancement; the redemption of Africa; racial identity; millenarianism; religious innovation.

•

Since at least the early 1800s there have been sectors of African Americans who have viewed the American social context as sufficiently inimical to black social fulfillment that breaking free from its structural and ideological hold has been an urgent concern. For them, the perspective has been that racism in America is too virulent and pervasive, and opposition to it too defined by "liberal" political and religious gradualism, to anticipate a dramatically different future for blacks within the American social framework.

Instead, these African Americans have pursued an alternative social and political footing; most often through spatial separation from white America, with a more ideologically radical version of this coupling separatist activities with millennialist expectations of a reconfiguration of the racial balance of power. The two inclinations have formed the sometimes converging, sometimes diverging components of a black religious nationalist tradition that has included nineteenth and early twentieth century black emigrationists and twentieth-century religious and cultural nationalist groups such as the Moorish Science Temple, the United Negro Improvement Association, the Nation of Islam, and black Hebrews (the latter two in assorted variations).

In important ways nationalists have advanced the cause of black resistance through their attempts to reconstitute black political and organizational space and reshape black world view in ways that situate black struggle in a redemptive historical framework. And though often criticized for an idealism that leads to the neglect of moderate, achievable political steps, black religious nationalists have refused to embrace strategies premised solely on contesting American laws, social policies, or social practices. Rather than confining black resistance to the substance of the oppressors' pre-established rules, these African Americans have opted for a resistance that attempts (as Karl Mannheim states) to step outside the room of contingent social reality altogether (192). Part of the significance of "orientations transcending reality," says Mannheim, is that they potentially "pass over into conduct [and] shatter, either partially or wholly, the order of things prevailing at the time" (192).

The record of black religious nationalists will not show that their efforts to overcome the limitations of their American surroundings have had a "shattering" effect on that social order. It will show, however, that by breaking intellectually and structurally from aspects of America's "socially constructed reality" (as Peter Berger and Thomas Luckmann would put it), they have pushed further than many toward embodying the Christian imperative of social nonconformism. Viewed in this light, their example will, it is hoped, prove instructive at a time marked by a spirit of inevitability toward the American status quo and domestication of religious resistance legacies by religious elites.

Religious and Political Content within Black Religious Nationalism

In a well-documented history of American religion by Martin Marty, the central metaphor employed to characterize the relationship between religion and race is "abyss." The description actually comes from a nineteenth-century French observer Marty cites named Andre Siegfried, who minced no words on the American race problem as he perceived it at the time. "No matter which way we turn in the North or the South, there seems to be no solution," Siegfried stated. And referring specifically to the nineteenth-century South, he observed: "Everything is poisoned, even religion" (Marty: 111). If Siegfried was clear on the irreconcilability of religion and race as framed within the American context, it is not surprising that quite a few African Americans were as well.

In fact, by the late eighteenth century, into the early nineteenth century, increasing numbers of African Americans had concluded that there was a virtual religious devotion to racial injustice in America and that, consequently, what was needed was black social space independent of white institutional and ideological control. Efforts in this direction during the period took the form of emigrationist movements, separate black community building inside the United States, and the creation of a diverse range of separate black institutions. Where there was freedom to separate—meaning outside the confines of the slave experience—spatial separations built upon pre-established social demarcations between blacks and whites. These demarcations became increasingly formalized and ideologized beginning in the first decades of the nineteenth century owing largely to a white, and mostly southern, Protestant discourse that advocated a "God-ordained" hierarchy of social ranks and spheres. For example, a prominent Presbyterian clergyman from South Carolina, James Thornwell, propagated the view that differentiations of authority between leaders and followers were not "artificial combinations to which men have been impelled by chance or choice" but were the "ordinance of God" (29). Another nineteenth-century minister, a North Carolina Methodist named Washington Chaffin, contended that nature had "drawn lines of demarcation between [blacks] and [whites] that no physical, mental or religious cultivation can obliterate" (87–88).

"Separate spheres" arguments provided ideological underpinnings for white hegemonic objectives but also for blacks skepticism regarding any possible common cause between blacks and whites into the foreseeable future. Although racist ideologizing by whites was neither unprecedented nor a critical precondition to black skepticism, the determinism of these "separate spheres" arguments could hardly have engendered much optimism among blacks about their American future. Nonetheless, it had been others—mostly well-intentioned clergy of both races—who had conceded years earlier that black social progress lay in the direction of separation from whites.

Samuel Hopkins, a white Rhode Island minister, laid the groundwork during the late 1700s for what became the American Colonization Society (ACS), an organization designed to resettle free blacks in Africa. And, as one historian notes, a curious bit of symmetry here was that the official founding of the ACS, which took place in 1816, coincided with the inauguration of the first of the historically black denominations, the African Methodists Episcopal Church (Wilmore: 102). The clergyman who pioneered this effort, an African American named Richard Allen, chartered a movement that would have even greater relevance to the cause of nineteenth-century black religious nationalism—the movement toward large-scale black ecclesiastical separation. Before the close of the century, the African Methodist Episcopal Zion church, the Colored Methodist Episcopal church, and the largest of the black Baptist conventions, the National Baptists, would also be formed.

Black churches provided institutional terrain independent of white control, but, like other black fraternal, civic, and educational institutions that developed during the period, their intent was to function ultimately as springboards for expanded black participation within the larger American society. The same could be said about another separatist initiative that emerged during the nineteenth century—the phenomenon of "organized Negro communities." These communities, comprised mostly of freed and fugitive slaves, were established mainly in the North and in Canada in the forty years prior to the Civil War and attracted about three thousand to five thousand participants in total.

Unlike most nineteenth-century black institution-and community-building activities, the ACS and subsequent emigrationist initiatives had no such long-term integrationist objectives. For emigrationists, physical separation from American space was to be maintained indefinitely. And although the ACS attracted significant criticism as a white organization committed to sending blacks out of the country, approximately twelve thousand African Americans left the United States under its auspices by the mid-1800s to establish colonies along the west coast of Africa. During the latter half of the nineteenth century, however, it was black clergymen and lay leaders such as Alexander Crummell, Henry McNeil Turner, Martin Delaney, and

Edward W. Blyden who were the leading proponents of black emigrationism. Through their efforts a number of additional sites for black colonies were explored, including the Niger Valley and non-African locations such as Haiti and Canada. Land was actually purchased in Haiti and Canada toward this end and about two thousand blacks were settled in each location (Essien-Udom: 19–23).

Black desires to relocate, whether inside or outside of the United States, conceivably drew inspiration from a climate of widespread utopian enthusiasms about the possibilities for recreating society.[1] These enthusiasms were reinforced by a larger sense of open frontiers and fluid resettlement within the United States and by colonial adventurism abroad. The appeal of relocation strategies endured into the early twentieth century, a period when both the possibilities and realities of such strategies intersected in mass migrations of blacks from the rural South to the urban North. But with the discovery that northern ghettos afforded scarcely more freedom than southern plantations, many who aspired ultimately toward some distinctively different grounding found themselves looking again toward Africa.

For the majority of twentieth-century nationalists, as was true of the emigrationists of the nineteenth century, American destinations were to be considered nothing more than stopover points. Marcus Garvey's United Negro Improvement Association (UNIA), the Nation of Islam and some black Hebrew groups built organizations that were to provide liberated space for their constituencies pending their eventual departure from American space altogether. Garvey's goal was that his followers, estimated at "several" million (Essien-Udom: 37), would return to Africa to redeem the continent from colonialism. The development of economic enterprises, including a factory and a steamship line of four ships, were to have facilitated this, but neither the economic nor the political dreams of the movement ever fully materialized.

The Nation of Islam (NOI), founded in the 1920s, has been just as outspoken in its separatist intentions. Listed among the points of the "Muslim Program" published continuously in the *Muhammad Speaks* newspaper of Elijah Muhammad and *The Final Call* newspaper of Louis Farrakhan is that African Americans "be allowed to establish a separate state or territory of their own—either [within North America] or elsewhere." With a membership that peaked at between 50,000 and 100,000 during the 1950s and 1960s, the Nation under Elijah Muhammad's leadership developed a financial empire valued at up to $46 million including "15,000 acres of farmland . . . several aircraft, a fish import business, restaurants, bakeries and supermarkets" (Barboza: 27; Holmes). After Elijah Muhammad's death in 1974 and a virtual collapse of the original organization, the group was reorganized under Louis Farrakhan's leadership and has since grown to a membership of over 20,000 with a sympathetic following of significantly more, as the 1995 Million Man March made clear. The NOI has also achieved a revitalized financial base that encompasses banking, insurance, food production, cosmetics, printing, and security operations worth tens of millions of dollars (Holmes).

Black Hebrew groups have also been quite successful in separatist community building in the United States and abroad. Three-hundred-fifty followers of a black Hebrew group led by a man named Ben Ammi decided in the late 1960s to relocate from Chicago's South Side to Liberia, where they established a settlement. Shortly thereafter, with a reduced number of 150, the group ventured on to Israel, where they organized a community in a southern desert of the country. The settlement, called Dimona, developed into a viable community of more than two thousand black Hebrews, successfully gaining official recognition from the Israeli government as well as $5 million in aid from the U.S. Congress. Referred to generally as the "African Hebrew Israelites," the group has communities in a number of U.S. cities and about six hundred members in satellite communities in Africa (Smallwood: 5–8; Lounds: 41–51). Perhaps the single largest group of black Hebrews, however, is the Nation of Yahweh, headed by a formerly Pentecostal preacher who goes by the name of Yahweh ben Yahweh (which translates "God, the son of God"). Ben Yahweh's group, primarily based in Miami but spread across forty-five cities and twenty states, had an early 1990s membership of approximately 20,00 people and property estimated variously at between $8 million and $100 million.

The self-contained, socially autonomous communities carved out by the UNIA, the NOI, and black Hebrew groups are not entirely different in certain respects from those of historic, rural separatist communities such as the Amish. For example, Walter Abilla notes in a study of the NOI in Cleveland during the 1960s that the obligations of NOI membership include: "regular attendance, giving charity to the temple whenever one can afford it, participating in organizational activities of the Nation of Islam, selling Muhammad Speaks, eating at Muslim restaurants, buying groceries from Black Muslim stores, taking your clothes for dry-cleaning and laundering to Muslim cleaning establishments, and living according to Muslim rules. . . ." One of the primary "Muslim rules" members must honor is disassociation from non-Muslims. Structurally, the only thing different here from what one encounters among the Amish—who also forbid business, marital, or other intimate connections with outsiders (Hostetler: 77)—is that the economic and social activity of the African American groups is urban in its contextualization.

What is also clear in these instances is that members must be highly motivated to submit to these levels of organizational discipline—but motivated by what? C. Eric Lincoln remarks in reference to the Nation of Islam that devotion of this sort derives from certain common characteristics on the part of the devotees, most importantly "a desire for personal rebirth—an escape to a new identity, in which they will be freed of their personal restrictions and oppressions" (100). Historically, motives of this nature have often carried religious believers in tragic directions. However, the type of transcendence black religious nationalists appear to be pursuing is not the world-rejecting kind that leads to a total loss of stake in temporal realities. Their rejection, while socially comprehensive, is of a different sort, premised more on objections to who has defined social reality and how black life has been specifically defined within that framework.

Transcendence has had a spatial component for nationalists, but it has also been concerned with overcoming American distortions and denigrations of the humanity and self-worth of black people. As Cornel West observes, black religious nationalists have recognized that "Black people will never value themselves as long as they subscribe to a standard of valuation that devalues them" (49). The religious nationalism that emerged by the early twentieth century was committed to throwing off these "devaluations" and providing new categories of religious and cultural definition for blacks to draw upon in their search for affirmation.

Groups like the Moorish Science Temple, the UNIA, the NOI, and the black Hebrews redefined black identity along the lines of African cultural content and, frequently, Islamic and Hebraic belief systems. In doing so, black religious nationalists have conveyed an awareness of abhorrent racial practices within American Christianity, but they also have appeared conscious of what Robert Hood (among others) contends are certain intrinsically anti-black dimensions to Christian scripture and historical theology. Hood writes: "Neither the images of blackness and blacks nor the control and shaping of those images by Europeans and Americans began simply with the fifteenth-century slave trade. . . . Images of blackness and blacks have deep primal roots that were established in the very formation of Western culture from its Greco-Roman antecedents and its Christian underpinnings" (182).

Black religious nationalists, well before the emergence of the black consciousness and black theology movements in the 1960s, innovated on Judeo-Christian themes, arguing for an historically privileged racial and religious status for blacks in ways intended to rebut American racial orthodoxies. The Moorish Science Temple, founded by Drew Ali in 1913, taught that "so-called Negroes" were actually Moors, that their true religion was Islam, and that Moorish nations were of divine origin. The NOI also instructed its followers that Islam was the authentic black faith, while expounding a racial and religious essentialism that promoted blacks as the original people of the earth and whites as devils. According to the NOI's teachings, these white "devils" were the result of laboratory experiments by a renegade black scientist named Yakub (Muhammad: 52–54, 100–102, 133–134). Black Hebrew groups, which emerged in the 1930s under Rabbi Wentworth Matthew and Prophet F. S. Cherry, promoted similar teachings. Black Hebrews contended that whites were created as the result of a curse and that the world would only be restored to its proper order through the political elevation of the true descendants of the original Hebrew people—the black Hebrew found within the ranks of black America (Fauset: 34–35).

Privileged status has also been conveyed through the notion that some of these black religious leaders were divine themselves. Drew Ali, for example, purported to possess a special divinity akin to Jesus, Buddha, Confucius, and Zoroaster (Fauset: 46–47). In a similar vein a central tenet of the Nation of Islam's belief system was that their enigmatic founder, W. D. Fard, was divine and that his principal lieutenant and designated prophet, Elijah Muhammad, may have been as well (Muhammad: 19–20). Yahweh ben Yahweh's name suggests that he too has been considered to have divine attributes. And in a slightly different variation on this theme a group called the Five Percent Nation contends that every black "man" is "his" own god, although only 5 percent have achieved a requisite level of enlightenment about their godly status. This group is comprised of young urban blacks, mostly in the Northeast, who subscribe to many of the teachings of the NOI, though steering clear of all formal structure and leadership (Ahern).

If taken literally (which was probably not the case), black claims of divinity probably struck all but the most ardent group members as far-fetched. A more plausible interpretation of this behavior could be that the claims of divinity were figurative, though quite problematical, components of a more serious concern with communicating what liberation theologians have referred to as God's "preferential" identification with the oppressed and downtrodden (Guttierez; Cone). Given the dramatically anti-black racial climate that existed in early twentieth-century America when nationalists first advanced these ideas, it is not surprising that they would assign theological and historical force to the urgencies of oppressed African Americans in similarly dramatic fashion.

Spatial and theological reconfiguration had one additional dimension for nationalists—a more explicitly teleological one. A conclusion reached by many nationalists was that there was little cause for faith in the kind of grand conceptions of evolutionary social progress written into America's entrenched "liberalist" political tradition. In particular, nationalists have rejected American liberal confidence that political and economic liberties, as construed by the U.S. Constitution, from the necessary basis for a fundamentally just social order. Though these liberalist beliefs provided much of the ideological force behind abolitionist successes and civil rights gains (Wills; Smith), religious nationalists, especially during the twentieth century, have felt that Christian millenarian teleologies were more resonant with their sense of the historical present and future.

Christian millenarian traditions, an extensive part of American culture for hundreds of years (Tyler: 68–78), have maintained that society is moving toward a final, decisive earthly battle between good and evil that will culminate in divine intervention and the establishment of a period of divine rule upon the earth. Nat Turner's slave insurrection was at least partly an effort to set this end-time scenario in motion (Aptheker: 33–56, 109–110). Black participation in the fatal undertakings of Jim Jones's People's temple and David Koresh's Branch Davidians represent contemporary examples of similarly disposed black millenarian involvements.

Nevertheless, it has been Elijah Muhammad's appropriations of millenarian concepts that have served largely as the model for other twentieth-century black religious nationalists. Elijah Muhammad began teaching in the 1930s that judgment upon white America was imminent and that blacks must ready themselves for the "re-establishment" of their temporarily interrupted rule over the Earth. Elijah Muhammad taught that an apocalyptic "battle in the sky" involving UFOs would initiate the "fall of America"—eventually predicting that this judgment would occur in 1965 or 1966 (Muhammad: 265–305; Lee: 47).

Farrakhan followed in Elijah Muhammad's footsteps, promoting the Nation's religious mission as one of acquainting blacks with their godly nature, with whites' diabolic nature, and with the need to separate themselves from the white devils who would soon face retribution for their evil deeds. This emphasis comes through in the following remarks from a 1989 Farrakhan speech: "the Honorable Elijah Muhammad . . . went to the roots of things. He's not interested in making you hate people, but he wants you to know people, to know yourself. . . . And it's clear . . . that we have not known the white man. . . . In your ignorance . . . you think that they are as you are, therefore you make demands on their nature that nature didn't put in them." He went on to say: "the caucasian people are different from the original people, or the black people, of the earth. . . . History shows us that from the very beginning . . .

these people have been troublemakers. . . . This is not a human being that is easy to live with in peace except you live on their terms. . . . What threatens them? Unity among us threatens them. . . . They are afraid of your rise because they believe that your rise is their fall" (Farrakhan). Farrakhan's millenarian views have been made more specific, even to the point of setting a date for the apocalypse, as evident in the following remarks: "The end of America is now in sight. You could save your miserable lives, but you're too filthy and wicked. You hate me for warning you. . . . Before 1986 comes in, we will close out both books—the Bible and the Holy Koran— and the world will be in the throes of that which will destroy every power that is on this earth in preparation for a new gospel . . . (Buursma and Curry).

A variety of millenarian themes have also been advanced by black Hebrew groups. The religious teachings of the African Hebrew Israelites, for example, have ranged from the racial essentialism of Israelite leader Prince Asiel Ben Israel, whose "chosen people" teachings have maintained a relatively nonthreatening tone (Moses: 88–90), to the retributionist millenarianism of Ben Ammi, who writes: "Black America, hear in these final hours . . . the end of this present world has come. . . . The perpetual irony of our history/fate is that the Euro-gentile, the rulers of America, Europe and the entire gentile world, know their end has come and know who the Black people truly are. Let us not once again be the last to know and be exploited even in these days of promised victory, prophesied championship, for our race. . . . We are the Chosen Race" (Ammi: 15–16). Retributionist millenarian tendencies have also been suspected within the Nation of Yahweh who during the 1980s had criminal charges brought against a number of group members accused of killing and dismembering a total of eight whites in Miami. The alleged motive was that the actions satisfied a group requirement that a "white devil" be killed and proof of the killing supplied as a condition for gaining status within the organization (Rohter).

White racism has clearly been viewed by black religious nationalists as a central evil in the world, and one so entrenched and diabolical that it cannot be accounted for in merely sociological terms. Particularly for nationalists with millenarian inclinations, white racism has been understood as a problem of cosmological proportions. And the race-specific millenarian doctrines out of which these nationalists have operated have provided an explication of causes and cures: whites and their actions are viewed as unwelcome aberrations in the created order, and their disruptive and destructive impacts on creation are seen as coming to a divinely mandated end.

Through these appropriations and innovations on Christian themes, nationalists attribute a significance to white racism rarely found in more conventional Christian frameworks. But they do so in a way that, in the end, rejects the power of white racism ultimately to define or shape either social or religious reality. Social reorientation must occur, no doubt, before social reconfiguration is possible. But while black religious nationalists have demonstrated significant creativity with respect to the former, a criticism which they must eventually respond to is that this "creativity" has been precisely the response for certain shortcomings in their efforts to effect real social change.

Symbol and Substance in the Nationalist Counter-Reality

With millenarian nationalists the hint of radical action has always been in the air, but their actual social practice has been mostly one of political disengagement. In this respect they follow in the footsteps of their direct predecessors—nineteenth-century emigrationists and a number of quietistic black churches. Despite sometimes noteworthy organizational and institutional achievements, these groups have considered systematic political engagement largely unnecessary—viewing black life in America as merely provisional pending some larger-scale liberation from white-controlled contexts through emigration, secession, transition from the temporal realm, or divine intervention within it.

Harold Cruse comments on tendencies toward a millennialist-minded disengagement within contemporary black nationalism, referring to nationalism as "a world that awaits the arrival of an Armageddon, a day of racial reckoning, but that rationalizes away every possible positive action on the political, economic and cultural fronts" (446). Cruse, a nationalist himself, does not criticize these nationalists for where they are trying to go politically, but his concern is that they shed the mythological and romantic dimensions, reverse their ineffectual isolationism, and draw more on the political and economic resources of the larger society in advancing their nationalist agenda.

Cruse voices the dissatisfaction some have had with religious nationalism's general failure to challenge concretely the terms of political and economic existence within America. The argument has been, correctly so, that abstentions from direct action against American power structures results in an acquiescence by default to its political policies and practices. There have been, however, important exceptions to this religious nationalist proclivity. Malcolm X, Elijah Muhammad's faithful lieutenant and national spokesman during the late 1950s and early 1960s, sought to move the NOI in a more militant and activist direction, though his efforts were largely rebuffed by Elijah Muhammad. He eventually broke ranks with the Nation in 1964 and went on to establish an alternative organization, the Organization of Afro-American Unity. He also embraced orthodox Islamic teachings and a more active leadership role on race issues, venturing into civil rights protest activities during the last year of his life and attempting to bring international attention to the issue of black political rights.

Exceptions to the pattern of disengagement also include Farrakhan's active involvement in the early stages of Jesse Jackson's 1984 presidential campaign and the emergence of a small number of Nation of Islam candidates for electoral office during the late 1980s and early 1990s. With respect to the broader record, however, the strategic focus and organizational activities of these nationalists have distanced them not only from white control but from American political engagement in general. Among nationalists this posture of political disengagement has been most evident on the part of the Nation of Islam, offshoot groups such as the Five-Percent Nation, and perhaps the Nation of Yahweh.

Measured solely by its impact on the social system, then, black religious nationalism's reputation of militancy would seem unwarranted. Its militancy claims, however, are rooted less in its actions than its attitude—a defiance of social meaning as defined by anyone but themselves. The ideas produced by these groups have not been entirely original, but available ideas have been appropriated and reshaped from existing social constructs into something unique and distinctive. Specifically, they have been re-shaped in ways that have promised to refute notions of black racial inferiority, of indefinite black social subjugation, and of the ultimacy of the oppressor's power.

Black religious nationalists have recognized that moderation in the face of the extreme urgencies of the oppressed and that conformity to categories of meaning and action dictated by one's subjugators betray the most vital social and spiritual instincts of oppressed populations. Therefore, from the perspective of these nation-alists, neither American Christian orthodoxies nor democratic liberalist traditions have been suitable for pointing the way toward black fulfillment. A grander, more complete transformation has been required, and race-specific millenarian innovations have proven particularly useful in this regard.

An ironic aspect of the millenarian dimensions within black religious nationalism is that the teachings have led to a heightened sense of group significance and political agency even though they have probably functioned more allegorically then literally for nationalists.[2] Paul Gilroy speaks of a "deliberately opaque" quality to the symbolic realms of some black nationalist groups. Theirs is an encrypted world, he states, "created under the nose of the overseer" where their "counter-culture . . . defiantly constructs its own critical, intellectual and moral genealogy anew in a partially hidden public sphere of its own" (134). In this case the symbolisms take the form of cosmological utterances that point to a deeper belief in a time of world reckoning (whatever form it may actually take)—a belief that binds the collective will of nationalists together around conceptions of a purposeful, orderly universe where divine justice prevails.

By stressing a higher ordering of reality in this way, millenarian nationalists have de-authorized the present order in important ways; yet the radicalizing potential of "transcendent orientations" that Mannheim speaks of has remained largely unreal-ized for them. This is due mainly to failures to proceed beyond consciousness to forms of action that concretely "shatter" the social order's power over their lives. As many of religious nationalism's critics have suggested, a consciousness that stops short in this way becomes compensatory. The consciousness becomes an end in itself and results in a politics that maintains more than transforms the actual situation of the oppressed. No doubt, this is not the political legacy black religious nationalists have aspired to, nor is it necessarily a political tradition incapable of regrouping in more politically instrumental directions. Nonetheless, it may be that rising above the current quagmires of social meaning and laying hold to new possibilities necessarily requires letting go of everything implicated in the largely discredited present order.

NOTES

1. Some of the better known utopian groups, such as the Shakers, emerged during the late 1700s and early 1800s, while 120 utopian communities were established in the United States between 1862 and 1919 alone; Kenneth Roemer, *America as Utopia* (New York: Burt Franklin & Co., 1981), 3. See also Tyler: 108–226.

2. Although operating on the presumption that the millenarian teachings were taken literally, Martha Lee's investigation of the impact of the failure of Elijah Muhammad's prophesied 1965 "Fall of America" on the Nation of Islam's followers finds that the reactions did not follow the expected patterns of a falling away or of other overt means of responding to cognitive dissonance. See Lee and Flanagan: 129–134.

REFERENCES

Ahern, Charlie. 1991. "The Five Percent Solution." *Spin Magazine* 6/11: 54–57.

Ammi, Ben. 1982. *God, the Black Man and Truth.* Chicago: Communications Press.

Aptheker, Herbert. 1996. *Nat Turner's Slave Rebellion.* New York: Humanities Press.

Barboza, Steven. 1992. "A Divided Legacy." *Emerge Magazine* 3/6: 26–27, 30, 32.

Berger, Peter, and Thomas Luckmann. 1967. *The Social Construction of Reality: A Treatise in the Sociology of Knowledge.* Garden City, NY: Anchor Books.

Buursma, Bruce, and George Curry 1984 "Farrakhan: Teaching Gospel of Revolution." *Chicago Times* April 15: V: 1, 6.

Chaffin, Washington S. Sermons, Jan. 1845–June 1862, in W. S. Chaffin Papers, Duke University Manuscript Department, Durham, NC.

Cone, James. 1975. *God of the Oppressed.* New York: Seabury Press.

Cruse, Harold. 1967. *The Crisis of the Negro Intellectual.* New York: William and Morrow Co.

Essien-Udom, E.U. 1962. *Black Nationalism: A Search for Identity in America.* Chicago: University of Chicago Press.

Farrakhan, Louis. 1989. Speech, Chicago: Mosque Maryam (November 26).

Fauset, Arthur. 1944. *Black Gods of the Metropolis: Negro Religious Cults in the Urban North.* Philadelphia: University of Pennsylvania Press.

Gilroy, Paul. 1993. *Small Acts: Thoughts on the Politics of Black Cultures.* London: Serpent's Tail.

Guttierez, Gustavo 1973 *A Theology of Liberation.* Maryknoll, NY: Orbis Books.

Holmes, Steven. 1994. "Farrakhan Groups Land Jobs from Government, Debate Grows." *New York Times* March 4: A1, 18.

Hood, Robert E. 1994. *Begrimed and Black: Christian Traditions on Blacks and Blackness.* Minneapolis: Fortress Press.

Hostetler, John A. 1980. *Amish Society.* Baltimore: John Hopkins University Press.

Lee, Martha. 1988. *The Nation of Islam, An American Millenarian Movement.* Lewiston, NY: Edwin Mellen Press.

Lee, Martha, and Thomas Flanagan. 1988. "The Black Muslims and the Fall of America: An Interpretation Based on the Failure of Prophecy." *Journal of Religious Studies* 6/1 and 2: 140–156.

Lincoln, C. Eric. 1961. *The Black Muslims in America.* Boston: Beacon Press.

Lounds, Morris Jr. 1981. *Israel's Black Hebrews: Black Americans in Search of Identity.* Washington, DC: University Press of America.

Mannheim, Karl. 1936. *Ideology and Utopia: An Introduction to the Sociology of Knowledge.* New York: Harcourt, Brace and Company.

Marty, Martin. 1991. *Modern American Religion: The Noise of Conflict, 1919–1941.* Vol. 2. Chicago: University of Chicago Press.

Moses, Wilson J. 1982. *Black Messiahs and Uncle Toms: Social and Literary Manipulations of a Religious Myth.* University Park, PA: Penn State University Press.

Muhammad, Elijah. 1965. *Message to the Blackman in America.* Newport News: United Brothers Communications System.

Rohter, Larry. 1992. "Sect's Racketeering Trial Is Set to Open." *New York Times* January 6: A16.

Smallwood, David. 1991. "The Hebrew Israelite Community—Forging a New Black Society in God's Land." *N'Digo, Chicago Sun Times* February. 5–8.

Smith, R. Drew. 1996. "African-American Protestants, Political Activism and 'Liberal' Redemptive Hopes." *Theology Today* 53/2: 191–200.

Thornwell, James H. 1850. *Thoughts Suited to the Present Crisis.* Columbia, SC: Publisher unknown.

Tyler, Alice Felt. 1944. *Freedom's Ferment: Phases of American Social History from the Colonial Period to the Outbreak of the Civil War.* New York: Harper Torchbooks.

West, Cornel. 1992. "Malcolm X and Black Rage." In *Malcolm X: In Our Own Image*, 48–58. Ed. by Joe Wood. New York: St. Martin's Press.

Wilmore, Gayraud. 1986. *Black Religion and Black Radicalism.* Maryknoll, NY: Orbis Press.

Wills, David. 1978. "Racial Justice and the Limits of American Liberalism." *Journal of Religious Ethics* 6/2: 187–219.

Chapter Thirty-three

The Dialectical Model of the Black Church

C. Eric Lincoln and Lawrence H. Mamiya

On the matter of protest and accommodation, there seems always to have been an array of postures and options attracting different members of the African American community, sometimes simultaneously pulling different ways on the same person. One discovers intermittent periods of assertiveness and quiescence, agitation for rights and concentration on achieving within the given conditions; or even withdrawing from the fray altogether. Because of its pivotal place in much of African Americans' history, one would expect rightly their religious life to have reflected this tension between protest and accommodation. And it has. In the twentieth century, we saw the tension reflected in the clergy, on the one hand whom Wilmore says turned the churches inward, and on the other hand, in the clergy such as Adam Clayton Powell, Pauli Murray, Ben Chavis, and Martin Luther King Jr., who were marshals of public advocacy for rights and justice. Author Donald Young says, 'One function which a minority religion may serve is that of reconciliation with inferior status and its discriminatory consequences . . . on the other hand, religious institutions may also develop in such a way as to be an incitement and support of revolt against inferior status.[1] *C. Eric Lincoln and Lawrence H. Mamiya suggest that the way to understand the divergent response postures observable in the African American community relative to its social circumstances is to see a people continually seeking to hold together competing but polar opposite values.*

•

In their important work, *The Black Church in the Sixties*, Hart Nelson and Anne Kusener Nelson have identified three different types of interpretive schemes or social scientific models found in the work of past researchers of the Black Church, which we have summarized as follows:[2]

1. The Assimilation Model—The essence of this view is the belief in the necessity of the demise of the Black Church for the public good of blacks. The Black Church is seen as a stumbling block to assimilation in the American mainstream. The assimilation model also views the Black Church as anti-intellectual and authoritarian. This model is found in the views and studies of E. Franklin Frazier.[3]

2. The Isolation Model—The Black Church is characterized by "involuntary iso-

lation" which is due to predominantly lower-class statuses in the black community. Isolation from civic affairs and mass apathy are the results of racial segregation in ghettos. Thus, black religion is viewed as being primarily lower class and otherworldly. The isolation model is found in the work of Anthony Orum and Charles Silberman.[4]

3. The Compensatory Model—The Black Church's main attraction is to give large masses of people the opportunity for power, control, applause, and acclaim within the group which they do not receive in the larger society, as St. Clair Drake and Horace Cayton asserted in *Black Metropolis*. This view is also related to Gunnar Myrdal's perspective in *An American Dilemma* that the black community is essentially pathological and black culture is a "distorted development" of general American culture, so black people compensate for this lack of acclaim and for lack of access to mainstream society in their own institutions.[5]

4. The Nelsens' fourth alternative (developed by themselves) is the "ethnic community-prophetic" model which gives a more positive interpretation of the Black Church. This model emphasizes the significance of the Black Church "as a base for building a sense of ethnic identity and a community of interest among its members." It also accentuates the potential of the Black Church or its minister as "prophet to a corrupt white Christian nation."[6]

Our own view of the Black Church, which is closer to the Nelsens' model, may be called the "dialectical model" of the Black Church. Black churches are institutions that are involved in a constant series of dialectical tensions. The dialectic holds polar opposites in tension, constantly shifting between the polarities in historical time. There is no Hegelian synthesis or ultimate resolution of the dialectic. Although this dialectical model is not completely new, we feel that it is time to reassert the dialectical tensions in order to obtain a holistic picture of black churches. The task of the social analyst is to examine the social conditions of any particular black church, including the situation of its leadership and membership, in order to determine what its major orientation is in relation to any pair of dialectical polarities. There are six main pairs of dialectically related polar opposites, which are discussed below.[7]

The dialectic between priestly and prophetic functions. Every black church is involved with both functions. Priestly functions involve only those activities concerned with worship and maintaining the spiritual life of members; church maintenance activities are the major thrust. Prophetic functions refer to involvement in political concerns and activities in the wider community; classically, prophetic activity has meant pronouncing a radical word of God's judgment. Some churches are closer to one end than the other. Priestly churches are bastions of survival and prophetic churches are networks of liberation. But both types of churches also illustrate both functions, which means that liberation churches also perform the priestly functions and priestly churches contain liberation potential. Much of the discussion of black liberation theology has tended to neglect the priestly element within black churches.

The dialectic between other-worldly versus this-worldly. While the previous dialectic referred to functions, other-worldly versus this-worldly project the orientation that believers have toward the world. "Other-worldly" means being concerned only with heaven and eternal life or the world beyond, a pie-in-the-sky attitude that neglects political and social concerns. "This-worldly" refers to involvement in the affairs of this world, especially politics and social life, in the here and now. Past studies have overemphasized the other-worldly views of black churches. The other-worldly aspect, the transcendence of social and political conditions, can have a this-worldly political correlate which returns to this world by providing an ethical and prophetic critique of the present social order. In some instances eschatological transcendence can help to critique the present. One example of this is found in the mysticism of Nat Turner, whose eschatological visions directed him to attempt a strategy of violence to over-turn the system of slavery.[8]

The dialectic between universalism and particularism. As ethnic institutions, the historic black churches reflected the dialectical tension between the universalism of the Christian message and the particularism of their past racial history as institutions emerging out of the racism of white Christianity and the larger society. While all of the historic black churches have maintained a universal openness to all races and proudly asserted a strong antiracial discrimination position, they have differed and varied in their views and support of particularistic racial views, especially in regard to black consciousness. After the watershed period of the civil rights movement and the rise of black consciousness, it is important to understand the dialectical tensions that exist in every black religious group in matters regarding the racial factor. Race has played a very important role in the lives of black people and in the history of black institutions. Assessments of the racial factor, both positive and negative, ought not to be avoided. For example, when confronted by the radical and particularistic demands of a phenomenon like black liberation theology, many white Christians, including theologians, have quickly hoisted the flag of a universal Christendom, as "brothers and sisters in Christ," while trying to escape responsibility for the contem-porary pain and suffering inflicted upon black people. Similarly, some black Chris-tians, including pastors, have felt uncomfortable in dealing with their racial past and present, and would prefer to assert the universalism of the gospel as an alternative to confronting the nettlesome problems of Christian racialism.

The dialectic between the communal and the privatistic. The communal orientation refers to the historic tradition of black churches being involved in all aspects of the lives of their members, including political, economic, educational, and social con-cerns. The privatistic pole of this dialectic means a withdrawal from the concerns of the larger community to a focus on meeting only the religious needs of its adherents. This dialectic is useful in assessing the degree to which the process of secularization has affected black churches. In sociological theory the effects of secularization are to push toward privatism, a more personal and individualistic sense of religiousness. Secularization also results in a psychologizing of religion, a focus on personal coun-seling and producing a sense of individual well-being.

The dialectic between charismatic versus bureaucratic. Max Weber's typology of organizational forms is useful in analyzing the organizational style of any black church or denomination. As an overall generalization, the majority of black churches and denominations tend to lean toward the charismatic pole of the continuum, especially when compared to white mainstream denominations and churches which tend to have more bureaucratic forms. This charismatic tendency is seen in the great difficulty that most of the historic black denominations have encountered in trying to establish a centralized national headquarters for their denominations. Among the seven black denominations, only the Christian Methodist Episcopal Church and the Church of God in Christ have been able to establish national headquarters, both in Memphis. The National Baptist Convention, U.S.A., Inc., established a national headquarters in Nashville in 1989. The charismatic tendency is also seen in the lower priority given by black churches and clergy to bureaucratic organizational forms like keeping accurate membership and financial records. From their beginnings in the "invisible institution" of slave religion, African Americans have invested far more authority in the charismatic personality of the preacher than in any organizational forms of bureaucratic hierarchy. The origins of this charismatic emphasis stemmed from the oral traditions of African cultures and religions, where people with the best speaking abilities were viewed as divinely gifted, and in the United States from the prohibition against teaching slaves to read and write, which resulted in a greater stress upon the development of an oral tradition in African American culture.[9]

The charisma of church leaders was demonstrated both in the appeal of their personalities and especially in their ability to preach and elicit a strong cathartic response. Rising educational levels and upward mobility among black people have not diminished the appeal of charisma in black churches. While middle-class black churches have been more careful in keeping better records and in adopting more efficient organizational forms, their pastors must not only possess the proper educational credentials but also a charismatic preaching ability. The nickname of a famous black preacher, Reverend Dr. Charles Adams of the Hartford Avenue Baptist Church in Detroit who is called the "Harvard whooper," is an illustration of this ideal. Dr. Adams is widely celebrated as an educated preacher who can still preach in the traditional black style. The "organization man and woman," those who embody the bureaucratic style, are seldom found among the pastors of the leading black churches in the United States.

The dialectic between resistance versus accommodation. The crucial axis of black history, according to Manning Marable, has consisted of two decisive political options, that of resistance versus accommodation.[10] Every black person and every black institution has participated in making compromises between these two poles. The pole of accommodation means to be influenced by the larger society and to take part in aspects of it, however marginal that participation may be. In their accommodative role, black churches have been one of the major cultural brokers of the norms, values, and expectations of white society. Black churches are viewed as "mediating institutions."[11] For example, after the Civil War the church was the main mediating and socializing vehicle for millions of former slaves, teaching them economic rationality, urging them to get an education, helping them to keep their families together, and providing the leadership for early black communities. Sometimes accommodation also meant that black preachers were manipulated and used by whites. But the pole of resistance meant that is was possible to resist the accommodative forces and pressures of the American mainstream. Resistance meant affirming one's own cultural heritage, in this case an African American or black heritage. As one of the few totally black controlled and independent institutions, black churches played a major role in resistance. Politically, resistance has included both self-determination and self-affirmation. Since the civil rights movement and the attempts to desegregate American society, the accommodative pressures on black people and black institutions have grown considerably. One of the major roles of black churches in the future will be as historic reservoirs of black culture and as examples of resistance and independence.[12]

These six pairs of dialectical polarities give a more comprehensive view of the complexity of black churches as social institutions, including their roles and functions in black communities.[13] The strength of the dialectical model of the Black Church is that it leads to a more dynamic view of black churches along a continuum of dialectical tensions, struggle, and change. The problem of single, nondialectical typological views of black churches is that they tend to categorize and stereotype black churches into rigid pigeonhole categories like "other-worldly"; they miss the historical dynamism of institutions moving back and forth in response to certain issues or social conditions. Besides allowing for institutional change, the dialectical model of the Black Church offers methodological flexibility. For example, six major polar dimensions have been mentioned above, but other polarities could be added to the model such as the dialectical polarities involved in sexual politics (male-female), or those of liberation theology (oppressor-oppressed). Whatever polarities are used, the most important aspect of the model is to stress the dialectical tensions and constant interactions.

The dialectical model of the Black Church is helpful in explaining the pluralism and the plurality of views that exist in black churches and black communities. For example, in regard to politics the dialectical model of the Black Church is helpful in understanding Gayraud Wilmore's statement that black churches have been "the most conservative" and "the most radical" institutions at the same time.[14] It also helps to clarify Manning Marable's political assessment of what he has called the "ambiguous Black Church."[15] Unless one understands that black churches are involved in a dynamic series of dialectical tensions, a serious misunderstanding of these institutions can occur because the usual tendency is to collapse the dialectic and assert one side of the polarity, which often results in a simplistic view. The models of black churches that were summarized earlier share the danger of oversimplification when certain insights about black churches are made the major defining categories.

The dialectical model allows for a more objective analysis of black churches as social institutions because it takes a broader, more comprehensive perspective. It moves beyond the simplistic positive or negative assessments of personal observation and places black churches along a dynamic continuum allowing for change in response to changing social conditions.

The dialectical model of the Black Church is reflective of W. E. B. Du Bois's phenomenology of consciousness, his poetic articulation of "double-consciousness" as summarizing both the plight and potential of the African and Euro-American heritage of black people; "two struggling souls within one dark body."[16] Du Bois did not provide any final resolution of this double-consciousness, but he did recognize the need for complete freedom for African Americans in order that their human potentials could be fully realized. The Black Church institutionalizes the dialectical tensions and constant struggles that Du Bois wrote about. The black churches are not reified social institutions, but they represent the collective double-consciousness of the African American subculture expressing itself as a religious community in the uncertain shadow of an established tradition.[17]

NOTES

1. See Gary T. Marx, "Religion: Opiate or Inspiration of Civil Rights Militancy Among Negroes?" Reprinted in August Meier and Elliot T. Rudwick, eds., *The Making of Black America*, Vol. II (New York: Atheneum Press, 1971), pp. 62–75.

2. Hart M. Nelsen and Anne Kusener Nelsen, *Black Church in the Sixties* (Lexington: University of Kentucky Press, 1975), pp. 8–13.

3. Although the Nelsens have combined their first model as the "assimilation-isolation model," we have separated them into two models to clarify their different sources. E. Franklin Frazier and C. Eric Lincoln, *The Negro Church in America: The Black Church since Frazier* (New York: Schocken Books, 1974), pp. 78–81, 85–86.

4. Anthony M. Orum, "A Reappraisal of the Social and Political Participation of Negroes," *American Journal of Sociology* 72 (July 1966): 33. Charles E. Silberman, *Crisis in Black and White* (New York: Random House, 1964), p. 144.

5. St. Clair Drake and Horace Cayton, *Black Metropolis: A Study of Negro Life in the North* (New York: Harper and Row, 1962) 2: 424. Gunnar Myrdal, An American Dilemma: *The Negro Problem and Modern Democracy* (New York: Harper and Row, 1944), p. 928.

6. Nelsen and Nelsen, *Black Church in the Sixties*, pp. 11–13.

7. These six main pairs of polar opposites are derived from some of the usual typologies used in the sociology of religion and from past studies of black churches which tend to overemphasize one pole of a dialectic, e.g., other-worldly.

8. John Brown was one of the few white to advocate the overthrow of the slave system via violent means; he also was a mystic like Nat Turner. See Gayraud Wilmore's account in his chapter, "Three Generals in the Lord's Army," in *Black Religion and Black Radicalism: An Interpretation of the Religious History of Afro-American People* (Maryknoll, NY: Orbis, 1983). Also see Wilmore's fine analysis of the tradition of eschatology in black religion in his *Last Things First* (Philadelphia: Westminster, 1982).

9. See John Mbiti, *African Religions and Philosophy* (New York: Praeger, 1969); and Ali Mazrui, *The Africans: A Triple Heritage* (Boston: Little, Brown, 1986). For the development of oral tradition among African Americans, see Lawrence Levine, *Black Culture and Black Consciousness* (New York: Oxford University Press, 1978).

10. See Manning Marable, *How Capitalism Underdeveloped Black America* (Boston: South End, 1983), p. 26.

11. For a sociological elaboration of the idea of "mediating structures" in society, see Peter L. Berger and John Richard Neuhaus, *To Empower People: The Role of Mediating Structures in Public Policy* (Washington, D.C.: American Enterprise Institute for Public Policy Research, 1977).

12. Alex Haley's story of his grandfather several generations removed, Kunta Kinte, is a poignant example of the themes of accommodation and resistance on an individual level. Although he always attempted to escape bondage but never succeeded, Kunta Kinte's masters

attempted to force him to take the name Toby. Even though he finally acquiesced to the name while he was being brutally whipped, Kunta Kinte never gave in spiritually; he resisted being "Toby-ized." See Alex Haley, *Roots: The Saga of an American Family* (Garden City, N.Y.: Doubleday, 1976). We are also indebted to Rev. Calvin Butts of the Abyssinian Baptist Church for coining the term "Toby-ize."

13. The "church-sect" typology, which is usually used in the study of black churches, has been omitted from this list because of its conservative tendency of emphasizing the inhibition of social change. The prophetic dimension tends to be left out. For a more elaborate critique, see Nelsen and Nelsen, *Black Church in the Sixties*, pp. 2–5.

14. Wilmore, *Black Religion and Black Radicalism*.

15. Marable, *How Capitalism Underdeveloped Black America*, chap. 7.

16. See Du Bois's famous elaboration of his phenomenology of African American consciousness in *The Souls of Black Folk* (New York: New American Library, 1969), pp. 45–46. It is significant that this description of "double-consciousness" is found in his essay, "Of Our Spiritual Strivings," indicating what he thought were the ultimate concerns of black people.

17. This view of a "collective double-consciousness" is similar to Durkheim's use of the concept "collective representation."

Part VII

Profiles of the Contemporary African American Church

Chapter Thirty-four

Rural, Urban Clergy and Churches

C. Eric Lincoln and Lawrence H. Mamiya

In the 1930s, Benjamin Mays and Joseph Nicholson undertook a major sociological study of African American religion. The results, published in such works as The Negro's Church *and* The Negro's God, *stood for decades as the only comprehensive sources of hard data documenting aspects of black religious expression. In the 1980s, sociologists C. Eric Lincoln and Lawrence H. Mamiya undertook to update and build upon the pioneering work of Mays and Nicholson. They led a team of researchers in a national investigation of the history, demographics, liturgical practices, and ministries of the seven (at that time) independent, historically black denominations: the National Baptist Convention, USA, Inc.; the National Baptist Convention of America; the Progressive National Baptist Convention; the African Methodist Episcopal Church; the African Methodist Episcopal Zion Church; the Christian Methodist Episcopal Church; the Church of God on Christ. Following are some of their findings relative to rural and urban churches.*

•

Black Migrations and Rural Churches

Migration has become a central social experience for African Americans. The 1890 census, the first to give an urban-rural breakdown of the black population, indicates that nine out of ten black people lived in the South and more than 80 percent of them in rural areas designated as the black belt.[1] By 1980, 85 percent of the black population resided in urban areas and only about 53 percent of them lived in the South.[2] The vast migrations from the rural South to the urban North and the West were clustered around the periods of the two world wars and the Korean War, transforming the demographic landscape as millions of African Americans relocated in search of jobs and a better life. Among the major causes for black migration were the mechanization of southern agriculture, the boll weevil attacks on the cotton crops, the lynchings and violence of a rigid system of Jim Crow segregation, the long-term decline of sharecropping and individual farm ownership, and the need for cheap labor in northern factories and industries.[3] Ironically, the exigencies of war opened up more avenues for labor mobility and improved standards of living for African Americans than all of the less sanguine efforts at economic parity combined.

From their beginnings in the mid-eighteenth century and throughout most of their history the majority of black churches in the South have been rural institutions, and the major effect of the migrations was to produce a largely "absentee pastorate" among these churches. Despite the conventions of a certain degree of itinerancy for the black clergy, due to the manner in which Christianity was spread on the plantations by traveling evangelists and circuit riders during the period of frontier revivalism, the migrations accentuated the situation of the absentee pastor. The studies by Richardson and Felton reflected the growing concern over the absentee pastor during the *World War II* period. As Richardson has pointed out, "there is a serious shortage of ministers in rural areas. Almost any pastor today can find a church of some kind. This is partly accountable for the fact that some ministers have three, four, and in a few cases even more churches. If a church is too greatly hampered by loss of members, the pastor can usually find another church without great difficulty."[4]

Since World War II, the ubiquitous use of the automobile, the paving of roads, and the building of parkways and interstates have led to the increased mobility of absentee rural pastors and they typically travel several hundred miles to preach in different churches. In fact, close to two thirds of the rural clergy in our study live in urban areas, away from their congregations. Our data indicate that the distances traveled by rural clergy to reach their churches range from one to 400 miles, with an average of 36.4 miles. When asked by an interviewer how he was able to pastor five different rural churches, a minister replied that he preached at services on Sunday morning, afternoon, and evening, and all he needed was "a fast mouth and a fast car." Although the case cited is not typical, the example does illustrate the logistical problems rural clergy face in serving their churches. In spite of the hardships involved, the majority of rural clergy are among the most dedicated of religious professionals.[5]

Despite his dedication, the phenomenon of the absentee pastor inevitably means that most black rural churches are inordinately dependent upon a network of loyal and devoted laypersons for their continued survival. Even if the congregation meets for worship only once a month, other church activities like weekly Sunday School, prayer meetings, choir rehearsal, and Usher Board meetings are frequently carried on by the laity in the interim. Rural church members seldom receive the kind of pastoral attention normally expected in other churches such as counseling, pastoral visits, and community leadership; but in spite of the dearth of conventional pastoral services and the impact of out-migrations, studies show that very few rural churches close their doors without a protracted struggle.[6] Consequently, in proportion to the total number of black churches in existence, a very large number of them are rural churches. Estimates are that 20 to 25 percent of all black churches are rural, close to double the percentage of the black rural population.[7]

The Civil Rights Watershed and Rural Churches

Besides black migrations, the period of the civil rights movement from 1954 to 1968 stands as a watershed in the annals of Black Church history and the sociology of black churches.[8] The past two decades of the 1970 and 1980s have dimmed the memories of the conflict and turmoil of the period, the complex picture of successes and failures, violence and nonviolence, of courage and cowardice. The dust has settled and Martin Luther King, Jr., has become the symbolic, mythic figure of that era. The movement has produced a lasting positive effect among black churches because many of them, especially rural ones, participated in the struggle.

Confounding the sociological prophecies of the decline of religion or black religion as the opiate of the masses, at the height of the conflict many black rural and urban folk stood up in their churches to be counted.[9] Although their exact numbers may never be known, from 1962 to 1965 in the South ninety-three churches, most of them rural, were burned or bombed.[10] The rural congregations fed and housed the voter registration volunteers and were the centers for political agitation and protests in their communities. Not all pastors and churches participated in the movement, but enough did so that they can point to that period of sacrifice and service with pride.[11]

The most important result was the desegregation of public accommodations and other aspects of southern life such as education and voting. Although housing and religious worship remain persistent bastions of segregation, any study of rural churches must take into account the impact of the civil rights movement. This movement, which had both visible and invisible repercussions, was largely southern, and it changed forever the social and political profile of life in the South. Rural churches were an agent and a catalyst in that change.

A Profile of Black Rural Clergy

In our sample of 363 clergy, 346 were males and seventeen were females. On marital status, 93 percent were married, while 2 percent were divorced, 3 percent were widowed, and only 1.7 percent were single. In the South, although there is the phenomenon of child preachers who began at age eleven or twelve, the tendency has been toward having older preachers in rural churches. For Felton's sample of 424 pastors, the average age was 51.1 years.[12] The results of our study showed that the median age was fifty-two. Despite the practice among several black denominations of placing beginning ministers or seminarians in rural churches to test their commitment and develop their skills in a less demanding environment, the clergy who continue in the rural ministry tend to be older.

The educational level of rural clergy in the current sample show an increase in the years of schooling completed in comparison with earlier studies by Richardson (1947) and Felton (1950). This change probably reflects the effects of the civil rights movement and the desegregation of education. In 1947, Richardson's survey of eighty rural ministers showed that 46.2 percent had eighth-grade schooling or less, and only 10 percent were professionally prepared with some seminary education.[13] Felton's 1950 study yielded similar results, with 43.3 percent of the ministers who had less than an eighth-grade education and 58.2 percent who had never gone beyond high school.[14] In this study the average educational attainment was "high school graduate," with the median education at one year of college. A significant finding is that the majority of rural clergy, 194 (58.3 percent), achieved at least some level of college education. Since desegregation, the expansion and proliferation of community colleges and junior colleges has enhanced the opportunities for black clergy to acquire some level of college education. Of the sample, 28.8 percent had some seminary training. The tendency of all the black denominations to place seminarians in rural churches probably skewed the higher educational achievement results to some degree.

Historically, black churches have been the most independent and stable institutions in black communities. Our survey of rural churches confirms this fact. Of the 619 churches, 566 (92.3 percent) reported that they owned their church building, 16 (2.3 percent) rented, and 31 (5.1 percent) had "other" arrangements. Of those churches that owned their property, 452 (76.9 percent) had paid up their mortgages and only 136 (23.1 percent) still owed on their mortgages. There are very few institutions in black communities that can match this record of ownership.

Internal Maintenance: Rural Church Programs

Mays and Nicholson once observed that all black rural churches have Sunday schools because "they are second in importance only to preaching."[15] Our study confirms this observation with 598 (97.4 percent) churches claiming Sunday schools. Roughly four-fifths, 442 (82.6 percent) said that their Sunday school met "every week," 59 (9.9 percent) churches said "twice a month," and 40 (6.7 percent) churches "once a month." The church schools are usually run by the laity; ministers seldom supervise or attend.

Besides worship services and Sunday schools, the internal life of rural churches is also sustained by midweek services, such as prayer meetings and Bible study. Seven out of ten churches claimed that they had midweek services, and 187 (30.2 percent) said they did not. Of those who have these services, 349 (79.1 percent) also reported that they met "once a week," 45 (10.2 percent) met "once every two weeks," and 34 (7.7 percent) met once a month. When asked "who leads the midweek services," 250 (56.9 percent) churches said the pastor led, while 189 (43.1 percent) replied that the laity did so.

The absentee nature of rural pastoral leadership means that church members are more independent and must develop their own networks of spiritual care and nurture. Lay leaders take active roles in midweek services with roughly half of the services unattended by the pastor. The fabled stories of strong and authoritarian deacons and deaconesses have their roots in the absentee and itinerant nature of the rural ministry. The lay leaders have developed a strong sense of ownership of their churches and the pastor is often regarded as a necessary but an occasional visitor. Conflicts between deacon or trustee boards and the pastor are found in many local communities; church splits are often the results of such conflicts.[16] As one of the few institutions that is completely owned and controlled by black people, the senses of possessiveness, pride, and power are unparalleled in other phases of African American life. Charles Hamilton noted that there is a complete identification with "my pastor, my church," not found elsewhere.[17] Black people very seldom speak of "my NAACP" or "my Democratic party," but they often speak of "my church."

The late summer months, and sometimes the early fall, comprise the "revival season" in black belt counties. This is the slack period when the crops have been "laid by," but are not yet ready for harvesting. The revival season is also the time when many lynchings have occurred in rural areas since white farmhands were also free to do their deadly deeds. The revival is the major form of religious renewal used by Protestant churches. Although urban churches and television evangelists also rely on revivals, the classic form of revival is still found in southern rural churches, both black and white. As a form and technique of religious renewal the revival can be traced back to the Great Awakenings, especially the Second Awakening during the early nineteenth century. Beginning in the frontier states of Kentucky and Tennessee, the camp meeting revivals swept up white masters and black slaves alike in a religious frenzy. It was, as Strout described it, "a jamboree and an awesome rite, a family picnic and a religious crisis" all rolled into one.[18] Our study shows that revivals were held in 542 (87.7 percent) churches; two thirds (67.2 percent) of the churches had one revival, the rest had two or more. Revivals can last from one day to two weeks or more. Churches that had revivals which lasted from "four to six days" numbered 394 (68.5 percent), while 154 (26.8 percent) claimed revivals of "seven days or more." Mays and Nicholson predicted that the "day of the professional evangelist" is rapidly passing.[19] While the professional evangelist who earned a living primarily by conducting revivals in churches may have suffered a demise, our data indicate that "guest evangelists" are still popular in black belt counties. The churches that had guest evangelists to conduct their revivals numbered 490 (85.8 percent), and only 73 (12.8 percent) churches relied on their regular pastor. Guest evangelists are often pastors of other churches who are known for their preaching or ability to elicit the emotional fervor necessary for religious conversion or reaffirmation of the spiritual life.

In revival evangelism all Black Church denominations make concessions to women preachers. Denominations, like the Church of God in Christ and some Baptist groups that have strict rules controlling or forbidding women pastors, will permit women to be evangelists. They can preach in revivals or special meetings, but they cannot pastor a church. One rural clergyman reiterated this view in his opinion of women as pastors: "Women have been preaching for years but [they were] not identified as preachers. That role [as] pastor has not been distinguished for her. As one within, I could not accept a woman pastor—a masculine role."

In this survey of groups and organizations in the church, 79.3 percent of the rural churches said that they had youth groups and 64.9 percent had women's groups. About half of the sample (49.4 percent) had organizations for men. Senior citizen groups (38.2 percent) seem to be the most neglected area. Rural churches have more active programs for young adults (49.5 percent) than the urban churches (22.8 percent) surveyed. Close to two thirds (63 percent) claimed that they had a lay group to help plan and conduct the worship service. The usual stereotype of rural churches as inactive, occasional meeting places is not sustained. They may lack continuous pastoral leadership, but many of them conduct a greater range of activities in the church and community than previously thought.

Rural Churches and Community Outreach

To assess the extent of participation of black rural churches within their communities, the survey examined interdenominational and interracial cooperation; cooperation with social agencies or non-church organizations; participation in any government-funded programs (city or county, state, and federal); and the church as a meeting place for nonchurch organizations.

Past studies of black rural churches have shown an extreme paucity of community activities initiated by the churches or held in church-owned buildings. For example, in Felton's study only 16.1 percent of the churches in his sample sponsored 4-H clubs, 13.9 percent had home demonstration clubs, and 12.8 percent were affiliated with the NAACP. These had the highest rates of participation in a list of eighteen community activities. Felton concluded that "these churches are lacking in community work. This type of work is doubly important because it is so greatly needed by these Negro families and because the Church is about the only organization to promote it."[20]

In this survey community outreach programs show mixed results. In some areas there are marked improvements in community participation over the past thirty years and in others black rural churches still lag in vitally needed community activities. On interdenominational cooperation with churches of other denominations on various projects, 357 (61 percent) claimed that they cooperated. The average number of projects in which churches participated was 4.34. The types of interdenominational projects that churches took part in were as follows: 152 (26.4 percent) churches had "fellowship with other churches and pulpit exchanges"; 139 (24.2 percent) conducted "evangelism programs with other churches (revivals, crusades, etc.)"; 17 (3 percent) were involved in "community-oriented service programs"; 9 (1.6 percent) sponsored "education programs with other churches"; 2 (0.3 percent) had "social problem-oriented programs"; and 21 (3.7 percent) claimed involvement in other projects. More than one third of the churches, 221 (38.4 percent), said that they did not participate.

Most of the interdenominational cooperation occurred between black churches denominations. Only 10 (1.7 percent) black rural churches said that they took part in "interracial cooperation with white churches." This finding confirms Felton's, for only 2 black rural churches in his study took part in "interracial relationships between churches."[21] These results continue to underscore the highly segregated nature of religion in American society.

Roughly 65 percent indicated that they cooperated with social agencies or other nonchurch organizations in dealing with community problems. There were 201 (32.5 percent) that did not cooperate. Table 34.1 shows the variety of social agencies and types of nonchurch programs in which black rural churches participated.

About half of the rural churches (50.1 percent) are involved with civil rights

TABLE 34.1

Cooperation with Social Agencies or Nonchurch Organizations by Rural Churches

Types of Agencies and Programs	Number	Percent
Civil rights organizations and activities	310	(50.1)
Employment agencies and problems	2	(0.3)
Day-care centers and nurseries	2	(0.3)
Drug and alcohol abuse agencies and problems	4	(0.6)
Senior citizen or elderly groups	13	(2.1)
Welfare rights and housing	2	(0.3)
Police community relations	5	(0.8)
Food programs and clothing banks	4	(0.6)
Tutoring and educational programs	5	(0.8)
Health-related agencies and problems	5	(0.8)
Local community crisis events and problems	4	(0.7)
Emergency land fund	2	(0.3)
Youth agencies (YM/YWCA, 4-H Club, Scouts, etc.)	4	(0.8)
Other agencies and programs	21	(3.4)
No cooperation	201	(32.5)
No response	35	(5.6)

$N = 619$

organizations and activities, such as the NAACP, in sharp contrast to Felton's earlier finding of only about 12.8 percent of the churches. The most obvious explanation for the difference is the tremendous impact that the civil rights movement had on all black churches. Mass-based organizations like the Southern Christian Leadership Conference with a largely all black church leadership, and the use of churches by civil rights groups for mass meetings and as bases of operation, contributed to a degree of involvement and activism that had not been seen before in rural areas. But much of the church's involvement in the community has remained with civil rights issues and organizations. Although there are many other pressing concerns, the results of Table 34.1 show a scattered and sparse degree of involvement. A little more than one third of the churches (35–38 percent) are consistently uninvolved in either interdenominational activities or community problems and agencies.

Our research shows that the vast majority of rural churches, 589 (95.2 percent), did not participate in any government-funded program, while only 17 (2.7 percent) claimed involvement in such programs. Of these participants, 8 churches (1.3 percent) received government funds as centers for Headstart programs; 11 (1.8 percent) sponsored day-care centers or nursery schools; 2 (0.3 percent) participated in other programs. The survey found no participation in government-funded programs like food services (breakfast or Meals on Wheels), CETA programs housing for the elderly and the indigent, and other tutorial and remedial education programs. In comparison, the black urban churches in our sample, 121 (7.9 percent) participated in government-funded programs at a higher rate. Probably the lack of knowledge and technique of applying to such programs and the absentee pastorate contribute to the lower rates for rural churches.

Historically, black churches have usually played a major role in providing a meeting place for community events. During the slavery period and after, *church buildings* were often the only large halls available for such events in black communities. As both Frazier and Lincoln have observed in their respective studies, black churches were multifunctional and multipurpose institutions.[22] The survey examined whether black churches continue to play such a role. The results show that 171 (28.9 percent) churches responded affirmatively, while 420 (71.1 percent) said no. For the churches that provided their buildings as meeting places, the following nonchurch organizations ranked in the top three: 122 (19.7 percent) churches permitted civil rights organizations; 52 (8.4 percent) allowed fraternity and sorority groups and lodges (Masons, Elks, and Eastern Star); and 71 (11.5 percent) allowed civic associations.

One of the unintended consequences of the civil rights movement and the desegregation of public accommodations is the decreased use of black churches as meeting places for community groups and events. If at one time they were the only meeting places available, desegregation has since opened up a wide range of choices like public schools, town halls, civic auditoriums, hotel conference rooms, and other facilities for large meetings. Secular nonchurch black organizations no longer depend on black churches for meeting places. A similar, unintended consequence has exacerbated the financial plight of black colleges because now a wider range of choices is available to black students. Yet, as ethnic institutions that have been the major carriers of African American culture, the churches and colleges will continue to play important but different roles in the future.

Conclusion: Present Trends and the Future of Black Rural Churches

Although there are a number of competent anthropological analyses of black church life in individual churches in recent years, a descriptive statistical social profile of black rural churches and clergy is missing.[23] Since 1950 the sociology of black rural churches has been largely neglected. Most contemporary scholarship has examined urban black churches where the majority of black people are now located.[24] However, rural churches have been and will remain as the historical and cultural reservoir of the "black folk" religious experience. Many of the distinctive features of black worship like styles of preaching, shouting, and falling out, spirituals and gospel music, and enthusiastic antiphonal audience responses were developed in the womb of the rural church. Black rural churches also played important historical roles in helping black people survive the dehumanization of slavery,[25] in providing economic and educational uplift after the Civil War,[26] and in acting as major centers for political activities like slave rebellions, civil rights protests, and, more recently, mobilizing the black vote.[27] Our study attempts to help fill the information gap which presently exists about black rural churches. Thus far, we have presented a profile of the present status of this institutional sector, but what of its future?

There are several present trends that will affect the future of black rural churches. First, the major financial crisis among farmers will affect the occupations of many black church members. There has been a continued rapid decline of small individual farms, tenant farming, and sharecropping, and an increase of large agribusinesses and farm factories like Frank Perdue's chicken industry. For example, census data on farm ownership show that there were 924,000 full- or part-time black owners of farms in 1910; by 1969 their numbers had declined to 104,000.[28] By 1989, black-owned farms had declined even more sharply, and they are quietly slipping away so that there soon will be few black independent farmers left.[29] Farm foreclosures, rising taxes, and the difficulty of obtaining bank loans created a major depression in farming and farm-related industries. Many blacks who remain in rural areas will work as managers, skilled workers, and common laborers in large farm industries and agribusinesses. Rural areas will not disappear but agriculture is changing, and the tenant farmers, sharecroppers, and small individual farmers who appeared in past studies of black rural churches will experience a change in occupations.

Another trend is the gradual but noticeable reverse migration among black people to the South and the sunshine states of the Southwest. Studies indicate that during the 1970s the South gained more than 259,000 black reverse migrants.[30] The causes for reverse migration are complex. Like their white counterparts who also are moving, the primary reasons are the search for jobs and the continued industrialization of the South. More heavy industries are moving away from northern states to escape high taxes and strong labor unions. For example, American and Japanese auto manufacturers have chosen rural southern areas to locate new plants. Besides jobs, there is also the growing disillusionment with the northern dream. In the black psyche, the North has always been historically associated with freedom, less violence, and greater opportunities. But drugs, crime, street gangs, depressing living conditions in urban ghettoes, cold weather, and rising fuel costs have taken their toll of the northern dream. Changes wrought by the civil rights movement have also made the South more tolerable. Finally, extended family ties provide another motivation to move. The majority of black people in the North have relatives in southern states, and many of them still regard the South as home. Although the reverse migration will probably not match the previous out-migrations, it is a trend that will increase the black population base of the South and provide a potential constituency for some rural churches.

These trends mean a mixed picture for the future of black rural churches. Those near southern cities and growing black suburban areas will probably experience a rise in membership. In the field we have seen scattered examples of rural churches that have constructed large, expensive new buildings. But there will also be a decline of some plantation churches and others in deep rural areas as young people seek their fortunes elsewhere.

A final trend that will affect rural churches is the growing class split in the black community. Studies are showing an increase in the black middle and working classes who have been the major beneficiaries of affirmative action and civil rights policies. But there is also a corresponding increase among poor black families and female-headed households.[31] Lower-class and uneducated black people have provided the major constituency for many rural churches. These churches will continue to have a needed ministry and services to provide. Since the pastor usually reflects to some degree the economic conditions of his members, the pattern of a part-time, absentee pastorate in black rural churches will continue.

One of the great strengths of black rural churches, which continued into the 1980s, is the loyalty of their members. In his reanalysis of the Gallup data on the "unchurched American," Nelsen has shown that black people residing in the nonmetropolitan South, or the traditional rural black belt, have the highest rates of being churched among all African Americans. Rural church members also tend to be among the poorest sector of the black population, having the lowest socioeconomic status.[32] In spite of the severe effects of urban migration upon rural churches, they have continued to hold the loyalty of a faithful remnant.

The high degree of racial segregation in religion and housing in the United States reflects the persistent difficulties that American society has had in adjusting to the realities of our racial and economic insensitivities. A total of 30 million African Americans are still trying to find a more comfortable place in their native land, a place they feel to be consistent with the expectations other Americans take for granted. The enduring search for respect and respectability, for acceptance and acceptability, takes many forms, and the fallout of the effort is not always predictable. Black rural churches became the first institutions to carry the hopes and dreams of an outcast people. If they were not always heroic institutions, they at least contributed to the survival of their people in the most extreme and violent circumstances. This study reflects the continuing saga and history of a neglected but remarkable institutional sector in the black community.

A Profile of Black Urban Clergy

A total of 1,531 urban clergy from the seven major black denominations were interviewed in fifteen major urban areas in the Northeast, Southeast, Southwest, Midwest, and West.[33] In terms of denominational affiliation, about 90 percent of all of the clergy respondents said that they identified with one primary black denomination. Only the Baptist groups (NBC, U.S.A., Inc.; NBC, America, Uninc.; and PNBC) had multiple denominational affiliations, either with another black Baptist denomination, usually between the NBC, U.S.A., Inc., and the PNBC, or with the white Southern Baptists and American Baptists. The black Methodists' groups (A.M.E.; A.M.E. Zion; and C.M.E.) remained within their primary denominational affiliation and so did the black Pentecostals (COGIC).

The gender distribution of our sample included 1,462 (98.8 percent) male and 149 (3.2 percent) female. Although our interviewers were instructed to oversample and to interview any woman pastor in the mainline black denominations they could find, even if they were not included in the original list for random sampling, only 3.2 percent of the urban clergy were found to be female. Our best estimate is that fewer than 5 percent of all black clergy in the seven historic denominations are female. The rural sample showed a similar result with 94.6 percent of the clergy who were male and only 4.6 percent female. In regard to marital status, 1,329 (88.7 percent) were married while 54 (3.6 percent) were divorced. Only seventy-five (5 percent) of the clergy were single, and forty (2.7 percent) were widowed. There are great social pressures and preferences within black churches for the pastor to be married or to get married. Because of the predominance of female members in black churches,

TABLE 34.2
Clergy Income

Income Categories	Total	Urban	Rural
Zero earnings	27 (1.4%)	27 (1.8%)	0 (0.0%)
$1–2,999	100 (5.3%)	78 (5.1%)	22 (5.9%)
$3,000–$5,999	191 (10.1%)	142 (9.3%)	49 (13.5%)
$6,000–$7,999	141 (7.5%)	106 (6.9%)	35 (9.8%)
$8,000–$9,999	135 (7.1%)	110 (7.2%)	24 (6.9%)
$10,000–$14,999	262 (13.8%)	228 (14.8%)	34 (9.4%)
$15,000–$24,999	350 (18.5%)	305 (20.0%)	45 (12.4%)
$25,000 and over	162 (8.5%)	151 (9.8%)	11 (2.9%)
No response	526 (27.7%)	383 (25.1%)	143 (39.2%)

Total *N* = 1,894
Urban *N* = 1,531
Rural *N* = 363

unattached single clergy, especially males, tend to be viewed as a threat to the stability of congregational life.

Clergy Income

Table 34.2 shows a comparative distribution of the gross income of both urban and rural clergy. As expected, the income of urban clergy tends to be higher than that of their rural counterparts. The median income for rural clergy was in the $10,000 to $15,000 range, while urban clergy reported a median income in the category of $15,000 to $25,000. It is interesting to note that about 151 (9.8 percent) of the urban clergy said that they earned more than $25,000, while only 11 (2.9 percent) of the rural clergy claimed that income level. The rural-urban difference reflects both a greater level of affluence in urban areas and the larger size of urban congregations. Questions regarding accurate income figures in black churches remain problematic. The large number of clergy (27.7 percent) who did not respond to the question on personal income indicates the need for caution in interpreting the results. The clergy income results of our study are comparable to the findings of Brown and Walters's study of twenty-one black churches in Washington, D.C. They reported a pastor's family median income of $13,000.[34] The slight difference between the surveys on clergy income is due to the fact that our study focused on clergy in the seven mainline black denominations, while theirs included all black churches in a census tract, without regard to denominational lines. The mainline black denominations probably include more middle-income church members than the small, independent Apostolic and Pentecostal churches and storefronts. A cross-tabulation of reported clergy income from the seven denominations showed no significant variations. Cramer's V was 0.12507 for 1,368 respondents. However, it is interesting to note that clergy from the three Baptist denominations (14 percent average) and from the Church of God in Christ (15.7 percent) tend to have slightly larger percentages of their clergy earning more than $25,000 per year than the three black Methodist denominations (8.37 percent average). This is probably due to the influence of the connectional polity among Methodists that tends to standardize salary scales for pastors in their churches. In the churches with an independent or congregational polity such as the Baptists, each church determines such matters. As mentioned earlier, the Church of God in Christ has a mixed polity. Although it is a connectional church with bishops, COGIC clergy are also encouraged to be independent spiritual entrepreneurs and establish their own churches rather than waiting for appointment by the bishop.

Education of the Clergy

In their 1934 study, Mays and Nicholson lamented the educational level of the Negro ministry. They reported that 80 percent of the urban pastors are not college trained and that 86.6 percent do not have the bachelor of divinity degree.[35] The educational level of both rural and urban clergy has risen considerably over the past fifty years, reflecting in part the desegregation of public education and the other social changes which have occurred in the black community since the Depression. The median level of education of our urban sample is close to four years of college. Moreover, 70.2 percent of the urban clergy have some level of college training. It is estimated that about one third (35.9 percent) of all black clergy, in both urban and rural situations, have had some seminary or Bible school training beyond the college level. Although the survey did not ask about completion of a master of divinity program or graduation from a theological seminary, it is estimated that only about 10–20 percent of the clergy nationwide have completed their professional training at an accredited divinity school or seminary.[36] Unfortunately, this rate of professional training for the ministry, as measured by a seminary degree, has not improved very much since the time of Mays and Nicholson's study. On the other hand, the requirements of modern technological society have made professional education for the ministry a prerequisite for pastors of the mainline black churches. As more and more African Americans are entering professions that were once closed to them, the pastors of black churches must have both the educational credentials and the ability to preach if they are to be acceptable to an increasingly well-educated clientele. While the black clergy overall have kept pace with the general rise in educational levels in the black community, they still lag behind in professional training when compared to other black professionals. It is difficult to imagine a profession, whether it is medicine, law, engineering, teaching, or social work, where two-thirds of the professionals have not had any advanced training, and more than 80 percent have not completed professional degrees. However, that was the case with the majority of the black clergy in the 1980s. Most black clergy have learned about pastoring a church through an informal system of apprenticeship which exists in all black denominations. But the days when pastors could brag about being "untrained" and still build a large church are rapidly passing. Similarly, the time when the minister was looked upon for leadership because he was the best-educated, or among the best-educated people in the black community, are also gone. To win the respect of the new black professionals and college-educated black people, the clergy must also, at a minimum, achieve professional parity.

If the Black Church is to have a viable future, the need for professional seminary education appears to be critical. As the results of our survey show, educational level has been a key variable in determining a pastor's awareness of social problems in the surrounding community, cooperation with social agencies, attitude toward politics, and awareness of internal problems in church structures. In our field interviews with black clergy, the churches that sponsor the most creative and innovative programs in the community and in the church usually have well-educated, well-trained pastors. The educational issue is problematic for most black churches because the historical evangelical background of the Baptists, Methodists, and Pentecostals did not have stringent educational demands but only required evidence of a personal call from God to the ministry. The anti-intellectual and fundamentalist strains of that tradition have made it difficult for innovative church leaders and bishops to make professional seminary education a requirement for the ministry. The response of nineteen clergy in the Brown and Walters's study of Washington, D.C., were similar to our results. Their median educational level was four years of college with 42 percent having had some level of college or postsecondary education, and 21.1 percent having attended graduate school.[37]

The age range of clergy in the urban sample was 18 to 92 years old with a median age of 51.5 years. There were no significant differences with the rural sample where the median age of clergy was 51.3 years and the age range was 17 to 89 years old. The majority of black clergy tend to be older, which probably reflects an economic situation where many pastors cannot afford to retire because of low or nonexistent retirement benefits and pension plans. In a profession where the median age is close to 52 years old, critical questions must be raised about the future of the ministry in the black denominations and the source of new recruits.

Pastoral Responsibilities

To assess which of their pastoral responsibilities the black clergy considered most important to them, we asked the ministers to give a rank order of common pastoral duties which were listed on a separate card handed to them. Only the clergy of black urban churches were given this task to perform since it became clear from our rural survey that the prevailing absentee pastorate in most black rural churches would obviate a listing of common pastoral responsibilities. The results in Table 34.3 show that for the black urban clergy, the task of preaching far outranks any other, 919 (60.0 percent). Second and third places, respectively, included teaching, 358 (23.4 percent) and church administration, 62 (4.0) percent. The least desired task among pastoral duties was fund raising, 3 (0.2 percent). This survey of pastoral responsibilities lends factual weight to the perceived importance of preaching in the ministry of black churches. Black churches have been far more charismatic than bureaucratic institutions in their general value orientation. A large amount of emphasis is placed on the black minister's personal charisma as reflected in his or her ability to preach. This stress on the central role of preaching in the Black Church underscores the continued importance of the oral tradition in black culture.[38]

It is remarkable that the institutional sector of the black churches has been able to attract some of the most talented people to its ranks over more than two hundred years, in spite of the often meager benefits and the precarious economic security that

TABLE 34.3
Pastoral Responsibilities (Urban Clergy Only)

Q. Please list the following pastoral responsibilities in order of their importance to you:
Civic leadership, teaching, preaching, leading worship, visitation and counseling, fund
raising, administration of the church, leadership of groups within the church.

Pastoral Responsibility	Urban	Rank Order
1. Civic leadership	14 (0.9%)	Sixth (tie)
2. Teaching	358 (23.4%)	Second
3. Preaching	919 (60.0%)	First
4. Leading worship	22 (1.4%)	Fifth
5. Visitation and counseling	14 (0.9%)	Sixth (tie)
6. Fund raising	3 (0.2%)	Seventh
7. Church administration	62 (4.0%)	Third
8. Leadership of groups within the church	38 (2.5%)	Fourth
9. No response	101 (6.7%)	

$N = 1,531$

the call to ministry often entails. To recite the litany of famous black preachers and church members is to recall the African American journey toward freedom in black history.[39] It is also a testimony to the deep religious commitment that was always a corollary of that pilgrimage. In spite of its venerable tradition, whether the Black Church will continue to attract the most talented men and women and whether it will continue to flourish in an increasingly complex urban society are serious questions for the future. Here we have presented a demographic profile of the urban black clergy with some comparisons with rural clergy data and among the denominations themselves. We now turn to a demographic profile of urban black churches.

A Demographic Profile of Urban Black Churches

It is a common convention in the black community that the church is the oldest and most stable institution. Our survey of 2,150 black rural and urban churches once again confirms that wisdom. The churches in our survey range from one to two hundred years old. The oldest church is the rural Silver Bluff Baptist Church in Beech Island, South Carolina, which claimed a much disputed founding date of 1750 on its cornerstone.[40] Among the oldest urban black churches were Bethel A.M.E. Church in Baltimore (1785); First African Baptist Church in Savannah (1787); Springfield Baptist Church in Augusta, Georgia (1788); Mother Bethel A.M.E. Church in Philadelphia (1794); Mother Zion in New York City (1796). The median age for all black churches in the study is one hundred years. Close to half of the urban churches, six hundred (47.6 percent), have moved only once, and another three hundred (23.9 percent) have changed locations twice. In other words, about 71.5 percent of the black urban churches surveyed have moved fewer than two times and have remained remarkably stable. The average number of years in the present location is 46.5. Black urban churches that change locations frequently tend to be storefront churches usually found in the poorest sections of black communities where the rents are lowest and the population transient. Here, their tenure may range from a few months to several years, while their unstable nature makes them difficult to study.[41] But like their more stable counterparts, the goal of many storefront churches and congregations is to move up to a regular church edifice in due time or to build one of their own.

The characteristic progression of building black churches is often from small meetings in private homes (usually the preacher's), to a rented hall or storefront, and finally to a regular church edifice. The distribution indicates that the vast majority of urban churches in the mainline black denominations, 1,326 (86.6 percent), worship in regular church edifices, 107 (7.0 percent) churches were storefronts, while 48 (3.1 percent) rented halls for their worship services from YMCAS or from other public or private institutions. Only 30 (2 percent) of the church groups were meeting in homes.

The type of building used for worship can also be used as an indicator of the class stratification among black churches. While the seven denominations include the broad range from abject poverty to upper middle class, much of their membership is composed of a coping middle-income strata, made up mostly of middle- and working-class people. Close to 88 percent of the churches surveyed worship in regular church buildings and about 12 percent use storefronts, rented halls, and individual homes. However, caution must be taken in regard to social class generalizations. From our field visits and observations, we know that even the most elite black churches tend to have some poor members on welfare in their congregations. Most of the large black churches tend to be the mixed type, composed of the middle class, working class, and poor. Depending on the church and the denomination, underclass members may range from 5 to 33 percent of the congregation. The black Methodist denominations, A.M.E., A.M.E. Zion, and C.M.E., tend to be more solidly middle class and have the fewest storefront churches.[42] Most of the storefront churches in the study were either Baptist or Pentecostal (COGIC).

Our survey found that 1,233 (80.5 percent) of the urban churches have incorporated and a little more than half, 354 (57.2 percent), of the rural churches have done so. It is probable that the lack of knowledge among church leadership about the benefits of incorporation accounts for the failure to utilize incorporation more widely. But the independent strain among some black churches contributes to the notion that the church is not the business of the state and that it should avoid the state's intrusion wherever possible.

In examining the incorporation status of black churches, our fieldwork discovered that relatively few institutional histories of local black churches have been written or preserved, but a number of these churches, urban ones in particular, have created their own archives and museums. For example, the First African Baptist Church of Savannah; the Springfield Baptist Church of Augusta; the Sixteenth Avenue Baptist Church in Birmingham, Alabama; the Abyssinian Baptist Church in New York; Mother Bethel A.M.E. Church in Philadelphia; and Bethel A.M.E. Church in Baltimore have extensive historical holdings in their archives. Some other smaller black churches have also attempted to collect fragments of their past history which they often publish in church bulletins or other literature to commemorate the anniversary of the founding of their church. A survey and catalog of these local historical materials and other yet undiscovered church archives is critical for the preservation of black institutional history. Unfortunately, among the major black denominations, only the Church of God in Christ has made some substantial progress toward creating a central archives and museum in its headquarters building in Memphis. To date, only COGIC and the C.M.E.s have established central headquarters, both in Memphis. The three Baptist denominations and the A.M.E. and A.M.E. Zion churches have not established denominational headquarters, although the National Baptist Convention, U.S.A., Inc., is in the process of establishing a world headquarters in Nashville. Perhaps as the major black denominations centralize and consolidate their denominational identities, the centralization of historical records and archives will follow in due course.

Black Urban Churches and Community Outreach Programs

In this section we will briefly present some of our data on the community outreach programs that black churches have sponsored. In examining these programs we asked, "Has your church cooperated with social agencies or other nonchurch programs in dealing with community problems?" The results show that 1,459 (67.9 percent) of the total sample of black churches responded affirmatively, while 596 (27.7 percent) said no. For urban churches 1,086 (70.9 percent) answered yes and 392 (25.6 percent) responded negatively, while the results for rural churches were 373 (60.3 percent) positive and 204 (33.0 percent) negative. Black churches and clergy, on the whole, were much more supportive of community outreach programs, thus undermining once more the stereotype of the Black Church as a withdrawn, insular, and privatized institution. Both urban and rural black churches cooperated with a wide variety of social agencies and programs that focused on problems within the African American community and in the larger society. As an overall generalization, the data show that black urban churches are far more active than rural ones in cooperating with social agencies and in dealing with community problems. The most popular nonchurch agencies were the civil rights organizations with which 625 (40.8 percent) of the urban churches and 310 (50.1 percent) of the rural churches indicated cooperation. The slightly higher rural rate of cooperation with civil rights groups is due to the fact that there is a paucity of social agencies in rural areas, and as we mentioned previously, many southern rural churches were heavily involved in the civil rights movement. This high rate of cooperation between black churches and the major civil rights organizations underscores the fact that black churches have been a key support system for these groups. Besides civil rights, black urban churches were also active in participating with youth agencies like the Scouts and YM/YWCA groups, 367 (23.4 percent); local community crisis events like school desegregation, local demonstrations, and closing of hospitals, 249 (16.3 percent); welfare rights and housing, 153 (10 percent); and police/community relations issues like crime and delinquency, recruitment of minorities, and police brutality, 158 (10.3 percent). Overall, the results of our survey were similar to the findings of Brown and Walters in Washington, D.C., where they found that 88.2 percent of the clergy replied that their churches had provided outreach services or worked in the local community. How-

TABLE 34.4
Use of Church Building by Nonchurch Groups

Q. Is the church building used by nonchurch organizations as a meeting place for special programs?

	Total	Urban	Rural
Yes	844 (39.3%)	673 (44.0%)	171 (27.6%)
No	1,221 (56.7%)	801 (52.3%)	420 (67.9%)
No Response	85 (4.0%)	57 (3.7%)	28 (4.5%)

Q. If yes, please list the organizations (more than one allowed, up to 3).

Organizations	Total	Urban	Rural
1. Civil rights organizations (NAACP, SCLC, etc.)	411 (19.1%)	289 (18.8%)	122 (19.7%)
2. Civic associations (block associations, neighborhood groups, citizens patrol, etc.)	542 (25.2%)	471 (30.7%)	71 (11.5%)
3. Political organizations (political meetings and rallies)	138 (6.4%)	114 (7.4%)	24 (3.9%)
4. Fraternal orders, lodges, fraternity and sorority groups	161 (7.5%)	109 (7.1%)	52 (8.4%)
5. Boy and Girl Scout troops, 4-H clubs, etc.	59 (2.7%)	57 (3.7%)	2 (0.3%)
6. Schools and educational groups	92 (4.3%)	74 (4.8%)	18 (2.9%)
7. Professional group meetings (teachers, social workers, etc.)	49 (2.3%)	45 (2.5%)	4 (0.6%)
8. Labor group meetings (labor unions, etc.)	41 (1.9%)	33 (2.2%)	8 (1.3%)
9. Other	190 (8.8%)	153 (7.1%)	37 (6.0%)

Total N = 2,150
Urban N = 1,531
Rural N = 619

ever, only 52.4 percent of the churches in their sample had cooperated with secular social agencies or organizations, compared to our rate of 70.9 percent for black urban churches.[43] The difference is explained by our focus on the seven mainline black denominations.

As part of our examination of community outreach, we inquired whether black urban churches continued the traditional historic practice of permitting nonchurch community groups to use the church building as a place for meetings and/or special programs. The data in Table 34.4 indicate that the practice still continues to some extent, particularly in black urban churches, 673 (44.0 percent), and to a lesser degree in rural churches, 171 (27.6 percent). At one time black churches were the only places where black nonchurch groups could hold a meeting or special event. That is no longer true since more options are available even in the rural South since the civil rights period. There is, however, a rural-urban difference in the types of groups allowed to use the church building. For black urban churches, civic associations like block associations, neighborhood improvement groups, citizens' patrols, and community organizations, 471 (30.7 percent) led the way, while for rural churches, civil rights groups, 122 (19.7 percent), were first. Civil rights groups came in second for black urban churches, 289 (18.8 percent), while the fraternal orders and lodges placed second for rural churches, 52 (8.4 percent). These fraternal orders and lodges, the Masons and Elks, and their female counterpart, the Order of the Eastern Star, seem to represent a declining phenomenon in black communities. At one time most of the members of the black elite in a town or city belonged to the lodges and they played a very important economic and service role. But many members of the contemporary college educated, black middle class have preferred to join the national black fraternity and sorority groups, thus leaving an aging and declining sector of secret societies behind; a parallel phenomenon has also occurred among whites. The urban churches which reported that the orders, lodges, and fraternity and sorority groups which used the church building for their meetings numbered 109 (7.1 percent). In regard to political meetings, urban churches, 114 (7.4 percent), were more active than rural churches, 24 (3.9 percent).

Our survey gathered the only known data about the participation of black churches in government-funded programs (federal, state, and city). Although the numbers were not large, the information is important because some politicians and government bureaucrats, as well as a growing number of black urban clergy, have begun to see black churches as important bases for the delivery of some government-related social services, educational, food, and housing programs. According to Table 34.5, 138 (6.4 percent) of all black churches have participated in government funded programs, including 121 (7.9 percent) urban churches and 17 (2.7 percent) rural churches. For the black urban churches the top four government funded programs were Day-care centers, 60 (3.9 percent); food programs like the federal breakfast/lunch programs, 47 (3.1 percent); Headstart programs, 30 (2.0 percent); and Federal Housing, 32 (2.1 percent). Rural churches participated only in the Headstart, 8 (1.4 percent), and Day-care center programs, 11 (1.8 percent). It is important to note that all of our survey data were collected before the twin crises of hunger and homelessness in the United States became major issues during the waning years of the Reagan administration. The data now would probably show a larger increase in participation by black churches in government programs. Many black churches, especially those in poor neighborhoods, became distribution points for the surplus cheese program, and a number of others have provided shelters for the homeless or set up soup kitchens. The participation of black churches in government funded programs is fraught with both opportunities and problems. On the one hand, black churches are a natural way of channeling federal, state, and city government resources and services into black communities because they remain one of the few stable social institutions with a broad base of support from the community. As we will show, some black church groups have brought about important changes in their surrounding neighborhoods through the use of government funds and programs. On the other hand, black clergy and churches that participate in government programs also face the dilemma of losing their prophetic voice; the proverbial problem of "biting the hand that feeds you" becomes a real one.

As a final item of community outreach, we also examined the attempts of black churches to reach out beyond themselves by participating in projects that required cooperation with churches of other denominations. Table 34.6 on interdenominational cooperation shows that 1,280 (59.5 percent) of all black churches participated in interdenominational projects, with 923 (60.3 percent) of the urban churches and

TABLE 34.5
Church Participation in Government-Funded Programs

Q. Does your church participate in any governmental program for which it receives funding?

	Total	Urban	Rural
Yes	138 (6.4%)	121 (7.9%)	17 (2.7%)
No	1,975 (93.5%)	1,386 (90.5%)	589 (95.2%)
No response	37 (1.7%)	24 (1.6%)	13 (2.1%)

Q. If yes, list the programs (can list more than one, up to four).

Government-funded Programs	Total	Urban	Rural
1. Headstart programs	38 (1.8%)	30 (2.0%)	8 (1.3%)
2. Food programs (breakfast, lunch, etc.)	47 (2.2%)	47 (3.1%)	0 (0.0%)
3. CETA (job training)	12 (0.6%)	10 (0.7%)	2 (0.3%)
4. Federal housing	40 (1.9%)	32 (2.1%)	8 (1.4%)
5. Day-care center	71 (3.3%)	60 (3.9%)	11 (1.8%)
6. Other educational programs	12 (0.6%)	12 (0.8%)	0 (0.0%)
7. Other government-funded programs	24 (1.1%)	20 (1.3%)	4 (0.6%)

Total N = 2,150
Urban N = 1,531
Rural N = 619

TABLE 34.6
Interdenominational Cooperation by Black Churches

Q. Has your church participated in any ongoing projects that required cooperation with churches of other denominations in the past year?

	Total	Urban	Rural
Yes	1,280 (59.5%)	923 (60.3%)	357 (57.7%)
No	776 (36.1%)	540 (35.3%)	236 (38.1%)
No response	94 (4.4%)	6 (4.4%)	26 (4.2%)

Q. If yes, briefly describe the programs.

Type of Program	Total	Urban	Rural
1. Fellowship with other churches, pulpit exchanges, etc.	572 (26.8%)	420 (27.2%)	152 (24.6%)
2. Evangelism	303 (14.2%)	164 (10.7%)	139 (22.5%)
3. Educational programs (Bible classes, vacation Bible school, etc.)	29 (1.3%)	20 (1.3%)	9 (1.4%)
4. Community service oriented programs (tutoring, day care, elderly, youth, etc.)	123 (5.7%)	106 (6.9%)	17 (2.7%)
5. Social program oriented programs (drug and alcohol abuse, crime, welfare, housing, etc.)	32 (1.5%)	30 (2.0%)	2 (0.3%)
6. Interracial cooperation with white churches	120 (5.6%)	110 (7.2%)	10 (1.7%)
7. Other	70 (3.4%)	40 (3.2%)	21 (3.4%)
8. No—no cooperation	741 (34.9%)	520 (34.0%)	221 (35.7%)
No response	160 (6.6%)	112 (7.5%)	48 (7.7%)

Total N = 2,150
Urban N = 1,531
Rural N = 619

357 (57.7 percent) of rural churches taking part. Slightly more than one-third of the churches, 776 (36.1 percent), responded negatively. The data indicated that two of the top three programs were the traditional types of interdenominational cooperation among black urban and rural churches such as fellowship with other churches and pulpit exchanges, 572 (26.8 percent), and evangelism programs (such as crusades and revivals) with other churches, 303 (14.2 percent). Interdenominationally sponsored community service-oriented programs (such as tutoring, day care, senior citizens, youth, counseling, and voter registration drives) ranked third with 123 (5.7 percent) churches.

The de facto segregation of American society has resulted in very little interracial cooperation with white churches, and the data indicate that only 120 (5.6 percent) of the total 2,150 black churches took part, with 110 (7.2 percent) black urban churches and 10 (1.7 percent) rural churches. The urban-rural difference is partly explained by the fact that black urban clergy have more opportunities to participate in interracial church councils or ministerial alliances in their areas. But rural areas in the South have also exhibited high degrees of racial segregation, as evidenced by a long history of lynchings and racial violence, especially during the civil rights era.[44] Lower-class whites have generally felt threatened by the gains of lower-class blacks. It is significant to note that less than 10 percent of all black churches have taken part in any kind of interracial cooperation with white churches. Racial segregation in American society is most clearly seen in religion.

Conclusion: Present Trends and the Future of Black Urban Churches

The major focus of this chapter has been twofold: to provide a summary overview of the impact of urbanization on black churches and a largely rural black migrant population, and to present a descriptive profile of black urban clergy and their churches from the data gathered through our national survey. The studies of black urban churches since the 1950s have consisted largely of detailed ethnographic and sociological studies of one or a few congregations, or focused on one issue such as civil rights militancy.[45] Only Brown and Walters's study of 21 black urban churches in Washington, D.C., paralleled our concerns, but even their study was limited to one city.[46] A much broader portrait of black clergy and churches of the mainline black denominations nationwide, especially a baseline statistical profile, was missing. We have attempted to fill that gap by a five-year survey consisting of face-to-face interviews with the pastors of 2,150 black urban and rural churches. For the remainder of this chapter we will discuss some present trends that may have an impact upon the future of black urban churches.

Black urban churches and the mainline black denominations have continued to attract and to hold the loyalty of a significant sector of the national black community. Gallup Poll data indicate that about 78 percent of the black population in 1987 were "churched," that is, claiming church membership and attending church within the last six months.[47] In their 1987 study of *American Mainline Religion*, Roof and McKinney have pointed to the "relatively strong socioreligious group ties" in the black community: "Black Protestants attend worship services more than any other group except white conservative Protestants: 56 percent are regular attenders and 25 percent are occasional attenders. . . . Generally blacks have a high level of denominational commitment, much higher in fact than most other groups."[48]

While black churches are still the central institutions in their communities, some cracks have begun to appear at the edges of the religious stronghold. Despite the universal claims of the Black Church for the whole black community, there has always been a small sector of unchurched black people. Mostly they were younger black males or other maverick types determined to resist the powerful social control of black churches in the small rural towns and in urban areas. They were given various names by past studies of black communities: Du Bois called them "criminal and vicious classes" in *The Philadelphia Negro*; Drake and Cayton referred to them as "the Shadies" and the "Non-Church Centered Respectables" in *Black Metropolis*. Liebow described them as "the street corner men" in *Talley's Corner*. In black folk terminology, they were simply known as "the low life," those who frequented the bars and clubs and listened to the "Devil's music."[49] More recent studies have begun to show a significant growth among young, unchurched blacks, especially males in northern urban areas.[50] From his reanalysis of the April 1978 Gallup study of "The Unchurched American" and the data of other studies, Hart Nelsen has found that "race," "residence," and "region" were among the most significant variables in determining the degree to which African Americans were churched or unchurched. Using the definition of "churched" mentioned earlier, Nelsen's study found that black people residing in rural areas of the South, or "non-metropolitan South," had both the highest rates of being churched (85.2 percent) compared to whites (48.8 percent) and the strongest degree of religious socialization. While African Americans in the northern and western urban areas—the "non-South metropolitan"—had the lowest rates of being churched, especially in central cities (28.4 percent). Black residents in the urban areas of the South, or "metropolitan South," had rates between 45.5 percent and 50 percent of being churched. Nelsen found no significant differences for education, occupation, or income. Because of the small size of the sample of black respondents ($N = 182$) in the Gallup survey, questions can be raised with regard to how representative the sample is, and the method of sampling.[51]

In spite of this trend of a small but growing population of unchurched blacks, it is a bit premature to conclude as Frazier, Mukenge, and Nelsen have that black churches in the urban environment have lost their major communal functions in politics, economics, education, and culture.[52] In other words, their argument is that differentiation has gone so far that religion has become a privatized matter and the Black Church has withdrawn into a sphere of religiosity. As Nelsen has written, "With the migration of blacks to the metropolitan area, the black church is subject to differentiation, to increasingly being coupled with religious motivation rather than being identified with meeting the whole panoply of black needs. Increasingly, religion becomes a private matter, with the black church not tied to meeting the many functions it once served."[53] In contrast to this privatization scenario and view of complete differentiation, we will point out in later chapters that there are far more interactions and interrelationships between black churches and the spheres of secular life such as politics and economics so that only a partial differentiation has taken place. Many black churches have not yet given up their communal functions and withdrawn from the "whole panoply of black needs." In fact, a holistic view of the ministry of the Black Church, of being involved with all aspects of life, has been one of the continuing major attractions for many black clergy throughout history; the holistic view represents a major historical stand among black churches that calls for continuous prophetic involvement in all phases of black communal life.[54] With the growing specialization of professions, ministry in black churches, both urban and rural, is one of the few vocations that has legitimated care and concern for all the needs in the black community.

Besides missing this theological self-understanding of the task of ministry in black churches, one of the major problems of the privatization scenario is that it tends to ignore the continuous and insidious role that racism in American society has played and the communal bonding effects that racism has stimulated in black communities. As one of the major bulwarks and voices against racism, black churches and clergy have played and will continue to play a far more communal role than they have been given credit for. The privatization scenario tends to project onto blacks the results of social processes from white ethnic groups, some of which may be relevant, but almost all have to be reinterpreted because of the racial factor. For example, while many white churches have tended to withdraw from an active role in the political and economic scene because there are strong, competing institutions that can fulfill those functions, in most urban and rural black communities there is a paucity of strong institutional alternatives. In many cases black churches have had to help create and nurture these institutions like banks, insurance companies, low-income housing projects, employment training centers, or political vehicles like the major civil rights organizations, and they still do so. Most black people do not feel a sense of ownership or of partnership with the major American political parties, even with the Democratic Party, as the Jackson candidacy in 1988 has shown; nor do they have a sense of ownership of a significant sector of American business enterprises, or the American economy. There may come a time when racial discrimination is completely eradicated in American society and African Americans are treated fairly and justly like any other American. When that happens, black churches and clergy may no longer feel compelled to involve themselves in all aspects of black life. But that point has not yet been reached in the late twentieth century. As Roof and McKinney have correctly argued,

> With respect to membership in a church group—perhaps the best measure of communal bonds—they (Black Protestants) exceed all the other families. They are the only family for which more than one-half claim involvement in a church group. Strong bonds to church and community have served to buffer the trends toward greater religious individualism dominant in the society.[55]

Just as social class factors cannot be adequately applied to black people without taking into account their "definition of the situation," as Billingsley cogently argued, a realistic assessment of the black religious situation must also take into account what black churches and black clergy have been doing and are doing.[56] To dismiss this side of the ledger is to miss more than half of the picture. We contend that the relationships between black churches and clergy and other aspects of black institutional life are far more interrelated and finely woven together—and more dynamic—than most social scientists have been willing to concede. The present picture of black urban churches is a complicated, mixed picture of some effects of privatization among unchurched sectors of the black population, and the withdrawal of some black churches into a sphere of personal piety and religiosity; but there are also numerous signs of a continuing tradition of activism and involvement in the political, economic, educational, and cultural aspects of black life among the majority of black clergy and churches. Much of the recent upsurge in activism by black churches can be traced to the legacy of the civil rights movement and the period of black pride and black power that followed it.

NOTES

1. U.S. Department of Commerce, *The Social and Economic Status of the Black Population in the United States: An Historical View, 1790–1978*. Current Population Reports. Special Studies Series, P. 23, No. 80 (Washington, D.C.: U.S. Government Printing Office, 1980).

2. Daniel M. Johnson and Rex Campbell, *Black Migration in America: A Social Demographic History* (Durham, N.C.: Duke University Press, 1981).

3. For some literature on the black migrations, see the following: Ibid.; Jacqueline Jones, *"To Get Out of This Land of Sufring": Black Migrant Women, Work and Family in Northern Cities, 1900–1930*. Working Paper No. 91 (Wellesley, Mass: Wellesley College Center for Research for Women, 1982); and Marcus E. Jones, *Black Migration in the United States with Emphasis on Selected Central Cities* (Saratoga, Calif.: Century Twenty-One Publishing, 1980).

4. Ralph Felton, *These My Brethren: A Study of 570 Negro Churches and 542 Negro Homes in the Rural South* (New York: Committee for the Training of the Negro Rural pastors of the Phelps-Stokes Fund and the Home Missions Council of North America, 1950); and Harry V. Richardson, *Dark Glory: A Picture of the Church among Negroes in the Rural South* (New York: Friendship, 1947), p. 65.

5. For example, see Ralph Felton's study of positive examples of rural black clergy, *Go Down Moses: A Study of 21 Successful Negro Rural Pastors* (Madison, N.J.: Department of Rural Church, Drew Theological Seminary, 1952).

6. Richardson, *Dark Glory*, pp. 65–66.

7. In their 1933 study, *The Negro's Church* (New York: Russell and Russell, 1969), Benjamin Mays and Joseph Nicholson raise the problem of "overchurching" as the central dilemma for black churches, both urban and rural. While there is the problem of depleting valuable resources in having too many churches, there are some deep cultural and economic reasons for this development. First, America's rigid system of racial exclusion made the job of "preacher" one of the few dignified roles with a large degree of independence and authority. The greater emphasis upon a charismatic personal style in the black community is one of the primary reasons for the origin of new churches. Second, for a long period of time black churches were the only institutions completely controlled by the people. The high degree of

personal investment in these churches makes it difficult to give up easily. Third, the variety of churches meet a pluralism of religious and social needs. Fourth, it is doubtful that the Roman Catholic strategy of one large parish church with twenty-five clergy would work in the black community. Decentralized centers seem to work best among the rural proletariat, although some degree of consolidation is desirable and perhaps inevitable.

8. Although the civil rights movement proper began with the organization of the Montgomery bus boycott in December 1955, the 1954 Supreme Court decision in *Brown v. Board of Education* provided the legal legitimation for the movement.

9. For the opiate thesis concerning black churches, see Gary Marx, *Protest and Prejudice* (New York: Harper and Row, revised edition, 1969).

10. Bruce Hilton, *The Delta Ministry* (New York: Macmillan, 1969), p. 182.

11. For a theoretical typology of the relationship between black religious groups, stratification, and social action, see the article by Hans Baer and Merrill Singer, "Toward a Typology of Black Sectarian Response to Racial Stratification." *Anthropological Quarterly* 54 (1981): 1–14.

12. Felton, *These My Brethren*, pp. 61–62.

13. Richardson, *Dark Glory*, p. 123.

14. Felton, *These My Brethren*, pp. 58–59.

15. Mays and Nicholson, *The Negro's Church*, p. 254.

16. These insights are based on field observances and the literature on power relations and schisms in black churches; cf. Mays and Nicholson, *The Negro's Church*, pp. 11–13, 278–98; Charles Hamilton, *The Black Preacher in America* (New York: William Morrow, 1972), pp. 19–23; Ida Rousseau Mukenge, *The Black Church in Urban America: A Case Study in Political Economy* (New York: University Press of America, 1983), pp. 125–26; and Melvin D. Williams, *Community in a Black Pentecostal Church: An Anthropological Study* (Pittsburgh: University of Pittsburgh Press, 1974).

17. Hamilton, *The Black Preacher in America*, pp. 19–28.

18. Cushing Strout, *The New Heavens and New Earth: Political Religion in America* (New York: Harper and Row, 1974), p. 106.

19. Mays and Nicholson, *The Negro's Church*, p. 254.

20. Felton, *Go Down Moses*, p. 97.

21. Ibid., p. 96.

22. E. Franklin Frazier and C. Eric Lincoln, *The Negro Church in America: The Black Church since Frazier* (New York: Schocken Books, 1974).

23. Williams, *Community in a Black Pentecostal Church*; Arthur Paris, *Black Pentecostalism: Southern Religion in an Urban World* (Amherst: University of Massachusetts Press, 1982).

24. Hart M. Nelsen and Anne Kusener Nelsen, *Black Church in the Sixties* (Lexington: University of Kentucky Press, 1975). Also see Mukenge, *The Black Church in Urban America*.

25. Eugene Genovese, *Roll, Jordan, Roll: The World the Slaves Made* (New York: Pantheon, 1974). Also see Albert Raboteau, Slave Religion: The *"Invisible Institution"* in the Antebellum South (New York: Oxford University Press, 1978).

26. Frazier, *The Negro Church in America*.

27. Gayraud Wilmore, *Black Religion and Black Radicalism: An Interpretation of the Religious History of Afro-American People* (Maryknoll, N.Y.: Orbis, 1983).

28. U.S. Department of Commerce, *The Social and Economic Status of the Black Population in the United States: An Historical View, 1798–1978*, p. 63.

29. The prediction is given in David Dybiec, ed., *Slippin' Away: The Loss of Black Owned Farms* (Atlanta: Glenmary Research Center, 1988). Also see "Nation's Farms Decrease: Black Farms Nearly Gone," *Jet 70* (April 7, 1986): 14.

30. In their 1981 study, Daniel M. Johnson and Rex Campbell point out that between 1970 and 1975, 238,000 blacks moved outside the South while 302,000 moved to the South with a net gain of 64,000 black population for the South. "The most significant change was the Northeast where for every one migrant to the Northeast, two were moving to the South" (Johnson and Campbell, *Black Migration in America: A Social Demographic History* (Durham, N.C.: Duke University Press, 1981), p. 170). Data from the National Urban League study of reverse migration indicate that between 1975 and 1980 some 415,000 blacks moved to the South, while only 220,000 left the South for a net gain of 195,000. James D. Williams, ed., *The State of Black America 1984* (New York: National Urban League, 1984), p. 172.

31. The title of William Julius Wilson's book, *The Declining Significance of Race*, unfortunately tends to obscure his important thesis of growing class divisions in the black community due primarily to the structural changes in the movement of American society from an industrial to a postindustrial, technological economy. The escalator opportunities in heavy industries are no longer available to the urban black underclass, and technological society demands more educational skills. National Urban League data indicate that 28 percent of 4.9 million black families in 1970 were headed by women; by 1982 almost 41 percent of 6.4 million black families were female-headed households (Williams, *The State of Black America 1984*, p. 173).

32. Hart M. Nelsen, "Unchurched Black Americans: Patterns of Religiosity and Affiliation," *Review of Religious Research 29*, No. 4 (June 1988): 402.

33. The fifteen major cities in the sample included New York, Newark, Philadelphia, Atlanta, Birmingham (Alabama), Jackson, Dallas, Houston, Chicago, Detroit, Kansas City, St. Louis, Oakland, San Francisco, and Los Angeles. The black churches in the Washington, D.C., area were surveyed in another study conducted by researchers from Howard University and our results will be compared with theirs. See Diane R. Brown and Ronald W. Walters, *Exploring the Role of the Black Church in the Community* (Washington, D.C.: Mental Health Research and Development Center and Institute for Urban Affairs and Research, Howard University, no publication date given, c. 1982).

34. Ibid., pp. 12–14.

35. Mays and Nicholson, *The Negro's Church*, pp. 54–55.

36. This estimate was given by Dr. James Costen, president of the Interdenominational Theological Seminary in Atlanta. His estimate also corresponds to the views of several denominational leaders who were interviewed as part of this project.

37. Diane R. Brown and Ronald W. Walters, *Exploring the Role of the Black Church in the Community*, table 2.1, p. 13.

38. For a historical overview of the importance of oral tradition in the formation of black culture, see Lawrence Levine, *Black Culture and Black Consciousness* (New York: Oxford University Press, 1978).

39. According to Bishop William J. Walls of the A. M. E. Zion Church, he started out to research the history of the church and he ended up with a history of the race. See Walls, *The African Methodist Episcopal Zion Church: Reality of the Black Church* (Charlotte, N.C.: A. M. E. Zion Publishing House, 1974). Using the metaphor of "river," Vincent Harding's historical reflections on the black journey toward freedom also follows a similar path of emphasizing the role of black churches and black religion. See Vincent Harding, *There Is a River: The Black Struggle for Freedom in America* (New York: Harcourt Brace Jovanovich, 1981).

40. Most scholars follow Carter G. Woodson's dating of the Silver Bluff Baptist Church between 1773 and 1775. However, during a field visit to Silver Bluff, we discovered that the cornerstone of the church had a founding date of 1750 inscribed on it. There has been an

ongoing dispute among the early black churches as to which one was first. Mechal Sobel in her classic work on early black Baptists, *Trabelin' On*, gave a founding date of 1758 for the African Baptist or "Bluestone Church" in Lunenberg, Virginia (now Mecklenberg). Cf. Sobel, *Trabelin' On: The Slave Journey to an Afro-Baptist Faith* (Westport, Conn.: Greenwood, 1979), pp. 250, 256. The Springfield Baptist Church in Augusta, Georgia, has claimed that it is an offshoot of the Silver Bluff congregation and therefore deserves to be considered the first continuous black church in existence, although its founding date was 1788. The First African Baptist Church of Savannah, established in 1787, has also made its claims to be the first black church.

41. There have been very few studies of urban storefront churches, which have usually been local in scope; there are no national studies. From field observations in a number of cities we have learned that storefront churches tend to appear in greatest frequency in some of the most depressed areas. For example, in 1982 in a two-block area on Fulton Avenue in one of the poorest sections of Bedford-Stuyvesant in Brooklyn, we counted twenty-two storefront churches.

42. In our national study we found only one Methodist storefront, which was an A.M.E. mission church.

43. Brown and Walters, *Exploring the Role of the Black Church*, pp. 31–33. Brown and Walters do make the important observation that the missionary societies within black churches often provided unspecified neighborhood services.

44. Ida Wells-Barnett was the prime mover behind the antilynching campaign in the late nineteenth and early twentieth-centuries. See Ida Bell Wells, *U.S. Atrocities* (London: 1892). On the civil rights period, see the following: Aldon D. Morris, *The Origins of the Civil Rights Movement: Black Communities Organizing for Change* (New York: Free Press, 1984). Thus far, the best film documentary on the civil rights movement is Henry Hampton's "Eyes On the Prize."

45. See the following: Williams, Community in a Black Pentecostal Church; Paris, Black Pentecostalism; Mukenge, *The Black Church in Urban America*; Nelsen and Nelsen, *Black Church in the Sixties*.

46. Brown and Walters, *Exploring the Role of the Black Church*.

47. *See Emerging Trends*, published by the Princeton Religion Research Center, Vol. 9, No. 5 (May 1987): 5. The only data that tend to contravene these findings are found in the Princeton Religion Research Center's study, *The Unchurched American ... 10 Years Later* (Princeton: Princeton Religion Research Center, 1979), p. 37. The church membership rate for black people was recorded as 64 percent, which is a 13 percent drop from the rate reported in 1987. Since this recent finding is so anomalous from other studies of black church membership over the past 20 years, including Gallup's own findings, we reserve judgement until other studies confirm or discount this result. Thus far, our church sources have not supported a large loss in church membership.

48. Wade Clark Roof and William McKinney, *American Mainline Religion: Its Changing Shape and Future* (New Brunswick, N.J.: Rutgers University Press, 1987), p. 91.

49. W. E. B. Du Bois, *The Philadelphia Negro: A Social Study* (New York: Schocken Books, 1970); see his analysis of "The Seventh Ward," pp. 58–72. St. Clair Drake and Horace Cayton, *Black Metropolis: A Study of Negro Life in the North* (New York: Harper and Row, 1962), 2: 524–25. The "Shadies" for Drake and Cayton were those who participated in illegal enterprises, a group which cut across class lines. Elliot Liebow, *Talley's Corner: A Study of Negro Streetcorner Men* (Boston: Little, Brown, 1967). Prior to the civil rights movement, the characterization of the unchurched in these community studies really meant those who were marginally

socialized into the Black Church tradition or those who were rebelling against it. It did not mean that they had virtually no contact with Black Church culture.

50. For a profile of this group, see Michael R. Welch, "The Unchurched Black Religious Non-Affiliates," *Journal for the Scientific Study of Religion* 17 (September 1978): 289–93.

51. Hart M. Nelsen, "Unchurched Black Americans: Patterns of Religiosity and Affiliation," *Review of Religious Research* 29, No. 4 (June 1988): 398–412. Nelsen's fine reanalysis of the Gallup study and of other data is a significant contribution to the field. However, we do have some questions about the adequacy of using a telephone survey in regard to lower-income or poor black Americans, who may be left out by such a method. It is estimated that only about 80 percent of Americans have telephones in their homes; most of the truly disadvantaged cannot afford the service.

52. Cf. Frazier, *The Negro Church in America*, p. 82. Mukenge tends to psychologize the functions of urban black churches because she sees their future role only in the area of mental health and psychological stability. Mukenge, *The Black Church in Urban America*, p. 204. Also, see Nelsen, "Unchurched Black Americans," pp. 408–9.

53. Nelsen, "Unchurched Black Americans," p. 408.

54. See Peter Paris, *The Social Teaching of the Black Churches* (Philadelphia: Fortress, 1985), for the continuous antiracial, ethical stance among the Black Baptists and Methodists. For the historical tradition of black religious radicalism or the prophetic stance, see Wilmore, *Black Religion and Black Radicalism*. As mentioned earlier, Vincent Harding has also written about the black journey toward freedom in *There Is a River*.

55. Roof and McKinney, *American Mainline Religion*, p. 91.

56. Andrew Billingsley, *Black Families in White America* (Englewood Cliffs, N.J.: Prentice-Hall, 1968), chap. 5.

Bishop Ida Robinson, founder of the Mount Sinai Holy Church, an independent denomination (1924). Courtesy of Elder Minerva Bell, Historian, Mt. Sinai Holy Church of America, Inc.

Chapter Thirty-five

The Black Denominations and the Ordination of Women

C. Eric Lincoln and Lawrence H. Mamiya

One of the important points of specific inquiry in the Lincoln/Mamiya study concerned the roles and official recognition of women in the ministries of the black churches. Following is what they discovered, including data on some of the issues and developmental directions related to black women as professional clergy.

•

The first black denomination to officially ordain women to the ministry was the African Methodist Episcopal Zion Church. In 1891 at the Second Ecumenical Conference, Bishop James Walker Hood defended the right of women to be elected delegates to the general conference of the denomination. He said that "there is one Methodist-Episcopal Church that guarantees to women all rights in common with men."[1] Several years later, he acted on his words. At the Seventy-Third Session of the New York Annual Conference held at the Catharine Street A.M.E. Zion Church in Poughkeepsie on May 20, 1894, Bishop Hood ordained Mrs. Julia A. Foote (who was a conference missionary) "deacon." On May 19, 1895, Mrs. Mary J. Small, wife of Bishop John B. Small, was ordained deacon by Bishop Alexander Walters at the Sixty-Seventh Session of the Philadelphia and Baltimore Conference. In 1898, Mrs. Small became the first woman of Methodism to be ordained "elder" by Bishop Calvin Pettey at the Philadelphia and Baltimore conference. After transferring to the New Jersey conference, Mrs. Foote was also ordained an elder by Bishop Alexander Walters in 1900.[2] Thus, Mrs. Small and Mrs. Foote became the first women to achieve the rights of full ordination to the ministry by any Methodist denomination, black or white. The A.M.E. Zion Church's ordination of women preceded similar action by the other black Methodist denominations and by the United Methodist Church by half a century.

The struggle for full ordination by black women in the other two black Methodist bodies, the African Methodist Episcopal Church and the Colored Methodist Episcopal Church, was considerably more protracted. Black women in the A.M.E. Church were not allowed full ordination until 1948. Prior to that time there were many attempts by A.M.E. women and their male supporters to obtain the rights of ordination for preaching women. At the 1868 General Conference the denomination created the post of stewardess, the first official position for women whose main task was to look after other women and to assist the male stewards, class leaders, and pastors. The 1884 General Conference approved of the licensing of women to preach but without ordination. In response to the growing pressure from women, in 1900 the A.M.E. Church created the position of deaconess, again without ordination, despite the fact that men were always ordained when they became deacons.[3] In creating the post of deaconess without ordination, the A.M.E. Church responded to women in the same manner as the northern and southern white Methodist bodies had done.[4]

The C.M.E. Church did not allow full ordination for women until 1954. On the issue of women, this southern black Methodist denomination was much more traditionalist and conservative than their northern counterparts. Partly due to its late organization as a separate denomination in 1870, it was not until 1902 that the women of the C.M.E. Church were able to organize the Women's Home Missionary Society, and only in 1918 did the Women's Connectional Missionary Council receive approval as an organization. As Bishop Othal H. Lakey described it in his history of the C.M.E. Church, "it is quite evident that neither the bishops nor the General Conference viewed an organization for women in the same manner in which they viewed other needs of the church." Further, the bishops and the General Conference would allow the women of the church to have their own connectional organization to run "as long as they did not conflict or interfere with the church itself."[5] With the concerns of women in the church given a low priority, the ordination of women as pastors and preachers in the C.M.E. Church would not occur until the beginning of the modern civil rights era in the 1950s.

For women in the three black Baptist denominations (National Baptist Convention, U.S.A., Inc., National Baptist Convention of America, Uninc., and Progressive National Baptist Convention), the struggle and quest for full ordination into the ministry has been even more difficult. The complete history of black preaching women among the Baptists is undocumented and difficult to trace because the independent church polity of the Baptists ensures the autonomy of each congregation in matters of faith and practice. However, in the earliest Separate Baptist churches of the South, women were ordained as deaconesses, and some unordained women were allowed to preach. As the Baptist faith spread during the First Awakening in the mid-eighteenth century, there was a "remarkable freedom of participation by women."[6] As Sobel has observed, "Black women found much room for involvement, expression, and leadership in the Baptist churches, which was in keeping with both the Southern Separatist tradition and earlier African traditions. . . . Women were given formal roles as deaconesses and served on committees to work with women who had violated Baptist ethics. . . . Southern black women even attended the meetings of the American Baptist Missionary Convention in the North."[7] However, in 1800 when the Separate and Regular Baptists merged, that freedom became far more restricted, and eventually in both black and white churches leadership became almost exclusively male. While women never lost the post of deaconess, their role as preachers was practically eclipsed. After the Civil War many of the black Baptist clergy became members of the Southern Baptist Convention, but due to unequal treatment and racism they began their movement toward independence in 1880, a process which was completed in 1895 with the formation of the National Baptist Convention (NBC).[8] Schisms among the black Baptists led to the formation of the National Baptist Convention of America (NBCA) in 1915 and the Progressive National Baptist Convention (PNBC) in 1961. While there is no specific policy against the ordination of women in any of the black Baptist denominations, the general climate has not been supportive of women preaching and pastoring churches. However, in recent years there has been a small minority of black clergymen who have sponsored women candidates for ordination in their associations. The Baptist principle of congregational autonomy has been helpful in these cases since the independence of each church and pastor cannot be challenged by any denominational authority.

Among the large variety of Pentecostal groups, the Church of God in Christ—the largest black Pentecostal denomination—has taken a firm policy stand against the full ordination of women as clergy. Although COGIC has recognized the numerous contributions that women have made in the affairs of the church, COGIC's *Official Manual* argues on scriptural grounds against ordaining women as elder, bishop, or pastor.[9] Although it has recognized that women were important in the ministry of the New Testament era, the denomination has found no mandate for ordaining women to the previously mentioned positions. COGIC has allowed women to preach in their churches but only as evangelists or missionaries, performing a teaching function that does not carry a mandate for ordination. There are, however, a few exceptions on record where widows have temporarily carried on the work of their deceased husbands. Many Pentecostal churches are kin-type churches, which are passed on in a hereditary manner from fathers to sons or, if sons are lacking, to wives. While proprietary churches are common among the Baptists where the congregation owns the church property, the mixed polity of COGIC has permitted the development of kin churches, which are often not only named after the founder but also passed on in the extended family. While COGIC is a connectional church with a hierarchical structure of bishops and strict denominational ties, the denomination also encourages its clergy to found and develop their own churches in the manner of the churches having an independent polity like the Baptists. There is no itinerancy requirement such as the Methodists have which requires pastors to be reassigned after a term of years. Hence, in COGIC the pastor's tenure in a particular church is usually for the long term, and may well be for life. In some cases a few congregations have preferred to have the wife of the founder continue as their minister instead of an outsider. In spite of its official policy of prohibiting women pastors, there seems to be a tacit understanding in the denomination which quietly tolerates such situations by allowing the woman to complete the ministry of her late husband as *shepherd sans portfolio.*

The official restrictions against ordaining women clergy in some of the major black denominations combined with sexist attitudes have often prompted many black women to start their own independent Holiness or Pentecostal churches. Such churches usually begin in private homes or apartments, eventually moving to storefronts. Some of the more charismatic women preachers have been able to attract substantial followings and build large churches. Elder Lucy Smith, who established the All Nations Pentecostal Church in Chicago in the 1930s, and Bishop Ida Robinson, who founded the Mount Sinai Holy Church of Philadelphia in 1924, come to mind. More recent examples include Reverend Dr. Barbara King of the Hillside International Truth Center in Atlanta, and Reverend Johnnie Colemon of the Christ Universal Temple in Chicago. Both King and Colemon, who have reputations as charismatic preachers, have several thousand members in each of their own congregations. In proportion to their respective numbers in the population, there have probably been more black women as preachers and pastors than there have been white women counterparts. White ethnic experience has not proved as fertile for the emergence of a strong preaching tradition among women, nor has there been the apparent reception that some black women preachers have found outside the structures of the major black churches.

Inevitably, this brief historical survey of the policies of the major black denominations toward women clergy raises questions about the contemporary attitudes of black clergy toward the issue of women as pastors and preachers and whether there has been any improvement in attitudes of clergy in the last quarter of the twentieth century with the growing pressures of the feminist movement. We turn now to an examination of the results of our survey on clergy attitudes toward women clerics.

Contemporary Black Clergy Attitudes Toward Women as Preachers and Pastors

In our nationwide survey of the black clergy of 2,150 churches, only sixty-six, or 3.7 percent, were female in spite of special efforts to interview black female clergy.[10] Our best estimate is that fewer than 5 percent of the clergy in the historic black denominations are female. Although there are probably more black women proportionately who are clergy than white women, the vast majority of them are found in storefront churches or in independent churches.

On the question of whether the clergy approved or disapproved of a woman as the pastor of a church, a Likert scale was used to measure the strength of the response. The results indicated that the following variables showed some relationship to the strength of the response: sex, age, education, and denomination. In regard to the sex of the clergy respondent, the eta coefficient of 0.16774 in Table 35.1 indicated a moderate degree of relationship with approval of women as pastors. For the women interviewed, fifty-two (81.5 percent) out of a total of sixty-four approved of women pastors, while twelve (18.5 percent) disapproved. For the men, the approval and disapproval rates were almost even, with only a slight majority 842 (50.8 percent) approved of women pastors, while 815 (49.2 percent) disapproved. Among the men there were some very strong feelings in the negative direction. For example, on the Likert scale 409 (24.7 percent) of the men strongly disapproved and only 249 (15.0 percent) strongly approved, while thirty-seven (58.0 percent) of the women strongly approved and five (7.1 percent) strongly disapproved. While it seemed a curious phenomenon to have women clergy who strongly disapproved of women as pastors, these women probably became ministers after their husbands' deaths, often reluc-

TABLE 35.1
Women as Pastors by Sex, Age, and Education

Variable		
SEX	Male	Female
Strongly approve	249 (15.0%)	37 (58.0%)
Approve	593 (35.8%)	15 (23.5%)
Disapprove	406 (24.5%)	7 (11.4%)
Strongly disapprove	409 (24.7%)	5 (7.1%)
Eta coefficient = .16774		
AGE	Under 30	Over 65
Strongly approve	18 (16.2%)	40 (13.1%)
Approve	60 (53.0%)	84 (27.5%)
Disapprove	18 (15.4%)	76 (25.0%)
Strongly disapprove	18 (15.4%)	105 (34.4%)
Eta coefficient = .17047		
EDUCATION	Less than High School Graduate	College 5 Plus
Strongly approve	28 (10.5%)	147 (23.2%)
Approve	87 (32.7%)	276 (43.6%)
Disapprove	68 (25,5%)	114 (18.0%)
Strongly disapprove	84 (31.3%)	97 (15.2%)
Eta coefficient = .23188		

tantly taking over their ministries. Further, despite their own roles as clergy, they may also be reflecting the official policies of their denominations against ordaining women as pastors, particularly in the Church of God in Christ and among some Baptist associations.

The results of Table 35.1 showed some symmetry with respect to age and the approval of women as pastors. Seventy-eight (69.2 percent) of those who were under thirty approved—and they were more liberal in their attitudes toward women pastors—while 124 (40.6 percent) of those over 65 approved and 181 (59.4 percent) disapproved. The eta coefficient of 0.17047 also indicated a moderate relationship between the variable of age and approval of women pastors.

However, a strong statistical and substantive relationship existed between the educational level of the clergy and their attitudes toward women as pastors. The eta coefficient was 0.23188. It is important to note in Table 35.1 that the majority of black clergy were negative in their attitudes until the category of those who have graduate training, college 5 plus, is considered. The data indicated that for those clergy who were less than a high school graduate, 152 (56.8 percent) disapproved of women as pastors and only 115 (43.2 percent) approved. But 423 (66.8 percent) of clergy in the college 5 plus category indicated their approval of women as pastors, while only 211 (33.2 percent) disapproved. The results were somewhat symmetrical with those in the lowest educational categories having the highest disapproval rates and those with the most education having the highest positive attitudes toward women pastors. The data also indicated that clergy with some college education have more positive views than those with only a high school education or less.

A very strong relationship existed between the variable of denomination and attitudes toward women as pastors (WP). Table 35.2 presents the results of chi-square cells, giving the breakdown of the seven black denominations and their rates of approval or disapproval of women pastors. The eta coefficient is 0.57607 with WP dependent and 0.26827 with denomination dependent. As the cells indicated, the three Baptist denominations and the Pentecostals (COGIC) tended to be highly negative in their attitudes toward women as pastors. The three Methodist denominations, on the other hand, were much more strongly positive. The A.M.E. Zion Church led with a 94.2 percent approval rate, the C.M.E. Church with 92 percent, and the A.M.E. Church with 88 percent.

Among the Baptists, the Progressive National Baptist Convention tended to be only slightly more progressive on this issue of women pastors than the other conventions. PNBC had a total approval rate of 42.7 percent and a total disapproval rate of 57.3 percent. The largest black Baptist body, NBC, U.S.A., Inc., was very strongly negative toward women pastors with 43.9 percent of their clergy strongly disapproving and a total disapproval rate of 73.6 percent. The total approval rate of the NBC, U.S.A., Inc., was 26.5 percent. The NBC, America, Uninc., had a total approval rate of 25.4 percent and a total disapproval rate of 74.6 percent.

The Church of God in Christ also had a high disapproval rate of 73.4 percent, with the second highest rate of 36 percent who strongly disapproved of women as pastors. The total approval rate was 26.6 percent. COGIC has an explicit denominational policy against the ordination of women as pastors. In COGIC women can become evangelists, an official church position, but not pastors. The few women who were pastors of churches in the denomination were widows who succeeded their husbands because their congregations felt more comfortable with the former pastor's kin leading the church, or because there are usually no survivor's benefits in the black churches, and succession may be an instrument of economic survival.

Among the major black denominations, a distinction is usually made between pastors and preachers, with pastor being the official ordained leader of a church, while a preacher may be anyone who preaches with or without benefit of ordination or denominational recognition as a pastor. There are instances of officially ordained preachers who may or may not be the pastor at any given time. They may teach in seminaries, or function as executives and administrators. Some Baptist churches permit women to be preachers or exhorters (that is, they can preach from the pulpit) but they are not allowed to carry out certain other pastoral functions, especially the rituals of baptism and communion. However, the distinctions are seldom rigid in conventional understanding, and the terms are often used interchangeably. A "jackleg preacher" is the pejorative idiom for a "self-called" preacher without credentials of any kind.

The Methodist-Baptist difference in our data is partly due to the fact that some of the black Methodists, like the A.M.E. Zion Church, have a longer historical and denominational tradition of allowing women to be ordained as pastors. The Zion Church began the official ordination of women as deacons and elders between 1894 and 1900. Furthermore, it did not develop euphemistic categories like "deaconess," which became an officially recognized but unordained subordinate office for women

TABLE 35.2
Women as Pastors by Denomination

Denomination	NBC, Inc.[a]	NBC, Uninc.[a]	PNBC	A.M.E.	A.M.E. Zion	C.M.E.	COGIC	Totals
WP								
Strongly approve	31 (6.6%)	10 (5.6%)	12 (9.2%)	74 (29.7%)	65 (33.6%)	50 (30.9%)	20 (6.9%)	262 (15.7%)
Approve	94 (19.9%)	34 (19.8%)	43 (33.5%)	146 (58.3%)	118 (60.6%)	99 (61.0%)	57 (19.7%)	591 (35.4%)
Disapprove	140 (29.7%)	76 (44.7%)	44 (33.6%)	24 (9.6%)	8 (3.8%)	4 (2.5%)	108 (37.4%)	404 (24.2%)
Strongly disapprove	207 (43.9%)	51 (29.9%)	31 (23.7%)	6 (2.4%)	4 (2.0%)	9 (2.0%)	104 (36.0%)	412 (24.7%)
Totals	472 (28.2%)	171 (10.2%)	130 (7.8%)	250 (15.1%)	195 (11.7%)	162 (9.7%)	289 (16.3%)	1,669 (100%)

Eta coefficient = .57607
Missing = 225 (11.9%)
N = 1,894

[a] These Baptist denominations are known more popularly by their "Inc." and "Uninc." designations. Their abbreviated titles are the NBC, USA Inc. and NBC, America Uninc.

in the other Methodist bodies, both black and white. The leadership provided by a small group of liberal feminist A.M.E. Zion bishops (Hood, Walters, Small, and Pettey) in the late nineteenth century was crucial to this process of legitimating women as pastors. Our survey results of contemporary black clergy nationwide reflected the continuing vitality of this liberal tradition. Zion clergy were the strongest supporters of women as pastors. Women in the A.M.E. and C.M.E. churches had a longer and much more difficult struggle, but the majority of clergy in these denominations also voiced support for women as pastors.

Black Clergy Views on Women as Pastors: Pro and Con

The qualitative section of the survey allowed the clergy who wished to do so to amplify their feelings and thoughts on one of the more controversial issues addressed by black churches. The following were some examples of verbatim pro and con statements made by the clergy who are identified only by interview number:

Negative Reactions

The clergy who disapproved of women as pastors of churches generally cited biblical support. Most frequent examples referred to the absence of women among the 12 disciples; Adam and Eve stories; and St. Paul's injunctions on the conduct of women in the church, that is, to keep silent. Others cited their denomination's restrictions, and still others the physical limitations of women.

No. 0358: "They do not have any business preaching. She has no voice. If she has any questions, let her ask her husband at home."

No. 1865: "Okay to preach but not as pastor. The doctrine of COGIC doesn't approve of the term preachers [for women]. [Call them] Evangelists."

No. 1935: "Women have been preaching for years but not identified as preachers. That role pastor has not been distinguished for her. As one within, I could not accept a woman pastor—a masculine role."

No. 1419: "She can be a 'pastor's helper—but God didn't make her job to be a pastor; they may have the educational ability, but they're not God-approved."

No. 1420: "Theoretically [they have] co-equal positions but no women are pastors. 'Spiritual leaders' or 'church mothers' are female counterparts to ministers; other positions [are] held—deaconesses, missionaries."

No. 1422: "[The] responsibility of the pastor is too strenuous for women. The pastor is on call 24 hours but there are certainly times when women are incapacitated, i.e., during pregnancy, during times of menstrual cycle. However, I feel a woman can be an 'evangelist.' Deacons must do 'dirty work'—How can you expect a woman to do such? She loses her femininity and it diminishes her womanhood."

No. 1725: "In order to pastor, one must be blameless and the husband of one wife, that's what the Bible says, and there is no way a woman can be the husband of one wife. I don't care what kind of operation she has."

No. 1836: "When a woman brings a message she is preaching. But when it comes to pastoring it's not her place, according to the Bible."

No. 1901: "In her discourse [she] can go whatever route she chooses to go to make plain the Gospel, but [do] not call it preaching, call it teaching."

Positive Reactions

The clergy who approved of women as pastors either cited biblical support or relied on the theological argument that God is all powerful and can do anything. Many of those who were favorable also had direct experiences with women who were preachers and pastors. Some pastors referred to the analogy between racial discrimination and sexual discrimination. In terms of biblical examples, Mary and Martha are called the first bearers of the good news of the resurrection.

No. 0125: "A woman minister shows more concern to her flock."

No. 1189: "If the Lord can cause rocks to cry out, surely he can call women."

No. 1403: "Adam and Eve—If [Eve] woman can lead men to hell, why can't she lead them to heaven."

No. 1507: "Value is not determined by sex."

No. 0101: "I don't think God is a sexist. Men must not do to women what whites have done to us on the basis of a false anthropological view of human nature in a backward sociology."

No. 1913: "I cannot restrict God to [the] male population of the church. The Holy Spirit on the day of Pentecost was not discriminatory. There are varied ministries and room in those also."

No. 1748: "I am a woman. I understand women to be more thorough and genuine in caring and nurturing."

No. 1506: "They are my fellow yokemen. I strongly approve. I would be happy to serve under a woman pastor."

No. 1249: "I think women have a place in the Christian ministry, although presently I am still mentally studying this situation in my own mind. I am convinced, however, God cannot be limited to who he might call into his service."

No. 1942: "The few [women] I have known were excellent speakers, good administrators and well educated."

No. 0324: "In Christ there is neither male nor female. The call is not a sex affair but a divine call for God. Women are doing a better job. In the last days all children shall prophesy. Women keeping silent in the church was a discipline and [has] nothing to do with preaching. God sees where he can use one."

The negative and positive reactions of the black clergy given above represented the range of feelings elicited in our open-ended interview section. Both the interview materials and data demonstrated that the struggle for black women to become preachers and pastors in the mainline black denominations is fraught with difficulty. Although there has been a long historical heritage of some black preaching women, the black religious tradition usually had a male as the authority figure, as preacher and pastor, with female as followers. This tradition, however, has been subjected to increasing criticism in recent years and it is slowly changing. In a field interview, Reverend Dr. Gardner C. Taylor, former president of the Progressive National Baptist Convention and pastor of Brooklyn's Concord Baptist Church, the largest black church in the United States, admitted that he had great difficulties with this question of the role of women as pastors. "I came to appreciate women," Taylor said, "as I taught women in school. I began to see an inkling of spiritual and religious leadership in them. I am open to this if a woman has been properly trained in the ministry."

In an interview with *The Cornerstone*, Reverend Dr. T. J. Jemison, president of the National Baptist Convention, U.S.A., Inc., said:

> It's not widely known that the National Baptist Convention, USA, Inc., has had three women pastors within the past twenty-five years. One of those pastors was Rev. Trudy Trim of Chicago, who assumed that role following the death of her husband. She too recently passed. Also when Rev. Plummer of Cleveland, Ohio became ill, his wife carried on in his absence. Many of our churches today have women assistants. The secretary of our convention, Dr. Richardson, is pastor of the Grace Church in Mount Vernon, New York. His assistant pastor is a woman, Rev. Flora Bridges. The editor of our convention's newspaper is Rev. Roscoe Cooper of Richmond, Virginia. The assistant in his church is also female . . . I welcome women and have nothing against them. Of course, most Baptists will come to accept this very slowly. My father was adamantly against this trend and so are most of my colleagues.[11]

Earlier generations of black preaching women during the urban migrations either founded independent churches, or they submitted to the secondary religious leadership positions created for them in the black denominations. The present generation of black preaching women, however, is insistent in their pursuit of leadership roles on parity with men, and they have won the support of some of their black clergy colleagues. About 51.1 percent of the black clergy interviewed in our study approved of women as pastors. However, our study also detected stronger, more intense feelings among the ministers who disapproved of women pastors. In spite of this intense opposition, which finds its primary focus among the Baptists and Pentecostals, the challenge of black women to open the doors of the Black Church to equal opportunities to serve shows no sign of abatement. In the next section we will examine some of the emerging trends among black women clergy.

Trends Among Contemporary Black Preaching Women

In contrast to earlier generations of their sisters who were often unlicensed or forced to found their own independent churches, black women preachers are far more likely to pursue the path of professionalization through full ordination. Two historical factors have influenced their search for official legitimation from black and white church denominations. One is that sudden postwar proliferation of Christian churches in the 1950s in the United States which led to an expanded need for professional clergy. Responding to this need, about one-third of the Protestant denominations in the World Council of Churches changed their disciplines to allow for the full ordination of women.[12] Second, the black consciousness movement of the late 1960s pushed the view of black leadership, and the feminist movement of the early 1970s fostered a quest for equality in all leadership positions and occupational arenas, including the church, as Delores Carpenter has pointed out in her study of black women clergy graduates of seminaries.[13] Because American women have a long tradition of church involvement in designated roles, the search for new involvements in positions of church leadership seemed consistent with the emerging ethos of sexual parity which was beginning to alter counterpart stereotypes in the secular world. For many women, the church was a comfortable and familiar environment in which to work.

The first major trend was a move toward professionalization among black clergy-women. From 1930 to 1980, the movement of black and white women into the professional ministry increased 240 percent.[14] But, according to Carpenter, the number of black women graduates from accredited theological seminaries increased 676 percent from 1972 to 1984.[15] The greater proportion of black women seeking theological credentials and ordination reflected both the paucity of their numbers in seminaries prior to the civil rights movement, and a tripling of the number of black college graduates who were twenty-five years and older, from 7 percent in 1960 to 20 percent in 1980. [16]

Another recent trend among black preaching women is their tendency to seek ordination and employment in the mainline, predominantly white denominations. More than half of the 380 ordained black women in Carpenter's study turned to the white denominations, partly because of the increased opportunity for ordination and employment, and the more rigid resistance and obstacles they experienced with the mainline black churches. Major white denominations like the United Church of Christ, the United Methodist Church, the Presbyterians, Episcopalians, Lutherans, and others have moved rapidly in the past two decades to include women among the ranks of ministers at almost all levels. Some of these white denominations have been more liberal and progressive on the issue of women clergy than most of the black denominations. Both white and black women have been attracted by these increased opportunities to move from the pew to the pulpit, and to the other leadership positions in their denominations. Carpenter has raised doubts, however, about how long this trend of black women preachers moving into white denominations will or can be sustained. The vast majority of these women are being assigned to the predominantly black parishes within these white denominations and it may only be a matter of time before these limited options will be filled and "the doors will shut."[17]

Furthermore, this projection is exacerbated by the suspicion of white paternalism and the resentment some black women feel at being showcased as evidence of white Christian liberalism. As one black United Methodist clergywoman pointed out in an interview, the cost of being a token person in a white denomination can be very high. She claimed that she was used as a "public relations piece," photographed and invited to dinners with the board of trustees of her seminary. Even as an ordained minister, she said, "I am viewed as a freak. Always singled out and critiqued, always asked to represent my race and/or my gender. I am always a minority—always without colleague support of the same gender/race."[18] Dr. Katie Cannon, an African American theologian, underscored the personal problems of tokenism in a white, male-denominated environment:

> I was quite successful in seminary because I knew how to behave in men's space so as not to threaten them. My stance was primarily that of the fly on the wall—a fly with many privileges granted to me as long as I remembered my place/space. Sometimes I was permitted to soar like a mighty eagle and other times I sat quietly like a bump on a log. Knowing the difference made me constantly feel as if I was driving with one foot on the accelerator and the other one simultaneously on the brakes. This meant that even though I was producing at top quality on one side of my brain, my soul sagged and ached with the heavy load of the precariousness of my tokenism.[19]

According to Cynthia Epstein, being black and female is one of the most cumulatively limiting of all the negatively evaluated statuses, and the majority of black women professionals in most occupations are often seen as inappropriate, or they are undervalued.[20] This view is common among professional black clergywomen in white denominations who must not only struggle with sexism but most do so against a backdrop of pervasive racial chauvinism.

A final trend found among both white and black clergywomen is their struggle to advance beyond entry level or auxiliary-style appointments or elections. While the reception of women as professional clergy has increased sharply over the last two decades, their advancement into positions of real power and prestige has been slow and dilatory. For example, while most newly ordained clergy can expect to begin pastoring in rural or small marginal urban churches, women are far more likely than men to move to second or third lateral appointments rather than truly promotive stations. Few women are chosen for the large established churches of the central city, or for posh, prestigious suburban churches. Interviews with men and women clergy and presiding elders in the Second District of the African Methodist Episcopal Church have confirmed the fact that the greatest challenge in the future is to have women move into the prestige churches in the district. The Second District, which encompasses the Washington-Baltimore region, is considered to be one of the most progressive in the A.M.E. Church and the clergy and laity have been receptive to women as pastors of churches. Yet one presiding elder confessed his skepticism regarding the future of women clergy:

> Acceptance has been terrific. We have not experienced any opposition to women as ministers. In fact, the women have turned the situation around in a number of problem churches. However, in this District all of the appointments have been beginning appointments. Some of the women are in their third and fourth years, the time of advancement. It remains to be seen whether they will experience the same kind of acceptance in larger churches as they did in smaller ones. It is a question in my mind.[21]

The apprehensions of the presiding elder are shared both by the women clergy in the Second District who want to move up, and by some of the male A.M.E. clergy who expressed concern about perceived competition for favorable posts in one of the few districts in the A.M.E. Church with a surplus of available ministers.[22]

Thus far, the only black women clerics to be elected as bishops are Leontyne C. Kelly of the United Methodist Church and Barbara C. Harris, who in 1988 was chosen a suffragan or assistant bishop for the diocese of Massachusetts of the Episcopal Church in an emotionally charged and highly controversial departure from tradition. None of the black Methodist denominations have yet elected a woman bishop and it will be some time before they do so. Bishop John Adams of the Second District of the A.M.E. Church probably speaks for most of his denomination when he predicts that "women will achieve the post of bishop in due time when they have accumulated enough experience as pastors and presiding elders and developed a reputation for leadership in the A.M.E. Church." But many women clergy in his church feel that his formula is a catch-22, and that the road ahead for women aspiring for the episcopacy is long and fraught with obstacles.[23]

In spite of the great difficulties and obstacles they have encountered in their attempts to become professional ministers, black women have forged ahead to answer their own spiritual calling to serve and to provide their own contributions to the church as a liberating force in American society. In Mozella Mitchell's study of black female religious professionals, 98 percent reported that they would not leave their vocation despite their feeling that they were heavily exploited and that coworkers often treated them with indifference or suspicion. The women are confident that they are qualified to minister to people's multidimensional needs and that God will support them in their ministry even if no one else does.[24]

The quest for professionalization among black preaching women has not only affected the practices of churches and church bureaucracies but it has also involved all of the intellectual fields concerned with the academic training of clergy in seminaries and divinity schools. Black liberation theology has also given rise to a new movement of black women who were concerned about critical theological reflections from their own perspective and context.

NOTES

1. William J. Walls, *The African Methodist Episcopal Zion Church: Reality of the Black Church* (Charlotte, N.C.: A. M. E. Zion Publishing House, 1974), p. 479.

2. According to Methodist Episcopal polity, the ordained ministers are of two orders, deacons and elders. A deacon can preach, *assist* at the administration of Holy Communion, baptize and administer matrimony, and try disorderly members. Eldership is the highest of holy orders. Only an elder can consecrate the elements of Holy Communion. Besides the duties of preaching, baptism, and marriage, and elder is usually the pastor of a church. Cf. Walls, *The African Methodist Episcopal Zion Church*, pp. 103–4.

3. For a summary of this history, see Jualynne Dodson, "Nineteenth-Century A.M.E. Preaching Women," Hilah F. Thomas and Rosemary Skinner Keller, eds., *Woman in New Worlds* (Nashville: Abingdon, 1981): 276–89.

4. The Methodist Episcopal Church, North, recognized deaconesses in 1888 and the Methodist Episcopal Church, South, accepted them in 1902. For both, deaconess is not an ordained position but the special status of a full-time church worker. See Jackson W. Carroll, Barbara Hargrove, and Adair T. Lummis, *Women of the Cloth: A New Opportunity for the Churches* (San Francisco: Harper and Row, 1981), p. 28.

5. See Othal Hawthorne Lakey, *The History of the C. M. E. Church* (Memphis: C.M.E. Publishing House, 1985), pp. 406, 408.

6. See the summary given by Carroll, et al., *Women of the Cloth*, p. 22.

7. Mechal Sobel, *Trabelin' On: The Slave Journey to an Afro-Baptist Faith* (Westport, Conn.: Greenwood, 1979), p. 233.

8. James M. Washington, *Frustrated Fellowship: The Black Baptist Quest for Social Power* (Macon, Ga.: Mercer University Press, 1986), part 3.

9. See C. F. Range, Jr., Clyde Young, German R. Ross, and Roy L. H. Winbush, eds., *Official Manual with the Doctrines and Disciplines of the Church of God in Christ* (Memphis: Church of God in Christ Publishing Board, 1973), pp. 144–46.

10. Our interviewers in the field were instructed to make special efforts to interview black female clergy of the seven historic black denominations even if they were not in the random sample.

11. Anqunett Fusilier, ed., "National Baptist Convention U.S.A., Inc., Socio-Economic Programs Sweep the Nation Under the Leadership of Dr. T. J. Jemison," *The Cornerstone* (San Antonio, Tex: Cornerstone Publishing, 1985), p. 22.

12. See John Lynch, "The Ordination of Women: Protestant Experience in Ecumenical Perspective," *Journal of Ecumenical Studies* 12 (1975), No. 2: 195. According to Lynch, most predominantly white denominations did not have to change their doctrines but only adjusted their disciplines to allow full ordination of women.

13. Delores Carpenter, "The Effects of Sect-Typeness Upon the Professionalization of Black Female Masters of Divinity Graduates, 1972–1984," Ph.D. dissertation, Department of Sociology, Rutgers University, 1986, p. 136. The authors wish to acknowledge and thank Rev. Dr. Delores Carpenter for sharing a copy of her dissertation with them.

14. Carroll, et al., *Women of the Cloth*, p. 4.

15. Delores Carpenter, "The Effects of Sect-Typeness," pp. 136ff. Also see Marjorie Hyer, "Black Women, White Pulpits," *Washington Post*, October 12, 1985.

16. Hyer, "Black Women, White Pulpits."

17. Interview with Carpenter in Hyer, "Black Women, White Pulpits."

18. Respondent no. 7 in a study by Deborah May, "The Impact of Racism and Sexism upon Black Clergywomen," unpublished study for a senior class thesis in Women's Studies at Vassar College, April 30, 1985, p. 44. The authors wish to thank Ms. May for permission to cite her excellent study.

19. Katie G. Cannon, in *God's Fierce Whimsy: Christian Feminism and Theological Education*, edited by Katie G. Cannon, Beverly W. Harrison, Carter Heyward, Ada Maria Isasi-Diaz, Bess B. Johnson, Mary D. Pellauer, Nancy D. Richardson (New York: Pilgrim, 1985), p. 44.

20. Cynthia Epstein, "Positive Effects of the Multiple Negative: Explaining the Success of Black Professional Women," *American Journal of Sociology* 78 (January 1973), No. 4: 917. Also see May, "The Impact of Racism."

21. Lawrence H. Mamiya, "The Second Episcopal District of the African Methodist Episcopal Church Under the Leadership of Bishop John Hurst Adams: Evaluations of the Leadership Training Institutes and the Phenomenon of Church Growth in the District," unpublished study funded by the Lilly Endowment, January 1986, p. 6.

22. Ibid.

23. Ibid.

24. See Mozella G. Mitchell, "The Black Women's View of Human Liberation," in *Theology Today* 39 (January 1983): 421–25. Also see May, "The Impact of Racism."

Chapter Thirty-six

The Churches and Broader Developments in Black Religion
Two Congregational Case Studies

David D. Daniels

The Religion in Urban American Program at the University of Illinois, Chicago, under the direction of Lowell Livezey, engaged in a multi-year case study of the greater Chicago area in examination of how religion configures itself in modern urban environments and addresses urban dynamics. A cross-section of congregations was selected for intense observation and analysis. Researcher David D. Daniels reflects on some of the characteristics and religio-cultural shifts discovered in African American congregations.

•

The churches in Chatham/Greater Grand Crossing represent the denominational diversity within American Christianity in general, and the Black Church in particular. While the denominations represented range from Baptist to Lutheran to Roman Catholic, the majority of churches belong to the Baptist and Methodist traditions, and the more prominent ones are members of black denominations within these traditions. Since Chatham/GGC is black middle-class community, the majority of congregations in previous decades exhibited various aspects of black middle-class religion, and some congregations continue to do so, which is sometimes highly contested within these congregations. Many of the congregations are undergoing a shift in religious culture as black middle-class religion was being redefined during the late twentieth century. This is the second major shift in religious culture for these churches in the twentieth century (Landry, 1987, 18–66, 67–93; Lincoln and Mamiya, 1990).

The first shift was the initial embrace of black middle-class religion by these churches in the early and mid-twentieth century. While these congregations stand in the revivalistic tradition of the eighteenth and nineteenth centuries which significantly shapes African-American ministry and informs its understanding of conversion, hymnody, and evangelism, they were in a part of the revivalistic tradition that had already distanced itself from the emotionalism often associated with African-American religion. These congregations exuded education and bourgeois values, and they promoted a learned and refined ministry. They represented a trajectory which historically countered the black religious stereotype by deemphasizing rhythmic music, religious dancing, and hooping by stressing note-perfect singing, quietness, and inspirational and intellectual preaching. Music structured the worship service with hymns representative of Protestant hymnody and choral selections drawn from anthems and spirituals, while the congregational singing reflected less of the urban gospel sound or the rural harmonies associated with long-meter hymns. These congregations prided themselves in their ability to worship in a manner as dignified as white middle-class Protestants. The preaching style was informational and inspirational with revelant biblical or theological applications on practical, everyday issues presented in an "intelligent" manner. The congregation's identification with the middle class resulted in its desire to attract middle-class blacks, especially professionals, and its tendency to restrict leadership positions in the church to middle-class members (Mays and Nicholson, 1969; Frazier 1962, 65–71).

The second shift in religious culture, which we are now witnessing in Chatham/ GGC, is precipitated by the emergence of the concept of the "Black Church" and the cultural identification of the Black Church with African American folk or popular religious culture. During the modern civil rights era, black congregations from diverse theological traditions ranging from Baptist and Methodist to Episcopal and Roman Catholic began to think of themselves as members of a racially defined Christian community, the Black Church, not simply of their ecclesially defined Christian traditions and denominations. They identified their commonality within the Black Church as their shared racial plight in the United States, their shared history of slavery and oppression, and their shared cultural heritage expressed in religion, arts, music, dance, and philosophy. Thus, the emerging identity of the Black Church encouraged a development of common liturgical forms and a sense of solidarity which united African American Christians across the theological and denominational spectrum. The impact of this has been that black middle-class religion now exhibits a religious culture previously identified with the folk or popular classes, as well as a loosening of the over-identification with the middle class accompanied by an expressed commitment to the black underclass (Wilmore, 1983, 192–219).

The redefinition of black middle-class religion is intensified by the introduction of afrocentricity within African American Christianity. Afrocentricity is a highly contested term within the academic and black communities. Definitions range from attempts to define knowledge and behavior in racial terms, through discussions of melanin, to projects that seek to reconstruct only the role of African peoples in history. The diverse definitions have sponsors in both the secular and theological disciplines (Dyson, 1993). Afrocentricity also echoes the earlier conversation within nineteenth- and early twentieth-century black nationalism which had cultural, social, political, economic, and intellectual expressions (Moses, 1978, 1990).

These earlier conversations stressed the racial uplift of African Americans and called for the development and use of black institutions to achieve racial progress. Central to the campaign were historical studies that refuted the claims of the racial inferiority of blacks by documenting the contributions of African peoples, especially African Americans, to science, literature, art, and human progress throughout human history.

The Ministries of Six Congregations

The congregations studied by RUAP find themselves in multiple contexts shaped by geography, history, demographics, economics, and culture.

The Chatham/GGC neighborhood includes approximately 177 churches, of which about eighty are "independent" churches, many of them "storefronts" not listed in the Yellow Pages or the city directory of churches. From these we selected six for in-depth study, one of which is independent, the others affiliated with major denominations.

All of these churches have their primary base in the neighborhood, that is, with the people who settled here in the 1950s and 1960s and their descendants. Some members are new residents and some are commuters (of the latter, some are former residents), but these churches are all rooted in the neighborhood. This is true of possibly all of the churches of Chatham/GGC.

The six congregations studied represent different constituencies within the Black Church. Two congregations are members of historically black denominations, the Christian Methodist Episcopal Church and the National Baptist Convention of America, respectively. One congregation is an independent black church, while the other three congregations are members of predominantly white denominations, the Roman Catholic Church, the Church of God (Anderson, IN), and the United Methodist Church. Four of the congregations were founded as black churches by African Americans. Two of the congregations began as white churches and experimented with integration for a period. The congregations vary in membership and attendance at Sunday worship. Over 1,000 people attend Sunday worship at two of the churches, while 500 and 600 attend two others, and 100 and 200 attend the remaining two, respectively.

Each of these congregations addresses many of the urban problematics we have found significant in other neighborhoods under study. While race and its interrelationship with religion is central here, it is not separated from the problematics of community, security, family, and others. We will introduce two of these congregations briefly and then comment on how they engage with the realities of the urban situation in their neighborhood.

Carter Temple

The church in our study that most explicitly invokes African symbols and traditions as a resource for redefining black religious culture is Carter Temple. The African heritage locates African Americans in the lineage of kings and queens of Africa, not of slaves of white plantation owners. It offers the model of the church as a village, where people share responsibility for rearing children (no matter whether a child's father is around) and where men take their rightful responsibility—even if the world around, including most of the churches, is caught up in "Eurocentric individualism." It provides a new, positive symbolic context for elements of African American culture (the extended family, intergenerational respect, even the village life of the American South) and of the structure and traditions of the Christian

Methodist Episcopal denomination (e.g., the responsibility of Steward in ministry to members). Rituals (rites of passage, black male role celebrations, African festivals), symbols (kente cloth, black liberation colors), new scholarship (the African biblical heritage, books by McCray and Felder) all are woven into a new collective self-image.

Located in the west central part of our study area, on the boundary between Chatham and Greater Grand Crossing in a relatively affluent and stable portion of the neighborhood, Carter Temple is a congregation of over 2,200 members and a major institution by virtue of its membership and neighborhood presence. Founded in 1921 in what was then Chicago's South Side, Carter Temple moved to this location and built the present edifice in the mid-1960s. Since Reverend Henry Williamson was appointed pastor in 1986, the church has grown by 1,000 members, and has added both a second Sunday service and a Saturday service.

Carter Temple builds community and promotes public security through a number of ministries. Especially connected to community and public security issues are its Save Our Sons, Project Essence, One-Church-One School, and Boys to Men conferences. These ministries play a double role of strengthening the congregational and neighborhood life and serving as forms of gang prevention. The One-Church-One-School ministry links Carter Temple to the Ruggles Elementary School. In each of these ministries one of the goals is to build the self-esteem of the youth so that they can develop into mature, responsible adults and reject destructive behavior such as gang involvement.

As noted, these same activities also build community. A distinctive element of Carter Temple's community building is its black male emphasis. In their attempt to reclaim the black male, they have stressed patriarchal roles for men and supporting roles for black women. They have also reached out to the prison population, which is predominantly male, in order to include these individuals in the reclaiming endeavor. Carter Temple strives hard to define community across class lines. They have moved in this direction by entering a partnership with the Olive Branch, a West Side homeless shelter, and holding a "Come As You Are" Saturday worship service designed to be a space where the homeless would feel comfortable. In addition to these innovative ministries, the church sponsors other extensive programs in Christian education and mutual support which strengthen the communal life of Carter Temple.

Carter Temple also participates in the redefinition of community, especially black community. The afrocentric symbolization at Carter Temple is only part of a deeper shift in the style of worship and collective identity in what has been a thoroughly middle-class church in a denomination identified with the black middle class and criticized (e.g., E. Franklin Frazier) for social stratification and paternalistic attitudes toward the plight of the poor. While Carter Temple celebrates and promotes the success of its members—especially males—in the mainstream society, it actively articulates an identification with and commitment to the African American community as a whole, including explicitly its more disadvantaged members. This is effected in part by the incorporation of styles of preaching (including "hooping") and music (gospel, percussion, rhythm), and "expressiveness" in a setting where inspirational preaching, note-perfect singing, and quietness (the "sweet hour of prayer") have been characteristic—and are still preserved as part of the new mix. The symbolic and stylistic innovations, most obvious in worship, cohere with attempts to broaden the constituency of the church. Social outreach programs to the disadvantaged include a monthly feeding and clothing giveaway activity which, along with its benevolence fund, forms a major component of the church's ministry to the poor.

Carter Temple actively supports the Christian Methodist Episcopal denomination, in which its pastor is a recognized leader.

New Covenant Missionary Baptist Church

This church is also actively engaged in the redefinition of black religious culture, but the central frame of reference of the innovation in this case is the Black Church in America, not Africa—although African symbols are sometimes invoked. At New Covenant, the heritage of the Black Church provides the assurance of God's love and saving power through "the mighty name of Jesus" in the midst of an oppressive dominant culture. The central lineage of New Covenant members is not kings and queens of Africa—although that may occasionally be mentioned—but Christian slaves who found salvation by trusting in Jesus and—this is crucial—organized a Black Church. Thus, if we are to find assurance that the Bible is true for us today, the minority in a white, secular culture that dominates us, we must remember that it was true for the slaves who trusted Jesus. If they had salvation under oppression, so can we. The Bible said so then, and it says so now. It was true then, so surely it is true now.

New Covenant is a growing church of 1,500 members with a weekly Sunday worship attendance of over 1,000. Established in 1934 on 44th Street by Pastor Thurston's grandfather, New Covenant moved to its present location in 1956, when only a few of its families lived in its new neighborhood. New Covenant engages in a large number of ministries, primarily in worship and evangelization, Christian education, and mission. Its pastor and prominent lay members are leaders in the National Baptist Convention of America, Inc.

It might reasonably be asked, where is the innovation? Nothing new here about the Black Church, at least not its history. The innovation is that New Covenant, a historically elite, "upper class church" (quoting the pastor) catering to the very black bourgeoisie Frazier wrote about, is now seeking to locate itself among the contemporary descendants of slaves who are still oppressed by the dominant culture their parents mainly sought to join. While we have only intimations of the worship style and class composition of this particular church in the 1930s, 1940s, and 1950s, it is clear that it is now providing an alternative to the liturgical life of the successful African Americans who settled neighborhoods like Chatham/GGC in that era. While Reverend Thurston's preaching is intellectually grounded, his style is expressive, he "hoops" and sings, and he constantly reminds his people that they have arrived not in the promised land but in an alien land, one in which the flesh pots are but the dominant culture's distractions from salvation through Christ, in which self-serving acquisitiveness competes with Jesus's model of service to others. Members of New Covenant are called upon to model an alternative to that culture, not to trust it and certainly not to join it. Those who have not crossed the church's threshold—which is social and cultural as well as physical—may hear its message on television or from a mission group member doing her time of service witnessing on the street or door to door. The newcomer will be welcomed into a cultural enclave that is continuous with a certain portion of the Black Church tradition, one that defines itself over against the predominant culture and is inclusive of all who trust Jesus and follow his ways. Music, preaching, education, and mission combine to define that enclave.

WORKS CITED

Michael E. Dyson, *Reflecting Black: African American Cultural Criticism.* (Minneapolis: University of Minnesota Press, 1993).

Cain Hope Felder, *Stony the Road We Trod* (Minneapolis: Fortess Press, 1991).

E. Franklin Frazier, *Black Bourgeoisie.* (New York: Collier Books, 1962), 65–71.

Bert Landry, *The Black Middle Class.* (Berkeley, CA: The University of California Press, 1987), 18–66, 67–93.

C. Eric Lincoln and Lawrence H. Mamiya, *The Black Church in the African American Experience.* (Durham, NC: Duke University Press, 1990).

Benjamin E. Mays and Joseph W. Nicholson, *The Negro's Church.* (New York: Arno Press, reprint, 1969).

Walter A. McCray, *The Black Presence in the Bible.* (Chicago, IL: Black Light Fellowship Press, 1990).

Wilson Jeremiah Moses, *The Golden Age of Black Nationalism.* (Hamden, CT: Archon books, 1978.

———, *The Wings of Ethiopia.* (Ames: Iowa State University Press, 1990).

Gayraud Wilmore, *Black Religion and Black Radicalism.* (Maryknoll, NY: Orbis Books, 1983), 192–219.

Part VIII

Claiming a Theological Voice
Black and Womanist Theologies in the Twentieth Century

Chapter Thirty-seven

Black Theology as Liberation Theology

James H. Cone

African Americans did not inherit from Western social philosophy nor from Christian doctrine the urge to freedom; it did not take Revolutionary War rhetoric nor liberation-oriented theology to confirm in them the legitimacy of their claim to an existence free from arbitrary, abusive restriction. The will to freedom is innate and pervasive. But biblical/Christian meaning symbols and conceptual language did provide avenues for locating that will in a transcendent ground, while articulating its claims in social/political discourse. The late twentieth-century appearance in academia and in church-related groups of formal statements consciously advancing a "black theology" had ample historical precursors: in writings and speeches of clergy and laity as far back as the eighteenth century; in the Negro Spirituals; in the many private and corporate acts of resistance and revolt, before and after slavery. In this chapter, James H. Cone offers a revealing account of the interactive development of civil rights, Black Power, and Black Theology.

•

Although I have discussed the impact of Black Power upon the creators of Black Theology, it may be useful to analyze the depth of their commitment to the civil rights movement and the events in it that produced such a radical change in their theological perspective.

Almost without exception (Albert Cleage being one), Black preachers and theologians had been thoroughly committed to Martin Luther King, Jr.'s method of nonviolent resistance as the only way for Blacks to achieve justice in America and they were proud to go to jail with him. They were strong advocates of integration and firm believers in King's dream that the United States would soon truly become the "land of the free and the home of the brave." Like King, their hope was deeply rooted in the Declaration of Independence, the U.S. Constitution, and the Christian claim that all human beings are created to be free. They, like other Blacks, including SNCC radicals, believed that they were living in the age in which freedom would be actualized and that their children would inherit a society that would be defined by justice and equality, not by oppression and slavery.

The successful "stride toward freedom" by King and the Blacks of Montgomery in 1955–56 marked the beginning of their hopeful struggle, motivated by the 1954 U.S. Supreme Court decision on the unconstitutionality of segregated public schooling, reinforced by the sit-ins and freedom rides of the early 1960s. The high point of their hope came with the 1963 march on Washington and King's "I Have a Dream" speech. After that speech, they firmly believed that the arrival of justice in America, long-awaited by black Americans, would soon be realized.[1]

Unfortunately we did not listen to Malcolm X and his analysis of the depth of racism in American society. After the march on Washington came Selma (1965) and then Chicago (1966). When King made his move to Chicago (1966), the first major northern urban riot had already happened—in Watts (Los Angeles), August 1965. It occurred only two weeks after Lyndon Johnson's signing of the Voting Rights Act. The Watts riot and the other eruptions like it should have told Black preachers something about the inadequacy of their analysis—both in terms of the method of nonviolence and the goal of integration.

In contrast to the South, Blacks "up North" had always been able to vote and use public facilities; the riots were dramatic indications that they had nothing for which to vote and they could not afford to live outside the ghetto. The riots were shocking evidence that the oppression of Blacks was much more complex and deeply rooted than had been articulated by Martin King. Its elimination would take more than a moral appeal to ideas of freedom and equality in the American liberal tradition or the idea of love in the traditional white view of the Christian faith.

A much more radical analysis was needed if the depth of racism was to be understood, and a much more radical method of change was needed if it was to be eliminated. Although the 1965 Watts riot clearly pointed to the bankruptcy of the ideas of integration and nonviolence, Black preachers still did not read the message. They continued along the same path of trying to achieve the "beloved community" by turning the other cheek.

However, when King took his nonviolent movement to Chicago and failed at almost every point, because he and Black preachers failed to analyze the complexity and depth of Northern racism, it began to dawn on many radical Black preachers that King's approach had serious limitations. Malcolm X began to make sense to them. It was while King was struggling against Richard Daly's racist political machine that James Meredith was shot in Mississippi, "marching against fear." The shooting of Meredith once again reminded Black Americans of the deep roots of white racism. They had a long way to go before its elimination would be a fact.

In what became the last attempt to publicly display a symbol of unity in the Black freedom struggle, King (SCLC), Stokely Carmichael (SNCC), Floyd McKissick (CORE), Whitney Young (NUL), and Roy Wilkins (NAACP) convened in Memphis in order to continue Meredith's march.[2] By the summer of 1966, SNCC and CORE members had already decided, *before* their leaders' meeting with King, Young, and Wilkins in Memphis, that a *new* day had come in the civil rights movement. Sharp conflicts between the members of the SNCC and King's SCLC had already surfaced in Albany, Washington, Selma, and other cities in the South. Differences in goals, methods, and personalities had always threatened the unity of the civil rights movement. But it was not until the Meredith-Mississippi march that everything came out in the open for the world to see.

SNCC and CORE members insisted that no whites be allowed to participate in the march and they insisted they would make no pledge of nonviolence as a response to whites' violence. Young, Wilkins, and King were truly shocked into disbelief at such a suggestion. The manifesto that defined the march stated: "This march will be a massive public indictment and protest of the failure of American society, the government of the United States, and the State of Mississippi to 'fulfill these rights' " (referring to a slogan of the Johnson administration).[3] Criticism of the Johnson administration, insistence on the exclusion of whites, and refusal to promise adherence to nonviolence were clearly viewed by mainline civil rights advocates as outside the bounds of acceptable rhetoric and behavior.

Young and Wilkins were so disturbed that anyone would make such proposals that they left, saying that they would have no part in such a march. They withdrew NAACP and NUL endorsement of it. How were they going to continue to appeal to whites for support of NAACP and NUL goals if they participated in a march from which whites were excluded, nonviolence was rejected, and the president of the United States was severely criticized? But to King's credit, he refused to leave. He debated with Carmichael and McKissick nearly all night trying to get them not to use the phrase "Black Power" and to allow whites to participate in the march under a pledge of nonviolence.

King succeeded in eliciting their commitment. The march began. But when the marchers reached Greenwood, Mississippi, the place where Carmichael had worked, he was arrested. Upon his release, Carmichael, who had been in many southern jails and the federal government had done nothing about it, mounted a platform and protested, "This is the twenty-seventh time I have been arrested—and I ain't going to jail no more!" He continued: "The only way we gonna stop them white men from whippin' us is to take over. We been saying 'freedom' for six years, and we ain't got nothin'. What we gonna start saying now is 'Black Power!' " At that moment, Willie Ricks, called "the preacher" because of his persuasive sermonic style, took over and brought the crowd to ecstasy, chanting "Black Power!" The crowd responded enthusiastically with the same phrase. Although King tried to stem the tide of the crowd's enthusiasm for "Black Power," he did not succeed and many of his own disciples followed Carmichael and Ricks. From that point on, "Black Power" replaced "freedom now," and "we shall overcome" was replaced by "we shall overrun" as slogans of young Black radicals.

The rise of Black Power created a radical change in the consciousness of many young radicals in the SNCC and their followers. Organized in the spring of 1960, they had adopted King's nonviolent direct action as a strategy for social change, even though most did not accept it as an ideology. They had used King's method throughout the South—Mississippi, Georgia, Alabama, and Arkansas. By 1966, after attending many of their comrades' funerals, after being beaten and shot as the FBI took notes and did nothing, the complexity and depth of white racism became clearer to them. They wryly noted that northern Blacks burned the cities even though they had the "rights" that southern Blacks risked their lives to achieve.

The Black power cry was the response of young Blacks to white power that had camouflaged itself in the Christian garb of love. It was their way of saying to whites that they were "on to their tricks" and thus would no longer allow them to use Martin King's idea of Christian love to keep the Black revolution in check. They now sang:

> I love everybody,
> I love everybody,
> I love everybody in my heart,

but they quickly added:

> I just told a lie,
> I just told a lie,
> I just told a lie in my heart.[4]

Young Black preachers were placed in an existential dilemma. Their faith was closer to King's but their politics closer to Carmichael's. In an effort to resolve the conflict, they began to reflect on how the gospel can be reconciled with the Black Power politics of liberation, especially as articulated by young Black radicals who claimed that Blacks should take their freedom "by any means necessary." Although they respected King and admired his commitment to justice, they could no longer embrace nonviolence as an ideology, nor could they affirm integration as the goal of the Black freedom struggle. But inasmuch as King, along with white churches and theologians, had defined Christianity as being identical with love, and love as being identical with nonviolence and integration, how could they retain their Christian identity and also support the Black Power claim that Blacks should take their freedom "by any means necessary"? That was their theological dilemma. How could radical Black preachers retain their Christian identity and also be as committed, as Black Power advocates, to Black liberation, refusing to accept white brutality with a turned cheek?

Black Power advocates made no claim to an identity derived from Christianity. Most were secular university students or adherents of African religions and all tended to define Christianity as "the white man's religion." Black preachers, in their struggle to be Christian *and* support Black Power, had to develop a theology that was distinctly Black and also accountable to our faith. It was in this context that Albert Cleage wrote the *Black Messiah* and I wrote *Black Theology and Black Power*.[5] I wanted to show that Black Power and the gospel were identical and that both focused on the politics of liberation.

It was not easy to connect Black Power with the Christian gospel. The advocates of Black Power were not only un-Christian, they were hostile to Christianity, viewing it as a white religion. Furthermore, most Christians, Black and white, were hostile to Black Power, viewing it as the opposite of everything that their faith represented. When Black Power advocates emerged as leaders in the Black movement, they de-Christianized the Black struggle for justice by emphasizing Black separatism and self-defense. As long as King was the acknowledged symbol and standard-bearer of the movement, it remained Christian, emphasizing love, integration, and nonviolence. But emergence of Malcolm's philosophy through Black Power meant the introduction of a radicalization that excluded Christianity.

Black Theology arose as an attempt to stem the tide of the irrelevance of Christianity by combining both Christianity and Blackness, Martin and Malcolm, Black Church and Black Power, even though neither side thought it was possible. The early interpreters of Black Theology were theologians "on the boundary" (to use Paul Tillich's self-evaluation) between integration and separation, nonviolence and self-defense, "love our white enemies and love our Black skins." They refused to sacrifice either emphasis; they insisted on the absolute necessity of both.

Black Church History

When Black preachers were confronted with the dilemma posed by Black Power, they began to search Black Church history for insights and models that would illustrate and support their claim that the gospel of Jesus is identical with Blacks' liberation from political bondage. Their search focused on their radical Black forebears, chiefly in the masculine line. To be sure, Black preachers sometimes mentioned Harriet Tubman and Sojourner Truth, but unfortunately Black women did not occupy a prominent place in their analysis.[6] Richard Allen, Daniel Payne, Andrew Bryan, George Leile, James Varick, and Christopher Rush emerged as significant advocates for an independent Black Church movement that began in the late eighteenth century.[7]

But these Black churchmen were not radical enough for the era of Black Power. It was Nat Turner, Gabriel Prosser, Denmark Vesey, Henry Highland Garnet, David Walker, Henry McNeil Turner, and others like them, who helped young Black radical preachers articulate a Black version of the gospel. It differed from an appeal to integration, love, and nonviolence and thus, to everyone's surprise, was quite similar to the message of Black Power in the 1960s.

Prosser, Vesey, and Turner were insurrectionists. They had organized slave revolts in 1800, 1822, and 1831, respectively, in the name of the gospel and Black freedom.[8] Garnet's "Address to the Slaves" in 1843 and David Walker's *Appeal* in 1829 sounded like Black Power music to our ears. They too had urged rebellion against the evils of slavery, comparing our condition in the United States with the Hebrew slaves' in ancient Egypt.[9] Henry M. Turner's claim that "God Is a Negro" (1898) suggested a historical and theological depth to the claim that God is on the side of Blacks for freedom.[10]

Black theologians and preachers of the 1960s began to realize that they were not the first to attempt to find theological meaning in Blackness and the gospel. Indeed, Blacks have a usable heritage, a revolutionary past, that can give direction in the search for the truth of the gospel in the struggle for Black freedom.

We also found out how little we knew about Black history, especially a Black history that correctly located the role of the Black Church. All we knew were a few denominational histories and as few names of nineteenth-century Black preachers.

Our denominational histories could hardly stand the test of critical scholarship, for they were written from the perspective of a particular ecclesiastical history and for the purpose of glorifying its leaders. Some few other personages were hardly known beyond a few historical references: not enough to give us substantive guidance in the age of Black Power.

Unfortunately no serious research had been done on the history of the Black Church since Carter G. Woodson's *The History of the Negro Church* (1921). E. Franklin Frazier's brief volume *The Negro Church in America* (1961) was helpful but was too much of a sociological reduction as defined by the University of Chicago school of sociology. "The Negro Church" (1903) by W. E. B. Du Bois in his Atlanta University Publications was useful, but it was even older than Woodson's work. Benjamin E. Mays's *The Negro's God* (1938) and his volume with J. W. Nicholson on *The Negro's Church* (1933), though not as old as the works by Du Bois or Woodson, did not adequately meet our historical needs. What we needed was a well-written, comprehensive, and scholarly history of the Black Church and religion that could meet the test of both critical historical scholarship and also be useful in our attempt to develop a Black Theology.

Gayraud Wilmore responded to that need by writing his *Black Religion and Black Radicalism* (1972). This text is one of the most important contributions emerging out of the Black Theology movement. A social ethicist by academic training and an ordained minister in the Presbyterian church, Wilmore has been the moving force behind the NCBC, serving as its historian and theologian. More than anyone else, he was deeply committed to uncovering our history, not just in the United States, but all the way back to our African past. He would not let young Black radicals remain content with sloganeering about Black Church heroes but pushed them to search for the religions of Africa before the whites came with their slave ships. He encouraged us to study African Traditional Religions, and he was one of the chief forces behind the NCBC creation of an African commission, which established dialogues with African church persons.

From the very beginning, Wilmore's concern was to create a Black Theology that was truly Black—that is, *African*—and not a white version of Western Christianity colored Black. He wanted the definition of Black Theology to be shaped by an African meaning of liberation and not simply by Western bourgeois ideas of freedom and equality or a Marxist idea of liberation. The key to Wilmore's new appreciation of the autonomy of the Black religious tradition—or at least one important and neglected stream of it—was W. E. B. Du Bois's *The Souls of Black Folk* (1903). It was Du Bois who pushed him toward Africa, and Wilmore then pushed us to read John Mbiti (*African Religions and Philosophy;*[11] *New Testament Eschatology in an African Background*),[12] Bolaji Idowu (*Olódùmare: God in Yoruba Belief;*[13] *Towards an Indigenous Church*),[14] Harry Sawyerr (*Creative Evangelism;*[15] *God: Ancestor or Creator?*),[16] and Kwesi Dickson and Paul Ellingworth (editors of *Biblical Revelation and African Beliefs*).[17]

Charles H. Long, then professor of the history of religions at the University of Chicago and later at the University of North Carolina at Chapel Hill, concurred with Wilmore as to the importance of the study of African religions.[18] Jerome Long,

Charles's brother, also supported the same emphasis, as did my brother Cecil Cone in his *Identity Crisis in Black Theology*.[19] We had many spirited debates about the role of African religions in Black Theology, with some advocating it as a source equally important as Christianity in the definition of Black religion and others defending biblical Christianity as its primary source.

Two meanings of liberation emerged from our historical past. One emphasized sociopolitical freedom as derived from the biblical theme of the exodus and nineteenth-century Black freedom fighters. The other emphasized cultural liberation as derived from the black nationalism of H. M. Turner, Marcus Garvey, Malcolm X, and especially the religions of Africa. No one wanted to exclude either emphasis entirely, but there was much debate about which should be normative for the definition of Black Theology.[20]

Although we debated our differences about the precise meaning of liberation, we all agreed that it had to be defined by our Black past. There can be no creative theology without a tradition upon which to base it. We knew that if we were going to sustain our attempt to make a Black Theology of liberation, we had to find persons in our history who had laid the groundwork for us. Therefore the attempt to create a Black Theology of liberation meant searching for its meaning in our historical past.

The Bible

In addition to Black Power and Black Church history, many Black theologians and preachers turned directly to the Bible for the content of the meaning of liberation as a theological category. Realization of the usefulness of the Bible as a support for the liberation of the Black poor came partly from our study of Black Church history. Henry Garnet, David Walker, Nat Turner, Gabriel Prosser, Harriet Tubman, Sojourner Truth, and many other Black freedom fighters used the scriptures in support of their resistance to and rebellion against oppression and slavery. In addition there were the Black spirituals and their emphasis on freedom—both here and hereafter. Although the Black spirituals had been interpreted as being exclusively otherworldly and compensatory, our research into the testimonies of Black slave narratives and other Black sayings revealed that the theme of heaven in the spirituals and in Black religion generally contained double meanings.[21] "Steal away" referred not only to an eschatological realm, but it was also used by Harriet Tubman as a signal of freedom for slaves who intended to run away with her to the North, or to Canada.[22] According to Frederick Douglass, the song "O Canaan" referred not only to heaven but also to Canada and the North.[23] In these slave songs were found also unambiguous demands for freedom:

> O Freedom! O Freedom!
> O Freedom! I love thee,
> And before I'll be a slave
> I be buried in my grave
> And go home to my Lord and be free.

A similar emphasis is found in "Go Down, Moses." While many Black leaders from Harriet Tubman to Martin King have been identified with Moses, almost all Blacks in America—past and present—have identified Egypt with America, Pharaoh and the Egyptians with white slaveholders and subsequent racists, and Blacks with the Israelite slaves:

> Go down, Moses,
> Way down in Egyptland,
> Tell old Pharaoh
> To let my people go.
>
> When Israel was in Egyptland,
> Let my people go,
> Oppressed so hard they could not stand,
> Let my people go.
>
> Go down, Moses,
> Way down in Egyptland,
> Tell old Pharaoh,
> "Let my people go."
>
> "Thus saith the Lord," bold Moses said,
> "Let my people go;
> If not I'll smite your first-born dead.
> Let my people go."
>
> Go down, Moses,
> Way down in Egyptland,
> Tell old Pharaoh,
> "Let my people go!"

With the Old Testament sharply in view, the New Testament Jesus was defined as the liberator whose ministry was in solidarity with, and whose death was on behalf of, the poor. In our investigation of our own Black Church history, we were driven to Scripture itself so as to analyze its message in the light of our struggle for freedom.

Because white theologians and preachers denied any relationship between the Scriptures and our struggle for freedom, we bypassed the classic Western theological tradition and went directly to Scripture for its word regarding our Black struggle. Although whites looked down with a condescending intellectual arrogance at our attempt to uncover a liberation theme in the Scriptures, we were not discouraged. Intuitively we knew that we were right, and they were wrong. Furthermore some of us had been trained by them, with a few doctorates to our credit, and we did not internalize everything we were taught. Besides, some things we had been taught in the seminary had far more revolutionary potential than our white teachers had envisioned.

For example, almost every biblical and theological teacher I had encountered in graduate school, as well as most of the well-known biblical scholars I read, claimed that revelation was not an abstract propositional truth but rather a historical event,

God's involvement in history. Many of us had read Ernest G. Wright's *Book of the Acts of God*, Oscar Cullmann's *Christ and Time*, Gerhard von Rad's *Theology of the Old Testament*, Bernard Anderson's *Understanding the Old Testament*, and many other neo-orthodox biblical scholars. We merely asked that if God is known by God's acts in history, what, then, is God doing in and through historical events? What is the meaning of salvation as an act of God? Basing ourselves on the exodus and the message of the prophets, we Black theologians agreed with our neo-orthodox teachers that God is known by God's acts in history and that these acts are identical with the liberation of the weak and the poor.

As long as we Blacks located the liberating acts of God for the poor in ancient Hebrew history, that was acceptable biblical exegesis from the viewpoint of white scholars. But when we tried to do systematic theology on the basis of our exegesis, applying God's liberating acts to our contemporary situation in the United States, focusing on the relations between Blacks and whites, white scholars vehemently rejected both the procedure and the message. They tried to get around our contemporary application of the biblical message by saying that there were other themes in the Bible besides liberation (which we never denied). Our concern was to locate the dominant theme in scripture and to ask what its message was for the Black struggle for freedom today.

We Black theologians contended that if God sided with the poor and the weak in biblical times, then why not today? If salvation is a historical event of rescue, a deliverance of Blacks from white American racial oppression? When we pressed these questions on white theologians and preachers, they always turned to the white, meek, pale-faced, blue-eyed Jesus, as if we Blacks were expected to embrace him as our Savior. But we vehemently rejected that Jesus.

In place of the white Jesus, we insisted that "Jesus Christ is Black, baby!" That sent shock waves throughout the white seminary and church communities. Whites thought that Blacks had lost their religious sanity. It was one thing to identify liberation as the central message of the Bible, but something else to introduce color into Christology. They could even keep their composure as we discussed together whether the title "liberator" can be appropriately applied to Jesus or whether he was a revolutionary. But to color Jesus Black, that was going too far, and they could hardly sit still during the discussion. "That is racism in reverse!" they said, "and such a claim has no biblical warrant." But we did not listen to them. We merely searched the Scriptures with the resources we had, knowing that in time the truth of our claim would be demonstrated so clearly that even whites would have to take notice of it!

The vehement rejection of the Black Jesus by whites merely reinforced the determination of Black clergy radicals to develop a Christology that took seriously Jesus's Blackness—both literally and symbolically.[24] The literal significance of Jesus's Blackness meant that he *was not* white! He was a Palestinian Jew whose racial ancestry may have been partly African but definitely not European. Therefore, white pictures of Jesus in Christian churches and homes are nothing but an ideological distortion of the biblical portrait. By making this point, Black clergy radicals wanted to show that the so-called scientific biblical exegesis of white scholars frequently was not scientific at all. For they have helped to maintain the white image of Jesus through their silence about his true color, thereby suggesting the European Jesus was the historical one.

The major importance of the claim that "Jesus is Black" rested on the symbolic meaning of that affirmation. We were strongly influenced by Bishop Henry M. Turner's claim that "God is a Negro" and Countee Cullen's poetic reflections on "The Black Christ" (1929), which Sterling Brown referred to as "a narrative poem about lynching."[25] The Blackness of Jesus had definite political implications that we derived from the New Testament witness. It was our way of saying that his cross and resurrection represented God's solidarity with the oppressed in their struggle for liberation. The oppressed do not have to accept their present misery as the final definition of their humanity. The good news is: God, the Holy One of Israel, has entered the human situation in Jesus and has transformed it through his cross and resurrection. The poor no longer have to remain in poverty. They are now free to fight for their freedom, because God is fighting with them. In the United States this claim meant that God was on the side of oppressed Blacks in their struggle for freedom and against whites who victimized them. For Black clergy radicals, the best way to describe that insight was to say that "Jesus is Black."

Of course, the Blackness of Jesus did not mean that he could not be described also as red, brown, yellow, or by some other characteristic that defined materially the condition of the poor in the United States and other parts of the globe. Black clergy radicals never denied the universal significance of Jesus's death and resurrection. We merely wanted to emphasize the theological significance of Jesus in the context of the Black liberation struggle in the United States. We wanted to expose the racism of white churches and also encourage Black churches to embrace the biblical Christ who looks much more like oppressed Blacks than white oppressors.

White theologians resented our refusal to listen to them, because they had taught us and they were the experts in the field. But I ask any fair observer, why should we listen to those who have done nothing to assist Blacks in their liberation struggle? White biblical scholars have not even bothered to train Blacks to acquire the skills that they regard as necessary for sound biblical exegesis. What right, then, do they have to say that our exegesis is unsound? We Blacks merely responded to white scholars by saying that the kingdom that Jesus embodied in his life, death, and resurrection was not promised to the learned but to the meek, the humble, and the poor. If white biblical exegetes think that the God of Jesus gave them a hermeneutical privilege in biblical interpretation, then they have not only misread Scripture but have substituted their scientific knowledge about the Bible for a genuine encounter with biblical faith.

Despite the prescientific approach by most Blacks to the Bible, we claimed that their focus on liberation was historically accurate and theologically sound.[26] A study of Black Church history, therefore, led us to a study of scripture, and once again the theme of liberation became the dominant emphasis.

European Political Theologies

In 1967, Jürgen Moltmann's *Theology of Hope*[27] was published in the United States. It emphasized the biblical theme of God's promise as embodied in the struggles of the poor for freedom. Later the works of Johannes B. Metz also stressed a similar eschatological theme.[28] The theology of hope with a political ingredient became a dominant theme in American theology, and many conferences were held in order to explore its implications. Moltmann and Metz lectured frequently in the United States.[29]

I remember well the excitement of reading Moltmann and Metz, one Protestant and the other Catholic. "Now," I said to myself, "my view of liberation in the Bible has some theological support from Germany—widely known as having the leading theological centers in the world. How will run-of-the-mill white North American theologians now be able to deny Black theologians' claims about the theme of liberation in the Bible?" The feeling that Moltmann's theology supported the liberation of the poor accounted for why he was quoted so liberally in my work; he provided "respectable" theological support for my claims regarding God's solidarity with the poor.[30]

Other Black theologians were also influenced by Moltmann and Metz. The title of the first book by Major J. Jones on Black Theology reflects this dependence—*Black Awareness: A Theology of Hope.*[31] The writings of J. Deotis Roberts refer frequently to Moltmann and Metz.[32] Black theologians quoted from European theologians because they had developed a theological language that appeared to support similar claims in Black Theology. White North American theologians could ignore our attempts to develop an argument for a Black Theology of liberation on the basis of our limited knowledge of scientific exegesis, but we knew that they would not (indeed, could not!) ignore major European theologians, for Europe is the continent of their origin and the place to which they and their students frequently return in order to deepen their theological knowledge. If a major European theologian said something, North Americans listened carefully, even if they strongly disagreed. As we Black theologians expected, white Americans did pay close attention to the European theology of hope (political theology).

But European theologians did not help us as much in developing a language for Black Theology as we had originally expected.[33] Indeed we Black theologians began to move away from the progressive theologies of Europe when we saw how easily they were adopted by white North Americans as a substitute for taking Black Theology seriously. How could white North American theologians devote so much attention to the hope thematized in European theology and completely ignore the hope emerging from the nearly three hundred and fifty years of Black struggle in North America?[34]

The songs of hope, the "Negro spirituals," seemed to be the logical place to turn for any North American theological reflection on hope. Why were they ignored by white North American theologians who claimed to be interested in applying the ideas of hope and promise to life in the United States? Their silence baffled me, because the spirituals played such a dominant role in the civil rights movement. Furthermore, many of these same theologians were present at the march on Washington and had marched with King in Selma, singing these songs as everyone else, because of the empowerment and the courage they bestowed upon the marchers. Why, then, did they ignore them when they sat down at their seminary or university desks to reflect on hope? Were white theologians too blinded by their own racism to hear the truth of the gospel that was erupting from the struggles of the Black poor?

It seemed that the silence of white theologians on Black Theology and religion was and is their way of saying that Blacks cannot think. But as Gustavo Gutiérrez has said, "Even the poor have the right to think. The right to think is the corollary of the human right to be, and to assert the right to think is only to assert the right to exist."[35] By ignoring our hopes and dreams in their theologies of hope, white progressive theologians were saying that Blacks cannot think, because they do not exist. That was why some of them could say, and still do, that there is no such thing as Black Theology.

The white theologians' claim that there is no such thing as Black Theology did not upset us; white acceptance was never our primary concern. Indeed, in one sense, I was pleased with their dismissal of Black Theology because it meant I was even more free to reread the Bible without having to answer the technical concerns of white theological academics. It also made me more determined to create a Black Theology of liberation that was not dependent upon my white theological mentors.

When whites asked me whether Black Theology was a "fad," I responded negatively, and with a theological confidence, and touch of arrogance that showed my disdain for anyone who asked such a question. I often said, "With over twenty million Blacks in the United States, most of whom are extremely poor, how can you be so insensitive as to ask whether reflection on their religious history is a passing fad?"

The Black theologians' move away from the political theologies of Europe was also motivated by our uneasiness over their tendency toward theological abstractions. Progressive theologians of Europe were not concrete; they did not name enemies.[36] It was the Latin American liberation theologians' critique of the progressive theologies of Europe that really demonstrated the Achilles' heel of European progressive theologies.

Gustavo Gutiérrez's distinction between the problem of the unbeliever as created by the European Enlightenment and the problem of the nonperson as created by European colonization and exploitation of the Third World clarified our unexpressed suspicion about the political theologies of Europe. "The poor," he writes, "are not, in the first instance, questioning the religious world or its philosophical presuppositions. They are calling into question first of all the economic, social, and political order that oppresses and marginalizes them."[37] And he also observes that "one of the best ways to refute a theology is to look at its practical consequences, not its intellectual arguments."[38] When we Blacks observed the practical consequences of European thought and its North American mirroring, it was quite clear that we could not base Black Theology on a liberation derived from Europe.

We then decided to incorporate into Black Theology the challenge of Frantz Fanon, a West Indian deeply involved in the Algerian war for independence from

France. Fanon helped us to realize that we must be suspicious of European intellectuals even when they use a language of liberation that appears to be supportive of the Third World. Not everything that is is what it appears to be. Underneath the European language of freedom and equality there is slavery and death. That was why Fanon said:

> Come, then, comrades; it would be well to decide at once to change our ways. We must shake off the heavy darkness in which we were plunged, and leave it behind. The new day which is already at hand must find us firm, prudent and resolute. We must leave our dreams and abandon our old beliefs and friendships of the time before life began. Let us waste no time in sterile litanies and nauseating mimicry. Leave this Europe where they are never done talking of [humanity], yet murder [human beings] everywhere they find them, at the corner of their own streets, in all the corners of the globe. For centuries they have stifled almost whole of humanity in the name of a so-called spiritual experience. Look at them swaying between atomic and spiritual disintegration.[39]

Fanon captured our imagination because his analysis rang true and he convinced us that Black thought could create no genuine future for its people by looking to Europe for support. Europeans created the problem that necessitated our need for liberation and it was naive of us to expect that our theological salvation could come from Europe: "That same Europe where they were never done talking of [humanity], and where they never stopped proclaiming that they were only anxious for the welfare of [humanity]: today we know with what sufferings humanity has paid for every one of their triumphs of the mind."[40]

Fanon's challenge involved more than turning away from Europe; it also involved a turning to the resources found in the victimized peoples of the world: "If we want humanity to advance a step further, if we want to bring it up to a different level than that which Europe has shown it, then we must invent and we must make discoveries.... For Europe, for ourselves, and for humanity, comrades, we must then turn over a new leaf, we must work out new concepts, and try to set afoot a new [humanity]."[41]

The application of Fanon's message to Black Theology affected our understanding of our theological task. We now realized it consisted in something more than simply ebonizing European concepts in theology. Gayraud Wilmore and Charles Long saw the necessity and complexity of this task much clearer than most of us. They took the lead in directing Black theologians to Africa first and then to Latin America and Asia.

Third World Theologies

When Black clergy radicals began to develop a Black Theology of liberation, they had no knowledge of a similar theological development going on in Africa, Asia, and Latin America. To be sure, like most civil rights activists, we had been influenced by the rise of the African movement toward independent nations during the 1950s and 1960s, and we had heard about a parallel movement in religion, creating a renewed interest in African Traditional Religions and indigenous churches. Missionary churches, implanted by European and white North American missionaries, were being critically evaluated through the newly created organization called the All Africa Conference of Churches (AACC). The AACC, founded in 1958, was similar to the NCBC in that it was ecumenical and it began to provide the context for the creation of an African theology that would question the Europeanization of the gospel.[42] But despite these creative political and theological irruptions in Africa, the early interpreters of Black Theology did not know much about them. Most of us had never been to Africa and had spent little time studying it.

Although Frantz Fanon's *The Wretched of the Earth* was the catalyst that drew our attention away from Europe, it was Gayraud Wilmore and Charles Long who accepted the radical implications of his challenge and pushed us toward Africa as the critical source for the development of a Black Theology based on Black religion. When we began to read African theologians, such as John Mbiti and Bolaji Idowu, their talk about "Africanization" and "indigenization" reinforced the importance of cultural liberation, which many North American Black nationalists had stressed.

Some of us, however, were greatly disturbed about the political conservatism of many African theologians. We knew that Fanon would not look favorably upon a cultural nationalism that did not radically transform economics and politics. But despite our reservations, we continued to listen carefully and viewed African theology as far more important to us than European political theology. When Black theologians of South Africa responded theologically to their situation of oppression by using the phrase "Black Theology," North American Black theologians became even more determined to learn from Africa in our efforts to develop a theology that was Black both politically and culturally.[43]

Many Black theologians were greatly surprised to discover that Latin American theologians were using the term "liberation" to define the heart of the gospel.[44] Almost none of us knew Spanish and thus were limited in our knowledge of Latin American theology. However, because American white religious radicals of a socialist bent (at least in language) adopted them, as liberal and neo-orthodox white theologians adopted the progressive theologies of Europe, we Blacks were very skeptical of this new liberation theology from Latin America.[45] Why were white religious radicals so interested in the poor in Latin America and so indifferent to the poor Black in North America? I was reminded of Sartre's comment: "The only way of helping the enslaved out there is to side with those who are here."

Furthermore, Latin American theologians' focus on classism and their silence on racism troubled many Black theologians. In Brazil alone, there are more than 40 million Blacks and in Latin America more than 70 million. Why, then, are there no Black or Amerindian theologies among them? I have written about the early encounters of Black and Latin American theologies elsewhere, and at another time I shall comment upon our mutual support, along with African and Asian theologies, in our efforts to create a common Third World theology.[46] My concern here is to emphasize that during the early development of Black Theology, we Blacks were much too suspicious to learn as much as we should have. An early incorporation of class analysis into Black Theology could have prevented some of its most obvious and excessive weaknesses, which I shall take up later.

Most of us did not know anything about Asian theology. Dialogue with Asian Christians is more recent, and it is quite promising.

Black clergy radicals began to develop a Black Theology of liberation springing from the particularity of our history, the urgency of our present struggles, and our creative hope for the future. Most of our ideas about liberation came from the depth of our political and spiritual struggle as we attempted to make sense out of Black existence in white America. Although Black preachers' formal theological knowledge may have been limited and most did not have the educational credentials that would have entitled them to teach in white universities and seminaries, yet they did have the prophetic vision that enabled them to discern the truth of the time. Black Theology, therefore, was created out of the sermonic imagination of Black preachers as they fought to establish the freedom for their people that white Americans had denied but that God had foretold and promised.

The Literature of Black Theology and Religion

Although Black clergy radicals were the chief initiators of the idea of a Black Theology, a small number of Black Theologians in seminaries, universities, and colleges were often present during their deliberations. Near the end of the 1960s, writings of Black professors began to be published.

The "dean" of Black scholarship in religion is without doubt C. Eric Lincoln, who was a professor of sociology and religion at Union Theological Seminary during the late 1960s and early 1970s and later took up a similar post at Duke University. He is the author of the classic study *The Black Muslims in America* (1961).[47] Additional texts include *My Face Is Black* (1964),[48] *The Sounds of the Struggle* (1967),[49] *The Black Church since Frazier* (1974),[50] and (as editor) *The Black Experience in Religion* (1974).[51]

In addition to his many published books and articles on Black religion, no one has done more than Lincoln in encouraging Black scholars to write and to publish. His C. Eric Lincoln Series in Black Religion made it possible for Black scholars to publish their radical ideas.

Although Joseph Washington's *Black Religion* was strongly criticized by almost all Black scholars and preachers, the importance of the text should not be minimized. Its importance is not simply the negative function it served in motivating Black theologians to develop a Black Theology. It served a positive function that is not often emphasized. Washington's *Black Religion* was the first text to demonstrate the uniqueness of Black Religion, separating it from Protestantism, Catholicism, Judaism, and secularism. This was a major scholarly achievement, and it should be recognized as such. Black scholars (Gayraud Wilmore, Cecil Cone, Henry Mitchell) used his arguments to demonstrate the uniqueness of Black religion even though they rejected his negative appraisal of it. Washington actually reconsidered his views in his next book, *The Politics of God* (1967).[52] His *Black and White Power Subreption* (1969)[53] was an important treatment of the theology of Black Power, and his *Black Sects and Cults* (1972)[54] represented a further investigation of the African roots of Black religion.

The first texts on Black Theology were my *Black Theology and Black Power* (1969) and *A Black Theology of Liberation* (1970). Both used liberation as the central theme of the gospel message and thus as the organizing principle for the systematic presentation of the Christian gospel from the standpoint of the Black struggle for freedom. The next volume, with a similar purpose in mind, was *God of the Oppressed* (1975).

J. Deotis Roberts is an important scholar in Black Theology; he has published several texts and many articles on the theme, the most important being *Liberation and Reconciliation: A Black Theology* (1971) and *Black Political Theology* (1974). Roberts is best known for an emphasis on reconciliation along with liberation in contrast to what he regarded as my one-sided stress on the latter.

A similar treatment to Roberts's was Major Jones's *Black Awareness: A Theology of Hope* (1971) and his *Christian Ethics for Black Theology* (1974).[55] His ethics and theology are closer to those of Martin Luther King, Jr., with an emphasis on love and reconciliation in black-white relationships. Although I have been critical of both Roberts's and Jones's views in Black Theology—because of what I considered as overemphasis on white theological norms for Black Theology—they will always be regarded as among the major interpreters of Black Theology, bridging the gap between the Martin King era and the rise of Black Power in religion and in the churches.[56]

No one has provided a deeper challenge to Black Theology than has the philosophical critique of William Jones. His book, *Is God a White Racist?* (1973),[57] shook Black theologians out of their "liberation complacency" and forced them to deal with the problem of theodicy at a deeper level. If God is liberating the Black poor from oppression, as Black theologians say, where is the liberation event that can serve as evidence of that fact? The question has not been answered to anyone's satisfaction, and thus continues to serve as a check against the tendency of substituting liberation rhetoric for actual events of freedom.

Another text that sparked a great deal of discussion was that by Cecil W. Cone, *The Identity Crisis in Black Theology* (1975).[58] Along with Wilmore's *Black Religion and Black Radicalism* (1972) and important articles by Charles H. Long, Cecil Cone's book criticized Black liberation theologians for their emphasis on political liberation and also for their dependence on white theologians, thereby separating them from the religion of the "Almighty Sovereign God" of the Black people. He claimed that an authentic Black Theology must use Black religion as its chief source.

Although Wilmore agreed with Cecil Cone regarding Black religion as the chief source of Black Theology, he disagreed with him regarding *who* had the identity crisis. According to Wilmore, "the crisis is not in black theology but in the contemporary black church."[59] Wilmore's perspective on Black religion and theology is persuasively argued in his *Black Religion and Black Radicalism*.

Differing with Cecil Cone at a different point was Charles Long, who questioned whether a Black Theology of liberation is possible in any sense if one takes Black religion seriously. He claims that theology is a discipline of European conquerors and thus alien to the experience of Blacks who have been enslaved by them.[60]

I have already discussed the significant impact of Albert Cleage's *Black Messiah* (1968); his *Black Christian Nationalism* (1972)[61] is a practical analysis of his theological program. Other early interpreters of Black Theology and religion included Henry Mitchell (*Black Preaching* [1970][62] and *Black Belief* [1975]);[63] Lawrence Jones, who wrote important articles in history;[64] Preston Williams, Herbert Edwards, and Carlton Lee, who made contributions in social ethics;[65] Robert Bennett in Bible studies;[66] Bishop Joseph Johnson and Warner Traynham in theology.[67] Leonard Barrett's *Soul Force* (1974)[68] is an important study of Black religion in the United States, Africa, and the West Indies.

No list of literature in Black Theology and religion of the 1960s and early 1970s would be complete without mentioning the outstanding work of Vincent Harding. His essay "No Turning Back?" is required reading for anyone interested in a critical interpretation of the documents of the NCBC. His "Black Power and the American Christ" and "The Religion of Black Power" are important for an interpretation of the mood that gave birth to Black Power and the challenge it presented to a religion of love based on the typical American theological perspective.

Since the late 1960s and early 1970s many Black scholars have been writing in the area of Black Theology, dwelling on different aspects and variations on the theme of liberation. The Fund for Theological Education and the Society for the Study of Black Religion, both then under the direction of C. Shelby Rooks (later president of Chicago Theological Seminary), did much to support and to encourage young Black scholars.[69]

Although the number of Black theologians has increased since 1966, there are still significant problems to be addressed in relation to the strengths and weaknesses of Black Theology in terms of its origin and present state. And if we Black theologians are hesitant to critically evaluate our work, then we should ask: For whom do we do theology—for ourselves or the Black poor? If the latter, then we must critically evaluate our work in order to assess whether it is accomplishing what we claim.

NOTES

1. King's dream that the "beloved community" could be accomplished through nonviolent direct action was shared by most Black Americans, including younger members of the SNCC, even though many of the latter did not share its Christian orientation. It is necessary to know the depth of the commitment of young Blacks to the achievement of justice through nonviolence and their perceived betrayal by white liberals and the federal government if one is to understand why they turned to Black power. See especially Clayborne Carson, *In Struggle: SNCC and the Black Awakening of the 1960s* (Harvard University Press, 1981). Julius Lester's "The Angry Children of Malcolm X," in Meier, Rudwick, and Broderick, *Black Protest Thought* (New York: Bobbs-Merrill, 1971) is required reading. Vincent Harding's *The Other American Revolution.* (Los Angeles: Center for Afro-American Studies, 1980) is also important. An excellent autobiographical account is that by James Forman, *The Making of Black Revolutionaries* (New York: Macmillan, 1972). See also the illuminating essay by Emily Stopher, "The Student Nonviolent Coordinating Committee: The Rise and Fall of a Redemptive Organization." *Journal of Black Studies 8*, no. 1, September 1977; and the important book by Howard

Zinn, SNCC: *The New Abolitionists* (Boston: Beacon Press, 1964). Lerone Bennett, "The Rise of Black Power," *Ebony* (February 1969): 36–42, is also useful. For an interpretation of the SNCC's move from Martin King's ideas to Black power, see Gene Roberts, "The Story of SNICK: From 'Freedom High' to Black Power," *New York Times Magazine*, September 25, 1966. An excellent interpretation of the need for Black power is Stokely Carmichael, "What We Want," *New York Review of Books*, Sept. 22, 1966.

2. For interpretations of the events surrounding the continuation of the Meredith march, see especially Harding, *The Other American Revolution*, chap. 28; Robert Brisbane, *Black Activism* (Valley Forge, Penn.: Judson, 1974), chap. 6; Harvard Stikoff, *The Struggle for Black Equality* (New York: Hill and Wang, 1981), chap. 7; Paul Good, *The Trouble I've Seen* (Washington, D.C.: Howard University Press, 1975): 247–72; Carson, *In Struggle*, chaps. 13 and 14.

3. Harding, *The Other American Revolution*, 186.

4. Ibid., 186–87.

5. Perhaps I should say a word about the differences between Albert Cleage and myself. There are many, but they all stem from one central difference: the theological value of skin color. I do not believe that God has created Blacks with more propensity toward the good than whites or any other people. All persons were created in the image of God and all have sinned against creation, claiming for ourselves more than we ought. Furthermore I do not share Cleage's historical judgment about the "Black Nation of Israel" or of the African origins of Jesus. Even if his interpretation was based on factual evidence; the theological conclusion must point to a God concerned about the salvation of all, including whites. Cleage's Black Christian Nationalism is such a reaction to white racism, as was Elijah Muhammad's Nation of Islam that influenced him, that he fails completely to recognize the oneness of all human beings. *Whatever else we may say about the methods that Martin Luther King, Jr., used in the civil rights movement, his "beloved community" is the goal of every genuine Christian, for without this element the gospel is no longer the gospel.* It is Cleage's inordinate focus on the particularity of Blackness that has led him to place the universalism of the gospel in jeopardy, turning it into an ideology. That is also why he rejects the letters of Paul and Jesus' resurrection as essential elements in his theological perspective. What Black Christian can take Cleage seriously when he appears to show no respect for genuine biblical Christianity?

Despite my differences with Cleage's theology, our similarities were and still are much more significant, the most important of which is the centrality of Blackness and its connection with liberation in the definition of the gospel for the Black community. This agreement between us made us allies in our common effort to make the Christian faith relevant to the Black struggle for freedom.

6. Sojourner Truth is best known for her speeches against slavery in the abolitionist movement, and Harriet Tubman has been called the "Moses" of her people because of her liberation of herself and more than three hundred other Blacks to freedom. See *Sojourner Truth: Narrative and Book of Life*, Ebony Classics (Chicago: Johnson, 1970); Jacqueline Bernard, *Journey Toward Freedom: The Story of Sojourner Truth* (New York: Dell, 1967); Hertha Pauli, *Her Name Was Sojourner Truth* (New York: Camelot/Avon, 1962). The best and most comprehensive treatment of Harriet Tubman's life is that by Earl Conrad, *Harriet Tubman* (New York: Paul E. Eriksson, 1969); see also Sarah Bradford, *Harriet Tubman: The Moses of Her People* (Secaucus, N.J.: Citadel, 1974, originally published in 1869).

7. Richard Allen was the founder and first bishop of the A.M.E. Church (1816). Daniel Alexander Payne was also a bishop and is best known for his emphasis on education and his initiative in purchasing and later serving as president of Wilberforce University, the oldest Black university in the United States. See his *Recollections of Seventy Years* (New York: Arno

Press, 1969); *History of the African Methodist Episcopal Church* (New York: Arno Press, 1969). George Leile was a significant participant in organizing the First Baptist Church in Silver Bluff, South Carolina, in the 1770s, and Andrew Bryan of Savannah was also a significant Baptist of the late eighteenth century. See James M. Washington, "The Origins and Emergence of Black Baptist Separatism, 1863–1897" (Ph.D. dissertation, Yale University, 1979). James Varick and Christopher Rush were significant participants in the founding of the AMEZ Church (1821). See Carol George, *Segregated Sabbaths* (New York: Oxford University Press, 1973), and Bishop William J. Walls, *The African Methodist Episcopal Church: Reality of the Black Church* (Charlotte, N.C.: A.M.E. Zion Publishing House, 1974).

8. See Herbert Aptheker, *American Negro Slave Revolts* (New York: International Publishers, 1943); idem, *Nat Turner's Slave Rebellion*; Arna Bontemps, *Black Thunder: Gabriel's Revolt, Virginia 1800* (New York: Macmillan, 1936); John O. Killens, *The Trial Record of Denmark Vesey* (Boston: Beacon Press, 1970); Robert S. Starobin ed., *Denmark Vesey: The Slave Conspiracy of 1822* (Englewood Cliffs, N.J.: Prentice-Hall, 1970). Particularly significant for Black theologians was Vincent Harding's research, "Religion and Resistance among Antebellum Negroes, 1800–1860," in A. Meier and E. Rudwick eds., *The Making of Black America I* :179–97; see also his more recent publication *There Is a River* (New York: Harcourt Brace Jovanovich, 1981). Gayraud Wilmore's "Three Generals in the Lord's Army," chapter 3 in his *Black Religion and Black Radicalism*, captured the emphasis of our concern and research. Although we rejected Joseph Washington's claim that Black churches had no theology, we did agree with his emphasis (in *Black Religion*) that Black faith had identified the gospel with the struggle for freedom. His book was often quoted with approval on this point. He served as a corrective to the widely held contention that Black religion was primarily otherworldly and compensatory. This view is strongly emphasized by Benjamin Mays in *The Negro's God*.

9. Walker's "Appeal" and Garnet's "Address" had an enormous impact on the thinking of the early interpreters of Black Theology. They were quoted more often than any other leading figures of the nineteenth century.

10. The impact of the rise of Black consciousness made Henry M. Turner especially important for the young Black clergy. He was a bishop in the A.M.E. Church, and the only mainline Black churchman whose radicalism was competitive with that of Garnet and Walker. He was a major critic of Booker T. Washington and was even isolated in his own denomination.

11. New York, Praeger, 1969. This book has a profound impact on Black theologians, and Mbiti, despite his conservative Western approach to theology, emerged as the most quoted and influential of all African theologians. See his controversial essay "An African Views American Black Theology," *Worldview* (August 1974), reprinted in Wilmore and Cone, *Black Theology*, 477–82. See my response to Mbiti, "A Black American Perspective on the Future of African Theology," in *Black Theology*, 492–502, and that of Desmond M. Tutu, "Black Theology/African Theology—Soul Mates or Antagonists?" ibid., 483–91. Mbiti does not like the stress on race and color in North American Black Theology.

12. London: Oxford University Press, 1971.

13. London: Longman, 1962.

14. London: Oxford University Press, 1965.

15. London: Lutterworth, 1968. Harry Sawyerr, an older African theologian, has not been friendly to Black Theology either; like Mbiti, he does not like the emphasis on race and color. Sawyerr wrote one of the earliest essays on African theology: "What Is African Theology?" *African Theological Journal* (August 1971): 7–24.

16. London: Longman, 1970.

17. London: Lutterworth, 1969. The collection of essays in this book was often referred to by young African American members of the clergy because of its influence in the development of an African theology.

18. Long was particularly influential as a teacher and lecturer on African religions in the Society for the Study of Black Religion. His most influential essay was "Perspectives for a Study of Afro-American Religion in the United States," *History of Religions* 2, no. 1 (August 1971): 54–66. This essay and his active participation in the SSBR provided the most challenging critique of the dependence of Black Theology on Western theology. See also his "Myth, Culture, and History: An Inquiry into the Cultural History of West Africa" (Ph.D. thesis, University of Chicago, 1962), and "The West African High God: History and Religious Experience," *History of Religions* 3, no. 2 (Winter 1964).

19. Nashville, Tenn.: African Methodist Episcopal Church Press, 1975.

20. I have referred to this debate in several places. See especially my interpretation of the debate among Black theologians in Wilmore and Cone, *Black Theology*, 615–20. See also Wilmore, *Black Religion*, chaps. 8 and 9.

21. Especially useful in this regard is Miles Mark Fisher, *Negro Slave Songs in the United States* (New York: Citadel, 1953), and John Lovell, Jr., "The Social Implications of the Negro Spiritual," *Journal of Negro Education* (October 1939), and his definitive study *Black Song: The Forge and the Flame* (New York: Macmillan, 1972). These works provided significant counter-interpretations of the typical view that the slave songs were exclusively otherworldly. The research of many Black historians also aided our this-worldly view of the spirituals and Black religion. See especially Vincent Harding's "Religion and Resistance" (note 9, above); "Beyond Chaos: Black History and the Search for the New Land." Black Paper no. 2 (August 1970, Institute of the Black World); and his "The Afro-American Past and the Afro-American Present," in Mitchell Goodman ed., *The Movement toward a New America* (New York; Knopf, 1970). No popular writer on the subject was more influential than the senior editor of *Ebony*, Lerone Bennett. See especially his *Before the Mayflower: A History of the Negro in America, 1619–1964* (Chicago: Johnson, 1966); and *Confrontation: Black and White* (Chicago: Johnson, 1965). The writings of W. E. B. Du Bois are particularly useful, especially his classic *The Souls of Black Folk* (New York: Fawcett, 1961; originally published in 1903); see also his *The Gift of Black folk* (New York: Washington Square, 1970; originally published in 1924). Another influential essay on the spirituals was that by Sterling Stuckey, "Through the Prism of Folklore: The Black Ethos in Slavery," in Jules Chametzky and Sidney Kaplan eds., *Black and White in American Culture* (University of Massachusetts Press, 1969). My *The Spirituals and the Blues* (New York: Seabury Press, 1972) was written in the light of this emphasis on *Black* rather than "Negro" history.

22. According to Richard Randall, "Once in America when we owned other men as chattels, Negro slaves chanted thinly-disguised songs of protest, set to the meter of spirituals— 'Go Down Moses,' the fighting song of Harriet Tubman who came like Moses to redeem her black kinsmen from the 'Egypt-land of the South'; 'Steal Away,' which invariably meant a summons to sneak off to the woods for a slave meeting; and the militant 'Follow the Drinking Gourd,' which meant following the Great Dipper to the Ohio River and freedom" ("Fighting Songs of the Unemployed." *The Sunday Worker Progressive Weekly*, September 3, 1939, p. 2). Earl Conrad made a similar interpretation of the spirituals: "Song, or the spiritual, as a means of communication, was a definite part of each of Harriet's campaigns. The spiritual, with its hidden meaning, was employed usually when the situation was the most dangerous. The idea of song was, in itself, disarming; thus, when the Negro sang he pampered his master's understanding of him as a 'loyal, satisfied, slave.' With a melody on his lips to cloak words

which held an important and immediate significance, it was possible to dupe the slaveholder" (*Harriet Tubman*, 76). Interpretations such as these gave us the perspective on the spirituals and Black religion we Black theologians needed to ground Black theology in the Bible and Black history. It is true that we were often not as careful in our interpretation as we perhaps should have been, but we achieved the *militant* reading of the Bible our times required and our own history suggested.

23. According to Douglass: "We were at times remarkably buoyant, sang hymns, and made joyous exclamations, almost as triumphant in their tone as if we had reached the land of freedom and safety. A keen observer might have detected in our repeated singing of 'O Canaan, sweet Canaan, I am bound for the land of Canaan,' something more than a hope of reaching heaven. We meant to reach the *North*, and the *North* was our Canaan" (*Life and Times of Frederick Douglass* [New York: Collier, 1962]: 159; a reprint of the 1892 edition).

24. A fuller exposition of my views on the Black Christ is found in *God of the Oppressed* (chap. 6); *A Black Theology of Liberation* (chap. 6); and *Black Theology and Black Power* (chap. 2). For a description of the controversy and a variety of views on the subject during the 1960s, see Alex Poinsett, "The Quest for a Black Christ," *Ebony* (March 1969). Albert Cleage was the most controversial with his emphasis on the literal Blackness of Jesus as a historical fact. See also Gayraud Wilmore, "The Black Messiah: Revising the Color Symbolism in Western Christology," *Journal of the Interdenominational Theological Center* 2, no. 1 (Fall 1974): 8–18; J. Deotis Roberts, *Liberation and Reconciliation: A Black Theology* (Philadelphia: Westminster Press, 1971); *The Black Messiah*, chap. 6; Vincent Harding, "Black Power and the American Christ," in Wilmore and Cone, *Black Theology: A Documentary History*, 35–42. For an exposition of the idea of a Black God, see chap. 4, "God in Black Theology," in my *A Black Theology of Liberation*. However, my *God of the Oppressed* is the most detailed explanation of my views.

25. See Sterling Brown, *Negro Poetry and Drama and the Negro in American Fiction* (1937; reprint, New York: Atheneum, 1969): 71. For an interpretation of Cullen's poem, see also Jean Wagner, *Black Poets of the United States*, trans. K. Douglas (Urbana: University of Illinois Press, 1973): 283–347.

26. It should be emphasized that the development of Christianity in both the New World and Africa among Blacks was inseparable from internal and external rejection of slavery. Black religions are unthinkable without this background since the sixteenth century. Hence whether the term "liberation" was used or not, Black Church history has been about liberation.

27. New York: Harper & Row.

28. See especially his *Theology of the World* (New York: Herder and Herder, 1969).

29. See the book that resulted from the Duke University consultation, "The Task of Theology Today," April 4–6, 1968, in which the major paper was given by Jürgen Moltmann: *The Future of Hope: Theology as Eschatology*, ed. Frederick Herzog (New York: Herder and Herder, 1970). Major responses to the Moltmann essay were by Harvey Cox, Frederick Herzog, Langdon Gilkey, John Macquarrie, and Van A. Harvey. Another conference was held in New York City, October 8–10, 1971, and a book was published with the title *Hope and the Future of Man*, ed. Ewert H. Cousins (Philadelphia: Fortress, 1972). Major speakers (whose essays were published) included Jürgen Moltmann, Wolfhart Pannenberg, Johannes B. Metz (all from Germany), John B. Cobb, Jr., Daniel Day Williams, Schubert M. Ogden, Carl E. Braaten, and Philip Hefner (all from the United States). More than a thousand persons turned out to hear the European theologians.

30. The influence of Moltmann's *Theology of Hope* and later his *Religion, Revolution, and the Future* (New York: Scribner's, 1969) was great. I read and then reread him: "The man who hopes will never be able to reconcile himself with the laws and constraints of this earth,

neither with the inevitability of death nor with the evil that constantly bears further evil. The raising of Christ is not merely a consolation to him in a life that is full of distress and doomed to die, but it is also God's contraction of suffering and death, of humiliation and offense, and of the wickedness of evil. Hope finds in Christ not only a consolation *in* suffering, but also the protest of the divine promise *against* suffering . . . Peace with God means conflict with the world. . . . If we had before our eyes only what we see, then we would cheerfully or reluctantly reconcile ourselves with things as they happen to be. That we do not reconcile ourselves, that there is no pleasant harmony between us and reality, is due to our unquenchable hope. This hope keeps man unreconciled, until the great day of the fulfillment of all the promises of God. . . . This hope makes the Christian church a constant disturbance in human society" (*Theology of Hope*, 21–22). As I read this and so many other passages like it, I concluded that this is exactly what hope in the spirituals means.

31. Nashville, Tenn.: Abingdon, 1971. Note especially chap. 1, "Introduction: The Case for a Black Theology of Hope," and chap. 7, "The Implications of a Theology of Hope for the Black Community." In both chapters, Jones quotes liberally from Moltmann's writings.

32. See especially his "Black Consciousness in Theological Perspective," in J. Gardiner and J. D. Roberts eds., *Quest for a Black Theology* (Philadelphia: Pilgrim, 1971), especially pp. 79–81; see also Roberts's *Liberation and Reconciliation*, and his *A Black Political Theology* (Philadelphia: Westminster Press, 1974). The title of the last book reflects Roberts's interest in hope theology, which was also called political theology.

33. J. Deotis Roberts was one of the first to note the problem with hope theology. That was why he asked: "How hopeful is the theology of hope?" (see his "Black Consciousness in Theological Perspective," 79). In most cases Roberts did not see much hope for Blacks in hope theology: "Some who have been the most vocal advocates of a theology of revolution have not touched the racial crisis in the United States. I am highly suspicious when Paul Lehmann, who teaches on the fringe of the largest black ghetto in the world, can wax eloquent concerning revolutionary theology, which is his answer to the situation in Latin America. Surely a political theology to be meaningful must be applied to the local crisis situation. . . . Another American, Prof. Richard Shaull of Princeton Seminary, has spoken on 'Revolutionary Change in Theological Perspective,' but he has selected Latin America. A black theologian, aware of the suffering of his people . . . has the responsibility to speak *first* to the American situation" (ibid., 79–80).

34. It was revealing that no Black theologians were invited as major participants in the conferences on hope; the issue of racism and the Black struggle against it were almost completely ignored. Jürgen Moltmann raised this problem at the New York conference, "Hope and the Future of Man," in his response to papers by Carl Braaten, John Cobb, and Philip Hefner. He asked: "*Whose* future do we mean? . . . Whose hopes are we giving an account of? . . . A future which does not begin in the transformation of the present is for me no genuine future. A hope which is not the hope of the oppressed today is no hope for which I could give a theological account. . . . If the theologians and philosophers of the future do not plant their feet on the ground and turn to a theology of the cross and the dialectic of the negative, they will appear in a cloud of liberal optimism and appear a mockery of the present suffering. If we cannot justify the theme of this conference, "Hope and the Future of Man," before the present reality of the frustration and oppression of man, we are batting the breeze and talking merely for our own self-satisfaction" (Cousins, *Hope and the Future of Man*, 55, 59). Many American theologians were upset with Moltmann's response and some considered it inappropriate and in bad taste. But I was very pleased and thought his comments would help American theologians to recognize that one cannot speak of hope without grounding that

speech in the struggles of Blacks for freedom. But American white theologians simply returned to theology as usual, even though they claimed to be *personally* concerned about justice. It was really strange to me, not to say disgusting, to listen to American white theologians speak of hope and ignore the hopes of the victims in their situation.

35. *The Power of the Poor in History* (Maryknoll, N.Y.: Orbis Books, 1983): 101.

36. Roberts writes:"At the Duke conference on the theology of hope, I put the question to Moltmann . . . as to the meaning of his theology for an oppressed people. His answer at that time was not very hopeful" ("Black Consciousness in Theological Perspective," 80). When Moltmann spoke at the hope conference in New York a few years later and in his later writings, as Roberts acknowledges, he was more explicit about the connections between his theology and the oppressed. But his concreteness and his naming the enemy still left something to be desired. José Míguez Bonino's critique of Moltmann caused a great stir, especially from Moltmann. See Míguez Bonino's *Doing Theology in a Revolutionary Situation* (Philadelphia: Fortress, 1975), chap. 7, especially pp. 144ff. See also Moltmann's response:"On Latin American Liberation Theology: An Open Letter to José Miguez Bonino," *Christianity and Crisis* 36, no. 5 (March 29, 1976): 57–63. To Moltmann's credit, he also went to Latin America and encountered Latin American theologians on their own theological turf. One important meeting was held in Mexico (October 1977), which I also attended. The issue between Moltmann and the Latin Americans focused on the use of Marxism—i.e., social analysis and the naming of one's enemies. It was a spirited exchange but with each learning from the other. See an account of the conference in Jorge V. Pixley and Jean-Pierre Bastien eds., *Praxis cristiana y producción teológica* (Salamanca, Spain: Sígueme, 1979).

37. *Power of the Poor*, 191; see also his "Two Theological Perspectives: Liberation. Theology and Progressive Theology," in *The Emergent Gospel*, S. Torres and V. Fabella eds. (Maryknoll, N.Y.: Orbis Books, 1978).

38. *Power of the Poor*, 196.

39. *The Wretched of the Earth* (New York: Grove, 1963), 252.

40. Ibid.

41. Ibid., 255.

42. Although the NCBC and the AACC were similar, they were also quite different. The AACC was made up of official representatives of churches. The membership base of the NCBC was individuals.

43. On black theology in South Africa, see Basil Moore ed., *Black Theology: A South African Voice* (London: Hurst, 1973); Allan A. Boesak, *Farewell to Innocence: A Socio-Ethical Study on Black Theology and Power* (Maryknoll, N.Y.: Orbis Books, 1977); and John W. de Gruchy, *The Church Struggle in South Africa* (Grand Rapids, Mich.: Eerdmans, 1979).

44. I have tried to demonstrate in this chapter that from its very origin Black theology was defined as liberation theology. We did not borrow the word "liberation" from Latin America. But because the problem of white racism has played the central role in creating the need for a distinctively Black theology; the word "Black" has been more visible in describing our theological enterprise than has the term "liberation." The focus on "Black" has provided many white North American and European interpreters with the option of identifying "liberation theology" as exclusively limited to Latin America, even though Blacks started using the word "liberation" in relation to theology about the same time as did Latin American theologians. The focus on liberation in terms of class in lieu of color gave white North American theologians yet another occasion for ignoring the problem of racism and what it means in the history of North America and Europe. As we Black theologians faced the problem of limiting our theological vision to issues of color, we felt that our perspective of the world, when seen

in terms of the immediate, existential needs of Blacks, required that we focus on color as our central starting point in theology, even though we recognized the obvious shortcomings in that initial point of departure.

45. For an introduction to the important theology of liberation movement in Latin America, see José Míguez Bonino, *Doing Theology in a Revolutionary Situation*. The classic and most important text on liberation theology in Latin America is still Gustavo Gutiérrez's *A Theology of Liberation*; see also his *The Power of the Poor in History*. For the best introduction to the variety of perspectives of the excellent theological work that is being done in Latin America, see Rosnio Gibellini ed., *Frontiers of Theology in Latin America* (Maryknoll, N.Y.: Orbis Books, 1979).

46. The dialogue between Latin American and African American theologians began in Geneva at the WCC in 1973; see *Risk* 9, no. 2 (1973). For my report on the history of our dialogue with Latin American, Asian, and African theologies, and important essays on the themes, see Wilmore and Cone, *Black Theology*, p. 4, "Black Theology and Third World Theologies," 445–608; see also my "From Geneva to São Paulo: A Dialogue between Black Theology and Latin American Liberation Theology," in Sergio Torres and John Eagleson eds., *The Challenge of Basic Christian Communities* (Maryknoll, N.Y.: Orbis Books, 1981): 265–81, and *My Soul Looks Back* (Nashville, Tenn.: Abingdon, 1982), chap. 4.

47. Boston: Beacon Press, 1973, rev. ed. (originally published in 1961).

48. Boston: Beacon Press.

49. New York: Morrow.

50. New York: Schocken Books.

51. New York: Doubleday.

52. Boston: Beacon Press.

53. Boston: Beacon Press.

54. New York: Doubleday.

55. Nashville, Tenn.: Abingdon.

56. See my *God of the Oppressed* and my "Interpretation of the Debate among Black Theologians," in Wilmore and Cone, *Black Theology: A Documentary History*.

57. New York: Doubleday. See my response to Jones in *God of the Oppressed*, chap. 8, and "Interpretation of the Debate among Black Theologians."

58. See my response to Cecil Cone in "Interpretation of the Debate."

59. Wilmore and Cone, *Black Theology*, 255.

60. See especially his "Perspectives for a Study of Afro-American Religion in the U.S." and his "Structural Similarities and Dissimilarities in Black and African Theologies," *Journal of Religious Thought* 32 (Spring 1976). See my response in "Interpretation of the Debate."

61. New York: Morrow.

62. Philadelphia: Lippincott.

63. New York: Harper & Row.

64. See especially his "Black Churches in Historical Perspective," *Christianity and Crisis* (November 2 and 16, 1970): 226–28; "They Sought a City: The Black Church and Churchmen in the Nineteenth Century," *Union Seminary Quarterly Review* 26, no. 3 (Spring 1971).

65. Preston Williams's most influential articles included "Black Church: Origin, History, Present Dilemmas"; "The Ethics of Black Power"; "The Ethical Aspects of the 'Black Church/ Black Theology' Phenomenon"; "Shifting Racial Perspectives," *Harvard Divinity Bulletin* (Fall 1968): 12–15; "Ethics and Ethos in the Black Experience," *Christianity and Crisis* (May 31, 1971); "Toward a Sociological Understanding of the Black Religious Community," *Soundings* (Fall 1971); "The Price of Social Justice," *Christian Century* (May 9, 1973). Herbert Edwards's most

important and insightful essay was his "Racism and Christian Ethics in America," *Katallegete* (Winter 1971). See also his "The Third World and the Problem of God-Talk," *Harvard Theological Review* 64, no. 4 (1971). Carlton Lee played a major role in the origin of the NCBC. One of his most important essays was his "Religious Roots of the Negro Protest," in Arnold Rose ed., *Assuring Freedom to the Free* (Detroit: Wayne State University Press, 1964).

66. See his "Africa and the Biblical Period," *Harvard Theological Review* (Oct. 1971); "Biblical Theology and Black Theology," *Journal of the Interdenominational Theological Center* (Spring 1976).

67. Johnson's essay, "Jesus, the Liberator" was the most influential. See also his *The Soul of the Black Preacher* (1970) and his *Proclamation Theology* (Shreveport, La.: Fourth Episcopal District Press, 1977). Warner Traynham has also written an important text on Black Theology, *Christian Faith in Black and White: A Primer in Theology from the Black Perspective*. This text is valuable not only because of its interpretation of the meaning of Black Theology but also because of the important documents in the appendices on the early development of Black Theology.

68. New York: Doubleday.

69. His most important written contribution to Black Theology is "Toward the Promised Land," *The Black Church* 2, no. 1 (1972): 1–48.

Chapter Thirty-eight

Statement by the National Committee of Black Churchmen, June 13, 1969

National Committee of Black Churchmen

The 1960s saw the assertion of the black theological agenda in many arenas. Black caucuses formed in predominantly white denominations; seminary students demanded enhancements and revisions of curricula to incorporate the black religious experience into theological education; clergy groups on the local and national levels came into operation with name identities and programs clearly indicating their focus on black concerns. For instance, in Seattle there was the Black United Clergy for Action. Another such group was the National Committee of Black Churchmen, which produced the two statements that follow.

The first statement articulates this ecumenical black clergy group's understanding of the nature and import of black theological claims.

•

Why Black Theology?

Black people affirm their being. This affirmation is made in the whole experience of being black in the hostile American society. Black Theology is not a gift of the Christian gospel dispensed to slaves; rather it is an *appropriation* which black slaves made of the gospel given by their white oppressors. Black Theology has been nurtured, sustained, and passed on in the black churches in their various ways of expression. Black Theology has dealt with all the ultimate and violent issues of life and death for a people despised and degraded.

The black church has not only nurtured black people but enabled them to survive brutalities that ought not to have been inflicted on any community of men. Black Theology is the product of black Christian experience and reflection. It comes out of the past. It is strong in the present. And we believe it is redemptive for the future.

This indigenous theological formation of faith emerged from the stark need of the fragmented black community to affirm itself as a part of the Kingdom of God. White theology sustained the American slave system and negated the humanity of blacks. This indigenous Black Theology, based on the imaginative black experience, was the best hope for the survival of black people. This is a way of saying that Black Theology was already present in the spirituals and slave songs and exhortations of slave preachers and their descendants.

All theologies arise out of communal experience with God. At this moment in time, the black community seeks to express its theology in language that speaks to the contemporary mood of black people.

What Is Black Theology?

Black Theology is a theology of black liberation. It seeks to plumb the black condition in the light of God's revelation in Jesus Christ, so that the black community can see that the gospel is commensurate with the achievement of black humanity. Black Theology is a theology of "blackness." It is the affirmation of black humanity that emancipates black people from white racism, thus providing authentic freedom for both white and black people. It affirms the humanity of white people in that it says No to the encroachment of white oppression.

The message of liberation is the revelation of God as revealed in the incarnation of Jesus Christ. Freedom IS the gospel. Jesus is the Liberator! "He ... hath sent me to preach deliverance to the captives" (Luke 4:18). Thus, the black patriarchs and we ourselves know this reality despite all attempts of the white church to obscure it and to utilize Christianity as a means of enslaving blacks. The demand that Christ the Liberator imposes on all men *requires* all blacks to affirm their full dignity as persons and all whites to surrender their presumptions of superiority and abuses of power.

What Does This Mean?

It means that Black Theology must confront the issues which are a part of the reality of black oppression. We cannot ignore the powerlessness of the black community. Despite the *repeated requests* for significant programs of social change, the American people have refused to appropriate adequate sums of money for social reconstruction. White church bodies have often made promises only to follow with default. We must, therefore, once again call the attention of the nation and the church to the need for providing adequate resources of power (reparation).

Reparation is a part of the Gospel message. Zaccheus knew well the necessity for repayment as an essential ingredient in repentance. "If I have taken anything from any man by false accusation, I restore him fourfold" (Luke 19:8). The church that calls itself the servant church must, like its Lord, be willing to strip itself of possessions in order to build and restore that which has been destroyed by the compromising bureaucrats and conscienceless rich. While reparation cannot remove the guilt created by the despicable deed of slavery, it is, nonetheless, a positive response to the need for power in the black community. This nation, and, a people who have always related the value of the person to his possession of property, must recognize the necessity of restoring property in order to reconstitute personhood.

What Is the Cost?

Living is risk. We take it in confidence. The black community has been brutalized and victimized over the centuries. The recognition that comes from seeing Jesus as Liberator and the Gospel as freedom empowers black men to risk themselves for freedom and for faith. This faith we affirm in the midst of a hostile, disbelieving society. We intend to exist by this faith at all times and in all places.

In spite of brutal deprivation and denial, the black community has appropriated the spurious form of Christianity imposed upon it and made it into an instrument for resisting the extreme demands of oppression. It has enabled the black community to live through unfulfilled promises, unnecessary risks, and inhuman relationships.

As black theologians address themselves to the issues of the black revolution, it is incumbent upon them to say that the black community will not be turned from its course, but will seek complete fulfillment of the promises of the Gospel. Black people have survived the terror. We now commit ourselves to the risks of affirming the dignity of black personhood. We do this as men and as black Christians. This is the message of Black Theology. In the words of Eldridge Cleaver:

> We shall have our manhood.
> We shall have it or the earth will be leveled by our efforts to gain it.

NOTE

This statement, produced by the Committee on Theological Prospectus, NCBC, was issued at the Interdenominational Theological Center, Atlanta, Georgia. It was adopted at the NCBC 1969 annual convocation in Oakland, California.

Chapter Thirty-nine

Statement by the National Committee of Black Churchmen, Third Annual Convocation, November 11–14, 1969

National Committee of Black Churchmen

The second statement of the National Committee of Black Churchmen is an elaboration of the first. It voices an apperception of black clergy's new tri-partite vocation: political, cultural, theological. It is, in effect, a theological agenda. Its language supports, among other things, the then current call for white churches to make material reparations to black Americans, as well as for black churches to get on with initiatives to address the needs of dispossessed blacks in the United States and abroad. Overall, the statement is a charge upon whites, especially white church bodies, for an equitable redistribution of power and resources to black Americans and to Third World peoples worldwide, from whose oppression white empowerment had derived.

•

We came to Oakland as an act of faith. We came seeking a deeper experience of the mission of God in the contemporary world than has ever been provided by the denominations and local congregations to which some of us belong, from which some of us have fled in profound disillusionment, and which some of us have observed, but only with doubt and distrust.

In a time of the increasing institutionalization and bureaucratization of the Church, we do not come to create a new institutional form of the Church. We are not here to invent a new denomination. Our primary and overreaching concern is to seek, through our common experience and consciousness of being black and powerless in a part of the world dominated by white racism and white power, a new religio-cultural, political, and economic vocation which can relate to our own deep alienation from a religious, cultural, political, and economic system which is not compatible with our own instincts and sensibilities but which has been commended to us and imposed upon us by white, bourgeois, European and American religious, political, and economic institutions interlocking and conspiring with one another to whitenize and subordinate black people.

This new vocation to which we are called is *political* in the sense that it seeks radically to change, by whatever means are necessary, the racist structures that dominate our lives; *cultural* in the sense that it seeks to identify, recreate, unify, and authenticate whatever traditions, values, and styles of life are indigenous or distinctive to the black community; and *theological* in the sense that we believe that it is God—however He chooses to reveal Himself today to oppressed peoples in America and in the Third World—who has chosen black humanity as a vanguard to resist the demonic powers of racism, capitalism, and imperialism, and to so reform the structures of this world that they will more perfectly minister to the peace and power of all people as children of One God and brothers of one another.

We black people are a religious people. From the earliest recorded time we have acknowledged a Supreme Being. With the fullness of our physical bodies and emotions we have unabashedly worshipped Him with shouts of joy and in the tears of pain and anguish. We neither believe that God is dead, white, nor captive to some highly rationalistic and dogmatic formulations of the Christian faith which relate Him exclusively to the canons of the Old and New Testaments and accommodate Him to the reigning spirits of a sociotechnical age. Rather, we affirm that God is Liberator in the man Jesus Christ, that His message is Freedom, and that today He calls all men to be what they are in themselves, and among their own people, in the context of a pluralistic world-society of dignity and self-determination for all. We believe that in a special way God's favor rests today upon the poor and oppressed peoples of the world and that He calls them to be the ministering angels of His judgment and grace as His Kingdom of Freedom and Peace breaks in from the future upon a world shackled to ancient sins and virtues and upon the present inequalities, imperialistic wars, and ambitions of privileged nations, classes, and power-groups.

This call of God which we in the NCBC hear in what we have been saying to one another in Oakland is a call to suffering and sacrifice. It is a call to identification with frustrated, emasculated, down-trodden men, women, and children, most of them black, to share their anguish and their hope and to work for their enlightenment and empowerment, not that they might in turn become oppressors, but that through them the world might be saved from the selfishness, greed, and subjugation that has characterized the centuries-old hegemony of the white, Anglo-Saxon, European civilizations of the West.

We therefore call upon the white, Christian churches of America and Europe, which have nurtured and sustained the systems of injustice that have driven the world to the present crisis, to submit themselves to radical reformation. We challenge them to psychologically and institutionally disengage themselves from the nations within whose boundaries they have so often baptized and sanctified racism, imperialism, and economic selfishness, and take upon themselves the kind of revolutionary posture that can force the transfer of requisite countervailing power to oppressed peoples wherever they may be found. We challenge them to divest themselves of their own great wealth—much of it ill-gotten—built upon the bodies of exploited races and classes wherever imperialistic political and economic influences have extended within and beyond national boundaries, and to make massive ecclesiastical resources of capital and technical assistance available to powerless people in Africa, Asia, Latin America, and the United States.

We believe that the Black Manifesto, which was issued this year to the churches of America and to several official church convocations in Europe by the Black Economic Development Conference, is a most significant and essentially accurate assessment of the guilt and reparational responsibility of white Christendom and the wealthy Jewish communions of the United States. We reaffirm our support of that document and particularly of its programmatic objectives with respect to the situation of black people in the United States, Africa, and the Caribbean area.

The NCBC will not desist from calling the white religious establishment of the United States to the full and immediate implementation of the demands of the Manifesto. Nor will we excuse from participation in the achievement of its objectives the historic black churches of America which have left undone many of the things they ought to have done in the slums and rural ghettos of the United States, Africa and the West Indies.

We do not shrink from the revolutionary, anticapitalistic implications of the Manifesto. While all of our members do not give unqualified endorsement to every strategy and tactic stated or implied in the original document issued in Detroit, the National Committee of Black Churchmen, as a body, is committed to the essential spirit and meaning of the analysis and proposals, and will continue to press them upon the churches and synagogues of America, upon the National Council of Churches in the U.S.A., and upon the World Council of Churches.

We demand that individual white church agencies and white brethren, who call themselves our allies, recognize the imperative nature and urgency of this task in light of the crisis that is upon us in the cities and depressed rural areas in this most affluent and powerful nation of the world.

By the faith of our fathers, by the faith of Nat Turner and Denmark Vesey, of Allen and Varick, of Delany, of Garvey and Du Bois and Martin Luther King, Jr., and Malcolm X, and by the grace of God, the NCBC has undertaken, in cooperation with IFCO and BEDC, to call this nation, beginning with the white churches, which have a clear and acknowledged moral responsibility, to the conference table to negotiate in good faith the transfer of power to those segments of society which have been deprived of freedom, justice, and self-determination. It *can* be done. It can be done peacefully. *It must be done* in any case, or peace, brotherhood, and reconciliation will remain empty, mocking words in an American wasteland of racial hatred and strife. Now is the time to act, for as the words of Isaiah 42 sternly remind us in every nation and generation: "He will not rest nor be silent until He has established justice in the earth."

Having thus analyzed our situation, and being ready and determined to respond to the promptings of this same God, we have been made to recognize that it is not enough simply to call the white churches to the negotiation table. Long, agonizing months of fruitless negotiations with these churches, in efforts to lead them to recognize and to fund the Black Economic Development Conference, have forced us sadly to acknowledge the harsh reality that the white churches and church structures are not capable of positive responses to the considered opinions of their black peers. We accept the defiance of us which this exposes; but we intend to do several things about that defiance. We are unalterably committed to the effecting of a more equi-

table power balance "by whatever means are necessary." Means additional to negotiation are now necessary. The time has come for us to resort to the use of unusual
forms of pressure upon the white church structures if we are ever to realize the
legitimate goal of a literal transferral of power.

One of the chief symbols of white church power is the institution known as the
National Council of Churches of Christ in the U.S.A. That institution—not unlike
the World Council of Churches, the myriad regional and local councils of churches,
and the white denominations themselves—is a sorry example of institutionalized
white decision-making power. This is true notwithstanding the fact that it has token
representation of blacks in executive capacity. The General Secretary is white; the
Deputy General Secretary is white; all of the Associate General Secretaries are white;
the heads of divisions which are of critical relevance to the black condition, such as
the Division of Christian Life and Mission, the Division of Overseas Ministries, and
the Division of Christian Education, are white. These are untenable and thoroughly
unacceptable realities. They comprise an affront to black churchmen everywhere.

We, therefore, announce our dedication to a battle which must culminate in the
appointment of a black General Secretary of the N.C.C., and in the designation of
black churchmen, in significant numbers, at the level of Associate General Secretaries
and division heads. These appointments must be black churchmen who come not
only from the ranks of the white denominations, but who presently labor within the
fold of the great, historical black communions. The day has passed when we can be
played one against the other. The NCBC, therefore, in concert with black churchmen
everywhere, will determine whom you shall appoint.

Time and circumstance have met in such a way as to place us, at this day, on the
virtual eve of the convening of the General Assembly of the National Council of
Churches. That assembly will meet in the city of Detroit during the first week of
December 1969. In the light of our deliberations in Oakland, and in view of the
stance which we have been forced by white recalcitrance to take, we declare our
intention to assure that that General Assembly is confronted with the serious issues
which here we have raised. One way or another, that General Assembly shall deal
with this aspect of the black agenda. We have neither the need nor the intention to
divulge the means by which we shall accomplish this end. We simply announce that
sufficient pressures shall be brought to bear upon the Assembly to cause it to deal
with these issues. Whether it deals wisely or foolishly with them is for the Assembly
to determine. We are persuaded that mere suggestions and reasonable arguments are
lost in the mires of verbiage and committee referrals which are so readily spawned
by white church institutions. To us "black empowerment" means, precisely, black
empowerment; it does not mean endless dialogue with persons and institutions have
demonstrated a propensity for eternal, infernal dialogue.

When the N.C.C., in 1967, spoke of a "Crisis in the Nation," it was speaking of
the black condition. It named that crisis as one of the two top priorities for programming and funding. Yet, as the N.C.C., and as every black churchman knows, little
enough has been done by that institution literally to re-order its priorities in line
with its eloquent statement. We are convinced that only the transfer of power, at
significant levels, can help to bring progress in this area of alleged concern. Detroit

must see the establishment of our efforts to accomplish this goal. The battle once begun, we pledge ourselves to the vigorous pursuit of these objectives, by whatever means are necessary, until victory is won. If it should be that racism and white negativism are, indeed, so vital a part of the reality of the N.C.C. that it would choose to destroy itself before acceding to these just insistences, then it is clear that the N.C.C. is incapable of becoming relevant to blacks, and, being thus irrelevant, would serve a more Christian purpose in its demise than it would in a continuation of its present disguise.

Let no white churches, church institutions, or churchmen seek comfort in the fact that we place our present focus upon the National Council of Churches. It is only the accidental timing of the meeting of the General Assembly which directs us so to do. Let the World Council of Churches know, assuredly, that it is programmed into our agenda; let every regional and local council of churches across this land know, without doubt, that our intentions and our agenda speak to them all; let all national and regional denominations, judicatories, dioceses and what-have-you know that this day we are speaking to them in tones of clarion sound. Our agenda for the white church structures is all-embracing. Fidelity to Jesus Christ, the Lord of all, informs us that none may be allowed the deceptive comfort of respite.

Our deliberations in Oakland have led us to know that it was for the clarification of these purposes that we were brought to Oakland, and it is with these resolutions and determinations that, under God's guidance, we return to our individual places and ramparts to work, to strive, and to fight.

Let all of the church of God say, "Amen!"

Mother Mary Elizabeth Lange, founder of the Oblate Sisters of Providence. Courtesy of the Josephite Archives.

Augustus Tolton as a young seminarian. Courtesy of A. Rankin.

Chapter Forty

African American Catholics and Black Theology
An Interpretation

M. Shawn Copeland

From colonial days, increasing numbers of African Americans have given their devotional loyalty to Catholic expressions of the Christian faith. They have formed orders of religious, such as the Oblate Sisters of Providence and the Sisters of the Holy Family. Several African Americans have been elevated to the episcopacy. Their presence in the Catholic communion has not been without conflict, however. Racial attitudes and their institutional manifestations have been the source of tension and discontent. One result was the organization in 1968 of the National Black Catholic Clergy Caucus, and subsequently the National Black Sisters' Conference. Another result was the breaking away of a contingent of black Catholics in 1989 under Father George Stallings and his establishment of the independent Imani Temple. Most black Catholics, though, have remained within the church, seeking avenues to racial reconciliation and the implementation of justice within the communion. Theologian M. Shawn Copeland reflects on the appropriation of Catholic piety among African Americans.

•

This is a report on the pastoral and intellectual appropriation of Black theology among African American Catholics. First, it will look backward to that thirty-five-year period between 1889 and 1924 that was the scene of two attempts by Catholics of African descent to enjoy the heritage of their faith; to win for themselves, their progeny, and their people, the attention, the respect, and the care of their church; and to help secure the rights of citizenship for their race. By the power and grace of the Holy Spirit, these men and women gave birth to an indigenous *African American Catholic church tradition of struggle for social justice.* The story of their dedication enriches the common memory of all African American Christians and provides the historical context for the current twenty-year-old movement of Black Catholics in the United States. Second, it will identify the chief catalysts that have promoted the resurgence of that tradition. Third, it will present some illustrations of African American Catholic pastoral and intellectual appropriation of the impulses and insights of Black Theology.

Contextualization

From 1889 until 1894, African American Catholic laity conducted an increasingly vigorous movement to importune their church to "take an active interest in what concerns, not only the spiritual but also the temporal welfare of all the people entrusted to your [its] care." The call for a meeting of "Colored Catholics . . . for the purpose of taking the status of the race in their relation to the church";[1] was the inspiration of Daniel Rudd, the publisher and editor of the *American Catholic Tribune*, the only national newspaper published by Catholics of African descent in the United States in the nineteenth century. On Tuesday, January 1, 1889, nearly one hundred Black delegates from thirteen states, the District of Columbia, and South America, along with invited and sympathetic members of the white clergy and the hierarchy, met in congress in Washington, D.C.

At the end of the nineteenth century, the general state of African American Catholics within their church mirrored their condition in the wider American society. Although unlike the Presbyterians, the Baptists, and the Methodists, the Catholic church did not split over the question of slavery, the church long had purchased the culture and custom of racism; and, but for rare exceptions, ignorance, benign neglect, and segregation obtained. Catholics numbered about two hundred thousand in an African American population of seven million. A survey taken by the first congress cited twenty churches—most with their own primary school; sixty-five other schools providing instruction for approximately five thousand children; nine orphanages; approximately one hundred fifty sisters in the two religious congregations founded for and by women of color[2]; seven seminarians; and one priest, Augustus Tolton.[3]

Four congresses followed, convening in 1890, 1892, 1893, and 1894, each assembly of delegates growing in confidence and in militancy. Their concerns and discussions were political and economic, social and religious, national and international in scope: an end to all forms of civic, economic, and political discrimination at home; the abolition of slavery abroad; the Back to Africa movement; just and equal treatment in their church. From the first, delegates had been eager for some permanent scheme, and at the third congress they organized the St. Peter Claver Union. However, neither the Union nor the congress movement lasted. It is not precisely clear why, but there were increasing clashes and differences with the white hierarchy and clergy over the identity, the direction, the purposes, and the leadership of the congress movement and the Union. Still, if their concrete accomplishments were few, this courageous group "recorded for posterity the perduring hopes and aspirations of the people they represented and left an embarrassing reminder of a plea for simple justice that would not be heeded."[4]

A broad-based movement among African American Catholics did not surface again until the second decade of the twentieth century with the concern of Dr. Thomas Wyatt Turner to meet the social, personal, and religious needs of Black Catholic servicemen during the First World War. The Committee for the Advancement of Colored Catholics, formed for this end, led to the Federated Colored Catholics. Turner had sought an action-oriented group dedicated to ending discrimination against Blacks within American society and within the church. For nearly a decade he was assisted by the Reverend John LaFarge, S.J., and the Reverend William Markoe, S.J. But rather than turn the Federated Colored Catholics in a less activist and practical direction, Turner parted company with the two Jesuits.

Catalysts in the Resurgence of the African American Catholic Struggle for Social Justice

The resurgence of an African American Catholic church tradition of struggle for social justice was catalyzed by radical change: change in the social, political, economic condition of Blacks in the United States and change in the Roman Catholic Church itself. The civil rights movement challenged the dominant ethos and pattern of accommodation to segregation; the Second Vatican Council challenged the historic intellectual, theological, and cultural insularity of the Catholic church. Change in the social mood without change in the ecclesial mood might have forced Black Catholics in the United States to abandon their centuries-old religious tradition; change in the ecclesial mood without change in the social mood might have compelled them to barter their racial-cultural heritage for silver. There was a propitiousness to these times. This was God's time; this was *kairos*.

The civil rights movement gave the U.S. Catholic church a singular opportunity to witness concretely at home to the meaning of unity in the faith and diversity in race, culture, and ethnicity. The nonviolent determination of Blacks for just and equal regard under law challenged the conscience. Catholic lay men and lay women, sisters and priests, marched at Selma. True, the Catholic hierarchy had denounced the sin of racism; and some, though not all, Catholic bishops had begun either to integrate those parochial schools under their direct control or to condemn publicly the worst examples of discrimination. But, as a whole, as an institution, the Catholic church in the United States made no significant contribution to the civil rights movement. Black Catholic scholar-priest Jerome LeDoux declared the failure of the church at this crucial moment as one of "the most shameful scandals of modern Christianity: the damning exposure of the Church as the taillight in matters of justice where the civil courts did not hesitate to be a headlight."[5] And writing from Gethsemani, Trappist Thomas Merton uncovered the dominant Catholic attitude as a "fake Catholicism." It was, he wrote, a "parody of unity which is no unity at all but a onesided and arbitrary attempt to reduce others to a condition of identity with ourselves . . . one of the most disastrous of misconceptions."[6]

If the silence and indifference of their church wounded Black Catholics, the cry "Black Power" galvanized them. At least one Black priest, Lawrence Lucas, joined the predominantly Protestant National Committee of Black Churchmen. Around the country Black priest, Black sisters, and Black laity began informal, nourishing conversations and study-groups. They retrieved and consumed the work of Black cultural theorists, historians, and artists. All over the United States, Black Catholics stood up.[7]

Fourteen days after the death of Martin Luther King, Jr., a group of Black priests stunned the white Catholic hierarchy by publicly and collectively naming their church as "primarily a white racist institution."[8] Women were not among delegates to the congress in 1889 and Robert L. Ruffin of Boston lamented their absence in his address to that body. But a woman was present at the priests' deliberations—Sister Martin de Porres Grey (now Dr. Patricia Grey Tyree). The priests urged her to organize Black sisters and she did. In August 1968, following a national gathering of 155 women from seventy-nine different religious congregations, forty-five cities, the Caribbean, and Africa, the National Black Sisters' Conference (NBSC) was born pledging "to work unceasingly for the liberation of Black people."[9] The National Office for Black Catholics (NOBC) along with national assemblies of seminarians and laity soon followed.

But the contemporary movement among Black Catholics was not without dissension and conflict. Black Catholics were never in complete accord over the function and organizational structure of the NOBC. There were heated objections to its presumed role as an umbrella agency for the various national groups. The clergy, sisters, and brothers were well-schooled in ecclesiastical protocol; at times they used this to disadvantage the laity. The new emphasis on lay leadership was no less threatening to Black clerics and religious than it was to their white colleagues. Long denied pastorates and other appropriate outlets for their talents, they were not always eager to share leadership with the laity. But still, always—then and now—our arguments focused on the best means to importune our church to address itself to racism, on the style and strategy of our self-determination, but never on the validity of these needs, on the legitimacy of our demands, or on their substance.

Pastoral and Intellectual Appropriation of Black Theolgy

The efforts at pastoral and intellectual appropriation of Black Theology by African American Catholics are, first of all, the products of the resurgence of an African American Catholic church tradition of struggle for justice in their church and in the wider society. Clearly the various projects and programs developed by African American Catholics derive inspiration from the pioneering theological and ministerial studies of Black Protestant theologians, church scholars, and pastors. But African American Catholic projects and programs also take impetus from the Black Power movement and Black cultural nationalism, from the Black separatism of the early Malcolm X and the Black Christian nationalism of Albert Cleage; from contact with the leaders and developments of post-Conciliar African Catholicism and the renewal of theology and pastoral ministry taking place in the universal church. On the other hand, two movements with deep Catholic roots, namely, the Theology In the Americas program (TIA)[10] and feminist theology, to date have exerted little influence on African American Catholic pastoral work and theological thinking as a whole.

The Black Catholic Clergy Caucus always has formed a visible and vigorous vanguard confronting ecclesiastical racism at every turn, collectively offering Black Catholics and our activities an offensive and defensive pastorate, and initiating communication with our counterparts in Africa. The increasing number and participation of Black bishops in the National Conference of Catholic Bishops keep the agenda of Black communicants before the wider American Catholic church. It is through the bishops' vigilance that the hierarchy issued the pastoral letter on racism, "Brothers and Sisters to Us."[11] But it was the establishment and staffing of the various national offices, especially those of the National Office for Black Catholics and the National Black Sisters' Conference, that put teeth and soul into the shaping of a distinctive African American Catholicism. These two organizations carved out space for the development of leadership, for study, for spiritual and psychological formation, for the creative intellectual and pastoral interpretation of the Black Catholic experience in the United States.

Pastoral Application of Black Theology

Liturgical Rites and Rituals. Catholics of African American descent will be forever indebted to the Reverend Clarence Joseph Rivers who singlehandedly revolutionized the hymnody, the ritual form, the symbols, the mood, and the atmosphere of their worship. Well before the Second Vatican Council, Father Rivers had begun to compose, perform, and lecture on Catholic church music in a Black cultural style. In his *American Mass Program, Mass Dedicated to the Brotherhood of Man*[12] and subsequent compositions and recordings, Rivers introduced the idiom of African American music into Catholic worship. In the late 1960s and early 1970s, in order to bring greater cultural coherence to the liturgy, he began to critically reexamine the relation of the various elements of the mass to the Black idiom. In his commitment to articulate an authentic African American Catholic liturgical aesthetic, Rivers challenged the diluted liturgical experimentation that attempted to pass for renewal in so many places in the wider U.S. Catholic church. To his achievements are joined the work of other Black Catholic composers including Rawn Harbour, Leon Roberts, Marjorie Gabriel-Burrow, Grayson Brown, Avon Gillespie, Eddie Bonnemere, and Ray East.

The earliest pastoral attempts of African American Catholics to incorporate the insights of Black Theology centered on the Sunday worship of the local parish. These individual and initially isolated efforts, usually by priests or sisters, to add Black cultural shadings to the Catholic liturgy distinguish a first phase of adaptation or acculturation. Under the directives of the Second Vatican Council, the process of acculturation opens the Roman liturgy to the inclusion, substitution, and symbolic representation of compatible elements from particular cultures.[13] Black Catholics dove into the treasure chest of African American sacred music lifting up the spirituals, plundering the Baptist hymnal, tracking down organists competent in the Black musical genre and idiom—often from the Baptist congregation across town! Ever so tentatively the laity began to sing these songs at the eucharistic liturgy, at prayer services, at Advent or Lenten devotions. The nationalist colors—red, black, and green—along with traditional African styles, patterns, and weaves were employed in the design of vestments, stoles, and altar linens used in the various ceremonies of the Roman rite. Crucifixes and statues of the mother of Jesus sculpted in African features, and Black cultural products began to appear on the walls and altars of Catholic parishes. Priests began to listen to and to appropriate the rhetorical style of their Black Protestant counterparts. It was not long before hand-clapping, call and response, the shout, the tambourine, and the drum sounded in the Catholic church.

This phase of adaption or acculturation began a process of psychic healing, as Cyprian Rowe observed:

> Catholics of African descent have suffered intensely from the sterility of liturgical rites, because they have somewhere in their bones a tradition of worship in which the sung and spoken word have been fused into celebrations of joy. Afro-Americans are therefore among the first to realize that it is a certain cultural ignorance, and even cultural imperialism, that have resulted in their almost total exclusion from worship, except as spectators.[14]

During this period there were widespread attempts simply to make Black culture welcome in Catholic parishes and among Black Catholics; but some measure of evaluation was needed so that parishes did not become "inauthentically Catholic in their scope while becoming authentically Black."[15] Under the leadership of its executive director, Brother Joseph M. Davis, S.M., and his successor, Brother Cyprian Rowe, F.M.S., NOBC's Program for Culture and Worship furnished the means to evaluate and to share liturgical activities; hence leading to the phase of indigenization. Through conferences, workshops, and the publications of monographs, the NOBC constructed a platform from which Black Catholic composers and liturgists could mold and direct an African American renewal of Catholic worship. The NOBC inaugurated an annual workshop, staffed by cultural specialists, dramatists, liturgists, musicians, gospel artists, and singers, to school liturgists, priests, musicians, choirs, and lectors in African American modes of worship. These workshops were attended by Black Catholic laity, sisters, brothers, and clergy, as well as white priests, brothers, and sisters who ministered in the Black community. Intensive sessions brought participants into contact with the slave moans and chants, the spirituals, traditional and contemporary gospel music, and freedom songs. Finally, these workshops created a climate for mutual exchange and collaboration among Black composer and musicians, as well as a stimulus for their professional growth.

The recent appearance of *Lead Me, Guide Me: The African American Catholic Hymnal*[16] is a sign of some maturity in this long and ambiguous period of indigenization. Thoroughly Black and thoroughly Catholic, the hymnal preserves spirituals as well as Gregorian plain chant, Black arrangements of Dr. Watts-style hymns as well as Catholic standards, traditional as well as contemporary Gospel Songs, Freedom Songs as well as African American Catholic compositions. The hymnal also recognizes and affirms both the commonality and plurality of the Black Catholic experience since "... a Louisiana Black Catholic is not a West Baltimore Black Catholic; neither is a New York Haitian Catholic a Los Angeles Black Catholic or a Chicago Black Catholic."[17]

The eucharistic liturgy is at the heart and center of Catholic worship. Given the nature of the doctrinal position held by the Vatican on the ordination of women, there resides at the core of Catholic liturgical life a putative theological bias favoring men over women. In the Roman Catholic church, only celibate males may preside at the eucharistic ritual. Inevitably, this taints Roman Catholic liturgical life with a patina of clerical-centricism. Black feminist theologians of other Christian traditions will find this situation not so different from their own: for even if their churches are logo-centric, preaching is dominated by the male voice. In the effort to nourish its own membership at retreats and to foster the gifts of women like Sister Teresita Weind, S.N.D., and Beverly Stanton, the NBSC encouraged the design of non-eucharistic rituals in a Black cultural style. Litanies and chants, African customs and symbols, stylized gesture and dance interplayed to express purification and dedication, to celebrate points of passage or commitment, to mark repentance of resolve.

Spiritual Formation. Christianity is, above all, a way of life. Catholicism marks that way of life with features that differentiate its expression from those of other Christians. And Black Catholics—lay women and men, sisters, brothers, priests—were not long in identifying the need and ways to ebonize features of a Catholic Christian way of life.

A retreat, the setting aside of sustained and uninterrupted time for prayer, for meditation, for examination or refreshment or renovation of one's relationship with God, was an opportunity to transform a common Catholic practice in the light of Black Theology. The NBSC sponsored retreats for its own members, but it was not unusual for married or single women, brothers, and priests to join them. (And in the last few years, retreats either have preceded of followed annual joint conferences of the permanent deacons and their wives, sisters, brothers, seminarians, and priests.) Retreats included a variety of spiritual disciplines—private and communal reflective reading and praying of the Scriptures, singing spirituals or other appropriate hymns, fasting, silence, quiet or guided meditation. Devotional conferences were the locus of nourishing formative reflection. From the perspective of Black Theology, these conferences examined such topics as prayer, spirituality, celibacy, suffering, loneliness, and the meaning of eucharist in the Black sociopolitical context. Often these conferences were prepared by nonordained women and men who had formal training in Catholic theology or spirituality or who were well read in Black Theology and in Catholic spirituality. These conferences attempted to work out new understandings of the Christian life by which Black Catholics could take their bearings.

In September 1969, Al McNeeley of Detroit's St. Bernard Parish, along with a team of lay leaders and priests, developed a pastoral training program to give Black men theological, spiritual, and personal formation and support to function in the Black community as lay or nonordained ministers within their parishes. The program took Scriptural impetus from the work of deacons (Acts 6:1–7); it took pastoral theological motivation from the pressing socioeconomic and cultural needs of the local Black community; and it took personal inspiration from the promotion and cultivation of Black self-concept and Black leadership. "Ministers of Service" fanned out into various city parishes, assessed needs, and generated innovative ways to meet them. They helped families cope with crises of all sorts, befriended Black youth, criticized crime and drugs, cheered bed-ridden and home-bound residents, comforted those confined to hospitals and nursing homes. They assisted at the eucharist, conducted Bible study classes, and prepared youth and adults for participation in the sacraments. These men carried the compassion, love, and mercy of God to people and places the institutional church neglected.

Theological Appropriation

The meeting of African American Catholic ministry and Black Theology has had fruitful results. Already, as I have indicated, this encounter has made distinctive and significant contributions to pastoral and social ministry by and among Black Catholics to the way liturgy is understood and celebrated by and among us, as well as to the wider renewal of liturgy and the liturgical arts in the Catholic church in the United States. In theology, however, the situation is quite different.

The work of thematizing a theology of African American Catholic spirituality has been carried on, in large measure, by Benedictine monk, scholar, and church historian Cyprian Davis. For nearly fifteen years he has presented monographs and lectures that retrieve, contextualize, and interpret both Black and Catholic models of sanctity and African American Catholic spiritual traditions of communal Bible study and prayer. By unsealing the neglected, antique and modern, history of Catholics of African descent and situating Black women and men within the stream of Catholic piety, Davis breaks open a tradition faithful to both Black religious experience and to multicultural Catholic spirituality. He suggests four characteristics of Black Catholic spirituality: it is contemplative, holistic, joyful, and communitarian. It is contemplative because the African American apprehension of religion mystically surrenders to the dark numinous power of God to hallow a home in the heart and soul, to infuse the whole person with awe at God's transcendent presence and with ecstatic joy at the intimacy of God's immanence. It is holistic because the African American personality is di-unital, and retains the capacity to manage ambiguity. This personality is gifted with a fundamental regard for person, for the human over products or things. Black spirituality is joyful resting in the power of God to protect, to defend, and to save; and this joy animates works of love and compassion, of reconciliation and peace. Black spirituality is communal and expresses itself in social concern and social justice; and this communitarian dimension opens Black Christians to all, excludes none. Davis's work displays a harmony neither artificial nor forced. He is a careful, painstaking historian able to tell the African American Catholic story in a style that emboldens and edifies. Currently Father Davis is at work on an extended history of African American Catholics.[18]

A Black Catholic theology of catechesis is one of the projects that occupies the scholarship of Toinette Eugene. Taking as her point of departure the African American religious experience as well as Roman Catholic church tradition, she sets evangelization and religious education in the place where revelation begins for Black people—in our own specific culture and ethos. Eugene's overall project in this area has been to lay out moral, ethical, and religious directions for Black Catholic catechesis. Those directions advocate Black culture as the "framework for embracing and synthesizing Church and community," a Christian love engaged in "meaningful and gracefull praxis within the struggle for liberation," and a prophetic "self-sacrificial love and concern for others."[19] Eugene has done additional studies that focus the moral and ethical imperatives of Black Catholic catechesis on specific questions—family, sexuality, love, images and roles of women. Her participation on the committee of women advising the U.S. Catholic Bishops' Committee on their pastoral letter on the status of women brings a nuanced and critical voice to predominantly white, middle-class, liberal feminist concerns.

Catholic theology as a whole still wants for dialogue with the social and human sciences. In exploring the psychosocial theme of Black self-concept, Black Catholic theologians contribute to furthering conversation with psychology. Dominican Sister Jamie Phelps has begun to delineate a prolegomenon to a fully differentiated theology of person that explicity adverts to and affirms Black self-concept.[20] Her doctoral studies were preceded by a graduate degree in psychiatric social work as well as extensive clinical experience; and her career has always included parish involvement. Hence, Phelps' writing and lecturing on Black self-concept are characterized by practical as well as theoretical relevance and a nuanced grasp of varieties of Black lived experience.

Canadian Jesuit philosopher-theologian, Bernard Lonergan has influenced the theological work of the Reverend Edward K. Braxton and me. Both of us have devoted doctoral research to Lonergan's work—Braxton on its relation to symbol and myth, me on its relation to contemporary political and theological thought on the common good.[21] Both of us are critical interpreters of contemporary theological movements and draw freely on the heuristic categories that Lonergan's reformulation of method in theology affords.

Reverend Braxton has written several articles analyzing and commenting on Black (Protestant) theology, as well as a lucid, thoughtful interpretation of changes in the church initiated by the Second Vatican Council.[22] James Cone has praised the potential Braxton's "theological imagination and discipline" to make a significant Catholic contribution to Black Theology. However, Cone suggests that classical and European theological motifs compete for Braxton's talent, evoking in him an "unresolved inner tension"[23] that prevents the flowering of his acumen. But, it is also possible that Edward Braxton is ensnared in that dilemma faced by all Black intellectuals seeking legitimation through an academy that is so inimical to their innermost concerns and so existentially and intellectually stultifying for them.

I served as Program Director for the first national consultation on Black Theilogy sponsored by the TIA Black Theology Project in 1977 and was Lonergan's teaching assistant during his final year at Boston College, where I have been associated with that university's group of Lonergan scholars. From the foundational categories of Bernard Lonergan's structure of the human good, I propose to rethink political theology in the American context with specific attention to issues of race, gender, and class.

Albert Raboteau's *Slave Religion*[24] is essential reading for an understanding of the Black religious experience. Here he made a study of the Herkovits-Frazier debate on the tenacity of African cultural elements in the life of the slaves. Raboteau argues a continuum of African influence, one of less degree in the United States than in Cuba, Haiti, and Brazil. And according to Raboteau, Catholicism accounts for this difference. In the Caribbean and Latin America, Catholicism offered points of contact with traditional African ritual and customs. In the United States, this was not the case as a deritualized Protestantism prevailed. Raboteau's historical interest in Black religion and Black religious experience complements the more specifically Catholic explorations of Cyprian Davis.

NOTES

1. *Three Catholic Afro-American Congresses* (Cincinnati: The American Catholic Tribune, 1893; Reprint. New York: Arno Press, 1978): 4, 13. See David Spalding, C.F.X., "The Negro Catholic Congress, 1889–1894," *The Catholic Historical Review* 55 (October 1969) 33–57, and Cyprian Davis, O.S.B., "Black Catholics in America: A Historical Note," *America* 142, no. 3 (May 1980) 378–80.

2. The first pre-Emancipation attempt to found a religious congregation for Black women was in 1824 through the work of Father Charles Nerinck in Kentucky. But the insensitivity of clergy and diocesan officials forced the dismissal of the group. In 1829, the Oblate Sisters of Providence was founded in Baltimore; in 1842, the Holy Family Sisters was founded in New Orleans. There is also a third Black religious congregation, the Franciscan Handmaids of the Most Pure Heart of Mary, founded in 1917 to work in Harlem, New York. True to the meaning of Catholicity, i.e., universality, each of these congregations opened their ranks to white women who have joined them over the years.

3. Father Augustus Tolton is generally recognized as the first Black American Catholic priest, but there were three others: the Healy brothers—James Augustine, Sherwood, and Patrick. Sons of a slave woman and an Irish Catholic planter, they had been isolated by their father's money and social associations from the brunt of racism, but this left them with little explicit race identification and consciousness. By the time of the congress movement, Sherwood, a canon lawyer and theologian, was dead; James Augustine was the Ordinary Bishop of the diocese of Portland, Maine; and Patrick, a Jesuit, had served Georgetown University as vice president and president.

4. Spalding, 357.

5. Jerome LeDoux, "Christian Pastoral Theology Looks at Black Experience," in *Theology: A Portrait in Black* (hereafter *TAPB*), ed. Thaddeus J. Posey, O.F.M., Cap. (Pittsburgh: Capuchin Press, 1980), 115.

6. Thomas Merton, *The Black Revolution* (The Southern Christian Leadership Conference in Atlanta, 1963?).

7. For some personal accounts see Saundra Willingham, "Why I Quit the Convent," *Ebony* (December 1968): 64–74; Lawrence Lucas, *Black Priest/White Church, Catholics and Racism* (New York:Random House, Inc., 1970); Sister Louis Marie Bryan, S.C., "History of the National Black Sisters' Conference," *Celibate Black Commitment: Report of the Third Annual National Black Sisters' Conference* (NBSC in Pittsburgh, 1971): 3–9; Sister Mary Roger Thibodeaux, S.B.S., *A Black Nun Looks at Black Power* (New York: Sheed and Ward, 1972).

8. First printed in *Freeing the Spirit* 1, no. 3 (Summer 1972); Reprinted in Gayraud S. Wilmore and James H. Cone, ed., *Black Theology: A Documentary History, 1966–1979* (Maryknoll, N.Y.: Orbis Books, 1979), 322–34.

9. "The National Black Sisters' Conference Position Paper," *Black Survival: Past, Present, Future, A Report of the Second National Black Sisters' Conference* (NBSC in Pittsburgh, 1970): 155.

10. The National Black Sisters' Conference was invited through me, its executive director, to participate in the 1975 Detroit meeting of Theology in the Americas. I was unable to attend because of conference business, and Sister Jamie Phelps, O.P., attended.

11. *Brothers and Sisters to Us* (Washington, D.C.: USCC, 1979).

12. World Library Publications, 1966. See also his *Soulfull Worship* (Washington, D.C.: NOBC, 1974), *Spirit in Worship* (Cincinnati, Ohio:Stimuli, Inc., 1978), "Thank God We Ain't What We Was: The State of Liturgy in the Black Catholic Community," TAPB: 66–74, and "The Oral Tradition Versus the Ocular Western Tradition," in *This Far By Faith: American Black Worship and Its African Roots* (NOBC and the Liturgical Conference in Washington, D.C., 1977): 38–49.

13. Vatican II, *Sacrosanctum Concilium*, Constitution on the Sacred Liturgy, 4 (December 1963): nos. 14 and 37.

14. Cyprian Lamar Rowe, F.M.S., "The Case for a Distinctive Black Culture," *This Far By Faith* 27.

15. Rivers, "Thank God," 73.

16. *Lead Me, Guide Me: The African American Catholic Hymnal* (Chicago: G.I.A. Publications, Inc., 1987). The hymnal was authorized in 1983 by the National Black Catholic Clergy Caucus; its compilation and editing were coordinated by Bishop James Lyke, O.F.M.

17. J. Glenn Murray, S.J., "The Liturgy of the Roman Rite and African American Worship," *Lead Me, Guide Me* (n.p.).

18. See Cyprian Davis, O.S.B., "The Christian Interpretation of the Black Experience," TAPB: 91–102; also his "Black Spirituality," paper presented at the meeting of the National Black Catholic Congress, Washington, D.C., May 1987; "The Holy See and American Blacks in the Files of the Apostolic Delegation, 1904–1919 (Paper delivered at the American Catholic Historical Association, Washington, D.C., December 30, 1987).

19. Toinette Eugene, "Developing Black Catholic Belief," TAPB: 14; see also her "Moral Values and Black Womanists," *The Journal of Religious Thought* 44 (Winter-Spring 1988): 23–34, and "White Love is Unfashionable: Ethical Implications of Black Spirituality and Sexuality," in *Women's Consciousness and Women's Conscience: A Reader in Feminist Ethics*, ed. Barbara Hikert-Andolsen, Christine Gudorf, and Mary D. Pellauer (San Francisco: Harper & Row, 1985), 121–41.

20. Jamie Phelps, O.P., "Black Self-Concept," *TAPB*: 52–65; "Doctrine: The Articulation of Soul," in *Tell It Like It Is: A Black Catholic Perspective on Christian Education* (Oakland, Calif: NBSC, 1983), 108–23; "Women and Power in the Church: A Black Catholic Perspective," Proceedings *Catholic Theological Society of America* 37 (1982): 119–23.

21. See Edward K. Braxton, "Images of Mystery: A Study of the Place of Myth and Symbol in the Theological Method of Bernard Lonergan" (Ph.D. diss. Catholic University of Louvain, 1975). My dissertation is still in progress and offers a more political interpretation of Lonergan's work. See my revision of *Prophesy Deliverance! An Afro-American Revolutionary Christianity* by Cornel West, *Cross Currents* 33 (Spring 1983): 67–71, "Black Theology," in *The New Dictionary of Theology*, ed. Komonchak et al. (Wilmington, Del.: Michael Glazier, 1987): 137–41; "The Interaction of Racism, Sexism, and Classism in Women's Exploitation," in *Concilium: Women, Work, and Poverty*, ed., Elisabeth Schussler-Fiorenza (Nijmegen, Edinburgh: Stichting Concilium and T. & T. Clark, 1987): 19–27.

22. See his essay on Black Theology in *America* (March 29, 1980): 274–77; "Reflections from a Theological Perspective," in *This Far By Faith*, 58–75; "Black Theology: Potentially Classic?" *Religious Studies Review* 4 (April 1978): 85–90, "What Is 'Black Theology' Anyway?" *The Critic* (Winter 1977): 64–70, and *The Wisdom Community* (New York: Paulist Press, 1980).

23. Cone, 52.

24. Albert Raboteau, *Slave Religion, The 'Invisible Institution' in the Antebellum South* (New York: Oxford University Press, 1978).

Chapter Forty-one

"Lifting As We Climb"
Womanist Theorizing about Religion and the Family

Toinette M. Eugene

As important as was the modern articulation of African American religious concerns in Black Theology, it repeated an error of past representations of African America's life: It subsumed women's thought and theologizing under the pronouncements of men; it assumed that when black men spoke genuinely for the community that black women's voice was being heard therein. In part this was attributable to a male blind spot: Men claimed to believe they were representing black women's concerns, not perceiving the category of black femaleness as one with experiences, perspectives, and concerns distinct from those of men with whom they shared the black experience. Even this blind spot, however, was traceable to the patriarchal, sexist attitudes and behaviors pervasive in the larger society and in which blacks as men participated. Black women have stepped forward to claim their own voice in theological discourse in a substantial and growing body of literature. Following is an example, from the writings of theologian and ethicist Toinette M. Eugene.

•

The central theses of this chapter, which traces the specific moral values of black feminism to their root within black religious traditions, are also theses derived in part from the highest expressions of moral and faith development as described particularly in the theoretical research of Carol Gilligan and James Fowler.[1]

By drawing on this psychological research and by reviewing black religious history, this chapter asserts that public activism and private endurance are paradigmatic black women's value indicators in both the black religious traditions and in womanist communities. Social activism, self-sacrifice, and other similar value indicators may be verified in the lives of Mary McLeod Bethune and Nannie Helen Burroughs, to name but two exemplary models. However, these value measures and these valuable models represent more than unusual courage and strength; they also represent realistic responses to economic deprivation and political and social inequality. Black women have been forced to perform labor and to take risks that few white women have been called on to do, either in the name of religious traditions or in behalf of the survival of their race.

Black women, however, are not special specimens of womanhood; rather, they are women of color who have been given less protected and more burdensome positions in society. As Michelle Wallace has so poignantly pointed out, this has resulted in the "myth" of the superwoman," which is not a description of black women but, rather, a measure of the difference between what is regularly expected of white women and what is essentially required of black women.[2] Womanists continue to lift as they climb.

It is obvious that black women have experienced the oppressive structures of racism, class bias, and male supremacy in both religion and society in this country. What is not always so obvious to a dominant white world view, and even to feminist theological understandings, is that African American culture and religion have generated alternative interrelated notions of womanhood that contradict those of mainstream American economics, sociology, and theology.[3] These alternative experiences, visions, and images of womanhood have been forged out of the furnace of a moral value system endemic to the black church, which is also undeniably the "domestic church" or home base for liberating revolutionary praxis. This chapter will explore aspects of the moral consciousness and value system that guide black women in their ongoing struggle for survival. It will do so through a commentary on black religious traditions that black women share. Within this commentary some reflections will also be made regarding black women's perspectives on feminism as a white women's movement, and on feminist theologies.

Black Women and Moral Values During Slavery

Historically, the domestic black church has been the fiery furnace through which systematic faith affirmations and liberating principles for biblical interpretation have been developed by black people. Within this "invisible institution," hidden from the observation of slave masters, black women and black men developed an extensive moral value system and religious life of their own. In the language of moral development theorist Carol Gilligan, they established and operated out of a web of network of relationships and intimacy with others in community. The moral values of care, compassion, and cooperation with other black and oppressed persons served as criteria for decisions and actions intended to lay hold of the good, the true, and the beautiful.

The biblical interpretations of the antebellum black church provided black people with webs of relationships centering on the God of justice and of liberation, and these made slaves incontestably discontent with their servile condition. In the case of black women, whose bodies and spirits were wantonly violated by the immoral sexual advances of white masters, the moral value system of black people in this period encouraged slave women to overcome the sources of their oppression in order to maintain and sustain their fragile nexus with God and community as valued and trusted friends.[4] Paula Giddings, in her text *When and Where I Enter: The Impact of Black Women on Race and Sex in America*, reports on the moral resistance black slave women offered:

So, by the early eighteenth century an incredible social, legal, racial structure was put in place. Women were firmly stratified in the roles that Plato envisioned. Blacks were chattel, White men could impregnate a Black woman with impunity, and she alone could give birth to a slave. Blacks constituted a permanent labor force and metaphor that were perpetuated through the Black woman's womb. And all of this was done within the context of the Church, the operating laws of capitalism, and the psychological needs of White males. Subsequent history would be a variation on the same theme.

In its infancy slavery was particularly harsh. Physical abuse, dismemberment, and torture were common. . . . Partly as a result, in the eighteenth century, slave masters did not underestimate the will of their slaves to rebel, even their female slaves. Black women proved especially adept at poisoning their masters, a skill undoubtedly imported from Africa. Incendiarism was another favorite method; it required neither brute physical strength nor direct confrontation. But Black women used every means available to resist slavery—as men did—and if caught, they were punished just as harshly.[5]

In the midst of this dehumanizing slave environment, black families, and thus the "domestic" church, survived. They overcame the slaveholders' attempts to reduce them to so many subhuman labor units, managing to create an ongoing system of family arrangements and kin networks. Domestic life became critically important, for it was the only place where slaves had any equality and autonomy as human beings in relation to one another.[6]

Regarding domestic life and labor, Angela Davis in *Women, Race, and Class* has observed a paradox of great significance for black women and men:

> The salient theme emerging from domestic life in the slave quarters is one of sexual equality. The labor that slaves performed for their own sake and not for the aggrandizement of their masters was carried out on terms of equality. Within the confines of their family and community life, therefore, Black people managed to accomplish a magnificent feat. They transformed that negative equality which emanated from the equal oppression they suffered as slaves into a positive quality: the egalitarianism characterizing their social relations.[7]

Harriet Tubman and countless others provided egalitarian images of slave women as strong, self-reliant, proud of their roots and of their ability to survive, and convinced of their right to a place in society through the liberation of all black people. Equally oppressed as laborers, equal to their men in the domestic sphere, they were also equal in their moral resistance to slavery, participating in work stoppages and revolts, fleeing north, and helping others to flee.

The ability of black people to cope in a hostile society endured into the twentieth century. Studies of black women in urban church situations show that the means by which black families survived slavery still enable black women and their families to survive today.

Within this historical framework of past and present hostility black women have always perceived networks of relationality in the liberation struggle differently from white women. Domesticity has never been seen as entirely oppressive but rather as a vehicle for building family life under slavery. Male/female relationships have always been more egalitarian. There has usually been less emphasis on women's work as different from and inferior to men's. And finally, slaves and freed persons, both male and female, have consistently rebelled against the sexual oppression of black women as well as the emasculation of black men. It is easy to understand why many black people today see the white feminist movement as an attempt to divide black people. Contemporary womanists caution against espousing more "radical" white feminist positions because they dismiss as irrelevant black men, black children, and black families. Consequently, a primary moral value for black people is articulated in this overarching and enduring womanist position: Solidarity among all black people is essential for survival.

A dramatic statement of black women's unique attitude toward solidarity with black men is found in the 1977 statement of the Combahee River Collective, a black lesbian feminist group from Boston:

> Although we are feminists and lesbians we feel solidarity with progressive Black men and do not advocate the fractionalization that white women who are separatists demand. Our situation as Black people necessitates that we have solidarity around the fact of race. . . . We struggle together with Black men against racism, while we also struggle with Black men about sexism.[8]

These black lesbian feminists explicitly rejected a feminist separatism that equates all oppression with sexual oppression, and which fails fully to acknowledge that black women and men are victims of shared racial oppression. Feminist separatism is not a viable political philosophy for most black women. Ethicist Barbara Hilkert Andolsen, in her remarkable assessment of racism and American feminism, *Daughters of Jefferson, Daughters of Bootblacks*, issues a strong caveat to white women who want to understand the black feminist experience:

> Those of us who are white feminists need to be careful that we do not articulate limited strategies for dealing with sexism as if they were the only legitimate feminist strategies. White feminist separatist theories or strategies that ignore the strong bond forged between many black women and men in a shared struggle against racism do not speak to all women's experience.[9]

White feminists have a responsibility to understand the perspectives of women of color on their own issues, to analyze how racist social structures may alter the impact of white feminist proposals, and to support black women in their own self-defined struggle for liberation. Womanists are creating their own analyses of sexism and of the interconnections between racism and sexism. White feminist theologians who wish to contribute to an inclusive feminist theology that respects and reflects the diversity of women's experience need to learn from the experiences, moral values, and feminist theology articulated by black women.

There is ample material for reflection in the records of black women's distinctive theological consciousness during slavery. For example, the biblical-exegetical abilities of Maria Stewart, coupled with her philosophical assumptions (that would later be known as modernist thinking), gave black women in 1832 a freer rein to express and act on ideas that liberated them from the oppression of both sexism and racism.[10] For Stewart, simple logic demanded that in light of women's past roles, "God at this eventful period should raise up your females to strive . . . both in public and private, to assist those who are endeavoring to stop the strong current of prejudice that flows so profusely against us at present."[11] Maria Stewart was sure enough of her moral values to admonish others not to doubt the validity of black women's mission: "No longer ridicule their efforts," she counseled, "It will be counted as sin."[12]

At a woman's rights convention in Akron, Ohio in 1851, several of the most celebrated examples of early womanist theology were rendered by the legendary abolitionist and mystic, Sojourner Truth, in her famous "Ain't I a Woman" speech. From the very beginning of the conference, the white women were overwhelmed by the jeering ridicule of men who had come to disrupt the meeting. Their most effective antagonist was a clergyman who used both the maleness of Jesus and the helplessness of the women to counter their feminist arguments. Sojourner squelched the heckler by correcting his theology first, noting that Jesus came from "God and a woman— man had nothing to do with Him."[13] Second, she asserted that women were not inherently weak and helpless.

Raising herself to her full height of six feet, flexing a muscled arm, and bellowing with a voice one observer likened to the apocalyptic thunders, Truth informed the audience that she could outwork, outeat, and outlast any man. Then she challenged: "Ain't I a Woman?"[14] She spoke of women's strength and moral abilities to set things aright: "If the first woman God ever made was strong enough to turn the world upside down all alone, these women together ought to be able to turn it back, and get it right side up again. And now they are asking to do it, the men better let them."[15] The moral values asserted by black women who give credence to the black Judeo—Christian tradition consistently honor reconciliation as highly as liberation. The praxis of "lifting as we climb" continues as a historically documentable theme.

The accumulated experiences and expressions of black women during slavery were nuanced by their differing webs of relationship within the institutional and patriarchal black church and its biblical interpretations of the salvific power of God. These women toiled under the lash for their masters, worked for the protected their families, fought against slavery and were beaten and raped; but, unsubdued, they passed on to their nominally free female descendants a rich legacy of their own moral value system. It was a legacy of hard work decidedly different from the WASP work ethic; it was a legacy of perseverance and self-reliance, a legacy of tenacity, resistance, and insistence on sexual equality—in short, a legacy of love spelling out standards for a new womanhood.[16]

Feminist Moral Values and Black Religious Traditions

The institution of chattel slavery in America was destroyed by the most momentous national event of the nineteenth century, the Civil War. Emancipation removed the legal and political status of slavery from approximately four million black people in the United States, which meant that, in principle, these blacks owned their persons and their labor for the first time. Unfortunately for the vast majority of African Americans, the traditional practices of racial and gender subordination continued to bring them incredible suffering after that war.

The black woman began her life of freedom with no vote, no protection, and no equity of any sort. Black women, young and old, were basically on their own. The pattern of exploiting the black woman as laborer and breeder was only shaken by the Civil War; by no means was it destroyed. Throughout the late nineteenth and early twentieth centuries, black women were strongly restricted to the most unskilled, poorly paid, menial work. Virtually no black woman held a job beyond that of a domestic servant or field hand. Keeping house, farming, and bearing and rearing children continued to dominate all aspects of the black woman's life. The systematic oppression and routinized exclusion of black females from other areas of employment served to confirm the continuing, servile status of black women. As Jeanne Noble describes it, "While freedom brought new opportunities for black men, for most women in augmented old problems."[17] After emancipation, racism and male supremacy continued to intersect with patriarchal and capitalist structures in definitive ways.

The religious consciousness of the black freedwoman in the latter nineteenth century focused on "uplifting the black community." The black female was taught that her education was meant not only to uplift her but also to prepare her for a life of service in the overall community. There was a general attitude, says Noble, that "Negro women should be trained to teach in order to uplift the masses."[18] This attitude provided an additional impetus for black women such as Nannie Helen Burroughs, Charlotte Hawkins Brown, and Mary McLeod Bethune to found schools. Although the curricula of these schools included academic subjects, there were large doses of industrial arts courses, particularly homemaking, and an environment that enforced codes of morality and thrift. Biblical faith, grounded in the prophetic tradition, helped black women devise strategies and tactics to make black people less susceptible to the indignities and proscriptions of an oppressive white social order.

Understanding the prophetic tradition of the Bible and of the black church has empowered black women to fashion a set of moral values on their own terms. It has helped them to master, radicalize, and sometimes destroy the pervasive negative orientations imposed by the larger society. It has also helped them to articulate possibilities for decisions and action that address forthrightly the circumstances that shape black life.

In light of black women's biblical faith grounded in the prophetic tradition, many black women have been inspired by the Bethune and Burroughs models to regard highly a diaconal model of black feminist theology, which is extremely consistent with their experience and identity. Without necessarily rejecting white feminist models of theology that focus principally or only on mutuality and equality as *sine qua nons* of liberation, the choice made by many black feminists is for a theology of servant-leadership as espoused by Christ. This biblical model of feminist liberation theology is principally focused on solidarity with those who suffer or are marginalized in any way. A much deeper examination, integration, and expression of this black feminist perspective and alternative to "mainstream" models of feminist liberation theology is needed.[19]

Rosemary Radford Ruether has been in the forefront of white feminist theologians who have insisted that confronting racism must be a high priority. She has produced particularly illuminating analyses of the interconnections between racism and sexism.[20] When discussing the future of feminist theology in the academic world, Ruether acknowledges that she speaks from a "white Western Christian context." She calls for an inclusive feminist theology that must emerge out of "a network of solidarity" existing among many feminist communities "engaged in the critique of patriarchalism in distinct cultural and religious contexts," rather than "one dominant form of feminism that claims to speak for the whole of womankind."[21]

During the mass migration of southern blacks to the North (1910–1925), tens of thousands of black women and men left home, seeking social democracy and economic opportunity. During this colossal movement of black people, the black church continued to serve as the focal point and center for maintaining the moral value system and the network of relationships that sustained community life.

Not surprisingly, this accelerated movement of blacks out of the South impinged on the black woman's reality in very definite ways. Black women migrated North in greater numbers than black men. Economic necessity required most black women who immigrated to the urban centers to find work immediately. In order to survive and to provide for their families, black women once again found only drudge work available to them.

The interaction of race and sex in the labor market exacted a heavy toll on the black woman, making all aspects of migration a problem of paramount religious significance. Her experience as a wife and a mother, responsible for transmitting the moral values, culture, and customs of the black community to her children, served as a decisive factor in determining how the Bible was read and understood by her. Simultaneously, while the black woman was trying to organize family life according to black traditional values, the white male-dominated industrial society required that she serve as a catalyst in their labor transition process. Her own culture shock and adaptation difficulties had to be repressed because she was responsible for making a home in crowded, substandard housing, finding inner-city schools that provided literacy training for her children, and earning enough income to cover the most elementary needs of her family.

The moral and religious value system of the domestic black church served as a sustaining force and as an interpretive grid to guide migrant black women in facing life squarely, and in acknowledging its raw coarseness. The white elitist attributes of passive gentleness and an enervated delicacy, considered particularly appropriate to womanhood, proved nonfunctional in the pragmatic survival of black women. Cultivating conventional amenities was not a luxury afforded them. Instead, black women were aware that their very lives depended on their being able to comprehend the various forces in the larger world; to hold in check the nightmare figures of terror; to fight for basic freedoms against the sadistic law enforcement agencies; to resist the temptation to capitulate to the demands of the *status quo*; to find meaning in the most despotic circumstances; and to create something where nothing existed before. The expression of a moral value system for black women meant and required a "sheroic" self-sacrifice and self-giving that could never allow for shyness, silence, softness, or diffidence as a response indicating subservience.

From the period of black urban migration through World War I and II black women, rooted in the strong moral values and prophetic tradition of the domestic black church, became religious crusaders for justice. Mary McLeod Bethune and her associates recorded and talked about the grimness of struggle among the least visible people in the society. Bethune was adamant about the unheralded achievements of black women, always encouraging them to "go to the front and take our rightful place; fight our battles and claim our victories."[22] She believed in black women's "possibilities," moral values, and their place on this earth. "Next to God," she once said, "we are indebted to women, first for life itself, and then for making it worth having."[23] In response to a hostile environment, deteriorating conditions, and the enduring humiliation of social ostracism experienced by black people especially during these war years, Bethune and company exposed the most serious and unyielding problem of the twentieth century—the single most determining factor of black existence in America—the question of color. In their strategic attacks against the ideological supremacy of racist practices and values, Bethune and her colleagues appealed to the religious traditions of black people that began in their invisible church during slavery.

From the period of urbanization during World War II to the present, women of color still find that their situation is a struggle to survive collectively and individually against the harsh historical realities and pervasive adversities of today's world. Federal government programs, civil rights movements, and voter-education programs have all had a positive impact on the black woman's situation, but they have not been able to offset the negative effects of inequities that are tied to the historical and ideological hegemony of racism, sexism, and class privilege.[24]

Precisely because of this reality and overwhelmingly oppressive national ideology, Rosemary Radford Ruether warns white feminists to give explicit attention to the ways in which they are involved in race and class privilege. If they do not, she says, they risk social encapsulation:

> Any women's movement which is only concerned about sexism and not other forms of oppression, must remain a woman's movement of the white upper class, for it is only this group of women whose only problem is the problem of being women, since in every other way, they belong to the ruling class.[25]

Moreover, both black and white feminist groups that do not give explicit attention to the need for yoking racism and sexism will find that they can easily be manipulated by dominant males, who often appeal to unexamined class and race interests to achieve economic exploitation of all women. Work and dialogue between feminists of color and white feminists in this essential area is, in some sense, just beginning. Meanwhile, black women and their families continue to be enslaved to hunger, disease, and the highest rate of black unemployment since the Depression years. Advances in education, housing, health care, and other necessities are deteriorating faster now than ever before.

Both in informal day-to-day life and in the formal organizations and institutions of society, black women are still the victims of aggravated inequities rooted in the tridimensional reality of race/class/gender oppression. It is in this context that the moral values of black women and the emergence of womanist consciousness, shaped by black biblical and religious traditions, must continue to make a decisive difference in a debilitated and nearly dysfunctional human environment.

Womanist Relationships, Moral Values, and Biblical Traditions

Because of this totally demoralizing reality, and because of the religious traditions from which most black women have come, the Bible has been the highest source of authority in developing and delivering a black moral praxis and a moral theology that is usable in all circumstances. By selectively utilizing the pages of revered Old Testament books, black women have learned how to refute the stereotypes that have depicted black people as ignorant minstrels or vindictive militants. Remembering and retelling the Jesus stories of the New Testament has helped black women to deal with the overwhelming difficulties of overworked and widowed mothers, of under-worked and anxious fathers, of sexually exploited and anguished daughters, of prodigal sons, and of dead or dying brothers whose networks of relationality are rooted deeply in the black community. Womanist consciousness and moral values grow out of and expand on liberationist, black biblical experience and hermeneutics.

Black feminist consciousness may be more accurately identified as black womanist consciousness, to use Alice Walker's concept and definition. In the introduction to *In Search of Our Mothers' Gardens*, Walker proposes several descriptions of the term "womanist," indicating that the word refers primarily to a black feminist and is derived from the older term "womanish," referring to outrageous, audacious, courageous, or willful behavior.[26] To be a faithful womanist, then, is to operate out of this system of black moral value indicators that flow from biblical understandings based on justice and love. It is to express in word and deed an alternative ontology or way of living in the world that is endemic to many black women. It is precisely the womanist religious responses of endurance, resistance, and resiliency offered in the face of all attempts at personal and institutional domination that may provide a renewed theological legacy of liberation for everyone concerned.

In exploring the implications contained in Walker's richly descriptive prose, it is possible to make some concluding reflections on black moral values and on the contribution of black women's life experiences as they interface with white feminist liberation theologies.

Womanist responses and black moral values gleaned from the domestic black church are meant to be alternative standards of womanhood contradictory to those of mainstream American society. Womanist images and black moral values are meant to be paradigmatic of an authentic Christian community of the oppressed, one embraces not only the story of the Resurrection but acts as a referent for the redemptive tribulations through which Jesus as Suffering Servant has come. Womanist moral values are expressed through radical healing and empowering actions in company with those who are considered the very least in the reign of God.

Walker adds that a womanist is "committed to the survival and wholeness of entire people, male *and* female." She is "not a separatist . . . [and is] traditionally capable."[27] The practical implications of such meanings for interaction and dialogue between black women's moral values and the diverse tenets of white feminist ethics are obvious and challenging. Womanist moral values can redeem the black community from naiveté regarding the nature and function of liberation, as well as deliver them from the simplistic, black pseudoexpression of providence that "de Lawd will provide." Nonetheless, a womanist religious tradition does subscribe to the black folk wisdom that God can make a way out of no way for those, like Zora Neale Huston and others, who simply refuse to resign from the human race.

Womanist moral values of "appreciation for the struggle, a love of the folk, and a love of self—*regardless*"[28] offer to black people as well as to others a continual and open means of interaction between those who claim diverse womanist and feminist identities and experiences. Such values are relevant to all who have a significant agenda for more authentic theologies of liberation. "Lifting as We Climb" remains the watchword and the praxis project for womanist theorizing and strategizing about religion and the family.

NOTES

1. Carol Gilligan, *In a Different Voice: Psychological Theory and Women's Development* (Cambridge, Mass.: Harvard University Press, 1982) and James W. Fowler, *Stages of Faith: The Psychology of Human Development and the Quest for Meaning* (San Francisco: Harper & Row, 1981).

2. Michelle Wallace, *Black Macho and the Myth of the Superwoman* (New York: Dial Press, 1979).

3. Toinette M. Eugene, "Black Women Contribute Strong Alternate Images," *National Catholic Reporter*, 13 April 1984, 4.

4. Carol Gilligan as described in James W. Fowler, *Becoming Adult, Becoming Christian* (San Francisco: Harper & Row, 1984), 39–40.

5. Paula Giddings, *When and Where I Enter: The Impact of Black Women on Race and Sex in America* (Toronto: Bantam Books, 1984), 39.

6. Herbert Gutman, *The Black Family in Slavery and Freedom*, 1750–1925 (New York: Pantheon Books, 1976), 356–57.

7. Angela Y. Davis, *Women, Race, and Class* (New York: Random House, 1981), 18.

8. Combahee River Collective, "A Black Feminist Statement," in *This Bridge Called My Back: Writings by Radical Women of Color*, ed. Cherrie Moraga and Gloria Anzaldua (Watertown, Mass.: Persephone Press, 1981), 213.

9. Barbara Hilkert Andolsen, *Daughters of Jefferson, Daughters of Bootblacks: Racism and American Feminism* (Macon, Ga.: Mercer University Press, 1986), 98.

10. Giddings, *When and Where I Enter*, 52.

11. Bert James Lowenberg and Ruth Bogin, eds., *Black Women in Nineteenth Century American Life: Their Words, Their Thoughts, Their Feelings* (University Park, Pa.: Pennsylvania State University Press, 1976), 149.

12. Ibid.

13. Ibid., 236.

14. Ibid., 235.

15. Ibid., 236.

16. Davis, *Women, Race, and Class*, 29.

17. Jeanne L. Noble, *Beautiful, Also, Are the Souls of My Black Sisters: A History of the Black Women in America* (New York: Prentice Hall Press, 1978), 63.

18. Jeanne L. Noble, as discussed in Paula Giddings, *When and Where I Enter*, 101.

19. Eugene, "Black Women Contribute," 4.

20. Rosemary Radford Ruether has written about racism many times. Two of her more detailed treatments of the topic are "Between the Sons of Whites and the Sons of Blackness: Racism and Sexism in America," in *New Women/New Earth: Sexist Ideologies and Human Liberation* (New York: Seabury Press, 1975), 115–33; and "Crisis in Sex and Race: Black Theology vs. Feminist Theology," *Christianity and Crisis* 34 (15 April 1985): 67–73.

21. Rosemary Radford Ruether, "Feminist Theology: On Becoming the Tradition," *Christianity and Crisis* 45 (4 March 1985): 58.

22. Elaine M. Smith, "Mary McLeod Bethune and the National Youth Administration," in *Clio Was a Woman: Studies in the History of American Women*, ed. Mabel E. Deutrich and Virginia C. Purdy (Washington, D.C.: Howard University Press, 1980), 152.

23. Ibid.

24. Davis, *Women, Race, and Class*, 231–32.

25. Ruether, *New Women/New Earth*, 116.

26. Alice Walker, *In Search of Our Mother's Gardens: Womanist Prose* (San Diego: Harcourt Brace Jovanovich, 1983), xi–xiii.

27. Ibid., xi.

28. Ibid.

Part IX

Looking Back to the Future

Chapter Forty-two

Survival, Elevation, and Liberation in Black Religion

Gayraud S. Wilmore

S. Gayraud Wilmore, one of the most knowledgeable and perceptive analysts of the African American religious experience, offers a critical recapitulation of that experience, with probing insights into black religion's role in the existential of struggles of African Americans.

•

> This then is the Gift of the Black Folk to the new world. Thus in singular and fine sense the slave became master, the bond servant became free and the meek not only inherited the earth but made their heritage a thing of questing for eternal youth, of fruitful labor, of joy and music, of the free spirit and of the ministering hand, of wide and poignant sympathy with men in their struggle to live and love which is, after all, the end of striving.
>
> —W. E. B. Du Bois, 1924

The three basic assertions are (1) that within American culture as a whole there was and continues to be an exceedingly complex and distinctive subculture that may be designated black or African American; (2) that despite sociological heterogeneity with respect to such secular factors as regional differences, education, gender, and socio-economic background, religion has been and continues to be an essential thread interweaving the fabric of black culture; and (3) that religiousness, oscillating between conservatism and radicalism, has been and continues to be a persistent characteristic of black life not only in the United States but also in Africa, South America, and the Caribbean—or wherever the animating spirits of Africa have touched the quick of the human heart.

Religious institutions such as the church, therefore, are of the greatest importance in these societies. To them accrue the primary responsibility for the conservation, enhancement, and further development of that unique spiritual quality that has enabled African and black people of the Diaspora to survive and flourish under some of the most unfavorable conditions of the modern world.

The African American Experience

We have focused primarily upon the African American experience without excluding its original locus in Africa and its historic relationship to that continent. From the earliest years of their captivity, transplanted Africans, denied access to other forms of self-affirmation and collective power, have used religion and its various institutions as the principal expression of their peoplehood and their will both to exist and to improve their condition. Black religion, fluctuation between moods of protest and accommodation, and protesting in the context of accommodating strategies, has contributed considerably to the ability of African American people to survive the worst forms of oppression and dehumanization. Beyond mere survival, as leaders and followers became more sophisticated about how to make the most of their religion, it has helped them liberate themselves, first from chattel slavery, then from ignorance and degradation, and finally—though still imperfectly—from civil inequality and subordination, to go on to greater heights of personal and group achievement.

African American religion has not always and in all circumstances functioned in this way for the advancement of the masses. But it is difficult to understand how even the most skeptical observers of the black religious experience in America could deny that, on the whole, religion and its ancillary institutions have served the people positively. One can scarcely imagine how they would have fared without them.

In a sense not true of any other immigrant group in America, the irreducible problem of the Africans brought here was survival. For two hundred years slavery in Protestant North America, unlike human bondage in the Caribbean and Latin America, was practically devoid of mitigating influences from the side of either the church or state. Blacks, scattered in relatively small, isolated groups, were reduced to the level of beasts of burden. With but few exceptions they were treated with slightly more regard than animals who were fed, clothed, and sheltered to no greater degree than was necessary to protect the original investment made to procure them. Owners exploited such human property for the maximum amount of selfish personal gain their bodies would tolerate.

There is no way to palliate this inhumanity. Force and violence were required to establish and maintain the system. The argument that slavery in the South was mainly a paternalistic institution should not be permitted to disguise the fact that blacks reciprocated the blandishments of their supposedly conscience-stricken *paters* in the most effective ways they could devise. Eugene Genovese, a major proponent of the paternalism thesis, acknowledges that it should not be interpreted as evidence of how benevolent slavery was for most blacks, or how readily they acquiesced to it:

> The slaves accepted the doctrine of reciprocity, but with a profound difference. To the idea of reciprocal duties they added their own doctrine of reciprocal rights. To the tendency to make them creatures of another's will they counterpoised a tendency to assert themselves as autonomous human beings. And they thereby contributed, as they had to, to the generation of conflict and great violence.[1]

The point needs to be made over and over. Paternalism, in fact, never really worked as it was supposed to. Slaveholders were obliged, sooner or later, to recognize that there was extreme insecurity in their situation. Only the most stupid among them could have mistaken the fact that they were not dealing with black "sons and daughters" who loved them as seignorial fathers and were willing to exchange that love for protection, but rather had on their hands sensible, thinking human beings who could never be trusted, precisely on that account, to respond in the same manner as children. Moreover, whatever feelings of warmth or tenderness may have been engendered in day-to-day relations, such feelings had to be subordinated to the hard, cold fact that the bottom line was the dollar. In the final analysis, the economic value was realistically calculated and made secure by the imposition of discipline and the monopoly of violent power that by law and otherwise remained in the hands of the masters. It is incredible that the slave did not know that the *noblesse oblige* of a fawning Christian master depended mainly on the slave's capability of producing wealth in the same sense that it was produced by the master's mule or cotton gin— a wealth to which the slave had no claim.

The Survival Tradition

Against this reduction to the status of a thing, enforced by unpredictable cruelty and ruthlessness, the slave's obsession was somehow "to make it"; to hold body and soul together for as long as possible; to engage in an unceasing interior struggle to preserve physical existence and psychological sanity—in short, to survive. Survival, therefore, became the regulative, moment-to-moment principle of the slave community, particularly among field hands. This single factor best explains the tenacity and functionality of black religion in the plantation South.

As a result of new research during the 1970s and 1980s we now have a better idea than previously of how this happened.[2] Drawn together in the quarters after sundown and on Sundays and holidays, the slaves pieced together the tattered remnants of their African past and new patterns of response to the American environment. They selectively chose for themselves attitudes of disbelief, codes of dissimulation and subterfuge, structures of meaning—in short, a view of reality and such coping skills that would make human survival possible under the conditions of their enslavement. Into this strategy of survival they invoked the protecting spirits of the gods of Africa, or in time, the new God of Christianity.

In the formation of a new common language, in the telling of animal tales and proverbs, in the leisure-time practice of remembered handicrafts, in the preparation of foods, homemade medicines, and magical potions and charms, in the standardization of rituals of birth, marriage, and death, in the singing, the use of instrumental music and the dance—by all of these and other means, the slaves wove for themselves the tapestry of a new African American culture. A culture of human survival in the face of legal oppression and forcible acculturation. A culture impregnated with spiritual and occult elements of African, European, and Native American origin, all integrated around a basically religious conception of human reality.

From the beginning, certain men and women who possessed power for both good and evil, skilled in sorcery and divination, exercised extraordinary influence over the slaves. In some slave narratives and reports of white missionaries, they occasionally appear as the first recognized leaders of the community, men and women respected and feared by both slaves and masters. Through these specialists in magic, conjuration, and the healing arts, what was left of the old African religions was transplanted and integrated into the new culture of enslavement.[3] To the misery and hopelessness of the slave quarters these specialists brought consolation and the possibility of transcending external circumstances to the extent that made physical and mental survival achievable. The invocation of mystical powers counteracted some of the magic of the whites and the wretchedness of daily existence. It gave a dimension of depth and ultimacy to the struggle for survival. At that deeper level the reinterpretation and synthesis of transplanted and newly acquired religious systems, mainly evangelical Protestantism, produced a distinctive African American religious consciousness.

Out of this mystical, survival-oriented consciousness, part African and part European, the shout songs and spirituals, expressing the loneliness and sorrow of a stolen people, emerged on the plantations. But with no less charismatic force the slaves' religion celebrated the sheer fact of survival despite constant brutalization in the fields and death and disease in the living quarters. The awakening of white evangelical Christianity during the second quarter of the eighteenth century made contact with this affirmative side of slave religion. Gradually a white-supervised black church evolved from the secret, shaman-led religious meetings in the cabins and brush arbors. But the white preachers and missionaries could never be sure what kind of religion their sermons and camp meetings were crafting.

The Christian faith did not sweep through the slave community with anything like the rate that some earlier scholars assumed.[4] The Society for the Propagation of the Gospel in Foreign Parts reported only 40 adult baptisms and 179 baptized children after some eight years of SPG labor among the relatively large slave population of New York City in the early 1700s. It is estimated that by 1750 there were only a thousand baptized slaves in Virginia—a mere 1 percent of the colony's black population.

Even those slaves who accepted white preaching and made a public profession of faith exasperated their mentors by the way they apparently drifted in and out of the state of grace, clinging to dreams, visions, belief in ghosts, good-luck charms, and the efficacy of the hoodoo man or root doctor. Some missionaries and travelers in the South simply branded black religion as childish superstition or insincerity, far distant from anything that they would call Christianity. They seem not to have been aware that the slaves were *surviving* rather than being swept away by the presumed cogency of Puritan theology.

If whites thought that they were dealing with children who could not discern the difference between white professions and white behavior, they were sadly mistaken. As John Lovell, Jr., has observed, "The slave relied upon religion, not primarily because he felt himself 'converted' [to white Christianity], but because he recognized the power inherent in religious things."[5] That power had to do, first of all, with the necessity of survival—with the creation of an alternative reality system that could keep a person alive and possessed of some modicum of sanity. The protest and resistance elements we found in early forms of black folk religious in the Caribbean and the southeastern United States express the determination of the slaves to "make it" against all odds.

We should not be surprised to find, therefore, a dark and contrary side of black religion as it developed under the most trying circumstances. In Haiti it was the difference between the Arada and Petro rites of vodun that separated a religion of survival from one with more affirmative possibilities for inner peace, sociability, and edification. The same thing can be said about myalism and obeah, or about the religion of the black Methodists of Philadelphia and New York and that of the rebellious black Methodists of Charleston. This was during the first quarter of the nineteenth century, when the example of Haiti was most vivid in the minds of African Americans throughout the nation, but particularly in towns on the Atlantic coast.

The dark and contrary side of black religion must be understood as an alternative form of spirituality. It is a fundamental aspect of what we may call the survival tradition and was indelibly imprinted on a persistently heterodox form of Christianity that came down through the African American churches, sects, and cults into the twentieth century. Although it was often expressed as a curiously divergent version of Christianity, this African American spirituality should not be confused with the kind of white spirituality that was eventually translated into benevolent social reform. It often had, rather, a bitter unsentimentality about it. It was more often cynical, manipulative, and at the very least, ambivalent about spiritual things. Horace Clayton and St. Clair Drake found it in the Chicago black ghetto during the Depression years of the 1930s.[6] C. Eric Lincoln observed the same spirit, in contrast to orthodox Islam, in the bitterness and hatred of the early Black Muslim movement.[7]

This harsh realism and irony, that comes strangley mixed with religiosity, antedated the Great Migration. There were the "upstart crows" in the Southland. Churchgoers circulated songs and saying that were irreverent of traditional religion:

> Our Father, who art in heaven
> White man owe me 'leven and pay me seven.
> Thy kingdom come, thy will be done,
> If I hadn't tuck that, I wouldn't got none.[8]

What Blassingame describes as making the best of a bad situation in the antebellum South is a good example of what we mean by the survival tradition in the literature.

> They simply had to make the best of the situation in which they found themselves. Henry Clay Bruce contended that there were many slaves "who though they knew they suffered a great wrong in their enslavement, gave their best services to their masters, realizing, philosophically, that the wisest course was to make the best of their unfortunate situation . . ." Frederick Douglass spoke for many of them when he asserted, "A man's troubles are always half disposed of when he finds endurance his only remedy." William Grimes indicated the brutal realism and the will to survive of many slaves

when he declared that slavery was a cruel institution, "but being placed in that situation, to repine was unless; we must submit to our fate, and bear up, as well as we can, under the cruel treatment of our despotic tyrants."[9]

There was a sense of the ironic and tragic in the slave secular songs and early blues. A sense that there is something out there that is in inexorable opposition to one's most ardent aspirations. But if we are not too "uppity, and remember that we are all, whether black or white, poor, ill-begotten creatures bound to die, it is possible 'to overcome someday.' " Other powers are always in the wings to help us survive.

W. E. B. Du Bois was probably the first to recognize this extraordinary duality in black folk religion. He speaks of "the peculiar ethical paradox" facing African American life at the turn of the nineteenth century that was transforming black Christianity. It was the paradox of the impotence, bitterness, and vindictiveness of migrants who still believed in God, but whose "religion, instead of worship, is a complaint and a curse, a wail rather than a hope, a sneer rather than a faith" as they faced the hopelessness and despair of the Northern ghetto.[10] The other side of the paradox was what he called the shrewd "Jesuitic casuistry" of the black farmhand who remained in the post–Reconstruction South, forced to take advantage of the inherent weakness of the white man by deception and hypocrisy, and willing, if necessary, to play the role of Uncle Tom—stooping in order to conquer.[11]

These two divergent tendencies in black ethics and religious life—the first tending toward a stubborn radicalism, the other toward a hypocritical compromise—represent two strands of the survival tradition. They belong to what Lawrence W. Levine differentiated from classical Christianity and called the slaves' "instruments of life, of sanity, of health, and of self-respect."[12]

Du Bois had an unfailing insight into this phenomenon. He recognized that what the white evangelical churches had passed on to African Americans had been thoroughly adulterated by the end of slavery and merged with a subterranean stream of African spirituality and the survival instincts of an impoverished and downtrodden people. In this condition, he wrote in his usual grandiloquent style, "broods silently the deep religious feeling of the real Negro heart, the stirring, unguided might of powerful human souls who have lost the guiding star of the past and seek in the great night, a new religious ideal."[13]

Perhaps it would be more accurate to speak of this form of African American religion as a tendency rather than an ideal toward which black believers strove. In any case, it was a persistent quality of the folk tradition that should disabuse us of the much too facile assumption that black religion was nothing more than an echo of nineteenth-century revivalism, a little louder, perhaps, and more given to raw emotionalism. Rather it had more to do with survival than with either elevation or liberation, although there is a complex relationship between the more aggressive form of survivalism and the left wing of the liberation tradition in the established black denominations. But the survival tradition was most characteristic of the "invisible institution," and gave the white missionaries much difficulty. By means of storefront religion and black Pentecostalism it laid the foundation for the paradoxical culture that Du Bois saw invading the Negro urban communities at the end of the nineteenth century.

He spoke of survival religion as the search for a "new religious ideal," breaking with the pietism and fundamentalism of the Southern Methodist and Baptist churches that tried to shape African American religiosity in its own image between the era of the plantation missions and the beginning of the Civil War. But whether powered by a "new ideal" or simply an instinctive recoil from white Christianity, the survival form was never completely domesticated by evangelicalism. It preserved an alternative tradition in the African American subculture that has served (to use Paul Lehmann's insightful phrase) "to make and keep life human."

Daniel Alexander Payne, the great patriarch of the A.M.E Church, fought against lower-class, survival-oriented folk religion throughout his long ministry. The passion with which he attempted to drive it out of his denomination is proof of its tenacity even in that bastion of black Christian respectability. Bishop Payne was not mistaken in his assumption that what he was witnessing was not conversion to the religion of John Wesley, or fidelity to the discipline of Asbury and Allen, but something very different and possibly heretical. He encountered a mysterious form of virtue, in the sense of the Latin word *virtus*, or the term *mana*, as used by anthropologists—a power or force of causal efficacy and creative vitality. Something of which it is of the greatest advantage to possess. It was what West African priest would have recognized as both proceeding from and capable of influencing the gods and the ancestors. A power that could be used to ward off evil, to perform good, and to keep body and soul together against every destructive element of the universe—in other words, the sheer power *to be*, the power to survive.

Leonard E. Barrett writes that this kind of religion, to the consternation of British missionaries, asserted itself in the great Jamaican revival of 1860–1861.[14] It also surfaced in several places in the United States in the early twentieth century: in the Azusa Street Revival of 1905, when Charles Fox Parham and his white followers split with William J. Seymour's black Pentecostals because of "heathen" manifestations; in the Universal Negro Improvement Association of Marcus Garvey, when West Indian survival religion sought synthesis with Anglo-Catholicism and Pan-Africanism in the African Orthodox Church; in the movement of the Cape Verdian prophet, Daddy Grace, who, from a small family congregation in New Bedford, Massachusetts, built one of the most powerful black religious organizations in the United States.

This survival motif is closely associated with authentic African American religion in its alternating phases of withdrawal from and aggressive opposition toward the white world. This is what the mysterious Detroit peddler W. D. Fard combined with a homegrown version of black orientalism to create the Nation of Islam. Elijah Muhammad's message attracted many alienated blacks because they recognized in it accents of a tradition they had known in the rural South where they and their ancestors had resisted the whitenization of the church. It is clear that Elijah Muhammad quoted as frequently from the Bible as from the Koran. His most gifted disciple, Malcolm X, whose father was a Garveyite Baptist preacher, received support from many black Christians who recognized those same accents when Malcolm drew upon a survival theme in folk religion to wean the masses away from evangelical Christianity.

The Harlem Renaissance poet Langston Hughes understood this survival tradition and used it as the basis of some of his most biting cultural criticism. He once wrote of those who were sustained by it:

> But then there are low-down folks, the so-called common element, and they are the majority—may the Lord be praised! The people who have their nip of gin on Saturday nights and are not too important to themselves of the community, or too well fed, or too learned to watch the lazy world go round. They live on 7th Street in Washington, or State Street in Chicago and they do not particularly care whether they are like white folks or anybody else. Their joy runs, bang! into ecstasy. Their religion soars to a shout. Work maybe a little today, rest a little tomorrow. Play awhile. Sing awhile. O, let's dance! These common people are not afraid of spirituals, as for a long time their more intellectual brethren were, and jazz is their child. They furnish a wealth of colorful, distinctive material for any artist because they still hold to their own individuality in the face of American standardization.[15]

The connective links between black secular culture and black religion, which were forged by the survival tradition, are explored in much of the literature of black America and the West Indies. They can be found in the poetry of Claude McKay, Countee Cullen, Nikki Giovanni, and Sonia Sanchez; the novels of Richard Wright, James Baldwin, and Toni Morrison; and the essays of Alice Walker, Andrew Salkey, Derek Walcott, and the so-called "public intellectuals" of the late twentieth century. As ever, creative writers often see more clearly than theologians the dimension of depth in life and culture that yields more truth than philosophical speculation and exposes the raw, mysterious edges of existence in the language and symbols of the folk, mediated by artistic genius.

The Elevation Tradition

What were the slaves trying to say when they mixed Old Testament allusions to Jacob's ladder and New Testament allusions to being "soldiers of the Cross," in the familiar words of one of the best-loved spirituals?

> We are climbing Jacob's ladder . . .
> Every round goes higher and higher . . .
> Soldiers of the Cross.

Most of us have assumed that the source of the inspiration for this song was the 28th chapter of Genesis where the patriarch Jacob names a lonely campsite in the desert, Bethel, because as he slept there he dreamed of angels ascending and descending a ladder stretched between heaven and earth. God stood at the top of that ladder and gave Jacob the solemn promise that the very land on which he lay would one day become his family's possession. That would seem clear enough to the slave poet, but John Lovell, in his monumental book on the spirituals perceives another, more profound meaning in the secret hearts and minds of the captive black men and women who first sang the lines of this spiritual. As humble as they were, they pictured themselves as climbing, one round at a time, out of their misery. They saw themselves, by the power of God and the dint of their own dogged determination, climbing out of downtroddenness, out of degradation, toward the God who called them to be soldiers of the Cross of Christ, working for a better world for themselves and their children. Lovell writes:

> The fact that there is a religious catchphrase in most songs (such as the name of the deity, or some other biblical character, or reference to a biblical event or to heaven) is not the significant thing at this point. The main thing is the pithy element of life suggested by the poetic grist of the title. For example, in "We Are Climbing Jacob's Ladder," the story of Jacob is just a point of departure. The really important expression the singer is pouring out is his determination to rise from his low estate and to progress up the material and spiritual ladder, "round by round." Jacob's experience has been chosen because it is the most available, the most dramatic, the most impressive and acceptable simile. And please note, his poetic point relates to his life on earth. In the mythical heaven, one is already as high as one can go.[16]

This spiritual, like many others Lovell analyzes, had a "morale-building function." Lovell compares it to other songs which suggest the slaves' determination to improve their earthly condition, to encourage individual and group initiative. He speaks of literally dozens of spirituals that focus on the perennial objective of both the slave and the free black—learning to read and write the English language. These spirituals include "My Lord's Writing All the Time," "My Mother Got a Letter," "O Lord, Write My Name," "Gwine to Write Massa Jesus," and "De Book of Revelation God to Us Revealed." "Jacob's Ladder" belongs to this genre of slave poetry. It expresses the longing and determination not to "go down," but rather to be "uplifted from slavery," by the power of God; to make a better life for one and one's children and grandchildren; to be "elevated" in body, mind, and spirit, above the vicissitudes and miseries of this life.[17]

The centrality of the idea of self-improvement, uplift, the "*advancement* of colored people," or elevation, is evident in much of the literature of the slave and the free African American in the nineteenth and early twentieth centuries. In many cases, it was closely connected with the comprehensive cultural vocation of the African American church. Elevation as a tradition is, of course, closely related to the tradition emphasizing liberation from slavery, for as A.M.E. Bishop Daniel A. Payne said he learned from the abolitionist Lewis Tappan, "slavery and education were antagonistic and could not exist together . . . the one must crush out the other."[18] But it is useful to differentiate between elevation and liberation in order to make a closer examination of each. Elevation emerges as a kind of second stage of self-development, for after the slave became conscious of the fact that despite the chains, he or she had a future, that there was something beyond mere survival—something better in this world as well as in the world to come—he or she began climbing the ladder of moral and material elevation. It was assumed that the church would lead the way.

Throughout the slave narratives, testimonies, letters, essays, speeches, sermons, and church resolutions, one finds the word elevation, or uplift, used profusely—and, more frequently than not, in the context of religion.[19] Most black preachers were opposed to the moral anarchy implied by slave carousing, indolence, feigned stupidity, or apathy, which made slaves not only the victims of their oppressors but also of their own ignorance and self-abnegation. The preachers, wanting desperately to read the Bible for themselves, tried to model the idea that belief in Jesus Christ puts a person's life on a foundation of good morals, manners, orderliness, and a growing ambition to learn and improve one's station in life. Those who became Christians began their elevation by learning how to read. The South Carolina slave James L. Bradley, who entered Lane Seminary in 1834, explains how his conversion started him on the Jacob's ladder of personal elevation:

> In the year 1828, I saw some Christians, who talked with me concerning my soul, and the sinfulness of my nature. They told me I must repent, and live to do good. This led me to the cross of Christ;—and then, oh, how I longed to be able to read the Bible! I made out to get an old spelling-book, which I carried in my hat for many months, until I could spell pretty well, and read easy words. When I got up in the night to work, I used to read a few minutes, if I could manage to get a light.... After I had learned to read a little, I wanted very much to learn to write; and I persuaded one of my young masters to teach me.[20]

C. H. Hall, a slave who was interviewed in Canada in 1863, intimates the connection between conversion, elevation, and anti-slavery:

> It was a rule in that country [Maryland], that a slave must not be seen with a book of any kind; but old madam Bean, my mistress, belonged to the Baptist Church, and she said we might all learn to spell and read the Bible. The old man fought against it for some time, but found it prevailed nothing.... [I] got to know too much for the old boss himself, and he said it wouldn't do. He said I was going just like my brother Bige, who had learned to read and was a preacher, and was raising the devil on the place. So after a little scorning, I stopped it, and gave up reading until I got to be 19 years old. But the more I read, the more I fought against slavery.[21]

Learning how to read and write did not, of course, work any magic for liberation, but it was the first rung of the ladder. The slave who could read soon discovered that there were other interesting things to read besides the Bible, such as Northern newspapers, pamphlets, and—if it was available—David Walker's insurrectionary "Appeal to the Coloured Citizens of the World." A whole new world was opened up and with it a new self-esteem, a new consciousness of identity and destiny.

In the North the independent black churches were freer to emphasize elevation and self-development. As a result they soon came together to uplift themselves by organizing burial clubs, lodges, churches, reading clubs, schools, and temperance and moral reform societies. The elevation motif stands out clearly in the statements of purpose and preambles of these fledgling organizations. They demonstrate how much freed men and women feared moral indifference and anarchy; how much they strove against ignorance, drunkenness, marital infidelity, and the neglect of widows and fatherless children. As we have seen, the Free African Societies or their counterparts in Boston, Newport, Rhode Island, New York, and Philadelphia, became the scaffolding of the black churches, particularly that preeminent instrumentality of African American self-help and self-development, the A.M.E. Church. On the occasion of its 100th anniversary, Bishop Richard R. Wright explained its raison d'être:

> The purpose in mind of the founding fathers of African Methodism... was, among other things, to exemplify in the black man the power of self-reliance, self-help, by the exercise of free religious thought with executive efficiency.[22]

Some of the most ardent champions of the doctrine of racial elevation were black women. Concerned about the stability of the family, the education of children, and the cultivation of Christian morality, they organized female societies and auxiliaries alongside of the churches and other male-dominated Institutions. The sermons and writings of Amanda Berry Smith, Maria Stewart, Frances Ellen Watkins Harper, Fannie Barrier Williams, Lucy Craft Laney, and Nannie H. Burroughs bear eloquent testimony to the special emphasis black women put upon uplifting black folk, making the church more responsible for "racial promotion," and training young women for parenting and leadership roles in church and community.

Delores Williams prefers to use the term "quality-of-life tradition" to describe essentially the same theme in African American religious history that we are calling "elevationism." Moreover, she links "quality-of-life" to survival as one of the primary contributions of biblically literate African American women to black culture and religion. Recent research in the writings of black women demonstrates that there is voluminous evidence to support her thesis. She writes:

> I concluded, then, that the female-centered tradition of African-American biblical appropriation could be named the *survival/quality-of-life tradition of African-American biblical appropriation*. This naming was consistent with the black American community's way of appropriating the Bible so that emphasis is put upon God's response to black people's situation rather than upon what would appear to be hopeless aspects of African-American people's existence in North America. In black consciousness, God's response of survival and quality of life to Hagar is God's response of survival and quality of life to African-American women and mothers of slave descent struggling to sustain their families with God's help.[23]

Before leaving the elevation, or "survival/quality-of-life tradition," we should note that women were the first to point out that the drive for self-improvement and uplift could be abused by selfish blacks who wanted only to distance themselves from those they considered beneath them. The very congregations that prided themselves on being models of respectability and uplift worthy of acceptance by whites were the ones that were cool to the bedraggled, poorly educated, and unsophisticated agricultural workers from the South who showed up at their doors on Sunday mornings. The elevation tradition was the lever by which some blacks lifted themselves up by their proverbial bootstraps and moved into the middle class, but when some of them shed the boots and donned the silk stockings and patent leather slippers, they regarded those not similarly blessed as unworthy of either their assistance or association. Maria Stewart, speaking in the African Masonic Hall of Boston in 1833, targeted the elevation-conscious black middle class:

> I am sensible that there are many highly intelligent gentlemen of color in these United States, in the force of whose arguments, doubtless, I should discover my inferiority; but if they are blest with wit and talent, friends and fortune, why have they not made themselves men of eminence, by striving to take all the reproach that is cast upon people of color, and in endeavoring to alleviate the woes of their brethren in bondage? Talk, without effort, is nothing . . . this gross neglect on your part, causes my blood to boil within me.[24]

While Maria Stewart in the antebellum period criticized the affluent class of blacks in the North for refusing to share their upward-bound energies with their enslaved brethren, Fannie Barrier Williams in 1893 bemoaned the fact that by the end of the century the leadership of the mass black church, because of apathy or incompetence, seemed woefully unprepared to elevate the race:

> It is not difficult to specify wherein church interests have failed and wherein religion could have helped to improve these people. In the first place the churches have sent among us too many ministers who have had no sort of preparation and fitness for the work assigned to them. With due regard for the highly capable colored ministers of the country, I feel no hesitancy in saying that the advancement of our condition is more hindered by a large part of the ministry entrusted with leadership than by any other single cause.[25]

When it came to the elevation of the race, no one was more critical of the defects of the black church than Booker T. Washington. By the time the great accommodationist of Tuskegee had reached the zenith of his power at the turn of the century, the ideals of moral elevation, self-help, and self-determination through industrial education had become the accepted antidote for the disappointment and despair that followed the rise of Jim Crow in every aspect of American life. Washington simply enunciated what almost all black religious leaders believed in both the South and the North: that rather than depend upon the political process to redress their grievances, blacks needed to get off their knees and elevate themselves morally, spiritually, and, especially, economically. Only then would God help them to help themselves and white America would relieve them of the onus of second-class citizenship.

The Liberation Tradition

Many scholars have commented upon the complexity of the character of Booker T. Washington. Washington is difficult to categorize. Notwithstanding the self-development tone of his famous autobiography, *Up From Slavery*, published in 1901, the man was probably more of a survivalist than an elevationist. He came up the hard way and was shrewdly distrustful of progressive ideas that were more high-flying flights of the imagination than the result of a hard, calculating logic. Certainly he was no liberationist in the sense that Bishop Henry McNeal Turner, W. E. B. Du Bois, or Ida Wells Barnett were. All three of these and many other leaders of the black church, particularly the Baptist churches of the 1830s and 1840s in Virginia, Ohio, Illinois, and the border states, and the African Methodists of the North, particularly the Zionites of New York and Massachusetts, were solidly grounded in the liberation tradition.[26]

The liberation tradition stands out as the single most important and characteristic perspective of black faith from 1800 to the civil rights movement. It could not have been otherwise. From the landing of the first twenty Africans on the wharf at Jamestown, Virginia, in 1619, to the Emancipation Proclamation on New Year's Day, 1863, African American consciousness and culture were permeated with the idea of freedom. As tensions mounted toward the Civil War, it was inevitable that the black quest for God and salvation would be greatly conditioned by an unquenchable desire to be rid of slavery. Even when individuals were manumitted, bought their own freedom, or escaped slavery and fled north, their consuming passion was to liberate the other members of their families who had been left behind. The main reason for the failure of the American Colonization Society was the refusal of free blacks, called to resistance by their churches, to leave the United States if that meant abandoning relatives and friends who were still in slavery.

Many of the spirituals speak about the yearning for liberation, and one of the most familiar expresses a willingness to die rather than submit to slavery:

> Oh, Freedom, Oh Freedom,
> Oh, Freedom over me,
> And before I'd be a slave,
> I'd be buried in my grave,
> And go home to my Lord
> And be free!

John Lovell, Jr., explodes with lyrical eloquence when he discusses this characteristic emphasis in so many of the slave songs and spirituals.

> No more passionate songs have ever been written to proclaim the concept of freedom. Perhaps the American slave knew more about freedom than anyone who has ever lived. Whether or not this is true, his songs declare freedom as well as or better than it has ever been declared: "No more peck o'corn for me, No more, no more," "And why not every man?" "Tell ol' Pharaoh, let my people go!" "If I had my way . . . I'd tear this building down!" "Before I'd be a slave I'd be buried in my grave," "Done wid driber's dribin'," "No second class aboard dis train"—for the concept of freedom, where can you find their superiors! Who speaks today for freedom in such glowing terms? Who understands so well the soul of freedom? Who better ties together the dream and the reality![27]

Whether or not Lovell's assumption about the superiority of the spirituals as songs of freedom is correct is less important than the incontestable fact that the slaves thought a great deal about freedom and made it the keystone of their religion. Talitha Lewis, a slave in North Carolina, born in 1852 and interviewed when she was 86 years old, recalled:

> My master used to ask us children, "Do your folks pray at night?" We said, "No," 'cause our folks had told us what to say. But the Lord have mercy, there was plenty of that going on. They'd pray, "Lord, deliver us from under bondage."[28]

Black preachers in the North and their congregants—having somehow survived the ordeal of slavery and having concentrated their efforts on the educational, moral, and spiritual elevation of the race—began about 1800 to focus all their energies and resources on emancipation. These churches literally pushed and pulled their white friends and supporters toward the great war between the states. It is no accident that the first black Baptist churches on the frontier renamed their associations "Friends of Humanity" to indicate that abolitionism was their first order of business, or that

Bishop William Paul Quinn of the A.M.E. Church said that the first black Methodist denomination was "a veritable antislavery society."

This extraordinary emphasis on the Christian religion as the foundation for a liberation movement and liberation itself as the primary message of the gospel is reflected in every African American institution of the nineteenth century. The Negro Convention Movement, which was an effective secular arm of the church from 1831 to the Civil War, brought together the leading men and women of the race in state and national conventions on political justice and economic issues. From its inception it was dominated by lay and clerical leaders of the churches. Nor did the black Methodists and Baptists have exclusive control of the Convention Movement. It was greatly influenced by clergymen like the three Presbyterians Samuel Cornish, Theodore Wright, and Henry Highland Garnet and the Congregationalists Charles B. Ray and J. W. C. Pennington. These ministers refused to spiritualize the concept of liberty as did so many white preachers and biblical exegetes of their day. They understood the freedom that Christ brought in very concrete terms. For them it was nothing less than freedom from chattel slavery. They ridiculed any attempt on the part of the white clergy of their denominations to use the Bible to spiritualize liberty, thereby making slavery a condition that referred primarily to being a slave of sin.

A white Methodist minister preaching to blacks in Charleston discovered later that he had completely misunderstood the meaning of the "Amens" they were giving him. A. M. Chreitzberg in his book on *Early Methodism in the Carolinas* published in 1897, describes what happened.

> Though ignorant of it at the time, he remembers now the cause of the enthusiasm under his deliverances [about] the "law of liberty" and "freedom from Egyptian bondage." What was figurative they interpreted literally. He thought of but one ending of the war; they quite another. He remembers the 68th Psalm as affording numerous texts for their declaration, e.g., "Let God arise, let his enemies be scattered;" His "march through the wilderness"; "the chariots of God are twenty-thousand." . . . It is mortifying now to think that his comprehension was not equal to the African intellect. All he thought about was relief from the servitude of sin, and freedom from the bondage of the devil. . . . But they interpreted it literally in the good time coming, which of course could not but make their ebony complexions attractive, very.[29]

The liberation tradition continued as a persistent emphasis through the years of the Civil War and into Reconstruction, when liberated black churchmen of the South became promoters of Radical Republicanism. Many pastors went into politics and enjoyed a brief if stormy tenure in state and national offices. Notwithstanding the bitter disillusionment over the withdrawal of federal troops from the South in 1877, the black churches continued to display the basic characteristics of the liberation movement—various forms of underground and open resistance to disfranchisement and racial segregation. While it is true, as we have already seen, that a wave of passivity and conservatism swept over African American churches in both the North and South between the First and Second World Wars, we are obliged to be cautious with that generalization when we examine more carefully the activity of what Carter G. Woodson called the "institutional churches" in many black communities.[30] These relatively large urban congregations across the country provided a social, economic, and political witness for liberation during the post–World War I period and into the Great Depression. They correctly understood that the vise of poverty and degradation in which the masses of their people were caught was the result of the deprivation of fundamental freedom and justice in the land of their birth. The liberation tradition slumbered in the black church from time to time, but it never slept.

Interrelationships between the Three Traditions

African Americans in the United States and the Caribbean are, for the most part, Christians. But they are Christian in a sense that is different from what the American public generally understands by the term. The nonsystematic, ambivalent Christianity of African Americans has been mistakenly identified by some scholars with occultism, otherworldliness, and primitive Protestant evangelicalism. Surely there is some of all three in black religion, but they have been transmuted by the experience of slavery and racism. That experience produced one of the most empirical, this-worldly, and culture-sophisticated religious traditions in the Western hemisphere. Moreover, the roots of this kind of religion are not in Rome, Geneva, or Canterbury, but in Calabar, West Kingston, Jamaica, and the plantation country of North America. It obscures the original, distinctive flair of this religion to equate it too easily with its subsequent institutionalization in the established black churches of the United States.

Many African Americans were converted to white Christianity, but many others were forced, by the sheer dint of an irrepressible humanity—and what Charles H. Long has called a "hardness of life"—to invent a religion of their own, a religion of survival.[31] As the Caribbean poet Walcott put the matter in an essay on black history, "What seemed to be surrender was redemption. What seemed the loss of tradition was its renewal. What seemed the death of faith was its rebirth."[32]

The liberation and elevation traditions began with the determination to survive, but they go beyond "make do" to "do more," and from "do more" to "freedom now" and "black power." All three strategies have to do with "making and keeping life human." They are basic to African American life and culture and intertwined in complex ways throughout the history of the Diaspora. All three traditions are responses to hard reality in a dominating "white man's world." All three arise from the same religious sensibility that crystallized in African American Christian, Afro-Islamic, and Afro-Judaic sects and cults since the mid-eighteenth century.

Elevation and liberation arise after successful survival. The people could not concern themselves with either until they first learned how to stay alive. Of course, elevationism was grounded in the will to live, but it rose above the constraining and pessimistic attitudes of slavery and established itself on the higher ground of individual and group improvement, the search for moral rectitude, and disinterested benevolence. William Hamilton, addressing the New York African Society in 1809 from the relative safety of lower Manhattan, could declare:

> The gloomy hermit we pity and the snarling synic [*sic*] we despise, these are men who appear to be rubbed off the list of men, they appear to have lost the fine fiber of the

mind, on which it depends for expansion and growth, they appear to be sunk into a
state of insensibility of the extreme happiness growing out of social life.[33]

Although the situation of most free blacks like Hamilton was little better than
slavery, the effort they made in Charleston, Boston, Philadelphia, and Baltimore with
groups like the Free African Societies demonstrates that their immediate interest was
not so much life and death as mutual encouragement along the path of "happiness
growing out of social life." The historic decision of Richard Allen and Absolom Jones
to transcend white denominationalism by organizing a nonsectarian society that
could solidify the community for morality and mutual welfare led directly to the
founding of the first black churches in the North. Allen and Jones were not, of
course, so easily to divest themselves of denominationalism, but Allen at least was
ultimately successful in wresting control from whites and establishing one of the first
national organizations concerned about the elevation and liberation of all African
Americans.

If the slave community of the South is where we find the most striking examples
of survivalism and can trace it through the Christian churches of the nineteenth
century to the heterodox sects and cults of the early twentieth, it is in the free
communities of the North, in Charleston, Richmond, Atlanta, and New Orleans that
we find incipient elevation and liberation traditions. They began, as we have seen, in
the quasi-religious benevolent societies and independent Protestant congregations.
They grew, side by side, in the Negro Convention Movement, the black press, black
abolitionism, missionary emigrationism, the mission to the freedmen during Reconstruction, the Niagara Movement, the NAACP, National Urban League, and the civil
rights movement.

It would be too simplistic to suppose that the survival tradition was exclusively
Southern, rural, and lower class, while the other two were exclusively Northern,
urban, and middle class. Such regional and economic compartmentalization breaks
down at several points. The connection between North and South, slave and free,
field hand and house servant, rural peasantry and urban proletariat, is too complex
for broad generalizations. And yet, with certain qualifications, it is instructive to
observe that the survivalist strand, neglected and repressed in the South for more
than two centuries, developed a stoical realism and inner strength consistent with its
plantation environment. In the North, on the other hand, where the church soon
found itself catering to a better-educated class, another set of religious norms and
values developed. Radical-aggressive and conservative-avoidance patterns cannot be
identified in the North any more than they can be shown among landless farm
workers and sharecroppers in the South, but the basic orientation of the elevation
and liberation traditions was not so much to survive brutality as to liberate by
uplifting and to uplift by liberating.

Nor can the latter two traditions be rigidly correlated with the division often made
between black separatism and black assimilationism. In the controversy among the
Baptists over the white American Baptist Publication Society and the development of
independent black schools, many ministers in the South, although steeped in the
survivalist tradition and the philosophy of Booker T. Washington, opted for cooper-

ation with the Northern white church.[34] On the other hand, liberation-oriented black Presbyterians in the North demonstrated strong separatist tendencies by organizing a race-conscious ethnic caucus as early as 1894 and supporting the black power movement of the 1960s.

The connections are intricate. All we can say is that there are both separatists and integrationists, or conservatives and progressives in the broad spectrum of each tradition. Nevertheless, the general direction of survivalist strategies seems to incline toward an indifference about interracial cooperation while having a stronger interest in self-help. The general direction of elevationist and liberationist strategies seems to be toward interracial cooperation, but with a willingness to use coercive secular politics rather than church-sponsored charity to address the needs of the race. We may speak of the former tradition as conservative-separatist and the latter two as progressive-integrationist, but such labels must be employed cautiously and will not hold up in all historical contexts.

The elevationist and liberationist church leaders of the nineteenth century sought to free themselves from white control without necessarily rejecting the proffered friendship of whites. Second, they tried to promote the moral and cultural advancement of blacks *within* the American political and economic system. Third, it was their purpose not only to free brothers and sisters in the South by nonviolent means, but to champion the cause of oppressed peoples throughout the world. These characteristics were fairly continuous among clergy during the nineteenth century, for most of them wanted to build self-respecting black institutions and believed that it could not be done without cutting the umbilical cord with whites while continuing, in some respects, to emulate them. But after the death of Allen in 1831, and a secular challenge to the control that preachers exercised over organizations that grew up alongside of the churches, there was an increasing deference to white leadership. The close relationship between Northern church leaders and white allies who promised to secure their full civil rights continued to be problematic. Except for periodic disengagements, as when several leading black ministers broke with William Lloyd Garrison and the American Anti-Slavery Society in the 1840s and 1850s, this ambivalent, semi-dependent relationship continued up to the founding of the NAACP and the National Urban League.

It is important to note, with respect to the survivalist tradition, that the Southern wing of the churches was often closer to a conservative, apolitical form of Christianity than Northern clergy like Reverdy Ransom and S. L. Corrothers, both A.M.E. leaders, or Elias C. Morris, J. Milton Waldrom and Sutton E. Griggs, leaders of the National Baptists in the border states.

In any case, there is persuasive evidence that the role of the major African American denominations in activities that can be identified within the elevation and liberation streams contradicts the allegation of E. Franklin Frazier that "the Negro church and Negro religion . . . have been responsible for the so-called backwardness of American Negroes."[35]

When we turn to the smaller denominations founded after the Civil War, most notably those that came out of the Holiness and Pentecostal movements, a somewhat different story emerges.[36] We know, for example, that most of their members were

Southern in origin, less educated, and of a lower socioeconomic status. When they migrated to the North and West the basic survivalism of their religion went in one of two directions: either it persisted with a strong neo-African and rural flavor in an essentially urban milieu, or became secularized toward a new alignment of folk religiosity with a radically alienated race consciousness.

These smaller sects and denominations deserve much more study than they have received. They represent an important transformation of traditional black religion under modern urban conditions. Unlike many of the mainstream black churches, they had little interest in integration or emulating the standards of whites. They took new form and expression in the storefront churches that multiplied rapidly after the First World War. The challenges they threw up to the established churches in communalism, styles of dress and worship, prohibitions against the new fashions and immoralities of the city, etc., must be understood as a judgment upon what they regarded as dechristianizing influences in mainstream Christianity. They were to find, however, a more formidable obstacle to their own brand of religiosity in the dechristianizing misery and despair of the poor than in the creeping secularism of the black bourgeoisie.

It should come as no surprise that members of "Holy and Sanctified" churches and Pentecostalism turned up in the Garvey movement, the Moorish Science Temple of Noble Drew Ali, Father Divine's Peace Mission, and many of the nationalist and revitalization cults that were spawned in the ghetto. The dechristianization tendency in African American culture after the First World War was partly due to the demor-alization of the masses by poverty and racism. If new sects and cults flourished it was because the survival mechanisms that their members found useful in the rural South went through a hardening process in the North that demystified black Christianity and produced a religiously motivated consciousness of color and racial destiny. The intellectuals and artists of the Harlem Renaissance perceived a rich, new culture developing out of this urbanization of survivalism. Their attempt to capture its aesthetic meaning and give it a voice helped create a new cultural nationalism.

Here we see the paradoxical interrelationship between the three traditions. What was happening in this development was their coming together in a new dialectic that was consonant with the demands of urban existence in a racist society. The black power movement, which emerged from secular activists in the North and a church-based civil rights movement in the South, was the ideological consequence of this three-way convergence. Martin Luther King, Jr., personified the dialectical relation-ship of the three strands of black religion and culture that coalesced in the black power movement which he, paradoxically, rejected. In Dr. King's development as a national leader, nevertheless, we see the interweaving of a moral sternness fueled by the emotionalism of the mass-based black church of the South with the pragmatic, social action orientation of the North. The fact that the Dexter Avenue Baptist Church which he pastored was in Montgomery, Alabama, should not confuse the issue. It had an elevationist and liberationist "Northern exposure," and stands at one end of King's orientation, while at the other end stands the Mason Temple Church of God in Christ, where his involvement with a garbage workers' strike, made up largely of the members of that survivalist denomination, led to his death. That is why King is such a pivotal figure in African American religious history. At the beginning and the end, if not throughout his remarkable ministry, he wove together in his own charismatic personality all three seminal traditions of black faith.

It was inevitable, therefore, that King would become a source of irritation to Joseph H. Jackson, the powerful leader of the National Baptist Convention, Inc., who was finally unseated from its presidency in 1982. Jackson represented the old-style, Bookerite leadership, essentially survivalist in character but certainly not opposed to racial advancement. This element of black Baptist leadership rather chose a nonconfrontational, conservative amelioration of the black condition. Such an orientation was bound to be threatened by a young Ph.D. from Atlanta who was educated at liberal Crozer Theological Seminary in Chester, Pennsylvania, and more liberal Boston University.

But it is also true, and points to the extraordinary character of King's leadership, that the more liberation-oriented clergy of the North—Adam Clayton Powell, Jr., of Harlem, Nathan Wright of the Episcopal Diocese of Newark, N.J., Bishop John D. Bright of the A.M.E. Church in Philadelphia, Bishop Herbert Bell Shaw of the A.M.E. Zion Church, and others—had their own questions about whether King's Southern Baptist piety was going to be tough and worldly enough to deal with the depths of white racism in the North. They supported his nonviolent strategy, but they still justified self-defense in a no-way-out confrontation with violent white power. In that regard these churchmen expressed, in a way that King made possible but never quite appreciated, the subtle interpenetration of the survival, elevation, and liberation perspectives among certain mainline clergy. These clergy opened the way to the convergence between the secular black power movement, the radical black studies movement, and black Christian theology.

Studies are still needed to show how black power and the mid-twentieth-century expression of black theology that was closely related to it illuminate the dialectical character of African American religion that was implied by King's leadership. He was never prepared to acknowledge those implications or admit that he had made a contribution to the radical rethinking of black Christianity. The new black theology, nonetheless, was grounded in the liberation tradition of one important segment of the mainstream church to which he belonged. It sought to learn from and assimilate the values of the black consciousness form of the survival tradition that King captured by his appeal to the urban masses.

The three traditions point to the diverse perspectives in the black theology movement. If that movement continues to hold together such divergent points of view as that of Jaramogi Abebe Agyeman, Cornel West, J. Deotis Roberts, and James H. Cone, it is partly because this way of doing theology in the post–civil rights African American community stands astride the shoulders of both Martin Luther King, Jr., the tender-hearted liberationist, and El-Hajj Malik El-Shabazz, the tough-minded survivalist.[37]

NOTES

1. Eugene D. Genovese, *Roll, Jordan, Roll: The World the Slaves Made* (New York: Pantheon, 1974), p. 91.

2. In addition to Genovese's monumental work (note 1 above), for a broad selection of books related to the themes of this chapter see John W. Blassingame, *The Slave Community: Plantation Life in the Ante-Bellum South* (New York: Oxford University Press, 1972), and Blassingame, ed., *Slave Testimony: Two Centuries of Letters, Speeches, Interviews, and Autobiographies* (Baton Rouge: Louisiana State University, 1977); Henry H. Mitchell, *Black Belief: Folk Beliefs of Blacks in America and West Africa* (New York: Harper & Row, 1975); Lawrence W. Levine, *Black Culture and Black Consciousness: Afro-American Folk Thought from Slavery to Freedom* (New York: Oxford University Press, 1978); Albert J. Raboteau, *Slave Religion: The "Invisible Institution" in the Antebellum South* (New York: Oxford University Press, 1978); George E. Simpson, *Black Religion in the New World* (New York: Columbia University Press, 1978); Sterling Stuckey, *Slave Culture: Nationalist Theory and the Foundations of Black America* (New York: Oxford University Press, 1987); Margaret Washington Creel, *"A Peculiar People": Slave Religion and Community-Culture Among the Gullahs* (New York: New York University Press, 1988); Vincent Harding, *There Is a River: The Black Struggle for Freedom in America* (New York: Harcourt Brace Jovanovich, 1981); Dwight N. Hopkins and George Cummings, eds., *Cut Loose Your Stammering Tongue: Black Theology in the Slave Narratives* (Maryknoll, N.Y.: Orbis, 1991); and C. Eric Lincoln and Lawrence H. Mamiya, *The Black Church in the African American Experience* (Durham: Duke University Press, 1990).

3. See Mechal Sobel, *Trabelin' On: The Slave Journey to an Afro-Baptist Faith* (Westport, Conn.: Greenwood Press, 1979), pp. 99–135.

4. See, e.g., Willis D. Weatherford, *American Churches and the Negro* (Boston: Christopher Publishing House, 1957), and Carter G. Woodson, *The History of the Negro Church* (Washington, D.C.: Associated Publishers, 1972).

5. John Lovell, Jr., *Black Song: The Forge and the Flame* (New York: Macmillan, 1972), p. 229.

6. St. Clair Drake and Horace R. Clayton, *Black Metropolis: A Study of Negro Life in a Northern City* (New York: Harcourt, Brace, 1945), pp. 650–57.

7. C. Eric Lincoln, *The Black Muslims in America* (Boston: Beacon Press, 1961), pp. 217–20.

8. Sterling Brown, Arthur P. Davis, and Ulysses Lee, *The Negro Caravan* (New York: Arno Press and the New York Times, 1941), p. 422.

9. Blassingame, *The Slave Community*, pp. 205–06.

10. W. E. B. Du Bois, *The Souls of Black Folk* (Greenwich, Conn.: Fawcett, 1961), p. 149.

11. Ibid.

12. Lawrence W. Levine, *Black Culture and Black Consciousness* (New York: Oxford University Press, 1977), p. 80.

13. Du Bois, *The Souls of Black Folk*, p. 151.

14. Leonard E. Barrett, *Soul-Force: African Heritage in Afro-American Religion* (Garden City, N.Y.:Doubleday, 1974), p. 115.

15. Langston Hughes, in Francis Broderick et al., *Black Protest Thought in the Twentieth Century* (New York: Bobbs-Merrill, 1970), p. 92.

16. Lovell, *Black Song*, p. 119.

17. Ibid., p. 122.

18. Cited by A.M.E. historian Paul R. Griffin, *The Struggle for a Black Theology of Education: Pioneering Efforts of Post Civil War Clergy* (Atlanta: ITC Press, 1993), p. 17.

19. The word "elevation" and cognates expressing the idea of moral and material uplift are sprinkled liberally throughout the many sermons, addresses, resolutions, and other documents in Dorothy Porter, ed., *Early Negro Writing, 1760–1837* (Boston: Beacon Press, 1971). For example, in that collection, see the address of Prince Saunders before the Pennsylvania Augustine Society, pp. 90–92; an 1828 address by William Whipper, p. 117; 1832 address by an unnamed woman to the Female Literary Association of Philadelphia, p. 128; 1833 address by Maria Stewart, p. 134; address in 1834 by Joseph M. Corr of Bethel A.M.E. Church in Philadelphia, pp. 150 and 153; address to the Moral Reform Society of Philadelphia in 1836 by William Watkins, pp. 156, 161, and 165; address of Bishop Richard Allen to the 1830 Convention of People of Color, p. 179; the Minutes of the American Moral Reform Society, pp. 202, 205, 209, 226, 229, 238, and 242. For similar emphases on elevation, uplift, and "promotion" of the race in writings by black women, see Bert James Loewenberg and Ruth Bogin, eds., *Black Women in Nineteenth-Century American Life: Their Words, Their Thoughts, Their Feelings* (University Park: Pennsylvania State University Press, 1976), passim. See also frequent citations of "elevation" from the *Christian Recorder*, in Clarence E. Walker, *A Rock in a Weary Land: The African Methodist Episcopal Church During the Civil War and Reconstruction* (Baton Rouge: Louisiana State University Press, 1982), pp. 16, 42, 44, 52, 90, and 93. As mentioned in Chapter 6 the concept of "elevation" is most fully developed by Martin R. Delany in *The Condition, Elevation, Emigration, and Destiny of the Colored People of the United States* (1852, Baltimore: Black Classic Press, 1993), pp. 36–48. In the revision of his 1982 doctoral dissertation Edward L. Wheeler used the term "uplift" in the same sense as Delany used "elevation," and examines its theological, sociological, political, and educational implications for the careers of black clergy after the Civil War; see Edward L. Wheeler, *Uplifting the Race: The Black Minister in the New South, 1865–1902* (Lanham, Md.: University Press of America, 1986).

20. Cited in Blassingame, *Slave Testimony*, p. 689.

21. Ibid., p. 417.

22. Richard R. Wright, Jr., *The Centennial Encyclopedia of the African Methodist Episcopal Church, 1816–1916* (Philadelphia: A.M.E. Church, 1916) p. 11.

23. Delores S. Williams, *Sisters in the Wilderness: The Challenge of Womanist God-Talk* (Maryknoll, N.Y.: Orbis, 1993), p. 6.

24. Maria Stewart, cited in Loewenberg and Bogin, eds., *Black Women in Nineteenth-Century American Life*, p. 196.

25. Fannie Barrier Williams, cited in ibid., p. 269.

26. See James Melvin Washington, *Frustrated Fellowship: The Black Baptist Quest for Social Power* (Macon: Mercer University Press, 1986), pp. 28–45; Benjamin Quarles, *Black Abolitionists* (New York: Oxford University Press, 1969), pp. 68–89; James M. McPherson, *The Negro's Civil War: How American Negroes Felt and Acted During the War for the Union* (New York: Vintage Books, 1967), pp. 33–53; David E. Swift, *Black Prophets of Justice: Activist Clergy Before the Civil War* (Baton Rouge: Louisiana State University Press, 1989), pp. 1–18 and passim; and Randall K. Burkett and Richard Newman, eds., *Black Apostles: Afro-American Clergy Confront the Twentieth Century* (Boston: G. K. Hall, 1978).

27. Lovell, *Black Song*, p. 386.

28. Talitha Lewis, cited in B. A. Botkin, ed., *Lay My Burden Down: A Folk History of Slavery* (Chicago: University of Chicago Press, 1945), p. 27.

29. Cited in William B. McClain, *Black People in the Methodist Church* (Cambridge: Schenkman, 1984), p. 37.

30. Carter G. Woodson; *The History of the Negro Church*, 3d ed. (Washington, D.C.: Associated Publishers, 1921), p. 251.

31. Charles H. Long, "Freedom, Otherness and Religion: Theologies Opaque," in the *Chicago Theological Seminary Register*, vol. 63, no. 1, Winter 1983, p. 23. Long speaks of a form of consciousness as "lithic" (Hegel) . . . "that mode of consciousness that in confronting reality in this mode formed a *will in opposition.* . . . The hardness of life or of reality was the experience of the meaning of their own identity as opaque."

32. Derek Walcott, in Orde Coombs, ed., *Is Massa Day Dead? Black Moods in the Caribbean* (Garden City, N.Y.: Doubleday, 1974), p. 7.

33. William Hamilton, "An Address to the New York African Society for Mutual Relief," in Dorothy Porter, ed., *Early Negro Writing*, p. 37.

34. Washington, *Frustrated Fellowship*, pp. 159–85.

35. E. Franklin Frazier, *The Negro Church in America* (New York: Schocken, 1964), p. 86.

36. The reference here is to the Colored Primitive Baptists (1865), the reunited African Union Methodists (1866), the Second Cumberland Presbyterian Church (1869), and the Colored Methodist Episcopal Church, about which considerably more has been written, founded in 1870. Among the Holiness and Pentecostal churches of the turn of the century were William Christian's Church of the Living God (1889), C. H. Mason's Church of God in Christ (1895), and William Crowdy's Church of God and Saints of Christ (1896).

37. For the best treatment of the significance of King's and Malcolm's lives and ministries for American religion and culture, see James H. Cone, *Martin & Malcolm & America: A Dream or a Nightmare* (Maryknoll, N.Y.: Orbis, 1991).

Chapter Forty-three

Fighting for Freedom with Church Fans
To Know What Religion Means

Vincent Harding

Vincent Harding follows the stream of African American history, plumbing the meanings of religion itself as the pulsing, agitating current in that stream—as Harding would see it, in the human *stream. He is particularly concerned with the intersection of religious faith and the movement for human freedom. As one deeply, personally immersed in the civil rights struggle of the King era, and a continuing important voice since, he reflects from the inside on that struggle, seeking instructive implications for those in present and future who must carry it on. He raises provocative questions toward a revisioning of our understanding of religion and its concrete imperatives for life in community.*

•

> My devotion to truth has drawn me into politics; and I can say without the slightest hesitation . . . that those who say that religion has nothing to do with politics do not know what religion means.
>
> —Mohandas K. Gandhi[1]

> After decades of shunning classroom discussion of religion, fearing that it was too divisive a subject or that church-state separation might be breached, many American public schools are now moving to incorporate it into their curriculums.
>
> The change results largely from a sentiment that schools have too long ignored religion as a force in American and world culture, and signs of it are far-flung.
>
> —New York Times, *March 19, 1989*[2]

For those of us who seek to anchor our teaching in the daily realities of the modern world, certain harsh encounters are difficult (and undesirable) to avoid. When we call the attention of our students to the possible presence of profound truths just beneath the surface of mundane events, none of us can escape the many times when great light, sometimes terrible beauty, is revealed to us through unspeakable tragedy.

That was certainly my response to the murder of the six Jesuit priests and their friends in El Salvador in 1989.

Those martyr deaths evoked both memories and anguished hope. For I saw not only Ignacio, Joaquin, Julia, and their companions but I remembered the Maryknoll women workers, and others who had been killed in service—as well as the assassinated Salvadoran archbishop. As a matter of fact, my memories went even deeper, longer, extending to other bearers of truth, embodiments of compassionate religion in the midst of life-affirming social movements. My memories embraced Martin and Malcolm. I heard Gandhi's dying chant of affirmation. I visited Steven Biko's grave, among so many other mounds of hope. I stumbled on the body of David Walker in nineteenth-century Boston. And these were only the tokens, representatives of the hosts.

It was in the midst of this great company of witnesses that I grasped again the meaning of Gandhi's words: "My devotion to truth has drawn me into the field of politics." For that is precisely what had happened to each member of the community of memories—their work for truth, for peace, for justice, for human solidarity had emerged naturally out of their deepest religious convictions. And these convictions, that work, had led them to identify with the expendable people, the exploited ones, the rejected stones. For each of them there came a time of discovery when, as King put it, "silence is betrayal," when they were faced with the impossibility of neutrality as a religious calling.

It is important to keep such persons close to us when we learn that there is a movement among America's school constituencies to find ways in which we can explore more fully the role of religion in our national past and present. We who are based in the classrooms are now being asked to consider and teach such subject matter in a richly pluralist—but often religiously biased—society. And although some of the proponents of this interest in religion may be more restrictive in their vision than we would like, the stirrings are important and need to be experienced and encouraged. They are signals of the return to a vaguely familiar, necessary, and wider-ranging search. For it is clear that ever since the time of the earliest, agonizing prayers on the African-laden slave ships, and the religiously founded civil compacts of the European settler-disrupters, the ubiquitous double-edged power of the search for the holy has been a source of both division and healing among us in our strangely native land.

Now, at this supposedly "secular" moment of our modernity, there is much evidence that we have begun to learn, again, that we cannot properly understand ourselves or others without some sense of the world of the numinous, that world which drives, defines, and shapes us, which frightens or repels us, and which feeds our deepest needs. Somehow we have come to see that the crossing places between religious faith and public action, between spiritual convictions and social commitments need to be explored if our classrooms—whether in public and private schools, community centers, or religious institutions—are to catch any real reflection of the vibrant, mysterious center of human life and struggle.

Indeed, what better way is there to teach and learn about religion than to explore the ways in which this sense of engagement with the ultimate has invaded and grasped human beings so fully that their lives have been transformed? And what happens when we are able to track the movement of those who live such lives, carefully watching as they move beyond their once accepted limits to become more fully realized persons and more compassionate participants in our common pilgrimage of responsibility? Might such explorations open our students to a richer, deeper sense of the meaning of religion than that which comes from the most famous of our religious television stars, or from mild and toothless Sunday school versions, or from soul-scarring introductions to deities of vengeance and fear? Is it possible that some serious exposure to the ways in which religious commitment can draw women and men into the task of creating a more just and humane society may be one of the best means for introducing children and adults in a pluralistic society to the amazing hope that so many persons find in the power and meaning of religion? In other words, rather than teaching only doctrines and comparative styles of worship, we may all learn more by also exploring compassionate lives on fire with faith and hope, human beings with beating hearts in search of a more just and loving society.

As we have already realized, there are witnesses from El Salvador to Romania and South Africa who can assist us in this approach to the places where religious faith and liberating social responsibility converge. But we are all served well at home. For by virtue of a sublime and tortured history lived out on the stage of our nation and the world, the Black struggle for freedom, at its best, provides just such openings into the power and mystery of a life-affirming religion at work. Carefully explored with our students, the freedom struggle—most obviously in its southern manifestations—not only provides us all an entry point to the world of Black religion in the United States (an important and deeply moving subject in itself), but also demonstrates some of the ways in which the humanizing force of any religion can draw to its side valuable companions from other religious traditions. We can also watch as these seekers are able both to embrace each other and to continue their search to find the best meanings and hopes in their own religious faith, to re-vision and re-experience their own essential ground of being. (Surely this was what Gandhi sought when he rejected the sometimes arrogant Christian calls to cross-religious conversions and urged instead that we stand in communion with one another, working sacrificially for the coming of a more just and loving social order, thereby developing the best possibilities and potentials of life in our own religious traditions. He said, "Our utmost prayer should be that a Hindu should be a better Hindu, a Muslim a better Muslim and a Christian a better Christian."[3]

As we reflect on the post–World War II African American freedom movement, nothing illustrates this powerful gathering and affirming tendency more fully than the vibrant interfaith mass meetings that were held at the height of the southern movement. Scenes from such explicitly religious (but not sectarian) meetings in Albany, Georgia, Birmingham, Alabama, Greenwood, Mississippi, and other similar settings are captured with great power in the *Eyes on the Prize* series and elsewhere. But many of our students of every chronological age will need us to help interpret the unfamiliar images, to call their attention to both the seen and unseen elements of the often ecstatic meetings. (Religious ecstasy in the midst of a dangerous sociopolitical freedom movement? What does that mean? Is it possible? Perhaps the deeper question is this: Can there be any real movement to freedom without deep ecstasy?) For they *were* meetings, deep engagements with things visible and invisible, with other human beings, both friends and oppressors, with fears and exultations. Sometimes they seemed to be great wrestling meetings between our lesser and better selves, shout-pierced, wing-spread engagements between humble men and women of the earth and the exalted spirits of the universe.

Usually the meetings were most powerfully experienced in the midst of times of crisis, when a local Black community had committed itself to struggle against the unjust system of segregation and white domination, and while public demonstrations were going on—often at great personal cost—in the area. In many cases the people who spoke and sang and prayed in those mass meetings had already begun to experience jailings, beatings, loss of jobs, and other forms of economic, physical, and psychological attempts at intimidation. Tensions and fears might be high. Dangers were real. That's why they *had* to sing, "Ain't Gonna Let Nobody Turn Me 'Round." That's why they had to sing songs taken from the deep reservoirs of their forebears' religious genius and then respond with their own revised versions of majestic hope. That's why they had to sing everything they could sing.

Dangers were real, but so were the great resources of their religious heritage. (Perhaps we should let our students hear those songs. Even better, let them try to break loose from inhibitions and fashionable disengagement—or lame adult excuses—to take on the songs, to take in the songs, to let out the songs themselves. Then perhaps there can be real conversations about the relation of singing and shouting and chanting to a variety of religious and liberating experiences. Perhaps it might even lead to an exploration of the holy vocal organs and cavities of our body and the tremendous power of breath which fills them with sounds that sometimes become more than we understand ourselves, sounds which some religious faiths believe are tying us to the breath of life, the breath of God. Maybe that's why they had to sing—in mass meetings, in jail, at funerals, on picket lines, in lonely times of prayer. Perhaps that's why Bull Connor heard the songs of life bursting out of crowded, rhythmically rocking police wagons in Birmingham and had to say, "If that's religion. I don't want no part of it." But perhaps it was too late. Perhaps some seven-year-old child on the way to "freedom jail" had already breathed on him.)

In the midst of such situations, the local movement leaders sometimes called in larger, more experienced organizations like SCLC, SNCC, the NAACP, and CORE. (What stacks of reports and papers and poems and songs, to be created by our students, lay hidden in those acronyms!) They in turn often called upon their Black and white allies in other parts of the country, and such persons soon flooded the relatively unsegregated airports and arrived on the scene. Almost always the movement leaders and others chose to organize mass meetings, sometimes every night, at least two or three times a week, depending on the intensity of the local struggle. On one level, the meetings were held to build cohesion, to convey necessary organizing information, to carry out planning—but there was always much more to them.

At the heart of the mass meetings was the experience of Black religion. The sessions were held in the Black churches, often changing location from night to night—partly for ecumenical purposes, partly for security. The powerful, roiling sessions brought together Baptists of all varieties, A.M.E.s, CMEs (the pregnant acronyms again!), Pentecostals and Black Lutherans, Roman Catholics, Methodists and Episcopalians. The mass meetings were, in other words, a great African American ecumenical revival-type gathering, where denominational rigidities and rivalries were temporarily cast aside. (Had they discovered "post-denominationalism" before the theologians and historians?) And beyond Black ecumenism there was more. Few things were more striking in these sessions than the sight and sound of Jewish rabbis, white priests and nuns, and visiting white Protestant ministers and lay people of many northern varieties, all singing, swaying, and shouting "Amens" in ways that probably surprised no one more than themselves. They had been drawn to a wondrous meeting place.

Here it was: The religious common ground so often sought at conferences, symposia, ecumenical services, and countless teas, was here on this ancient southern ground. Breaking—at least temporarily—against bloodied barriers of human construction, women and men of many faith persuasions had been brought to a sacred space of struggle, sacrifice, and hope. In small, simple church buildings, lined up on streets facing dogs and guns and fire hoses, sharing Mason jars of tepid water in sweltering prison cells, the human temple of the divine Creator had been drawn together, perhaps by the breath of hope. And the mass meetings expressed it all, reminded people of the central promises that appear in so many manifestations of the divine, promises that said we human seekers would be met most urgently by the great spirits not in the magnificent and fabled temples of religion but at those beleaguered places of most urgent human need, where struggling, hoping, committed women and men were willing to risk their safety for the sake of a compassionate quest for justice, reconciliation, and peace.

Perhaps we can help our students to sense the constantly surprising, often jarring, role of religion, and encourage them to recognize the power of its call, especially when that summons emerges out of the lives of men and women who have committed themselves to the creation of a more humane society. To introduce them to these mass meetings, this freedom religion, this divinely obsessed search for our separated kindred, this spirit-filled movement toward a righteous community, has nothing to do with proselytizing, but it has even less to do with "neutrality" in our teaching. Rather, it takes a stand with all those who have sought a compassionate way toward the release of the best, most humane, and life-affirming qualities in us. And it certainly at least calls attention to those tendencies or institutions (even within a freedom movement) that stifle the grace of creativity, self-reliance, and mutual responsibility in any of us. So we discover anew that it is impossible to study "religion" without serious examination of our own values and visions, without facing King's question: What are we prepared to die for?

In that spirit we take our students again to the mass meetings as a central paradigm for the meeting of religion and social responsibility (a better term for "politics"). We remind them of the ways in which the movement context was always presenting the nightly participants with an opportunity "to live the life I sing about," to "walk your talk," as the old folks admonished. This, of course, is central to the teachings of heart-deep religion everywhere—faith and work, beliefs and action, walking our talk. So at the mass meetings there was praying and singing ; there were women, men, and children testifying to divine assistance when they were in jail, or facing the billy clubs or the hoses; there were songs and more songs. There were solos, quartets, and choirs leading the singing. But when they had sung "Go Tell It on the Mountain," or "Leaning on the Everlasting Arms," or "We Shall Overcome," then they had to go out into that dangerous night or prepare for the next morning when they would test the faith and courage they had proclaimed, offering themselves as living, public witnesses to the power of the religion which so moved them inside the churches.

Eyes on the Prize caught one of the most vivid and revealing testimonies to the power and meaning of such religion as it told the story of the Albany, Georgia, freedom movement. There the cameras caught the face of a Black woman in a mass meeting as she sang and fanned herself with one of the ubiquitous cardboard church fans. Soon after, in another scene, probably the next day, she was present again, now kneeling with others in prayer, visibly moved by the spirit, right in front of Albany's combination jail and City Hall. As she rose to be arrested and escorted into jail this woman of faith and action was still waving the church fan, testifying in that simple motion to the fact that the religion that moved her life was one and the same in the church building and in the public square—and it would remain the same in the city jail. (Meanwhile, she and other such nonviolent freedom fighters would find some of the priests and rabbis and white Protestant allies also in prison, joining in the singing about "Paul and Silas bound in jail. . . ." Certainly it would be good to encourage our students to ask what were the elements in those other religious traditions that might prepare their practitioners for voluntary entry into jail, for serious response to the call of the Black freedom movement. Perhaps we should also entice them into the longer history of the movement, encourage them to investigate the African and earlier African American sources for its stirring combination of religion and political struggle, to understand why they felt the authority to call others and expect a positive response.)

There is a good chance that such scenes from the struggle would help our students to understand the significant statement by Gayraud Wilmore, one of our most perceptive historians of Black religion in America, when he wrote, "Between 1955 and 1960 the South experienced a revival of black religion—a revival that did not break out with sawdust trails and mourners' benches, but with picket lines, boycotts and marches through the downtown sections of scores of southern towns and cities." For Wilmore, the hundreds of Black preachers involved in the struggle, "most of them unknown and unsung, were there only as the instruments—sometimes the reluctant instruments—from which the theme of freedom rose like a great crescendo from the depths of the people."[4]

It might be helpful to take Wilmore's statement into our varied classrooms and build on it, opening for exploration some of the many meanings of religious revivalism. What has that experience meant in American history, going back as far as the eighteenth century? What does revivalism mean as we see it in other-than-Christian religions in the world today? Such questions are important, for even as the African American, Christian-led "revival" was taking place in the Deep South, for instance, we might ask how it was related to the parallel "revival" of the Black American version of Islam, most widely known as the Black Muslims. Opening the world of Islam through the Black Muslim experience offers many important pathways, including an opportunity to understand why people change their names, like Kareem Abdul-Jabbar and Muhammad Ali—or like many Roman Catholic sisters and monks. What is the spiritual significance of new names? All of which might bring us back to revival, for some of our students may want to know what actually happens in the lives of people who are "revived" or renamed.

Against the background of such crucial questions, one of the discoveries we may make with our students as we move into the religious core of the Black freedom movement is that religion, when taken with heartfelt seriousness, presents a great challenge. At its best it is a challenge to its practitioners, to their immediate communities and to the world around them. So we can begin to understand why the Black religious expressions of the freedom movement participants were often so threatening to their sisters and brothers in the southern white churches, parishes, and synagogues. Perhaps we can also help each other to understand some of the reasons why there should have been such turmoil in the northern-based religious institutions when Brother Martin Luther King, Jr., moved into their precincts to challenge urban poverty, American militarism, some of the northern varieties of white racism—and the acquiescence of religious people in all these betrayals of human community.

In the same way, it would be fascinating for students to discover James Forman, the former SNCC executive secretary who led what was called the Black Manifesto Movement of the late 1960s and early 1970s. Forman's movement was an audacious and often powerful (and slightly revolutionary) attempt to face the northern churches of the United States with their responsibility for white American racism. It was also a demand on them to make concrete financial amends in the form of reparations for the wrongs and exploitation suffered by Black people over many generations. But perhaps the most difficult part for the churches and other institutions to deal with was the Manifesto's call for the interracial redistribution of power in white-dominated religious institutions and the encouragement of Black self-determination everywhere. Comparing the responses to the call for money to the call for shared power, comparing the responses of the northern white churches and those in the South to the challenge of Black demands for justice—all this would be a marvelous lesson in the ways of religion, as well as other important American institutions. Of course, it also provides an excellent opportunity for our students to investigate the explosive rise of Black theology in the United States, not as an arcane academic or ecclesiastical set of formulations, but as a vibrant, controversial expression of judgment and hope, surging forth from the daily experiences of the African American communities, annealed by fire. Once they see this American development, then the global rise of liberation theologies in the quest for democratic transformation becomes easier to comprehend.

The sources for such larger explorations are legion. For instance, the story of the Black freedom movement can take us into fascinating realms of history, sociology, and gender studies when we explore the long tradition of men and women in the

African American experience who combine the role of political and spiritual leader. Beginning with Africa before the slave ships, then remembering the ministries of survival and hope that were shared beneath the decks of those floating nightmares, we are eventually brought face to face with persons like Frederick Douglass, Sojourner Truth, Nat Turner, Harriet Tubman, Bishop Henry McNeill Turner, the Honorable Elijah Muhammad, Malcolm X, Adam Clayton Powell, Jr., Reverend Herbert Dougherty, and Martin Luther King, Jr. In this generation the tradition flourishes even more formally with pastors who are members of Congress, such as William Gray of Philadelphia, Floyd Flake of New York, and Walter Fauntroy of the District of Columbia (who was a youth leader with King and SCLC at the outset of his career). Can our students eventually meet one or more of them, and people like them, in local political and religious leadership?

From another, related perspective, the rise of Black caucuses in predominantly white churches (and everywhere else) in the period of great rage and hope at the end of the 1960s and beginning of the 1970s presents one more fascinating subject for study. When the members of these ubiquitous caucuses were charged with "separatism" by a majority of their white Christian sisters and brothers, why did so many of the African American leaders remind the white (and Black) churches that Jesus of Nazareth had taught people to love their neighbors *as* they love themselves? Is healthy self-love really a religious imperative? If so, how does a society, a school, a religious institution encourage self-love among those who have been told for so long that their racial ancestry automatically makes them inferior to whites (or is it their overly long exposure to "the culture of poverty" that disqualifies them?)? Is this powerful quest for self-affirmation and self-determination really more than a matter of social issues or court cases?

In a society increasingly populated by peoples of color, by those who have known the disdain and domination of the Euro-American world, it would be fascinating to ponder self-love as a religious calling. How are people, beginning in their earliest years, nurtured to act with self-respect and self-responsibility? How are they/we encouraged to move through the world with a spirit which unselfrighteously challenges everything that threatens to crush the human spirit, the human ability to love ourselves and others? Can we explore such fundamental questions with our students, wondering aloud with them about the fascinating possible spiritual connections between the capacity to love ourselves and the willingness to love and serve others? As we begin the twenty-first century in the United States, how can we afford not to engage such essential human issues with our best resources, with our greatest and most imaginative energies?

These quests for the human truths opened up by the religion of the Black freedom movement could help us to understand why Malcolm X, with his insistent call for self-affirmation and self-determination, became the "Black shining prince" to so many of those he left behind. They might explain the scene in *Eyes on the Prize II* when a Black Roman Catholic priest in Chicago bursts with joy as he recounts the experience of hearing a room full of young African American children affirm their special sense of identity with Fred Hampton, recently martyred Black Panther leader.

The study of religion, like religion itself, is surely filled with surprises, and they come from every direction. For instance, as we linger over the image of the African robes of the Black priest, as we see Carl Stokes of Cleveland and Harold Washington of Chicago campaigning—and receiving blessings—in the familiar precincts of the African American churches, we may be tempted to miss a powerful fact of the northern-based freedom struggle: From many outward appearances, the Black churches of the North seemed less central to the movement there than had been the case in the South. Now, that is not an undebated issue, and exposure to the debate would surely be helpful to our students. However, if it is true, then what does it mean, not just about the Black churches of North and South, but about our understanding of the basic similarities and differences between the northern and southern Black experiences? For now we must look back and ask, How much did the evocative, central power of the Black churches, their beliefs and their rituals, their life rhythms and their leaders, have to do with the character of the southern freedom movement? How did the shifting, perhaps less central, role of those churches in the northern Black communities help account for the more episodic, relatively unfocused and physically explosive movement that developed in the North?

In other words, when it comes time to carry on a struggle for fundamental social change, is it better to start from a setting in which you have known your "place" for a long time, where you have had ample opportunity to nurture networks of both resistance and accommodation? Is it also important to ask what kind of religious manifestations are developed within experiences of uncertainty and uprootedness, in the crisis of migration and the search for place? Or are the differences we see as the movement moves north more a function of Black people's entering more deeply over time into all the antic unknowing of the twentieth century, paying the century's hard price for our passage into the ambiguous world of modernity?

Of course, none of these questions must be allowed to drive our students, or ourselves, away from our wrestling with one of the most important elements of all explorations of religion. In our search for the Black churches, it *is* certainly crucial that we remember that religion at its deepest levels has never been confined to churches, synagogues, mosques, or any places made with human hands. Indeed, it may be that some of our most fascinating and searching discussions will grow out of an attempt to discover how much of the deepest religious undercurrents of the northern freedom movement are to be found among its ever-expanding non–church-going (sometimes church-bashing) participants, women and men with no apparent current connections to any religious institutions at all.

This path may lead us to sentiments like that expressed by Langston Hughes in his poem "Personal":

> In an envelope marked:
> > *Personal*
> God addressed me a letter.
> In an envelope marked:
> > *Personal*
> I have given my answer.[5]

Even more importantly, and publicly, we may all begin to understand religion as being every truly compassionate expression of the great human longing for participation in the wholeness of the universe. Thus, we may absorb more fully Gandhi's equation of the religious quest with the search for truth. We can explore with our classes the religion of the Hebrew prophets, hear the powerful announcement that true religion consists of love for God and humanity, that true love leads to service, especially to the poor, the weak, the oppressed. They may look through the window of the Black freedom movement and discover a religion beyond buildings and institutions that is a profound personal and collective recognition of the oneness of humankind. They may see that religion is that commitment to give our best self to the work of nurturing and defending the great connectedness, through personal disciplines, collective work, and public witness. If students apprehend the ways in which the human quest for meaning most often begins in the depths of our own truth-seeking lives and emerges into a sense of connection with the cosmos, then they may see fascinating things, beyond the churches, beyond all institutions (and also within them), at the heart of the northern-based freedom movement.

For instance, from such a point of view we may recognize the emphasis on Black self-love that rose out of the late 1960s and moved into the next decade as a necessary preparation for the love of neighbor and of God. They may grasp the possibility that the affirmation of God's blackness (so puzzling and offensive to some), of Jesus as a man of color, may have been crucial openings to an authentic sense of African American oneness with the Divine (as well as an important recognition of the color realities of the Middle East). As they explore the renascence-like movement that grew out of the post-assassinations decade, students may find religion in strange places: the magnificent, creative outpouring, exploding out of saxophones and trumpets, resounding from drums, singing from guitars, lifted up by poets and playwrights, unfurled in living colors on Black community "walls of respect," focused on canvas squares by artists of many talents and visions, the sculpturing of every conceivable material into throbbing statements of the heart. Perhaps all this rediscovery and reshaping of the African American creative forces of that period can be recognized as a re-encounter with the image of the divine Creator within us, a reclaiming of our best selves, a statement of our ultimate hope.

When religion is seen with new eyes, we may re-vision all the Panthers (and others like them) who really believed their lives were meant to be lived for "the people," especially the poor and intimidated among the people. Then our students may recognize these apparently strange, often cursing, angry, and defiant young women and men in the light of the story that appears in the twenty-fifth chapter of the Gospel according to Matthew. For it may well be that some day, somewhere, some of the young Panther folks who often seemed so frightening to so many people in their time will be surprised and sustained by the joy of the timeless, simple words, "I was hungry and you gave me breakfast . . . Come."

Who knows? Perhaps religion really is about the fact that all of us, by the very reality of our humanity, are called to serve the poor, to open doors for prisoners, to work on behalf of the exploited, to seek for a new order of sharing, forgiveness, and compassion in this world. If that is the case, then Gandhi is teacher to us all, and religion really cannot be separated from responsible public participation in the shaping of our community—politics at its best. Exploring such insights, our students will have every right to ask about where love-possessed "doers of the word" might be today. They might ask who has been called in our own time (and what does *calling* mean, does it have anything to do with making as much money as possible?) to release and serve, to heal and bring good news? And which of our students will wonder aloud about what is "good news" in the last decade of the twentieth century? Does it have anything to do with the tumbling of walls, with the opening of borders, with the freeing of prisoners of conscience? Or is it the invasion of a small, helpless nation? What can we say?

Somewhere in the exploration of the various expressions of the African American freedom movement, somewhere in our attempt to understand the convergence of religion and politics in that singular experience, such reflections and questions may well arise. The least we can do is prepare ourselves and our students for surprises, from within and without. Religion has a way of doing that, especially when we track its movement among people who have nothing to lose but their pain. Finally—or is it initially?—if we are open and caring, our students may well ask about our own religion, our own hope, our own commitments. Are we ready?

NOTES

1. Quoted in Eknath Easwaran, *Gandhi the Man* (Petaluma, CA: Nilgiri, 1978), 2d ed., p. 60.

2. "Trend Gaining in Public Schools to Add Teaching About Religion," Peter Steinfels, *New York Times*, March 19, 1989, p. 1.

3. Mohandas Gandhi, *All Religions Are True*, ed. Anand T. Hingorani (Bombay, India: Bharatiya Vida Bhavan, 1962), pp. 83–84.

4. Gayraud S. Wilmore, *Black Religion and Black Radicalism* (New York: Anchor Press, 1973), pp. 177–78.

5. Langston Hughes, *Selected Poems* (New York: Knopf, 1959), p. 88. Apparently this was one of Hughes favorite poems. It is found in many published collections, edited by Hughes and by others.

Appendixes

TIMELINE OF THE AFRICAN AMERICAN RELIGIOUS EXPERIENCE

Early Slavery 1526–1775	Slavery in the Era of Abolition 1776–1865	Reconstruction and Jim Crow 1868–1900	Migration and The New Negro 1901–1929

African American Community

Spanish explorers bring Africans to what are now the Carolinas; they escape in what is the first recorded slave revolt in North America (1526).	As part of the "Great Compromise" between northern and southern states, a slave is counted as 3/5 of a free man (1787).	14th Amendment guarantees former slaves citizenship (1866).	Nearly 2 million African Americans migrate to the North (1900–1930)
The population of British North American is 1.1 million people, 1/5 of whom are slaves (1678).	Denmark Vesey plans a revolt in Charleston, SC; many members of the First A.M.E. Church are involved (1822).	15th Amendment guarantees African American men the right to vote (1869).	The NAACP (1909) and the National Urban League (1911) are founded.
Pennsylvania Quakers abolish slavery among themselves (1758) and organize the first Abolition Society of Philadelphia (1775)	Nat Turner leads a 2-day rebellion, claiming the spirit of the Old Testament called on him to deliver his people; lower southern states forbid blacks to preach (1831).	14 African Americans serve in the House of Representatives; two serve in the U.S. Senate (1869–1877).	Marcus Garvey organizes the Universal Negro Improvement Association in New York (1917).
	Harriet Tubman of the A.M.E. Zion church leads more than 300 slaves to freedom (1850s).	Literacy among blacks climbs to 18.6% (1870).	Racial violence of the "Red Summer" (1919).
	13th Amendment abolishes slavery (1865).	Booker T. Washington founds Tuskegee Institute (1881).	The "Harlem Renaissance," a flourishing of art, fiction, and poetry (1920–1935).
		90% of all blacks live in the South (1890).	
		Plessy v. Ferguson declares "separate but equal" accommodations constitutional (1896).	

TIMELINE OF THE AFRICAN AMERICAN RELIGIOUS EXPERIENCE (*continued*)

The Depresion and WWII 1930–1949	Civil Rights Era 1950–1964	Black Power 1965–1979	End of the Century 1980–

African American Community

The Depresion and WWII 1930–1949

Over 2/3 of African Americans in professional jobs are teachers or ministers (1931).

Educator Mary McLeod Bethune establishes the National Council of Negro Women (1935).

Congress of Racial Equality (CORE), based on Gandhi's principles of nonviolence, is formed (1942).

Rev. Adam Clayton Powell, Jr. is elected to the House of Representatives (1948).

President Truman orders "equality of treatment and opportunity" in the armed forces (1948).

Civil Rights Era 1950–1964

The U.S. population is over 15 million; 10% are African Americans, of whom 52% live in cities (1950).

In *Brown v. Board of Education,* the Supreme Court declares "separate but equal" public education unconstitutional (1954).

The Montgomery bus boycott is led by Baptist minister Rev. Martin Luther King, Jr. (1955).

The Sixteenth Street Baptist Church in Birmingham, AL, is bombed, killing four young girls (1963).

Black Power 1965–1979

March from Selma to Montgomery in support of voter rights (1965).

Congress passes Voting Rights (1965).

The Black Panther Party is founded (1966).

Kwanzaa created to restore and reaffirm African heritage and culture (1967).

National Black Power Convention in Gary, IN (1972).

NAACP decries worsening economic conditions for African Americans; 12% of adults and 40% of eligible youth unemployed (1976).

End of the Century 1980–

Rev. Jesse Jackson runs for President, getting 6.1 million primary votes (1988).

Speaking at the Riverside church in NYC, Nelson Mandela thanks American churches for their support during S. Africa's struggles (1990).

A Harvard University study indicates that racial segregation is rising to levels not seen since 1968 (1993).

Between 400,000 and 1 million black men join the Million Man March, organized by the Nation of Islam's Louis Farrakhan (1995).

TIMELINE OF THE AFRICAN AMERICAN RELIGIOUS EXPERIENCE (*continued*)

Early Slavery 1526–1775	Slavery in the Era of Abolition 1776–1865	Reconstruction and Jim Crow 1868–1900	Migration and The New Negro 1901–1929

African American Religion

LEADERS AND INSTITUTIONS

Estevan, the first identified Muslim in North America, lands in Florida as a Moroccan guide to the Spaniards (1527).	Richard Allen establishes the Free African Society, which will become the African Methodist Episcopal Church (A.M.E.), the first major black institution in America (1787).	The Augusta Institute, which becomes Morehouse college, is founded in the basement of the Springfield Baptist church in Augusta, GA (1867).	The Azusa Street Revival, an integrated "24-hour church" led by William Seymour, is regarded as the genesis of the American Pentecostal movement (1906).
A group of slaves in Massachusetts seek to form their own separate Christian meetings; Puritan cleric Cotton Mather draws up *Rules for the Society of Negroes* (1693).	Jarena Lee begins her evangelical ministry, traveling hundreds of miles on foot; because she is female, she is never officially recognized by he A.M.E. Church (1809).	Colored Methodist Episcopal church (C.M.E.) is founded by freedmen (1870).	C. H. Mason, founder of the Church of God in Christ, is beaten and jailed for his pacifist stance and statement, "The Kaiser is not my enemy" (1918).
The earliest black churches are founded: the African Baptist Church in VA (1758), and the Silver Bluff Baptist Church in SC (c.1773).	The Oblate Sisters of Providence is established as the first permanent community of black Catholic nuns (1829).	James Augustine Healy is made the first African American bishop by Roman Catholic Church (1875).	Howard Thurman becomes pastor of Mount Zion Baptist Church in Oberlin, OH (1928).
	A.M.E. minister Henry McNeal Turner becomes first chaplain of U.S. Military's colored troops (1863).	Prophet F. S. Cherry, leader of the Black Jewish Movement, founds the Church of the Living God (1886).	

PROGRAMS AND PRACTICES

An estimated 7–8% of West African slaves brought to North America are Muslim.	Alabama passes legislation making it illegal for slaves or free blacks to preach the gospel unless five "respectable" slaveholders are present (1833).	"Lining-out," an African tradition in which the preacher chants a line that the congregation repeats, is common where congregations are illiterate and lack hymnals.	In an Atlanta University study, W. E. B. Du Bois cites the black church, particularly church women, as the greatest source of social benefit for African Americans (1909).
"Ring shout," the African-derived sacred dance, is practiced by slaves during religious gatherings.	The first known lay society of black Catholics is formed in Baltimore (1842).	Vodun, brought by slaves from the French West Indies, flourishes, particularly, though not exclusively, in New Orleans (late 1800s).	Migration to urban areas brings about the rise of the "storefront church," often for poor or newly formed congregations (c.1910).
Santa Teresa de Mose in Florida is established as a town for freed slaves converted to Catholicism (1738).		In the wake of Emancipation, the A.M.E. church increases tenfold to 200,000 members (1876).	

TIMELINE OF THE AFRICAN AMERICAN RELIGIOUS EXPERIENCE (*continued*)

The Depresion and WWII 1930–1949	Civil Rights Era 1950–1964	Black Power 1965–1979	End of the Century 1980–

African American Religion

LEADERS AND INSTITUTIONS

W. D. Fard begins preaching in Detroit (1930); his ideas will inspire Elijah Muhammad in founding the Nation of Islam.

Interracial religious communes, known collectively as the "Peace Mission," are developed under the guidance of Father Divine (1932).

FBI takes Bishop Ida Robinson off the radio for her pacifist declaration that she has nothing against the Japanese (1942).

Rev. Martin Luther King Jr. leads 300,000 in March on Washington (D.C.) (1963).

The Ministers Committee for Job Opportunities for Brooklyn leads 3-week protest for fair hiring practices in local facilities (1963).

Rev. Milton Galamison leads boycott of NYC schools to force the Board of Education to integrate schools (1964).

Malcom X breaks from the Nation of Islam and embraces Orthodox Islam (1964).

Malcolm X is assassinated (1965).

Martin Luther King, Jr., is assassinated (1968).

James Forman reads *The Black Manifesto* at the Riverside Church in NYC (1969).

While serving time in prison, activist H. Rap Brown converts to Islam; later he will become Imam Jamil Al-Amin (1971).

Pauli Murray is named the first black female priest in the Episcopal Church USA (1976).

Warith Deen Mohammed and Louis Farrakhan split over the ideology of the Nation of Islam (1978).

Rev. Barbara Clementine Harris is consecrated as first female bishop of the Episcopal Church (1980).

Rev. Floyd Flake of Allen A.M.E. Church in Jamaica, NY, is elected to the 100th Congress (1986).

George A. Stallings is consecrated as bishop of the African American Catholic Church (1991).

Imam Siraj Wahhaj is the first Muslim to give opening prayers at the U.S. House of Representatives (1991).

Imam Warith Deen Mohammed gives opening prayers at the U.S. Senate (1992).

PROGRAMS AND PRACTICES

Solomon Lightfoot Michaux, believed to be the first radio evangelist, goes on the air (1933).

After a trip to India, Howard Thurman begins teaching Gandhi's philosophy of nonviolence to his students, who will include Martin Luther King Jr. and James Farmer of CORE (1937).

The Nation of Islam grows to an estimated membership of 100,000, in part due to Malcolm X's message and charismatic style (1960).

Civil rights activists kneel outside many all-white churches in protest of segregation (1960s).

James H. Cone, professor at Union Theological Seminary, publishes his seminal *Black Theology and Black Power* (1969).

The segregated Central Jurisdiction of the United Methodist Church is officially disbanded after a 20-year fight (1972).

The seven largest black Christian denominations organize the Congress of National Black Churches (1978).

Black Baptists constitute the 4th largest U.S. religious group, with 8.7 million members (1990).

Several Muslin organizations begin the Islamic Prison Foundation (1991).

The Church of God in Christ claims 6.3 million members, making it the largest Pentecostal denomination in the world (1993).

Early Slavery 1526–1775	Slavery in the Era of Abolition 1776–1865	Reconstruction and Jim Crow 1868–1900	Migration and The New Negro 1901–1929

African American Religion (*continued*)

MUSIC AND ARTS

Job Ben Solomon, an enslaved African Muslin, writes several copies of the Qur'an from memory (c.1733).	Richard Allen compiles first collection of African American spirituals, songs, and hymns (1801).	The first major collection of Negro songs, *Slave Songs of the United States,* is published (1867).	Record companies record sermons and spirituals for their "race records," targeted at the African American market (1920s).
One of the first known publications by an African American is Jupiter Hammon's poem, *An Evening Thought, Salvation by Christ, with Penitential Cries* (1760).	*The Narrative of Sojourner Truth,* slave missionary and leading abolitionist, is published (1853).	The Fisk Jubilee Singers perform black spirituals throughout the United States and Europe (1870s).	James Weldon Johnson's *God's Trombones,* seven sermons in verse, celebrates the tradition of the old Negro preacher (1927).
The same year she is freed Phillis Wheatley publishes *Poems on Various Subjects, Religious and Moral* (1773).	Elizabeth, a former slave, preaches among the Quakers. Her testimony is later published as *Elizabeth, a Colored Minister of the Gospel Born in Slavery* (late 1700s).	Painter Henry O. Tanner, whose works contain black and religious themes, receives the Medal of Honor at the Paris Exposition (1900).	Countee Cullen publishes *The Black Christ,* a book of poems (1929).

World and American Religion

The English Crown charters the Society for Propagation of the Gospel in Foreign Parts of the Anglican Church (SPGA) to convert slaves and Native Americans (1701).	First Amendment to U.S. Constitution provides for separation of church and state and protects citizens' freedom of religion (1789).	The Holiness Movement, involving both black and white worshippers, organized by Methodists (1867).	Era of mainstream Protestant support for an ideology of the Social Gospel (1910s).
Charles and John Wesley develop evangelical style of worship, focusing on the poor in London (1720s).	The "Second Great Awakening" begins (c.1800).	"New Immigrants" from Sothern and Eastern Europe, mostly Catholics and Jews, encounter hostility and discrimination in U.S. (1880s).	The interracial period of Pentecostalism ends with the formation of the all-white Assemblies of God (1914).
Successive waves of religious revival known as the "Great Awakening" begin (1740s).	The Methodist church splits over the issue of slavery (1844). The Baptists follow suit (1845).	The World's Parliament of Religions held in Chicago brings Buddhists, Hindus, and Jains into contact with American religious leaders (1893).	The Ku Klux Klan is resurrected and more than 4 million Americans join this anti-Catholic, anti-Semitic, anti-immigrant and anti-black organization (1915–1920).
The founding of Mission San Diego de Alcala marks the expansion of Spanish Catholicism in the American West (1769).	1.5 million Irish and 1 million German immigrants vastly increase the American Catholic community (1845–60).	*The Woman's Bible,* edited by Elizabeth Cady Stanton, offering alternative readings about the role of women in the Bible, is a best seller (1895–1898).	
	Antoinette Brown Blackwell is made the first woman minister in the U.S. by the Congregationalist Church (1853).		

TIMELINE OF THE AFRICAN AMERICAN RELIGIOUS EXPERIENCE (*continued*)

The Depression and WWII 1930–1949	Civil Rights Era 1950–1964	Black Power 1965–1979	End of the Century 1980–

African American Religion (*continued*)

MUSIC AND ARTS

Thomas Dorsey, the "Father of Gospel," writes his most famous song, "Take My Hand, Precious Lord," and co-founds the first publishing house for the promotion of Black American gospel (1932).

The Golden Gates Record "No Segregation in Heaven" (1942), a highlight in the golden era of *a cappella* quartets that dominates gospel music in the 1930s and 1940s.

Mahalia Jackson is featured in the first large gospel concert at Carnegie Hall (1950).

Alvin Ailey's dance company debuts *Revelations*, based on black religious heritage (1960).

The nation's first black-owned and operated radio station airs daily gospel and all-day Sunday religious programming in Atlanta (1962).

The Amen Corner by James Baldwin opens on Broadway (1965).

The Edwin Hawkins Singers record the crossover gospel hit "Oh Happy Day" (1968).

Bernice Johnson Reagon forms the women's group *Sweet Honey in the Rock* (1973).

Aretha Franlkin releases *One Lord, One Faith, One Baptism,* in a renewed celebration of her gospel roots (1987).

Rap artist Kirk Franklin and his group Stomp stir controversy with his "popgos" that brings some young people back to church (1990s).

World and American Religion

Mahatma Gandhi is arrested for leading a 200-mile march to the sea to protest government's salt tax (1930).

The Jewish state of Israel is established (1948).

The National Council of Churches is formed, representing over 33 million members (1950).

Members of the "Mother Mosque" in Cedar Rapids, Iowa, organize the first national Islamic organization, later known as the Federation of Islamic Associations (1952).

The Revised Standard Version of the Bible is issued (1952).

Three white ministers are beaten in Selma, AL; the Reverend James Reeb dies from his injuries (1965).

The Episcopal Church ordains women (1976).

The Mormon Church ends its policy excluding black men from the priesthood (1978).

910 members of the "People's Temple" commit mass suicide in Jonestown, Guyana (1978).

Bishop Desmond Tutu wins the Nobel Peace Prize (1984).

Pope John Paul II apologizes for the Catholic Church's support of slavery (1993).

More than 100 Christian leaders from diverse traditions join "Cry for Renewal," a group dedicated to social justice that "transcends old categories of Right and Left" (1995).

THE AFRICAN-AMERICAN RELIGIOUS EXPERIENCE: FILMOGRAPHY

Title	Year	Length (min.)
A Time for Building	1969	—
A Time for Burning	1965	16
A Time for Reflections	1995	16
Achievements in American Black History: Black Religion	—	40
African Religions and Ritual Dance	—	18
Black Church: Bethel AME Baltimore (McNeil Lehrer News)	—	13
Black Delta Religion	1972	15
Cast the First Stone (ABC Close-Up)	1960	30
Climbing Jacob's Ladder	—	—
Fire in the Pews	—	30
God's Alcatraz: Reconstructing a Community in Despair	1993	36
He Never Sent Women: The Ordination of a Female Priest	1992	58
How Open This Door? Black Pioneers in a White Denomination (Unitarian Universalist Association)	1986	35
Keeping the Faith (Frontline)	—	58
Let the Church Say Amen (St. Clair Bourne)	1973	70
March of Time: Father Divine's Deal	1938	9
March of Time: Harlem Heaven's Headman Pinched!	1937	6
Nation of Islam, The: A Portrait	—	60
Performed Word, The	1982	59
Reunion With the Spirit (Say Brother)	1990	29
Rev. Audrey Bronson	—	90
Rev. Floyd Flake (CBS News)	1997	—
Rev. Leon Sullivan (ABC Americans All)	1973	15
Say Amen, Somebody	1985	100
Sojourner (Sojourner Truth)	1975	—
Take Away This Anger: Children, Violence, and the Church	1996	58
The Story of Gospel Music	1996	90
Upon This Rock: The Black Church in Kentucky	1982	—
Voodoo	1956	—
What If Jesus Was Black? (Phil Donahue)	—	—

Acknowledgments

We gratefully acknowledge those who have given us permission to reprint the following:

Charles H. Long, "Perspectives for a Study of African American Religion," in *History of Religions* No. 11, 1971, 54–66 (Chicago: University of Chicago Press), © 1971 by the University of Chicago Press, reprinted by permission; Albert J. Raboteau, *A Fire in the Bones*, 28–36, 66–72, 113–116, © 1995 by Albert J. Raboteau, reprinted by permission of Beacon Press, Boston; Gayraud S. Wilmore, *Black and Presbyterian* (Louisville: Witherspoon Press, 1998), 1–4, used by permission; C. Eric Lincoln and Lawrence H. Mamiya, *The Black Church in the African American Experience*, 5–8, 10–16, 105–114, 126–163, 285–301, © 1990, Duke University Press, all rights reserved, reprinted with permission; Maulana Karenga, *Introduction to Black Studies*, 2nd ed. (Los Angeles: University of Sankore Press, 1993), 211–220; Albert J. Raboteau, *Slave Religion: The "Invisible Institution" in the Antebellum South*, 152–155, 157, 62, 175–180, © 1978 by Oxford University Press, Inc., used by permission of Oxford University Press, Inc.; Mary R. Sawyer, *Black Ecumenism*, 199–208, 236–237, © 1994 (Harrisburg, PA: Trinity Press International); Richard Brent Turner, "Pre-Twentieth Century Islam," *Journal of Religious Thought*, 51:1 (summer/fall 1994): 28–35, Washington, DC: *Journal of Religious Thought*, reprinted by permission; Jon F. Sensbach, *A Separate Canaan: The Making of an Afro-Moravian World in North Carolina*, 1763–1840, 309–311, © 1998 by the University of North Carolina Press, Chapel Hill, used by permission of the publisher; Monroe Fordham, *Major Themes in Northern Black Religious Thought*, 1800–1860 (Hicksville, N.Y.: Exposition Press, 1975), 85–92; 98–107; Delores C. Carpenter, "Black Women in Religious Institutions: A Historical Summary from Slavery to the 1960s," *Journal of Religious Thought* 46:2 (winter/spring 1989–90): 7–15, Washington, DC: *Journal of Religious Thought*, reprinted by permission; Leon F. Litwack, *Been in the Storm So Long*, 451–476, © 1979 by Leon F. Litwack, reprinted by permission of Alfred A. Knopf Inc.; Manning Marable, "The Black Faith of W. E. B. Du Bois: Sociocultural and Political Dimensions of Black Religion," *Southern Quarterly*, 23:3 (spring 1985): 15–33; St. Clair Drake, *The Redemption of Africa and Black Religion*, 41–53, 71–74, © 1970 by St. Clair Drake, reprinted by permission of Third World Press Inc., Chicago, Illinois; Blackside, Inc., *This Far by Faith*, 3–8, © 1998, used by permission of Blackside, Inc., Boston, MA; Martha Fowlkes, from a proposal for video documentary *This Far By Faith*, © 1998 Blackside, Inc.; St. Clair Drake and Horace Cayton, *Black Metropolis: A Study of Negro Life in a Northern City*, 412–429, © 1970 by St. Clair Drake and Horace Cayton, reprinted by permission of Harcourt, Inc.; Lawrence W. Levine, *Black Culture and Black Consciousness: Afro-American Folk Thought from Slavery to Freedom*, 174–188, © 1977 by Oxford University Press, Inc., used by permission of Oxford University Press, Inc.; Iain MacRobert, "The Black Roots of Pentecostalism," in *Pentecost, Mission, and Ecumenism*, edited by Jan A. B. Jongeneel, 73–84 (Peter Lang: Frankfurt/M., Berlin, Bern, New York, Paris, Wein, 1992); Gordon Melton, "The Second Emergence of Islam," in the *Encyclopedia of African American Religious Experience*, edited by Larry Murphy, Gordon Melton, and Gary Ward, 379–382 (Garland Publishing, 1993); Erdmann Doane Beynon, "The Voodoo Cult Among Negro Migrants in Detroit," *American Journal of Sociology* (Chicago: American Sociological Society, 1938), 894–907; Gary Ward, "Father Major Jealous Divine," in the *Encyclopedia of African American Religious Experience*, edited by Larry Murphy, Gordon Melton, and Gary Ward, 236–237 (Garland Publishing, 1993); Merrill Singer, " 'Now I Know What the Songs Mean!': Traditional Black Music in a Contemporary Black Sect," *Southern Quarterly*, 23:3 (spring 1985): 125–140; Hans A. Baer, *The Black Spiritual Movement: A Religious Response to Racism*, 17–30, © 1984 by The University of Tennessee Press, reprinted by permission of The University of Tennessee Press; Anthony B. Pinn, *Varieties of Religious Experience*, 76–88, 160–75, © 1998 Augsburg Fortress, reprinted by permission; Tracey Hucks, "The Historical Roots of African American Yoruba Expression," 7–12 (unpublished paper, delivered at the annual meeting of the American Academy of Religion/Society for Biblical Literature, 1998); Bruce Jackson, "The Other Kind of Doctor: Conjure and Magic in Black American Folk Medicine," in *American Folk Legend: A Symposium*, edited by Wayland Hand, 259–72, © 1971 by The Regents of the University of California, reprinted by permission of the University of California Press; Mary R. Sawyer, "Black Religion and Social Change: Women in Leadership Roles," *Journal of Religious Thought*, 47:2 (winter/spring 1990–91): 16–29, Washington, DC: *Journal of Religious Thought*, reprinted by permission; Mary R. Sawyer, "The Black Church and Black Politics: Models of Ministerial Activism," *Journal of Religious Thought*, 52:2 (1996): 45–62, Washington, DC: *Journal of Religious Thought*, reprinted by permission; R. Drew Smith, "Black Religious Nationalism and the Politics of Transcendence," 533–547, © 1998; David Daniels, "The Churches and Broader Developments in Black Religion: Two Congregational Case Studies," in *RUAP Final Research Report*, edited by Lowell W. Livezey (Office of Social Science Research, University of Illinois at Chicago, 1995): 191–196; James H. Cone, "Black Theology as Liberation Theology," in *For My People*, 53–77 (Orbis, 1984); National Committee of Black Churchmen, "Statement by the National Committee of Black Churchmen, June 13, 1969," in *Black Theology: A Documentary History, 1966–1979*, 2nd ed., edited by James H. Cone and Gayraud Wilmore (Orbis Books, 1993), 100–107; M. Shawn Copeland, O.P., "African American Catholics and Black Theology: An Interpretation," in *African American Religious Studies: An Interdisciplinary Anthology*, ed. Gayraud S. Wilmore, 228–236; 239; 241–243; 246–248, © 1989, Duke University Press, all rights reserved, reprinted with permission; Toinette M. Eugene, " 'Lifting as We Climb': Womanist Theorizing about Religion and the Family," in *Religion, Feminism, and the Family*, edited by Anne-

Carr and Mary Steward Van Leeuwen, 331–343, © 1996 Westminster John Knox Press, used by permission of Westminster John Knox Press; Gayraud S. Wilmore, *Black Religion and Black Radicalism*, 3rd rev. ed., 220–234 (Orbis Books, 1998); Vincent Harding, *Hope and History*, 75–90 (Orbis Books, 1990).

Index

About the Editor

Larry G. Murphy is Professor of the History of Christianity at Garrett-Evangelical Theological Seminary/Northwestern University. He was also Senior Researcher, Religion in Urban America Project, at the University of Illinois and an editor of *The Encyclopedia of African American Religions.*